An Anthology of
Jewish-Russian Literature

Volume 1: 1801–1953

An Anthology of Jewish-Russian Literature

Two Centuries of Dual Identity in Prose and Poetry

Volume 1: 1801–1953

Edited, selected, and cotranslated, with introductory essays by

Maxim D. Shrayer

M.E.Sharpe
Armonk, New York
London, England

Copyright © 2007 by M.E. Sharpe, Inc.

Detailed notes on sources, publication history, and copyright appear with each selection
and on pages 607–19 and 1185–98.

The EuroSlavic fonts used to create this work are © 1986–2002 Payne Loving Trust.
EuroSlavic is available from Linguist's Software, Inc.,
www.linguistsoftware.com, P.O. Box 580, Edmonds, WA 98020-0580 USA
tel (425) 775-1130.

Library of Congress Cataloging-in-Publication Data

An anthology of Jewish-Russian literature : two centuries of dual identity in prose and
poetry / edited, selected, and cotranslated, with introductory essays by Maxim D. Shrayer.
    v. cm.
Includes bibliographical references and index.
Contents: v. 1. 1801–1953 — v. 2. 1953–2001.
ISBN 978-0-7656-0521-4 (cloth : alk. paper)
    1. Russian literature—Jewish authors—Translations into English. 2. Jews in literature.
3. Russian literature—19th century—Translations into English. 4. Russian literature—
20th century—Translations into English. I. Shrayer, Maxim D., 1967–

PG3213.A55 2007
891.708'08924'009034—dc22   2005012792

Printed in the United States of America

The paper used in this publication meets the minimum requirements of
American National Standard for Information Sciences
Permanence of Paper for Printed Library Materials,
ANSI Z 39.48-1984.

BM (c)   10   9   8   7   6   5   4   3   2   1

for Karen and Mirusha, with all my love

in loving memory of Bella Breydo
                     Pyotr (Peysakh) Shrayer
                     Arkady (Aron) Polyak

CONTENTS

Volume 1: 1801–1953

THE BEGINNING

GAINING A VOICE: 1840–1881

EMIGRATIONS: 1917–1967

ACKNOWLEDGMENTS

This anthology has been in preparation for almost eight years. I would like to thank Boston College for its continuous support of my research through a Research Incentive Grant and several Research Expense Grants awarded me between 1997 and 2003, and for granting me leave time through an 80 percent sabbatical in 2002–3 and a faculty fellowship in the fall of 2004, both of which were crucial in the completion of this anthology. The Boston College Undergraduate Research Assistant Program enabled me to work with six gifted young men and women, whose contributions to the realization of this anthology I gratefully acknowledge: Adam Fuss, Patrick Kelly, Peter Rahaghi, Lisa Senay, Rachel Skiba, and Tim Tranchilla. Cathleen "Cat" Olson, a former graduate student in Boston College's Department of Slavic and Eastern Languages, helped me during the final months of working on the anthology.

Some of the initial research was conducted during the academic year 1998–99, when I enjoyed a year-long respite from my teaching duties thanks to a National Endowment for the Humanities Fellowship for University Teachers. I was also fortunate to have the support of The Lucius N. Littauer Foundation (1998) and The Memorial Foundation for Jewish Culture (1998–99). Harvard University's Davis Center for Russian and Eurasian Studies provided library and collegial support by making me a center associate. A portion of this anthology was completed in November–December 2002 at the Rockefeller Foundation's Study and Conference Center in Bellagio, Italy, and I thank its staff for their thoughtfulness and kind attention during my stay there. A fellowship from the Bogliasco Foundation and the staff of the Centro Studi Ligure per le arti e le lettere (Bogliasco, Italy) provided me with the peace and comfort that I so needed to complete most of the writing and editing of this anthology in October–November 2004. *Mille grazie!*

The staff of the Interlibrary Loan Office of Boston College's O'Neill Library was absolutely splendid in obtaining thousands of pages of materials, and I would like to thank Daniel Benedetti, Anne Kenny, Ellen Maher, and Daniel Saulean for all their tireless efforts, which are very much appreciated. Stephen Vedder and Michael S. Swanson of Boston College's Media and Technology Services have done a splendid job with the cover art.

Patricia Kolb, vice-president and editorial director of M.E. Sharpe, has been an enthusiastic supporter of this project from the very beginning, when it was only an initial proposal for an anthology half the size of the present two volumes. She has encouraged me through all the stages of research, editing, and writing. I have benefited from Pat's editorial talent and wisdom, and I wish to thank her for having been the anthology's doting godmother. Amy B. Albert was most helpful during the preparation of the manuscript for production and copyediting. The copyeditor, Dobrochna Dyrcz-Freeman Fire, herself an accomplished translator, has done a superb job, and I very much appreciate her linguistic acumen, her commitment to this large and complex project, and also her graceful and tactful resistance to my authorial folly. My thanks go to Ana Erlić, to proofreaders Paula Cook and Irina Burns, Diana McDermott and the entire staff of M.E. Sharpe for giving the anthology a warm and loving home.

I would like to extend my gratitude to all the writers and writers' families and executors who have responded to my queries and kindly supplied the information I requested. Three of the writers featured in this anthology passed away during the time that I was working on it, and I would like to remember them here: Semyon Lipkin (1911–2003), Ruth Zernova (1919–2004), and Bella Ulanovskaya (1943–2005).

I would never have been able to undertake this anthology without the passion and dedication of the gifted translators who worked with me toward its completion. Their contributions are labors of love, and their commitment to the cause of making Jewish-Russian literature available in English translation knows no comparison.

John D. Klier, who wrote the two-part outline of Jewish-Russian history for this anthology, generously responded to my questions. Vassili Schedrin kindly read and critiqued a draft of the general introduction.

Viktor Kelner and his associates from the Russian National Library in St. Petersburg kindly supplied copies of several texts unavailable in North America and furnished me with important bibliographical data.

In working on the anthology, I drew on numerous published and some unpublished sources and materials. The following encyclopedias and dictionaries proved invaluable: *Encyclopedia Judaica*, 16 vols. (Jerusalem, 1972); *Evreiskaia entsiklopediia*, 16 vols. (St. Petersburg, 1906–13); *Kratkaia evreiskaia entsiklopediia*, 10 vols. plus 3 supplements (Jerusalem, 1976–2001); *The New Standard Jewish Encyclopedia*, new revised edition (New York, 1992); *Russkie pisateli 1800–1917: biograficheskii slovar'* (4 vols. published to date; Moscow, 1989–1999).

Some of my translations and cotranslations featured in these pages previously appeared in periodicals. The complete information about these publications is found in the bibliographies in the back of each volume. Here I would like to thank these periodicals and their editors and staff: *Absinthe*, *Agni*, *Bee Museum*, *Commentary*, *Descant*, *Mantis*, *Nedge*, *Salmagundi*, and *Sí Señor*.

* * *

A number of colleagues, friends, and family members in America, Europe, and Israel have provided professional advice, information, logistical support, and hospitality at various stages of the making of this anthology. I gratefully acknowledge their professional courtesy, kindness, generosity, and friendship: Ivan Akhmetiev; Arna B.

Bronstein; Marco Caratozzolo; Dwayne E. Carpenter, M. J. Connolly; Richard D. Davies; Gennady Estraikh; Rainer Goldt; Andrzej Herczynski; Zsuzsa Hetényi; Vladimir Khazan; Yakov L. Klots; Radislav Lapushin; Joan Lasser, Maksim Mussel and Olga Mosalova; Alice Nakhimovsky; Ruth Rischin; Lisbeth Tarlow; Ekaterina Tsarapkina and Zakhar Smushkin; Andrew Sofer; Franck Salameh, Aleksandr Senderovich; Cynthia Simmons; Rifat Sonsino; Evgeny Soshkin; Evgeny Vitkovsky; Bella Ulanovskaya and Vladimir Novoselov; Andrew Von Hendy; Yekaterina Young.

* * *

I would like to dedicate this anthology to the memory of my paternal grandparents Bella Breydo and Pyotr (Peysakh) Shrayer and my maternal grandfather Arkady (Aron) Polyak. My maternal grandmother, Anna Studnits, is here in America to celebrate the publication of this book with me and the members of our family.

My wonderful parents, David Shrayer-Petrov and Emilia Shrayer, raised me as both a Jew and a Russian in the former Soviet Union. Living through almost nine hellish years as Jewish refuseniks, my parents made countless sacrifices to protect me from the persecution they both endured in 1979–87. I owe to them not only my life but also all the opportunities and freedoms I have enjoyed since we came to America in 1987. This anthology is theirs inasmuch as I am theirs.

* * *

My beloved wife Karen E. Lasser joined her life with mine in 2000, when this anthology was already under way. Believing in me and in the importance of this project, Karen has loved, sustained, and supported me for the past seven years. Without her I would never have been able to complete this anthology, and there are no words in Russian or English to express my love and gratitude.

Our daughter Mira Isabella Shrayer was born on February 9, 2006, as I worked on the copy-edited manuscript of this anthology. Mirusha is more perfect than anything I will ever write or edit.

M.D.S.

March 8, 2005–June 14, 2006
Chestnut Hill, MA

NOTE ON TRANSLITERATION, SPELLING OF NAMES, DATES, AND NOTES

A significantly modified (and we hope reader-friendly) version of the Library of Congress system for transliterating the Russian alphabet is used throughout the editor's general introduction, the editor's introductions to individual authors and their works, and the English translations of works. Exceptions are Russian words and geographical and personal names that have gained a common spelling in English, such as Ossip Dymow instead of "Osip Dymov," Maxim Gorky instead of "Maksim Gorky," Joseph Brodsky instead of "Iosif Brodsky," Osip Mandelstam instead of "Osip Mandelshtam," Vladimir Jabotinsky instead of "Vladimir Zhabotinsky," and so forth. Bibliographical references, including titles of Russian-language periodicals, in the main text, footnotes, and the bibliography of primary sources, are rendered in the standard Library of Congress system of transliterating the Russian alphabet, without diacritical marks.

We have adopted the transliteration system established by YIVO commonly used in English contexts for the spelling of all Yiddish words and expressions, including those using Cyrillic in the Russian originals. *The Yiddish Dictionary Sourcebook: A Transliterated Guide to the Yiddish Language* by Herman Galvin and Stan Tamarkin (Hoboken, NJ: Ktav, 1986) has been a useful resource for verifying spellings. Hebrew words and expressions have been transliterated to conform to English-language rather than Russian-language standards.

While the bibliography of primary sources lists transliterated Russian titles of all literary works, the editor's general introduction and the editor's introductions to individual authors and their works provide transliterated Russian titles or transliterated quotations from the Russian originals only where the editor has deemed it absolutely necessary. Otherwise, English translations, as literal as possible, are provided instead. Where a Russian periodical is mentioned for the first time in a particular entry, the English translation is followed by the Russian title in parentheses. In some cases, however, major Russian periodicals, such as *Pravda* or *Novy mir*, are known in English-language scholarship by their original names and have gained common spellings. These titles have not been translated.

All quotations from the Hebrew Bible are from *Tanakh: A New Translation of the Holy Scriptures According to the Traditional Hebrew Text* (Philadelphia: The Jewish Publication Society, 1985); all quotations from the New Testament are from *The Revised English Bible with Apocrypha* (Oxford/Cambridge: Oxford University Press/ Cambridge University Press, 1989).

Unless otherwise specified, the dates in the table of contents and at the end of each individual text refer to the completion of the work; in some instances, the date of first publication follows if it differs significantly from the date of completion. Unless otherwise specified, a parenthetical date in the editor's general introduction, the editor's introductions to the individual authors and their works, or the notes refers to the first publication of a work; in some cases, the date of completion precedes if it differs significantly from the date of first publication. Parenthetical dates for nonliterary works always refer to the date of publication. Where two dates are provided for an historical event, the first refers to the Julian calendar, used in Russia prior to 1918, and the second to the Gregorian calendar.

For information about the primary sources that have been consulted and the history of the publication of all the works included in the anthology, please see the bibliography of primary sources for volumes 1 and 2.

Unless otherwise indicated, all bibliographical notes, introductory essays and headnotes, explanatory notes, and bibliographies are by Maxim D. Shrayer.

NOTE ON HOW TO USE
THIS ANTHOLOGY

This anthology is simultaneously a Jewish-Russian literary history, an encyclopedic compendium, and a collection of individual literary works. One would certainly benefit from reading the anthology sequentially: first volume 1, then volume 2, in the order in which the more than 130 authors and their works appear in the table of contents. However, in addition to a chronological and consecutive reading, this anthology yields itself readily to selective reading in accordance with the reader's predilections, literary interests, or fascination with a specific author or a particular period of nineteenth- or twentieth-century Jewish and Russian (and Soviet) history. Individual sections of the anthology and works by particular authors can be read out of sequence or one at a time.

In addition to the editor's general introduction (in volume 1) and introductory essays preceding each of the eleven sections, the anthology includes a two-part concise survey of Jewish-Russian history written by the historian John D. Klier exclusively for this anthology. Readers less familiar with the main historical events that shaped the destinies of Russia's Jews would especially benefit from consulting Klier's outlines and bibliographies, found in the back of volumes 1 and 2.

A critical essay highlighting principal biographical events, artistic contributions, and place in literary history introduces each individual author. The introductory essays focus primarily on the writers' artistic careers, while their other professional and/or social occupations are referenced only insofar as they directly pertain to their literary works. Additionally, each work or selection of works by a given author is prefaced by a headnote containing information about the work's conception and publication and outlining some of the historical and literary contexts that might help the reader understand it better. Throughout the individual introductory essays and headnotes, efforts have been made to introduce a system of cross-references: every time another author or work featured in the anthology is mentioned or a major historical or literary event discussed elsewhere is evoked, a parenthetical reference points to its appropriate place or places in the anthology. This cross-referencing approach also emphasizes instances of dialogue among authors and of interplay among their texts. A comprehensive index of names, works, and selected subjects referenced in the anthology, located in the back of volume 2, should be especially helpful to readers who wish to trace these connections.

The editor's general introduction outlines the details of the periodization of Jewish-

Russian literature and the organizing principles behind the anthology's division into eleven separate sections. The chronologically and historically oriented organization of this anthology could never achieve perfect order and transparency simply because writers' lives do not fit too neatly within external boundaries, however carefully conceived. This is why the order of writers and works in the anthology and within its individual sections is based in part on the time of a work's creation and in part on its year of publication. The latter circumstance is especially valid for the post–World War II sections of the anthology. To those writers whose works span beyond the chronological confines of a given section, such as Genrikh Sapgir or Yan Satunovsky in volume 2, the editor has applied the notion of a critical mass of the composition dates (for example, the majority of the author's works were composed in the late 1960s) or publication dates (such as, the works were composed in the 1970s in the USSR but published in the 1990s in emigration).

Finally, given the limited available space and a desire to feature a diversity of authors and works and to illustrate each of the historical periods with adequate and representative works, hard choices had to be made in the final selection of the included texts. It is therefore important to keep in mind that length and number of works in and of themselves do not represent a value judgment of a given author's status and contribution. Furthermore, some longer prosaic or poetic texts yield themselves poorly to abridgment and had to be included almost in their entirety. Where a selected text could be included only in extracts, ellipsis points [. . .] within brackets indicate the location of the abridgment. In a few cases, the editor felt that longer introductions were necessary in order to do justice to the complexity of the critical debates surrounding the career of a particular Jewish-Russian author (Boris Slutsky, for example). Additionally, the historical and cultural backgrounds of several individual works called for longer headnotes (such as Lev Levanda's *Seething Times*). But only in four instances (Ilya Ehrenburg, Vladislav Khodasevich, Vassily Grossman, and Boris Slutsky) are the author's works represented in more than one section of the anthology. These four exceptions are the result of the special circumstances of these authors' lives and the indispensability of their works to the sections of the anthology in which they appear. In these four cases, separate headnotes introduce the works by the same author found in the different sections.

For the reader's convenience, both volumes contain an alphabetical index of writers included in the anthology, with volume and page numbers following each writer's name. Also found in the back of each volume are detailed bibliographies that reflect the history of each work's publication. In some cases, obtaining complete information on a given work's original publication, either in periodical or in book form, was an arduous task, and the editor and publisher would be grateful to readers for any additional information they might have. At the bottom of the last page of each individual author's selection, the reader will find information on copyright. In several cases we have been unable to obtain information on the present copyright owner, and we invite anyone with knowledge thereof to contact us.

In preparing this anthology, the editor was lucky to have worked with a team of excellent literary translators. A separate index of translators is found in the back of each volume and lists all contributions of each translator by author and volume. Faithfulness to the originals' meaning and design, precision in places bordering on literalism, and commitment to safeguarding the "strangeness" of the original texts' appearance and provenance have shaped the editor's formal expectations. This applies particularly to the efforts to rescue and preserve the originals' prosody and versification. In places going against the grain of the currently dominant practices in Anglo-American verse, the editor and the translators have sought to protect the originals' intactness, their structural accoutrements and formal vestments. At the same time, the editor has done his best to shield the translators' artistic autonomy. Where translators have introduced substitutions and accommodations, notably in some of the verse translations (such as one inspired British translator's reasonably justified avoidance of trochaic pentameter), they have made those choices not as acts of cultural violence but in the belief that art does stand to gain something in translation.

M.D.S.

EDITOR'S GENERAL INTRODUCTION

Toward a Canon of Jewish-Russian Literature

Maxim D. Shrayer

Jewish Culture in Diaspora and the Case of Russia

Dual Literary Identities

What are cultures measured by? Cultural contributions are difficult to quantify and even harder to qualify without a critical judgment in hand. In the case of verbal arts, and of literature specifically, various criteria of formal perfection and originality, place in literary history, and aspects of time, place, and milieu all contribute to the ways in which one regards a writer's contribution. In the case of Jewish culture in Diaspora, and specifically of Jewish writing created in non-Jewish languages adopted by Jews, the reckoning of a writer's status is further riddled by a set of powerful contrapositions. Above all else, there is the duality of a writer's own identity—both Jewish and German (Heinrich Heine) or French (Marcel Proust) or Russian (Isaac Babel) or Polish (Julian Tuwim) or Hungarian (Imre Kertész) or Brazilian (Clarice Lispector) or Canadian (Mordechai Richler) or American (Bernard Malamud). Then there is the dividedly redoubled perspective of a Diasporic Jew: both an in-looking outsider and an out-looking insider.[1] And there is the language of writing itself, not always one of

---

1. In the context of Jewish-Russian history and culture, the juxtaposition between a "divided" and a "redoubled" identity goes back to the writings of the critic and polemicist Iosif Bikerman (1867–1941?42?), who stated in 1910, on the pages of the St. Petersburg magazine *Jewish World* (*Evreiskii mir*): "Not dividedness [*razdvoennost'*] but redoubledness [*udvoennost'*]"; quoted in Shimon Markish, *Babel' i drugie*, 2nd ed., 186 (Moscow and Jerusalem: Personal'naia tvorcheskaia masterskaia "Mikhail Shchigol'," 1997). I am increasingly aware of the body of scholarship, most notably Caryn Aviv and David Shneer's *New Jews: The End of the Jewish Diaspora* (New York: New York University Press, 2005), which argues that one is no longer justified to speak of the Jewish Diaspora—and, by implication, of the Jewish culture in Diaspora. Such controversial arguments are bound to challenge future scholars of Jewish-Russian literature to rethink some of their concepts and precepts.

the writer's native setting, not necessarily one in which a writer spoke to his or her own parents or non-Jewish childhood friends, but in some cases a second or third language—acquired, mastered, and made one's own in a flight from home.

Evgeny Shklyar (1894–1942), a Jewish-Russian poet and a Lithuanian patriot who translated into Russian the text of the Lithuanian national anthem and was murdered in a Nazi concentration camp outside Kaunas, wrote in the poem "Where's Home?" (1925):

> . . . In Judaism fierce, hidden strengths appear
> To nurture twice exile's flowers
> And deep within the heart's most buried bowers
> To pick amongst them and to make it clear
> You're going either where all's alien but dear
> Or where the majestic past regales the hours . . .[2]

(Trans. Maxim D. Shrayer and Andrew Von Hendy)

The poem, which appears in the first volume of this anthology, was composed at a time when dreams of a Jewish state were becoming much more than a poet's parable. The land "where all's alien but dear" is, of course, Shklyar's native Pale of Settlement, while the place where "the majestic past regales the hours" is Shklyar's vision of Israel. The duality of a Diasporic Jew's dividedly redoubled loyalties is both political-ideological and cultural-linguistic. In the poem's final line, envisioning his own life as a Jewish-Russian poet and translator of Lithuanian poets into Russian come to Israel to hear children "greet [him] with words of welcome in *ivrit*," Shklyar employs the italicized (and transliterated) Hebrew word for the ancient Jewish tongue. The poet's word choice in the final, rhyming position also underscores the duality of his identity: linguistically and culturally at home in the east European abode where "all's alien but dear" and spiritually, if symbolically, traveling to the land of Israel, "where the majestic past regales the hours," and yet where Shklyar's Jewish-Russian poet is culturally a foreigner.

"Exile" in Shklyar's poem is the Diaspora, where Jews have added Hebrew-Farsi, Ladino, and Yiddish to their Hebrew, while also translating their identities, albeit never fully or completely (but is translation ever?), into Arabic, Spanish, Italian, French, German, English, Polish, Russian, and many other languages spoken in the places of their dispersion. But Shklyar's "exile" is also the Jewish poet's exile from his literary home, his Russian tongue, and this duality renders nearly meaningless debates about the legitimacy of "Jewish" literatures in "non-Jewish" languages.

In the late nineteenth and the twentieth century, the torrents of history, coupled with personal artistic ambitions, thrust Jewish writers across the globe in numbers far greater than ever before. In their adopted countries, some continued to cultivate writing only in their native non-Jewish languages, while others became bilingual or multilingual authors. Using the Jewish languages to define the "religion," "identity," or

---

2. Hereinafter, unless indicated otherwise, all translations from the Russian are my own.

"nationality" of a Jewish writer's work becomes especially knotty in the twentieth century, when a critical mass of the Jewish population shifted from the use of Yiddish to the use of modern European languages or Modern Hebrew. The Shoah then completed the undoing of Yiddish as the transnational language of Ashkenazic Jews, the undoing that the rigors of modernization, acculturation, and integration had been performing both in the USSR and in the West for almost a century.[3]

"All writers immigrate to their art and stay therein," stated the Russian-American writer Vladimir Nabokov (1899–1977) soon after having fled to America from war-stricken Europe with his Jewish wife and son aboard a ship chartered by a Jewish refugee agency. One is tempted to ask where Jewish writers immigrate, whence they emigrate, and where they stay. One also wonders how the dualities of the Jewish writers' selves change in their travels across time and culture, and, finally, what these Jewish writers share in their comings and goings. A Jewish poetics, perhaps? Some of the answers to these questions lie in the many nineteenth- and twentieth-century works gathered in this anthology of Jewish-Russian literature.

In the two centuries that followed the spread of the Haskalah (Jewish Enlightenment) in the late eighteenth century, linguistic self-expression in non-Jewish languages was central to the Jewish experience and Jewish survival in Diaspora. The experience of working on this anthology has taught me that, especially in the nineteenth and twentieth centuries, Jewish literary culture created in non-Jewish languages increasingly served as one of the main receptacles into which the traditions of Jewish spirituality were poured. Varieties of Jewish self-awareness are channeled and transmitted through what is called, for lack of a better term, "secular literature." Quite often, while an uninformed reading of a Jewish text created and published in the literary mainstream reveals only superficially Jewish references, a rereading shows how much of the Judaic heritage is captured and preserved in its pages. A classic example of such a dual, non-Jewish and Jewish, model of (re)reading is Isaac Babel's novel-length cycle of stories *Red Cavalry* (first book edition 1926). A recent example is Saul Bellow's novel *Ravelstein* (2000), where a dying Jewish-American gay neoconservative intellectual finds himself truly at home only in one book, *The Book*, if in any place at all.

As I think of the ways Jewish literature transgresses and transcends the boundaries of history, politics, and culture, I am reminded of an essay–testament by one of the

---

3. A few examples will suffice: Abraham Cahan, born outside Vilna in 1860, died in 1951 in New York; wrote in Yiddish and English; Gertrude Stein, born in Allegheny, Pennsylvania, in 1874, died in Paris in 1946, wrote in English; Stefan Zweig, born in 1881 in Vienna, died by his own hand in 1942 in Petrópolis, Brazil, wrote in German; Rahel, born Rahel Bluwstein in 1890 in Saratov, died in Tel Aviv in 1931, wrote in Russian but mainly in Hebrew; Paul Celan, born Paul Antschel in 1920 in Czernowitz (then Romania, now Ukraine), a suicide in Paris in 1970, wrote in German; Joseph Brodsky, born in 1940 in Leningrad (now St. Petersburg), died in 1996 in New York, wrote in Russian and English.

protagonists of this anthology, Lev Levanda (1835–1888). Titled "On Assimilation," Levanda's polemical essay appeared in the St. Petersburg Russian-language *Weekly Chronicle of Sunrise* (*Nedel'naia khronika Voskhoda*) in 1885. "The Jewish nationality, that is, the universal doctrine known as Judaism, does not particularly need a strictly assigned territory: its territory is the entire wide world!" wrote Levanda. ". . . Jews do not consider themselves a living people; they consider themselves a living *nation* that lives and must live, namely, a *Jewish* nation, that is, a doctrine, an idea. As an *idea*, Judaism does not necessitate a particular territory. . . ." By implication, as it embodies aspects of Jewish spiritual life both directly and obliquely, Jewish literature is perhaps also not bound to a particular local philological terrain and retains its Jewishness in translation. While translation from a non-Jewish language into a Jewish one, or into another non-Jewish language, may either enhance or obscure a writer's subterranean Judaic references, Jewish literary culture itself is both national and transnational. One of the reasons to study Jewish literature is that it preserves and reveals aspects of the Jewish condition that a Jewish religious mind would commonly seek elsewhere and a non-Jewish mind might not at all be conscious of during the act of reading. Among the letters between the Russian poet and thinker Vyacheslav Ivanov (1866–1949) and the Jewish-Russian philosopher of culture Mikhail Gershenzon (1869–1925), gathered in *Correspondence from Two Corners* (1920; published 1921), one of the most tragic of Gershenzon's letters underscored a survival of Jewish memory in the works that acculturated Jews address to the cultural mainstream: "How can I forget my native Jewish Kishinev of the spring of 1903!" Gershenzon cried out to his non-Jewish interlocutor. "Perhaps this Kishinev is outside of Russian history, perhaps the Krushevans are outside the history of Russian society [the journalist Pavel Krushevan incited anti-Jewish violence in the Kishinev pogrom], but they live on in my memory, and I am their judge. . . . And my people is outside history, and its history is outside the schemas of the world historians—but I know the price of all these historical constructs by writers who do not wish to know the truth."

In Russia

This anthology tests our conception of Jewish literature in Diaspora on its most extreme case: the case of Russia and the former USSR. In *Jewry and the Christian Question,* written in 1884, three years after Fyodor Dostoevsky's death, the Russian religious philosopher Vladimir Solovyov (1853–1900) posited three main questions about the interrelation between Christianity, and specifically Russian Orthodoxy, and Judaism. Solovyov's questions also apply to the survival of Jewish identity and culture in Russia:

    1. Why was Christ a Jew, and why is the stepping-stone of the universal church taken from the House of Israel?
    2. Why did the majority of Israel not recognize its Messiah, why did the Old Testament church not dissolve into the New Testament church, and why do the majority of the Jews prefer to be completely without a temple rather than join the Christian temple?

3. Why, finally, and for what purpose was the most solid (in the religious aspect) part of Jewry moved to Russia and Poland, placed at the boundary of the Graeco-Slavic and Latin-Slavic worlds?

Solovyov, who on his deathbed prayed in Hebrew for the Jewish people, did not live to see the pogroms of 1905, the 1917 revolutions and the ensuing civil war, the destruction of traditional Jewish life during the first Soviet decades, and the horrors of the Shoah. With slight adjustments, Solovyov's fundamental questions still hold true: Why, despite all the misfortunes and pressures, have the Jews of the Russian Empire and the Soviet Union survived without losing their selfhood, even though so many have lost their religion and living ties to Yiddish and Hebrew? One of the most fascinating cultural paradoxes of Russian Jewry is that, against all the historical odds, even during the post-Shoah Soviet decades, it continued to nurture its dual sense of self, both Jewish and Russian, and Russian letters became its principal outlet for articulating this duality.

Russia was the last European nation to gain—through western expansion—a large Jewish minority and also the last to free its Jews of oppressive legal restrictions. Since the 1860s the Jewish question has occupied a prominent place in Russian—and later Soviet —history. The Jewish question in Russia involved the mostly prejudicial attitudes of both the Russian government and the general population toward the Jews but also the attempts of the Jewish community to preserve its spiritual and cultural identity as a minority without a territory of its own. The double bind of anti-Jewish attitudes and policies during the tsarist era presented a contradiction: on the one hand, the Russians expected the Jews to assimilate if not convert to Christianity; on the other, fearful of a growing Jewish presence, the Russians prevented the Jews from integrating into Russian life by instituting restrictions and not discouraging popular antisemitic sentiments.

By the early twentieth century, the Russian Empire had the highest concentration of Jews in the world: in 1897, about 5.2 million (about 47 percent of the world's Jewish population), and in 1914, at the beginning of World War I, still about 5.5 million, including Poland's 2 million (about 41 percent of the world's Jewish population). According to the same census of 1897, 24.6 percent of Jews in the Russian Empire could read and write in Russian, but only 1 percent considered Russian their mother tongue. In growing numbers, the nonemancipated Jews strove to enter the Russian social and cultural mainstream. Anton Chekhov (1860–1904), an astute student of the Jewish question, remarked as he sketched a southern provincial town in "My Life" (1896) that "only Jewish adolescents frequented the local . . . libraries." In the story "Ionych" (1898), Chekhov stressed again that. ". . . the people in S. read very little, and at the local library they said that if it hadn't been for unmarried ladies and young Jews, one might as well close the library." The Jewish question certainly preoccupied the creator of *Ivanov* (1887), "Steppe" (1888), and "Rothschild's Fiddle" (1894), and during his final years in Yalta, Chekhov was likely to hear from his acquaintances among the Jewish-Russian intelligentsia about the mesmeric and polarizing impacts of both Zionism and Marxism.

Russia offers the student of Jewish literature and culture a challenging case study of contrasting attitudes, ranging from philosemitic dreams of a harmonious fusion to antisemitic fabrications and genocidal scenarios. To measure the enormity of the religious, historical, and cultural baggage that the Jews brought to Russian letters would mean much more than merely to examine Jewish history through the prism of Russian literature created by Jews. And to state, in keeping with the genre of anthology introductions, that the Jews have made a major contribution to Russian literature would be to commit a necessary truism. Of the four Russian writers to have been awarded the Nobel Prize in literature, two were born Jewish: Boris Pasternak, whom the Soviet authorities forced to turn down the prize in 1958; and Joseph Brodsky, a Russian poet and American essayist banished from the USSR, who received the prize in 1987. For a Jew in Russia or the Soviet Union, the act of becoming a Russian writer often amounted to an act of identity revamping. In some cases, a Jewish-Russian writer's gravitation to Christianity and abnegation of his or her Jewish self completed the process of becoming Russian (e.g., Boris Pasternak [1890–1960]). In other cases, deeply devotional Judaic thinking (Matvey Royzman [1896–1973]) or a militantly Zionist worldview (Vladimir [Ze′ev] Jabotinsky [1880–1940]) was combined with an acute aesthetic sense of one's Russianness. Jewry gave Russia its arguably most European poet of modernity, Osip Mandelstam (1891–1938); its most talented and controversial mythologists of the Revolution and the civil war, Isaac Babel (1894–1940) in prose and Eduard Bagritsky (1895–1934) in poetry; its mightiest voice of the people's resistance during the years of the Nazi invasion, Ilya Ehrenburg (1891–1967); its savviest herald of the Thaw, Boris Slutsky (1919–1986); the greatest underground keeper of avant-garde freedom in the late Soviet era, Genrikh Sapgir (1928–1999); and even Russia's most admired literary comedian of the late Soviet decades, Mikhail Zhvanetsky (b. 1934). And Jewry also gave Russia many distinguished Jewish-Russian authors, such as Mark Aldanov (1886–1957), Dovid Knut (1900–1955), and Friedrich Gorenstein (1923–2002), who later became exiles and émigrés while remaining Russian writers. Others yet, like Elsa Triolet (1896–1970), had started in Russian but in exile switched to writing in western languages. By writing in Russian, a Jew becomes a Russian writer.[4] But to what degree does he or she also remain a Jewish writer? This anthology investigates the dilemma of cultural duality by attempting a story, a history—and an encyclopedic overview—of Jewish-Russian literature.

History, Periodization, and the Scope of the Anthology

The first anthology of its kind, *An Anthology of Jewish-Russian Literature: Two Centuries of Dual Identity in Prose and Poetry* outlines the canon of Russian-language writings by Jewish authors and introduces to the western reader a major

---

4. I am indebted to Alice Nakhimovsky's observations about Jewish-Russian writers made in connection with the career of David Aizman, whose work is featured in this anthology. See Alice Stone-Nakhimovsky, "Encounters: Russians and Jews in the Short Stories of David Aizman," *Cahiers du monde russe et soviétique* 26, no. 2 (April–June 1985): 175–84. I previously discussed the subject of a Jew becoming a Russian (and/or Soviet) writer in *Russian Poet/Soviet Jew: The Legacy of Eduard Bagritskii* (Lanham, MD: Rowman and Littlefield, 2000).

branch of Jewish creativity, until now largely unavailable in translation.[5] Exemplary works of poetry and creative prose, both fiction and nonfiction, by more than 130 authors are featured here, some in their entirety, others in an abridged form or in the form of representative excerpts. The anthology includes no works of drama because drama yields itself very poorly to excerpting and anthologizing. Much to the editor's regret, even such major works of Jewish-Russian theater as Nikolay Minsky's *The Siege of Tulchin* (1888), Isaac Babel's *Sunset* (1928), and Friedrich Gorenstein's *Berdichev* (1975) do not appear in these two volumes. (An anthology of Jewish-Russian theater is much needed.)

Comments are in order about the way historical considerations have affected the structure of this anthology. John D. Klier's two-part concise overview of Jewish-Russian history, written for this anthology, is found in the back of these two volumes. Klier highlights the main historical developments from the eighteenth century to the present, and there is no need to summarize them here. For purposes of this

---

5. The following extensive Russian-language anthologies published in the 1970s–90s have featured Jewish motifs in the works of both Jewish and non-Jewish Russian-language poets: Aleksandr Donat, ed., *Neopalimaia kupina. Evreiskie siuzhety v russkoi poezii. Antologiia* (New York: New York University Press, 1973); Tamar Dolzhanskaia, ed., *Na odnoi volne. Evreiskie motivy v russkoi poezii* (Tel Aviv: Biblioteka "Aliia," 1974); Ada Kolganova, ed., *Menora. Evreiskie motivy v russkoi poezii* (Moscow: Evreiskii universitet v Moskve; Jerusalem: Gesharim, 1993); Mikhail Grozovskii, comp., Evgenii Vitkovskii, ed., *Svet dvuedinyi. Evrei i Rossiia v sovremennoi poezii* (Moscow: AO "KhGS," 1996). Kuzminsky's and Kovalev's monumental anthology includes works by a number of Jewish-Russian poets: Konstantin K. Kuzminsky and Gregory L. Kovalev, eds., *The Blue Lagoon Anthology of Modern Russian Poetry* [in Russian], 5 vols. in 9 [of the projected but suspended 13] (Newtonville, MA: Oriental Research Partners, 1980–86). A recent anthology has collected works by Russian-Israeli authors of the 1990s: Margarita Shklovskaia, ed., *Orientatsiia na mestnosti. Russko-izrail'skaia literatura 90-kh godov. Antologiia* (Jerusalem: Assotsiatsiia po izucheniiu evreiskikh obshchin/ "Biblioteka 'Aliia,'" 2001). At various stages of the making of this anthology, the editor also took inspiration, both positive and negative, from the following anthologies of Jewish writing: Harold U. Ribalow, ed., *A Treasury of American Jewish Stories* (New York: Thomas Yoseloff, 1958); Irving Howe and Eliezer Greenberg, eds., *A Treasury of Yiddish Poetry* (New York: Holt, Rinehart and Winston, 1969); Abraham Chapman, ed., *Jewish American Literature: An Anthology of Fiction, Poetry, Autobiography, and Criticism* (New York: New American Library, 1974); T. Carmi, ed. and trans., *The Penguin Book of Hebrew Verse* (Harmondsworth: Penguin, 1981); Homutal Bar-Yosef, Zoia Kopelman, eds., *Antologiia ivritskoi literatury. Evreiskaia literatura XIX–XX vekov v russkikh perevodakh* (Moscow: Rossiiskii gosudarstvennyi gumanitarnyi universitet, 2000); Miriyam Glazer, ed., *Dreaming the Actual: Contemporary Fiction and Poetry by Israeli Women Writers* (Albany: State University of New York Press, 2000); Jules Chametzky, John Felstiner, Hilene Flanzbaum, and Kathryn Hellerstein, eds., *Jewish American Literature: A Norton Anthology* (New York: W.W. Norton, 2001); Joachim Neugroschel, ed. and trans., *No Star Too Beautiful: Yiddish Stories from 1392 to the Present* (New York: W.W. Norton, 2002); Ken Frieden, ed., *Classic Yiddish Stories of S.Y. Abramovitsh, Sholem Aleichem, and I.L. Peretz* (Syracuse, NY: Syracuse University Press, 2004).

discussion, it will suffice to say that the lower historical boundary, 1801, is the year Alexander I ascended the Russian throne; the upper boundary, 2001, exactly two hundred years later, was the first year of Vladimir Putin's presidency after the Russian election of 2000. Within the glare of two hundred years, other historical boundaries serve as historical demarcation points. Some are major events of Russian and world history: 1917, the year of two revolutions; 1939, the beginning of World War II; 1953, Stalin's death and the beginning of the Thaw; 1964, the ousting of Khrushchev in a Kremlin coup and the beginning of Brezhnev's rule; 1991, the end of the Soviet Union. Other boundaries bear particular significance to Jewish-Russian history: 1840, the year of the imperial ukase establishing, as part of Nicholas's reforms of Russia's Jewish community, "The Committee to Develop Measures for the Fundamental Transformation of the Jews"; 1881, the beginning of the first wave of ferocious pogroms following Alexander II's assassination; 1902, the year preceding the Kishinev pogrom and summoning the start of the second wave of pogroms; 1967, the Six-Day War and the breaking off of diplomatic relations with Israel by the USSR. In three cases, 1881, 1917, and 1953, the boundaries are equally important to Russian and Jewish history and make for particularly suitable places to close one section of the anthology and open the next one. The aftermath of the Shoah and Stalin's death in 1953 seemed the most logical place to divide the anthology into two volumes of nearly equal length.

While historically based, the structure of the anthology also presents the major artistic periods and trends in Jewish-Russian literature. In the brief introductory essays placed before each individual section of the anthology, I will focus on the various intersections of historical events and aesthetic developments. In doing so, both in the introductory essays and here, I will draw examples mainly from the authors and works featured in the anthology's two volumes.

Debating Jewish-Russian Literature

The Principal Issues

This anthology has been in the making for a period of almost eight years. Prior to conducting the final selection of the materials, I had read and considered works by as many as 300 authors. To this day, with some questions still unanswered, I fundamentally agree with Alice Nakhimovsky's definition of a Jewish-Russian writer as formulated in her *Russian-Jewish Literature and Identity* (1992): "any Russian-language writer of Jewish origin for whom the question of Jewish identity is, on some level, compelling." Through example and commentary, this anthology seeks to present the many "levels" of the figuration of Jewishness in the diverse texts collected in its pages. Throughout this presentation, the anthology highlights the dual identities of Jewish-Russian writers writing in the nineteenth and twentieth centuries.

My term of choice is "Jewish-Russian literature," by close analogy with such terms (and the respective phenomena they describe) as African-American literature, French-Canadian literature, and Jewish-American literature. I prefer the term "Jewish-Russian literature" to "Russian-Jewish literature" or others because it strikes me as the most direct and transparent one: the first adjective determines the literature's distinguishing aspect (Jewishness) and the second the country, language, or culture with which this literature is transparently identified by choice, default, or proxy.[6] Later in this introduction, in the section "The Texture of Jewishness" and elsewhere,[7] I will have more to say about my choice of the term "Jewish-Russian literature."

I came to this project with a specialist's avid interest in the possibility of elaborating a "Jewish poetics." I also approached this anthology with a generalist's skepticism toward the idea that seemingly universal and all-encompassing laws of artistic creation vary for the artistic imaginations of the representatives of the different ethnic, national, and religious groups. Simply put, my working hypothesis rested on three premises: first, that at different stages Jewish-Russian writers displayed varying types of duality; second, that Jewish-Russian writers are by nature at least bicultural; and third, that any noninclusive and reductive approach to the selection of material is likely to result in twofold cultural violence. My ensuing working method has been to steer clear of any advance generalizations about the canon of Jewish-Russian literature. Rather, the canon wrote itself as I gradually selected the materials while also parsing an approach to Jewish writing in Diaspora, an approach that invites complexity and evades categorization.

The results of my investigation are in the texts themselves—and to some extent in my introductions and headnotes to the sections of this anthology and the individual Jewish-Russian authors and their works included here. Before outlining what I have learned through the process of working on this project, I find it necessary to offer an overview of the critical discussions that have surrounded Jewish-Russian literature from the 1880s–1900s, when it came into the larger public's eye, to the present. From the very beginning, the debates about Jewish-Russian literature have focused on three main issues: the definition and criteria of Jewish-Russian literature; the validity of the

---

6. In the introduction and throughout the entire anthology, the term "Jewish-Russian literature" will be used, except in those cases where I quote other critics and authors who have used a different term.

7. I am certainly not the first author to use the term "the texture of Jewishness," and I do not wish to claim having invented it. A last-minute Google search, conducted as this anthology was going through copyediting, revealed one reference, in an essay by the Jewish-American writer Rebecca Goldstein. "I have found," Goldstein wrote in 1997 in the pages of *Tikkun*, "like several others linked in this suggested revival of Jewish-American letters, that my Jewish dreams, at least sometimes, take me backward in time, into a past in which the texture of Jewishness was more richly felt"; see Rebecca Goldstein, "Against Logic: Jewish Author's Reflection on Her Work and Jewish Literature," *Tikkun* (November–December 1997); http://www.trincoll.edu/~rgoldste/Tikkun_Against_logic.htm, 8 June 2005.

very notion of Jewish-Russian literature; and its artistic merits relative to the Russian literary mainstream, on the one hand, and to Yiddish and Hebrew writing, on the other. In this overview (and in the selective bibliography that concludes this general introduction), I seek to present both a diversity of critical approaches to Jewish-Russian literature and a history of their formulation and publication.

The Tsarist-Era Debates

The first major statement on Jewish-Russian literature belonged to the journalist and prose writer Mikhail N. Lazarev (1851–1912, also known under the pen name Optimist). Titled "The Goals and Significance of Russian-Jewish Belles Lettres," Lazarev's two-part "sketch" appeared in 1885 in the St. Petersburg Jewish-Russian magazine *Sunrise* (*Voskhod*; for information on the history of Jewish-Russian periodicals, see the editor's introduction to the section "Gaining a Voice: 1840–1881" in volume 1). Lazarev argued that "[Russia's Jews] simultaneously experienced the feeling of being both Russians and foreigners, were interested in all-Russian political and social concerns and, at the same time, in living their own uniquely Jewish life. This dividedness [*razdvoennost'*] in the life of Russia's Jews was inevitably going to be reflected in their literature." Writing of the "gap"—huge, "in their eyes"—that the early writers had to fill by writing about the Jew in the Russian language, Lazarev characterized this literature: "the literature of Russian Jews, like their life, is strange and abnormal," a literature of a "transitional time in the life of Russian Jewry." Regarding Jewish-Russian belles lettres as a kind of barometer of the prevalent sentiments of the Jewish intelligentsia in Russia, Lazarev argued that the early writers found themselves in the nearly impossible predicament of trying to be artists faithful to truth and reality and to be defenders of their fellow Jews. The polemical and tendentious thrust of early Jewish-Russian literature, Lazarev claimed, stifled the development of great prose while stimulating the growth of lyrical poetry.

The issues fleshed out by Lazarev continued to be debated in the Jewish-Russian press for the next two decades before bursting into the Russian mainstream in the 1900s. The so-called "debates of 1908" deserve special attention because their participants included both renowned Russian critics and prominent Jewish thinkers and activists, several of them featured in this anthology. (Coincidentally or not, the 1908 debates about Jewish-Russian literature occurred during the same year as the Czernowitz Conference, whose participants produced an authoritative statement on Yiddish as a Jewish national language.) In January 1908, Korney Chukovsky (1882–1969), then a leading Russian book critic and subsequently a major Soviet children's author, published the essay "Jews and Russian Literature" in the St. Petersburg newspaper *Free Thoughts* (*Svobodnye mysli*). Chukovsky's essay was reprinted at least twice in 1908, an abridged version appearing in the Jewish-Russian review *Dawn* (*Rassvet*, known as *Dawn* "3"). "[The Jew] is so close to Russian literature," Chukovsky wrote, "and yet he has not created in it any eternal values. This is almost a mystery:

Tolstoy, Turgenev, Dostoevsky, Pisemsky, Leskov, Andreev—among them there is not one Jew." Speaking admiringly of what he knew, in Russian translation, of Hayyim Nahman Bialik's (Hebrew) poetry and Sholem Aleichem's (Yiddish) fiction, Chukovsky asserted with deep regret that the "heirs of David's Psalms" played "auxiliary roles" in Russian literature: not the "birth mother" but the "midwife." Apparently failing to see that Jewish literature in Diaspora is both multilingual and multicultural, Chukovsky maintained that the "national spirit" cannot be expressed except in the "national language." His essay stirred up a polemic, extending even to the pages of the right-wing Russian press. The status of Jewish-Russian literature was hotly debated by Jewish-Russian authors and critics, among them S. An-sky and N.A. Tan (Bogoraz). The person to publish the most important response to Chukovsky was none other than Vladimir Jabotinsky. Sharing Chukovsky's skepticism about the Jewish contribution to Russian literature, Jabotinsky, in his feuilletonistic essay "On the Jews in Russian Literature," took issue with Chukovsky's view of what determines the "nationality" of literature. "In our complex times," Jabotinsky wrote, "the 'nationality' of a literary work is determined not nearly by the language alone in which it is written. . . . A decisive factor is not the language, and . . . not even the author's origins, nor even the story; the decisive factor is the *disposition* [*nastroenie*] of the author—*for whom* he writes, *to whom* he addresses his works, *whose* spiritual aspirations he has in mind when creating his works." Thus, Jabotinsky insisted on figuring both the Jewish-Russian author's intent and his or her intended audience into a critical judgment of his or her works. In 1985, perceptively reexamining the legacy of the debates of 1908, the émigré scholar Ilya Serman, husband of the writer Ruth Zernova, who is included in this anthology, commented that the original critics of Jewish-Russian literature would have been better served by "proceeding from the literature itself, and not from schemas, however thoughtful and persuasive."

The first encyclopedic assessment of Jewish-Russian literature was written, emblematically, by one of the founders of the New Hebrew poetry, Saul Tchernichovsky [Chernikhovskii] (1875–1943). Tchernichovsky's article in the sixteen-volume Russian-language *Jewish Encyclopedia* (*Evreiskaia entsiklopediia*), published in St. Petersburg in 1908–13, in which a number of Jewish-Russian, Hebrew, and Yiddish authors took part, echoed Lazarev's largely unenthusiastic view of Jewish-Russian prose: "in Russian-Jewish literature, there is not a single truly artistic work." Like Lazarev, Tchernichovsky also asserted that "while devoting his works to his people, the Jew who was a writer [*evrei-pisatel'*] never forgot that his reader lived not only in [a Jewish] environment but also in the surrounding society, and because of this he weighed his every word out of a fear that he would be misunderstood; not infrequently he was given to apologetic rage, owing to which he deprived himself of objectivity in creative writing and became tendentious." Only when Jewish-Russian literature repudiated tendentiousness, Tchernichovsky argued, when it "believed in the need for its existence as an expression of the spiritual life of an independent group, which has a right to its independent existence . . . [did it] reach its highest artistic importance." It seems clear that the skepticism and low assessments stemmed mainly from the fact that many of the critics, both Jewish and non-Jewish, measured the emerging Jewish-Russian writers of the 1860s–1900s by the highest standards, looking for and not finding, as it were, the Jewish Tolstoys and Dostoevskys. At the same time, they refused to characterize as *Jewish* those several notable writers of Jewish origin who, like Nikolay Minsky (1855–1937), had entered the Russian cultural mainstream in the 1880s, 1890s, and early 1900s.

The Early Soviet Years

By the time Vasily Lvov-Rogachevsky (1874–1930), a non-Jewish critic of Marxist convictions, embarked on the first book about Jewish-Russian writers, a number of them had made themselves known to the Russian public during the Silver Age of Russian culture. Lvov-Rogachevsky started his book during World War I and completed it after the 1917 revolutions. Published in 1922 in Moscow, *Russian-Jewish Literature* was a thematic and chronological survey, from the 1800s to the 1910s, from Leyba Nevakhovich to Andrey Sobol. Lvov-Rogachevsky treated the works by Jewish-Russian authors mainly in light of history and with a shallow knowledge of the Jewish background, but his book was a critical milestone. In some respects, Lvov-Rogachevsky's argument echoed Jabotinsky's: "The nationality of a literary work is determined not by the language in which it was brought to life but the author's dominant mood, his commitment to a particular nation, the affinity of the author's soul with the soul of his native people, with its culture, its capturing of the past, the present, and the future of this people; it is determined by [his] response to the question of whom he works for and whose national interests he defends." Lvov-Rogachevsky's optimism heralded the arrival on the early Soviet literary scene of Jewish-Russian writers of the first magnitude (see the section "Revolution and Betrayal: 1917–1939" in volume 1): "The thrice-shackled people has created a literature in which its shackles manifest themselves too much. A free people in a free land will have new bards who will sing new songs. . . . And this will happen. And this cannot but happen."

The next major critical statement appeared, not surprisingly, as a polemical response to Lvov-Rogachevsky's book. In 1923, critic and translator Arkady Gornfeld (1867–1941) contributed "Russian Letters and Jewish Creativity" to the Petrograd-based *Jewish Almanac* (*Evreiskii al'manakh*). Here Gornfeld criticized Lvov-Rogachevsky for focusing on the contribution of Jewish-Russian writers to the Jewish social consciousness, not to Russian literature. Gornfeld argued that Jewish contributions to Russian culture ought to be measured by their cultural self-worth rather than by their love and enthusiasm, as the philosemitic Russian critics often did, some patronizingly. Gornfeld went on to make a crucial if debatable point that "a given literature is an *otherbeing* [*inobytie*] of a given language; that national literature is a carrier and a creation of a national tradition." Gornfeld consequently advanced a distinction between the "belonging" of Jewish authors to Jewry and their works in non-Jewish languages to the literatures in those languages: "Meïr Aron Goldschmidt [1819–1887],

Catulle Mendes [1841–1909], and Bernhard Kellermann [1879–1951] belong to Jewry, and Jewry has a right to speak of their creations in its cultural history, but the writings of Goldschmidt belong to Danish literature, the poems of the Parnassian Mendes, to French, Kellermann's novels, to German." Gornfeld's ideas colored his assessment of Jewish-Russian writers:

> While they are not too significant . . . they have said in Russian literature what without them no one would have said. They came from the Russian (more from the semi-Russian) periphery, from an alien cultural world; in their families they still spoke Yiddish; they brought with them their memories, their skills, their linguistic irregularities and peculiarities, their world vision, and their images. In an alien tongue, which through school and peers, through literature and the press became for them their native tongue, they certainly could not have been independent; on the contrary, the alien literary tradition remained for them an unsurmounted law. . . . They were themselves, and thus, being Russian writers, they were Jews. They introduced novelty into the Russian literary language; this novelty may horrify the purists and infuriate nationalists, but it is more enduring than the horror and the fury.

Notes of eulogizing may be heard in Gornfeld's essay, as though he thought that the history of Jewish-Russian literature had already ended. In 1922 Iosif Kleinman and Boris Kaufman, the future coeditors of the landmark 1923 collective *Jewish Almanac*, tried to jump-start the Jewish-Russian press in Petrograd on the platform that "there is a practical need to restore the Russian-Jewish press . . . [since], besides the national and popular press [in Yiddish], we should continue the work for Jewry in the Russian language." Kleinman's and Kaufman's monthly magazine, *The Jewish Messenger (Evreiskii vestnik)*, failed after having released seven issues. By the early 1930s, discussions of Jewish-Russian literature had disappeared from the pages of Soviet publications. Hebrew had been suppressed, while Yiddish was (temporarily) given the go-ahead as the "national" language of Soviet Jews. With astonishing speed Jewish-Russian literature was reduced to a nonentity in the Soviet critical and academic discourse of the late 1920s and early 1930s as literary production itself became a part of the government apparatus on the eve of the First Congress of Soviet Writers (1934). Only a writer working in Yiddish would be officially recognized as a "Jewish writer" (*evreiskii pisatel'*); Jews writing in Russian could only be "Russian writers" (I discuss this distinction in the editor's introduction to the section "Revolution and Betrayal, 1917–1939" in volume 1). Some of the early Soviet students of Jewish-Russian literature did not anticipate that the official days of Jewish-Russian writing were numbered, as becomes apparent when one considers the essay by Iosif Kleinman "Jews in the Newest Russian Literature," published in Moscow in 1928. After surveying the previous debates, from Lazarev all the way to Gornfeld, Kleinman turned to the Jewish-Russian writers who had gained acclaim in the 1920s. Kleinman echoed Lvov-Rogachevsky in his enthusiasm and faith in the future of Jewish artistic expression in the Russian language:

> many pages of [Isaac] Babel, and even in places [Ilya] Ehrenburg, and even Iosif Utkin, must be perceived by us and are perceived as an enrichment of Russian-Jewish literature.

But, in truth, this Russian-Jewish literature has had a happier destiny than the works of [Osip] Rabinovich, [Lev] Levanda, [Miron] Ryvkin [not in this anthology], [S.] An-sky. It does not live under the sign of Russian doubting. It is not deprived of common acceptance, it does not live outside the sphere of Russian literature proper, and it does not exist solely for the Jewish ghetto. . . . But because it is artistic, it is true literature, and it is earning this right for itself both for Russian literature and for the Jews. The Revolution has destroyed many divisions and partitions, also removing the drastic boundary between Russian and Russian-Jewish literature. And it has called new active forces to the creation of art. Jewish creative forces also participate in this movement. They flow widely into the sea of Russian artistic life, as equal and equally valued creators of Russian letters. And if this is the case, and if Russian-Jewish literature is alive, then it needs its own literary receptacles, it needs its organs and tools of dissemination—and it needs the Russian-Jewish audience, its compassion and concord."

Buoyant with Bolshevik rhetorical clichés, Kleinman's hopes that the Soviet state would support the new Jewish-Russian literature came to naught. The silence about Jewish-Russian writers of the prerevolutionary past and the Soviet present continued from the 1930s until the late 1970s. While Jewish-Russian literature was, one might say, one of the ill-kept secrets of Soviet literary scholarship and Russian culture of the Soviet period, critical discussions did not spring up until the rise of the samizdat underground press in the late 1960s–early 1970s. And, ironically, the first officially condoned or official remarks about Jewish-Russian writers entered the public discourse in the late 1970s in the speeches and publications of representatives of the emerging ultranationalist Russian cultural movement, who were then embracing openly antisemitic positions. Arguing that Jewish-Russian writers were, in most cases, incompatible with the "humanistic" (and Christian) traditions of Russian culture, the poet and essayist Stanislav Kunyaev, the critics Pyotr Palievsky and Vadim Kozhinov, and other Russian authors on the cultural right inadvertently acknowledged the existence of a large (and to them threatening) body of Russian literary works by Jewish writers. A systematic study of Jewish-Russian literature did not resume in Russia and the former USSR until the post-Soviet years.

Western and Émigré Scholarship

In the west, Jewish-Russian writing was brought to the larger critical attention in Joshua Kunitz's pioneering book *Russian Literature and the Jew* (1929). Although his main focus was on Russian writers' treatment of Jewish characters and topics, Kunitz also surveyed works by a representative group of Jewish-Russian writers from the beginnings and until the Soviet 1920s. It fell to émigré critics to introduce western students of Russian and Jewish literature to the rich body of Jewish-Russian literature. The émigrés served as conduits between the severed scholarship in Soviet Russia and western scholarship. For example, consider "Reflections on Russian Jewry and Its Literature" by Y. Kisin (1886–1950), a Yiddish poet, translator, and critic.

Writing in 1944 in *Jewish World* (*Evreiskii mir*), the organ of the Union of Russian Jews in New York, Kisin, after Lazarev and other early students of Jewish-Russian literature, emphasized that from the beginning, from the "hapless [*sic*] versicles" of Leon Mandelstam, the works had expressed a "dividedness." In his essay, Kisin paid tribute to the splendid book *Spanish and Portuguese Poets, Victims of Inquisitions* by the poet and translator Valentin Parnakh (1891–1951). Originally created for publication in France but published in Moscow in 1934, Parnakh's book was both a critical study and an anthology of translations. Adroitly drawing a parallel between Jewish-Russian writers and Spanish and Portuguese Marranos, Kisin quoted from Parnakh's introduction: "Some Marrano writers gave their lives simultaneously to the Jewish cause and the cause of Spanish [and Portuguese] literature. . . . *Odi et amo*: I hate and I love! In exile, some of the members of the Jewish-Spanish and Jewish-Portuguese intelligentsia did not wrest their gazes from Spain and Portugal." Kisin's pathos is particularly well placed, considering that he was himself a Jewish exile writing these lines during the Shoah on America's shores. Other émigré critics and scholars were less eager to consider Jewish-Russian literature as a "spiritual home" of the Jewish people. Writing in 1944 in the same issue of *Jewish World*, the émigré critic turned American professor Marc Slonim (1894–1976) was skeptical of the idea of a contemporary Jewish-Russian literature: "There is not and there cannot be any distinct 'Russian-Jewish' literature in the USSR. Only one question may concern the historian and student of art: What influence have the writers who are Jews [*pisateli-evrei*, in contrast to *evreiskie pisateli*, "Jewish writers"] had on Russian literature? . . . One can only assess them within the framework of Russian literature, and segmenting them into a separate group is aesthetically incorrect." Slonim's skepticism had its roots in the prewar émigré discussions of Jewish culture. Prevalent in the Jewish-Russian émigré milieu were versions of Korney Chukovsky's position (of 1908, see above) that language and language alone determines the literary identity of a writer. It is illuminating to consult the short essay "Do Writers Who Are Jews Exist?" by the notable Jewish-born émigré Yuly Aykhenvald (1872–1928), printed in 1927 in Riga's Russian daily *Today* (*Segodnia*), one of the leading émigré newspapers of its day. "In particular, the writer who is a Jew ceases to be a Jew when he becomes a writer," Aykhenvald declared.

> He remains a writer who is a Jew only when he writes in [a Jewish language]. Having accepted the power of another language over himself and entrusted his soul to this other language, he is thereby the other [*drugoi*], no longer a Jew [*uzhe ne evrei*], and his pages are no longer the pages of Jewish literature. . . . With his Jewish head [the Russian original also implies 'his Jewish mindset'] the Jew *does not* betray himself if he writes not in [a] Jewish [language] but in a European one. . . . In German literature there are no Jews, only Germans, just as there are no Jews in Russian literature, only Russians.

The study of Jewish-Russian literature nearly came to a standstill during the 1950s and 1960s. The New York–based émigrés Sofia Dubnova-Erlikh (1885–1986) and Vera Alexandrova (1895–1966) were almost the sole advocates for Jewish-Russian writers. Writing in 1952, Dubnova-Erlikh was not hopeful about the future of Jewish-Russian literature in the USSR after World War II. A decade and a half later, Alexandrova was considerably more positive about the growth potential of this literature in the Soviet Union. Her great insight was to suggest that the sources of Jewish-Russian writers' creativity, even among the most assimilated and acculturated authors of the second and third Soviet generations, continue to emanate from Jewish spirituality and culture:

> It would be erroneous to suppose that the humanistic strand woven into Soviet literature by Jewish writers was merely a tribute to the ancient tradition of Russian classical literature, with its humanitarian thirst for justice. The sources of Jewish humanism must be looked for more deeply: they are embedded in the most ancient humanitarian culture of Judaism. Quite independently of the personal inclinations and the literary methods of the Jewish writers, these profound wellsprings impregnated their creative work, and thus enriched contemporary Russian literature of the Soviet period.[8]

After the Shoah and postwar Soviet antisemitic policies had threatened the very survival of Jewishness, Alexandrova's argument justly called for a broad and inclusive approach to Jewish-Russian literature of the Soviet period. A conviction that Jewish culture survives and endures even under the greatest historical threats and pressures also resounded through the scholarship of Maurice Friedberg, arguably the only American Slavist in the 1970s to write with care and attention about Jewish-Russian writers.

Shimon Markish

Jewish-Russian literature enjoyed its most prominent student in Shimon Markish (1931–2003), the son of the martyred Yiddish classic Perets Markish (1895–1952) and the brother of the writer David Markish (b. 1938). In his latter years as a professor at the University of Geneva, Shimon Markish demonstrated a passionate commitment to the systematic incorporation of Jewish-Russian literature into the curricula of both Russian and Jewish studies. Despite the residual indifference if not resistance of many Western Slavists to the study of Jewish-Russian literature, by the 1990s Markish's ideas had won supporters. An exilic keeper of the flame of Jewish-Russian writing, Shimon Markish died without publishing a book-length history. However, his numerous articles, including an extensive survey (1995) and a monographic 1994 entry, "Russian-Jewish Literature," in *The Short Jewish Encyclopedia* published in Israel, amount to a cumulative history of Jewish-Russian literature. In 1995 Markish offered this definition of Jewish-Russian literature: "Jewish literary creativity (broadly conceived) in the Russian language . . . one of the branches of the New Jewish letters." One of Markish's premises was the fundamental notion of a unity of Jewish culture

---

8. Alexandrova's essay had originally appeared in Russian in 1968, but I quote its modified, English-language version of 1969.

across the languages in and of Diaspora. This premise was in many respects an application of the argument of the great Jewish historian Shimon Dubnow (1860–1941), specifically as Dubnow expressed it for the émigré audience in the essay "The Russian-Jewish Intelligentsia in Its Historical Aspect" (1939):

> We must remember that inadvertent language assimilation in Diaspora does not yet mean inner assimilation and departure from the national unity. In all epochs of our history, many of the best representatives of our people spoke and wrote in alien tongues, which had become their own, and expressed in them ideas that became the foundation blocks of Judaism. From the cohort of the builders of Judaism one cannot exclude Philo, Maimonides, [Moses] Mendelssohn, [Heinrich] Graetz, Hermann Cohen, and many other thinkers. The future generation will not forget the contributions of the newest Russian-Jewish intelligentsia, which has created a national literature [in Russian] alongside the literature in both languages of our people [Yiddish and Hebrew].[9]

It is hardly surprising that Shimon Markish poured much of his energy into making the works by Jewish-Russian writers available to readers in the West and in the post-Soviet states. He edited *The Native Voice* (2001), the only reader of Jewish-Russian literature to have appeared to date in Russian. Featuring works by twenty-four writers of the nineteenth and the first three decades of the twentieth century, from Osip Rabinovich to Isaac Babel and Dovid Knut, *The Native Voice* was meant to serve as a text to introduce today's readers and students to the heritage of Jewish-Russian literary culture. Along with a collection of his essays gathered in *Babel and Others* (1997), *The Native Voice* stands as a monument to Shimon Markish's peerless contribution. Markish's widow, the Hungarian scholar Zsuzsa Hetényi, has continued her husband's work.

I will return to Markish's position in the pages to follow. Markish's views, as is usually the case with solitary thinkers of his fervor and caliber, are not free of internal contradictions. Perhaps his most emblematic shortcoming was his unwillingness to extend, save for a few exceptions, the history of Jewish-Russian literature beyond the boundary of the 1930s. Markish considered 1940, the year of Babel's execution in Moscow (and Jabotinsky's death in America), to be the end of Jewish-Russian literature. Whether or not one disagrees with some of Markish's precepts and aesthetic predilections, the legacy of Shimon Markish will continue to enlighten and inform us in the decades to come. His achievements are legion.

The Late 1980s to the Present

Three ground-breaking studies of Jewish-Russian literature appeared within three to four years of one another in the late 1980s and early 1990s. Danilo Cavaion's Italian-language *Memoria e poesia: Storia e letteratura degli ebrei russi nell'età moderna*

---

9. See Semen Dubnov [Shimon Dubnow], "Russko-evreiskaia intelligentsia v istoricheskom aspekte," *Evreiskii mir. Ezhegodnik za 1939 god*, 11–16 (Paris: Ob"edinenie russko-evreiskoi intelligentsii v Parizhe, 1939).

(1988) has not received the attention it solidly deserves for its analysis of the early Soviet decades. Alice Stone Nakhimovsky's *Russian-Jewish Literature and Identity: Jabotinsky, Babel, Grossman, Galich, Roziner, Markish* (1992) was the first book in the English language devoted entirely to the subject, providing a systematic introduction to as well as in-depth investigations of the careers of six literary figures from the 1900s to the 1980s (all six are in this anthology).[10] Efraim Sicher's *Jews in Russian Literature after the October Revolution: Writers and Artists between Hope and Apostasy* (1995) focuses on the post-1917 period in the history of Jewish-Russian literature and explores the radical transformations of Jewish-Russian writers under the impact of revolutionary ideology. Sicher also delved into the cultural aspects of Jewish writers' religious conversion. Additionally, no survey of the modern debates about the Jewish contributions to Russian literary culture should ignore the work of Viktoria Levitina on the Jewish-Russian theater.

In the late 1990s and early 2000s, capitalizing on the advances in the study of Jewish-Russian literature, a number of scholars based in the West, in Israel, and in the Soviet successor states have probed some of the more specialized or nuanced aspects of Jewish-Russian literature. Arlen V. Blium's study of the Jewish question and Soviet censorship (1996) provides a wealth of information about the Jewish writers' mounting publishing difficulties in the USSR. Carole B. Balin's *To Reveal Our Hearts: Jewish Women Writers in Tsarist Russia* (2000) analyzes, for the first time within one study, the careers of five Jewish women writers from Russia, two working in Hebrew and three in Russian (two of them, Rakhel Khin and Sofia Dubnova-Erlikh, are featured in this anthology). In *Russian Poet/Soviet Jew* (2000), Maxim D. Shrayer explored the architectonics of Jewish-Russian literary identity and the limits of cultural assimilation during the first two Soviet decades. Gabriella Safran, in *Rewriting the Jew* (2000), examined "assimilation narratives" of the last third of the nineteenth century, comparing the treatment of the Jewish question in works by three prominent Russian and Polish authors to the self-presentation of the Jew in the work of Grigory Bogrov (1825–1885), one of the first Jews to reach a Russian mainstream audience. The year 2000 also marked the publication, in Budapest, of Zsuzsa Hetényi's two-volume *Örvényben (In the Whirlpool)*, a concise Hungarian-language history of Jewish-Russian prose from 1860 to 1940 and a companion anthology of prose by seventeen authors in Hungarian translation.[11]

---

10. Alice Nakhimovsky has recently revisited the history of Jewish-Russian literature in an encyclopedic overview forthcoming in 2008, which I had the privilege of reading in manuscript form.

11. I am grateful to Zsuzsa Hetényi for having furnished me with an English translation of her book's table of contents, and I only regret being unable to read the book. Hetényi's Hungarian anthology includes works by Osip Rabinovich, Lev Levanda, Grigory Bogrov, Yakov Rombro (pseud. Philip Krantz, 1858–1922; not in this anthology), Ben-Ami, N. Naumov (Kogan, 1863–1993; not in this anthology), Sergey Yaroshevsky (18??–1907; not in this anthology), S. Ansky, Aleksandr Kipen (1870–1938; not in this anthology), David Aizman, Semyon Yushkevich, Isaac Babel, Andrey Sobol, Lev Lunts, Semyon Gekht (1903–1963; not in this anthology), Mikhail Kozakov, and Vladimir Jabotinsky.

Taking its title from a line in a well-known poem by the émigré Dovid Knut, included in this anthology, Vladimir Khazan's *That Peculiarly Jewish-Russian Air . . .* (2001) investigates the cultural ties and thematic transpositions between Jewish-Russian and Russian writers in the nineteenth and twentieth centuries. Additionally, a small but growing number of monographs dealing with individual authors and the problematics of Jewish writing and identity have appeared in the 1990s and 2000s, giving hope that the study of Jewish-Russian literature has indeed entered the stage of systematic academic inquiry.[12] What we still need today is a detailed history of Jewish-Russian letters from its beginnings to the present. We are also in great need of more in-depth studies of individual authors. Finally, we need to make the heritage of Jewish-Russian literature available in translation to non-Russian readers.

The Texture of Jewishness

From the earliest debates to the present, critics both Jewish and non-Jewish have mainly crossed swords over the definition of Jewish-Russian literature and the inclusiveness of the criteria one employs in constructing its canon.[13] A terminological diversity reflects some of the fundamental problems a student of Jewish-Russian literature still faces today. In this anthology, the transparent term of choice is "Jewish-Russian literature." In the critical literature, one commonly encounters the expression "Russian-Jewish literature." The English-language term "Russian-Jewish literature" is a literal, and at that imperfect, rendition of the Russian hyphenated term *russko-evreiskaia literatura*, which, in turn, corresponds to the expression *russkii evrei* ("a Russian Jew"), in which "Russian" is an adjective and "Jew" a noun. To the same family of terms belong such contortedly descriptive expressions as "Jewish Russian-language literature" (Mikhail Vainshtein), "Jewish literature in the Russian language" (Dmitri A. Elyashevich), or even "*la littérature juive d'expression russe*" (Shimon Markish 1985). In opposition to the terms that put stock in the complex cultural standing of Jewish-Russian literature, one also comes across variations on

---

12. See, for instance, Laura Salmon, *Una voce dal deserto: Ben-Ami, uno scrittore dimenticato* (Bologna: Pàtron, 1995); Vladimir Khazan, *Dovid Knut: Sud′ba i tvorchestvo* (Lyon: Centre d'études slaves André Lirondelle, Université Jean-Moulin, 2000); Matvei Geizer, *Russko-evreiskaia literatura XX veka. Avtoreferat na soiskanie uchenoi stepeni doktora filologicheskikh nauk* (Moscow: Moskovskii pedagogicheskii universitet, 2001); Leonid Katsis, *Osip Mandel′shtam: Muskus iudeistva* (Moscow–Jerusalem: Mosty kul′tury–Gesharim, 2002); Harriet Murav, *Identity Theft: The Jew in Imperial Russia and the Case of Avraam Uri Kovner* (Stanford: Stanford University Press, 2004). Due to limited space, I am unable to acknowledge all the recent scholarship. The outcropping of recent scholarship on early Jewish-Russian literature, especially on the Jewish-Russian writers from Odessa and the south of Russia, is informed by the work of the historian Steven J. Zipperstein, particularly his *The Jews of Odessa: A Cultural History, 1794–1881* (Stanford: Stanford University Press, 1985).

13. Ruth R. Wisse offers illuminating comments about the making of the canon of Jewish literature in her book *The Modern Jewish Canon: A Journey through Language and Culture* (New York: The Free Press, 2000).

the term "Jews in Russian literature," such as "writers who are Jews [*pisateli-evrei*] in Soviet Literature" (Marc Slonim), and so forth. It is both difficult and awkward to render in English such Russian expressions as *evrei-pisatel'* (literally "a Jew who is a writer") or *pisatel'-evrei* (literally "a writer who is a Jew"), both of which stand for a writer who is Jewish or of Jewish origin and are sometimes used in contrast to *evreiskii pisatel'* (literally "Jewish writer"), commonly understood in Russian to mean a writer in a Jewish language and only to a lesser degree a writer with a manifest "Jewish" agenda. The two opposing sets of critical terms thus reflect either their user's conviction that Jewish-Russian writers constitute a bicultural canon or their user's dismissive view of Jewish-Russian literature as a cultural and critical category.

In this anthology, I have been guided by Shimon Markish's understanding of Jewish-Russian literature as bicultural and binational: "A dual, in this case Russian and Jewish, and equally necessary in both its halves, belonging to a civilization . . . A double belonging of a writer means that, among all else, his creativity belongs to two nations equally." Biculturalism is one of the key aspects of the artistic vision of Jewish-Russian writers (and, for that matter, of any Jewish writer in Diaspora who is conscious of his or her origins). In 1994 the St. Petersburg scholar Aleksandr Kobrinsky illustrated this point splendidly with examples from Isaac Babel's *Red Cavalry* stories.[14] For instance, in Babel's story "The Rabbi's Son," included in this anthology, much of the Judaic religious background is lost on non-Jewish readers, but the story still works well with both audiences:[15]

> Here everything was dumped together—the warrants of the agitator and the commemorative booklets of the Jewish poet. Portraits of Lenin and Maimonides lay side by side. [The nodulous iron of Lenin's] skull and the tarnished silk of the portraits of Maimonides. A strand of female hair had been placed in a book of the resolutions of the Sixth Party Congress, and in the margins of communist leaflets swarmed crooked lines of Ancient Hebrew verse. In a sad and meager rain they fell on me—pages of the Song of Songs and revolver cartridges. [Trans. David McDuff]

---

14. Several Western scholars, including Maurice Friedberg and Ephraim Sicher, have made similar points about the place of the Judaic texts and traditions in Babel's bicultural fiction. Remarkably, the author of a postrehabilitation Soviet book about Babel's life and works, Fyodor Levin, had been able to signal this point; see F. Levin, *I. Babel'. Ocherk tvorchestva*, 7–9 (Moscow: Khudozhestvennaia literatura, 1972).

15. In this regard, the way non-Jewish Russian readers approach works of Jewish-Russian literature remains a fascinating subject of inquiry. My personal experience at teaching works by Jewish-American writers at a Jesuit university to a predominantly Catholic student audience confirms that these texts yield a bicultural model of reading. The non-Jewish students read them in English translation as native works and yet intuitively recognize in the strangeness of these texts the presence of another, Jewish culture.

One of the central implications of the inherent biculturalism of Jewish-Russian writers is that their works should not be defined oppositionally, whether to Yiddish and Hebrew or to Russian letters. Furthermore, through the experience of perusing thousands of pages written by Jewish-Russian writers in search of both balance and representativeness, I have come to believe that only the most inclusive definitions of Jewish Diasporic literature are fundamentally indisputable.

In the preceding pages, I have aimed to show how, in the cannonade of the critical debates of the 1880s through the 1920s, critics have deemed an author's language (Russian) and identity (Jewish) and the works' thematic orientation (related to Jewish spirituality, history, culture, or mores) as cornerstone criteria determining an author's assignation to Jewish-Russian literature. Two more criteria have been proposed and have met both acceptance and opposition. Some critics, going back to Jabotinsky, insist on the criterion of the text's Jewish addressee, either implied or real. Other critics have argued that a work of Jewish-Russian literature constructs a unique insider's perspective on both Jews and non-Jews: "No matter what the attitude of the writer toward his material," Shimon Markish remarked in 1995, "his outlook is always an outlook from within, which represents the principal difference between a Jewish writer and a non-Jewish one who has turned to a Jewish subject (regardless of how they treat the subject)."

Those who believe in Jewish-Russian literature ask that, in addition to the author's identity, Jewish or Judaic aspects and attributes, such as themes, topics, points of view, reflections on spirituality and history, references to culture and daily living, and the like, be present in the writer's texts. And yet, one is frequently left with the impression that not everything has been accounted for, that a Jewish something is slipping through one's fingers. Which brings me back to my opening questions about the possibility of a Jewish poetics and about developing more precise criteria for measuring the Jewishness of a literary text. Aleksandr Kobrinsky has advanced the notion of a Jewish text's "mentality," although he readily admits that "calculating" it would be a grueling task. Consider Kobrinsky's argument:

> When we place side by side and compare two works in the Russian language, written on a Jewish theme by a Jew and a Russian, respectively, then the main criterion would be the system of values calculated on the basis of the author's angle of vision: fluctuations of style and stylistic play, the level of the narrative subject or a poem's lyrical hero, varieties of narration, background of the action and its shifts, lyrical and philosophical digressions, and so forth. In Jewish literature, a Jewish system of values either is accepted as a given . . . , or one (traditional) Jewish system is juxtaposed with another Jewish system [of values].

The principal implication is a need for "calculable" formal criteria of judging the Jewishness of a text in Russian or another language that Jews have adopted as their own. If there is a Jewish poetics, it certainly encompasses much more than theme, subject matter, or system of textual references. Born at the intersection of the author's identity and aesthetics, a Jewish poetics is often buried in plain view. Its real measure is "not text, but texture," to borrow Vladimir Nabokov's mysterious phrase from *Pale*

Fire. By this I mean not only that the Jewishness of the text may not be reduced to its author's Jewish self-awareness and the awareness of his readers or to the text's thematic and topical parameters. For example, in a text such as the poetic cycle "Kol Nidre" (1923; in this anthology) by Matvey Royzman, the Judaic topos overwhelms the reader, facilitating the recognition of the texture of Jewishness:

> On the Torah these bells
> Tremble like a fallow deer.
> Held as by a knifepoint spell,
> Congregants chant pure and clear.
>
> This is David's rising shield
> Like the true new moon tonight,
> And of all the fast has healed,
> Freed, the shofar sings delight.

> *(Trans. Maxim D. Shrayer and J.B. Sisson)*

Another common device of signaling to the reader the texture of Jewishness is the emulation of Yiddish speech or the introduction of Yiddish lexical items, as in the story "Sarah and Rooster" (1988) by Philip Isaac Berman (b. 1936): "Marusya stayed in our room and paid the rent. You know what a room in Moscow means? Now one has to pay thousands and thousands to get one in the city. So when we returned [from Kazakhstan] in 1943 we had a place to live in. I had left her as much money as I could. What was money then? Nothing, *gornit!* A *shtikl* paper!"[16]

At the same time, readers frequently respond to a work by a Jewish author in a non-Jewish language, lacking apparent Jewish clues, with comments such as "I hear a Jewish intonation in this text" or "There is something Jewish between the lines." A number of works in this anthology, especially in its second volume, elicit such responses, not only in their Russian originals but also in translation. Those comments are but a reader's way of trying to put his or her finger onto something quite real. The main challenge that students of Jewish-Russian literature face, both theoretically and practically, is to develop an approach that investigates and measures the texture of a work's Jewishness. But for purposes of this anthology, the only ethical choice I have in seeking to present in its maximum fullness, unity, and diversity the canon of Jewish-Russian literature is to apply the most transparent and all-inclusive criteria.

The Criteria of Jewish-Russian Literature: The Sufficient and the Necessary

By 2001, I had concluded a preliminary review of hundreds of texts by Jewish-Russian writers. Believing—as I still do today—that the only representative anthology of a

---

16. *Gornit* (Yiddish) = nothing; *shtikl* (Yiddish) = bit.

literary canon is a full unabridged canon (and the digital revolution may soon allow for just that), I had to make difficult, at times agonizing decisions in my final selection of materials. I favored transparency over obscurity and inclusivity over exclusivity. In selecting many materials for this anthology from a large pool of texts, I found useful the position of Aleksandr Kobrinsky, who stated in 1994, "A writer's unequivocal self-identification as a Jewish writer appears to be necessary, although not sufficient, to qualify a Russian-language writer as a Jewish one."

Two main criteria, a sufficient one and a necessary one, govern the selection of texts chosen for this anthology. First, in regard to the author's origin or identity, it suffices that a given author be Jewish either in Halakhic terms (in terms of Judaic law) or in any other terms (ethnic, national, etc.) in which Jewishness was legally defined or commonly understood in the Russian Empire, the Soviet Union and its successor states, or any other country of the writer's residence either during the author's life or in subsequent periods. The fact of a Jewish-Russian author's conversion to another religion does not automatically disqualify him or her from being included in this anthology. At the same time, the fact of having been born Jewish does not automatically qualify an author, however important his or her place may be in the Russian literary tradition, for inclusion in this anthology. Here the necessary criterion must be applied: engagement of Jewish subjects, themes, agendas, or questions in the writing. While I have considered works by about 300 authors who satisfy the sufficient criterion of Jewish origin or identity, I have only included works that in some way engage or touch on Jewish agendas. The latter point has already been addressed at some length in the previous pages, whereas the former calls for further clarification.

Apostasy, Assimilation, and the Changing Types of Duality

Quite impermeable to historical and geopolitical changes, the Halakhic configuration of Jewishness could not have drastically changed over the past three centuries of Jewish-Russian history. At the same time, the radical political transformation of Russian society after the 1917 revolutions brought on a transition from the religiously based official legal definition of Jewishness to an ethnically based one. Jewish assimilation, whether real or marranic, forced or voluntary, within the context of tsarist Russia meant religious conversion, a Jew's formally ceasing to be someone of Mosaic confession.

In his model study "Jewish Apostasy in Russia: A Tentative Typology" (1987), the historian Michael Stanislawski pointed out that "in the nineteenth century more Jews converted to Christianity in the Russian Empire than anywhere else in Europe; this is not too surprising, of course, since Russian Jewry was by far the largest Jewish community in the world."[17] Treating the available statistics with a "healthy dose of skep-

---

17. See Michael Stanislawski, "Jewish Apostasy in Russia: A Tentative Typology," in *Jewish Apostasy in the Modern World*, ed. Todd M. Endelman, 189–205 (New York: Holmes and Meier, 1987).

ticism," Stanislawski cited the data of the Russian Holy Synod, which "establish that 69,400 Russian Jews were baptized in the Russian Orthodox Church during the entire nineteenth century." "Western historians of Jewish apostasy," Stanislawski noted, "have claimed in addition that some 12,000 Jews, most probably in the Polish provinces, converted to Roman Catholicism, and 3,100 to various forms of Protestantism, especially Lutheranism." One example, directly relevant to this anthology, was the Jewish-born Catholic mother of the poet Vladislav Khodasevich (1886–1939), whose husband, the poet's father, was Polish and Catholic. Remarking that the "statistics on Jewish conversions to Roman Catholicism, and especially to Protestantism, seem low," Stanislawski further noted that "in total, [Western historians of Jewish apostasy] assert, the 84,500 Russian Jews represented 41 percent of all Jewish converts to Christianity in nineteenth-century Russia." The Russian Empire had gained about 900,000 Jews in 1773, following the first partition of Poland. In 1815, when the so-called Kingdom of Poland became a part of the Russian Empire, there were about 1.5 million Jews in Russia. According to 1897 census data, the Russian Empire had 5.2 million Jews, or about 41 percent of the world's Jewish population (about 4.9 million of those in the Pale of Settlement). Given these statistics, one would have to conclude that the total number of Jewish converts to Christianity (Russian Orthodoxy, Catholicism, Protestantism) in nineteenth-century Russia (69,400) was fairly low.

Overall, historians describe a correspondence between rates of conversion and the dynamics of imperial Russia's political climate and anti-Jewish restrictions. During the reign of Nicholas I, from 1825 to 1855, and the lifetime of the institution of *kantonisty* (Jewish youths forced to become military recruits), which coercively encouraged the baptism of Jews in army schools, one sees higher rates of conversion to Russian Orthodoxy. After a period of decline during the rule of the more liberal Alexander II, from 1855 to 1881, the rates of conversion increased again in the 1880s and early 1890s, following the pogroms of the 1880s and the introduction of further anti-Jewish restrictions. Emblematic of this historical trend is the timing of conversion by members of the swelling ranks of the Jewish-Russian intelligentsia, such as the poet Nikolay Minsky, who converted to Russian Orthodoxy in 1882. Of the subsequent tsarist decades, Stanislawski writes, "While the heady years of 1905–06 saw the number of converts decline, and the astonishing return to Judaism of recalcitrant apostates, between 1907 and 1917 a new, and even larger, wave of baptism was reported to have swept Russian Jewry." For example, the conversion of Osip Mandelstam to Methodism in 1911 exemplifies both a response to the post-1907 climate and a desire to circumvent anti-Jewish institutional quotas. The wave came to a halt in 1917, and in fact, soon after the February 1917 Revolution, one observed a reaffirmation of the Jewish faith by some reluctant Jewish converts to Christianity.

The imperial Russian definition of Jewish (Judaic) identity was replaced by the imperial Soviet one, in which Jews were conceived of as a national minority in ethnic, ethnolinguistic and, to some extent, in historical terms, with the religious components of Jewishness forcefully disavowed. Tsarist-era legal discrimination against Jews, epitomized by the notorious Pale of Settlement, had been abolished after the February 1917 Revolution. In the Soviet state, anti-Jewish restrictions were never given legal status, but from the 1940s they did gain a state-sponsored status. Even prior to the 1940s, the popular antisemitism, which had decreased in the first Soviet decade but had risen again by the early 1930s, had been driving ethnic assimilation. In 1936, when passports were replaced after the passage of "Stalin's" 1936 Soviet Constitution, a wave of Jews took advantage of the opportunity to change their official nationality in the new document. Such ethnic (self-)obliteration and assimilation was particularly manifest in mixed marriages of Jews and non-Jews. Jewish parents and parents in mixed marriages were likely to register their children's "nationality" not as Jewish but as Russian (or Ukrainian, Belorussian, Armenian, and so forth) so as to protect them from discrimination. While official papers might have eased the plight of half-Jewish individuals registered as not Jewish, the Soviet-era popular antisemitism was commonly directed at phenotypic or visible linguistic and cultural markers of one's Jewish origin. "They hit you not on the passport but on the face"—so went a popular Soviet adage. At the Soviet crossroads of Jewish history and Russian culture, identity scenarios such as the one of the poet Inna Lisnyanskaya (b. 1928) were not uncommon. Born to a Jewish father and an Armenian mother, Lisnyanskaya was baptized in her infancy by her Armenian grandmother. Raised in a Russian-, Yiddish-, and Armenian-speaking household in Baku, Azerbaijan, during the most antireligious Soviet years, Lisnyanskaya declared her official nationality as Jewish in 1944, when she turned sixteen. "And I thought . . . if I'm baptized as a Christian, then I must register myself as a Jew, because so many have been annihilated . . . ," Lisnyanskaya explained to me in January 2000. Remaining a Christian, Lisnyanskaya treated Jewish subjects in her lyrics. Her example illustrates how during the Soviet years both the official rhetoric on Jewish identity and antisemitism might have enhanced a Jewish-Russian writer's self-awareness.

The official definitions of Jewishness have changed not only from epoch to epoch but also from country to country. The latter circumstance is of some weight, given that from the 1917 revolutions until the Soviet late 1980s emigration was a prominent feature of this twentieth-century Jewish-Russian cultural experience. Moreover, in their lifetimes a number of authors in this anthology have changed countries or lived in a country whose regime and geopolitical status changed not once but twice, sometimes even three or four times. Characteristic is the experience of Grigory Kanovich (b. 1929), the Jewish-Russian writer who grew up in prewar independent Lithuania, survived the Shoah by escaping to the Soviet hinterland, returned and lived for five decades in Soviet Lithuania, then for two more years in the newly independent Lithuania, only to make aliyah and move to Israel in 1993. The official status of one's Jewishness would sometimes undergo rapid and cataclysmic transformations, especially during transition and emigration. The careers of Jewish-Russian writers provide a number of such examples.

To illustrate the polyvalent figurations of the sufficient criterion of Jewishness, I turn below to a few individual cases from the anthology. Among the authors included here, the reader will find the poet Semyon Nadson (1862–1887), the son of a non-Jewish mother and a father who was born Jewish but who was baptized as a child when his own father converted to Orthodox Christianity. If one takes a broad and inclusive view of the canon of Jewish-Russian literature, the prose writer Yury Trifonov (1925–1981), the son of a Cossack father and a Jewish mother, would also belong in it. Consider also two émigré examples that naturally call for a comparison: the lives of two contemporaries, the poets Anna Prismanova (1892–1960) and Raisa Blokh (1899–1943). Born Anna Prisman in Libava, in Kurland Province (now in Latvia), Prismanova converted to Russian Orthodoxy at the age of eighteen and spent much of her adult life in France. Prismanova survived the roundups of thousands of Jews in occupied wartime France, partly on a technicality: she had entered France on papers listing her as Russian Orthodox. Blokh was born in St. Petersburg to the family of a Jewish lawyer who, as far as one can tell, had converted to Russian Orthodoxy so as to be able to practice law. She immigrated to Germany in 1922 and to France in 1933. Blokh perished in a concentration camp in 1943 after Swiss border guards returned her to the Nazis.

Additionally, consider three examples from the late Soviet and post-Soviet years. Featured in this anthology is the fiction of Ludmila Ulitskaya (b. 1943), a convert to Christianity and a former Jewish cultural activist who made her mark in contemporary Russian prose with stories about the survival of Jewish-Russian memory and identity. Also included is the work of Aleksandr Melikhov, who was born Aleksandr Meilakhs in 1947 to a Jewish father and a Ukrainian mother and became well known after the publication of his novel *The Confession of a Jew* (1994). And finally, there is the intriguing case of the poet Tatyana Voltskaya (b. 1960), who developed a visible interest in Jewishness after learning, apparently as an adult, that her maternal grandmother was Jewish, "which means that I'm actually a real Jew. . . . Without asking my permission, they had deprived me of my origins," Voltskaya wrote to me in 2002.

The openness and broadness with which I have sought to conceive of cultural Jewishness throughout this anthology even leaves open the possibility of becoming a Jewish-Russian author by taking on a Jewish identity. Such cases are quite rare, but there is the fascinating example of Elisheva (Elizaveta Bikhovskaya, born Zhirkova, 1888–1949), who became a Zionist and a Hebrew poet after a brief but intense career as a poet in the Russian language and a translator of Hebrew verse. "I am a Jew in my heart and soul," Elisheva wrote to a Jewish correspondent in 1919. In an article in the sixteen-volume *Encyclopedia Judaica* (1972), the Israeli scholar Gedalyah Elkoshi characterized Elisheva, who moved to the territory of the British Mandate of Palestine with her Jewish husband in 1925 and died there in 1949, as "a non-Jewish Hebrew poet."[18] Such an austerely Halakhic-based approach to Jewish culture strikes me as reductionist and not always warranted.

---

18. Gedalyah Elkoshi, "Elisheva," in *Encyclopedia Judaica*, vol. 6, 672 (Jerusalem: Keter Publishing House, 1972).

As a student of Jewish-Russian culture and an anthologizer, I have tried to be sensitive to the complexity of the architectonics of a Jewish identity during the tsarist but especially during the Soviet years and also in emigration. And yet I believe that Jewish apostasy takes on a very different meaning and significance during the late Soviet decades. As such, it is likely to have much more of an impact on one's judgment of a writer's Jewishness than Jewish conversion during the tsarist period. In assessing the phenomenon of Jewish apostasy in the postwar Soviet Union, it is important to make clear that one is dealing with a conversion by choice and without visible gain in legal status or career advancement, in contrast to either the forced conversion of Jewish teenaged recruits under Nicholas I or the unenthusiastic, frequently marranic conversion of Jews during the later tsarist years for purposes of bypassing official restrictions. Conversion to Russian Orthodoxy (and, to a much lesser degree, to Catholicism) became a notable phenomenon in the 1960s and 1970s among artists and intellectuals from urban Jewish families, mainly in Moscow and Leningrad (St. Petersburg). In contrast to the perilously inaccessible Judaic sacred texts and religious traditions, Russian Orthodox religious texts and religious practices were more easily accessible to an average Soviet citizen. Furthermore, degrees of interest in Christian spirituality on the part of the second and third Soviet generations of acculturated Jews were part of the general shift toward God searching among the Soviet intelligentsia during the years of stagnation.

Conversion to Russian Orthodoxy by choice among the postwar Jewish-Russian intelligentsia has been the subject of the fascinating research of Judith Deutsch Kornblatt.[19] Kornblatt's approach is qualitative, based on interviews with over thirty individuals, including artists and writers, whose anonymity Kornblatt has protected. Quantitative data on apostasy among Jews from the USSR (including the émigrés of the 1960s through the 1980s) would be difficult to obtain. It is my estimate that the number of Jewish apostates in the Soviet Union of the last three decades would be in the range of several thousand. The individuals in question would have come predominantly from the middle and upper echelons of the intelligentsia and would be especially visible among the artistic milieu. They include, to take examples from different generations, the pianist Maria Yudina (1899–1970), the author and dissident Feliks Svetov (Fridliand, 1927–2002; not in this anthology) and the "last Jewish joker" Mikhail Zhvanetsky (b. 1934; Alice Nakhimovsky's expression). The person who stood at the helm of the movement for Jewish conversion to Christianity in the Soviet 1960s–80s was the Jewish-born Russian Orthodox priest and theologian Father

19. See Judith Deutsch Kornblatt, "Jewish Converts to Orthodoxy in Russia in Recent Decades," in *Jewish Life after the USSR*, ed. Zvi Gitelman, Musya Glants, and Marshall I. Goldman, 210–23 (Bloomington: Indiana University Press, 2003); *Doubly Chosen: Jewish Identity, the Soviet Intelligentsia, and the Russian Orthodox Church* (Madison: University of Wisconsin Press, 2004).

Aleksandr Men (1935–1990), who, through personal example and proselytizing among the Jewish-Russian intelligentsia, advanced a platform of the "double chosenness" of Jewish-born Christians.

Although my personal view of the argument about the "double chosenness"— and double mission—of Jewish-born Christians is negative, it was absolutely necessary to represent in this anthology the cultural contribution of apostates among Jewish-Russian writers. I have proceeded on the premise that both an author's confession and an author's change of confession can be private matters. As one might expect, information of this sort is not always available about writers, especially those from the former USSR. While I sent no questionnaires to the living contributors to this anthology, I did request biographical information from those with whom I have had direct contact, and some writers have volunteered facts about their religious life. I have also garnered information in the course of extensive interviews and shorter conversations with some of the featured contemporary authors. The émigré fiction writer Philip Isaac Berman (b. 1936), one of the most overt Jewish metaphysicians in this anthology, told me in 2004 that even in the postwar Soviet years his late father used to go to *shul* every morning before going to work as a Moscow civil servant, thus providing me with an important fact about his Jewish upbringing in the postwar USSR. What I learned helped explain the roots of Berman's fervent Judaism. When the émigré poet and former victim of Stalinism Naum Korzhavin (b. 1925) told me, also in 2004, of his conversion to Russian Orthodoxy in Moscow in 1992, years after he had begun to explore Christian themes in his writings, this information, too, constituted a literary fact.

While I did not deliberately seek out private information unless the fact of a Jewish-Russian writer's conversion had already been established or publicly stated, I did seek out clarification as to when, where, and under what circumstances the conversions took place. In the careers of about half a dozen authors representing the postwar Soviet and émigré years in this anthology, cultural identity and spiritual identity are much further apart than in the cases of other Jewish-Russian writers. From a cultural (bicultural, transcultural) standpoint, those writers are part of a canon of Jewish-Russian literature and an aspect of this discussion. While Jewish apostates by choice opt to remove themselves from the Judaic religious community, they are still part of the Jewish cultural patrimony, whether or not they choose to recognize it. Finally, they are a part of Jewish culture not only because one cannot fully leave one's home but also because they might still choose to return. In refusing to write off this group of writers among living Jewish-Russian authors, I was partly guided by the emblematic twentieth-century example of the composer Arnold Schoenberg and his return to Judaism.[20]

---

20. Marc Chagall was one of the two witnesses who signed Schoenberg's reaffirmation certificate in Paris in 1933. See the certificate facsimile in *Schoenberg, Kandinsky, and the Blue Rider*, ed. Esther da Costa Meyer and Fred Wasserman, 62 (New York: The Jewish Museum; London: Scala Publishers, 2003).

In selecting the materials for this anthology, I also faced a number of additional problems concomitant with the sufficient criterion of a Jewish identity and the necessary criterion of a Jewish subject matter. While most of these supplementary problems will become apparent from my introductions to the individual authors and the headnotes contextualizing their works, below I will talk about three issues. The first two deal with the selection of materials and judgments of their quality and representativeness, and the third, with Jewish-Russian literature in Israel.

Selection, Representativeness, and Excerptability

How many works by a given Jewish-Russian author are enough to satisfy the necessary criterion? What if, out of his entire oeuvre, an author has left only one or two Jewishly marked poems, as was the case with Semyon Nadson, but their presence and impact on the Russian literary mainstream has been vital? Conversely, what if a writer of the Soviet period shunned Jewish subjects throughout his successful public career and yet could not help reflecting, in the secrecy and privacy of his diaries and notebooks, on his own shedding of Jewishness in the Stalinist 1930s and later, in the 1970s, during the rise of Judeophobia among the Russian cultural right? This was the case of the gifted poet and translator David Samoylov (born Kaufman, 1920–1998), especially lionized by some circles of the post-Thaw Jewish-Russian intelligentsia. Following Samoylov's death, the publications of his previously unprinted verse have confirmed that, even in what Samoylov wrote for his "desk drawer," one finds only two or three faint and tired Jewish motifs, such as a Jewish fiddler playing in the fringes of one of the poems. Yet in Samoylov's reflections, which his widow published in the late 1990s–2000s, one finds seminal passages about the trauma of the poet's failed assimilation and Russianization. Samoylov's notebooks and diaries might have helped me understand the place of Jewish poems in his oeuvre—had Samoylov indeed written such poems. But he did not; he *chose* not to write them, and it is with regret that I am unable to include him in this anthology. I am certainly aware that an author's meaningful silence about a particular topic or subject may be regarded as a "minus-device," as Aleksandr Kobrinsky has suggested, applying Yury Lotman's term to the study of Jewish-Russian literature. However, when set against the background of some discussions of Jewish questions in his diaries and notebooks, Samoylov's virtual silence about Jewishness in verse amounts not to a minus-device but rather to a "plus-device." This example is hardly an exception for the Jewish-Russian writers of the postwar Soviet years. In working on this anthology, I had to draw the line based not only on the relative weight and singularity of a given work in the author's entire known oeuvre, whether published in the author's lifetime or posthumously, but also on the historical weight and recorded impact of a given work on Russian and Soviet society and the public imagination of both Jewish and non-Jewish readers.

Both the general conditions of state control over culture in the USSR and the specific situation with the post-1930s official Soviet taboo on Jewish topics complicate the study of Jewish-Russian literature because some works remained unpublished for various reasons until the period of reforms and the fall of the Soviet Union. It was common for a Soviet author, Jewish or otherwise, to go to the grave without publishing a single work in the official press, and a Jewish-Russian writer was likely to have lived most if not all of his or her life without ever publishing a single work displaying Jewish features. In some cases, such works were disseminated in *samizdat* (underground, unauthorized but limited circulation) or in *tamizdat* (abroad), both bearing risks for their authors. In other cases, the presence of such works would not come to light until their discovery among the writers' papers. Important works still remain unpublished, unknown, and buried in archival obscurity. Such is the case of Feiga Kogan (1891–1974), whose work is not represented here. A student of the symbolist poet and philosopher Vyacheslav Ivanov, Kogan was a poet in her own right, a gifted translator, and a theorist of versification and literary declamation. Drawing on Ruth Rischin's trailblazing research, Carole B. Balin has traced Kogan's career from her first poetry collection, *My Soul* (1912), to her peerless Russian translation of all 150 Hebrew Psalms, completed in the Soviet 1950s. Kogan left a trove of unpublished materials, which include, in addition to the translations, poems and extensive diaries that chronicle what Balin has called "a Jewish life behind the scenes." Unfortunately, even knowing what I know about Kogan, I was unable to justify the inclusion of her unpublished poetry in this anthology, whereas her early, published verse does little justice to her contribution as a Jewish-Russian poet.

In the Soviet period, especially its postwar years, writers would live to be old and grey, or even pass away, before their principal works were made available in print at home, owing to censorship and a ban on their publication. Genrikh Sapgir, the patriarch of the Moscow poetic avant-garde of the 1960s–90s and a famous author for children, could not publish a single line of poetry for adults, including his own renditions of the Psalms, in the USSR until 1989, although his works for adults were widely circulated in the underground and abroad. During the late Soviet and post-Soviet years, Sapgir became one of Russia's most admired *published* poets. Much information about unpublished or underpublished works came to light during the perestroika and post-Soviet years and is still emerging, putting the anthologizer's task to the test. While the Soviet-era sections of this anthology are largely concerned with works disseminated through publication in the cultural mainstream, I did attempt to correct for the censorship factor and the factor of delayed cultural recognition by paying attention to works published out of the desk drawer, as it were. It is a fairly common feature of Jewish-Russian texts from the Soviet period that decades separate the date of composition and the date of first publication. For instance, the poem "Ghetto. 1943" by Aleksandr Aronov (1934–2001), written in the 1960s and polemically commemorating the Warsaw Ghetto Uprising, did not appear until 1989, having first become known in the Soviet literary underground. Moreover, such significant delays and deferrals in publication of literary works complicate the periodization of Jewish-Russian literature during the Soviet period. As writers' lives do not always fit neatly within chronological and classificational boundaries, the approach employed here is based in part on the year of composition and in part on the year of publication. The latter is especially valid for the postwar Soviet and émigré sections, and compromises had to be made in order to accommodate the anthology's general structural principles as well as the sometimes intricate history of an individual text's publication. To use one example, the short novel *The King's Hour* (1968–69) by Boris Khazanov (b. 1928) first appeared in the Russian-language *samizdat* magazine *Jews in the USSR* in 1975 and was reprinted in 1976 in Israel. Khazanov did not immigrate to and settle in Germany until 1982, and yet the featured excerpt from *The Hour's King* appears not in the section on "The Late Soviet Empire" but in a different section, "The Jewish Exodus." This decision, incongruous with the chronology as it may appear, reflects Khazanov's personal view, as expressed to me, that his career best fits in the section on the legacy of the Jewish emigration.

Finally, there are the practical difficulties of excerptability. Some works simply do not excerpt well, and constraints of space have forced me to leave out not only all the works of the Jewish-Russian theater but also several very important works of prose and epic and narrative poetry. The example that comes to mind most immediately and painfully is the tale *In a Backwater Small Town* (*V glukhom mestechke*) by N. Naumov (N. Kogan, 1863–1893), which was published in 1892 in the major Russian monthly *The Messenger of Europe* (*Vestnik Evropy*) and received immediate and wide recognition. Of the writers who left the former USSR in the years immediately following its disintegration, I especially regret not having been able to feature an excerpt from the memoirist work *Hellenes and Jews* (1996) by Yuri Gert (b. 1931; emigrated 1992), parts of which anatomize the rise of Russian ultrapatriotism. Only in a handful of disappointing cases was I unable to include a work either for complicated copyright reasons or because its living author did not consent to its inclusion for reasons ranging from financial to ideological and religious.

The Dilemma of Literary Quality

For each of the works in this anthology, in addition to the affirmative answers to the anticipated questions "Is this Jewish literature?" and "Is this Russian literature?" one should ideally be expected to answer "yes" to the question "Is this good literature?" However, and especially given the history of the bicultural canon of Jewish-Russian literature with its modest beginnings and subsequent aesthetic explosions, the expectation of quality is neither simple nor safe. Prior to the 1900s–1910s, when a number of writers firmly entered Russian culture, an assessment of their literary quality warrants a double reckoning. On the one hand, these works are to be regarded vis-à-vis writing that was mainly confined to the Jewish-Russian press, that served Jewish-Russian readers, and that was not known to a wider non-Jewish audience. On the other hand, they are to be construed in terms of the Russian national literary mainstream. The poetry of Simon Frug (1860–1916) serves as a telling example of such a teetering double judgment. Widely published in the Jewish-Russian press of his day, Frug, whom Shimon Markish has called the "national poet" of Russia's Jews on several occasions, was immensely popular among Russia's Jewish population. As a Russian-language poet (he also wrote Russian prose and Yiddish poetry and prose), Frug met a social need of the growing ranks of Russia's integrating Jews by bringing them accessible Russian-language lyrics at a time when the mainstream Russian poetry did not exactly converge with the Jews' dual sensibilities. If judged by the formal standards of Russian poetry of Frug's day, his unoriginal verse is of average quality, but it certainly accomplished enough to have gained recognition among readers in Russia's cultural mainstream—had this, and not writing in Russian for Russia's Jews, indeed been Frug's ambition. What distinguishes Frug's Russian-language verses is the way they exhibit an awareness of their Jewish-Russian reader. Judging by the accounts of Frug's Jewish contemporaries, including such great artists as Hayyim Nahman Bialik, Frug's Russian poems must have touched chords that would have left most non-Jewish readers indifferent. When the critic Arkady Gornfeld stated that Frug's contribution to "Jewish thought" was great and to Russian poetry "modest," he pinpointed the discrepancy between Frug's recognition by Jewish-Russian readers of his day and the place Frug the Russian-language poet has earned for posterity. At the same time, as a result of Frug's almost exclusive focus on the Jewish-Russian audience, to this day he remains practically unknown to historians of Russian poetry. Frug's poetry has not been featured even in the largest and most representative anthologies of Russian poetry, where it undoubtedly belongs, with the exception of a few specialized anthologies devoted to Jewish and Biblical themes or motifs. Even more modest was the aesthetic place of Frug's contemporary, the Russian-language poet Mikhail Abramovich (1859–1940), the son of the Yiddish classic S.Y. Abramovich (Mendele Mokher Sefarim, 1835–1917). Frug, Abramovich, and the other poets populating the pages of Jewish-Russian publications in the 1890s–1900s have not been recognized in the Russian literary canon.

I would maintain that for Jewish-Russian writers the issue of quality as we judge it today and as the Russian literary mainstream judged it at the time only became relevant around the turn of the nineteenth century, during the Russian Silver Age. The bicultural imbalance caused by almost a century of virtual isolation and both legal and cultural fencing was finally righted in the first two decades of the Soviet period. From that point, the judgment of literary quality becomes truly relevant in the assessment of the place of a Jewish-Russian writer in both canons. In the 1920s, Jewish-Russian literature finally had a prose genius of the first magnitude, Isaac Babel, as well as the peerless poetry of Osip Mandelstam, Boris Pasternak, and Eduard Bagritsky. Centered as they were in the Russian-language literary mainstream, these writers set the highest imaginable formal standards, which enabled Jewish-Russian writers to measure themselves not only against the non-Jewish Russian classics or contemporaries but also against these and other resplendent authors of Jewish origin. Not having had its Tolstoy or Dostoevsky in the nineteenth century, Jewish-Russian literature gained its uneclipsable stars in the twentieth. When Korney Chukovsky, in his polemical essay of 1908 considered earlier, lamented the dearth of genius among the Jewish contributions to Russian letters, he probably had no idea that in his own lifetime a score of major writers would become a looming cultural reality during the early Soviet years and would enrich Jewish culture outside Russia.

Writers in Israel and the Canon of Jewish-Russian Literature

Speaking earlier of the poet Elisheva, who made aliyah in 1925, I outlined the scenario of a Jewish-Russian author turned Hebrew author. Perhaps the most famous example of such a transition was the poet Rahel (1890–1931), who permanently resettled to the territory of the British Mandate of Palestine in 1919 to leave Russian writing behind. Other writers remained actively bilingual practitioners of both Russian and Hebrew letters, notably Leyb Jaffe (1878–1948), who arrived in Palestine in 1920 and edited the newspaper *Ha'aretz*. During the 1920s–40s, both before and immediately after the founding of the state of Israel in 1948, several Jewish-Russian writers of the first and second waves immigrated there. With a few exceptions, however, they were quite minor even for the context of Russian émigré writing. The two major exceptions featured in this anthology are the prose writer Yuly Margolin (1900–1971) and the poet Dovid Knut (1900–1955). Both permanently settled in the land of Israel at advanced points in their literary careers, Margolin in 1946 after spending the interwar and wartime years in Poland and the USSR, and Knut in 1949 after having lived in France for nearly three decades. The real influx of numerous and diverse Jewish-Russian writers did not start until the exodus of the late 1960s and the 1970s, when a stalwart Russian-language culture began to take shape in Israel, armed with its own literary journals such as *Zion* (*Sion*), *Twenty-two* (*Dvadtsat' dva*), and others. A number of Russian-language authors entered the cultural scene after having moved to Israel. Consider, for instance, the intriguing career of Eli Luksemburg (b. 1940; not in this anthology), who came to Israel from Tashkent in 1972 and incorporated into his fiction the traditions of Jewish mysticism and Judaic holy texts. It is the changed cultural and ideological status of these authors that fascinates me the most, as emigration to Israel and becoming new Israelis cannot but alter these writers' position vis-à-vis Jewish writers remaining in Diaspora. In some cases, the writers would subsequently leave Israel, usually seeking larger artistic spaces or broader horizons for self-expression, after spending there the initial or transitional years following emigration from the USSR. In the pages to follow, three writers epitomize this trend: Henri Volohonsky (b. 1936), who lived in Israel from 1973 until 1985, when he moved to Germany; Yury Kolker (b. 1947), who spent the years 1984–89 in Israel before alighting in England; and Felix Roziner (1936–1997), who was very active in Russian-language Israeli culture from 1978 until 1985, when he chose to emigrate again, to the United States. Does secondary immigration to Western Europe or North America immediately restore their status as Jewish writers in Diaspora?

In this anthology, four writers represent the extensive Russian-language literary community that had formed in Israel by the 1980s and was replenished by new arrivals in the 1990s: the poets Ilia Bokstein (1937–1999; in Israel since 1972) and Michail

Grobman (b. 1939; in Israel since 1971) and the prose writers David Markish (b. 1938; in Israel since 1972) and Ruth Zernova (1919–2004; in Israel since 1976). All four came to Israel old enough to have been shaped as Russian-language authors in the USSR, and their careers underwent aesthetic and ideological transformations as they became Israelis. During the reform-era and post-Soviet years, Jewish-Russian writers of the older generations (in this anthology, Grigory Kanovich [b. 1929; in Israel since 1993] and Sara Pogreb [b. 1921; in Israel since 1990]) as well as the already published younger authors (Dina Rubina [b. 1953; in Israel since 1990]) made Israel their home. Finally, there is a group of young Russian-language Israeli authors whose entire careers have unfolded in Israel, such as Anna Gorenko (1972–1999), who immigrated to Israel in 1990 and died there.

Can Israel's Russian-language authors be considered Jewish writers in Diaspora? Do they carry with them their Diasporic Jewish-Russian culture? Felix Roziner, a former Muscovite, said this in a 1983 interview to the Tel-Aviv Russian-language magazine *Circle* (*Krug*): "[A Russian writer in Israel] begins to create Israeli culture—in terms of his belonging to the cultural environment of which he is becoming a part." Russian-language writers in Israel are a formidable force, although perhaps not as replete with talent as some of the contemporary Jewish-Russian writers in Europe and America. Not to have featured them in this anthology would have been a great mistake, but I also sought not to overrepresent them. In 1985, in a brief essay, the writer David Markish suggested that he and the others writing in Russian in Israel "prefer to call themselves [Israeli-Russian] writers." Markish also admitted that "our colleagues, Israeli writers writing in Hebrew, while not doubting that we belong to Israeli literature, call us none other than 'Russian writers,' as they marvel quietly that in our work we do not pay sufficient attention to Russian bears, gypsies, and other proverbial boners [*razvesistaia kliukva*, literally 'branchy cranberry plant']."

Canon Making, Canon Breaking

Canons take form slowly, which is to say that our ideas about a particular body of artistic works shape themselves over a period of time, sometimes long enough for a living canon to have become a necropolis. This sobering possibility is quite real in the case of Jewish-Russian literature, and one way of beating time, the merciless canonizer, at its own game is to anthologize.

What then is this anthology? A collection of landscapes of Jewish-Russian literature over the past two centuries, complete with its mountain peaks, crumbling hills, mounds and hummocks, dales, valleys and ravines, rivers, streams, dams and irrigation canals, lakes and ponds, forests, fields of wheat, cherry orchards, orange groves and olive gardens, swamps, deserts, steppes, and even its taiga and tundra? A gallery record of Jewish survival and a debate about Jewish selfhood? A series of dual literary selves? A grand experiment in canon making? I hope it is all of the above and much more, but I am also aware of this anthology's limitations and shortcomings.

To reiterate: This anthology aims at inclusiveness but does not aspire to be exhaustive and complete. It seeks to represent many artistic movements and thematic trends, many genres and forms of prose and poetry, both traditional and experimental, both archaic and avant-garde—in a word, many different Jewish textures of the Russian verbal artistic experience. As with any anthology—and especially the first of its kind—this is not only a creation but also an interpretation of the Jewish-Russian literary canon.

Any anthology is always and inevitably a record of its compiler's predilections of various sorts, of the anthologizer's own self. In this sense, the only objective anthology would be one that includes all works by all authors, a kind of virtual library project that, as I have already suggested, may become possible in the future. I hope that this aerial view of Jewish-Russian literature is accurate while maintaining sufficient distance and perspective. If I have erred in my judgment in some cases, it is in the direction of inclusiveness. While I would like to think this anthology is to some extent authoritative, it is also an invitation to other critics and readers to join the dialogue.

In Closing

In a 2003 demographic study of the dwindling Jewish population in the former USSR, Mark Tolts has provided these statistics: in 1959 there were 2,279,000 Jews in the USSR (880,000 in Russia); in 1989, 1,480,000 (570,000 in Russia); and in 1999, 544,000 in the former USSR (310,000 in Russia). Echoing the population data with a culturological commentary on the place of the Jewish question in Russian intellectual life in 1985–95, the contemporary Russian thinker Sergey Lyozov (Lezov) argued in 1996 that "Jews as enemies or simply as protagonists have been dropped from the central Russian myths of the 1990s." Lyozov suggested that "what one might call a 'normalization' of the Jewish question in Russian culture is taking place 'before our eyes.'" "There is," Lyozov indicated, "no direct linkage between this normalization and the level of our anti-Jewish sentiments [sic]."[21] There is perhaps some truth to such Russian-centric arguments as Lyozov's, or, at the very least, they reflect a post-Soviet picture of the Russian cultural mainstream, where openly Judeophobic and antisemitic views occupy something of a marginal and provincial niche. But the suggestion that the Jewish question captivates post-Soviet Russian culture to a lesser and lesser degree must have to do primarily with a disappearance not of the anti-Jewish myths, which tend to outlive both their subjects and their makers, but of the Jews themselves from the mainstream of Russian culture in the former USSR.

Which is not to say that Jewish-Russian writers have disappeared from today's Russia. Quite a few of the authors of Jewish origin born in the 1930s–50s are visible in post-Soviet Russian letters. One of the authors featured in this anthology, Evgeny Reyn (b. 1935), received most of his country's highest laurels and prizes in

---

21. See Sergei Lezov, " 'Evreiskii vopros' v russkoi intellectual'noi zhizni (1985–1995)," *Znamia* 9 (1996): 182–87.

the 1990s and early 2000s. In 2005 the poet and critic Aleksandr Kushner (b. 1936), also featured in these pages, became the first recipient of Russia's Poet Prize. The winners of the annual Russian Booker Prize, established in 1991 and now known as the Booker–Open Russia Prize, included three Jewish-Russian writers, two of whom, Ludmila Ulitskaya (b. 1943) and Vassily Aksyonov (b. 1932), are in this anthology; over the years, a number of the authors longlisted and shortlisted for the prize have also been Jewish. Moreover, in addition to the writers of the older generations who could not publish under Soviet conditions, the post-Soviet literary culture in Russia has gained new authors of Jewish descent born in the 1960s–80s. While too little time has passed to draw safe assumptions, my preliminary conclusion is that Jewish-Russian writers whose careers were formed during the Soviet years continue to address Jewish topics in their works, some due to a renewed personal interest as well as the freedom to write and publish about it, others out of cultural inertia. At the same time, younger authors of Jewish origin in today's Russia have tended to be more assimilated and Russianized, resulting in a dearth of Jewish consciousness in their writing.

Jewish-Russian literature in the former USSR might have found a temporary domain on the pages of such periodicals as the Moscow-based magazine *Lekhaim*, which claims a larger circulation than the leading Moscow and St. Petersburg literary monthlies—so-called "thick" journals. From a cultural standpoint, today's Jewish Russian-language press in Russia resembles the Jewish-Russian publications of the 1870s–1900s, which almost exclusively served the Jewish readership. The difference is that the latter were a springboard for bringing Russian Jews into the cultural mainstream, while today's Jewish-Russian publications attempt to consolidate, perhaps artificially, a critical mass of writers and readers even as Jewish-Russian culture itself spirals toward disappearance. The critical mass of the Jewish-Russian intelligentsia presently resides outside Russia, in Israel, North America, and Germany, but of these it is only in Israel that Jewish-Russian literary culture is surviving with some degree of vibrancy and continuity. In the United States and Canada, the older émigrés continue to write and publish in Russian, while the younger literary generation of Russian Jews is naturally turning to writing in English. In the decades to come, Jewish-American writers born in the former USSR and raised in North America will become increasingly visible in the English-language cultural mainstream.

It is disheartening to observe that the xenophobic prayers of Russian ultranationalists about cleansing Russian culture of Jews might have been answered.[22] While Jew-

---

22. Consider the opening sentence of a recent book, *Judeans in Russian Literature of the Twentieth Century (A Book without a Subtext)*, by one Aleksandr Andriushkin of St. Petersburg: "Jews, a senseless and uncontrollable [*nevmeniaemaia*] race, moved by a blind loyalty to its monstrous god Yahweh (or more simply put—the devil), set themselves an insane task: to capture the power in Russia and to annihilate the Russian people . . . [the Jews] instinctually understand that to annihilate Russia it is necessary above all to desecrate [*ispokhabit'*] and vandalize one of our main sanctities—Russian literature"; see A. Andriushkin, *Iudei v russkoi*

ish names will not have been erased from the Russian literary scene of the decades to come, a Russian cultural chauvinist might soon be hard pressed to speak of the alleged dominance of Jews and Judaism in Russian letters.

Students of Jewish history and culture have been talking for quite some time, and louder and clearer since the collapse of the Soviet Union, about the end of Russian Jewry and its bicultural heritage. Jewish time in Russian culture seems to be almost over, or perhaps Jewish-Russian culture of the post-Soviet period is living on borrowed time. Celebrating almost 200 years of Jewish-Russian literature, does the upper chronological boundary of this anthology, 2001, also close the page on the canon of Jewish-Russian literature? I would not want this introduction to become an obituary.

In closing, I would like to turn to the work of the distinguished St. Petersburg ethnographer Natalya V. Yukhneva. Yukhneva has advanced the notion of "Russian Jews" (*russkie evrei*) as a "subethnic group," "with the Russian spoken language and a simultaneous belonging to two cultures: Jewish and Russian."[23] Emphasizing the bicultural, "bicivilizational" character of Russian Jewry, Yukhneva posited that "Russia at the beginning of the twentieth century saw the formation within the Ashkenazim of a subethnic group characterized by Russian as the conversational and secular language, Hebrew as the language of religion and national traditions, a combination of Russian and Jewish culture in professional and daily life, Judaism (it is quite likely that within the group one version of reform Judaism or another would eventually have become widespread), and, finally, the emergence of a group consciousness at whose foundation lies not religious but ethnic identity." It is difficult to speculate how Yukhneva's scenario might have continued to develop in the twentieth century had Soviet history not made different arrangements. The Soviet period witnessed a state-sponsored attempt at eradicating the religious aspects of the Jewish identity. The Soviet rhetoric on Jewish identity promulgated a view of Soviet Russian Jews as an ethnic group whose belonging to the community of world Jewry was severed and denied, except when it was politically and economically advantageous to the Soviet government (e.g., during World War II). And yet, in the final analysis, I find myself taking exception to the position of Yukhneva and other historians and ethnographers who speak of the predominantly ethnic self-consciousness of Russian Jews by the end of the Soviet period and of the disappearance of Jewish religious self-awareness among Russia's Jews. In terms of the fifty-eight centuries of Jewish spirituality, the seventy Soviet years are but a flicker of time, and millennia of Jewish religious culture could not have been erased from the identities of Russia's Jews during the

---

literature XX veka (Kniga bez podteksta) (St. Petersburg: Svetoch, 2003). The book appeared in an obscure publishing house, in a print run of two hundred copies. Loath as I am to cite this opprobrious book, it gives an idea of the openly and virulently Judeophobic thinking that continues on the fringes of post-Soviet culture in Russia.

23. See, for instance, Natalia V. Yukhneva, "Russkie evrei v XX v.: osobennosti etnicheskogo razvitiia." Preprint of a paper delivered at Plenary Session 4b at the Sixth World Congress of Central and East European Studies, Tampere, Finland, 2000.

seventy Soviet years. The works gathered in this anthology of Jewish-Russian literature tell a different story, amassing a record of Jewish religious, cultural, and ethnic
endurance.

Throughout the Soviet years, Jewish-Russian writers have been the carriers of an
unsuppressed Judaic culture and spirituality expressed through the Russian language.
Jewish-Russian writers have been the double if divided voices of both Jews and Russians, and only in this sense, not in reference to Jewish-Russian apostates, am I prepared to use the term *doubly chosen.* Jewish-Russian writers, as this anthology aims
to show, have been doubly chosen to be voices, heralds of their two peoples in the
second half of the nineteenth and especially in the twentieth century. In Jewish writers, however assimilated they may seem at first glance, the breath of God manifests
itself not so much because they are chosen to say something to their audiences but
because—and I hesitate only a little to say this—they are the material, textual evidence of God's artistic powers. This is largely what I meant when I spoke earlier
about the *texture of Jewishness* in the texts by Jewish-Russian writers.

As the problem of identity has been a central one throughout the millennia of
Jewish Diaspora, this *Anthology of Jewish-Russian Literature* goes to the very heart
of Jewish culture and history. Moreover, in our age, when people and even whole
countries are increasingly concerned with defining and redefining their identity, this
anthology tells the story of attempts by writers to become Russians while also remaining Jews. It makes me particularly happy that here in my adopted country, the
immigrant America of the late twentieth and early twenty-first centuries, bicultural
Jewish-Russian literature has found its home, in English translation and in the memory
of readers.

Jewish-Russian Literature
A Selected Bibliography

Far from a complete or exhaustive bibliography, this list of books and articles mainly includes works referred to in the general introduction. The purpose of this bibliography is to present a history of the study of Jewish-Russian literature from the 1880s to the present and to highlight the dynamics of the principal debates about the contents and criteria of its canon. If a work is available in the original language and in English, preference has been generally given to English versions.

Aikhlenval'd, Iu[lii]. "Sushchestvuiut li pisateli-evrei?" *Segodnia* [Riga], no. 202 (9 September 1927).

Alexandrova, Vera. "Jews in Soviet Literature." In *Russian Jewry 1917–1967*, ed. Gregor Aronson et al., trans. Joel Carmichael, 300–327. New York: Thomas Yoseloff, 1969.

Aronson, G[rigorii]. "Evrei v russkoi literature, kritike i obshchestvennoi zhizni." In *Kniga o russkom evreistve ot 1860-kh godov do revoliutsii 1917 g. Sbornik statei*, ed. Ia.G. Frumkin et al., 361–99. New York: Soiuz russkikh evreev, 1960.

———. "Russko-evreiskaia pechat'." In *Kniga o russkom evreistve*, ed. Frumkin et al., 548–73.

Balin, Carole B. *To Reveal Our Hearts: Jewish Women Writers in Tsarist Russia.* Cincinnati: Hebrew Union College Press, 2000.

Blium, A[rlen] V. *Evreiskii vopros pod sovetskoi tsenzuroi, 1917–1991.* St. Petersburg: Peterburgskii evreiskii universitet, 1996.

Cavaion, Danilo. *Memoria e poesia: Storia e letteratura degli ebrei russi nell'età moderna.* Rome: Carucci editore, 1988.

Chernikhovskii, S[aul]. "Russko-evreiskaia khudozhestvennaia literatura." In *Evreiskaia entsiklopediia.* Vol. 13, 640–42. St. Petersburg: Obshchestvo dlia Nauchnykh Evreiskikh Izdanii; Izdatel'stvo Brokgauz-Efron, [1906–13].

Chukovskii, Kornei. "Evrei i russkaia literatura." *Svobodnye mysli* (14 January 1908).

Dubnow-Ehrlich, S. [Sofia Dubnova-Erlikh]. "Jewish Literature in Russian." In *The Jewish People: Past and Present*, ed. Rafael Abramovich. Vol. 3, 257–67. New York: Central Yiddish Cultural Organization, 1952.

El'iashevich, D[mitrii] A. "Russko-evreiskaia kul'tura i russko-evreiskaia pechat'. 1860–1945." In *Literatura o evreiakh na russkom iazyke, 1890–1947. Knigi, broshiury, ottiski statei, organy periodicheskoi pechati. Bibliograficheskii ukazatel'*, ed. V.E. Kel'ner and D.A. El'iashevich, 37–78. St. Petersburg: Akademicheskii proekt, 1995.

————. "Russko-evreiskaia pechat' i russko-evreiskaia kul'tura: k probleme genezisa." In *Trudy po iudaike* 3 (1995). St. Petersburg: Peterburgskii evreiskii universitet, 1995. www.jewish-heritage.org/tp3a7r.htm, 10 February 2005.

Friedberg, Maurice. "Jewish Contributions to Soviet Literature." In *The Jews in Soviet Russia since 1917*, ed. Lionel Kochan. 3rd ed., 217–25. Oxford: Oxford University Press, 1978.

————. "The Jewish Search in Russian Literature." *Prooftexts* 4, no. 1 (1984): 93–105.

Gornfel'd, Arkadii. "Russkoe slovo i evreiskoe tvorchestvo." In *Evreiskii al'manakh*, ed. B.I. Kaufman and I. A. Kleinman, 178–99. Petrograd and Moscow: Knigoizdatel'stvo Petrograd, 1923.

Hetényi, Zsuzsa. *Örvényben.* 2 vols. (1. *Az orosz-zsidó próza története, 1860–1940.* 2. *Az orosz-zsidó próza antológiája, 1860–1940*). Budapest: Dolce Filológia II, 2000.

Kel'ner, V[iktor] E. *Dopolneniia k ukazateliu "Literatura o evreiakh na russkom iazyke, 1890–1947."* Moscow: Evreiskoe nasledie, 1998.

Kel'ner, V[iktor] E. and D.A. El'iashevich, comp. *Literatura o evreiakh na russkom iazyke, 1890–1947.* St. Petersburg: Akademicheskii proekt, 1995.

Khazan, Vladimir. *Osobennyi evreisko-russkii vozdukh: K problematike i poetike russko-evreiskogo literaturnogo dialoga v XX veke.* Moscow: Mosty kul'tury; Jerusalem: Gesharim, 2001.

————. "Sovetskaia literatura." In *Kratkaia evreiskaia entsiklopediia*. Vol. 8, 97–142. Jerusalem: Obshchestvo po issledovaniiu evreiskikh obshchin; Evreiskii universitet v Ierusalime, 1996 [the entry is unsigned].

[Kheifets, Mikhail]. "Russkaia literatura v Izraile." In *Kratkaia ervreiskaia entsiklopediia.* Supplement 2, 324–34. Jerusalem: Obshchestvo po issledovaniiu evreiskikh obshchin; Evreiskii universitet v Ierusalime, 1995 [the entry is unsigned].

Kisin, I. "Razmyshleniia o russkom evreistve i ego literature." *Evreiskii mir* 2 (1944): 164–72.

Kleinman, I[osif] A. "Evrei v noveishei russkoi literature." In *Evreiskii vestnik*, ed. S.M. Ginzburg, 155–66. Leningrad: Obshchestvo rasprostraneniia prosveshcheniia mezhdu evreiami, 1928.

Kobrinskii, A[leksandr]. "K voprosu o kriteriiakh poniatiia 'russko-evreiskaia literatura.'" *Vestnik evreiskogo universiteta v Moskve* 5 (1994): 100–114.

Kunitz, Joshua. *Russian Literature and the Jew: A Sociological Inquiry into the Nature and Origin of Literary Pattern.* New York: Columbia University Press, 1929.

Lazarev, M.N. "Zadachi i znachenie russko-evreiskoi belletristiki (Kriticheskii ocherk)." *Voskhod* 5 (1885): 28–42; 6 (1885): 24–42.

Levitina, Viktoriia. *Russkii teatr i evrei.* Jerusalem: Biblioteka "Aliia," 1988.

————. . . . *I evrei—moia krov'. (Evreiskaia drama—russkaia stsena).* Moscow: [Izdatel'stvo Vozdushnyi transport], 1991.

L'vov-Rogachevskii, V[asilii]. *Russko-evreiskaia literatura.* Intro. B[oris] Gorev. Moscow: Gosudarstvennoe izdatel'stvo; Moskovskoe otdelenie, 1922. Reprint, Tel

Aviv, 1972; English edition, *A History of Russian-Jewish Literature*, ed. and trans. Arthur Levin. Ann Arbor: Ardis, 1979.

Markish, David. "Russko-evreiskaia literatura v Izraile." *Cahiers du monde russe et soviétique* 26, no. 2 (April–June 1985): 255–56.

Markish, Shimon. *Babel' i drugie*. 2nd ed. Moscow and Jerusalem: Personal'naia tvorcheskaia masterskaia "Mikhail Shchigol'," 1997.

———. "À propos de l'histoire et de la méthodologie de l'étude de la littérature juive d'expression russe." *Cahiers du monde russe et soviétique* 26, no. 2 (April–June 1985): 139–52.

———. "Eshche raz o nenavisti k samomu sebe." *Dvadtsat' dva* 16 (December 1980): 177–91.

———. "O nadezhdakh i razocharovanii (usykhaiushchaia vetv')." In *Babel' i drugie* [1993], 188–93.

———. "O rossiiskom evreistve i ego literature." In *Babel' i drugie*, 194–211.

———. "O russkoiazychii i russkoiazychnykh." In *Babel' i drugie* [1990], 182–88.

———. "The Role of Officially Published Russian Literature in the Reawakening of Jewish National Consciousness (1953–1970)." In *Jewish Culture and Identity in the Soviet Union*, ed. Yaacov Ro'i and Avi Beker, 208–31. New York: New York University Press, 1991.

———. "Russkaia podtsenzurnaia literatura i natsional'noe vozrozhdenie (1953–1970)." In *Babel' i drugie*, 213–34.

———. "Russko-evreiskaia literatura." In *Kratkaia evreiskaia entsiklopediia.* Vol. 7, 525–51. Jerusalem: Obshchestvo po issledovaniiu evreiskikh obshchin; Evreiskii universitet v Ierusalime, 1994 [the entry is unsigned].

———. "Russko-evreiskaia literatura: predmet, podkhody, otsenki." *Novoe literaturnoe obozrenie* 15 (1995): 217–50.

Markish, Shimon, ed. *Rodnoi golos: stranitsy russko-evreiskoi literatury kontsa XIX–nachala XX vv.: kniga dlia chteniia.* Kyïv: Dukh i litera, 2001.

Nakhimovsky, Alice Stone. *Russian-Jewish Literature and Identity: Jabotinsky, Babel, Grossman, Galich, Roziner, Markish.* Baltimore: The Johns Hopkins University Press, 1992.

Nakhimovsky, Alice. "Russian-Jewish Literature." In *The YIVO Encyclopedia of Jews in Eastern Europe*, ed. Gershon D. Hundert. New Haven: Yale University Press, forthcoming 2008.

Safran, Gabriella. *Rewriting the Jew: Assimilation Narratives in the Russian Empire.* Princeton: Princeton University Press, 2000.

Sedykh, Andrei (Iak. Tsvibak). "Russkie evrei v emigrantskoi literature." In *Kniga o russkom evreistve, 1917–1967*, ed. Ia.G. Frumkin et al., 426–47. New York: Soiuz russkikh evreev, 1968. [Vol. 2 of the 1960 edition.]

Serman, Il'ia. "Spory 1908 goda o russko-evreiskoi literature i posleoktiabr'skoe desiatiletie." *Cahiers du monde russe et soviétique* 26, no. 2 (April–June 1985): 167–74.

Shrayer, Maxim D. *Russian Poet/Soviet Jew: The Legacy of Eduard Bagritskii.* Lanham, MA: Rowman and Littlefield, 2000.

Sicher, Efraim. *Jews in Russian Literature after the October Revolution: Writers and Artists between Hope and Apostasy.* Cambridge: Cambridge University Press, 1995.

Slonim, Mark. "Pisateli-evrei v sovetskoi literature." *Evreiskii mir* 2 (1944): 146–64.

[Timenchik, Roman]. "Russkaia literatura." In *Kratkaia evreiskaia entsiklopediia.* Vol. 7, 489–525. Jerusalem: Obshchestvo po issledovaniiu evreiskikh obshchin; Evreiskii universitet v Ierusalime, 1994 [the entry is unsigned].

Vainshtein, Mikhail. *A list' ia snova zeleneiut . . . Stranitsy evreiskoi russkoiazychnoi literatury.* Jerusalem: Kakhol-Lavan, 1988.

Zhabotinskii [Jabotinsky], V[ladimir (Zeev)]. "Pis'mo. (O 'evreiakh i russkoi literature')." *Svobodnye mysli* 24 (March 1908). Reprinted in *Izbrannoe,* 61–68. Jerusalem: Biblioteka "Aliia," 1978.

Zinberg, Israel. *A History of Jewish Literature. Part Twelve: The Haskalah Movement in Russia.* Cincinnati: Hebrew Union College Press; New York: Ktav, 1978.

———. *A History of Jewish Literature. Part Thirteen: Haskalah at Its Zenith.* Cincinnati: Hebrew Union College Press; New York: Ktav, 1978.

An Anthology of
Jewish-Russian Literature

Volume 1: 1801–1953

✳ The Beginning ✳

Although their population in Russia had been miniscule before the partitions of Poland, Jews created important works in the Russian language as early as the beginning of the eighteenth century. In 1817, Baron Pyotr Shafirov (1669–1739), a Russian vice-chancellor and top diplomat, the son of a converted Jew, and a close cohort of Peter I, published *Discourse Concerning the First Causes of the War between Sweden and Russia*. While it would be a big stretch to call Shafirov's book a literary text and feature it in this anthology, one finds the first genuine work of Jewish-Russian literature in the *Lament of the Daughter of Judah* (St. Petersburg, 1803) by Leyba Nevakhovich (1776–1831). One of Russia's earliest *maskilim* (followers of the Haskalah, the Jewish Enlightenment movement), Nevakhovich resorted to artistic devices in his prose so as to persuade the members of the Jewish Committee, then deliberating in St. Petersburg, to "look for the human being in the Jew." For the next several decades, Nevakhovich's would remain the lone Jewish-Russian literary voice among his generation of the *maskilim*. The Haskalah was born in the German lands in the second half of the eighteenth century, and the news about the teachings of Moses Mendelssohn (1729–1786) and his followers spread into the Pale of Settlement from Prussia. Copies of *The Gatherer (Ha-Meassef)*, the Hebrew monthly founded in 1783 in Königsberg (now Kaliningrad) and subsequently published in Berlin and other German cities, quickly reached Kurland and the neighboring northwestern provinces. As was to have been expected, therefore, the early *maskilim* in Russia looked to the German lands for inspiration, while the principal early writings by the Russian *maskilim*, most notably the "Russian Mendelssohn," Isaac Ber Levinson (1788–1860), were in Hebrew and occasionally Yiddish, not in Russian. Between Nevakhovich's *Lament* and the year 1841, when Leon Mandelstam (1819–1889) published his *Poems* in Moscow, hardly anything of note by Jews appeared in Russian. Of historical interest only is the publication, in 1846 in Vilna, of *Thoughts of an Israelite*, written in awkwardly manipulated Russian by Abram Solomonov (1778–18??), a Jew of the generation of the early Russian *maskilim*.

LEYBA NEVAKHOVICH

Leyba (Lev) **Nevakhovich** (1776–1831) was the Russianized name under which Judah Leib ben Noah published *Lament of the Daughter of Judah* (1803), arguably the first work of Jewish-Russian literature and the one that opens this anthology. Born in the Podolian town of Letichev, Nevakhovich was one of the earliest Russian *maskilim*—proponents and champions of the Haskalah, the Jewish Enlightenment movement. Proficient in several European languages, by the 1790s Nevakhovich had fallen under the influence of Moses Mendelssohn (1729–1786) and the Haskalah. He moved to St. Petersburg together with the family of his former pupil, the naval contractor Abram Perets, and became part of what John D. Klier called the "informal triumvirate" of Jews influencing the Russian policies on the Jew in the early 1800s, the other two being Perets himself and Nota Notkin, a promoter of Jewish economic reform. Nevakhovich worked as a government employee and translator from the Hebrew (e.g., preparing the materials on the arrests of Rebbe Shneur Zalman ben Baruch of Lyady in 1798 and 1800; Rebbe Shneur Zalman was finally released in 1801). As Andrey Rogachevsky recently demonstrated, Nevakhovich composed an ode in Hebrew on the ascension of Alexander I to the throne (12 March 1801), accompanied by a Russian translation. It was not published but has survived in the archives.

Nevakhovich contributed to the discussions of the Jewish Committee, which was established by Alexander I in November 1802 (see Klier's "Outline of Jewish-Russian History: Part I") and to which *kahal* deputies gave testimony in the summer and fall of 1803 in St. Petersburg. He wrote his *Lament of the Daughter of Judah* specifically for the deliberations of this committee. Dedicated to Prince Viktor Kochubey, at the time the Minister of Internal Affairs, it was printed in St. Petersburg in 1803. In 1804 an expanded Hebrew edition appeared in Shklov, Belorussia, under the title *Kol Shavat bat Yehudah*.

Disillusioned by the 1804 "Statute for the Jews," which fell far too short of his hopes and expectations and in effect confirmed the Pale of Settlement, Nevakhovich gave up writing on Jewish issues. His next work was a philosophical treatise, *Man in Nature. Correspondence between Two Enlightened Individuals* (1804). In 1804–6 he contributed to the Russian journals *Northern Messenger* (*Severnyi vestnik*) and *Lyceum* (*Litsei*), and in 1809 the Imperial Theater staged his drama *The Suliots, or Spartans in the Eighteenth Century*. Although in the *Lament* Nevakhovich did not posit conversion as a sine qua non of Jewish modernization, he was baptized around

1806. News of his apostasy, as well as of Abram Perets's baptism in 1813, contributed negatively to the spread of the Haskalah among the masses of Russia's Jewish population, who regarded the movement as a threat to Judaic traditions. Nevakhovich subsequently served as a civil servant in Warsaw in the field of finances and translated from the German. In 1832 his drama *Sword of Justice* was staged in St. Petersburg.

His descendants made contributions to Russian culture and scholarship: Mikhail Nevakhovich was a cartoonist and the founder of *Mish-Mash (Eralash)*, the first magazine of humor in Russia; Aleksandr Nevakhovich was a playwright and a repertory director of the emperor's theaters in St. Petersburg; and Nevakhovich's daughter Emilia was the mother of Ilya Mechnikov (1846–1916). A great Russian microbiologist and a disciple of Louis Pasteur, Mechnikov shared the 1908 Nobel Prize for Physiology or Medicine with Paul Ehrlich.

In addition to the opening essay, which lent its title to the entire book, Nevakhovich's *Lament* included two other parts: "Conversation among Sinat-Hadat [Intolerance], Emet [Truth], and Shalum [Peacefulness]" and "The Feelings of a Loyal Citizen, On the Occasion of the Institution by the Highest Order of His Royal Majesty Emperor Alexander I, the Russian Monarch, of the Committee Concerning the Accommodation of the Jews in Accordance with the Needs of the State and Their Own Needs." The latter parts of the book are believed to have been composed in Hebrew and then translated into Russian. They differ stylistically from the opening essay, which is composed in the style of Russian neoclassical prose, in competent albeit aging eighteenth-century Russian. Nevakhovich advocates religious tolerance and the extension of equal civil rights to the Jews, pleading with the Russian authorities to regard them as loyal citizens and patriots. His arguments are imbued with the ideas of the European Enlightenment and the Haskalah, and he pays tribute to two cornerstone texts: Gotthold Ephraim Lessing's *Nathan the Wise* and Moses Mendelssohn's *Jerusalem*. A brief note, "From the Author," precedes the text of the *Lament of the Daughter of Judah:* "Love for the Emperor and the Fatherland, enchantment with today's enlightened times, pleasure and a certain sense of dignity and pride in being able to call the Russians my compatriots, compassion consuming my heart as I judge the fellow members of my tribe—this is the portrayal of the spirit that here guides my feeble pen!" The following excerpt (about one-third of the entire *Lament of the Daughter of Judah*) comes from the middle section of the essay.

From *Lament of the Daughter of Judah*

[. . .] Centuries and nations accuse the Jews—but why are these accusations not consistent? Just look at history and you will see many contradictions: one minute they are accused of sorcery,[1] the next of lack of faith, the next of superstition. The centuries had not yet had time to discover the futility of the intrigues against them before new ones were already arising. Like the links in an unbreakable chain, they have been welded together for the oppression of this nation alone, which in its lot resembles an unhappy son suffering in the bosom of a family that hates him. His brothers interpret all his acts in a bad light; and if, nay, when his innocence is revealed to them, they strive, as if ashamed of their former errors, to level new accusations against the sufferer in order to prolong his torments and stifle the reproaches of their conscience, so palpable and striking, for those acts of oppression which they have inflicted upon him hitherto. Has it been long since the heads of the innocent children of Israel ceased to fall beneath the sword of the vile libel that accused them with unshakable assurance of using Christian blood during their festival called *Pesach* (Passover)?

O Russians, you who love your fellow men! You would shudder from the bottoms of your kind hearts if you saw the effect of that terrible accusation which Jews who were eyewitnesses to the unjustified deaths of fellow members of their race cannot call to mind without trembling. More than once during my childhood my tears mingled with those of my mother, who used to tell me, with grief in her voice, of the terrible events that broke the nation's heart. Almost the whole world knows how many thousands of victims this unjust accusation cost.

The festival of Pesach just mentioned is that in which Jews remember the time of their forefathers' exodus from Egypt, a time that they revere as a memorial of the first era of their free existence. During this festival, they mentally share in the joy of their forefathers.

Noble children of the north! Your mild monarchs have taught you to look with a calm and impartial eye upon the rites of worship of the different nations living under your shield, upon the various festivities that make up their happiness—and you do not disturb this! But in those days Jews did not yet have the good fortune to be Russia's subjects; in those days hatred, that hellish Fury, managed to convince many that Jews supposedly have need of this horrific evil on the day of that festival. Then the credulous and simpleminded were incited by cunning and wily souls to place a dead and mutilated infant surreptitiously by night beneath some house of a

---

1. A certain German book describes extremely heatedly how great a number of Christians perished through the supposed sorcery of the Jews—a hellish fabrication for simple folk, but how much blood that fabrication cost in days gone by. [L.N.]

Jew, which malice was pleased to designate. The next morning that house is surrounded by a crowd of people demanding vengeance. A grizzled patriarch is plucked in the most contemptuous and violent manner from the circle of his innocent family; the rabbi (teacher of the law) and the most venerable of the Jews are taken; and finally, without further investigation, without the acceptance of any protestations of innocence from the victims, they are subjected to the most brutal executions. Children are robbed of a father, the wife of a husband, the brother of a brother . . . The joy and festivity they had hoped to enjoy at that time gave way to lamentation, sobbing, and despondency. And so afterward, as this festival approached, each of them was seized by a terror that some sort of similar misfortune would descend on his house. But when this terrible lot was drawing to a close and some of the persecuted had fallen victim to the fury of the misguided plotters devoted to their devilish delight, the rest, with grief-stricken hearts, counted themselves safe for that year. What a pitiful solace! What a sorrowful comfort!

The Polish king Augustus Poniatowski of blessed memory, a wise and benevolent ruler, was moved to tremble at such inhuman outrages and through his wisdom brought them to an end. At last the dead bodies of infants ceased to be found beneath the houses of Jews, which still further demonstrated the absurdity of the past calumnies. Alone the mighty hand of Empress Catherine the Great of Russia was able to ease the lot of this nation, which had previously been the plaything of arbitrary deeds. Under the peaceful protection of Russian power, those hounded by fate found respite from earlier oppressions and began to feel to the full extent their former woes, the recollection of which even now forces whole floods of tears from their eyes. Alas! Now that the blows have ceased, these people begin to feel the pain of their wounds, which previously in their fever-like suffering they could not feel![2]

Oh, Christians! You who live in community with them, you must know that virtue is just as sacred to them as it is to you—just look! But how do you look upon them? . . . Do you look for the Jew in the human being? No. Look for the human being in the Jew, and you will find him without a doubt. Only look. You will see among them many people who keep their word sacredly. You will see many compassionate people who give alms to the poor, not only of their own tribe but of other tribes too. You will see that many of them

---

2. It is well known that the Jewish people were everywhere oppressed for several centuries, being driven out of Spain, France, and Portugal . . . They were oppressed in Poland before its annexation to Russia. And to what humiliation they were brought there! Even schoolchildren had some appointed days on which they attacked Jews and their homes, beat them, and reviled them mercilessly, with no respect even for old people. Those days were known among Jews as *shiler gelauf*, that is, school children running wild, and during those days the Jews would take cover and not ply their trade. In some towns mayors, by then Russian appointees, still noticed such willful disturbances, but, having at their disposal the Statute of Good Order, the Constitution of the Provinces, and the Civil Command, they put a stop to them; some schoolchildren were imprisoned, and Jews saw for the first time that being cruel is not the duty of a Christian. [L.N.]

magnanimously pardon wrongs. You will see in them gratitude, restraint, and respect for the old. Likewise you will see with what feeling they revere those people of other faiths who show them kindness and do good to them—and with what veneration they bethink themselves of the sovereign. Lessing puts it splendidly this time: "Are a Christian and a Jew really first and foremost a Christian and a Jew rather than human beings?"[3] I do not doubt that there are many among you who, in having dealings with Jews, have witnessed the generosity of their behavior and their sentiments of gratitude. The trouble is, the only trouble is, that no one discloses observations of this kind. And if anyone happened to observe something repugnant in certain of them, you still cannot form an opinion about the generality of people on this basis, just as I, if I see many depraved people among Christians, similarly cannot make a judgment about all of their coreligionists.

I also make so bold as to say this to you: If you have observed depravity in some Jews close to you, take a good look at yourselves and do not be upset that I am going to ask, "Are you yourselves not perhaps the cause of it?" Forgive the Jews if the torments inflicted upon them over several centuries have given them an unfavorable opinion of the Christian nations. Might it be that a Jew of upright principles will in fact not establish close ties with you but will seek to distance himself, just as the Americans avoided the Spanish? In those close to you, then, you do not for the most part see the image of the real Hebrew but only the depraved one. Have a long hard look at yourselves, I say, do you yourselves perhaps support their outrages with your patronage? . . . So you live with a nation without knowing its heart. I swear that a Jew who observes his religion faithfully cannot be a wicked person, or a bad citizen!

I will extend further the lament of my burning heart. The religion professed by the Jews is harmless to any citizenship. This can be very clearly seen from the fact that in many well-ordered states it is not proscribed. The main purport of this religion is that each person, of whatever faith, is capable of achieving perfection, even if not well-versed in the Jewish religion's rites, which, according to its canon, have been established by God solely for the Jews in commemoration of the covenant made between them in the wilderness of Horeb.[4] And in Jewish traditions it is enjoined to pray for the prosperity of the czar,[5] it is laid down that the state law[6] is the substantive law, it is likewise forbidden to transport goods without paying

---

3. See *Nathan der Weise*. [L.N.] Nevakhovich is referring to *Nathan the Wise: A Dramatic Poem in Five Acts* by Gotthold Ephraim Lessing (1729–1781).

4. See Mendelssohn's *Jerusalem*. [L.N.] Nevakhovich is referring to the treatise of 1783 by the prototype of Lessing's Nathan the Wise, Moses Mendelssohn (1729–1786), a major figure of the Jewish Enlightenment, a philosopher and publicist, translator of the Pentateuch into German.

5. See the Jewish legends called *Pirke Avos*. [L.N.] Pirke Avot (lit. "Ethics of the Fathers") is the fourth tractate of the Mishnah in *Nezikin*, without any halakic commentary. Containing teachings and maxims of the sages dating from the third century B.C.E., Pirke Avot is a part of the liturgy that is read by Ashkenazic Jews on Sabbath afternoons in the summer and by the Sephardic Jews at home on Sabbaths between Passover and Pentecost.]

6. See the *Talmud* in the tractate *Bava Kama*, last *pereq* [chapter]. [L.N.]

duties, and so forth. If the law is honest, then the true followers of it must be honest.[7]

It is indisputable that the morals and manners of nations are different and that each nation has its own particular moral propensities. Yet I cannot allow that these propensities are innate in a nation. Does Nature really produce people already glued to those things whose charm depends only on prejudices? What! A person has just been born and already understands that a piece of metal can afford him many benefits if it has upon it some image of which he is as yet ignorant! No, nurture is the cause of everything, nurture dependent on the disposition and habit of those who are responsible for it and whose disposition depends likewise on nurture. What an amazing mutual dependence: nurture on disposition, disposition on nurture! And what is the origin of this interdependence? There is in nature no effect without a cause and no cause without an effect. The morals and manners of nations are formed by a concatenation of different circumstances. The state of morals and manners is just as necessary in relation to the course of things in the moral world as are natural effects in relation to [the course of things] in the physical world.[8] When we do not feel animosity toward a person weighed down by physical ailments but only feel sorry for him, have we any reason to hate a person suffering from ailments of the heart? Moral ailments lend themselves to healing as much as physical ones; all that is necessary is to discover their true causes. And really there is no reason to feel hatred for a depraved person: after all, the punishment of

---

7. For the reader's curiosity, I impart here an extract from a morning prayer offered by Jews that encompasses the whole doctrine of the Jewish faith: "Exalted is the living and most glorious God, the Being whose existence is independent of time, the One like unto whom there is none other, the Unfathomable whose Oneness has no successor, who has no likeness with beings corporeal nor yet incorporeal. His holiness is beyond investigation. He is the precursor of each created being, the First without antecedent; this Lord of all the World shows His grandeur and dominion to every creature. Part of His foreknowledge He vouchsafed to men deemed worthy of His love and loveliness. No prophet, nor any contemplator of His image, arose in Israel like Moses. God gave the true law to His people through His prophet and willing servant. God will not alter His law or replace it with another through all eternity. He sees into us and knows all that is hidden there. He foresees the end of an act even in its beginning. He dispenses grace to man according to his deeds and casts misfortune upon the unrighteous according to his iniquity. He will send us our anointed one at the end of the age for the redemption of those who rely upon His salvation. God will resurrect the dead according to the abundance of His mercy. May His name be blessed and glorified for all eternity." [L.N.] This is a literal translation of Nevakhovich's Russian-language rendition of Yigdal, the traditional Jewish hymn based on Maimonides' "Thirteen Principles of Faith"; in the Ashkenazic rite, Yigdal serves as an opening hymn of the weekday morning service.

8. If a nation is kept under oppression for a long time, it degenerates in its morality. The Greeks, who were an example to the whole world, finding themselves under the oppressive yoke of the Mohammedans, transformed into something outlandish. . . . Jews in England, Holland, Prussia, in short, where they have more rights and freedom, are far superior in moral behavior to those who had, or still to this day have, no such things. [L.N.]

lawbreakers is not an act of vengeance or malice but has as its object the averting of a greater evil; the punishments laid down for lawbreakers are necessary for keeping society within the due bounds of law and order, and in the opposite instance they deserve to be deplored. Dear compatriots! Let us kiss the divine book[9] of the immortal sovereign Empress Catherine II, in which it is confided to us that punishment beyond the measure needed for correction is a tyrannical punishment! [. . .]

1803

Translated from the Russian by Brian Cooper

---

9. Instruction for Composing the Draft of a New Law Code. [L.N.] Russ. "*Nakaz dlia sochineniia proekta novogo ulozheniia.*" Nevakhovich is here referring to (and misquoting the title of) "*Nakaz Eia Imperatorskogo Velichestva Ekateriny Vtoroi o sochinenii Proekta Novogo Ulozheniia*" ("Instruction of Her Imperial Majesty Catherine II Concerning the Composition of the Draft of a New Law Code"), which Empress Catherine II presented to her celebrated Legislative Commission of 1767.

❋ Gaining a Voice ❋
1840–1881

In 1840, the Imperial Committee endorsed a proposal by Count Sergey Uvarov, minister of public education, addressing the question of Jewish education and calling for the creation of government elementary and secondary Jewish schools in the Pale. After Rabbi Max Lilienthal (1815–1882), Uvarov's first point man, quit in frustration and departed for America in 1844, Leon Mandelstam (1819–1889) essentially took charge of Uvarov's reforms. The first Jew to graduate from a Russian university, Mandelstam also holds the distinction of publishing the first collection of Jewish poetry in Russian (Moscow, 1841). Leon Mandelstam, Ruvim Kulisher (1828–1896), and other members of the second, Russian-oriented generation of the Russian *maskilim* showed a great interest in the public education and integration of the Jewish masses. With the exception of the singular case of Afanasy Fet (1820–1890), the featured writers in this section constitute the very first, still fragile and thin, layer of the Jewish-Russian intelligentsia of the 1840s–1860s, for whom writing in Russian became an intellectual imperative and a great artistic ambition. For the history of early Jewish-Russian letters, the landmark year, after 1803 and 1841, will always be 1859, when a tale by Osip Rabinovich (1817–1869), *The Penal Recruit*, was published in *Russian Messenger (Russkii vestnik)*, a leading Russian review of its day. A Jewish writer had entered the Russian literary mainstream and enjoyed favorable reception. Writing of the founding fathers of Jewish-Russian literature, such as Rabinovich, Lev Levanda (1835–1888), and Grigory Bogrov (1825–1885), the émigré critic Grigory Aronson suggested in 1960 that "during the initial, pioneering period, the [Jewish-Russian] writer was cognizant of the fact that his readers are not only Jews but also new readers from the Russian milieu, for whom Russian Jewry appeared as a mysterious sphinx, either in the magisterial but abstract image of the Eternal Wanderer Ahasuerus or in the rather uncouth, miserable, ugly, and repulsive image that a number of renowned Russian authors had nevertheless associated with the Jews residing in poverty, oppression, and unbearable toil in the Pale of Settlement." In the 1860s, one observes the rise of the Jewish-Russian panoramic novel, such as Lev Levanda's rutted *Seething Times* (published 1871–73), which was set during the Polish Uprising of 1863–64 and at first glance advocated a Jewish alle-

13

giance to Russia and Russianness. Writing of the aspirations of the Jewish-Russian writers and political thinkers in the 1860s and 1870s, not only of Rabinovich and Levanda but also of Leon Pinsker (1821–1891), the future author of *Autoemancipation* (1882) and founder of the Palestinophilic Hibbat Zion (Hebrew "Love of Zion") movement, the ranking historian of Jewish-Russian letters Shimon Markish noted that they "tried to tear their way, their arms thrust open, into the greater but inhospitable world, only to return to the narrow, crowded, and untidy Jewish street and limit themselves to its interests." The idea that in the 1860s and 1870s the early current of Jewish-Russian writing might have been too weak for the larger Russian literary mainstream and therefore carried the writers back to their limited Russian-language Jewish audience calls for a brief digression about the early Jewish-Russian periodicals, where much of the work by Jewish-Russian authors was appearing until the late 1890s.

Dawn *(Rassvet)*, the first Jewish-Russian serial publication founded in Odessa in 1860, only lasted for a year. Two other short-lived periodicals, *Zion* (*Sion*, 1861) and *Day* (*Den'*, 1869–71), also appeared in Odessa, the unrivaled center of the Russian Haskalah in the 1860s. In the 1870s the center of Jewish-Russian publishing shifted to St. Petersburg; according to the data of Dmitri A. Elyashevich, between 1871 and 1916 a total of forty-three Jewish-Russian periodicals appeared in St. Petersburg. An important step was the founding in 1863 in St. Petersburg of the Society for the Dissemination of Education among Jews (OPE). The four principal St. Petersburg publications, where a lion's share of Jewish-Russian writing appeared in the 1870s and 1880s, were the magazines *Dawn* (1879–84, known as *Dawn* "2"), *Messenger of Russian Jews* (*Vestnik russkikh evreev*, 1871–79), *The Russian Jew* (*Russkii evrei*, 1879–84), and the collective volumes of *Jewish Library* (*Evreiskaia biblioteka*, altogether eight volumes in 1871–80 and two more in the 1900s). Running ahead of myself, I should note the publication of the major monthly *Sunrise* (*Voskhod*, 1881–1906) and its weekly supplement. After 1884, *Sunrise* would remain the only regular Jewish-Russian periodical for fifteen years, its print run growing, according to Elyashevich's 1995 survey, from 950 copies in 1881 to 4,397 at its peak in 1895. This information gives one a sense of the dimensions of the immediate audience of Jewish-Russian writers in the 1860s–90s. Perhaps the commanding Jewish-Russian journal of the late czarist era was *Dawn* (known as *Dawn* "3"), founded in St. Petersburg in 1907 as the official Zionist weekly and widely consumed by Jewish-Russian educated circles. With a print run of 10,000 copies, *Dawn* "3" was certainly the most read and the most influential of the periodicals; its publication stopped in 1915 in the atmosphere of wartime censorship. Finally, I should mention the rise of provincial and local Jewish-Russian publications in the Pale and the south of Russia in the 1900s–1910s. For instance, the young Samuil Marshak (1887–1964) published his early, Zionist verse in the Yalta-based magazine *Young Judea* (*Molodaia Iudeia*, 1906).

LEON MANDELSTAM

Leon (Arie-Leib) **Mandelstam** (1819–1889), Hebraist, Jewish educator, multilingual author, was born in Novo-Zagory, Vilna Province (presently Zagare, Lithuania). Mandelstam's father, a reader of the *The Gatherer* (*Ha-Meassef*), a Haskalah journal founded in Königsberg in 1783, made sure that his son learned languages and general subjects. The teenaged Mandelstam discovered Maimonides's *Guide for the Perplexed* and Spinoza and composed his first literary opuses. Mandelstam was married at seventeen and went to live with his wife's parents. In their strictly Orthodox household, where any subject beyond the study of Talmud was regarded as blasphemous, Mandelstam suffered a nervous breakdown. Moving back home, he obtained a *get* (annulment of marriage) and pursued the study of foreign languages and literatures.

In 1839 Mandelstam petitioned Russian authorities to be allowed to take the examination for a gymnasium* diploma and was permitted to enter Moscow University. In his *Notes of the First Jewish Student in Russia*, Mandelstam reminisced:

"Thus I stand now—a wild, strong, free son of nature, loving his fatherland and the language of his native land, but miserable with the misery of his coreligionist brothers. [. . .] The goal of my life is to vindicate them before the world and to help them earn this vindication. They are not mean nor incurably afflicted and corrupt, but they lie supine like a desperate patient with clenched teeth and do not wish to accept curative drops from the hands of the physician; but perhaps their native son, someone of their own soul, suffering with them, will succeed in persuading them" (published 1908). Mandelstam entered Moscow University in 1840, and his Russian-language collection *Poems* was published there in 1841. Mandelstam transferred to St. Petersburg University, to the Faculty of Philosophy, and in 1844 was the first Jew to graduate from a Russian university, although both Derpt University and Vilna University had had Jewish students who were not apostates.

After graduating Mandelstam went abroad to continue his philological training. Upon his return, he was appointed by Prince Sergey Uvarov, Russia's minister of education, to the post of "expert Jew" at his ministry following the departure of Rabbi Max Lilienthal (1815–82) for the United States in 1844. Mandelstam's task was to implement a plan of Jewish education reforms. He was also charged

---

*Gymnasium = high school based on the classical model of liberal arts education.

15

with preparing materials to replace the Talmud in state-sponsored Jewish schools. While in effect running the official Jewish educational program between 1845 and 1857, Mandelstam put together *A Maimonides Reader* (1848), an instruction on civic duties (*Shene Perakim*, 1852), and other texts. Of great importance were Mandelstam's *Hebrew–Russian Dictionary* (1859) and *Russian–Hebrew Dictionary* (1860), used at government yeshivas. Mandelstam also undertook to translate the Pentateuch into Russian. Inspired by Moses Mendelssohn's German translation of the Pentateuch (1783), the first Russian translation by a Jew was a major accomplishment of Mandelstam's career. The first edition of his translation was published in 1862 in Berlin. Permission was finally granted in 1869 for the publication of his translation of the Pentateuch and the Psalms, with parallel Hebrew and Russian texts, and was printed in 1872 in Berlin for distribution in the Russian Empire.

In 1857 Mandelstam left his post at the ministry. He lived abroad for a period of time, publishing books on the Bible and the Talmud and contributing to foreign and Russian periodicals. A brochure with two of Mandelstam's polemical essays was printed in St. Petersburg in 1859 under the title *In Defense of the Jews*. His tale in verse, *The Jewish Family*, which was published in Berlin in 1864, was blocked by the censors and only appeared in Russia, in expurgated form, in 1872. In 1880 a German-language volume of Mandelstam's poetry appeared in London. Initially successful, Mandelstam's publishing ventures eventually failed. Forgotten and impoverished during his last years, he died in St. Petersburg in 1889. Writing in 1944 in the New York magazine *Jewish World* (*Evreiskii mir*), the Yiddish poet and critic Y. Kisin (1886–1950) commented that "the lonely Mandelstam of the 1840s expressed a grievance that was 'eternally Jewish, eternally human', while at the same time predicting and defining the dividedness [*razdvoennost'*] of a member of the Russian-Jewish intelligentsia."

More than half of Mandelstam's *Poems* (1841) were his own translations of what he had originally written in Hebrew. The collection was a landmark of Jewish-Russian literature, the first Russian-language poetry collection by a Jew. Compositely autobiographical for the growing numbers of Jews breaking into the ranks of the Russian intelligentsia in the 1840s and 1850s, the Jewish Student of the book's programmatic poem "The People" meekly dialogues with Olga, a young Russian woman or feminized Russia herself, asking for pity, understanding, and tolerance. Olga appears as a lyrical addressee in several other poems in the collection.

Pleading with the Russians to recognize the humanity of Jews, "The People" constitutes the volume's penultimate section and was probably composed directly in Russian; it exhibits the greatest formal sophistication and hints at Mandelstam's knowledge of Russian Romantic poetry. Fascinating is Mandelstam's likening of his fellow Jews to a messy poem in need of a good (Russian, perhaps even Christian) editor.

Mandelstam's patriotic and apologetic collection is the work of a gifted imitator who did not start writing in Russian until after the age of fifteen. The poems, some stilted and wan and others stylistically old-fashioned already in the 1840s, stand in vast contrast to Ruvim Kulisher's punchy and zesty, Pushkinian *An Answer to the Slav* (1849, in volume 1).

The People

1.

Olga
    There where you live no flower blooms,
    No stream flows—all is desolation;
    It must be that your hearts are numb,
    Your souls devoid of aspiration . . .

Student
    In life I know no bliss or leisure—
    Around me naught but emptiness;
    But I do know a song's sweet pleasure,
    And lofty dreams are my bequest!

    In dreams I leave the plains of exile,
    In dreams I join the ranks of men;
    I step inside the promised temple,
    The homes of brothers and of friends.
    In dreams my soul keeps hope alive,
    Through dreams of nation Jews survive!

2.

Olga
    How to tame them? How to curb them?
    Their savage customs breed contempt.
    No matter how we teach them, spurn them—
    They keep intoning "Talmud" and "Reb"!

Student
    The wind once made the sun a wager:
Who had such might over the stranger
'To take the coat from off his back . . .
    And flapping its powerful wings in attack
    It swooped down in thirty-two onslaughts of black:

    Storms rushed like malevolent criminals, churning
And shrieking with frenzy, with murderous wrath,
They surged and they whirled, stirring up in their path
The water of rivers, the earth on the banks,

    While gusts seized the arms and the legs of the stranger,
His chest and his shoulders . . . How tough was the man! . . .
He wrapped himself tight and he walked with eyes shut;
He struggled, he fell—but held on to his coat! . . .

    The winds die down; the sun in splendor
Sows blossoms on the gloomy track;
It soothes, it strokes the weary stranger,
Calms his suffering, warms his back . . .

    He feels the sunshine's rich abundance
And breathes more freely in its rays.
His clothing now hangs hot upon him—
His winter coat he casts away! . . .

3.

Student
    Our people in essence is much like a poem,
There are errors in form and the whole is perplexing;
Its end comes before it begins incorrectly;
Its parts are untidy, the sense does not hold! . . .

    But a powerful critic, loving the heathen,
Glibly amends the disorganized verse,
Revealing the true spirit of poetic words—
Until heartrending melodies penetrate, seething . . .

Olga
Please tell me some more of your national traits,
Tell me your failings and also your strengths;
And although you alone are the rule's one exception,
For me one's sufficient—your people's redemption
From my scorn is assured; may Christ hold you all dear
And forgive you—you're worthy of genuine tears! . . .

1840

Translated from the Russian by Alyssa Dinega Gillespie

AFANASY FET

Afanasy Fet (1820–90), poet and translator, was born in Novoselki, the estate of the affluent nobleman Afanasy N. Shenshin in Orel Province. The critical literature and literary mythology have led many Russian readers and writers to believe to this day that one and perhaps both of the poet's birth parents were of Jewish extraction. For example, in his memoir *People, Years, Life*, Ilya Ehrenburg (in vol. 1) reported Fet's Jewish origins on the basis of what he had allegedly learned from Fet's nephew. To cite a more recent example, as early as 1977, the poet Stanislav Kunyaev, a leader of what was then the emerging Russian ultranationalism, juxtaposed the poetic sensibility of the Odessa Jewish-Russian poet Eduard Bagritsky (in vol. 1), in Kunyaev's view a Jewish alien in the groves of Russian poetry, with that of two major Russian poets of Jewish origin, Afanasy Fet and Osip Mandelstam (in vol. 1), both of whom somehow satisfied Kunyaev's criteria of cultural "Russianness." Laden with controversy both old and new, the question of Fet's origins remains open, and it is not the editor's purpose in this anthology to resolve it one way or the other. Shenshin, a retired Russian officer, came to Darmstadt in 1820 for the waters and met Charlotte Foeth (née Becker), the wife of the local tax assessor Johann Peter Karl Wilhelm Foeth, who was also a minor poet. Charlotte Foeth (Fet is the Russianized spelling), who was twenty-two at the time and pregnant with her second child, left her husband for Shenshin, came to Russia with him, and about two months later gave birth to a boy. Out of respect for the landowner, the parish priest who baptized the newborn recorded him as Shenshin's own son; in 1822, after the divorce of Charlotte and Johann Foeth had been finalized, the child's mother and Shenshin were married in a Russian Orthodox ceremony. Twelve years later, in 1834, the Orel Ecclesiastical Consistory conducted an inquest and ruled that Afanasy was not Shenshin's lawful son. Until that time, the boy had reportedly assumed that he was a Shenshin and a Russian nobleman; now he had to identify himself as "Afanasy Fet, subject of Hessen-Darmstadt." Although Fet's teenage years were not lacking in privilege, the experience traumatized him, motivating his career choices and his reluctance to disclose what he knew, or thought he knew, of his origins.

Fet entered Moscow University in 1838 and became part of a circle of gifted students centered around the future poet and critic Apollon Grigoriev. Fet's first collection, *Lyrical Pantheon*, released in 1840, was signed "A.F.," but by 1842 he began to sign his poems "Fet." A number of Fet's early lyrics (e.g., "Don't wake her at dawn . . .") became instant classics, and in 1843 the leading critic Vissarion Belinsky (1811–1848) called Fet "the most gifted" of the Moscow poets.

Fet entered military service in 1845 and spent eight years in a cuirassier regiment in Kherson Province, writing and publishing little. His second volume, *Poems*, did not appear until 1850. His transfer to the guards in 1853 enabled him to spend time in St. Petersburg and to become close to such literary figures as Ivan Turgenev, who regarded his verse as "higher" and "freer" than Heinrich Heine's (Turgenev's comparison with the Jewish-born German poet may not have been gratuitous) and edited a volume of Fet's poems in 1856. During this time, Fet contributed to *The Contemporary* (*Sovremennik*), a leading review, and in 1857 married Maria Botkina, the sister of the critic Vladimir Botkin. The following year Fet retired from the military as a captain, without earning the desired hereditary nobility. In 1860 he purchased an estate in his native Mtsensk District and became an enthusiastic landowner. After releasing a two-volume edition of his works in 1863, Fet published no other books of verse until 1883 and contributed little to periodicals during these two decades. He engaged in local politics and was elected to the post of public arbitrator in 1867. By the late 1860s, he had developed a profound interest in Arthur Schopenhauer's thought, eventually publishing a translation into Russian of volume 1 of *The World as Will and Representation* in 1881.

In December 1873, following Fet's appeal to Alexander II, a royal edict admitted him "to the family name of his father Shenshin with all the rights pertaining to his title and name." At last Fet had achieved his lifelong goal for himself and his children. "Now that it's all over, thank God, you cannot imagine how much I loathe the name Fet," Fet wrote to his wife on 10 January 1874. "[. . .] If one asks for the name of all my suffering, all the woes of my life, I will then answer: the name Fet." Shenshin became his legal name, but he kept Fet as his literary name. In 1877 he bought a larger estate and, in 1881, a house in Moscow, where he wintered. He returned to literary life in the 1880s, and his 1883 collection, *Evening Lights*, was lauded by critics. Fet was given the court title of *Kammerherr* (Chamberlain) in 1889. He died in Moscow in 1892.

Even in his memoirs, published in the 1890s, Fet failed to tell the full story of his origins. In *My Reminiscences* Fet described as a moment of great relief his discovery, in the papers of his deceased father, an 1820 document, apparently a forgery, that Shenshin and Fet's mother had been married in a Lutheran church prior to his birth, which proved that he had not been born out of wedlock. While one should not discount Fet's emotional response to the secret of his birth, the stigma of bastardy alone can hardly explain why Fet continued to obfuscate his origins even after Alexander II granted him the full privileges of nobility. Fet's actions appear incommensurate with the way noblemen's illegitimate children were perceived in Russian society. In a letter to Fet, Tolstoy responded to the news of the 1873 royal edict: "I was very surprised, having received your letter, dear Afanasy Afanasievich, although I had been hearing . . . for a while the history of this whole mess, and I am glad at your courage to unravel it, however long it has taken. I have always observed that this tormented you, and although I myself could not understand what there was to be tormented by, I felt that this must have had an enormous impact on your whole life." Whether Tolstoy's "this whole mess" alluded only to Fet's illegitimate birth or to another secret, his words underscored a bewilderment with Fet's reaction. What else was behind Fet's response to what he knew of his own birth, compelling him to resort to such obfuscatory measures?

One may never be able to reconstruct what exactly Fet and his intimates knew and did not know. Even in a letter to his future wife (16 July 1857), Fet passed over some aspects of his background and embellished others: "My mother was married to my father, the Darmstadt scholar and attorney Foeth . . . and was pregnant with me. At that time my stepfather, Shenshin, came to stay in Darmstadt and took my mother away from Foeth . . . Several months after Shenshin came to his country estate, my mother gave birth to me. About half a year or a year later Foeth died, and Shenshin married my mother. This is the story of my birth."

Fet's inability to put the matter of his origins to rest may have been a response to an alternative version of his birth that circulated among his contemporaries. It was rumored that Shenshin saw a young, "beautiful Jewess" in a roadside saloon in Königsberg, East Prussia, "bought" her from her husband, took her home, and later married her, and that Fet was the fruit of that marriage. In his autobiography, the artist and art historian Igor Grabar (1871–1960) referred to this version as "Pulcinella's secret," claiming that Fet's friends, including the poet Yakov Polonsky (1819–1898), knew about his alleged Jewish origins. Fet himself made compensatory (or self-hating?) remarks of the most stereotypically antisemitic sort: "The Yids cheated me and short-changed me. They stalk Russians and Swedes the way a raven stalks blood" (*From Abroad: Travel Impressions*). Regarding himself in the mirror, did the phenotypically sensitive Fet see a Semitic face (several of Fet's photographic portraits survive) or imagine the face of a Russian nobleman, be he of Slavic or Germanic stock?

A number of Soviet scholars, including Grigory Blok, Yakov Bukhshtab, and Dmitry Blagoy, have treated the subtleties of Fet's origins in academic and popular publications. In 1942, the German Slavist Reinhold Trautmann published a note in volume 18 of *Zeitschrift für slavische Philologie* entitled "The Mother of A. Fet-Shenshin." Aiming to dispel the opinion that Fet's mother was of "German Jewish origin" (Deutsche jüdischer Abstammung), Trautmann claimed that the parents of Charlotte Becker were Lutherans (evangelischer Konfession) and that Fet's maternal grandmother came from an old German noble family, the von Gagerns. Reporting that Fet's father, Johann Peter Karl Wilhelm Foeth (1789–1825), was of "the Catholic creed" (katholischen Glaubensbekenntnisses), Trautmann stated that his baptismal certificate could not be found in Köln, where Foeth was born.

An incomplete Russian translation of Trautmann's article appeared in the reform-era USSR in 1990 in the newspaper *Literary Russia* (*Literaturnaia Rossiia*), a stronghold of Russian nationalists. It was furnished with an introduction, "On the Mysteries of Afanasy Fet's Origins," by Vadim Kozhinov (1930–2001). The *éminence grise* of the Russian ultranationalist cultural movement since the 1970s, Kozhinov subsequently published antisemitic books such as *Mysterious Pages in Twentieth-Century History* (1995), where chapter 4, a defense of the Black Hundreds, is entitled "The Truth about Pogroms." Kozhinov had been keen to debunk the theories of Fet's Jewish origins since the late 1970s. Convinced that Fet's biological father was not Foeth but Afanasy Shenshin, Kozhinov argued nonetheless that Johann Foeth himself was not a Jew but an illegitimate son of "one of the sons of the Archduke of Hessen-Darmstadt, Ludwig I [*sic*]." Kozhinov was obviously threatened by the possibility that the great Russian poet Fet might have come of Jewish stock.

In *The Poetics of Afanasy Fet* (2002), the American Slavist Emily Klenin aptly characterized Trautmann's 1942 article as a "worthy testament to the Zeitgeist that engendered it." Klenin deemed "rumors [. . .] of Fet's Jewish origins" to be "apparently false." Allowing for the possibility of Fet's "perhaps now knowing the truth himself," she detailed the incongruities in Fet's reporting of his background. Admitting that "the apparent mystery of Fet's parentage is odd, since Fet was in contact with his German relatives throughout his life," Klenin deferred to the research of Rainer Goldt.

In 1988 Rainer Goldt, a German Slavist, published an illuminating essay in German entitled "Burden and Bond: Afanasy A. Fet as Mediator and Critic of German Culture." Goldt checked the Lutheran church records in Darmstadt and confirmed that neither the marriage record of Charlotte Becker and Johann Foeth nor the birth record of Charlotte Foeth (née Becker) mentioned their Jewish origins. Goldt also corroborated Trautmann's 1942 statement that no information about Johann Foeth's baptism could be located in the archives in Köln. Major gaps thus remain in our knowledge of Fet's origins.

The identity of a Jewish-Russian writer is defined not only by questionable bloodlines or confession but also by one's self-awareness as a (former) Jew and an (aspiring) Russian. Such an identity is also forged by the perception of the writer and his legacy by the public and the literary community. In the case of Afanasy Fet, the poet's dual awareness betrayed itself primarily not through self-expression but through both obfuscation and compensation. Fet's legacy will remain intricately linked with the Jewish presence in Russian culture and history, and his poetry will continue to raise questions about his origins—questions that may never be answered.

Lyrical and confessional, Fet's best verses articulate a soul's turmoil in tremulous words. He continued to write post-Romantic poetry in the 1880s with little anticipation of modernism. His landscape lyrics, such as "Chudnaia kartina . . ." ("Wondrous picture . . ."), are among the finest in Russian classical prosody, inviting a comparison with the landscapes of Isaac Levitan (1860–1900), a Jew and one of the most "Russian" of Russian painters.

With two notable exceptions, Fet's original poetry exhibits no explicit Jewish themes. The first of the two selected poems, "When my daydreams cross the brink of long-lost days . . . ," appeared in *Notes of the Fatherland* (*Otechestvennye zapiski*) in 1845. In 1892, not long before his death, Fet included the poem in the outline of an edition of his collected works. Fet published the second poem, "Sheltered by a crimson awning . . . ," in his *Poems* (1850), a volume that also contained translations of a number of poems by Heinrich Heine. Fet intended to include the second poem in the 1892 outline of his collected works.

Although Biblical references were standard fare in Russian poetry of Fet's age, the two poems deserve special attention. Fet's identification with the "first Hebrew" and his fashioning of the Jewish matriarch as both an "odalisque" and an "houri of the prophet" may signal an attraction of Fet the poet (and possibly a Jewish alien) to what Shenshin the person (and the hopeful Russian nobleman) had shunned his whole life.

*   *   *

When my daydreams cross the brink of long-lost days
To find you there again, within the mist of memory,
I weep sweet tears, like the first Hebrew who gazed
Upon the promised land beyond the boundary.

I don't regret the childish games or quiet dreams
Stirred up so painfully and sweetly by your presence
During those days when I discovered what first love means:
A chaotic rush of feelings, restless

Hours, the pressure of a hand, and shining eyes,
The murmur of our innocent, senseless patter
Accompanied now by giggles, now by tender sighs—
These seemed to us the echo of true passion.

1844

*   *   *

Sheltered by a crimson awning,
All alone, his slaves dismissed,
A lord is bidding farewell fondly
To a black-browed odalisque.

"Sarah, houri of the prophet,
My sunshine, comfort, strength, delight,
Sarah, morning's not far off now—
Azrael will soon alight.

"After battle on the morrow
Will I still walk the earth somewhere,
Or, forever freed from sorrow,
Rest my head without a care?

"Another night and tabernacle
Soon may take the place of these;
Then despite my ardent rapture,
I won't touch your rosebud cheek.

"I won't smoke my lazy hookah
Idly as you bide nearby,
Will not pensively sit looking
Into your gazelle-like eyes.

"Nor will I with weary fingers
Plait and twist your tresses black
Along the scarlet fez and fringes
Into a shining, scaly snake."

1847

Translated from the Russian by Alyssa Dinega Gillespie

RUVIM KULISHER

Ruvim (Reuben) **Kulisher** (1828–1896), essayist, poet, and Jewish communal leader, was born in Dubno, Volhynia, in 1828. His father, a follower of the Haskalah, insisted on giving him a systematic European education along with a solid grounding in Judaism. Kulisher, therefore, studied at the Zhitomir classical gymnasium. He entered St. Petersburg University in 1848 and was, to the best of our knowledge, the third Jewish student (after Leon Mandelstam and Mavriky Rappoport) to graduate from a Russian university. Kulisher studied at the Medical-Surgical Academy in St. Petersburg in 1852–56, whereupon he joined the Russian army's medical corps as a physician, one of the first three Jews to be given such a position. Starting in 1860, Kulisher was on the staff of the Kiev Military Hospital, and he spent 1869–76 in western Europe on a research fellowship, specializing in public health. He published several medical articles, including an analysis of skin diseases mentioned in the Bible.

A close disciple and friend of the "Russian Mendelssohn," Isaac Ber Levinson (1788–1860), Kulisher contributed essays on Jewish history, communal living, and education to Jewish periodicals in both Hebrew and Russian. In 1892–94, the Jewish-Russian periodical *Sunrise* (*Voskhod*) serialized the first part of Kulisher's memoirs, *Summing Up. The Hopes and Expectations of Russian Jews over the Past 50 Years, 1838–1888*, expanded and published as a separate book in 1896. He died in Kiev in August 1896.

Kulisher created one of the earliest works of Jewish-Russian poetry, the polemical poem *An Answer to the Slav*. He composed *An Answer to the Slav* in November 1849 while a student at St. Petersburg University. Hand copies of this poem of nearly 400 lines circulated and were known to Kulisher's contemporaries. Attempts by Kulisher and his friends to publish the poem in the 1840s and 1850s failed, most likely owing to government censorship. One stanza made it to print in 1861, quoted in the Jewish-Russian weekly *Dawn* (*Rassvet*). In 1911 Saul Ginsburg (1866–1940), a Jewish historian and journalist, founder of the Yiddish daily *The Friend* (*Der Fraind*, St. Petersburg), obtained the text of *An Answer to the Slav* from Kulisher's son and published it with a biographical introduction in issue 3 of the collection *The Bygone* (*Perezhitoe*). In *Tsar Nicholas I and the Jews* (1983), the historian Michael Stanislawski described the poem as expressing "bitter disillusionment with the basic axioms of the Haskalah's political ideology." Kulisher's poem was a daring response to the Judeophobic commonplaces of Russian literature and journalism of the 1820s–40s, where the Jewish question was habitually treated with a mixture of ignorance, antisemitic stereotyping, and crude Christian supersessionism. The writings that were likeliest to provoke Kulisher's answer were not such works as *The Avaricious Knight* (1830), the "little tragedy" by the national Russian author Alexander Pushkin, whom Kulisher mentions, but rather the works of Faddey Bulgarin (1789–1859), a popular middle brow novelist and journalist, especially his novels *Little Esther* (1828) and *Ivan Vyzhigin* (1829), and his article "Polish Jews" (1838). What is particularly important, and especially if compared to the shyly apologetic argument of Leon Mandelstam's "The People" (in vol. 1), is not only the demand for legal equality for the Jews but also the poem's attack on the Slavs' Christian, religious antisemitism. "The Jews have always treated us in accordance with the Jewish faith," the Russian religious philosopher Vladimir Solovyev would write thirty-five years after Kulisher in *Jewry and the Christian Question* (1884). "We Christians, on the contrary, have yet to learn to treat the Jews in the Christian fashion."

The Romantic-ironic detachment and the formal makeup of Kulisher's poem point to its sources in Pushkin's *Eugene Onegin* (1833). Both the iambic tetrameter of Kulisher's poem and use of stanzaic structure and rhyme (quatrains in which conjoining and enclosing rhymes alternate with couplets) recall the Onegin stanza. Additionally, Kulisher includes several deliberate allusions to and borrowings from Pushkin's novel in verse. In places skillful and well tempered, in others a composition of an imitator–apprentice, *An Answer to the Slav* showcases instances of elegant versification alongside those of heavy-handed rhymestering. But it is the work of a Russian poet, and nothing in its composition and language bespeaks a Jew timidly making his entrance into the forbidden corridors of Russian literature. The unapologetic, militantly satirical Jewish-Russian voice of Kulisher's poem makes it absolutely unique for its time and anticipates Vladimir Jabotinsky's feuilletons of the 1890s–1900s (see "An Exchange of Compliments" in vol. 1). Had Kulisher's poem been published soon after its composition, it would have given other aspiring Jewish-Russian authors a model to follow: learn from the Russian masterpieces and infuse your work with Jewish subject matter.

From *An Answer to the Slav*

Introduction

I hesitate to sound immodest,
So I must warn you in advance,
If you will listen now in earnest,
Then please excuse my stance.

More startling than other words,
And I will use this frightening word—
It is as novel to your ears
As the whistle of steam that I first heard.
Perhaps your ears are all too tender,
Unused to terrifying sounds,
Then you'll immediately consider
My speech so spitefully unbound.

Not ancient ghosts or petty demons,
Nor the old mounted wicked witch,
Nor even Satan's evil sermons
Contribute to the subject which
I wish to talk to you about:
Those themes have long since been portrayed,
And even cannibals no doubt,
To some will seem a bit too staid.
I wish to introduce the *Jew.*
Please don't be scared, I beg of you,
Oh, how you trembled, turning pale—
I'll either smash the frightening tale
Or for a time put it aside
So fragile souls can feel no fear
While those with moral strength decide,
To love the truth with hearts sincere.

[. . .]

III.

In exile I was given shelter,
For loads of money, by the Pole;
My sufferings grew manifold
With wild assaults by Polish *szlachta*[1]
Beholding my endless torments
How many times the Pole rejoiced:
His crops were watered by the torrents
Of Jewish blood upon his fields!
From Little Russia came the raids
By Cossacks threatening to erase me,
And for my gold the Pole repaid me
With nothing but profound contempt.

Those people had no God, although
They wanted to appease him so;
And knowing neither Faith nor Love
They sought those virtues in my blood.
And though the people have improved
And they no longer torture Jews,
We still cannot sigh with relief,
The road to peace is long and steep.
It's been my lot to stand there waiting
At Russia's still unopened gate.
For bread and salt upon a plate
In vain I stood anticipating.
I'm just allowed to share the pain
Of this vast empire and its nation:
Your brother in war and desperation,
In peace you treat me with disdain.
Enlightenment brings me only torment,
I see without any adornment:
With others enjoying naught but bliss
What misery for me exists.

[. . .]

---

1. *Szlachta* (Pol.) = Polish rank-and-file landed gentry.

Why is my lot much more ill-fortuned
Than even the fate of the Tatars
Whose gifts to you were yoke and torture,
Who kept you debtors from afar?
Is it because you hate and envy
The fact your Savior was a Jew?
Whatever may say the mob of enemies
He's *mine*, and He has suffered for *you*.
There is no need to force upon us
And fiercely teach the law of love:
For generations we have followed
What our forebears gained from above!

When will the freedom of our conscience—
The spirit's priceless treasury—
Be finally granted to the nation
That heeds its ancestors' decrees?
Too few still victims of coercion[2]
And violence defying reason?
Does spiritual apostasy burgeon
Amid the riches bought with treason?
Or maybe God has willed this daily
Defilement of our holy rights?
Should we blaspheme in public sight,
And abnegate our family?
A child will disavow his mother,
A father will disown his son,
And then 'til death they'll weep and suffer . . .
Behold the plight of the martyred nation!

IV.

No longer stalwart in his ways,
The Jew is subject now to changing;
So in advance I have portrayed—
And you may well find this estranging—
A previous image of my nation:

---

2. The Jewish *kantonisty* (conscripts) and recruits are subjected—of course, without the knowledge of the government—to treatment that hardly disposes the Jews toward fulfilling their military service . . . [R.K.]

The way they had existed prior
To '46, when regulations
Compelled a change in their attire.
And wearing garb of German style;[3]
Back when the trepid brides would fear
The matronly matchmakers' wile;
The Jewish girls would not come near.
The Hussar and his enticing tricks;
The Jew had not discovered the theater,
And actresses and the coulisse,
And hearing a female singer
Was not a negligible sin.
His thoughts converged upon one thing:
On gaining bliss through faith and care,
On acts of goodness one has wrought,[4]
On bettering his heart through prayer,
And reaching God in lofty thought.

[. . .]

Here is for you a salient feature
Of my portrayal, with its help
I understand the total picture,
The mystery reveals itself.
But there is yet another trait
My nation's everlasting fate,
The Holy Land we left behind,
The unforgettable, the cherished,
The one that never leaves our minds,
The land whose image never perished.
This high abode of dreamy visions,
Lays claim to us our whole life long;
This dream we yet again revisit,
Transported on the wings of song.
There everything heartfelt abounds,
The sky vault's nearer to the ground.

---

3. In 1844 the government of Tsar Nicholas I abolished the *kahal* communal structure of Jewish life in the Russian Empire. According to the 1846 regulations that followed the abolishment of the *kahal*, Jews were required, among other things, to modernize their medieval garb.

4. *Tora u-maasim tovim* [Heb. = Torah and good deeds.]. [R.K.]

One does not seek the heavens there—
Where heaven and earth are merged forever.[5]
The Jew has carried into exile
His feelings for the holy land,
He'll bear them throughout every trial,
And every hardship he'll withstand.

[. . .]

Behold his main characteristics:
My sketchy portrait of the Jew
Is a defense, and bold logistics
To show how slanders are untrue.
I know the day will finally come
When Slavs embrace us all as one.
The Russian and the Polish nation
Will offer us reconciliation.
For all the ancestors' offense
Their heirs will show me tolerance,
And having heard my tale of torments
Will willingly tear down the fences.

I hope the face that I have shown
The Jew acknowledges as his own.
I hope he shows his future children,
And tells of me without chagrin.
And if he's worthier than I
And more enlightened he is made—
May he appreciate my aid
When I was fighting for his rights!

1849

Translated from the Russian by Maxim D. Shrayer

---

5. Especially remarkable among the beliefs the Jews have about the Holy Land is the one that attributes to this land the capacity to purify of sins those who are buried in it. Therefore many Jews move there in old age so as to await death. [R.K.]

OSIP RABINOVICH

Osip (Yosef) **Rabinovich** (1817–1869), fiction writer, essayist, and editor, was born in Kobeliaki in Poltava Province and received a broad education in the home of his affluent father. After his marriage at the age of eighteen, he studied law independently before entering Kharkov University in 1840. Because of a government prohibition against unconverted Jews on the bar, Rabinovich was unable to study law and enrolled instead at the Faculty of Medicine, but he left without taking a degree after his father's affairs deteriorated. In 1845 Rabinovich settled in Odessa, where he served at the Commercial Court. He was elected a notary public in 1848 and participated as a city councilman in the drafting of Odessa's new civil code.

The publication in 1847 of Rabinovich's Russian translation of the poem *The Battle (Ha-Krav)* by the Hebrew poet Jacob Eichenbaum (1796–1861) showcased his impeccably perfect command of literary Russian. It was reprinted in St. Petersburg by the very popular magazine *Library for Reading* (*Biblioteka dlia chteniya*), edited by the Polish-born Orientalist and author Osip Senkovsky, whose literary penname was Baron Brambeus. Two essays published in *The Odessa Herald* (*Odesskii vestnik*), "The New Jewish Synagogue" (1847) and "Apropos the Kind Word" (1848), defined the agenda of Rabinovich the polemicist. His principled if conflicted position of "fighting on two fronts"—defending Jews from antisemitism while also exposing their own flaws—influenced a whole generation of Russianized Jewish intelligentsia.

Rabinovich's first work of fiction, *The Story of the Trading Firm Firlich & Co.* (1849), was free of Jewish thematics, but his next short novel, *Morits Sefardi* (1850), is commonly considered the first work of Jewish-Russian fiction. In terms of Russian literary history, there were many "firsts" in *Morits Sefardi:* a young maskilic protagonist; a traditional Jew rendered not through antisemitic caricature or abstract humanism but with deep knowledge and understanding; Jewish speech represented in Russian not via imitation of accent but through Jewish sayings translated almost literally. Rabinovich's next novel, *Kaleidoscope,* published in its entirety in 1860, featured Odessa's multiethnic life and a poet as one of its protagonists. Jews in it have speaking albeit not principal parts. In the years following the ascension and reforms of Alexander II, Rabinovich gained a national reputation as a writer on Jewish issues. In 1859 his most famous work, *The Penal Recruit,* appeared in the Moscow review *The Russian Messenger* (*Russkii vestnik*). Russian Jewry hailed Rabinovich's tale, and it was read publicly in Jewish homes where no other non-

Jewish books were allowed. Legends describe gatherings of Jews where makeshift Yiddish translations of *The Penal Recruit* would be improvised and read on the spot. An 1860 volume with the German translation, published in Leipzig, sold several thousand copies.

The Penal Recruit (excerpt below) was the first in a two-part work entitled *Pictures of the Past*, set in the era of Nicholas I. The second part, the tale *The Hereditary Candlestick,* appeared serially in 1860 in the new magazine *Dawn (Rassvet)*, which Rabinovich cofounded in Odessa with Yoachim Tarnopol (1810–1900; on the history of the Jewish-Russian press, see the section introduction). *Dawn* was the first Jewish-Russian weekly magazine, although several Jewish periodicals with the same title appeared subsequently. As the magazine's editor, Rabinovich contributed thirty-nine front-page articles. He was hopeful that Russia's Jews would ameliorate themselves with the government's support. However, *Dawn* was closed down after a year, both under government pressure and also due to Rabinovich's own realization that his arguments were lending wind to the sails of Judeophobes. Disillusioned with his own powers as a Jewish-Russian spokesman but also with the extent of Alexander II's liberalizing reforms (the Pale, a chief impediment of Jewish opportunities in the Russian Empire, was never dismantled), Rabinovich divided his latter years between the tasks of a journalist for the mainstream Russian press and those of a Jewish-Russian belletrist. His most formally accomplished work is *The Tale of How Reb Hayyim-Shulim Feiges Traveled from Kishinev to Odessa and What Transpired with Him on the Way* (Odessa, 1865). Rabinovich's maskilic scorn had metamorphosed into warmth and sympathy, and the narrator's Jewish perspective was no longer encumbered by the contradictions of being both an advocate for and a critic of his people. Rabinovich was seriously ill in his last years and died of consumption in Merano, Tyrol, in 1869.

Almost nothing in the style of *The Penal Recruit* betrays a nonnative Russian writer, and for a Jewish writer composing prose in Russian in 1859, this is one of its significant achievements. The subject and the narrator's outlook are deeply Jewish, though, and the tone, both dispassionate and naïve, is perfectly chosen to depict the recruitment of Jews under Nicholas I. Rabinovich presented Jewish suffering neither sentimentally nor ethnographically. The Russian reader of Rabinovich's age would find Rabinovich's tale both strange and gripping, while the Jewish reader would feel the bittersweet pleasure of recognition.

From *The Penal Recruit*

CHAPTER 2

The entire next day I couldn't get the recruit out of my mind. Taking pains to wait until evening, I then set off to see him. This time he greeted me more kindly; I could even tell that my visit gave him pleasure.

"Do you know, I've been waiting impatiently for you," he said to me. "Since the time this disaster struck me, I have not seen a friendly face to take an interest in me, a person to whom I could pour out my sorrow. I only managed to see my wife and daughter once . . . for a very short time, but now how can I see them? God Almighty! I wouldn't wish such a situation on anyone."

"When did you see them?" I asked.

"When they were putting the gray overcoat on me," he answered, "an hour before they sent me on my long journey. But that's the end of my story, and you don't yet know the beginning. Now listen to this."

We sat down across from one another; he rested his elbows on the table, crossed his hands, and in a drawn out, quiet voice began his story:

"The town where I lived, grew up, and became a man is inhabited nearly entirely by Jews and located not far from the border. We have a fairly large community. Although I was not one of the very rich men, I was still well off. I was involved in trade like the majority of our people and managed to earn enough to maintain my position thanks to hard work and thriftiness. I lived happily with my family, my wife and two daughters; God did not give me a boy. For a long time I complained, but now I see that it was for the best. In my free time, and there was quite enough of it, since my business did not demand constant work—I bought up wool and sold it to foreign merchants who came for it—I liked to read and study non-Jewish subjects. These were accessible to me thanks to a natural inclination, which had been developed in me by my late father. You know that for the most part we all study on a shoestring since we are intended to engage in trade. Actually only someone who wants to devote himself exclusively to scholarship studies seriously and systematically; the merchant class considers serious study secondary. With us in the western provinces in any case, that's the way it is. There is certainly no point in looking for scholars or highly educated men among us—that's a luxury, and we are condemned to work. We have to exist, and it isn't easy to exist, because we are crammed in large communities and restricted in most of our actions, as you know. So there is no point in looking for well-educated men among us, but at the same time, total ignorance, a lack of at least some knowledge, this, too, is a rarity among us. Many of us have more or less studied a bit, and one doesn't feel embarrassed to meet with them, as we Jews say. That is, among us there are well-cultivated individuals, in a Jewish, limited way, of course, since they are still far from true European enlightenment, and this applies not only to them but to many others, too, who are much higher than they are on the social ladder and enjoy far better living conditions. I am speaking about civil servants and proprietors. Of course, the exceptions do not change this fact.

"I had my own small circle of friends, which consisted of what we call *autodidacts*, that is, the self-taught. We used to get together and discuss Jewish literature, which in recent years has achieved great success abroad, or new works in Polish and German. Few in our midst knew Russian well—for the most part only those who had direct contact with the government knew Russian, for example, the tax farmers, their lawyers, contractors, and those who carried out official duties. I was happy, surrounded by my small family and friends. Our time was divided between our respective business affairs and the tranquil evenings spent at one of our homes, where ignorant Jewish businessmen, unknown to the world at large, sometimes discussed the latest questions of science and literature from the far corners of Europe. Our town and its outlying small towns, it seems, enjoyed as much prosperity as we could, given the periodic invasions of the municipal and rural administrations, for whom a place populated by Jews makes up a profitable source of revenue. There's no point in telling you about it since I think it must be the same where you live too, right?"

"Unfortunately, yes," I answered.

"Of course!" the old man continued with vigor. "Whether it's a fair, a dead body, a deserter, or a new ordinance concerning synagogues or private schools—all of it is turned into a pretext for bribery, making a solid source of income for certain people. The end is always the same: a sum is collected by members of the community, the representatives go off with the offering and the drumbeat of disaster subsides until the next time. And we are used to it. You know how easily a Jew reconciles himself to his fate. A warm hearth, an onion, a piece of bread and a piece of fish or meat on the Sabbath, and he's happy. Recalling that persecution is his fate from the cradle on, that it is predestined from above, he hums his *zemiros* (mealtime songs)[1] and wipes a random tear with his fist in expectation of a better future."

He stopped and for several minutes sat in deep silence.

"But our community was afflicted by one misfortune from which we could never extricate ourselves," the soldier began again. "And it affected not just our community but everyone, as far as we know. It is the shortfall in our quota of military recruits. We constantly expended huge sums on bribes in the provincial capital, hired replacement recruits from other towns, jumped out of our skin, but were always in arrears. Since I enjoyed an honorable reputation in our town and was known as a selfless man, I, among others, was chosen as a *kahal* representative and served in this position over ten years. Do you know what a *kahal* representative does? He is either a robber or a martyr, there is no in between. He has to endure the cries of a poor man who, because

---

1. *Zemirot (zemiros)* = traditional Hebrew songs sung during the Sabbath meal; see David Aizman's "The Countrymen" (vol. 1).

of his debts, has just been deprived of his last blanket, which had served as a shield from the cold for his naked family. He has to endure the screams of a widow from whom her last son has been taken as a recruit. He has to put up with persecutions from rich Jews, if in some way he has inconvenienced their distant relatives in the effort to collect debts or meet other obligations; the rich always have defenders on call. He is vulnerable to the persecution of the authorities if, out of pity for poor Jews, he thinks of stopping the daily robbery of the tax collector, who sells meatless bones as though they were meat, and at the double price, no less. If the *kahal* representative has a heart, he is apt to experience torture daily. If he has a rock in his chest instead of a heart, he joins the oppressors and makes a sizeable profit. Either a criminal or a martyr, I tell you! Fortunately or unfortunately, I belonged to the latter group. Only God Almighty knows what I endured and experienced.

"The eviction of Jews from the countryside and villages, their restriction to a few occupations and to living in the Pale of Settlement, and other laws, coming at the same time as the growth of the population, brought on terrible poverty. You could barely count one wealthy Jew for two hundred poor ones. Pauperism and homelessness increased every year. Our custom of marrying children at an early age contributed a great deal to this poverty. This stupid custom has done a great deal of harm! If for a rich man a large family increases the number of workers and brings beneficence, for a homeless man who has no specific employment it is an absolute curse. [. . .]

"With each year and each recruitment selection, our community's monetary and recruitment arrears kept accumulating. Earlier selections had quite depleted us; many families ran away and disappeared without a trace, and many of those capable of working fled abroad. There was not a single middle-class family that was not short of a brother, a son, a grandson, a husband. Some went into hiding, while others had already been handed over to the recruitment. Some families had already given recruits two or three times, but soon their turn would come again, since there was no one left. Recruitments came often in our parts. If there was one in the *Western Region*, we gave recruits; if there was one in the *Eastern Region*, again we gave recruits—and each time, ten for every thousand. An impossible task! And how many among the thousand were underage, already deceased, aged, sick, or infirm? How many had run away or, in the end, had already been drafted for military service but had not been removed from the recruitment list as they should have been!

"For us, the elected representatives, this was pure torture. God is a witness how we were tortured as we tried to fulfill the government's demands. And what could we do? It was completely beyond our power. Whenever we saw an orphan, an unmarried man, a drunkard, we turned them over. Families fought with us, and they were right; they had fulfilled their quota long ago with one and even two recruits. We collected money, sent it off to various places, and hired recruits, but that was always connected with extreme difficulties and expenses, and rarely was crowned with success. The government officials would nag us, threaten us. We had to go down to the capital of our province, get down on our knees, beg, give present after present, incur terrible expenses. Documents and reports flew in all directions: 'such and such urban community cannot fulfill . . . owing to cholera or recent fires' . . . or something else, and meanwhile time would pass and the storm would die down for a few months, but the costs were huge! Our strength and money perished in vain because our arrears not only did not diminish but grew larger.

"Don't even ask about the district officials and inspectors for God's sake! Whether one of them had a paper from the provincial authorities or didn't have one, if we had to send recruits or not, what business was it of his? He would roll into a small town, and the small town would shake as though in a fever. 'Close the shops . . . punish someone . . . drive everyone into the synagogue . . . light black candles . . . swear in both young and old!' Why? For what reason? God only knows! Of course, the outcome was the same: another deputation, more bows, and the usual presents.

"I must confess that this constant fear and worry made life repulsive. I implored the community to relieve me of the duties of *kahal* representative and choose someone in my place. I wanted to leave the town, even the region, so as to move far away and not see scenes that outraged my soul and occurred more and more frequently as we failed to manage.

"I've already told you that I had two daughters. One was seventeen at the time, already engaged. Her fiancé was an orphan, without money, but he had great talents. He was studying medicine at a distant university, at my expense. The end of his course of studies was still three years away, but when he got his diploma we were going to have a wedding. My other daughter was only a child of thirteen. My daughters were pretty . . . or perhaps it just seemed that way to a father's eyes. Did I see them as obligations? They were my children, my blood, my joy and consolation in this world. They made up a part of my being. It seemed impossible to separate them from me, just as it would be impossible to tear my heart from my breast . . . Oh my God, my God; they have been ripped away from me, and I am still alive! . . ."

He jumped up and in inexpressible despair began to swing his arms and hit himself in the chest, letting out hollow moans. I let him get all his crying out. Perhaps I also cried, I don't remember. After a few minutes he calmed down somewhat and sat down again.

"Excuse the tears of an unfortunate father," he began again, taking my hand. "I cannot remember my children without shedding tears. Right here, this is where I feel terrible pain!"

He pointed to his chest.

"I understand your grief," I replied, "but I—"

"—but you cannot ameliorate grief with tears," he interrupted, without letting me finish, "you cannot return the past. You're right. I'll go on with my story. My daughters had received a modest education, corresponding to my financial position. I asked the community if I could retire in order to devote the remainder of my days to the happiness of my children. Influential people in the community were prepared to grant me my wish. They took into consideration my old age and long service, which, whether you judge it good or bad, I had carried out and which, besides worry and distress, brought me nothing. But suddenly new circumstances came to the fore, and my liberation from service became entirely impossible.

"An order was received to the effect that, in order to avoid any future lapse in fulfilling the quota, we would now have to give the following: two recruits as a penalty for each no-show and a recruit for each debt of two thousand rubles. In the event that we did not fulfill these conditions, we had to yield up the *kahal* representatives and community elders as soldiers, putting them on the list as part of the penalty. They listed our debts as forty recruits, so now, imagine, we had to hand over one hundred twenty. Then add another one hundred twenty or so future recruits in the next selection, not to speak of the tens of thousands of rubles of debt, which we also had to replace with people, and you will understand the predicament. Horror paralyzed us, even more so when we realized that if we didn't manage to deliver the penal recruits, then a *new penalty* would be levied upon us, two recruits for one, and so on in a progression until our entire town turned into one huge recruitment. We couldn't have any doubt about the consequences because we had no hope of fulfilling the new order.

"What happened to us then I am incapable of describing to you. Our representatives went posthaste to the provincial capital, money flew about like useless throwaway trash. We begged for mercy, a delay . . . Again papers were sent to various places. And we weren't napping in the meantime, we began to grab whomever we could. Whoever did not have someone to defend him was our recruit. We took children of eight as recruits, we chained them in pairs and sent them off. We were deaf to shrieking and wailing. It was a terrible time. Let God the merciful forgive those who invoked Him against us."

"But I don't understand the despair," I remarked. "Our fatherland needs soldiers; it is a sin to refuse to serve when the tsar orders it."

"Without the slightest doubt, it's a sin," answered the old man. "The tsar's will is the will of God. We are obliged to sacrifice our lives for our fatherland if need be. Who would argue with that? But our people are still not used to military service. And, moreover, there's military service and there's military service. If there was any hope of promotion, that would be something else, but a Jew cannot get promoted. In addition, look at his treatment from his ignorant fellows. On whom do they vent their anger and irritation if not on the *damn kike*? Whom should they kick for no reason at all if not the kike? To whose mug should they hold out a piece of pig fat if not to the kike's? Not to mention that the officers look at him differently, knowing that no accomplishment will propel the kike upward. There are exceptions, of course, but I'm speaking of the rule. Don't forget this was happening to adults, who sometimes can stand up for themselves, can complain to the officers; but what about the children? What can a poor child barely out of diapers do in a foreign land among boorish and cruel people who hate his religion, his tribe, among people who don't even treat their own any better and whose language he often does not understand at all? What kind of service can you expect from such a child? He is supposed to herd the military settlers' pigs and endure beatings and shoves if by chance he doesn't manage to fall into his grave quickly enough. No, real service is something else. One must serve if one is ordered to serve, and it's a shame that the treatment is not always tolerable, especially from the lower-ranking officers. The higher officers are always well meaning and respect God's creation in every man, but one is far from the higher-ups, and the lower officers are always at hand . . . Anyway, that's not the point . . . back to my story.

"We wore ourselves out like fish knocking against the ice. We already began to accept those with only one eye, or no teeth, and cripples, and old men too. But the costs of each recruit! How much the doctor cost, the military recruitment committee, legal clerks! It's terrible even to speak of it. And still there was little sense to it since we didn't even get half of the full number. The recruitment arrears gradually increased and reached several hundred. I don't remember the exact figure, but even counting them up was frightening. We stopped even answering orders from the provincial capital. We couldn't fulfill them, and trying to explain that we didn't have enough recruits was futile. Then somehow it let up. Everything was quiet for a time, as though dark clouds were thickening over our heads. That illusory peace they gave us terrified us more than the former strict instructions. We felt that an unavoidable storm was gathering over us, and we weren't wrong. It soon broke out in the most terrible way.

"One morning—it was the fourth day of Hanukkah (the holiday of the Maccabees), when we were readying ourselves to celebrate the victory of our heroic ancestors, which was the capture of Antioch—the sound of many bells rang out through the town. Our hearts sank. Government officials came from the provincial and district recruitment offices. A detachment of armed soldiers entered the town. A few troika carriages rode straight to the synagogue. Our people were herded to the synagogue like sheep. They drove the old and young, women and children, drove everyone with their rifle butts. They ordered the entire population of the town to gather together. We, *kahal* representatives, tax collectors, and elders, all those who held a position, were immediately placed in chains and pushed along with everyone else. A lot of people were collected. Not only were the men's and women's sections filled, but so was the entire courtyard and street in front of the synagogue. An official stepped onto the podium and began to read from a piece of paper. He read for a long time and berated us for persistently disobeying the government. When he finished reading, he began to curse us. He abused everyone, everyone without distinction. Everyone silently listened with anxiety and trepidation. But when in conclusion he yelled out threateningly, 'You've picked the wrong people to trifle with! You know, you contemptuous and insignificant people, that in an instant we can wipe you from the face of the earth, crush you underfoot like a foul worm!'—when he pronounced these words, loud weeping broke out from the listeners' breasts. And those who were in the courtyard and those in the street, hearing the sobs of their brothers in the synagogue, also began to weep, having a premonition of something terrible. Shrieks filled the air. It was terrible to see how the entire population sobbed uncontrollably.

It seemed that the deaf walls of the houses were also ready to break out in tears.

"But that was still only the beginning. The order was to grab whomever they could, whoever looked at all like a suitable recruit. People ran in all directions like a frightened herd. The soldiers ran after them. There was terror on everyone's faces. Everyone scattered wherever they could, hiding in basements and in attics. All the stores were locked, all activity ceased, the confusion was indescribable. But those who were snatched up in the streets still did not come close to making up the needed number of recruits. Orders were given such that the panic could die down a bit by evening. Then at night houses were searched, and men were dragged from their beds. Scream as much as you like: 'I'm old' or 'I'm alone and can't possibly be a candidate' or 'I already have a brother and a son in the service' or 'I'm transferring to the merchant class and soon will be certified' or what have you, they didn't pay any attention to it. They shackled and sheared you in the twinkling of an eye.

"Our town could not emerge from its stupor for a long time, they say. For a long time no one dared show his face on the street, and whoever absolutely needed to would sneak by back alleys and under fences like a thief. Shops were closed for two months, markets were empty, no life, no movement could be seen. Moans and sighs, moans and sighs, this was all that you could hear. Everyone mourned someone: here there was no father, or no brother, or no son or husband, and elsewhere one and the other or all three together were gone.

"That is how it ended, the raid we brought upon ourselves because of our unintentional, unavoidable failure to provide recruits. The raid struck our town with paralysis because everyone had both hands and legs taken away, everyone lost his energy; this unprecedented event and fear for the future lay on everyone's breast like a lead weight.

"And those of us who held administrative positions—and there were fifteen of us—they added to the group of *penal recruits* and, placing us in chains, sent us to the capital of our province and from there to jail. Some of us couldn't take it and soon died in jail.

"You can imagine the mournful condition of my family. My wife, an old woman, who felt boundless attachment and respect for me and, according to her own understanding, considered me an untouchable person; my engaged daughter, who seemed to have the brightest future of happiness with a loving husband; the other, younger daughter, the darling of her parents, who found it difficult to imagine someone superior and more important than her father—all of this was somehow left hanging and in a single second was bereft of its leader and guardian. The entire past dissipated like fog, broke into tiny pieces. I can't even tell you anything about myself. It seemed to me that the whole thing was untrue, that it was a bad dream. But unfortunately the chains and prison reminded me that it was not a dream but merciless reality.

"My wife and eldest daughter soon followed me to the provincial capital. My wife collected as much money as she could, hoping to free me. They went everywhere together, begged and didn't spare any expense. There were good people who became involved in my case, who took money from them and promised their help.

But as it turned out, they could not help. Sometimes they permitted me to see my wife and daughter in my cell. They gave me strength, consoled me, and mixed their tears with my own. Worry and sleepless nights exhausted them, but they did not lose heart and gathered all their energies to ease my situation. Nothing came of it. One morning my beard was cut off, my head was shaved, and I was led outside, where several wagons were standing. A crowd, recruits and police officers, were moving about. I didn't see anything, my mind somehow grew muddled. They took off my coat and began to put a soldier's overcoat on me. Suddenly I heard a terrible scream . . . my wife and daughter threw themselves at me . . . I stood as though turned to stone. Pity expressed itself on the faces of all those who surrounded me. Even a few soldiers and policemen said in an undertone, "Poor women!" My wife hung on my chest like a hundred-pound weight . . . another scream and she fell like a lump at my feet. An apoplectic fit struck her down.

"I asked for a delay in order to hear my wife's last breath. They gave it to me. In an hour my wife was dead, and a few minutes after her death our eldest daughter went insane."

The old man fell silent. His tears poured down his face in two streams. I felt as though my own hair was cutting into me. I was inwardly amazed that such a feeble old man, tormented by being confined in jail and tortured by the fate of two beings dear to him, a fate that befell them in his presence, could still remain alive after this.

"But here I am, you see, I have not gone crazy, and I'm still alive," he continued after a short silence and as though responding to my hidden thought. "I am a useless vessel, a broken dish, and must endure all the torments of a mind that has not become muddled; but *she,* such a beautiful and innocent girl, who had just begun to blossom, had to say goodbye to her dreams and hopes. . . . What can one do? God is just. He gave and He took away, let His name be blessed!"

"So what happened then?" I asked, seeing that he had calmed down a bit.

"What could happen then?" he responded bitterly. "Wasn't this alone enough for me? I was sent far to the north; there I spent several months. With the help of good people I was later transferred to the garrison here and given good recommendations. With the help of these same people, my business was properly closed down, since my misfortune came upon me suddenly and my affairs were in disorder. Whatever could be collected from my property and whatever remained after my wife's last large expenditures and theft by various clerks they turned into cash and transferred into trustworthy hands. They assigned an old female relative to care for my youngest daughter and from the interest on the money give her enough for her needs. My eldest daughter, as I was informed in a letter, is at death's door in a hospital in the provincial capital. I pray to heaven to take her away quickly. I am also often sent money here, and for that reason I don't lack for funds; anyway I don't need much here. The officers treat me well. They allow me to rent an apartment and are not too concerned with the service. Let God, the patron of all unfortunates, give them their due. They are respectful toward me, the senior officials that is.

The younger ones sometimes give me trouble, although I know what I have to do and to whom I should give my offerings. Anyway, nothing can be done, I endure. Sometimes I even become energetic and reconcile myself to my situation, but this does not last long. The thought of my unfortunate child, the only dear being who is left to me, torments me constantly. The girl is growing up, developing . . . what is going to happen to her, an orphan, without a mother, twelve hundred versts away from me!"

He dropped his head onto his chest and yielded to his heavy sorrow. For a long time I walked back and forth in the room, at times glancing at the penal recruit. He continued to sit in the same position and seemed to have forgotten entirely about my presence. I came up to the window and opened it. The summer evening was at the height of its charming beauty. In the dark-blue sky full of millions of stars, now sparkling with brilliant blinding light, now barely glimmering as though shaking in the unimaginable distance, there swam a barely visible full moon, which gave off a pale, calming light. The town was long since asleep. Everything in nature was quiet and triumphal.

I approached the old man and placed my hand on his shoulder. He got up. I took his hand and led him over to the window.

"Look how beautiful everything is here," I said to him. "Is even this not capable of consoling you?"

"You are speaking of the beauty of nature," he answered, "and asking whether it consoles me. No . . . You are young, you have still not encountered misfortune. Your eyes perceive differently and send their impressions to your heart in a different way. I was young, too, and I looked at the world and nature differently then . . . but not now. I remember," he added, pointing at the horizon, "I remember that there should be happiness and brightness here, but my eyes don't see it, and my heart doesn't feel it. The sky is dressed in the colors of mourning, the moon is a funeral candle for me, the stars seem to me open gaping ulcers on a tormented body from which blood is about to start pouring out, and the trees seem to be whispering about the horrors that occur in silence . . . No, whatever is visible is black for me, and what is *beyond,* what is ahead, what is invisible to my earthly eyes, what is covered by mystery for all of us—that is what consoles me. *There*, beyond what appears to you as bright images, beyond what appears to me as dark ghosts, *there*, where thought does not dare to reach—there it is, my consolation." [. . .]

1859

Translated from the Russian by Brian Horowitz

LEV LEVANDA

Lev (Yehuda Leyb) **Levanda** (1835–1888), fiction writer, essayist, and journalist, was born in Minsk to a poor family. He studied at a reformed Talmud Torah in Minsk and at a government-sponsored Jewish school. In 1849 he entered the Vilna Rabbinical College, at the time a hub of maskilic thought, graduating in 1854 with a teacher's diploma and a knowledge of several languages and both Russian and western literature. Levanda taught at a government-sponsored Jewish school in Minsk until 1860, and from then until his death he served as an "expert Jew" (*uchenyi evrei*) at the office of the governor-general of Vilna. In this capacity, Levanda submitted reports on Jewish life and education in the Northwestern Region and in the late 1860s participated in the Vilna Commission on the Organization (*ustroistvo*) of Jews.

Levanda's literary talent was most evident in his partially memoirist *Sketches of the Past* (1870), *Travel Impressions and Notes* (1873), and *Schoolfear* (1875), which invite a comparison with *Notes of a Jew* by Grigory Bogrov (in vol. 1). Exciting from a historical point of view are Levanda's novels and tales *Friend Bernard* (1861), *Samuil Gimpels* (1867), and *Avraam Iezofovich* (1887). Levanda's satirical fiction, *Confession of a Dealer* (1880) and *The Great Fraud* (1880–81), betrays an influence of the dominant Russian satirical novelist Mikhail Saltykov-Shchedrin (1826–1889). The mastery of Levanda's prose grew toward the end of his career, especially in his discursive works, but Levanda's language never lost its patina of being not quite native. Some pages of Levanda's fiction read like slightly imperfect translations, exhibiting a stiffly over-correct usage, or an unwarranted Polonism, or a faint misuse of Russian verbal aspect. The language of his fellow pioneers of Jewish-Russian literature Osip Rabinovich and Grigory Bogrov (both in vol. 1), who were exposed to Russian under different circumstances, is more pure and elegant.

Levanda wrote for *Zion* (*Sion*), which replaced *Dawn* in 1861–62, and after *Zion*'s closing contributed articles about the Northwestern Region to the central newspapers *The St. Petersburg Gazette* (*Sankt-Peterburgskie vedomosti*) and *New Time* (*Novoe vremia*). In 1864–65 Levanda edited *The Vilna Province Gazette* (*Vilenskie gubernskie vedomosti*). In 1878 a collection of his sketches and feuilletons, previously published in *The Vilna Messenger* (*Vilenskii vestnik*), came out under the title *Vilna Life*. Levanda's best-known novel, *Seething Times*, was serialized in the St. Petersburg–based *Jewish Library* (*Evreiskaia biblioteka*, founded 1871) in 1871–73 (excerpt below). Many of

Levanda's belles lettres appeared in that periodical and in the Jewish-Russian magazine *Dawn (Rassvet*, known as *Dawn* "2"), founded in 1881.

While he was in Minsk, Levanda contributed feuilletons to *The Minsk Province Gazette* (*Minskie gubernskie vedomosti*) under the anagrammatic pen name Ladneva. Alexander II's reforms fueled Levanda's optimism about the amelioration of the Jewish condition and sharpened his desire to fight for an improvement of the Jewish civil status. He was hopeful that Russia's Jews would quickly be granted equality. Joining arms with Osip Rabinovich (see vol. 1), Levanda became a leading contributor to the Odessa-based *Dawn* (*Rassvet*, 1860–61), the first major Jewish-Russian periodical (see general introduction). Levanda's first work of belles lettres, *The Warehouse of Groceries. Pictures of the Jewish Life* (book edition, Vilna, 1869; Hebrew translation, 1874), which was serialized in *Dawn*, tendentiously portrayed much in Jewish life as dark, stagnant, and fanatical while presenting the mainstream Russian life uncritically.

From 1879, Levanda poured most of his energies into polemical essays. In a letter published in 1879 in the first issue of *The Russian Jew* (*Russkii evrei*), he advanced an assimilationist platform: "to effectuate energetically all that leads to the irrevocable rebirth of the Russian *Jew* into a Russian citizen with a shade of religious particularity." The pogroms of 1881–82 transformed Levanda's vision, making him skeptical of the idea of a fusion (*sliianie*) with the Russian people and putting him, as Brian Horowitz remarked in an article in 2004, "into an ideological cul-de-sac." After having been an avid proponent of the transformation of Russia's Jews into "Russians of Mosaic law," Levanda became a devotee of the Hibbat Zion (Love of Zion) movement. In his later essays, especially "The Essence of the So-Called 'Palestine' Movement (Letter to the Publishers)" (1884), Levanda discussed the emerging ideas of Jewish self-preservation (*samosokhranenie*) and self-assistance (*samopomoshch'*) in keeping with the proto-Zionist position of Leon Pinsker (1821–1891) and his *Autoemancipation* (1882). Levanda's last testament was his essay "On 'Assimilation,'" published in the *Weekly Chronicle of Sunrise* (*Nedel'naia Khronika voskhoda,* 111885).

Levanda died in 1888, in a mental clinic. He was the best-known Jewish-Russian essayist and literary polemicist in the 1870s and 1880s, and his articulation of the most pressing issues made Levanda's fiction successful with Jewish-Russian readers. Shimon Markish called Levanda, along with Osip Rabinovich, a "founding father" of Jewish-Russian literature.

Written possibly as early as the mid-1860s, Lev Levanda's *Seething Times: A Novel from the Last Polish Uprising* was serialized in *The Jewish Library* in 1871–3; a separate revised book edition was issued in 1875 in St. Petersburg by *The Jewish Library*'s publisher, A.E. Landau. At the historical center of Levanda's colorful if artistically flawed novel lie the events of the Polish Uprising of 1863–64. Several of Levanda's other fictional works, a number of his essays, and his 1885 sketches *Wrath and Mercy of the Magnate* deal with Jewish life in the former Polish–Lithuanian Commonwealth. Recognition by Jewish historians in our time, including John D. Klier and Brian Horowitz, underscores the novel's documentary value.

The uprising began as a protest against the conscription of Poles into the Imperial Army. The January 1863 manifesto issued by the Polish Provisional Government declared "all sons of Poland free and equal citizens without distinction of religion, condition, and estate," which theoretically applied to the Jews in the historically Polish lands. The insurgents, whose force of about 10,000 faced regular Russian troops of about 200,000, persisted with armed struggle. The uprising, in which some Jews fought on the side of the Polish rebels, was crushed by September 1864; Polish losses were estimated at 20,000 dead, with thousands of rebels deported to Siberia.

Spanning the period from the summer of 1861 through the summer of 1864, *Seething Times* is set partly in the city of G. (Grodno) and largely in the city of N., actually Vilna, both the Jerusalem of eastern Europe and a stronghold of Polish culture and national spirit. The Jews of the Northwestern Region are experiencing anxiety over their future and allegiance. One of the novel's characters, Jules Perets, wonders whether the liberated Poland would be "fairer toward us [i.e., the Jews]." The travails of the Jewish intellectual Sarin, the privileged if schematic protagonist, reflect Levanda's opinion that Jews ought to be neutral in the Russian–Polish conflict while proceeding to acculturate after a Russian fashion. Pavel Lavrinets argued in 1999 that, in keeping with the conventions of the Russian "antinihilist novel" of the 1860s and 1870s, Sarin comes to realize that the future lies with Russia while seeing only "hypocrisy" in the Polish "courtship of the Jews," aimed at winning their support in the uprising against Russian rule.

In the words of Shimon Markish, despite a lack of both verisimilitude and an "organically unfolding fabula," *Seething Times* presents "a decisive answer to the question . . . what is a Jew to do who had chosen the path of enlightenment and realized his humiliating inequality." On the surface of it, the novel's thesis advocates Jewish civil and cultural allegiance to Russia, not Poland. However, there is enough polyphony and ambiguity in the novel to represent other perspectives and to show the existence of a degree of closeness among Polish-educated (or western-educated) Jews and members of the Polish intelligentsia. As Brian Horowitz has argued, "by showing the political failures of Sarin, the author's ideological mouthpiece, and by drawing the Poles as fully developed characters as opposed to the one-dimensional Russians, Levanda subverts the positive message of Russification." Particularly fascinating is Levanda's depiction of amorous relations between Polish aristocrats and members of the Jewish intelligentsia (e.g., Vaclav Zaremba and Polina Krants; Julia Staszycka and Arkady Sarin), which serve to embody, through desire, the Jewish–Polish attraction and confrontation.

Seething Times does not yield itself well to excerpting, especially its thriller-paced sequences portraying the uprising. The excerpts below all come from the first of the novel's four parts. Entitled "To the Right or to the Left?" it captures the Polish national upheaval of 1861 mainly through the eyes of the female protagonist Sofia Aronson and her circle of young Jewish women from privileged N. families. The narrative mode alternates between pages of Sofia Aronson's journal (chaps. IV, VII, XI, XVI) and letters sent to their mutual Jewish acquaintance in N. by Arkady Sarin from G. (chap. XVII) and to Sofia by her friend Mary Tidman (chap. XXI). The text below follows the original serial publication of *Seething Times*, not the revised book edition.

From *Seething Times*

PART 1

IV.

27 July

I could not have expected that the scene with Vaclav in the garden would get so deep inside my head.[1] [Vaclav's] words: "Is not Panna[2] Sofia as much a Polish lady as you are?" have not left my memory now for several days. They distress me, for some reason persistently demanding my response. No matter what I apply myself to, the question is right there, waiting. It screens off everything else I try to focus on. Why did this Vaclav pronounce such a phrase, which, most likely, will leave me restless for a long time? Did he know how much unrest he would introduce into my soul with this seemingly innocent phrase?

Who am I in fact? A Pole? I have received a predominantly Polish education. I studied at a Polish boarding school. My governesses were all Polish. I love Polish literature, my library collection consists of Polish books, and I am writing this journal also in Polish. But I feel that between me and a Polish lady there's a whole abyss; I have always felt that a Polish lady looks upon me as a *żydówka*,[3] and I look upon a

---

1. In this journal entry, Sofia Aronson is referring to her own birthday party, which took place six days earlier, on 21 July 1861. In addition to the members of her circle, young Jewish women and men educated after a western fashion, Sofia also invited her former Polish tutor, Izabella, who brought her cousin, Vaclav Zaremba; both Izabella and Vaclav come from the Polish gentry (*szlachta*). The party culminated in the garden, where Vaclav made a philosemitic speech and a passionate, if self-serving, plea for Polish–Jewish unity.

2. *Panna* (Pol.) = Miss; *Pan* (Pol.) = Sir.

3. *Żydówka* (Pol.) = Jewess; *Żyd* (Pol.) = Jew; neither has the same pejorative usage as the Russian *zhidovka* or *zhid*.

Polish lady with the same feeling as a despised person does upon the one despising her, that is, with concealed malice. I have never been conscious of this feeling, but it has existed and exists nonetheless. I have had occasion to lose myself in Polish society, that is, to think and even to feel that I and *they* are the same, especially since I was also taken with their intelligentsia and understood the works of Polish literature not only no worse but actually better than many of the noble Polish ladies; but it would suffice for one word to be uttered, most likely without any unkind intention, by one of the *aristocrats*, it would suffice for one glance to be cast in my direction, one flattering but in truth tactless compliment, and I would wake up from my quick reverie only to feel, of course with pain in my heart, that I am one thing and all of them another, that, as the Jews say, I am dancing at the wrong wedding. No, I am not Polish and will never be Polish!

Who am I then, a German? But this does not make any sense whatsoever. The land we live on is not at all German land, and all our surroundings have nothing to do with things German. I know the German language, German literature, but this does not at all make me German, as though I could become a Chinese woman because I knew Chinese. I find Jules Perets laughable, he who has learned French and imagines himself to be a Frenchman, or John Berkovich, who has mastered English and contorts himself into a native Englishman. Messrs. Perets and Berkovich are, perhaps, good teachers of French and English, but what kind of Frenchman and Englishman are they! Just the same for me: although I know German, I find it difficult to imagine myself a German. Pretending to be one would be stupid and silly. I have always been amazed at the educated Jewish families where the entire domestic life has been fashioned after Germany. This would have made at least some sense if they themselves, or their near ancestors, had come from Germany; but no, they and their great-great-grandfathers were born here. Why then, on what grounds, do they make themselves into some sort of a German colony here, on Lithuanian soil? Of course one cannot blame them: there probably were, and still are, reasons for this, perhaps very important, legitimate ones. But their position is nevertheless false and at times even comical.

So then, what am I, a Jewess? Without a doubt. But day after day the meaning of this word gets narrower and narrower. Abroad, they say, this word now only refers to one's confession. In time, the same will probably happen here. But confession is only one part of life, not all of life. My mother, for instance, is a Jew, a complete, full Jew, by faith, notions, customs, feelings, hopes, and aspirations, while I am already only half, or even one-fourth of a Jew. So who am I in the remaining three-fourths of my being? Many Jewish women like me probably ask themselves the same question. We feel that the Jewish ground is getting narrower and narrower under our feet; we feel that it is becoming crowded and uncomfortable for us to stand on this ground. It will likely reach a point when we will not be able to be there. To whom should we attach ourselves?

So we attach ourselves, each of us as God allows, one to one people, another to another people. Mary [Tidman] is predominantly a German, and I am predominantly a Pole. Perets is French. Berkovich is English. Children of one tribe and one city, we have spread ourselves around different peoples. And this all happened by accident. Mary ended up in Riga by accident and came out of it a German woman; by accident I ended up at a Polish boarding school and emerged a Polish woman. Perets, I imagine, chanced upon a good textbook of French and felt that he could easily become a Frenchman, and Berkovich pretty much says that Robertson[4] and *The Vicar of Wakefield*[5] made him an Englishman.

This position is strange, abnormal, false, and unpleasant. In essence, Mary is not a German, I am not a Pole, Perets is not a Frenchman, and Berkovich is not an Englishman. In each of us there is only a fraction of that which we pretend to be. I am judging by myself. In analyzing my feelings, I discover that of all things Polish I love only Polish literature, and everything else is alien to me. I am indifferent toward the Poles, their destiny, their interests, and their homeland. Who is to blame? Is it I, who do not know how to love Poland, or they, who have not succeeded in teaching me this love? It is enough that it makes me so sad to be asking myself the question "Who am I?" and not to be able to find a direct answer in my heart.

How happy our mothers were, who did not ask themselves such questions and wrack their brains over their resolution. They knew they were Jewish, and that was sufficient for them . . .

VII.

9 August

This morning I met Vaclav on the street.

"God himself has arranged our meeting," he continued after the usual greetings and inquiries about health. "Walking here, I thought of you."

"Might I be able to find out the reason for your thinking of me?" I asked.

"I wanted to convey to you an interesting piece of news," he replied, twisting his thin moustache.

"News, and even interesting news! That's very interesting. Speak without further delay."

"Aha! So you are curious as well!"

"Surely I am! Am I not Eve's daughter? Do please go on, do not torment me."

"Fine, I shall not. But allow me first to ask if you read newspapers."

"No," I replied. "What is the use in reading them, particularly for women?"

---

4. Perhaps William Robertson (1721–93), prominent British eighteenth-century historian.
5. Best-known novel by Oliver Goldsmith, first published in 1776.

"You at least find out what happens in the whole wide world."

"In the whole wide world everything happens without us," I objected.

"How could it be without us?" Vaclav asked, hurt. "Not angels, but people do everything in the world, the same kinds of creatures as us. It stands to reason that we, too, can do something—and we shall do it. Please believe me that we shall do it and do it well! The sky will be feeling the heat!"

"Oh, Jesus and Mary! How terrifying!" I said jokingly, wringing my arms.

"Have you the pleasure of joking, Panna Sofia?" Vaclac remarked with reproach.

"Why then are you tormenting me? Where is the news you promised?"

"Here it is," he said, removing from his side pocket a folded issue of a Polish newspaper. "In here you will find, marked with a red pencil, an article that I recommend you read carefully."

"And who is the author of this article, not Pan Vaclav Zaremba by any chance?" I asked slyly.

"I don't know," he replied with an author's modesty. "It is unsigned."

"Never mind. I promise to read it with great attention."

"And if you like it," Vaclav added, "then please do read it to your girlfriends, and especially the ones whom I had the good fortune of meeting at your birthday party."

"And to Panna Polina Krants?" I asked suggestively.

"Naturally," he responded, blushing and starting to bid me adieu.

Upon returning home, I poured over the newspaper. The article marked with a pencil was a long contribution from our city, in which—whoever would have expected it!—the celebration of my birthday was described with all the details and in such colors! Names were not revealed, only identified with initials. Even conversations, even jokes were not forgotten. Pan Vaclav must have an excellent memory and also must be quite observant. At the forefront is, of course, Panna P.[6] He calls her now a "pearl in an eastern princess's diadem," now the "main flower in the arrangement." The correspondent comments with delight on our pure Polish pronunciation, our purely Polish *dowcip*.[7] But even more than by the article itself, I was struck by the following editorial commentary:

> In this interesting article, which, we hope, every good Pole will read with contentment, the unharmonious word *starozakonni*[8] has unpleasantly struck our ears. Does not our esteemed contributor know that we do not have and should not have *starozakonni* but only *Poles of Mosaic persuasion*? If he does not know, then be it known to him and to all *those who ought to know*, that the word *starozakonny* is as old as are those harmful prejudices that we must repudiate forever if we want to go apace with the century, if we want the

---

6. Polina Krants, Sofia Aronson's friend who, in their Vilna circle of young Jewish women and men, is most taken with Polish patriotism.

7. *Dowcip* (Pol.) = wit.

8. *Starozakonny* (sing.), *starozakonni* (pl.) (Pol.; cf. Russ. *starozakonnyi*) = lit. "of the old law"; a traditional supersessionist Polish-Catholic reference to the Jews ("those of the Old Testament").

enlightened world to be with us and not against us. Do you understand, brothers of ours in
Poland, Lithuania, Volhynia, and Podolia? . . . If you obstinately persecute an honest man
with the label "thief," he will become a thief, not because of his nature but through your
doing. If you continue to call Israelites Yids, *starozakonni*, they will never become Poles.
We do not intend here to enter into an inquest about which of you are right and which are
wrong. Maybe they are at fault, but maybe we ourselves are even more at fault than they
are. We nullify the old scores and extend our hands to them in *zgoda, jedność,
braterstwo*.[9] Those to whom we feed our bread must not be and cannot be our enemy.
Jews are a historical people, tremendously capable and energetic, not a crowd of gypsies but a civilized society with a significant culture. In them there is an abyss of
patriotic feelings. The proof is their two-thousand-year-long attachment to their former
fatherland, religion, customs. If we succeed in taking advantage of this feeling, we
shall not lose. If we make this land a second Palestine for them, they will go through
fire to lay down their lives for it, they will shed their blood for it. With what self-
sacrifice, worthy of imitation, did they defend their holy city from the victorious
Roman legions! Read Josephus Flavius, and you will be convinced of how much
military valor, courage, and fearlessness this people had. Reaching our hands out to
today's Israelites, we extend our hands not to the heirs of the despicable Russians or
to the traitors of their fatherland but to the successors of brave *knights*, defeated only
by the will of Providence. *Sapienti sat . . .*[10]

It is difficult for me to express in words what I felt when I read these fiery
lines. My heart began to pound. . . . My head was spinning. . . . I kept reading and
rereading it, and I could not believe my eyes. . . . A language completely new to
me. . . . It arouses my blood. . . . I am all atremble. . . . And a Pole saying this? And
he is not joking, not teasing? . . . . Go away, doubts! . . . . I want to believe, I want
to love! . . . . Cannot we indeed grow to love our motherland the way our ancestors loved Palestine? Yes we can! A thousand times we can! . . . . Are we monsters
of some kind? We are "successors of brave knights, defeated only by the will of
Providence!" Does this mean we have not always been greedy buyers and sellers,
spendthrifts, egoists? Give us a chance to love, and we will not be calculating
everything in cold blood. Do you think we enjoy not loving anything, not belonging anywhere, always feeling ourselves among strangers? The old generation may
have found pleasure in this, but it burdens us, the young. Belonging to our people
alone does not satisfy us; we do not find in it that which our parents did. Our
needs are entirely different. . . . They must be satisfied. So satisfy them! Do not
push us away with words, glances, for we so morbidly understand your words
and glances. Give us a fatherland, give us a nationhood! . . . . We are loathe to be
Germans on Polish soil. . . . I want to be, must be, and can be a Polish woman. A
Pole just like my fellow countrywomen! . . . . Do you hear what your elder brother

---

9. *Zgoda, jedność, braterstwo* (Pol.) = concord, unity, brotherhood.
10. *Sapienti sat* (Lat.) = [This] will suffice for the intelligent.

is telling you? "If we succeed in taking advantage of this feeling, we shall not lose. If we make this land a second Palestine for them, they will go through fire to lay down their lives for it, they will shed their blood for it." Yes. We shall show you that a Jewess can be no less of a patriot than an aristocratic Polish lady. And woe be unto you if you take away from us the chance to love our fatherland the way you love it! . . .

My hand trembles . . . I cannot go on . . .

XI.

14 August

The city has put on mourning. This, as they say, is mourning for our fatherland. In cathedrals they sing some patriotic hymns. The Poles demand that the Jews also wear mourning, which means we have a common cause. Poland is our common fatherland. All of us are called to its defense. We shall all go, we must go. We must not spare any sacrifices. How sweet it is to have a fatherland, to love it, to worry about it, to shed tears and blood for it. Our old ones never knew this feeling, but they also did not know many other things; times were different. The old ones say things used to be better, but I believe they were worse. A meaningless attitude toward life might be healthier, but it humiliates one. Yes, such an attitude toward life is actually impossible, unimaginable in our times. Our times push us forth; they do not let us lose track of time or meaninglessly stare around. Thank God, the wheel of time has caught us Jews at last. We cannot stay forever behind the onward-moving procession. Where the Poles go, we go also. In a society of living beings, we might be resurrected, especially since we are not quite dead yet. . . .

I have just received a note from Polina. She writes: "Poland, enslaved and oppressed, stretches out to us her motherly embrace. Let us hasten to press ourselves to her love-giving breast. She is crying; let us dry her tears, rejoice along with her, our wet nurse! Have you read the proclamation addressed to us? Today we received it in the mail. Father, after reading it, wanted to rip it up, but I did not let him.[11] It is in my possession. Tomorrow I will bring it to you. Tomorrow my dress will be ready. Today I shall not go out—I do not want to appear in the streets in colorful garb. It is uncouth for us to lag behind our sisters of Catholic persuasion. By the way, invite over all our girlfriends and close acquaintances tomorrow. We shall read to them the paper and the proclamation. We must now act in concord.

Out motto: "Long live Poland!"

---

11. In earlier chapters, Levanda describes how the fathers of these young Jewish women, especially Sofia Aronson's and Polina Krants's fathers, reacted with skepticism and hostility to the Polish overtures toward the Jews. "Let them do what they want, but we are not their companions," Sofia's father says in chapter XI. "We shall pray to God for our present Tsar [Alexander II], who is merciful to us, and Poland . . . Let it rebel, to its own detriment."

XVI.

31 August

The whole city has not stopped talking about the great honor Countess Staszycka bestowed upon us in the public garden.[12] Acquaintances have been congratulating us and asking about details of that stroll [in the garden]. Many cannot believe that Countess Staszycka, that proud Polish aristocrat, would forget herself to such an extent as to stroll in public almost arm in arm with young Jewish women. Many see in this most significant fact a great change for the better for us Jews. Yet many treat this fact with skepticism. "Deception! Fakery!" they say. "Poles will not love us; all this fraternization with Jews is but a comedy, politics. They seek our friendship because they have been ordered to do so from Warsaw and Paris. In their hearts they still hate us and detest us as always. Poles are very cunning and adept at pretending."

On whose side is the truth? O God! Can people really be so false? What good would it do for the Poles to deceive us? Why cannot they love us sincerely? What good would it do for them and for us to hate each other? . . . No, this is not deception, not fakery! . . . Go away, you miserable thought!

Many of our other girlfriends, on whom the honor of Countess Staszycka's graces has not been bestowed, envy and disparage us. M-lle Zakman, for example, is beside herself and is acting sulky. Such a fool! How can she not understand that the Countess has shed her grace through us onto all of Jewish youth, which includes her as well?

What is good in this whole occurrence is that M-lle Zakman and many other young Jewish women have finally understood a need to know Polish, the study of which they have now seriously taken up. Thank God! They have finally heard reason. To be Polish women at least of some kind in our region [i.e., the Northwestern Region] makes much more sense than to contort ourselves into Germans. I have recently referred five new students to Panna Izabella. Yesterday, when we met, she informed me that her new students are making incredibly rapid progress in the Polish language. She cannot praise their diligence, their intelligence enough. If it were up to me, I would make it obligatory for all Jews to learn Polish. Without the Polish language we shall never understand and come to love each other. Language is the first step in the rapprochement of peoples.

It is strange that Jews do not understand this or do not wish to understand. Even my father has a very strange perspective on the Polish language. The other day he put it to me directly that he was very sorry I had been taught Polish, and he would be very happy if I did not know this language. He said this to me in connection with my account of the encounter [with Countess Staszycka] in the public garden. I thought he would be glad for me, but it turned out the other way around. He furrowed his eye-

---

12. Countess Julia Staszycka, a wealthy and influential aristocrat and one of the leaders of the city's pro-independence movement.

brows and advised me to try to avoid Polish company, as such company, in his opinion, would not lead to anything good.

And Polina has had to endure a more tempestuous scene with her father and even her brother. There they could not do without screaming, threats, and even tears. "You want to bring yourself down and me as well!" old Krants screamed. "I will put you on a chain; I will banish you to a small town," and so on.

Even intelligent old people sometimes hold very strange beliefs.

I have just received a note from Izabella, who has invited Polina and me to her nameday party. I have almost forgotten that her nameday is the day after tomorrow. I must prepare a present.

XVII.

Arkady Sarin to Morits Mozyrsky[13]

G., 2 September 1861

. . . So then, where you are, everything is sleeping like the dead and no trumpet's blare has managed to awaken you? Does this mean that everything is well with all of you? Lucky you! It is as though you were living in Arcadia. And we, for some reason, have been unable to sleep, and how can we sleep now? Everything around us is stirring, bustling, making noises. All across the expanse of Russia a general breakage is taking place, from above and from below. A breakage of old ideas, obsolete principles, petrified institutions and customs eroding the flesh. Noise, cracking sounds, and rattling. Everything hurries to renew and purify itself, everything strives ahead, toward something new, heretofore unseen, almost unexpected. Even our coreligionists have gotten on their feet and are ready to go. . . . Except they still do not know where. Are the pleasing calls of the trumpet reaching you from the south? It appears not, because from your city no response has followed. Please tell me, for God's sake, could it be that the incredible noise of all that is happening has not reached your ears? Have the past five years really rushed over your heads completely without a trace? Could it be that your thirty-thousand-strong community is still the same disorganized, unflustered, and lazy mass we knew five, ten years ago?[14] Are the activities of your sated ones still limited to nothing more than their afternoon walk? Do your hungry still expect manna

---

13. Arkady Sarin, a teacher and a charismatic leader of a circle of young Jewish people, advancing a program of cultural Russification in G. (Grodno), is writing to his friend Morits Mozyrsky in N. (Vilna), where Sarin is soon to be transferred. This letter is one of the novel's most famous and programmatic episodes.

14. Sarin's number is fairly accurate for Vilna's Jewish population; at the time of the novel's publication, Vilna's Jews constituted about 38,000, or about 46 percent, of the city's total population.

to fall from the sky—or yet another Old Testament miracle? Do your petty capitalists still consider themselves candidates to succeed Rothschild and your mean bankrupts still consider themselves clever entrepreneurs? Do your learned still think they are unrecognized geniuses, and do your littérateurs still dream of resurrecting the Jewish tongue through their rhymed gibberish? Do your women still imagine themselves to be Germans by origin and marquises by manner? Do your maidens still dream of ardent love and marry in keeping with a no less ardent attraction to pockets stuffed full of money? Is your newly fashionable prayer house, which held so much promise at its founding, still as rich in promises alone? Do your progressives still stand in the rear, waiting for a bomb of some sort to push them forward? In a word, is your community still dwelling in munificence, as the Israelites did in the days of Solomon, not worrying about anything and not knowing anything?

But please know that the times are coming, *seething times*, when your vineyards and fig trees will no longer offer shade and relief to those resting beneath them. A time is coming when they will demand of us, with a knife pressed to our throats, a categorical answer to the questions: "Who are you? What are you? Who do you stand for? Whose side are you on?" In the Polish camp something serious is in the making, and it smells of blood. For a year now some fermenting has been visible in it. It was just not known what it would burst into. Now this fermenting is making itself clearer and clearer. The centuries-old domestic quarrel enters the stage again. We do not know when the battle will begin, but we do know that this battle will be to the death. This battle will, one way or another, touch us as well. We have been getting rather transparent hints in this regard. The Poles have been sniffing around, courting us, perchance we could be tempted, since we have also not been living too freely under the Russian law. They sense in us or presuppose a spirit hostile to Moscow, and this is why we come in handy to them. A population of two million with a significant economic position is indeed no joking matter. They have sized us up pretty good. What is silly is that they have come to their senses too late. But we know that *Polak mądry po szkodzie. . . .*[15] Therefore it is not our fault that reason only paid them a visit a few days ago. And do you know what is going on in Warsaw? Since 1831 we have grown older by thirty years.[16] They now regard us as adults. They count on us, appeal to us. And so, have you figured out already where we should turn, *to the right* or *to the left*? Do not forget that the future of our tribe rests on this decision. This means that it would be worth your while to wrack your brains over this decision.

We here have thought and decided to go to the right, to stick to Moscow. Our instinct, considerations, and, finally, sense of gratitude lead us there. We must never

---

15. Sarin, whose knowledge of Polish might be less perfect than his command of Russian, seems to misquote slightly the expression "*Mądry Polak po szkodzie*," which may be translated as "A Pole is wise after the damage is done."

16. Sarin is referring to the Polish Uprising of 1830–31 (the November Uprising) against Russian rule.

forget that *barbaric* Russia, not *civilized* Poland, first started to concern itself with our education and upbringing. We owe to Russia, not Poland, the awakening of our self-consciousness. Emperor Nicholas I was for us Jews in some ways what Peter I was for the Russians. What has Prince Czartoryski[17] done for our education? For him we did not exist at all. But we did exist for Count Uvarov;[18] he selected us for Russian education; he did a lot for us, and he *wanted* to do even more. We must not forget it and shall not forget it.

Poland has given us neither fatherland nor nationhood—what should we love in her? Having given us shelter, Poland has turned us into a horde of petty traders, which she badly needed, so let her now look for patriotism in this horde. She will not find it? Of course not, and it would be odd if she were to find it. What you have not sown, you will not reap. We will perhaps have more luck with Russia. Having received from her the key to education, we shall, God willing, unlock Russian nationhood, a Russian sense of citizenship, a Russian fatherland with this key. . . . True, they do not much favor us in Russia either. But my heart tells me that in time the Russians will love us.[19] We shall *force* them to love us! With what?—With love itself. The Russian nation is a healthy, happy nation, and in a healthy nation there is more love, more benevolence, and, finally, more intelligence than in a languishing, miserable, dying tribe. The Poles *cannot* love us:

That heart will never learn to love,
Which has grown tired of loathing and hating.[20]

Poland has done nothing but hate: the aristocracy hated the common folk; the common folk, the aristocracy; and both hated other Slavs, Russians, Swedes, Germans. Why should she start to practice loving on us Jews? . . . History moves in mysterious ways. It is quite possible that the Poles will emerge victorious from the upcoming struggle. In that case we who have not sided with their banner will have it tough. I suppose they would not be opposed to annihilating us completely. Well, so be it: this way we shall once and for all end our impossible existence. I experience hell-

---

17. Prince Adam Czartoryski (1770–1861), a descendant of Polish-Lithuanian royalty, was a prominent associate of Czar Alexander I during the early years of his rule and served as the Russian foreign minister in 1803–6. Czartoryski was instrumental in obtaining the 1815 Polish Constitution at the Congress of Vienna. After the Polish Uprising of 1830–31, during which he headed the Polish Provisional Government, Czartoryski fled to France, where his Paris home became a center of the Polish independence movement.

18. Count Sergey Uvarov (1786–1855)—Russia's minister of education in 1833–49; see introductions to Lev Levanda and to Leon Mandelstam (vol. 1).

19. Compare the ending of Ruvim Kulisher's "An Answer to the Slav" (1849) in vol. 1.

20. The last two lines of the fifth and final quatrain of the poem "Grow quiet now, Muse of revenge and sorrow . . ." (1855) by the major Russian poet Nikolay Nekrasov (1821–1877). Concluding Nekrasov's 1856 collection of poetry, this poem was perceived by his contemporaries as being both a new manifesto and a boundary marker in Nekrasov's life and creative work.

ish torments each time I think that I am like a dog without a master, forlornly wandering the streets without anybody to love, to be loyal to, to show tenderness for. Such a dog, have you noticed, has even lost the habit of barking, because he has nothing to guard, nobody to protect. He walks silently and indifferently by a nighttime thief creeping into a sleeping peasant hut. "Let him steal, what do I care? Whereas if I find a bone, I will gnaw on it and be sated. I need no more than that."

I am sick and tired of being such a stray, free-roaming dog, and that is why I am very happy to decide once and for all who we are and with whom we are. In determining the centuries-long strained relations between the Poles and the Russians, this struggle will also determine our ambiguous position amid these two peoples. Neither the Poles nor the Russians will let us get away with such phrases as "we do not know, we do not understand," because now we must *know*, we must *understand*.

Do you know, do you understand, my dear Morits, and you, my treasured comrades in arms? . . . Beware that approaching events do not catch you by surprise. Stand guard, be vigilant. The education we have received, and our calling of the people's mentors and therefore leaders of the young generation, commit us to go consciously where we ought to go and not where the blowing wind would push the senseless crowd. They look at us as at the vanguard, and thus we must go onward, to a specific goal, firmly, consciously; they will not forgive us any spineless deviations to the side.

XXI.

[Mary Tidman to Sofia Aronson][21]

G., 12 September 1861

Just imagine, chère Sophie, I have been taking Russian lessons. You did not expect it? I also did not expect it. And this is, indeed, strange: I wear mourning for the *Polish* fatherland and study the *Russian* language! But what else was I supposed to do? Sarin insisted, coaxed, and so did Mrs. Lipman, I could not refuse and agreed to acquaint myself with the Russian language, which, as you know, until recently I had not been able to bear. Sarin reassures me that in due time I will grow to love both the Russian language and Russian literature. Do you hear this, *literature*? The Russians have literature! A completely new discovery for us, is it not? From translations we know that there exists Spanish literature, even Swedish literature, even Persian, but to suppose that there is Russian literature—this we never suspected, or at least I had never heard of it in Riga. If I did not know Sarin to be a very serious person, one who does not allow himself to say something untrue, even jokingly, I

---

21. After her father had lost his fortune, Mary Tidman left N. (Vilna) to live with her aunt's family in G. (Grodno).

would think he was making a joke in order to mystify me. But since Sarin is talking about Russian literature, then such a thing must exist in the world, and now I am burning with impatience to get to know this thing as quickly as possible. This impatience of mine slightly sweetens the tedium of the first lessons. My God, what words! What letters! My teeth start aching from pronouncing them, as if I were nibbling on rocks. Sarin says this is from unfamiliarity. Perhaps, but that does not make me feel any better. But without the Russian language, as Sarin says, I would not be of use to the circle of which I have the honor to be a part, since all the business, all the correspondence of our circle is conducted in Russian. Besides, since I live here, I cannot lag behind the locals—*mit den Wölfen muss man heulen*.[22] All the local young Jewish women know Russian and gladly use this language. I cannot just sit with them and stare with incomprehension.

A few days ago I had the following conversation with Sarin:

"To whom are you handing over command?" I asked, half-seriously, half-jokingly.

"In our circle there has never been and can never be a command," he replied. "Besides the idea we serve, we do not accept any power over us, any personal will. We, all of us, are fellow workers at the same factory: one does one thing, another does something else, and from our common work something whole emerges, more or less in keeping with the plan we put together. Even as I depart, I do not cease to belong to the local artel. I am only changing my place of residence, not my mode of operation."

"So this means you will not cut off your ties with us?"

"So this means you have not familiarized yourself enough with the spirit of our circle, if you can ask me such a question. No matter where destiny casts me or any one of us, we will not stop working for as long as we have strength, in the spirit of our defined program."

"What is this program?" I asked.

"Our program is to pull our coreligionists from the bewitched circle into which unfavorable circumstances have thrust them and to place them on a course toward becoming citizens of Russia. In a word: our program is to make Jews into Russians."

"Why Russians and not Germans?" I asked, a bit frightened by the circle's program. "Do you not acknowledge that German civilization is incomparably higher than Russian?"

"We could not care less which civilization is higher," he replied. "For now we are talking not about civilization but nationhood, that is, spirit and language. We live in Russia, and therefore we must be Russians."

"What will the Poles say?"

"The Poles have already had their say. Their entire past policies toward us have proved that it is not desirable to them that we be Poles."

---

22. (Ger.) = literally "When with wolves, one must howl," meaning that one must learn to adapt to a hostile environment.

"But are they not singing a totally different song now?"

"What they sing now they should have sung at least one hundred years ago. Then it would have made sense. And now we have no use for their swan song; it touches us like the voice of a dying man, but it does not compel us to lie down in the grave next to Poland as it passes away into eternity. Destiny has ordained for us to live, and this is why we must and shall live. We shall live and sing: Do we want to be Russians?"

"But what happens if your new song does not find a response with the Russians as well?" I asked.

"This cannot be," he replied firmly.

"Why?"

"Because the Russian nation is no fool, and also we should not jump too far ahead of ourselves. Let us try—trying is not a crime."

"But what if your attempt fails, that is, what if it proves that the Russians also do not want to know you? What then?"

"Then . . . ," Sarin began, slightly pensively, "then we know what will happen. But why such skepticism? If you think it will shake our determination, you are mistaken. We are very firm in our hopes and convictions, firmer than you think, especially since we have had no reason to doubt them. We are convinced that we can become Russians, and therefore we must strive for it with all that is in our power. We are doing our job, so you do the job you have been entrusted with: learn Russian! We have so far not asked more of you, but not for anything in the world would we free you of the little you have already promised us. Study Russian—and *basta!*"

How do you like such despotism? They have simply enslaved me. I do not have a choice now: I *must* study Russian because I gave them my word.

P.S. Sarin is leaving in a few days. I shall give him a letter for you. This will give you the opportunity to meet him. I hope you two will get along well.

1860s

Translated from the Russian by Maxim D. Shrayer

GRIGORY BOGROV

Grigory Bogrov (Beharav, Bagrov) (1825–1885), fiction writer, memoirist, and essayist, was born in Poltava, a Ukrainian provincial capital, to a rabbi's family. His father, revered by the local Jewish community as a tzaddik, left scholarly notes on astronomy. From childhood, Bogrov received rigorous Talmudic training, while at the same time developing a passion for Russian, which he taught himself, hiding Russian books from his parents because he feared punishment. After his marriage at the age of seventeen, Bogrov lived separately and pursued the study of Russian, German, and French as well as music. Bogrov spent the 1850s and 1860s serving as a government tax farmer, underwhelmed intellectually, surrounded by provincial civil servants and businessmen, and unhappy in his first marriage.

In 1863 he composed the three opening chapters of what would become his famous memoir, *Notes of a Jew*, set in the 1830s and 1840s. Bogrov unsuccessfully sought a publisher for a number of years, until Nikolay A. Nekrasov (1821–1878), editor of the esteemed review *Notes of the Fatherland* (*Otechestvennye zapiski*), opted to print the chapters. Sharing some of the populist rhetoric on the Jewish question of the 1860s, the poet, nobleman, and liberal Nekrasov was given to imagining ubiquitous Jewish tentacles on the innocent communal body of the Russian people (see Michail Bezrodnyj's discussion of Nekrasov's long poem of 1875, *Contemporaries*, in vol. 2). Nekrasov serialized Bogrov's entire memoir—about one thousand pages total—in his journal in 1871–3. It was the first time that a Jewish author had contributed such a vast text—a text that provided not only a broad panorama of Jewish life in the Pale of Settlement but also a wealth of anthropologically valuable explanations and footnotes—to a leading mainstream Russian publication. *Notes of a Jew* was favorably received by the Russian press and public and was known in western Europe through the 1880 German translation, *Memorien eines Juden*. An English translation of the entire memoir would be a welcome addition. Following the success of his memoir and the novel *The Captive* (1873), Bogrov moved to St. Petersburg and devoted himself to writing. Among his other works of the 1870s, besides *The Captive* (Hebrew trans., *Ha-Nilkad*, 1877), were the historical novel *Jewish Manuscript: Before the Drama* (1876; Hebrew trans., *Ketav-Yad Ivri*, 1900), set in Ukraine during the Bohdan Khmelnytsky rebellion (1648–54), and several shorter works, such as the stories "The Mad Woman," "The Vampire," and "Who Is to Be Blamed?"

In St. Petersburg Bogrov came in contact with Jewish-Russian authors and partici-pated in the editing of the Jewish-Russian periodicals *The Russian Jew* (*Russkii evrei*) and *Dawn* (*Rassvet*), and in his latter years he served as a contributor to—and one of the coeditors of—the magazine *Sunrise* (*Voskhod*). His complex position was power-fully expressed in an 1878 letter to Lev Levanda: "In the broad sense of the term, I am an *emancipated* cosmopolitan [Bogrov's italics]. If Jews in Russia were not subjected to such abuse and systematic persecution, I would perhaps cross over to the other shore, where alternative sympathies and alternative ideals smile at me. But my fellow members of the [Jewish] nation, actually four million people, suffer without guilt—can a decent person wave off such an injustice?" Bogrov spoke out against anti-Jewish discrimination while advocating the abandonment of Talmudic mores and favoring rapid acculturation. In his novel *Maniac* (1884), he even crudely satirized the proto-Zionist Hibbat Zion (Love of Zion) movement. Yet in his novel *Scum of the Century* (1879–81), he wrote compassionately of traditional Jewish values and derided "su-perficial assimilation" (Shimon Markish's expression). Not long before his death, Bogrov published the essay "Of Mixed Marriages," adumbrating his own apostasy. Several months prior to his death he converted to Russian Orthodoxy in order to marry a Christian woman with whom he had been living. He died in Derevki, Minsk Province, in 1885.

Jews have accused Bogrov of contempt for centuries-old Jewish life; Russian antisemites have quoted Bogrov's *Notes of a Jew* in support of their arguments. Bogrov's belletristic recollections of his childhood and youth may strike a vigilant Jewish reader as bordering on hatred of one's past self and origins. At the same time, blaming the Jewish victims for their own victimization hardly seems to have been an objective of Bogrov's work. In his dry and analytical prose, Bogrov su-perbly articulated the anxieties of acculturated Russian Jews of the 1860s, who were suspended between past and present, tradition and modernity, the forbidding Talmud and the slithery promises of conversion.

From *Notes of a Jew*
Childhood Sufferings

PART 1, CHAPTER 2*

There is nothing duller than attending the birth of the hero of a story and fussing over him until the commencement of his conscious life. Not wishing to bore my readers for no special reason, I will pass over my first seven years and turn immediately to the time when I became dimly conscious of myself and of the bitter fate that has burdened me my entire life. If Jews attain moral maturity unusually early, they owe that unnatural precociousness to the merciless blows that fortune deals them from their earliest youth. Misery is the best instructor.

My first seven years are not particularly interesting. I suppose my mother loved me a great deal, although I often felt the weight of her heavy hand on my feeble body. My father was always strict and serious; he almost never hugged me, though at the same time he never hit me. [. . .]

We lived in the countryside, in a deep forest. Some cottages, some huts, the ever-smoking distillery in the distance, a rivulet winding through tall pines, horned cattle, boars grown fat on the waste from the distillery, eternally grimy peasant men and women—that picture is etched in my memory and has not faded to this day. [. . .]

Once I turned five, an assistant of my father's, a gangly Jew, began to teach me the Hebrew alphabet. How I hated my teacher and his notebook! But I was afraid of my strict father and sat at my writing for hours, although the sun shone so brightly in the yard, the pretty little birds chirped so merrily, and I so wanted to run away and dive into the thicket of tall, succulent grass!

I turned seven. I was already reading the language of the Bible fairly fluently. My gangly teacher had passed on almost all that he knew. I was proud of my learning and very happy. But what happiness is ever solid or long-lasting?

One truly beautiful summer day, my father returned from town. Seeing him from afar, I grew suddenly bold and ran to meet him. He ordered the young coachman to stop.

"Srulik! Do you want to ride up to the house with me?"

Instead of answering, I clambered onto the wagon. My father's tenderness surprised and delighted me—it was so rare.

"And Srulik, I brought you a new outfit and shoes!"

Knowing nothing of the custom of thanking people for attention, I just looked at my father and smiled joyously.

---

* The text has been slightly abridged.

How happy I was that day! I was free of the teacher, I had a new outfit, my father was paying attention to me, my mother kissed me so often, and no one kicked me that whole long day! [. . .]

Three days later, they put me sobbing into the wagon. My father sat down next to me. The boy Tryoshka, in his ill-fitting deep astrakhan hat, made a smacking sound, shook his long stick, and we were off on our long journey. "Don't cry, my poor Srulik," my mother, sobbing no less than me, repeated for the hundredth time. "Soon I'll come to you, or I'll bring you home!"

My father did not even try to comfort me. He knew what he was doing, and that was enough for him. How I hated him then!

Nothing amused me during the journey. My father was deep in thought or else dozing, and I tried to divine my future. Where was I going? And why? What would I do there? And as for the old dragon, the witch—as my mother called her—would she beat me often? My thoughts were heavy and sad. My childish mind imagined a new, unknown world, full of sorrow, sadness, boredom, suffering. And the instinct of a child did not betray me.

Shaken up, spent, and exhausted, we arrived one cloudy evening in P. For the first time in my life, I saw a series of straight streets, bordered with wooden sidewalks and tall poplars, through which I saw big, clean, beautiful houses. For the first time I saw well-dressed people sauntering back and forth. I felt frightened in this new world; I suppose I felt like a country dog brought to a market square bustling with a crowd of unfamiliar people: it thinks each of these people is busy only in order to hit it as deftly as possible.

Eventually we turned from one of these wide streets onto an alley and finally stopped at a broken-down gate. My father went into the courtyard. Right past the gate, a small clean house stood out facing the alley. Could it be, I wondered, that an old witch lives in that pretty house? [. . .]

However modestly my parents lived in the country, however little I was used to luxury and every comfort, at least at home I was used to cleanliness and order, to unbroken if simple pieces of furniture. Here I saw something completely different.

The room was fairly big and irregularly shaped. Two wide-open doors on the sides, leading into dark spaces, reminded me of the open mouths of toothless old men. The room was lit by a single tallow candle-end placed in a tall, dusty copper candlestick. The furniture consisted of a simple table, three or four unpainted chairs, and a low cupboard. In the eastern corner was a small ark covered by a faded brocade cloth.

A stooped old Jew sat at the table in front of an enormous open book. When we entered, he slowly lifted his head and lazily turned it toward us. I met his eyes meekly and was startled by his face. Under a pair of bushy gray brows, I saw gray eyes. Almost his whole face was covered by his long thick *peyes*[1] and beard; what was not covered by

---

1. *Peyes* (Yiddish) = sidecurls.

growth was ashy yellow. Innumerable wrinkles traced his flat brow. A faded, soiled, velveteen yarmulke on the back of his head made a greasy, dirty spot on his bald skull.

"Well, sit down, Reb Zelman, you are welcome here," he greeted my father in a hoarse, guttural voice. "Ah, so this is your kid? Looks like a weak little thing . . . What has he been taught at home?"

"He can read the Bible a bit, but nothing else yet."

"That's very little, very little; you'll have to work hard, kid! You can't be lazy here; I don't spoil anyone."

I kept quiet, but a sob caught in my throat. It took all my child's willpower not to start wailing. I would undoubtedly have failed but for another person who darted in through one of the side doors and caught my attention. I saw a stooped, wrinkled, small old woman with a face like a soaked apple, eyes small and black like thorns, no trace of eyelashes, and a nose like the beak of the most bloodthirsty bird of prey.

"There you are, Zelman! Thank God!" the old woman said in an unpleasant treble. "I'd already concluded that you changed your mind about bringing your little boy!"

"Why did you think so, auntie?" my father asked.

"God knows what kind of people you are! Your Rebecca is such a fashion plate that she may have decided it's not necessary to have her son educated." [. . .]

"My dear auntie," father said with a conciliatory smile, "let's not quarrel the first time we all meet."

During this whole unpleasant scene, I seemed not even to exist; they had completely forgotten about me. Finally, the nasty old woman noticed me, seemingly by accident.

"Aha! That's your son? He looks so delicate! He must have been raised on gingerbread! If I'd known he was so sickly, I'd never have agreed to take on such a burden. He could get sick and die, and I'll be held responsible. Come here, kid," Leah called me in the most commanding of tones.

I went to her unwillingly and timidly. She took my chin in her dry wrinkled hand and roughly raised my head.

"Are you spoiled? Huh? Tell the truth, kid. You watch out here . . . By God, I don't spoil anyone; I don't tolerate any nonsense around here." [. . .]

The reception we were given presaged nothing good. It was hard to sleep, but physical and emotional exhaustion brought me into that deep slumber that children attain after crying for an hour.

The next morning my father turned over my few belongings, gave me a few silver coins, said an unusually tender farewell, and left. I was now alone.

From that day I began to go to the *heder* (school), where my stern guardian and teacher ruled despotically. The heder was in a shack that my uncle rented from a poor Jewish woman. We studied in a low, dim room with sooty walls and a gigantic stove with a shelf on top. That shelf was our oasis in the desert: there we huddled in the dim light and rested; there we ate the provisions that each of us had brought; there we told frightening tales about dead people and witches; there we made merry. As soon as the thin one-kopeck tallow candle was lit and a light pierced the darkness of the shelf, we jumped down; the light was a signal to gather around the table and bend again threefold over our books until late at night. We followed this same routine every day. The numbing monotony lay on our souls like a dead weight, with no distraction, not a minute of rest during the entire day; how nice it would have been to run around, how we wanted to stretch our aching limbs!

There were about fifteen of us students. We lived more or less in harmony and friendship. The Jewish heder is an unusual kind of school, where all the students are equally intimidated, equally timid, equally scared, equally suffocated by the dreadful power of the teacher, who punished us at whim and was partial to no one. A kind of fellow feeling developed among the heder students, as among prisoners taken together to captivity and put in the same cell. The more the *melamed* (teacher) persecuted any one of the students, the more affinity the others felt for this student. Then again, the lucky one who was the teacher's favorite and suffered less from his cruelty would awaken envy, expressed in open enmity, from his classmates. This trait is so deeply etched into the Jewish character from childhood that it does not leave him even when he and his fellow heder students enter adult society. A Jew would give his last shirt to his suffering fellow, share his last piece of bread with him in a time of trouble, but is suffused with poisonous envy and malice when his fellow Jew succeeds. He is prepared to destroy the other's happiness with his own hand, at no benefit to himself, just to bring him down to the same level. For the Jew, fate is just such a vile, fickle *melamed*.

My teacher was pleased with me: I did my lessons dutifully and, thanks to my fair memory, could translate the Bible into Yiddish[2] fairly fluently. I acknowledged, however, that I understood nothing at all of what I was saying: I was a parrot. It didn't matter, so long as he was satisfied. I did get the occasional kick, pinch, or slap, which I soon learned to endure stoically. In our heder we thought it dishonorable to cry over such trifles. There were stoics among us who smiled with tears in their eyes after being dealt a deafening slap. Contempt for the teacher's bony hands was our revenge.

Of all my fellow students I became closest to a poor, pale, blue-eyed boy named Erukhim. I was charmed by his kindness, tenderness, and sincerity. I loved him as my own brother, and we shared everything that weighed on our hearts. My life became much more bearable once we had become close. Now I had a modest, understanding, and kind friend to whom I related all my feelings and complained about the fate that deprived me so early of my mother's affection and placed me in the hands of a cruel old dragon.

Erukhim told me all about his parents, whom he loved dearly. He described his father as a pious and legendarily honorable person. In spite of his poverty and his large family (my friend had several brothers and sisters), he never sent a hungry person away without food, and whenever he could help a poor family he would go

---

2. In Bogrov's Russian original, "into Jewish jargon" ("*na evreiskii zhargon*").

around untiringly night and day, taking time away from his own work, gathering kopecks for those in need. My friend's mother, he said, was a beautiful and quiet woman who worshipped her children and gave all her energy to them, and she loved and cosseted Erukhim the most. Erukhim told her of our friendship and about me and my sad position in the home of my mean relatives.

One day, one of our classmates was not in heder. The teacher was furious and planned one of his special punishments, casting frequent glances at the three-pointed whip that hung in a place of honor. Suddenly the door opened and a synagogue official entered with a tin collection box in his hand.

"Charity saves from death," he said through his teeth in a monotonous, apathetic voice.

"Who died?" the teacher asked, just as unconcerned.

"Shmul, the shopkeeper."

This was the father of our missing friend.

The teacher pulled on his hat and sped to the home of the dead man to attend him on the journey to that place from which no one returns.

This event saddened all of us. Erukhim and I climbed onto our beloved stove shelf. We sat in silence for a long time, lost in sad thoughts of death and its consequences.

"Erukhim! What would happen to you if your mother died?" I asked suddenly.

Erukhim started and paled. Clearly I had voiced his very thought.

"Don't say that, Srulik, for God's sake, don't! If they buried my poor mother, I'd jump into her grave and die there. What about you?" he asked after a silence.

"Me? I don't really know. I'd cry, for sure, but as for dying—I wouldn't want to."

The gloomy autumn with its fogs, rains, and morning frosts was long over. Winter had been raging for a long time, with hard frosts and sharp winds that froze my ears and hands. My life continued monotonously: prayers and the old woman's curses in the mornings, the walk to heder, there cramming, the teacher's kicks and scolding, the walk home, prayers, a scanty lunch, the old woman's curses, prayers, the walk to heder, cramming, shoves, evening prayers, a rest on the shelf, cramming, prayers, the return home, prayers, a scanty cold supper, prayers, the old woman's curses at bedtime, a last prayer before bed, and then sleep on a buckled trunk. That routine varied only on the Sabbath with the addition of a garlicky dish to our meal, extra prayers, and attendance at synagogue. [. . .]

In my free moments at home—if my teacher, who wanted to turn me into a scholar at the age of eight, wasn't torturing me by making me repeat the lessons I hated—my favorite occupation was sitting at the window, looking at the deserted yard covered in snow, and thinking. I can no longer remember what I thought about with such concentration, but I know that unchildish questions and reveries stirred within me. The harsh school of life was obviously forcing me to develop, setting my immature mind in motion. My teacher was not only a scholar but a well-known kabbalist. He owned some ancient, thick, strange books in a reddish binding. Jewish men and women frequently asked him to heal them from the evil eye or toothache. He possessed some trick and occult remedies for epilepsy; he could charm away toothache and stop bleeding by

casting a spell on the wound. Sometimes he would make wax figures, murmuring incessantly. While this secret work went on, which was always in the evenings, the shrewish
old woman would keep quiet, following the movements of the old man's hands with
her frightened eyes. I was always sent to my bedroom and ordered to sleep. The mystical atmosphere of the old couple always terrified me. I trembled on the trunk in my
dark empty room. There was no one to hear my complaints. I would pull my little coat
over myself and press my face into the pillow; fortunately I always fell asleep quickly
and slept soundly till morning. My teacher, in a talkative moment, told me that among
his books was one that guarded him against fire by its presence alone. Another unprepossessing book could be touched only by a person who had prepared himself by fasting, prayer, and righteous living. He assured me that he who took the name of a certain
spirit in vain risked death. He insisted that there was no miracle that could not be
performed by Kabbalah. For instance, one could expose any theft, see whomever one
wanted to in a dream, tap wine from a wall, and even make oneself invisible.

While I looked distractedly at the snowdrifts adorning our yard, importunate thoughts
would fill my young mind. Why does the government waste money on fire companies?
Why doesn't every householder keep books that guard against fire? Then there would
be no more fires. Why did my teacher buy watery wine every Friday when it would cost
him nothing to get it from a wall? How I wanted to become invisible! Then . . . of
course, first of all I would run away from this accursed house, I would get on the first
carriage that passed—after all, no one would see me!—and go far, far away. If I got
hungry, I'd go into the first house I saw and eat whatever I wanted. If I needed money
I'd go to a money-changer and take as many shiny ten-kopeck coins as I wanted! My
thoughts went on in this vein God knows where; I lived in a world of fantasy, and time
passed without my noticing. In those moments I was very happy. [. . .]

On Fridays we were released fairly early from heder so that they could prepare for
the approaching Sabbath. On one of those relatively free days, I sat before evening at
my dull window, looking at the yard, admiring the matte golden disk of the setting
sun, which gave the winter scene a special, enchantingly soft color. A boy of about
twelve shot out of the back door of a pretty house and began to run around, executing
various jumps as he went. I admired this lively boy. His full fair face, flushed from the
cold, was enlivened by two big blue eyes, and his pretty mouth wore a happy smile.
His every movement, every jump expressed strength, suppleness, and health. He was
well proportioned; a broad, prominent chest made it seem that he would become a
very strong man. His clothing was plain: thick knee-high boots, a lined sheepskin
coat, a gymnasium uniform cap with a red band, wool gloves.

"Mitya!" I heard a long-drawn-out, sweet female voice.

The boy stopped in midjump and whirled in the direction of the voice. I, too,
looked that way. On the porch that faced the yard stood an attractive middle-aged
lady, a short-sleeved jacket carelessly tossed over her shoulders.

"Mitya dear, come here!"

The boy bounded toward her.

"Naughty boy!" the woman reproved him, a smile on her lips. "Look, your jacket's undone, and you're running around as if nothing's wrong!"

With those words the woman bent toward the boy and began to fasten his jacket, but the boy spun out of her hands with a ringing laugh.

"Mama," he said, "I want to make a snowman, a really tall one!"

"Then make one, darling."

"But Mama, don't tell Olya about it until I'm ready."

"All right, dear."

Mitya rushed into the yard, lifted a shovel that was lying there, and started to dig up the very deepest snowdrift.

"What did he want to do? What's a snowman?" I wondered and began to watch him with special interest.

Meanwhile, Mitya's strong arms were at work. He dug out a pile of snow, then began to carve away the sides of the pile, throwing some snow aside. [. . .] Within fifteen minutes the pile of snow looked like a human figure without legs or arms, like the crudest ancient stone idol. A round head of the same sort appeared on the snow figure's shoulders. Mitya finished his work, ran a few steps back, and, checking his results, stood for a moment, clearly satisfied with his work. Then he ran back into the house.

"Why has that foolish boy been working so hard?" I thought. I had barely finished formulating that question when Mitya was back in the yard clad in a gymnasium student's gray overcoat with its red collar and metal buttons. He looked around and dashed to his snowman, quickly threw the overcoat on it, took off his cap, and adroitly put it on the snowman's head. In such respectable clothes, the snowman resembled Mitya himself, standing there and seeming to look at the sunset. Mitya stood for a few minutes with his head bare, rubbing his ears with his hands, which were red from cold and work. It was clear that he was quite chilled. He kept looking at the door, clearly expecting someone, and then back at his snow twin, but no one came. Mitya impatiently stamped his foot, turned decisively, and ran straight to our cottage. I was so interested in his movements that I jumped from my observation point and ran to the hallway. Mitya arrived at the same moment.

"Olya isn't coming," he said in a voice quivering from excitement, "and I'm cold. Please run to our place and call Olya. Tell her Mitya wants her as soon as possible."

I understood very little Russian and could barely speak at all, except for a few Ukrainian words. The only thing I understood of what Mitya said was that he was cold. Not thinking long, I took off my inelegant fur hat and offered it to Mitya.

"Yuck!" he yelled, pushing the hat away with loathing. "I don't need your beanie. Go over to our house and call Olya. I can't . . ."

At that moment a girl appeared in the doorway of the house where Mitya had been steadily looking. Without finishing his sentence, Mitya fell silent, hid behind the door, and eagerly, barely breathing, watched the girl's every movement.

Shading her eyes with her hand, the girl looked around the yard and paused when she saw what seemed to be Mitya. She stood for a few seconds, smiled, and then carefully, soundlessly, went down the three steps of the low porch and toward the snowman, walking in the funniest way, rolling from one foot to the other, making faces, worried that her feet would make a sound by scraping against the snow. Meanwhile, behind the door, Mitya was overcome by irrepressible, soundless laughter, and in the passion of amusement grabbed my hand and squeezed hard. Wearing a big black hood and snugly wrapped in a fur, Olya crept two paces away from the snowman and, wanting to scare what she took for Mitya, suddenly threw herself at him and grabbed him from behind.

"Oh!" she cried in a frightened voice when she felt that she was holding a pile of snow under the gymnasium student's overcoat. She jumped away awkwardly and fell face forward in the snow.

I ran headlong toward her, Mitya behind me, but I got there first and lifted her up. She looked at me with fear and then, seeing the frightened Mitya behind me, burst into ringing childish laughter.

"Oh, you're so bad, Mitya! I'm not hurt. But I thought it was you, and I wanted to scare you."

"You're so brave! But then you got scared yourself and fell down."

"That's not true! I wasn't scared, I just stumbled."

I was silent during this whole conversation and stared at Olya. I can't account for what I saw in her young face, but I know that it charmed me. There was so much kindness and tenderness in the girl's dark blue eyes, her delicate mouth, and her round, dimpled chin.

"Mitya, put on your cap!" called the frightened voice of the woman who had been fastening up his jacket half an hour ago. "Mitya! Olya! Come inside!"

"We're coming, Mama, we're coming," Olya answered. Grabbing the cap off the snowman, she put it on the boy's head, seized his hand, and playfully pulled him along. Then she stopped abruptly, released Mitya's hand, and ran to me.

"Thank you for lifting me up," she said, looking me warmly in the eyes. I felt that I was blushing up to my ears; I lowered my eyes and did not answer.

"Will you come and visit us?" Mitya in his turn asked remarkably tenderly. "Come over, brother, we'll play together."

Hand in hand, the children ran off and disappeared behind the door of the house. I stood where I was for a long time. Something fresh and kind emanated from these children. Could these really be Christian children? Could it really be that they did not despise me? Why was I so afraid of Russian boys? And I would perhaps have stood for a long time asking myself these kinds of questions if the old hag's shrill voice hadn't roused me from my thoughts with a harsh call.

"Why are you standing there like a stone idol? What are you doing trying to strike up an acquaintance with the *goyim?*[3] Get away, you moron, before you get a beating!

---

3. The word *goyim* translates as *tribe*, but since almost all the tribes in ancient times were idol worshippers, the word became an insult. [G.B.]

He takes every opportunity to hang around and gape. Good boys have already been in synagogue for a long time, and he's hanging around with all sorts of scum."

I hung my head and went back into our quarters. I had long since ceased to be affected by my tormenter's insults and threats, but her abuse was especially unpleasant at this unusually sweet moment. In my mind I compared the joyful life of those happy, playful, free children, bursting with health, and my tormented existence, full of degradation, deprivation, and confinement. With an inexpressibly bitter feeling of envy and dissatisfaction, I went into my room. Without meaning to, I glanced into the fragment of unpolished mirror glued to the wall: I saw my own reflection and started. My inordinately long, irregular, pale yellowish face, with sunken cheeks and prominent cheekbones, shadowed by long, lank, thin *peyes* that looked like worms, my ridiculously gangly neck with no tie, my whole thin, bent body on my skinny legs, and my clumsy shoes filled me with such overwhelming disgust that I turned away and spat, but I did this so awkwardly that the spittle landed on the old woman's cheek. She turned green with anger and slapped my cheek so hard with her dry hand that I saw sparks.

"Go to synagogue, you scoundrel!" she screamed, pushing me out and slamming the door loudly behind her.

"To synagogue again," I whispered with a deep moan. "God! When will this ever end?"

Covering my burning cheek with one hand, I went off to synagogue. On the porch of his house Mitya was whimsically jumping around. I came even with him.

"Where are you going?" he asked. I heard teasing in his voice and walked by silently.

"Fool!" he called at me. I began sobbing and, to hide it, ran away without looking back.

It is painful to bear an insult, but to be insulted by a happy person is unbearable.

1863

Translated from the Russian by Gabriella Safran

❉ First Flowering ❉
1881–1902

Following the government's palliative efforts at "ameliorating" the position of the Russian Jews during the period of the Great Reforms in the 1860s, Jews began to leave the Pale in larger numbers through education, military and civil service, and conversion, and enter the mainstream of Russian society. The first Jewish-Russian authors to reach a position of prominence in the Russian cultural mainstream emerged from their ranks in the 1880s–90s, including Nikolay Minsky (1855–1937) and the first major Jewish-Russian woman writer, Rashel Khin (1861–1928), who was encouraged in her youth by the aged Ivan Turgenev. The half-Jewish Semyon Nadson (1862–1887), Russia's most popular poet of the 1890s–1900s, brought into the Russian mainstream an awareness of the growing Jewish cultural presence. As early as 1880, Russian xenophobic authors and publicists began to decry an alleged Jewish takeover of the mainstays of Russian society—professional life and culture—and the paranoia has not quite subsided to this day. "The Yid Is Coming," a programmatic essay by Aleksey Suvorin, the editor of the newspaper *New Time* (*Novoe vremia*), set the tone for the antisemitic retrenchment. Emperor Alexander II was assassinated on 1 March 1881; among the populist terrorists was Gesya Gelfman, a Jewish woman. A wave of about one hundred fifty pogroms in 1881–82, among them the particularly violent pogroms in Elizavetgrad (15 April 1881) and Balta (29 March 1882), changed the course of Jewish-Russian history. The 1881–82 pogroms weaned the second-generation Russian *maskilim*, such as Lev Levanda, of their illusions and of their false hopes for an integration into and fusion (*sliianie*) with the Russian people.

During the next several decades, four principal factors defined the thematic thrust of Jewish-Russian writing: the outburst of Russian antisemitism in the 1880s–1900s, punctuated by pogroms and blood libels; the introduction of further discriminatory regulations and quotas, which were not abolished until 1917; the massive flight of Russian Jews to North America; and the rise of the Jewish worker's movement, especially after the founding of Bund, the Jewish socialist party, in 1897 in Vilna.

Census data indicate that, of about 5.2 million Jews in the Russian Empire in 1897, 24.6 percent could read and write in Russian, but only 1 percent considered it their mother tongue. These data, combined with the data on the Jewish-Russian periodicals given in the introduction to the previous section, help quantify and qualify the still small but growing readership of those Jewish-Russian writers who, like the popular belletrist Ben-Ami (1854–1932), targeted the audience of Russian-reading Jews. The emergence of Jewish-Russian lyrical poetry, exemplified by the ascent of Simon Frug (1860–1916), who was celebrated by Russia's Jews and unknown to the general Russian reader, occurred as a response to an elemental need for accessible Russian-language Jewish poetry. Frug and his lesser contemporaries and epigones published in the Jewish Russian-language press of the 1880s–1900s. The 1890s made imminent the arrival of Jewish-Russian writers in the Russian national mainstream.

Introduction copyright © by Maxim D. Shrayer.

RASHEL KHIN

Rashel (Rachel) **Khin** (1861–1928), belletrist and playwright, was born in Gorki, Mogilev Province. Khin enjoyed opportunities that were denied to the vast majority of Russia's Jews; her father, a wealthy entrepreneur, moved his family to Moscow and gave his children a first-class European education. He may have financed his children's acculturation, but Khin's father was adamant about remaining Jewish. In Moscow Khin attended the Women's Third Gymnasium in 1877–80 and went to St. Petersburg in 1880 to train as a midwife; her brief medical studies informed the novella "From Side to Side" (1883). In a career change, she moved to Paris to study literature and history at the Collège de France. In Paris Khin met Ivan Turgenev (1818–1883), who became her mentor. She would later dedicate her collection of seven tales, *Downhill*, published in Moscow in 1900, to Turgenev's memory.

Khin debuted in 1881 in the magazine *Friend of Women* (*Drug zhenshchin*) and during the next two decades published fiction in mainstream journals, such as *The Messenger of Europe* (*Vestnik Evropy*), and in the Jewish-Russian review *Sunrise* (*voskhod*), some under the penname R. M-khin. Her fiction, while stylistically timid, articulated the anxieties of the Jewish-Russian intelligentsia and one-sidedly critiqued the Jewish nouveaux riches. Her most fascinating work is the short novel *The Misfit*, which was published in 1886 in *Sunrise* and was included in Khin's well-known collection *Silhouettes* (Moscow, 1895). Her other notable Jewish fiction is "Makarka," published in *Sunrise* in 1889 and reprinted in 1895 in the same "cheap edition" as the short novel *In a Backwater Small Town* by N. Naumov, the penname of the important Jewish-Russian writer Naum Kogan (1863–1893).

In the mid-1880s, unhappy in her marriage and unable to obtain a divorce from her Jewish husband, she converted to Catholicism, which under Russian law at the time resulted in the dissolution of her marriage. She later married Osip Goldovsky, a lawyer and a convert like herself. In the late 1890s she became acquainted with leading Russian writers and intellectuals, including Vladimir Solovyov and Anatoly Koni. In addition to being a "salon Jewess of sorts," as she was called by her American student Carole B. Balin, Khin also distinguished herself in the 1890s–1900s as a playwright. Two of the five plays she wrote, *Young Sprouts* and *Heirs,* were staged by the Maly Theater in Moscow. *Young Sprouts* (1905), the better known of the two, deals with women's emancipation. In 1905 Khin moved to France, returning to Russia in 1914. Her fifth play, poignantly titled *Ice Drifting* (1917), appears to have been her last published work. Little is known about her latter years in Russia and her death in 1928. Khin was the best-known Jewish woman in nineteenth-century Russian letters.

Several of Khin's works, among them the tales "Makarka" and "Dreamer," address burning Jewish issues. In *The Misfit*, written in 1881 Khin fictionalized her sister's, and perhaps her own, story of conversion. In 1881 Khin's sister, a governess with an aristocratic family, converted to Orthodoxy. The novel's protagonist, Sara Berg, finds herself on the verge of apostasy and is helped by a French teacher who suggests Gotthold Lessing's *Nathan the Wise* as a model of Jewish dignity. She is determined to help poor Jews, but too much separates her from them. Abandoned by her Jewish husband, she loses a daughter to death. A double outsider, she eventually experiences the love of a wealthy aristocrat who wants to marry her—but she refuses.

Included below is the opening scene of Khin's novel, which depicts a painful confrontation between eleven-year-old Sara Berg and her father. A reader of Fyodor Dostoevsky will note a likely allusion to the problematic discussion of blood libel (*krovavyi navet*) by Liza Khokhlakova and Alyosha Karamazov, which occurs in chapter 3, book 11, of part 4 of *The Brothers Karamazov* and was written in May 1880. Published as a book in 1881, *The Brothers Karamazov* appeared serially in *Russian Messenger* in 1879–80 not long before Khin wrote *The Misfit*. In the scene in question, which has bewildered many a Dostoevsky student, Liza asks Alyosha, "Alyosha, is it true that at Easter [in Russian the same word, *paskha,* is used for both Easter and Passover] Yids [*zhidy*] steal children and kill them?" And Alyosha replies, "I don't know." A possible allusion to this discussion in *The Brothers Karamazov* makes it so much more difficult to regard Khin's novel merely as a Jewish "fathers and daughters" tale of the times. *The Misfit* was one of the very first works by Jewish-Russian writers to negotiate Jewish self-hatred.

From *The Misfit*

CHAPTER 1

Pavel Abramovich Berg paced angrily up and down his lavish study, which was crammed with all kinds of fine objects and resembled a fancy haberdashery store. He finally stopped, put his hands in his pockets, and, frowning, turned to his wife:

"So now you don't want to send *her* to a boarding school?"

His wife, a beautiful pale brunette with timid dark eyes, about thirty years old, sighed, looked down, and in confusion began to run her fingers over the fringe on a silk pillow.

"This is intolerable!" Pavel Abramovich fumed. "Not only do I run around from morning to night, bustle about trying to make a living, wear myself out, I still have to take care that my children don't grow up to be shopkeepers. Do you really think that love for one's children consists of stuffing them with food from morning to night? I'm telling you that you don't love your children, you hate them, you're ruining them, you . . ."

Seeing his wife sniffle, Pavel Abramovich lost his temper completely.

"Tears again!" he cried. "What the devil is this? I can't say a word. It's as if I'm a beggar come in from the street. You'll all be the death of me, I'm leaving the house . . ."

"But I'm not saying a word," said Berta Isakovna, quickly wiping away her tears. "Do as you wish."

The cause of this domestic scene was a very small person, the Bergs' daughter, Sarah, a delightful girl of about eleven, with fiery dark eyes, a dark complexion, and perfect features. The girl was hot tempered, playful, and impressionable and caused her parents—that is, her father (her mother was always able to win her over with kindness)—no end of trouble. But Pavel Abramovich! He was the embodiment of a type of wealthy Jewish autodidact that appeared in Russia about thirty years ago. Quite intelligent, proud, and capable, he had borne since birth the heavy burden of poverty, even penury, had encountered people of the most varied disposition and social status, and got on well with everyone. Gradually, he turned from Peysach into Herr Paul and from the latter to Pavel Abramovich, and passing, as they say, through fire and water, he had reached that ideal state when it's no longer the Jew who obsequiously looks into the policeman's eyes but the policeman who sweetly murmurs to the Jew, "How may I help you?" But Pavel Abramovich had not forgotten the bitter days of his youth. His dream, his ambition, his *idée fixe* was his children. His main goal was that no one should "recognize" them, and, at the same time, he would not allow even the thought that they might formally convert to Christianity. In general, all his actions were ruled precisely by a hidden desire for revenge—to prove to *them,* that is, Russians, that "look at us, we're no worse than you," a natural desire, characteristic of a slave who has gained his freedom. And now what! A child, a girl, is hindering his plans. Told to recite poetry for guests, she clams up, while in the nursery she declaims to her nurse with such fervor that the nurse's head pounds. Sarah had a new governess almost every week. She usually bombarded them with questions—what for, why, how come—and when not satisfied with the answers, she abandoned her books and, instead of learning her lessons, played with her favorite poodle, Valday, for hours on end. The only thing that attracted her was music. One of her governesses was a thin, old, almost illiterate Russified Englishwoman. One evening, as usual, Sarah had quickly deserted her for her poodle, but when she heard her abandoned governess playing some passionately pensive Scottish ballad, she left the dog and quietly sat down next to the piano.

"What are you playing, miss?" she asked.

The governess began to explain.

"Play some more," the girl said peremptorily.

The governess obeyed.

When she finished, the girl was silent and seemed to continue listening.

"I want to play like that, too. Teach me," she announced at last.

Thanks to her music, the governess lasted about a year with the Bergs. Sarah learned to chatter fluently in English, and she played the ancient ballads with such inexpressible and deep feeling that tears came to the eyes of the elderly miss when she listened to her. Still, Sarah did not betray Valday, her favorite, and he became the unintentional cause of her removal from her parents' home.

Pavel Abramovich had a servant, a crafty, sneaky fellow, a fop and a tattletale, who enjoyed the unlimited trust of his master. There was no one in the house, beginning with the mistress, for whom Aleksey (that was the servant's name) did not cause trouble. Sarah hated him so much that she wouldn't take anything from his hands. The servant took revenge on her in his own way. One day he stepped on Valday's paw right in front of her. The unhappy poodle began to yelp. Sarah burst into tears and ran to him. The dog limped for several days. The girl cared for him tenderly, bandaged his paw, brought food to him herself, and then, one day, when she was making her way to Valday carefully so as not to spill his bowl of soup, through the half-opened door she saw Aleksey, who had tied the poodle to the leg of the sofa and was whipping his injured leg with a hunting whip. Valday just howled and tried helplessly to jump out of the way. Sarah felt faint. Beside herself, she dropped the bowl, dashed into the room, tore the whip from the hands of the terrified lackey, and began to whip his face with it in some kind of frenzied rage. . . . A week after this incident she was taken to the aristocratic boarding school of Mme. Roget in Moscow to "change her character."

The boarding school was no better and no worse than other institutions of this type, but it differed from them in its extreme seclusion, which the girl's lively nature found impossible to accept. She loved her mother passionately, missed her terribly and suffered from her absence, and revived only on Sundays, when her mother visited the school. As soon as she saw her carriage approach the porch, she would run into the reception room as fast as her legs would carry her, throw herself onto her neck, kiss her pale hands and cheeks and beautiful dark eyes, and complain that "Ugly Puss"—Mme.

Roget—gave them nothing to eat and had not let her have dinner three times that week. "She was stingy with her 'slop' so I stole two hunks of bread and cheese," she would say about her exploits.

Her mother would shake her head reproachfully, and her daughter would begin to justify herself.

"Oh, mother, I know myself it's not right, but why don't you want me to live at home? If you sent me to the gymnasium I would be an excellent student, while here it's so revolting that I can't do anything except think of how to make someone mad. Take me back home."

"It's impossible, my angel," her mother would usually reply to this pestering. "You know papa doesn't want that."

But then vacations were such a joy! On Christmas Eve Mme. Roget had a Christmas tree and gave presents to all the pupils. The pupils, in turn, had to show their solicitude with various surprises—and how angry she would get if the surprise was not on the expensive side. Classes ended about three days before the holiday. The baking of meat pies from sweet dough began early in the morning; the girls would steal it right out from under Mme. Roget's hands and eat it raw in the dormitory. But now, thank God, the last candle on the tree has gone out . . . the pupils begin to leave for home. Sarah's heart sinks at the thought that they might come for her tomorrow instead of today.

Finally Amalia Karlovna, the housekeeper, arrives.

"On vient te chercher," Mme. Roget says to Sarah, "*mais il faut tard; veux tu pas aller demain, petite?*"[1]

Such thoughtfulness makes Sarah's temples throb.

"Oh, madame, il ne m'arrivera rien, bien sûr,"[2] she mumbles and, without waiting for a reply, runs off; in a minute, already dressed, she runs down the stairs, skipping several steps and stumbling in her hurry. Amalia Karlovna keeps her from falling, but she does not calm down until she's in the sleigh. "Now they won't leave me," she thinks aloud, and almost throws herself on the coachman's neck and begs him to go "faster, for God's sake." "There are four streets left, three, two," she says to Amalia Karlovna, who shares her impatience rather calmly.

The horses stop at a gray stone house with an imposing cast-iron awning. Sarah almost knocks over the servant, bursts right into her mother's room in her coat and boots, and throws her arms around her neck. The laughter and horseplay of the girl— who is trying to enjoy her freedom as fully as she can, bothering and nagging everyone she encounters, from her mother to her five-year-old sister Lidochka, who bursts into tears from her caresses—sounds strange in the quiet, decorous house. The two weeks of vacation seem infinite to her, the boarding school disappears in some kind of hazy distance; who knew what can happen in two weeks: maybe they would keep her at home for good. But the hours fly by, and the last evening comes. Sarah's father, who

---

1. "They've come for you . . . but it's late; wouldn't you like to go tomorrow, my little one?" (Fr.)
2. "Oh, of course I'll be fine." (Fr.)

usually leaves for his club after dinner, stays home purposely to be with his daughter, but she, knowing that *he* was the one who was forcing her to stagnate at "Ugly Puss's," reacts to his kindness rather coldly. She even has an irresistible desire to anger him.

"Papa, we're Jews, right?" she says.

"Of course," answers her father, "as if you didn't know."

"And is it true that all Jews are such vile swindlers that after death every single one of them burns in hell?"

"Who told you that, Sarah? Not Mme. Roget, I hope."

"No, not her; I've heard it from a lot of people."

"It's pure rubbish. I advise you not to repeat such nonsense," says her father.

"I've also heard," continues Sarah, unruffled, "that Jews drink human blood with matzoh on Passover."[3]

"Have you ever drunk it on Passover?" her father asks angrily.

"There you are," the daughter replies resentfully, "we're not real Jews."

"And what kind are we?"

"I don't know what kind, only not real ones; real ones are all dirty."

"Jews, like Russians, are dirty when they are poor and uneducated. If you don't want to be dirty, study. I spare nothing for your education, as you must realize."

"And I can't stand kikes and will certainly get baptized when I grow up," Sarah blurts out, vexed that she's unable to make him angry.

"Get out of here, you nasty girl. You'll stay at the boarding school all summer."

She leaves but pauses in the corridor. She hears her mother's meek voice.

"Those are the fruits of bringing her up away from home, in someone else's house," she says. "It had to end like this."

"Leave it alone, please," says her father. "I know what I'm doing. She has to stay at the boarding school for at least three years. I want her to know languages fluently and to have manners fit for society. She can't get that at home. And as for her philosophy, I don't give a damn about it. We just have to tell Mme. Roget to keep a stricter watch over her."

Upon hearing this verdict, Sarah threw herself on her bed and cried until she fell asleep.

1881

Translated from the Russian by Emily Tall

---

3. Sarah Berg here invokes the blood libel, the charge that Jews allegedly use the blood of Christian babies to make matzos, of which the Jews of Europe had been accused from the twelfth century (the William of Norwich affair) by their persecutors in order to justify anti-Jewish violence and restrictive measures. The accusation had a history in Russia in the Velizh affair of 1823, for example, and others.

SEMYON NADSON

Semyon Nadson (1862–1887), poet and essayist, was born in St. Petersburg in 1862. His father, a civil servant who came from a Jewish family and was baptized after his own father had converted to Russian Orthodoxy, died in a lunatic asylum when Nadson was two. His mother, a private teacher descended from the Russian nobility, died of consumption in 1873, whereupon his uncle, I.S. Mamontov, became the boy's guardian. In his autobiographical notes, written in 1880 and published in 1902, Nadson described the humiliation of being a ward in the household of his antisemitic uncle, who called the impressionable, sensitive boy "kikish ninny." After graduating from a military high school in 1879, he entered a cadet school and then, in 1882, the 148th Caspian Regiment as a lieutenant. In 1884, the consumptive Nadson retired and left for European resorts with his companion Maria Vatson, who abandoned her husband to be with him. Returning to St. Petersburg in 1885, Nadson soon went to live in the Ukraine. He died in Yalta in 1887 and was buried in St. Petersburg. A large crowd turned up for Nadson's funeral; students carried his casket to the Volkov cemetery, where it was laid to final rest next to Nikolay Dobrolyubov (1836–1861), a leading "civic" critic of his time, who also died young of consumption.

Nadson's first poem was published in 1878 in the magazine *Light* (*Svet*). In 1881 he met the prominent poet Aleksey Pleshcheev, who published Nadson's poems in *Notes of the Fatherland* (*Otechestvennye zapiski*), a leading journal, forging the young poet's literary reputation. Nadson later referred to Pleshcheev as his literary "godfather." Nadson's essays of 1882–86 were gathered in the volume *Literary Sketches* (1887). In 1886 he was awarded half the Pushkin prize for his *Poems*, a tremendous distinction in and of itself, and all the more so when accorded to a poet of Jewish origin. In the last two years of his life, Nadson enjoyed phenomenal popularity, yet these years were also poisoned by ostracism, especially in the implicitly xenophobic feuilletons of Viktor Burenin.

Semyon Nadson was Russia's most popular poet throughout the three decades preceding the 1917 revolutions. His first collection, *Poems* (1885), was reprinted twenty-nine times before 1917 and sold over 200,000 copies—a bestseller by any account. Nadson was the first Russian poet of Jewish descent to achieve national fame, emerging as a "captor" of the souls of younger readers in the period of Alexander III's rule following the defeat of the populist revolutionary movement of the 1870s. In the decades that followed Nadson's death, educated Russians were very likely to know one or two of his poems by heart.

Oscillating between the poetry of "pure art" (e.g., Afanasy Fet [in vol. 1] and Aleksey Apukhtin) and the poetry of social reflection, Nadson was a link between the civic poetry of Nekrasov and early Russian symbolism. A number of critics and poets were condescending toward him, due in part to his Jewishness, yet such major Russian writers as Lev Tolstoy, Mikhail Saltykov-Shchedrin, Vsevolod Garshin, and Anton Chekhov thought very highly of his gift. When he was starting out in literature, Dmitry Merezhkovsky (1865–1941), one of the founders of the Russian Symbolist movement, regarded Nadson, his senior by only three years, as his literary master. Metrically quite traditional, narcissistically melodious and sonorous, many of Nadson's verses showcase a disillusioned poet's quest for an enduring liberal ideal of humanity. A central theme in a number of his poems is the poet's place in society. Nadson's love lyrics speak with verve and affectation of lost or unrequited love.

In the late 1880s–90s, Nadson was a cult figure among young adults and university students, and his influence is distinctly notable in the early verses of such original poets as Ivan Bunin (1870–1953, the first Russian writer to win the Nobel Prize in Literature for his fiction in 1933). Russian composers—Anton Arensky, Cesar Cui, Arthur Rubinstein, and Sergey Rachmaninoff among them—have set Nadson's lyrics to music, and to this day they remain a solid part of the repertoire of Russian classical *romansy*.

Semyon Nadson wrote one poem with an explicit Jewish theme ("I grew up shunning you, O most degraded nation . . .") and also a poem ("The Woman") where the auto-biographical motifs of a Jewish child's loneliness and alienation are entertained, albeit never quite explicitly. However, the relative importance of Nadson's "Jewish poem" is tremendous, as he, being Russian Orthodox, openly identified with the people of his father and their plight at the time of the pogroms and the new antisemitic restrictions of the 1880s. Composed in 1885, "I grew up shunning you, O most degraded nation . . ." first appeared in the famous collection *Aid to the Jews Devastated by Poor Crops* (1901).

From "The Woman"

(PART 2)

I grew up all alone. No family's gentle care
Gave shelter from early storms or first misfortune.
My mother did not kneel beside me giving prayer,
Nor nanny whisper meekly into my sleeping ear,
Making the cross above me, her passionate devotion . . .
. . . .
    I recall an ancient temple, glittering with lights,
I remember, too, my mother: all bestrewn with flowers,
With clenched and bloodless lips and hands clenched tight she lies,
So silent, in her coffin above our timid height—
Beside her bier, in tears and disbelief, we cower.
My little sister's hand I take in my hand firmly . . .
Dressed in her mourning gown, she's doubly sad and pale,
She presses close against me, so trusting and so small,
Unchildlike anguish floods her eyes as she observes me . . .
We are afraid . . . Death's grisly silences appall,
As do the murky shadows gathering in corners,
The staircase draped in black, and black uncommon garments,
And mother in her coffin, so mute, and cold, and frail.
We want to fly away, into the deepening azure,
Where heaven arches wide and cloudlets gently sift,
Where on the garden path the fragrant green is lavish,
And moths with gaily patterned wings winnow and drift . . .
But yet we do not dare escape, and, hardly knowing
Why we are here amidst the stern and alien crowd,
We listen as the chorus's last hymn resounds
And fades, then solemnly swells again to overflowing . . .

1883

*   *   *

I grew up shunning you, O most degraded nation,
'Twas not to you I sang when inspiration called.
The world of your traditions, the scourge of lamentation
Are alien to me, as are your laws.

And were you, as in times of yore, robust and thriving,
And were you not humiliated everywhere,
But warmed and animated by other, cheerful striving,
I would not hail you then, I swear.

Yet in our times, when, humbled by the weight of sorrow,
You bow your head, await salvation all in vain,
These times when just the name "Jew" keenly harrows,
Or hangs in the mouths of masses like a symbol of disdain,

And when your enemies, a pack of rabid dogs, endeavor
To tear you all to pieces—snarling, wroth with greed—
Then let me also join the ranks of your defenders,
O nation scorned by destiny!

1885

Translated from the Russian by Alyssa Dinega Gillespie

NIKOLAY MINSKY

Nikolay Minsky (1855–1937), poet, essayist, playwright, and translator, was born in Glubokoe, Vilna Province (now in Belarus). His real last name was Vilenkin, and his pen name was derived from Minsk, where he grew up and attended a gymnasium. Minsky graduated in law from St. Petersburg University in 1879.

A remarkable gift for self-refashioning fueled Minsky's career. He began to publish poetry in 1876, his early poems (e.g., "A Slav's Dream") lending support to Bulgaria's struggle against Turkish dominance. His poetry of 1878–80, emulating the civic verses of Aleksey Pleshcheev and Semyon Nadson (in vol. 1) and showcasing self-reflexive populist-revolutionary intellectuals, gained wide recognition; notable was the novelty of the poet's presentation of the working masses as surrounded by an aura of dark mystery. Minsky's epic poem *White Nights* (1879) was praised by Ivan Turgenev, and his *Last Confession* (1879) inspired a painting by the great Russian artist Ilya Repin (1844–1930), who came from the family of a (Jewish) *kantonist*. In 1879–80 Minsky published essays in the Jewish periodical *Dawn* (*Rassvet*) under the pseudonym "Nord-West" and others, arguing for the creation of a Jewish farming class as a way of ameliorating the economic and social condition of Jews and what he deemed the "impurities" of Judaism. Minsky's essays acknowledged his debt to the ideas of Peter (Peretz) Smolenskin (1842–1885; also see Ben-Ami in Vol. 1), while also distancing Minsky from Smolenskin's influence. In 1882 Minsky converted to Russian Orthodoxy and married Yulia Yakovleva (Bezrodnaya); later they divorced, and he married the writer Lyubov Vilkina. Following Vilkina's death in 1920, Minsky married the littérateur Zinaida Vengerova.

The print run of Minsky's volume *Poems* was destroyed by the censors in 1883. The following year Minsky's long poem *The Garden of Gethsemane* was banned by censors as "distorting" the Gospels, but it was circulated in handwritten copies. Minsky's freedom in treating the Gospels stemmed from his self-awareness of being genetically connected to Jesus and a Jewish outsider.

The year 1884 marked Minsky's shift to antiutilitarian aesthetics. His landmark essay "The Ancient Argument" was the first open declaration of aestheticism and decadence in Russian literature. When a modified version of his *Poems* appeared in 1887, the book and its author were ostracized in the xenophobic press. Perhaps these antisemitic attacks inspired Minsky to create his most important Jewish work, *The Siege of Tulchin* (1888). A masterpiece of Jewish-Russian theater, this drama in verse was set during the Khmelnytsky rebellion of 1648–54. Contemporaries immediately recognized the obvious parallels between the pogroms of 1881–82 and the anti-Jewish violence perpetrated by Khmelnytsky's troops. Some readers also identified parallels in the play with the post-1881 debate about the creation of Jewish self-defense against pogromists.

In 1890 Minsky published the treatise *Under the Light of Conscience*, where his doctrine of meonism was elaborated. The term "meonism" comes from the Greek *mè on* (nonexistence, Plato's term), and Minsky's esoteric theory posits nonbeing as the inwardly revealed "unearthly truth." Minsky expounded upon his meonistic ideas in the book *Religion of the Future. Philosophical Conversations* (1905). Although meonism had little long-term impact, it earned an important place in cultural history as the first religious-philosophical system of early Russian modernism. In the 1890s Minsky was among the principal leaders of Russian decadence and the early Symbolist movement, preaching a cult of beauty and pleasure. In the early 1900s, he cofounded the Religious-Philosophical Society with Dmitry Merezhkovsky, Zinaida Gippius, Vasily Rozanov, and others.

In 1905, during the first Russian revolution, Minsky was taken with the revolutionary mood, then regarding himself as an "appointee of the proletariat" and composing a "Workers' Anthem" as a free rendition of the "Internationale." Minsky, together with Gorky and Lenin, headed *New Life* (*Novaia zhizn'*), the newspaper of the Bolshevik faction of the RSDRP (Russian Socialist Democratic Workers' Party). He was arrested, was released on bail, and, facing a prison term, escaped abroad in December 1905. He stayed abroad until the 1913 amnesty, contributing journalistic articles to Russian newspapers. His literary reputation steeply declined. Following the 1917 Bolshevik Revolution, Minsky became an émigré. In 1921 he moved to Berlin, where *From Darkness to Light*, a summing-up of his poetry, appeared a few years later. He died in Paris in 1937 and was buried at Père Lachaise cemetery.

The poem "To Rubinstein" (1887) was dedicated to Anton Rubinstein (1829–1894), the famous pianist and composer who founded the St. Petersburg Conservatory of Music in 1862. His younger brother, Nikolay Rubinstein (1835–1881), founded the Moscow Conservatory. The Rubinstein brothers came from a family of Jewish-German converts to Christianity, which did not vouchsafe them against accusations of not being sufficiently "Russian" in their musical endeavors. Anton Rubinstein set several of Minsky's poems, including "Serenade" (1879), to music. The heroic Biblical past was a source of Minsky's inspiration and Judaic pride. Given Minsky's status as a lapsed Jew, irony stems from the identification of Anton Rubinstein with young David and the audience with David's predecessor, King Saul.

To Rubinstein

When before the eager Petersburg crowd
You come onstage augustly as a lion, treading proud,
And the public greets the striking figure you present—
So full of grandeur—with roars of ecstasy, enthralled,
    It seems to me: David again
    Has reappeared to play for Saul,
Has reappeared in our diseased and desperate time
So as to flood coarse minds with the charms of blissful languor,
So as to vanquish nightmares, lull enmity and anger,
Illumine stubborn hearts with hopes of realms sublime.

And now you sit to play—the notes awake, expand
To flow in crystal streams, in murmuring cascades,
As music, sight unseen, extends its burning rays
Toward every heart from under your mighty hands
And melts in each the stubborn ice of fears and worries.
Amidst the teeming capital's stormy sea, like God,
You conjure a sapphire island out of naught,
You give new wings to dreams—and send Youth in a flurry
Forth on those very wings, to flutter onward
Into the land of hope, where striving knows no bounds,
Where happiness has no end, and lovers never wander
Or betray—while mournful Age retreats to that profound
    Abode of memories grown deaf,
Of erstwhile sweet confessions, innocent tears once wept.
And high above the abyss of social tumult,
Unclasping from your soul, the poet's soul goes soaring
To regions where immortal beauty reigns in glory,
To Edens of unending summer.

You've breathed the fire of love into hearts grown dead and cold;
You've resurrected what the truth may oft destroy,
And the crowds pray and weep, as Saul did long ago,
    And bless your genius as they cry.

1886

Translated from the Russian by Alyssa Dinega Gillespie

SIMON FRUG

Simon (Semyon, Shimen, Shmuel) **Frug** (1860–1916), poet, essayist, and translator, was born and grew up in Bobrovy Kut, a Jewish agricultural colony in the Kherson Province, and his love for the rural landscapes of his childhood and youth would later manifest itself in his poetry. At fifteen Frug moved to Kherson and worked in the office of a government rabbi; in 1881 he moved to St. Petersburg with the support of the Jewish public figure and philanthropist Mark S. Varshavsky. Frug's Russian poems began to appear in *Sunrise* (*Voskhod*) in 1879 and soon became popular. His "Legend of the Goblet" (1882) won a major prize, and its Yiddish translation, "Des Kos," by Isaac Leyb Perets was set to music and sung worldwide. By the mid-1880s, Frug's poems had made their way into mainstream Russian periodicals, including *European Messenger* (*Vestnik Evropy*) and *Russian Wealth* (*Russkoe bogatstvo*).

Frug's early verses capture the upheavals and aspirations of the Jewish-Russian intelligentsia in the 1870s. Later, shaken by the pogroms of 1881–82, Frug joined the Hibbat Zion (Love of Zion) movement; his poem "Jewish Melody" ("And the eye is sharp . . .") was an anthem of the Russian Palestinophiles in the 1880s. While he never abandoned his youthful ideals of a *maskil*, he championed a Jewish national revival on Israeli soil. Frug's first collection, *Poems,* appeared in 1885 to sympathetic reviews by Russian critics and accolades in the Jewish press; it was reprinted twice. The first volume was followed in 1887 by *Thoughts and Songs* and by multivolume editions in the 1900s–1910s. The First Zionist Congress (1897) gave Frug's poetry a great boost, resulting in an impressive body of verse, which was published in 1902 in *Zionides and Other Poems, 1897–1902* and in 1908 in *Songs of Exodus.* Struggling to make a living in the 1890s–1900s, Frug contributed light verse and feuilletons pseudonymously to Russian tabloids.

Frug also wrote in Yiddish for newspapers in Europe and America, contributing to (*Dos Yiddishe Folksblat*) *The People's Jewish Paper* from the middle of the 1880s. Many of Frug's Yiddish poems, such as "Song of Labor" (Lid fur der Arbet), were used as lyrics for popular songs; Jewish protesters sang and chanted the lyrics of his "Have Pity" (Hot Rakhmones), written in 1903 after the Kishinev Pogrom. A volume of his Yiddish poems was published in 1896, followed by a two-volume edition in 1902. Yiddish author though he was, Frug stated, in an article in the Yiddish daily *The Friend* (*Der Fraynd*), "One of the two: either we are a nation, then Yiddish is not our national language; or Yiddish is our national language, then we are not a nation." At the age of thirty-eight, Frug returned to writing Hebrew verse and became close to the writers of the new Hebrew literature after moving to Odessa in 1909. His Russian translation of

Book of Legends (*Sefer Ha'Aggadah*), edited and collected by Hayyim Nahman Bialik and Yehoshua Ravnitzky, appeared in Odessa in 1910. A spectacular reader, Frug toured Jewish communities giving recitals. He died in Odessa in 1916; a crowd of 100,000 people from many parts of the Russian Empire followed Frug's casket to the cemetery, mourning the loss of the first Jewish-Russian poet of national fame.

"Carry my soul to that faraway blue,/Where the golden steppe far extending,/As wide as my fateful sorrow,/As my bottomless woe . . ." Rendered literally, at the expense of both its meter and its rhyme, the opening of one of Frug's best-known poems, which reportedly moved his Jewish audiences to tears, epitomizes the appeal as well as the limitations of his poetic diction. Although to this day historians identify Frug as the first Jewish-Russian "national poet," his voluminous legacy presents a literary scholar with a dilemma of judgment. Frug's reception by Jewish-Russian readers in the 1880s–1910s was much more enthusiastic than the intrinsic merits of his Russian poetry should have warranted. Quite pedestrian when placed in the broader contexts of Russian poetry and literary history, Frug's poems call into question Bialik's well-known comment, made in an interview with *Odessa News* (*Odesskie novosti*) on 8 September 1916, on the occasion of Frug's death and possibly misquoted: "In my view Frug wrote not in Russian [. . .]. Reading his Russian verses, I did not notice the Russian language. I felt in each word the language of [his] ancestors, the language of the Bible." A doubly "national" poet of Russia's Jews, for the liminal Jewish-Russian intelligentsia as well as the Yiddish-reading masses, Frug the Russian poet may have motivated the admiring new Hebrew poets Bialik, Tchernikhovsky and others not to write in Russian.

Frug's best Russian poems are lyrical and confessional. Suffused with the pain of Jewish suffering, they borrow Russian Biblical intonations from Aleksandr Pushkin ("scorching people's hearts with the Word," as in Pushkin's 1825 "Prophet," based on Isaiah 6) and derive civic pathos from Mikhail Lermontov and Nikolay Nekrasov. Less successful are Frug's epic poems based on the Bible and the Aggadah.

In the first of the two poems translated here, "Song," Frug refers to the Aeolian harp, which in Greek mythology was the instrument played by the god Aeolus, using the winds of which he was custodian rather than his hands. European poetic references to the Aeolian harp, which is currently sometimes known as a wind harp, date back to the seventeenth century. Frug's work is opposite in mood to Samuel Taylor Coleridge's tranquil poem of 1795, "The Aeolian Harp."

In the second poem, "Shylock," Frug was not translating but rather approximating, adapting, and recreating in Russian a free version of Shakespeare's *The Merchant of Venice*. The epigraph is the exception, being a translation of lines 179 and 183–84 in scene 1 of act 4 of Portia's speech in Shakespeare's play.

Song

Aeolian harp am I, voice of my people,
I echo my people's heartache.

You see how those ghosts tread the darkness so steeply?
You hear their chains clatter and scrape?

Now phantoms of sadness, now specters of suffering
Bequeath me their doleful refrains . . .

And I have forgotten dawn's roseate blushing,
Forgotten the nightingale's strains.

Should hope kindle brightly, despair sends its worries
To ravage my soul in a throng.

Whatever I've gleaned from my people through fury
And poison, I'll give back through song . . .

1890s

Shylock

The quality of mercy is not strain'd . . . it becomes
The thronèd monarch better than his crown.
Shakespeare

I.

Dry as a pole, with sparse and patchy whiskers,
The hoar of early aging in his curls,
And on his bloodless lips a caustic and malicious
Smirk stealthily unfurls.
He steps inside the court of dazzling Venice . . .
Clutched in his hand, a knife blade gleams . . .
And the majestic, haughty Duke soon seems

To tremble at this terrifying menace:
Not really? . . . Can it be? . . . But resonantly
As the clang of tempered steel,
The voice of Shylock, mercilessly scathing,
Sounds, full of enmity and hatred:
"O Duke! Esteeming our Venetian laws as blest,
Pronounce your just decree—
Without delay or mercy, sir, let me
Cut out my bloody debt from yon Antonio's breast . . .
Give me my pound of flesh, O judge, my pound of flesh!"

II.

Ages have passed. The dukes' palazzo
Is derelict, forgotten. The parade
Of centuries has pitted its colossal
Granite pedestals, windblown its marble colonnades.
Both those who were judged, and those who sat in judgment
Repose in death's eternal dungeon,
And all are lulled beneath the gravestone slab
By a chilly but attentive hand . . .
The blades of the rapacious dagger
And noble saber both have rusted from disuse;
In the turbid fog of time lie scattered
The thorn plant's prickles, the petals of the rose . . .
But you, who cannot sleep when night is desolate and mute,
Your soul tormented by a searching thought
As the shadow of a fable flits across,
Though never shutting out the fatal truth—
Do you not sometimes seem to see
A vatic vision, at first confused, that slowly sharpens,
And does there not appear to you beyond the age-old darkness
The living incarnation of a fantasy?

III.

Here is the judgment chamber . . .
Before that selfsame mighty Duke there stands
An aged man. Not with a passionate demand
But in bitter supplication does he linger.
In his eyes—the yoke of centuries emblazoned,
And in his hands—no dagger, but a book now blazes,
Held open to the judge's face . . .

The letters in that tome resemble white-hot coals,
They spark and burn. Sharper than swords
That smite to the marrow are its flaming words.
Both the disdainful stare of the adjudicator,
And humble gaze of him whom judgment binds,
The book's prophetic page has captivated
With its chastising lines . . .

IV.

The old man speaks:
"O Duke! Once in this very chamber
I stood beside Antonio.
My blood was boiling then with rancor,
The fire of enmity flared in my soul.
I thirsted vengefully to carve out from his hateful
Breast a pound of flesh . . . O judge, behold
What people have done to me since that fateful
Day—not, like myself, downtrodden folk,
But proud and mighty in the world's opinion,
Pray ask them—why am I now a skeleton repining?
Ask—who has stripped my bones of flesh,
And swallowed all the blood that warmed my breast? . . .
And if I was considered once a debtor,
Then is this recompense worthy of them
Who pride themselves midst all the universe of men
On their compassion and their gentle temper?
Ask, O judge! . . ."

V.

But the Duke is speechless . . . Silence
Reigns all around . . . Only the undying
Letters marching across the page bear living witness,
Burn in the darkness. . . . Like transplendent swords
Those fiery symbols daze and glitter,
Fill up the dusky hall with flaming words . . .

1890s

Translated from the Russian by Alyssa Dinega Gillespie

Frug's serious Russian prose was collected in *Meetings and Impressions* (1898) and *Sketches and Fairy Tales* (1898), and later in his *Collected Works*. Whether they showcase images of Jewish colonies in his native Kherson Province or discuss vital Jewish issues of his time, Frug's atmospheric and colorful sketches are more stylistically accomplished than his Russian poems.

An Admirer of Napoleon

Look, there's the tombstone that has the inscription "Here lies Israel-Moses, son of Yehuda, a Levite." Israel-Moses, or Sruel-Moishe, came into the world in one of the unattractive little houses of the colony. For sixty-three years he trod life's path and covered only some 300–400 *sazheni*[1]—precisely the distance between the log hut where he was born and the knoll beneath which he lay to rest after his long arduous journey. Sruel-Moishe was a squat, rotund little man with a thick jet-black beard and a broad muscular face who stammered slightly when he grew excited. He was married three times, first at thirteen years of age and for the last time at thirty-six. He served for thirty years as the village policeman attached to the rural district office, safely survived the scurvy and cholera that raged in the region (in 1847–48 and 1853), cut and threshed with his own hands during his lifetime, by his reckoning, about 1,350 acres of wheat, rye, and so forth, and died in the firm belief that there was and would be no one wiser, mightier, and nobler than the emperor Napoleon I. Nobody knows where Sruel-Moishe picked up his knowledge about the French emperor and on what he actually based his belief about his wisdom, might, and nobility. Perhaps he would not have been able to answer that sort of question himself, but this did not in the least prevent him from defending his belief on every conceivable occasion. Sruel-Moishe had, in fact, an extremely vague conception of the road that his beloved emperor traveled, of the events that are closely associated with his name, and of the sad fate that befell him at the end of his celebrated epic journey. In the chronicle that Sruel-Moishe kept, the French emperor appeared in all manner of situations of aggressive and defensive politics, quite often performing feats of an utterly legendary nature but always remaining unfailingly mighty and impeccably noble. I could not help recalling this strange inclination of Sruel-Moishe's for "politics" precisely because of its

---

1. A *sazhen* is a Russian unit of distance, now obsolete, that is equal to about seven feet (2.134 meters).

strangeness. As he had been born in the colony and been a policeman since the age of thirty-three, Sruel-Moishe was a direct, natural product of the sphere of life that, in the eighty years that the agricultural colonies existed in Novorossiia,[2] had produced a certain type of Jewish farmer who was very far removed from any philosophizing on abstract subjects in general and political ones in particular. The *lovchiki*,[3] the *kantonisty,* and the birch, these were the only terms around which all tales of a recruit's life revolved in this environment and to which all notions of "politics" were effectively confined. As regards the manifestations of ordinary everyday life, the Jewish colonist is a copy of his Slavic peasant neighbor. The land and the tools with which it is worked, domestic animals and the constant concern for them—these are the main items toward which the thoughts and attention of the colonist are directed and that are the source of all his joys and sorrows. True, his "bond" with the land is not yet as firmly established as that observed in his peasant neighbor. Two or three years of crop failure in succession and the general loss of cattle from disease that usually follows them disturb the Jewish farmer's routine and shake him to his foundations to a considerably greater degree than is apparent in the peasant milieu. However, this is fostered by reasons that lie not in any particular characteristics inherent in the Jewish colonist but in certain economic and administrative conditions that, from the very first moments when the category of Jewish farmers came into being in Novorossiia, placed the Jewish farmer in an exceptional and far from advantageous position. Yet in ordinary everyday life, as I have already said, the Jewish colonist is in no way different from his peasant neighbor.

Such a colonist was Sruel-Moishe. The position of policeman could not harm his interests as a farmer because it did not deprive him of virtually a single hour of his work in the fields. This will become clear if I say that during ploughing and reaping almost no village meetings usually take place at which the work of the policeman, as the tax collector and guardian of law and order, is overridingly in evidence. As for internal work on the tasks of village self-government, although it is carried out constantly by the *shultse* [village headman] or one of his two *beisitsern* [assessors], it is of a sort that in no way requires the obligatory presence of the policeman. The *shultse* or his *beisitser* would just sit there of a hot summer's noonday and click away at the beads of a large, ink-stained abacus, working out the totals for tax assessments or checking the figures for revenue from land-rent account items. The office room, decorated with portraits of members of the imperial family and two or three ministers of state property and with various "tables," "charts," and lists with long, narrow columns

---

2. Novorossiia (lit. "New Russia")—area in the south of Russia encompassing the northern and northeastern coasts of the Black Sea and the Crimean peninsula. In the late eighteenth century, Novorossiia became part of the Russian Empire (parts of it had been captured from the Ottoman Empire), and Jews were allowed to settle there.
    3. *Lovchiki* (Russ.) = lit. "catchers," those in charge of delivering the Jewish recruits into the hands of the authorities.

of numbers, was quiet and fairly cool thanks to the curtains drawn at the windows on its sunny side. The bead-clicking "boss" would raise his head at times and, turning to the door into the hall, yell, "Mendl, ho Mendl!" "What is it?" would come the reply in a child's voice, and Mendl, Sruel-Moishe's son, with a sleepy face and disheveled hair would emerge from the hall. "What?" "Did you fall asleep again?" the "boss" would say to him. "Go and fetch some cold water to quench my thirst, go to the well and draw some fresh. . . . What a thirst I have!" Or he would say, "Go to my house, Mendl, and find out whether our people are back from the fields and ask how many sheaves there are still left in the cornfield that's beside Tyaginskaya Road. Oh, and while you're at it ask them to hang out to dry the breast-band and reins that I tarred yesterday."

And the "boss" would become absorbed again in his abacus and calculations. In this way matters were managed without the presence of Sruel-Moishe, who was at that time in the field doing his work, as were the other residents. He did not differ in any way from any of his fellow villagers, unless one counts his incomprehensible penchant for politics, with its total and unswerving admiration for the political genius of Napoleon I, and then his minor passion for the reputation of a jurist or "legal eagle," as residents of the colony jocularly nicknamed him. "The law says"—that was the usual device to which Sruel-Moishe resorted whenever he had occasion to argue about some problem or other concerning the colony's self-government, and to the policeman's credit it should be noted that, as he had long years of experience behind him and, furthermore, knew the personal characteristics of the most immediate authorities who controlled the colonists' destinies, he was rarely ever wrong. To make up for it, Sruel-Moishe would become inimitably comic in the matter of his other weakness, Napoleon I.

For example, once in an argument with Reb Gersh, a man of the strictest devotion and piety, he ventured to express the opinion that the Temple of Zion might still be standing today if Napoleon and not Nebuchadnezzar had been the king of ancient Babylon because Napoleon was too wise and noble to bring himself to destroy such a mighty building.

"What!" exclaimed the indignant Reb Gersh, "you've taken leave of your senses, Sruel-Moishe! I like that, the Temple would not have been destroyed! So in your opinion it comes to this, that the Ninth of Av, when even the Eternal One Himself weeps, could have been eliminated by Napoleon and . . . and. . . . But what can one say to such an ignoramus and atheist as you!" And Reb Gersh waved his hand and turned away, unable to control his agitation.

Reb Gersh's indignation was entirely natural, for he profoundly believed that all the wisdom and might of all earthly rulers were pitiful and insignificant compared with the "finger of God" alone and that consequently the point was not who was at war with Israel but that the Temple of Zion had to be destroyed, and no Napoleons or even Alexanders of Macedonia would have been able to preserve it.

The argument occurred on one of those fine July evenings, on the stone steps by the doors of the synagogue, where the minyan had begun to gather for evening prayer. Along the wide street overgrown here and there with grass, the cows and goats returning from pasture toiled along, filling the air with their lowing and bleating, and among them noisily bustled the lads, puffing and panting from running and the heat, most of them barefoot and in short tattered trousers. Directly opposite the synagogue building, a dramatic scene of sorts was being enacted in Tevye Khaikin's homestead: a roan cow, as she crossed the yard, sank her teeth into a child's short-tailed shirt that had been hung out to dry on the garden fence and, chewing inanely, dragged it along with her in the direction of the stalls. Tevye's wife, who was standing at the door, busy at the time putting a bag of curd under the press, was about to rush to recover the shirt, but at that same moment a calf broke loose from its tether, ran up to its mother, and began to suckle ravenously, which plunged the thoroughly flustered mistress of the house into despair. Motya Khaliper's cart piled high with sheaves was trundling along the same street, and the driver's shouted reprimands at the weary horses were mingled with the lowing of the cows and the voices of the youths scurrying round and about. Some young lad was clambering up the wall of the public barn built inside the synagogue fence, striving to reach his hand into a nest of house-martins nestling right under the eaves. Twice already he had contrived to fall to the ground and badly bruise his shoulder, but each time he set to work again with increasing vigor. A lively flock of sparrows flitted about the yard, one minute descending and hopping around on the grass, the next soaring suddenly up into the air with a song. From somewhere to the left came the thud-thud of the threshing stone and from the other direction, the hum of the winnowing fan. The dying rays of the sun illumined this whole motley scene, tingeing with gold the long gray beard of Reb Gersh and leaving their reflection on the badly crumpled yet still shining visor on the cap of Sruel-Moishe—those two who were arguing at the time about the might and nobility of Napoleon I.

Which of them was right they simply failed to establish, either then or on subsequent occasions, as with many other questions to which they found a single common answer, each beneath one of the tombstones that dot the small dispiriting graveyard.

1890s

Translated from the Russian by Brian Cooper

Simon Frug, "Poklonnik Napoleona." English translation copyright © by Brian Cooper. Introduction and notes copyright © by Maxim D. Shrayer.

BEN-AMI

Ben-Ami (1854–1932), fiction writer, journalist, and Zionist activist, was born Mark Rabinovich in Verkhovka, near the town of Bar, Ukraine, presently in Vinnitsa Province. In Hebrew, "Ben-Ami" literally means "son of my people"; in Genesis 19:30–38, Lot's daughters lay with their father and later gave birth, the elder to Moab, the younger to Ben-Ami. The writer chose the latter as his *nom de plume* to sign his fiction.

Ben-Ami attended a yeshiva in Odessa. There he experienced the powerful influence of Peter (Peretz) Smolenskin (1842–1885), the Hebrew-Russian novelist and essayist who founded the Vienna-based *The Dawn* (*Ha-Shahar*) and advocated eastern Jewry's rapprochement with the west. Becoming a *maskil* on Smolenskin's model, Ben-Ami studied at a Russian gymnasium and later Novorossiysk University. He debuted in 1881 in *Sunrise* (*Voskhod*) with the essay "On the Necessity of Special Textbooks of the Russian Language for Jewish Schools." During the 1881–82 pogroms, Ben-Ami took part in organizing Jewish self-defense. He subsequently journeyed to Paris seeking assistance for the pogrom victims from the Alliance Israélite Universelle. Ben-Ami contributed "Letters from Paris" to *Sunrise* under the pen name "Reish-Geluta," a term that, first, referred to the leader of the ancient Jewish semiautonomous government in Babylonia and Persia and, second, must have been a bilingual phonetic pun on the Russian *rech' galuta*, meaning "speech of exile." Ben-Ami here voiced a profound admiration for enduring Jewish values and a critique of assimilationism. After moving to Geneva in 1882, Ben-Ami began a series of Russian-language stories and tales celebrating the spirit of Jewish festivals and legends, including "The Tzaddik's Arrival" (1883) and "Baal Tefila" (1884). Appearing regularly in *Sunrise,* his stories were in great demand, and Ben-Ami was the first major Jewish writer of popular fiction in Russian for the growing ranks of Russianized professionals and businessmen.

In 1887 Ben-Ami returned to Odessa, remaining there until the eruption of the first Russian revolution in 1905, when he moved back to Geneva. He published Russian fiction, such as the cycle *Stories for My Children*, and essays, decrying governmental antisemitism while also condemning the Jewish intelligentsia for its abnegation of the oppressed Jewish masses and its assimilationist tendencies. Remaining one of *Sunrise*'s principal's authors until its termination in 1906, Ben-Ami also published a collection of Russian-language *Biblical Stories for Jewish Children* (Odessa, 1903) and a cycle of stories in Yiddish, one of which appeared in the second issue of Sholem Aleichem's

The Jewish Popular Library (*Die Yiddishe Folksbibliotek*) in 1889. Several of his works have been translated into Hebrew by Hayyim Nahman Bialik. Written in Yiddish, Ben-Ami's short novel *A Night in a Small Town* (A nacht in a kleyn shtetl, 1909) stemmed from his Russian-language "shtetl" fiction of the 1880s. Ben-Ami's literary output dwindled after his return to Geneva in 1905.

Ben-Ami was a member of the central committee of Hovevei Zion (Lovers of Zion) in Odessa from its founding in 1890 and a delegate to the First Zionist Congress and to the subsequent congresses presided over by Theodor Herzl. In 1923 Ben-Ami moved to Palestine, where he died in Tel Aviv in 1932. Except for Laura Salmon's Italian-language monograph of 1995, modern scholarship about Ben-Ami remains scarce.

Narrated in the first person, Ben-Ami's Russian fiction is set in the 1860s. One wonders if Ben-Ami's idealization of his childhood and youth did not betray some nostalgia for the epoch when the majority of the Jewish masses in Russia had not fully confronted the problems of modernization and acculturation. Sentimental and free of authorial irony, Ben-Ami's narratives minimize dramatic conflict and underrate structures of desire; many are not stories but actually long sketches or pseudoautobiographical recollections. In contrast to the *maskilim* who are the heroes in the works of his contemporaries, Ben-Ami's characters are run-of-the-mill Jews in the Pale. A typical example is "A Little Drama" (1893), in which the protagonist, a righteous but poor bookbinder, manages to scrape together enough money to buy his son a pair of new boots. On the eve of Passover, as the father and son wash themselves in the communal bathhouse, the new boots are stolen and the boy's heart is broken. In its dramatic collision, the story recalls the well-known tale of a poor Baltic-German musician in the St. Petersburg of the 1830s, "A Story of Two Galoshes" by Vladimir Sollogub (1813–1882).

There is reason to believe that Ben-Ami was keenly aware of both his dominant reader's expectations and level of linguistic and cultural preparation. His mission was to depict the beauty of the Jewish past and to lift his reader's spirits, and shorter fiction was just a convenient medium, not his form of choice. Ben-Ami's achievement as an essayist eclipses his own contribution as a fictionist; his essays were punchier and tighter, displaying a greater degree of authorial self-reflection. Romanticizing as it does the "soul of the *Jewish* folk," the following preface to a volume of his Russian fiction was a credo of Ben-Ami the Russian writer and a testament of Ben-Ami the Jewish activist.

Collected Stories and Sketches (1898)
(Author's Preface to Volume 1)

The Jewish reading public is more or less familiar with the stories that follow[1]—I am referring, of course, to Jewish readers who are interested in the life of their people.

In these stories I have tried, to the best of my strength and ability, to reproduce the life of our national masses or, to be more precise, those sides of this life with which I am more familiar and the way I know them; to reproduce them not as an indifferent outside observer but as a coparticipant who has experienced it all and suffered along with others. This, however, does not mean in the least that the author actually appears throughout these stories as a character. If the story is told for the most part in the first person, that is because such a form seems to me the most straightforward and natural.

Actually, I am imprecise in speaking about the "life of the national masses," for the overwhelming majority of Jews live their lives without knowing a division into estates.

Woven of woe and privations, this life is sorrowful and joyless. But the severe, impossible struggle to earn one's daily bread, which gets harder and more ruthless every day, every hour, has not murdered the people's soul, which is still alive and receptive to anything lofty and noble. The ancient national ideals still linger at the bottom of the people's soul, the ancient hopes and aspirations still live—the great heritage of our nation's great grievers, the prophets.

And that is the only solace, the bright light that shines in the life of Jewry, bright in the realm of the spirit, in the realm of ideals. A dark fathomless ocean of suffering, over which up on high, here and there amid thick black storm clouds, little stars sparkle . . .

At a time when different individuals and groups are prepared to make various "adjustments" of their selves, supposing thus to ease their lives and in doing so pretend to be now zealous Germans, now flaming Poles, Czechs, Magyars—in a word, whatever they need to pretend to be—our people in its vast majority continues to live its *own* life. And it does not even think about or care to know whether its existence is pleasing to anybody else. Quite the contrary, it is fully conscious of the fact that it is not pleasing. And this, I believe, serves as a significant stimulus for the people to value its own existence. For the people's instinct is in general nobler than all the premeditated and

---

1. With the exception of the story "At Night on the Eve of Goshano Rabot," which previously appeared in a general-interest magazine, all the other stories were originally published in *Sunrise*. Of the three stories included in this volume, only "Baal-Tefila" has undergone substantial reworking. [B-A.] The third story included in vol. 1 was "A Little Drama."

deliberate punditry, nobler just by virtue of being an *instinct,* that is, a natural phenomenon, inborn and not something artificial, devised for a particular occasion.

It is common for the Jewish writer, if he devotes his literary work to Jews, to regard himself for the most part as a "defender" of the Jews. No matter to what area of literature he contributes, he above all has such a "defense" in mind. And even when he addresses an exclusively Jewish audience, often even when he writes in a language that is completely inaccessible to the non-Jewish world, in Hebrew for instance, even then his spiritual gaze inadvertently remains shackled to "them," these visible and invisible "enemies" of Israel. And in nearly every passage can be seen the clear intention to persuade "them," to prove to "them," to vindicate in "their" eyes, to solicit "their" compassion, and so forth.

I confess that in me all these types of "defense," these strivings to "prove," and so on, have always elicited the heaviest, most unpleasant feelings. I know nothing more insulting to or more humiliating for a person's dignity than the sense that everyone for whatever reason believes it his duty to vindicate or defend the person before whomever, almost apologizing for the person's unforgivable desire to exist. The thought of appearing as a "defender" is therefore not only alien to me but also antithetical to my beliefs. I think least of all about proving or demonstrating something to someone. I decisively do not believe that we are guilty before anyone, and I could not care less what somebody thinks of us.

What opinion people have about us does not depend on us, and even less on our obsessive explanations and appeals.

If I really sought to instill sympathy for the deeply miserable masses of our population, which alone bear the oppressive burden of Jewish sorrow and Jewish dire need, that would be above all and mainly in the Jews themselves, those numerous "cultured" Jews who have suddenly become the keepers of the vineyards of others while leaving their own to the cruel mercy of fate.

I am not speaking of those vile reptiles from the ranks of our own gilded house servants who, out of pitiful, despicable vanity, and expecting to receive the master's patting or the master's smile, thrust themselves as benefactors upon those who need them the least. They can shell out tens of thousands for the publication of works they do not understand and hundreds of thousands for the establishment of various schools, homes, shelters, and so forth, which can well be organized without the help of the Jewish Derunovs.[2] They will not blind anyone, nor deceive anyone with their rich

---

2. Osip Derunov is the protagonist of "Pillar" ("Stolp"), a chapter in *Speeches of a Loyal Citizen,* a cycle of essays that the novelist, satirist, and essayist Mikhail Saltykov-Shchedrin (1826–1889) published in *Notes of the Fatherland* in 1872–76. The subject of "Pillar" is the post-1860s reforms for the development of capitalism in Russia. A small-time trader prior to the abolition of serfdom in 1861, Osip Derunov becomes, by hook or by crook, a wealthy businessman and major power broker in his province, making his capital off the impoverished peasants and ruined gentry. Derived etymologically from the Russian verb *drat'* ("to rip"), Derunov became a name in Russian culture that denoted a ruthless individual who would stop at nothing to increase his capital and power.

offerings. These offerings belong to the sort that in ancient times were not admitted to the Temple . . . Everybody knows perfectly well that it is not nobleness but rather the baseness of their souls that motivates them, for nobleness makes its sacrifices for the weakest, not the strongest.

I speak not of the renegades who are a subject of contempt both by the ones they have abandoned and the ones upon whom they force themselves.

I have in mind those who have dedicated themselves to the vineyards of others because they do not suspect the existence of their own or else do not know of its woeful state.

Yes, may the Jews themselves be filled with a genuine love for the Jewish people and for Jewry—and that would be perfectly sufficient.

Not from the others must we expect salvation.

This eternal anticipation of the mercy of others, this eternal standing on our hind paws before the table of others and awaiting their crumbs is what completely paralyzes our moral strength and corrupts our character, developing in us so many lowly, unworthy traits.

Our help, our salvation is in ourselves. We can and must help ourselves. And only such help, coming from within ourselves, is capable of strengthening us morally and spiritually, elevating us both in our own eyes and in those of others, and making us equal to other nations.

Only those rights are valid and valuable that accord a nation the opportunity to develop its spirit freely and independently and that by their very nature alone cannot be offered as a gift.

1897

Translated from the Russian by Maxim D. Shrayer

Ben-Ami, "Ot avtora," *Sobranie rasskazov i ocherkov,* vol. 1 (Odessa, 1898). English translation, introduction, and notes copyright © by Maxim D. Shrayer.

AVRAAM-URIA KOVNER

Avraam-Uria (Albert, Arkady) **Kovner** (1842–1909), critic and memoirist, was born in Vilna to a poor teacher's family; he studied at a number of Lithuanian yeshivas in the 1850s. Kovner married in 1860, but he soon left his wife and moved to Kiev and in 1865–69 lived in Odessa. An autodidact, in the early1860s he discovered the works of the Russian radical critics of the 1850s. In the 1860s he contributed to Odessa's newspaper *The Advocate* (*Ha-Melits*) and the Vilna journal *Carmel* (*Ha-Karmel*). Kovner accused the Haskalah Hebrew-Russian authors of futile romanticism and remoteness, both stylistic and topical, from the contemporary life of the Jewish people. He called on Hebrew writers to treat current subjects and considered literature in Hebrew and Yiddish to be a stage on the way to the assimilation of the Jewish writers into the language of their native country. Kovner gained the reputation of a nihilist and a "Jewish Pisarev" (after the influential critic Dmitry Pisarev, 1840–1868). Kovner's critical essays appeared in two volumes, *Investigation of the Issue* (1865) and *A Bunch of Flowers* (1868).

In the 1860s and early 1870s, Kovner spoke out against traditional Jewish life in the Odessan Jewish-Russian weekly *Day* (*Den'*), attributing the "Jewish problem" in Russia largely to socioeconomic, not religious, factors. An outcast in Odessa's Jewish community, he relocated to St. Petersburg in 1871, where he contributed to the Russian press, writing next to nothing about Jewish issues. In 1872–73, Kovner was staff feuilletonist for the newspaper *The Voice* (*Golos*), lashing out against complacent journalists and crooked, in his view, financiers. His Russian-language novel *Without a Label* was banned in 1872 for "wild socialist attacks against the affluent classes." In 1873 Kovner joined a large bank in St. Petersburg as a clerk. He conceived, not without the influence of *Crime and Punishment*, of a crime that would lift his family out of poverty and enable his consumptive fiancée to go abroad for treatment. In April 1875, he forged a check for 168,000 rubles—an enormous sum for his time. Arrested in Kiev and tried in Moscow, he was sentenced to four years of hard labor, which was replaced with a jail term due to his weak health. Kovner's fiancée died after the trial.

Kovner owes his place in Russian literature mainly to his correspondence with Fyodor Dostoevsky, whose novel *Possessed* (1871) he had previously attacked in print. Leonid Grossman (1888–1965; also see Leonid Tsypkin in Vol. 2) unearthed Kovner's correspondence with Dostoevsky in his remarkable 1924 book, *Confession of One Jew*. From jail, in January 1877, Kovner sent Dostoevsky a long polemical letter. "No, alas you know neither the Jewish people, nor its life, nor its spirit, nor, finally, the forty millennia of its history," Kovner wrote, "[. . .] a sincere, completely honest person, you end up involuntarily wronging the huge masses of the Jewish people living in abject poverty [. . .]." A Dostoevskian character, a Jew and an atheist, an idealistic embezzler who stole exactly 3 percent of the annual profit of Russia's richest bank, Kovner made a strong impression upon Dostoevsky, compelling him to speak of the Jewish question in the March 1877 issue of his *Diary of a Writer*. Dostoevsky quoted Kovner's letter, calling him an "educated and talented man," but Dostoevsky's discussion of the Jewish question was largely disappointing: a crude rhetoric of the "Yid is coming" variety crowned by an opaque scenario of a Jewish–Christian reconciliation at the funeral, in Minsk, of a Protestant German obstetrician who dedicated his life to helping the poor of all creeds, including Jews.

After two years in jail, Kovner was sent to Siberia, eventually spending thirteen years' exile in Tomsk and Omsk. In 1893 he married a young Russian woman, taking baptism just fourteen days prior to the wedding. Kovner left Siberia in 1897 and settled in Łomża, Poland, where he became a civil servant with the auditor's department, although the Jewish question continued to preoccupy him. In 1901 he wrote to Vasily Rozanov (1856–1919), their ensuing correspondence (1901–08) focusing on two main topics: antisemitism, especially in the aftermath of the Kishinev pogrom, and atheism. Rozanov, the future author of the notorious treatise *The Olfactory and Tactile Attitude of Jews to Blood* (1911–13), included Kovner's essay "Why I Do Not Believe" in his two-volume book *Near Church Walls* (1906). In 1908 Kovner's essay *Language of Facts. A Propos the Jews' Discreteness* was published as a separate brochure. He died in the spring of 1909.

Kovner's memoirs, including "My Ordeals" (1894), "Jail Memoirs" (1897), and *Memoirs of a Jew* (ca. 1900), appeared in prominent Russian periodicals. Kovner had originally intended to call the longest and most significant of his memoirs *From the Memoirs of a Former Jew*. In 1903 *Memoirs of a Jew* appeared in two installments in *Historical Messenger* (*Istoricheskii vestnik*) under the initials "A.G." It is especially notable for the atmospheric depiction of Kovner's childhood and youth and of the changing worldview of the young acculturating Jews in the 1850s and 1860s.

From *Memoirs of a Jew*

CHAPTER 5

Change of rulers—New wanderings—Kovno—Distant relatives—With the Hassids—
The tzaddiks—Girsh Nesvizhsky—Private banknotes—Catching the bridegroom—
Punishment with lashes—Composing verse—Town of Merets—The "Epicureans"—A
beautiful girl—Return to Vilna

Emperor Nicholas I, whom the Jews heartily disliked, had passed away; Emperor
Alexander II, on whom the Jews pinned great hopes, had ascended the throne; the
Crimean War had ended, and the Jews had a slight respite from continuous military
service and began to live their usual bustling life. I had turned sixteen. It was still too
early for me to be married, but at the same time several new members had been added
to the family at home. I was one mouth too many to feed, so father decided that I
should again be sent off somewhere to live at someone else's expense.

The choice fell on Kovno, where we had distant relatives. Father provided me with
"tearful" letters to them, and off I went. There was as yet no railway then, and how I
traveled to Kovno I can't remember.

I liked the town very much, with its straight streets and the cleanness that the so-called
Newtown district in particular flaunted. Here all the houses were built of stone in the latest
architectural style, here lived the governor and the rest of the provincial authorities, and
here were concentrated the Jewish nouveaux riches, of whom I had the haziest of notions.

First of all I had to take care of my daily bread. I gave father's letters to "the
relations" and secured agreement from them to feed me one day a week each. One of
my benefactors was a Hassid, and, thanks to his influence, I obtained shelter in a
Hassidic prayer house.

But the Hassidic sect needs explaining.

The word *Hassid* in Hebrew means "pious, modest, ascetic"; but why this name
was adopted by a small Jewish sect that broke away from mainstream Jewry in the
eighteenth century has still to this day not been explained. Essentially the Hassidic
sect does not differ in anything substantial from the rest of the Jews as regards its
fundamental religious principles. Both adhere strictly to the ordinances of Moses, of
the Talmud, and of the later Jewish authorities. The only difference is that the Hassids
are more ignorant, more fanatical, more inclined to mysticism, and without fail believe in the holiness of some *tzaddik* (righteous man), some descendant of a supposed
miracle worker of Israel who became famous among the Jews early in the 1700s, the
"Baal Shem Tov" (master of miraculous power).[1]

---

1. Baal Shem Tov, Israel ben Eliezer (1700–1760)—founder of Hassidism; in Hebrew,
Baal Shem literally means "miracle worker" or "master of the name."

These tzaddiks, of whom more below, horribly exploited and still today exploit the benighted mass of Hassids, bolstering the difference between them and the rest of the Jews.

And since the original founder of Hassidism made some, incidentally very slight, changes in the prayer ritual and in the text of the prayers, the Hassids ceased to pray in company with other Jews and built their own special prayer houses.

So, it was in one of these houses that I found myself for the first time, and it was there that I was to find shelter and sustenance.

Yet living in this nest of Hassidism, I did not find the horrors that their opponents (*Mitnagedim*) reported about the Hassids. Here I became convinced that the Hassids, just like the mainstream Jews, did not deviate by a whisker from the basic tenets of the Jewish religion: they prayed, fasted, went forth and multiplied, devoting all their thoughts to God and to His service. The essential difference lay in only two points.

Whereas non-Hassidic Jews lived perpetually in fear of God, forever dispirited, believing that the dread God of Israel is the enemy of all merriment and high spirits—hence their renunciation of every joy of life—the Hassids in contrast did everything joyfully, with singing, jumping, and dancing in ecstasy, believing from the words of their tzaddiks that the God of Israel is also in merriment, in dances, and even in carousals, which they permitted themselves at every opportunity. Hence the irreconcilable difference between non-Hassidic and Hassidic Jews. The former, being ascetic, could not but look with contempt and even hatred upon the latter, considering them almost possessed by the devil, while the Hassids in their turn despised and pitied their "opponents" for condemning themselves to suffering and sorrow, which God did not need, and to dejection and gloom.

The second main point of difference is that the Hassids sincerely believed in the holiness and miracle working of their tzaddiks descendants of the above-mentioned Israel, the Baal Shem Tov, and other self-styled miracle workers, whereas the non-Hassidic Jews did not allow any manifestations of miracles by mortals, even learned and righteous ones, after the prophets and compilers of the Talmud, and despised the tzaddiks for their ignorance in interpreting the Talmud and their merry, at times luxurious, lifestyle.

For example, some tzaddiks were said to live in palaces and have their own orchestras and bodyguards of Jews and their own "Cossacks" from among the Jews as well, armed with lances and accompanying the tzaddiks on horseback on all their journeys. All this luxury, all these feasts, was of course paid for by voluntary offerings from the tzaddik's devotees, who would come to him from all corners of Poland and Volhynia, confide in him their life's sorrow, seek advice and comfort, and take their leave of him reassured and cheered for life's struggle in complete faith that the tzaddik would pray for them and solicit of God all manner of earthly and heavenly blessings for them.

Audiences with the tzaddiks are not open to everyone. Tzaddiks have their *gabbayim* (wardens),[2] who extort a separate payment for each audience, and the duration of the

---

2. *Gabbai* (Heb.) = synagogue official, nowadays mainly assigned a particular role during the service.

audience depends on the size of the payment. Poor people, however, who are not in a position to give anything, are not granted the honor of a face-to-face meeting with the tzaddik at all.

Nevertheless, it must be said that there were exceptions among the tzaddiks, though not many. For example, the Hassidic sect in whose prayer house I found shelter regarded as their tzaddik a rabbi from Libava [Liepaja], who was famous at the time and had a reputation for piety even among non-Hassidic Jews. According to the beadle of the prayer house, who visited the Libava tzaddik repeatedly, he led a modest life noted for holiness and the simplicity of his relations with people. And although there was no open access even to him without gifts exacted by the *gabbayim* prior to the audience, these were very moderate and showed no particular instances of extortion.

Yet even this tzaddik, whom the Hassids called simply Rebbe (teacher), in contrast to the rest, encouraged faith in himself as a miracle worker and promised the fulfillment of their desires to all his numerous followers coming to him from Poland and the western territories: recovery from illnesses, fertility for the childless, a profitable contract, a good match, lucidity of mind, and so forth.

The promises, of course, were rarely fulfilled, but the tzaddik's adherents believed steadfastly in his holiness and omnipotence—and it only needed one of the tzaddik's fancies to come about by chance for news of this "miracle" to spread among all his devotees, increasing his fame.

Although faith in the tzaddiks comforts many and strengthens them in their struggle for survival, in general it is a real canker among the Hassids, encouraging superstition and sowing dissension among the Jews. Especially harmful are those tzaddiks who have proliferated considerably in Galicia and our southwestern territories, who for the sake of their whims and dissipated life, for the enrichment of their kin and cronies, fleece the living and the dead, spread ignorance, and hunt down every glimmer of enlightenment among the Jews.

I soon grew sick of the fusty atmosphere of the small Hassidic prayer house, in which I had no possibility of reading "forbidden" books, and I made up my mind to move to a more lively center of Jewish life. By repute, such a center in Kovno was the prayer house of the wealthy Girsh Nesvizhsky, whose congregants were more or less affluent and educated, in the European sense, Jews. Through the good offices of one of my distant relatives, I managed to move to this house, where I soon made friends who secretly supplied me with various "little books" to which I devoted all the time I had free from studying the Talmud. At that time I was particularly keen on Jewish poetry and was even catching the bug myself. I began to write verse on different themes, imitated many recognized Jewish poets, and soon seriously considered myself one of them. My friends gave my rhymed lines their approval and flattered me outrageously. I subsequently accumulated several notebooks of these verses and had already begun to dream of publishing them as a separate slim volume. But after a few years, when I had gained an understanding of true Jewish poets and come to know the artistic pearls of German and Russian poetry, I realized the weakness of my muse and, without regret, burned all her fruits. Only a very short poem of mine was ever published, in 1861, in the Jewish newspaper-magazine *Ha-Karmel*,[3] and it was even honored with a German translation, so I was told.

I will mention in passing that many Jewish poets brought their art of writing poetry in Hebrew to an extraordinary degree of perfection. Despite the fact that this biblical language is long dead, knows no modern concepts, and furthermore has at its disposal a very limited number of words, Jewish poets contrive to write in it philosophical, lyrical, erotic, narrative, and satirical poetry that in many instances is notable for its uncommon strength, beauty, and felicity. Some poets have such a command of the language that they permit themselves various tricks in it, with no loss of beauty. So, for example, even without mentioning the requirement for all poems to have eleven syllables in a line and not to include words beginning with two consonants, many poems are simultaneously acrostics and, in addition, the sum of the letters in each line (it is well known that each letter of the Hebrew alphabet has a numerical value) corresponds to the number of the year in which the poem was written, according to Hebrew chronology.

Of all the congregants of the Nesvizhsky prayer house, the most original was the proprietor himself. A tall, fit, spry old man of about sixty, very rich, with several stone houses and a considerable grain trade in Kovno, Girsh Nesvizhsky often passed the night in his prayer house, sleeping fully dressed on a bare bench, with the sole aim of spending several hours during the night mechanically reading some religious books. I say "mechanically" because Nesvizhsky was *am ha-aretz*, that is, a man of the land, an uneducated man, one who understands nothing in the Bible and the Talmud but just about manages to understand the Midrash, which are religious collections containing many legends from Jewish history, various fables and anecdotes and fantastic tales of the life to be. Nesvizhsky would leaf reverentially through these collections, although he understood little in them, reckoning, like all religious Jews, that the very process of reading religious books is pleasing to God and a means of salvation for the soul.

Nesvizhsky was far from an ascetic. His ruddy face and flourishing constitution were evidence that he permitted himself much excess at home, but in his prayer house he subjected himself to all the deprivations that we *bahurim*,[4] lacking a home of our own, experienced. The only luxury in which this rich old man indulged himself in his own prayer house was that he contended with me for the bench by the stove, which was considered my privilege and which I had to surrender to him on his nocturnal visits.

Nesvizhsky enjoyed unlimited credit among the Jews of Kovno, and his own banknotes were accepted by Jews like the national currency. These notes, written on ordinary pieces of paper and furnished only with Nesvizhsky's signature and his name

---

3. *Ha-Karmel* was a weekly magazine in Hebrew published in Vilna under the editorship of S.-Y. Fin (S.-J. Fünn) during 1860–80, with additions in Russian, and later published monthly without Russian additions.

4. *Bahurim* (Heb. pl; sg. *Vahur*) = young men.

stamp, had values ranging from five kopecks to five rubles. Nesvizhsky's cash office scrupulously paid out ready money to honor them in full without any delay. Incidentally, similar banknotes were issued also by other rich Jews, and not only in Kovno but in all the towns of the Northwestern Region populated by Jews, so that at one time genuine banknotes almost completely disappeared from circulation. But, as was to be expected, many fake private banknotes appeared and many home-grown bankers, after issuing a vast quantity of banknotes, defaulted on their payments. The Jewish beggarly folk became distraught, the matter came to the attention of the authorities, and improvised banknotes were permanently banned, to the benefit of indigent Jewry.

Among the benefactors who fed me for one day a week was one who was the keeper of a tavern, frankly speaking a drinking den. I was instinctively repelled by the tavern. My many relatives in Vilna did not include a single innkeeper, and I considered this way of life shameful. For this reason I did not care for my benefactor's family either, and the whole situation was very depressing: a constant commotion, and the food doled out to me was meager and unpalatable. I had long wanted to forgo this "day," but needs must when the devil drives, and one doesn't look a gift horse in the mouth.

Then suddenly, to my surprise, I began to notice that I was being fussed over. The landlord's wife took to sitting at the table on which my food was usually served, and the food itself improved appreciably. She would ask me about my parents, about their social position, and about my relatives. I could not begin to guess why this change came about. But the key to this mystery was not hard to find. It turned out that they were trying to hook me as a match for the landlord's daughter, a young woman of around fifteen or sixteen who constantly hung about near the bar with the drinks and snacks and to whom I had earlier paid no attention at all, though I found time to notice that she was very unprepossessing and wore grubby clothes. Now that they had got to know about my aristocratic relations, my benefactors were not at all averse to marrying their plain Jane of a daughter to me. Even though I had not yet even turned sixteen, I nevertheless entered the matrimonial stakes, but I negotiated them so diplomatically that the tavern keepers immediately backed off. First, I demanded a dowry of four hundred rubles (I did not rate myself any higher); second, presents to the value of one hundred rubles; and third, four years' decent maintenance, with board and lodging all provided, in my future father-in-law's house.

"What a high opinion you have of yourself!" remarked the landlord's wife maliciously and broke off negotiations.

After that, of course, I had to forgo the tavern keepers' food.

However, I soon left Kovno altogether and moved to the small nonadministrative provincial town of Merets on the Neman River. I am absolutely unable to reawaken in my memory the reasons that prompted me to change my life in the lively town of Kovno and choose such a backwater as Merets. But before I speak of my life in the latter town, I want to describe the ceremony of public whipping of a certain criminal, at which I was present and which left an indelible impression with me for the whole of my life . . .

As I walked through the horse market each day I noticed that a scaffold was being erected on it. This meant that the public punishment of a criminal was being prepared. The scaffold took several days to build. At last it was ready, and I learned that the ceremony was fixed for the following day at 8 A.M. When I turned up in the market square at 7 o'clock, it was already completely full to overflowing with dense swarms of people and many sumptuous carriages in which sat elegant Polish ladies. The entire upper aristocracy of Kovno is made up of Poles. The procession appeared at 8 o'clock sharp. At its head were the gendarmes on stately horses, followed by the escort officer, the drummer who beat out a ruffle the whole way, and an escort of about twenty to twenty-five men surrounding the whipping cart, in which, bound to it with his back to the horses, sat the young criminal, about twenty-three years of age, fit, tall, and very handsome. On his chest hung a black board with an inscription indicating the crime he had committed, but I could not read this inscription and so did not gather the reason for the imminent punishment. Immediately behind the whipping cart walked two fellows in convict smocks. These were the flogger and his volunteer assistant drawn from among the prisoners. The procession came to a halt by the scaffold; the officer gave a command; the prisoner was untied and led to the scaffold, onto which he was followed by the clerk—there were not yet any public prosecutors in Kovno at that time—who unsealed a long narrow box in which the three-tailed whip was kept, unwound it, and inspected it carefully. Then he descended the scaffold, the officer gave the command "Present arms!" and the clerk read out loud the sentence of the court, from which I understood only that the criminal had been sentenced to sixty lashes. After the sentence was read, the flogger fastened the criminal to the pillory and left him in that position for some minutes (ten minutes, according to the law), while he himself adjusted the bench on which the man to be punished is placed. Then the flogger unfastened the criminal, removed his smock, and, when he had brought him to the whipping bench, began to undress him. After he had laid him on the sloping bench, the flogger, with the help of his amateur assistant, tightly strapped the criminal hand and foot to the places adapted for that purpose, stripped him naked from his waist to his feet, unfurled the whip, and awaited the command.

When the clerk called out "Begin!" the flogger flicked the whip high above his head and brought down the first lash. A heart-rending cry rang out . . . The flogger, counting the lashes, continued his work; the howls of the man being punished filled the whole square . . . But suddenly, at the twentieth stroke, the flogger stopped and called his assistant over. The problem was that the criminal, as I said, was very tall. Bound hand and foot to the bench, he was able to move his whole body, so that after each lash he had been flinging himself from side to side with the terrible pain so much that he had almost turned belly upwards. Without unstrapping his hands, the flogger and his assistant straightened his legs, secured his lower extremities more tightly, fastened straps round his waist as well, and the dreadful corporal punishment was resumed to the sound of the criminal's cries, which drowned out the drum beat.

I could not watch this spectacle any more and turned away. I intended to leave altogether, but, surrounded on all sides by a continuous crush of people, I had to stay to the end, and it was only at this point that I noticed the refined and elegant Polish ladies actually standing up in their carriages, the better to see the torture of this man . . . It seemed to me then outrageous and beyond comprehension how these delicate ladies, who were probably wont to swoon if their pet dog's paw was accidentally nipped, who never of course allowed a single male stranger to remove his frock-coat in their presence, were here publicly looking with obvious pleasure at a naked criminal, whose back the flogger was turning into bloody beefsteak . . .

When the flogger had finished his scourging, he unfastened the criminal, removed him from the bench, perfunctorily put his clothes back in order, drew him a little to one side right there on the scaffold, made him kneel and proceeded to the ritual of branding. It involved the flogger thrusting into the criminal's face a kind of sharp stamp with embossed letters that dug into the skin. Blood was drawn by the blow and the bloody marks of the letters were smeared with some compound which supposedly could never be washed off, so that the brand remained throughout his life . . . After this, the criminal was led from the scaffold, laid face down in the cart standing there, and taken away to the prison hospital. So ended the "triumph" of justice.

It is a good thing that the ceremony of public attestation of the sentence of the court upon criminals and indeed corporal punishment by whipping have now been abolished. But our lawyers and jurists really did think at that time that there was some need for such a ceremony, that public punishment of someone frightens and deters people from crimes. Judging by my own feelings, I am sure that all this ceremonial served merely to provide the idle crowd with a free "show," which excited only bloodthirsty instincts. I was certain that if suddenly, just before the punishment was due to be carried out, an order from the appropriate authority had supervened rescinding it, the crowd would have been displeased and disappointed. Even the elegant Polish ladies watching the punishment from high up in their carriages would not have agreed to a cancellation of the "show" if they had been asked and if it had depended on them . . . Otherwise they would not have risen so early from their beds, would not have hurried to take the best places near the scaffold, and would not have striven to have a better view of everything, the peasant being stripped and his bare back being flogged . . .

Yes, there were some dreadful times!

My life in Merets did not differ in any way from that in Kovno and other towns: permanent residence within the walls of a prayer house, meals with different townsfolk one day each a week, study of the Talmud by day, sleep on bare boards at night, and no supervision of me at all.

The inner life of the Jewish anthills in which I moved was unknown to me. What this unfortunate mass of Jewry saw as giving meaning to their lives, how and where they earned their living, whence came the prosperity and wealth that some of them had—all this remained obscure to me and did not particularly interest me. But I saw that all of them were constantly working, constantly bustling about, that on a certain day of the week lots of peasants would come into town and gather at the market; the Jews would surround them, gabble noisily about something, spend the whole day fussing around them; and the peasants would drink—the inns were a veritable Tower of Babel—yell, fight; and toward evening all would go their separate ways, and peace and quiet would settle on the town.

By chance I learned that there was a young epicurean poet in the town, and I endeavored to make his acquaintance despite the fact that dealings with epicureans were considered blameworthy, especially for a poor *bahur* living at the expense of religious benefactors. It must be said that it was not a follower of the philosophy of Epicurus who was deemed an epicurean (*apikoires*) among the Jews but anyone deviating from the strict regime of the Talmud. If anyone dressed in a slightly European way, trimmed his sidecurls and beard a little, wore starched linens and polished boots, did not pray as fervently as others, read German books, occasionally went to the theatre or a concert, he was considered among Orthodox Jews an apostate, an epicurean. Life for an epicurean like that would sometimes grow unbearable. Pious Jews shunned him, avoided any contacts with him, and sometimes played all sorts of mean tricks on him: did not admit him to prayer houses, would not bury him with due dignities, delivered him up to the recruitment office out of turn, and so on.

Yet my epicurean poet from Merets, by virtue of being married to the daughter of a local man of substance who had all the Christian authorities of the locality on his side, was afraid of no one, held his head high, freely wrote poetry, and openly read all kinds of forbidden books.

Yet *quod licet Jovi, non licet bovi.*[5] Mere acquaintance with an epicurean was enough to put me under a cloud, but reading the forbidden books with which he provided me and writing poetry upon various occasions severely damaged my reputation; people began to look askance at me, and my benefactors were reluctant to feed me. The beadle (*shames*) of the prayer house, a coarse and fanatical old man, kept an eagle eye on me, snatched forbidden books out of my hands, and threatened that I would be driven from the prayer house and deprived of my "days" of sustenance if I did not devote myself zealously to studying the Talmud and give up foul books.

I had to toe the line, circumvent my Cerberus's vigilance, and read the books outside of town, in the fields, on the Neman.

In Merets I almost became betrothed again. Two brothers lived in the town, one of whom spent all his life in the prayer house studying the Talmud and leaving his home and extensive family to the care of his wife, who ran a business of some sort, while the other brother, who was reputed to be a rich man, lived permanently in Prussia, where he had commercial interests, and rarely returned home to his family. I had a "day" with the first brother and therefore often met his eldest daughter, a young woman of about 18, very plain looking but spirited and vivacious. I surmised that my bene-

---

5. *Quod licet Jovi, non licet bovi* (Lat.) = What is permitted to Jove is not permitted to an ox.

factor would not mind marrying his daughter to me. As we studied together in the prayer-house, he repeatedly dropped transparent hints to this effect. I said neither yea nor nay, finding on the whole that it was still too early for me to think about marriage.

But one day in my benefactor's house I met a young woman of about 17 who stunned me with her unusual beauty and grace. She proved to be the daughter of the other brother, the businessman. When I compared the two cousins, I abandoned any idea of ever marrying the daughter of my patron and immediately became the beauty's admirer. Although I could not in the least hope or claim to be liked by her, never uttered a word to her, and did not dare even to dream of the possibility of marrying her, I would daily pass her father's house, watching with my heart in my mouth for the window to open in her little room, which I imagined as a veritable Eden-like nest, for even a lock of her wonderful hair to come into view, for a celestial ray to sparkle from her enchanting eyes, for a smile to light up her delightful little face. I thought that there was nothing more charming in the whole world, at bottom, than her father's modest little house, bordered by its small front garden in which bright flowers bloomed, and I was convinced that the future husband of this graceful fairy would be the happiest man alive.

Yet my beauty to all appearances did not even suspect that she had such an unprepossessing passionate admirer, and nothing troubled her innocent sleep, the sleep of a modest, simple Jewish girl.

Soon I returned to Vilna, and that was the end of the first glimmers of my veneration for feminine beauty and grace.

ca. 1900

Translated from the Russian by Brian Cooper

❋ On the Eve ❋
1902–1917

By the 1890s the Jewish-Russian authors had come to the Russian national mainstream; one of these was David Aizman (1869–1922), the "Jewish Chekhov," who published in such leading magazines as the populist *Russian Wealth* (*Russkoe bogatstvo*).The pogroms of 1903–6, especially the 1903 pogrom in Kishinev, Hayyim Nahman Bialik's "city of slaughter," brought Russia's Jewish problem to the world's attention while propelling masses of the Jewish population to emigrate. For Jewish-Russian writers, S. An-sky (1863–1920), for example, the 1900s were a time of greater involvement in Russian politics and revolutionary activity. Both the wave of pogroms and the failed 1905–7 Russian revolution pushed Jewish-Russian writers, notably such neorealists as Aizman or Semyon Yushkevich (1869–1927), to depict anti-Jewish violence and the daily lives of the Jewish working masses. Zionism and revolutionary ideology (Marxism and other types of radical thought, such as agrarian socialism and anarchism) were the two gravities that pulled apart Russia's Jewish community, leaving major imprints on the lives and works of Jewish-Russian writers. In the words of Shimon Markish, whose contribution to the study of Jewish-Russian literature is discussed in the general introduction, Zionism gave Jewish-Russian literature "a new generation of literary polemicists [*publitsisty*] and a new polemicist style. The unrivaled primacy in this field . . . belongs to Vladimir Jabotinsky [1880–1940]." A gifted author and subsequently a Zionist leader, Jabotinsky particularly excelled at the literary feuilleton in the 1900s. The Jewish question had become so vital to Russian life and culture in the first decade of the twentieth century that Jewish-Russian authors articulated it in the pages of mainstream newspapers and magazines. A telling example is the special "Jewish" 1909 issue of *Satyricon,* a leading highbrow magazine of humor, where Sasha Cherny (1880–1932) published his sharp and witty poem "The Jewish Question." This was also the time when both Jewish and non-Jewish writers started arguing on the pages of popular publications about the status and criteria of Jewish-Russian literature, as is particularly evident from the so-called "debates of 1908," which is also considered in the general introduction.

The 1900s–1910s, known as the Silver Age of Russian culture, witnessed the emergence of a number of talented Jewish-Russian poets, prose writers, playwrights, translators, and critics. This period also set the stage for an explosion of Jewish-Russian creativity during the first Soviet decade. For the first time during the Silver Age, Jews were visible in all the principal Russian literary and artistic movements, first in symbolism and then in futurism, acmeism, imagism, and other groups and trends. At this time, from the ranks of acculturated or partly acculturated Jewish families, Russian culture gained one of its most important twentieth-century poets, Osip Mandelstam (1891–1938; in the section "Revolution and Betrayal: 1917–1939"), and the "Russian Sappho," Sofia Parnok (1885–1933).

Finally, in the late 1900s and then again in the late 1910s, one observes the beginning of a brief but fascinating cultural dialogue, to crescendo in 1917–18, between Hebrew and Russian authors, in which Jewish-Russian authors such as Leyb Jaffe (1878–1948) were the bicultural harbingers of cross-pollination and translation.

Introduction copyright © by Maxim D. Shrayer.

DAVID AIZMAN

David Aizman (1869–1922) was born in Nikolaev, a coastal city in Ukraine where Isaac Babel (in vol. 1) spent his childhood. Aizman spent most of his adult life as a perpetual wanderer. In an autobiographical note penned in January 1914 in Odessa and reminiscent of the tearful laughter of Sholem Aleichem's Tevye, Aizman wrote: "What else can I say? To this day I have no certain place of residence. . . . A nomad, I live in hotels and paltry furnished apartments. I suffer a great deal from the absence of a residence permit. . . . I would like to be able to visit my native city of Nikolaev, but I cannot: it is now also outside the 'Pale.' . . . It is unethical to give bribes. I give bribes. It is dishonest to bypass the law. I bypass the law. I am a writer. I pass myself off as a shop assistant. It is only as a shop assistant that I can legally stay in Petersburg, if only temporarily."

Aizman left Odessa and went to Paris in 1896 to study painting. In 1898 he and his wife, a Jewish-Russian physician, moved to the French countryside, to the Haute-Marne region. While living in France, Aizman gained his own literary voice and made his debut in *Russian Wealth* (*Russkoe bogatstvo*), then a leading Russian monthly with a *narodnik* (populist) stance. Two of David Aizman's most original works of fiction, "In a Foreign Land" (published 1902) and "The Countrymen" (published 1903), were composed and set in France. Aizman returned to Russia in 1902. Despite two lengthy stays, first in France (1896–1902) and later in Italy (1907–9), he never became an émigré and died in Russia in 1922. During the 1900s and 1910s, Aizman's stories and novellas appeared regularly in the leading Russian periodicals, and major theaters staged his plays; Maxim Gorky's Znanie was among his publishers. An eight-volume edition of Aizman's works was released in 1911–19. As unknown today as he was famous then, Aizman was characterized by the writer Aleksandr Amfiteatrov in 1908 in the following terms: "After Dostoevsky and also partly [Vsevolod] Garshin, we have not had a verbal artist who would know how to 'strike the hearts with an unprecedented force' more poignantly, consistently, and effectively than David Aizman." From his early stories, notably including "In a Foreign Land" and "The Countrymen," a Chekhovian power of understatement distinguishes Aizman's best works. In his other well-known works, especially in "Ice Breaking" (published 1905), "Anchl's Morning" (published 1906), and "The Bloody Deluge" (published 1908), with its harrowing account of a pogrom, Aizman succumbed to the osmotic pressures of Gorky's and Leonid Andreev's neorealist fiction of social upheaval. In 1907,

Gorky himself reproached Aizman for writing of the anti-Jewish violence with "much screaming and no wrath."

The open and naturalistic portrayal of Russian and Ukrainian antisemitism and the anti-Jewish violence of 1905–6 made Aizman too unpalatable for the Soviet literary canonizers. Starting with the early 1930s, his books went out of print in the Soviet Union, and he was chiefly remembered there as a playwright (his most significant play is the 1907 *Thorny Bush*) and in connection with Gorky's circle of writers. Neither a Zionist nor a Jewish revolutionary writing about both Zionists and revolutionaries, Aizman has fallen prey to cultural amnesia by both Russian and Jewish readers. In 1985, in a passionate reassessment of his career, Alice Stone Nakhimovsky described Aizman's early stories as works of "a Jewish Chekhov." Despite the efforts of the past two decades, by Nakhimovsky, Claudia Colombo, Shimon Markish, and Mikhail Weinstein, David Aizman remains vastly forgotten by the reading public both in the former Soviet Union and outside of it. No books by Aizman are in print in Russia or available in English translations. If distant echoes of Aizman's acclaim have reached the ears of the American public, these would be through *Sima* (1976), Leonard J. Lehrman's excellent opera based on Aizman's novella "The Krasovitsky Couple," and a recent publication of his story in *Commentary* in English translation.

Written in 1902 in Paris, Aizman's "The Countrymen" is a poignant story of the Jewish-Slavic unburdening of guilt in exile, indeed a gem of Jewish writing in Diaspora. Of "The Countrymen" and "In a Foreign Land," Shimon Markish wrote in 1985 as he replied to an antisemitic Russian émigré journalist, "I do not know a more penetrating and heartfelt depiction of the irrational, obsessive love for the land, the people who, it would seem, have done everything to instill [in the Jews] hatred for them."

* * *

The Countrymen*

I

For the first week, Varvara Stepanovna Klobukova[1] felt simply splendid in her new surroundings. Above all, she was tickled by the knowledge that a miracle had occurred and she was abroad, in France. Making her no less happy was the thought of her salary: 700 francs a month, plus room and board—more than she would have earned in a year at home in Mertvovodsk.[2] Finally, there was pleasure to be had from living in luxury and comfort of a kind she had never known.

Varvara Stepanovna had been given two wonderful rooms and a *cabinet de toilette* with a bath, a shower, and a very large three-section mirror in which one could admire oneself from every angle.

The furniture was all truly "royal," and what astonished Klobukova most of all was the bed, an edifice with carved rosewood columns, silk covers, and lace curtains.

Her chambermaid was "a thousand times" more elegant than that "faker" Oberemchenko—Mertvovodsk's first social lioness—and at dinner a stately footman in stockings and white gloves served her innumerable dishes of the most refined taste.

Varvara Stepanovna had gotten her job in the following way.

Count de Saint-Blin[3] was a rich and enterprising French industrialist who owned shares in a number of Russian factories and visited Russia several times a year. His wife, a heavy, rotund woman, famous in her youth for parties and wild sprees, usually stayed home, either in Paris or at their castle in the provinces, giving herself over to pious exercises such as knitting jerseys for the poor or subjecting herself to treatments for illnesses she did not have. But it so happened one day that the countess took it into her head to tour her Russian properties, and off she went.

Naturally she was accompanied by a whole staff of servants: chambermaids, footmen, coachmen, and a secretary for her philanthropic activities as well as two lady's companions and a Swedish masseuse, Mlle. Norcelius.

The countess spent two weeks in Ekaterinoslav[4] Province and a month in Kherson

---

* The text has been slightly abridged.

1. Varvara Stepanovna Klobukova—Varvara is the Russian equivalent of Barbara, and it points directly to "barbarian" (*varvar*). Klobukova derives from *klobuk*, referring to the head-gear of an Orthodox monk.

2. Mertvovodsk—a fictitious name, literally, "[Town] of Dead Waters." Varvara's home town of Mertvovodsk possibly hints at the town of Zheltye Vody (literally, "yellow waters") in the upper western corner of Kherson Province and some thirty miles north of Krivoy Rog.

3. Saint-Blin—the name of a French village in the Haute-Marne region where Aizman and his wife, a physician, lived from 1898 to 1902.

4. Ekaterinoslav—now Dnepropetrovsk, in Ukraine.

Province, visited St. Petersburg, and stopped for a while in Moscow before, excited and enchanted by everything she had seen, in particular our people—*"ils sont si soumis, les russes"*[5]—she started making arrangements to return home.

All of a sudden, the Swedish masseuse announced she was staying. In Mertvovodsk she had met a compatriot who owned a fish store, and she was marrying him.

The countess gasped.

So shaken was she by the girl's untoward behavior that for a whole week she could not knit a single charitable jersey. But somehow she managed to calm down and initiated a search for a replacement.

Varvara Stepanovna was chosen.

The countess immediately took a strong liking to her. First, she was *soumise* and, second, she excelled in her work. Or at least so the countess said. She declared that no one had ever given her as good a massage as this *petite russe*. When the moment came to pack for home, she found she could not part from Varvara Stepanovna, not for anything in the world; trebling her salary, she took her back to her castle.

Varvara Stepanovna's duties occupied her for exactly one hour each day, from nine to ten in the morning. The rest of her time was hers to dispose of as she would. But how to spend it, she did not know.

She had brought with her a few issues of *Virgin Soil* magazine and a volume of Vonlyarsky's[6] writings, and though she was no lover of books, she now spent long hours reading. But that could hardly fill up an entire day, and when the writings had been read, Klobukova quickly became bored.

She strolled in the park, vast and strikingly beautiful; she took long walks to neighboring villages; she spent hours feeding the swans in the village pond and the rabbits in their sheds. All the while, she never ceased being bored.

She could more or less understand French—she had studied it back home at her progymnasium, where her education had safely ended—but she spoke it very badly. Still, when she had to, she was capable of expressing herself and making some sort of conversation, and the countess had made her solemnly swear not to engage in conversation with any of the castle's servant staff. "Mlle. Norcelius used to chat with everyone," the countess complained. "She was a socialist, and I'm very happy she's finally gone. . . . You, I hope, are not a socialist?"

Klobukova reassured the countess.

Her father, she said, was a retired captain and prison warden, her brother was a police officer, and she herself professed quite moderate beliefs.

"Je vous en félicite," the countess responded, adding that in November her grandchildren with their two governesses would be arriving, and then Klobukova would have people to talk to, for they would all have breakfast and lunch together.

---

5. *Ils sont si soumis, les russes* = They are so pliant, the Russians.
6. Vonlyarsky, Vasily (1814–1852)—a popular Russian belletrist of the 1840s–1850s.

But in the meantime, Varvara Stepanovna had to sit at the table alone, and she was unbearably lonely from having nobody to talk to. Nor did she find palatable the *suprême de volaille à l'Elysée* or the aromatic fine wines she was served. She longed for the sweet taste of cabbage, for dried salty fish.

At home in Mertvovodsk, she had known how to fill her day—visiting clients, doing things around the house, mending, embroidering, knitting doilies and other totally useless objects; on summer evenings she would walk to the main boulevard where officers and post-office clerks courted her; in winter she would go skating or visit friends or attend balls at the club.

Never before had she been away from her hometown or her family. Now she languished in the grip of sadness.

The alien French faces, so different from the Russian type; the quick, nasal speech, which made it hard to discern what was being said; the cheery beauty of the landscape; the strangeness of the peasants' garb—all this made Klobukova uncomfortable and sometimes angry. . . .

"The devil only knows why they need wooden shoes!" she would exclaim crossly.

Day by day, she grew more sullen and grim. She lost weight and became pale. She even wept a few times.

"I'm such a fool," she would say, trying to stop herself. "A twenty-two-year-old crying like a school girl. . . ."

But admonitions did not help. Tears streamed down her face as she climbed into her huge rosewood bed a little after nine in the evening, thinking angrily and bitterly how lousy her life was. For the sake of a few hundred francs she had left her native land and all of her loved and dear ones, parted with all her old habits and customs, gone God knows where to live with God knows whom, sold herself into servitude.

In her dreams, when she would finally fall asleep, she would see Mertvovodsk—the market square littered with horse manure; a soldier standing in the watch tower; pigs strolling on the boulevard; the tipsy sexton, Lavrenty; the firm, oak-brown legs of Gorpyna, the dishwasher; and other people, vistas, and objects close to her heart. . . .

If, of a nighttime, Russia or things Russian failed to fill her dreams, she would arise in the morning more subdued and somber than ever. . . .

Everything around her was more beautiful, more graceful, more fanciful, more costly, and more cheerful than in Russia, and still they elicited only vexation, ennui, and longing.

"When the governesses come I'll feel better, happier," she tried to console herself.

But she knew that the governesses could not help and that the longer she stayed, the more acute and unbearable her yearnings would become. Every day she wrote lengthy letters—even to people she wasn't close to—counting the days ahead and marking down when she should expect a reply.

"I should leave everything, run away!" would sometimes flash in her head.

But then she would immediately recall her family's dire finances, soon to worsen when her brother Vasya went to university, and her parents' little old house, mortgaged and remortgaged and upon the very point of foreclosure. . . .

And, gathering all her strength and courage, Varvara Stepanovna would chase away the enticing thought of escape and go on bearing her cross with ever increasing anguish.

II

One day after breakfast, she was taking a walk in a meadow along the bank of a stream. It had just rained, and tousled scraps of storm clouds, blackish-blue and softly silver, rushed across the sky, ceaselessly changing shades and shapes. Now the sun hid away, now it emerged, causing light effects that followed each other in sharp rapidity. First the poplars lining the stream's banks sparkled in the bright sunshine, while the pine forest behind them was enveloped in gloomy, listless shadow; a moment later, hot rays of light fell upon the forest, while the poplars grew dusky and almost black. But the landscape's brighter and happier hues escaped Varvara Stepanovna's notice; her longing soul was fixed on the gloom of the cold shadows.

"God, how unbearable," she said with a sigh. "A penal colony . . . worse than any penal colony."

"*Comment?*" someone unexpectedly spoke up from the other side of some tall blackberry bushes girding the stream.

Varvara Stepanovna raised her head.

Sitting on the bank, angling, was a decrepit old man wearing brown satin trousers and a navy blue shirt. Klobukova muttered something and made as if to continue on her way. Removing his hat, the old man greeted her.

"*Bonjour, mademoiselle!* Taking a walk? Well, the weather today isn't too shabby. Would you care to do some fishing? Please, have a seat next to an old man."

He spoke rapidly, mumbling and lisping as old people do, and Varvara Stepanovna was unable to follow what he was saying.

"Sit down, *mademoiselle!*" The old man ran his hand along the grass next to him.

"If only this were old Nikanorych!" she thought. Neither sitting down nor leaving, she stared with distaste at his foreign face, beardless as an actor's.

"Here, I'll set up a rod for you," said the old man merrily. "It's a rather amusing thing, fishing. You, I suppose, are pretty bored here, right?"

"*Vee,*" Varvara Stepanovna replied with a sad smile.

"Sure! A foreign place. . . ." The old man glanced quickly at the water before lifting his eyes to Klobukova. "You see, I think this: our country isn't bad, but if one isn't from here, one has got to be pretty bored."

Varvara Stepanovna stood in silence. . . .

"Yes. I, for instance, am about to be eighty-three years old, and I've never been farther than fifty kilometers from my village. The town of Chaumont[7] is only six kilometers away, and yet I haven't been there more than ten times. You know, home's best."

---

7. Chaumont—a town in the Haute-Marne region of France.

The old man moved his lips and fell silent.

Varvara Stepanovna still did not walk away from him.

"But tell me please, *mademoiselle*, how does one get to your country? By way of Spain?"

Varvara Stepanovna explained the route from there to Russia.

"Oh, I see! Well, Austria is okay, too. A nice place. What isn't good is being away from home. My son Ernest has been abroad—in Prussia, as a prisoner of war. And what do you think? He wants some grape vodka, and he cannot say 'grape vodka' to a Prussian. A Prussian wouldn't get it; he has a totally different word for it. And fish, for instance, isn't fish to him, but something else. Everything's different."

A bitter smirk twisted Varvara Stepanovna's mouth. The gentle words of this compassionate oldster had given her a surge of warmth but also pain.

"*Mademoiselle*," he started again. "Have you met your countrymen in town?"

"*Comment?*" Varvara Stepanovna asked, listening more closely.

"Your countrymen, in Chaumont. Have you met them already?"

What's he saying? Klobukova thought, alarmed. Are there Russians in Chaumont?

"Ah, you don't know?" the old man sang out. "I can't believe they haven't told you. Oh, those people at the castle! They don't even know what to tell a person. Of course, you have fellow countrymen living in Chaumont, Russians."

"*Pas possible!*" Varvara Stepanovna exclaimed. "Are you sure?"

The old man made a face and shrugged his shoulders.

"*Parbleu!* On Sunday I was in their shop buying hats for my grandchildren. Why don't you go see? Go to the square where the prefecture is, and there on your left is Rue Sadi Carnot. Walk up the street, past a dozen houses or so, and there, opposite the lycée, there's a millinery shop."

In agitation Varvara Stepanovna stared at the old man. Russians? she thought. In Chaumont? Oh, my God! This cannot be true. What would they be doing in Chaumont, a nothing little town in central France? No, this is nonsense. The old man has it all wrong.

"Yes, and the hats are splendid, too. Expensive but very good, real felt. These countrymen of yours were banished from Russia," grunted the old man, stretching his legs that had fallen asleep. "They were banished, and they came to live here. From your country they chase away the Israelites. They don't want them, but we don't mind. We let them stay."

Oh, they're kikes! Varvara Stepanovna drew it out in her mind.

And suddenly taking umbrage, she started to walk away.

"We let them stay," the old man repeated, studying the surface of the water. "Nothing wrong with it, selling hats. Why should we kick them out? Real felt. They charged me an arm and a leg, but they gave me real felt, shiny. When I sell them fish, I'll charge *them* an arm and a leg."

Having taken five or six steps, Varvara Stepanovna composed herself. She felt that she had acted discourteously. Turning toward the fisherman and trying to sound friendly, she yelled out, "*Au revoir!*"

One could not say that Varvara Stepanovna hated Jews. She had never had a significant encounter with one, never observed them closely, did not associate them with anything specifically bad, could not justly feel any animosity toward them. But she found them ridiculous and deserving of contempt, if not revulsion: they were repulsive, chafing creatures. Along with her father—and probably all of Mertvovodsk—she knew and could explain to you that Jews cared about nothing but commerce and moneylending, that they ate garlic and something called kugel, that they gave off a foul smell and had crooked noses, and, finally, that the Russian people suffered on their account. If she ever saw a ragged Jew on the street, she would hold her nose and think "dirty Jew"; and when she came across smartly dressed Jews promenading on the boulevard or at the club, she would mock their lack of taste and remind herself that their silks and velvets had been paid for with stolen cash.

And now, under the label of fellow countrymen, she was to be served up these same stinking Jews? . . . For the rest of the day Klobukova felt a depressing mixture of chagrin, bitterness, and a gnawing disappointment. It was as if she had read in the newspaper that she had won the lottery and then it turned out to be a misprint, she hadn't won anything at all. . . .

Still, she thought, what if there really were Russians living there? Yes, a remote corner of the world, the sticks, the middle of nowhere—but didn't she, Klobukova, end up here? So why couldn't others? And how good that would be, how fortunate! She would have someone to talk to, to give her heart a rest. She could visit these Russians in town, and they would come to see her in the castle. Life would assume a totally different course! She could stay longer with the countess then: a year, even two. After all, no matter how you looked at it, life here was comfortable and the pay was excellent. She could order books on embroidery, study French, subscribe to a Russian magazine. Sure, Klobukova concluded, I could arrange my life here better if there were people, Russians, even a single family. Otherwise I'll die of longing.

Up until today it had never even occurred to her that there might be Russians in Chaumont; now, the lack of them struck her as strange, almost unfair. She was getting angry. Now Jews are all over the place; you find them everywhere. But Russians? They're so inert, afraid to move; they sit by their stoves and never take so much as a step anywhere.

At night, before falling asleep, Varvara Stepanovna sat on her bed and cried. She was thinking about her family, who just like that had let her go off to a foreign land. They should have struggled, suffered, borrowed money, done anything, but they should never have sent her so far away, to this cursed castle. They had acted greedily, selfishly.

It took a letter six days to reach Russia, crossing three borders and all of Switzerland and Austria. What if she were to die here? It could happen—no one was insured against death—and there would be no one to bury her. "I'll go to town, to see those kikes!" Klobukova suddenly decided. She was overcome by a desire to spite some-

one, to have her revenge. "What's the big deal! I swear I'll go. By God, I'll go."
The windows of her bedroom lay open to the park. The moon shone brightly; listless shadows fell along the winding paths and across the lawns. The pond slept, as did the trees and birds, and a deep, untroubled silence reigned all around.

Like a cemetery, Klobukova thought, and I'm all alone. She got down from the bed, put out the candle, and sat by the window.

"The town lies just beyond this forest. On foot, I could get there in an hour and a half." She sat still, her eyebrows raised, and stared out at the forest and at the road to Chaumont that flanked it like a magical, shining stripe. Varvara Stepanovna could not take her eyes off that stripe. "*Zdravstvuyte*," she suddenly said in Russian, smiling softly. And then, changing the pitch and tone of her voice, she responded to herself, "Hello . . ."

Tomorrow she might hear somebody else say this same word to her. And, "What good fortune brings you here!" And many other such things. And she would speak Russian, a lot, and for a long time! "Why shouldn't I go see them?" she asked herself. "Why not? Of course I'll go."

In the morning, when she awoke, her first thought was that today she would be going to town to see the Jews. "So what if they are kikes? They are still almost my own people. And what if they turn out to be decent? There are occasionally decent Jews. Take Dr. Morgulis—all of Mertvovodsk receives him, the best homes; he even gets invited to General Skripitsyn's Christmas party. A very decent person, no worse than your average Russian."

From nine to ten in the morning she gave the countess her massage. Immediately thereafter, she started to ready herself for her journey. But since the mailman did not make his second round of the day until two in the afternoon, and since she had marked in her notebook that today, 18 October, two letters were due—one from Semyon Ivanovich and one from her Aunt Anfisa—she decided to wait. She ate her lunch with appetite, her face considerably less gloomy than before. She couldn't stop thinking about the Jews who lived in Chaumont, whom she envisioned looking exactly like Dr. Morgulis—neatly dressed, not misrolling their *r*s too badly, their noses not at all crooked.

The mailman came at the usual hour, but there were no letters. This small misfortune, which recurred almost daily and customarily plunged her into a black mood, left Klobukova unmoved. "No problem. Tomorrow I'll have three letters, including one from Vasya."

Hurriedly she put on her hat and veil and headed to town.

III

The road traversed several hamlets. The peasants were threshing grain, and the rumbling whistle of the machines could be heard everywhere. Every so often huge carts clattered by carrying loads of straw or bags of grain. The fat, strong horses harnessed in teams of four, sometimes six, stepped slowly, tranquilly, effortlessly. Along the way, the peasants bowed to Varvara Stepanovna and struck up a conversation. She spoke to them cheerfully, bravely, although she did get confused and befuddled at every phrase, and she laughed aloud when, failing to comprehend something or other, she answered them at random.

She was in a strange mood.

She felt happy, and she knew that the best and most interesting part was yet to come. But at the same time she was still vaguely offended at the idea that here she was, going to see Jews.

She was doing something wild, unbecoming, and somehow it humiliated her in her own eyes.

"If I have to associate with kikes, I wish they'd come to see me first. But there they are, sitting at home, happy as clams, and I'm running after them."

Her thoughts unsettled and confused her, but she brushed them away and with all her strength tried not to give in to the anger that flared up in her.

"What can you do," she asked herself. "No wonder the Ukrainians have a saying: 'In a foreign city, seeing a dog is almost as good as seeing your own father.' And besides, they couldn't really have come to see me. How would they have known I'm here? Besides, they wouldn't dare. And anyway, it's only me who's such a ninny as to need fellow countrymen. Someone else in my place wouldn't even *want* to see them."

As she approached the town, her offense gave way to a pleasant rush of anticipation. "Funny, isn't it," she thought, an involuntary smile appearing on her lips. "How strange! How terribly strange!" And then, entering the town, crossing a railroad bridge, she had a new and jarring idea. "What if the Jews refuse to see me? What if they treat me coldly or even rudely? Didn't they emigrate from Russia because things were bad for them there, because they were oppressed? That must mean they don't like Russia and Russians. They could, perhaps, insult me, offend me."

"They wouldn't dare!" Varvara Stepanovna was becoming angry again, though she realized her anger was misplaced. "Why shouldn't they, after all? What's to prevent them? Here they have nothing to fear." And suddenly she herself was overcome by fear. More than ever before, she felt lonely, abandoned, forgotten. Aunt Anfisa wasn't writing, . . . and Vasya wasn't either.

She stopped.

Her eyes filled with sadness and self-pity as they fixed on the tall building of the police prefecture, which was where she was to turn onto Rue Sadi Carnot. For a couple of minutes she stood stock still. "No, it's okay. I'm going!" She shook off her stupor. "I'm going. What will be, will be!"

She hastened across the square in front of the prefecture, her heart trembling as she saw a dark blue sign, Rue Sadi Carnot, on the yellowish wall of the tall corner building. She stared at the white letters, which seemed to smile and bow to her. "Strange," she thought, walking up the street, "so strange."

Having taken about a hundred steps, Varvara Stepanovna stood in front of the lycée. The building was set back from the street, surrounded by a large garden, and she could see only heavy gates and an ornate fence. Klobukova walked along the length of the fence as shadows from its wrought-iron ornaments swam across her face and bodice. At the end she saw a large gray house with balconies. Next to it stood another house, a white one. Across the road, in a squat brick building, there was a glass door and over the door a sign: *Chapellerie moderne.*

"Of course, it's here," Varvara Stepanovna said out loud. "Here!"

She ran across the street and, after climbing the front steps, peered inside. A short, stooped, scrawny man with completely gray hair stood behind the counter, staring sorrowfully at the street through the window. He had only one eye, a blemish that was imperfectly concealed by the big round spectacles placed athwart his short, fleshy nose. His left hand was gripping a shelf cluttered with hat boxes, while his right hand drummed lazily on the counter.

"Well, isn't this strange?" Varvara Petrovna said to herself. "It's as though he were Uncle Afanasy Petrovich, and I'm about to surprise him by turning up." She pushed open the door and, hardly over the threshold, called in a resounding voice: "*Zdravstvuyte!* Well, hello!"

The gray-haired man behind the counter made a strange, jerking motion. His glasses jumped, the large round lenses sparkling.

"*Oy . . .* what's this?" he exclaimed, startled.

And for a moment he froze.

Then he swiftly turned his face to the dark-red curtain behind the counter and yelled for all he was worth, "Dvoyra! Dvoyra! Come here right away, Dvoyra! Oy, look what's happening here!" He was speaking in Yiddish, and Varvara Stepanovna's heart smiled at the guttural sounds that she could not understand but recognized so well.

"You're Russian? You're from Russia? When did you come from Russia?" The old man threw himself at Klobukova. "Oh, how wonderful! So you're from Russia! Where from? What province? Taurida? No? From Kherson? Oh, my God! That's incredible! That's so rare!"

With both hands he shook Varvara Stepanovna's small hand, still shouting in agitation, "You know, we've been here eleven years now, and this is only the third time I've seen a Russian person. Only the third time. In eleven years! Well? What do you say to that? Dvoyra! Come now! Come, look, just look who's here!"

"Well, no, they won't hurt me," Varvara Stepanovna thought, smiling gently at the agitated Jew. "How excited he is to see me! What a funny little fellow!" The red curtain fluttered, and Dvoyra entered, a short plump woman wearing a dark-brown dress. Hers was a typical Jewish face, with a large curved nose and big beady eyes. With composure, carrying herself with cold pride, she bowed to Klobukova and stood by the counter.

"A Russian, you see! She's Russian!" the excited old man pointed to Varvara Stepanovna.

Dvoyra made a wry face. "What are you so happy about?" she asked him in a half-whisper, in Yiddish. "Did you get an inheritance or something?"

The old man cast a baffled look at his wife, then turned again to Varvara Stepanovna and began to jabber, "My name's Shapiro. We're from Russia. . . . Why, we're from Krivaya Balka.[8] Oh yes! We used to live in Krivaya Balka. And you? Permit me to ask, are you here visiting? Passing through town? And how much longer will you stay? Oh, what a wonderful thing! Simply incredible! But please pass through into the parlor. Why are we standing here? Please, please come in!"

"She's fine where she is," Dvoyra grumbled in Yiddish, angrily pursing her lips. "She can go back where she came from."

Bewildered, Shapiro glanced at his wife. "Ah, you'd better be quiet," he mumbled softly but very dramatically. "My God, what's come over you?"

"Please, come into the dining room," he called out to Varvara Stepanovna, dashing to the curtain and pulling it open with an energetic motion. "Oh, how did it all happen, that you went so far from home? Here, please, sit here, in the armchair, by the light, by the window, please! Dvoyra, invite her, *nu!*"

"Well, sit down," Dvoyra said gloomily as if forcing herself to speak. "I guess we can sit for a while."

All three entered the dining room and sat, and Varvara Stepanovna started to tell them the story of where she was from and how she ended up in France. "Ah, forgive me, please," Shapiro suddenly jumped up from his chair. "Forgive me for interrupting . . . Just one moment . . . I should call for a samovar."

"Why a samovar?" Dvoyra confronted her husband in a deep low voice. "No need, the water boils faster on gas."

"Oh no, Dvoyrochka! Gas? Don't you understand? This is a Russian person. She needs tea from a samovar!"

"We don't have any coal," Dvoyra muttered.

"No coal?" Shapiro grabbed his head with both hands and made a comically pitiful face. "*Oy*, what a misfortune! Can there be any coal in this town? Is this possible? In the whole town they've burned up all the coal? Georgette! Georgette!" he dashed to the door. "Georgette, run quick to Monsieur Petitjean's shop and bring some coal. And put on the samovar, quick! And do it in one minute, in one second!" He was speaking in some extraordinary, homegrown, French–Russian–Yiddish dialect. Varvara Stepanovna couldn't help smiling.

---

8. Krivaya Balka—like Varvara's Mertvovodsk, the Shapiros' Krivaya Balka is an invented name. Most likely it refers to Krivoy Rog, a town in Kherson Province of the Russian Empire, presently in Ukraine, where anti-Jewish violence took place in 1883. At the turn of the nineteenth century, Krivoy Rog had a Jewish population of almost 3,000 out of a total of about 15,000 residents. The name also evokes Balta, a town in the former Podolia Province, where a well-documented pogrom erupted in 1882. Shapiro's further comments betray Aizman's detailed knowledge of the region, as the village of Starye Krinitsy, which Shapiro mentions, most likely alludes to Belaya Krinitsa, halfway between Kherson and Krivoy Rog.

"This little old Jew is all right," rushed through her head. "He seems to be hospitable and kind." But her feelings were moving faster than her thoughts, and her feelings did not care for her mind's condescending tone. Her entire being was drawn to this noisily bustling Jew and even to his gloomy, pouting wife. Happy and excited, she continued her tale about life at the castle, speaking with complete openness, concealing nothing, and all the while feeling as though she were addressing members of her own family or people she had known for a long time. . . .

Dvoyra maintained her harsh expression, but her husband could not tear his eyes away from Varvara Stepanovna, nor, like her, could he stop smiling. At times he lost his self-control, exclaiming, "Oh, my God," "*Nu! Nu!*" or "That's wonderful!" And these exclamations reflected not so much the stories Varvara Stepanovna was telling as the marvelously delightful and joyful state that had suddenly gripped his heart and soul.

Turning to the subject of her loneliness and longing, Klobukova tried to sound humorous, but Shapiro, it seemed, knew well the bitterness and anguish that lay beneath this humor. Sorrowfully he looked at Varvara Stepanovna, sighing with compassion and rocking his head. "Of course, of course," he said under his breath. "What do you expect, being so far from home. And besides, it's your first time. And you are still a child. Just a child. When a person is thrown like this into a foreign place, surely he is the most miserable individual in the whole wide world. . . ."

IV

Then Shapiro, in turn, started telling her about his business and his children. Their son Solomon worked as a *chef d'atelier* at "the biggest" hat factory in Lyon. Their daughter was doing well in school and, God willing, would become a doctor. Dunechka was now visiting her brother in Lyon, but in a few days she was coming back, "and you'll see for yourself what a beauty she is and how well educated." As he talked about their children, his wife Dvoyra's face became less gloomy, and she even put in a few words. Cheered, her husband brightened still more and began to speak even more openly and loudly.

"Why did you leave Russia?" Varvara Stepanovna asked.

Shapiro became flustered. "It just turned out that way." An embarrassed, guilty smile appeared on his face. "Do I know why? Silliness. I got it into my head and I left."

"Did you have a hard life in Krivaya Balka?"

"Hard?" Shapiro lifted his eyebrows. "Not hard, but you know . . . We lived the way everybody does. But you know, well, how could I explain this to you? Well, for instance, fish seek deeper waters, and man . . ."

"Why are you telling tales?" Dvoyra suddenly interrupted, noisily pulling up her chair and planting both elbows on the table. "'Fish seek deeper waters . . .' Did she ask you about fish? We escaped from Krivaya Balka because of the pogroms. There's the answer for you!"

"Please, Dvoyra. Leave it be!" Shapiro said in a shrill, almost frightened voice. "Leave it be. This isn't the right time."

"It's always the right time! What kind of secrets are these? Why leave it out? You think we had a sweet life there? We suffered, we endured, our entire life we were just trying to survive. And then came the good people—your Russian people—and made a pogrom, and everything we had in the house they destroyed instantly."

"Well, they destroyed it. Well, well, what's to be done about it now?" Shapiro beseeched his wife. "Please let's not talk about it."

"And they whacked him in the eye with an iron," Dvoyra raised her voice. "And he's been blind ever since. He lost his eye. Why would we stay there after that? Tell me, please. So they could torment us some more? You think it wasn't enough? I think we'd had plenty. So that's why we left. We were going to America, but on our way my brilliant husband's other eye started to hurt—the eyes are connected, and when one hurts, the other responds—and he nearly went totally blind. So we couldn't go any further, and when we got to Chaumont he had to be hospitalized. And I and my two children were left on the pavement. And it looked like our only option was to lie down and die or else throw ourselves under a train. Well? What were we to do? But let me tell you, maybe the people here aren't as nice as in Russia . . . don't interrupt!" Dvoyra yelled, casting a furious glance at her husband. "Don't interrupt, I'm telling you, be quiet! I, thank God, haven't gone mad yet! I, too, am allowed to say a few words!

"Here the people didn't take out our eyes, you know," she went on, turning toward Varvara Stepanovna. "And they didn't rob us either. They gave us shelter and a job—sewing visors on hats. My Solomon and I, we worked day and night, first visors, then ribbons, and when this president of mine left the hospital, not only did we have food on the table but we also had an apartment and had managed to save up seventy francs. You see?"

Dvoyra sat with her arms akimbo and proudly nodded her head. "Could we possibly have had all this in Russia? What do you think? And so we settled here, and thank God, we're happy here."

"Happy, eh?" Shapiro moaned in a quiet voice, looking sadly at the plush frames with pictures of Chaumont hanging on the wall in front of him.

"Yes, happy! Just so you should know, we're happy. In Russia he was a tailor. There we were always hungry. And now, look at our store. This is no small thing! And no one abuses us or hurts us, and no one makes our life miserable, no one yells 'stinking kike!' at us. We're treated like people here, so there!"

And Dvoyra spread her arms in an expressive gesture and leaned back against her chair. Having gotten everything off her chest in front of Varvara Stepanovna, she evidently felt relieved. Her face had lost its gloomy pout, and instead she shone with an air of independence and proud contentment.

Varvara Stepanovna was looking at the Jewish woman timidly, out of the corner of her eye.

For the first time in her life, she had had occasion to have a conversation with Jews; for the first time, she had listened carefully and seriously, without a desire to mock. Dvoyra's seething words made her feel quietly sad and vaguely self-reproachful.

"But tell me, please," Shapiro asked in a small voice. "Do you happen to know how the crops are now in our Kherson Province?"

"Bad, I think. Everything got scorched."

"Scorched again!"

Dvoyra shrugged her shoulders contemptuously.

"So what's going to happen now?" the old man continued, as if thinking out loud. "Well, in Krivaya Balka they do have some retail stores, although now, of course, what sort of sales can they expect? But what's going to happen in the villages? In Korenikha, for instance? Or in Chervonnoe, in Starye Krinitsy?"

He grew silent for a minute. Then he sighed. "People are going to die," he answered his own question.

"*Vey!*" Dvoyra burst in, derisively pressing her lips together. "What's the great sorrow? Let them . . ."

Shapiro swiftly raised his head. "Dvoyra!" he moaned, folding his hands on his chest. "Why are you doing this? Why, I ask you?" And turning to Varvara Stepanovna he said, "You know, this is all a show. You're sitting here, a Russian, and she wants to show you that she's angry with the Russians and cannot stand them. But actually," Shapiro glanced at his wife with a sad smile, "actually, she's the one who thought of calling our daughter Dunya, Dunechka."[9]

"That means nothing," Dvoyra said, taken aback.

"In Russia we called our little girl by her Jewish name, Branka. And the Russian kids would yell 'banker,' 'wanker,' 'tanker,' and other rhymes they'd come up with."

"When a Russian needs to offend a Jew, he knows how to find good rhymes," Dvoyra added.

"But no matter how much they insulted our little girl, we paid no heed and continued to call her our way—Branka. But since we went abroad, my wife started calling her Dunya . . . What? Isn't it true?"

Dvoyra was silent. A sorrowing smile played faintly on her full lips. Varvara Stepanovna looked at Shapiro, then at his wife. She wanted to say something nice, tender, warm, but for some reason she felt awkward, and the words would not come.

But then Georgette rolled into the room, a round old French lady in a white apron and bonnet, and set a samovar and glasses on the table.

---

9. Dunya, Dunechka—diminutives of the Russian Christian name Evdokiya.

"Nous voici à Moscou maintenant," she burbled in a kindly voice. *"Du thé, le samovar, une belle demoiselle russe . . . Ah, que j'aime la jeunesse!"*[10]
Dvoyra started pouring tea.

No doubt she was tired of being dour, and her husband's words had knocked the wind out of her sails. . . . Gradually her face lost its final traces of grimness, and she was becoming more and more friendly. Ceremoniously, with a certain affectation, she waited on Varvara Stepanovna, insisting that she take four—no fewer than four—lumps of sugar with her tea and diligently spooning first sour cherry and then apricot preserves onto her plate, followed by brown pastries with honey that she had baked herself. As the conversation grew livelier, they jumped from topic to topic, but no matter what they talked about—people, buildings, weather, hat making—everything was connected with Russia and Russians. Dvoyra's tongue was finally untied, and she jabbered loudly in a singsong. Varvara Stepanovna's face, a typical, good Russian face, white with rosy cheeks, clear blue eyes, and a fresh, affectionately smiling mouth, was an invitation to open up, and within half an hour Dvoyra no longer held back any secrets from her guest. She was pouring out her whole heart.

And Varvara Stepanovna also talked, talked, and smiled, listening to her own voice and her words in quiet wonderment. How unexpected this all was! How strange! How unusual! And how long it was since she had been in such pleasant and entertaining company!

Now Shapiro was the only one with little to say. Three times he went back to the store to wait on customers, and when he returned he sat quietly and listened to the women talk. His expression had grown pensive, gently doleful, and now and then a quiet, forgiving smile surfaced on his bloodless lips.

Dvoyra took Klobukova to look at Dunechka's room, showed Klobukova her daughter's photograph, her books and notebooks, and then started taking her trousseau out of the closets and trunks. She had already put away four eiderdown comforters, and a fifth was in the works; there were dozens of different chemises and blouses, cuts of silk and satin. "She says she doesn't need all this," Dvoyra said. "All she worries about are her studies. Does a child understand? She wants to be a doctor. With pleasure! But a down comforter cannot hurt."

"Haven't you had enough?" Shapiro stopped his wife. "Put away the rags, why don't you talk of something else?"

"No, about this, about this," Varvara Stepanovna yelled playfully, digging into a new pile of lingerie. "If you would please not interrupt us. This is women's business."

"That's right!" Dvoyra agreed. "Women's business. And you—sit here and listen, philosopher!"

For a while longer the women went through clothes and chatted away. Varvara

---

10. *Nous voici à Moscou,* etc.—"Now here we are in Moscow. Some tea, a samovar, a young Russian beauty . . . Oh, how I love youth!"

Stepanovna liked Dvoyra more and more. She now thought that, both in appearance and in character, this new acquaintance resembled her cousin twice removed Vasilisa Efremovna, the wife of the rural deacon from Novopokrovsk. Her cheeks, too, were chubby and red, and her waist started under her shoulder blades, and she laughed just the same way, raucously and heartily. A little funny, but dear, very dear.

V

About an hour and a half later, Klobukova picked up her hat and announced she was leaving. But Dvoyra, bowing ceremoniously and pulling a face, tried to take the hat out of her hands.

"Let's say," she said in a sugary falsetto, "let's say we won't let you go, and you'll stay for supper. Today, by the way, is Friday."

The invitation both gladdened and confused Varvara Stepanovna. She had no desire whatsoever to hurry back to the castle, but she didn't want to take advantage of her new acquaintances' hospitality. "It will be too late to return," she objected indecisively.

"And why should you return late when you can return early?" Shapiro asked with a sly smile.

Varvara Stepanovna thought she knew what he meant, but it only added to her embarrassment. "Yes, exactly," the old man went on. "Your countess gets up at nine, so if you sleep over and leave here bright and early, you'll surely make it back in time."

"Oh, how wonderful!" Dvoyra splashed the air with her hands. "That's the best thing to do. Makes the most sense. You'll sleep in Dunechka's room."

A half-hour later all three settled around the festively set table. Six candles stood lit in new nickel-plated candlesticks, and in front of them, under a starched, snow-white napkin, loomed two large challahs. Customarily the Shapiros' Friday-evening meal was accompanied by solemn rituals, but this time, for the sake of their guest, Shapiro simplified matters considerably, and after a brief prayer he sat down at the head of the table. A fish course—stuffed carp—was served, followed by a traditional broth with noodles, then chicken and compote.

"And where's the kugel?" Varvara Stepanovna inquired.

Dvoyra explained that one ate kugel on Saturday, at midday, and that the tasty dish in question was still baking in the oven. "There's no kugel for you," Shapiro chimed in, "but you will get to sing *zemiros*."

"What's that, *zemiros?*"

"They're Sabbath songs. We sing them between courses, in Hebrew, the ancient Jewish tongue."

"Oh, please sing, please!"

"Will you help with the high notes?"

"Yes, yes. Please start."

Shapiro cleared his throat, rubbed the outside of his windpipe with a finger as if to clear it, and started singing an ornate oriental-sounding song in a trembling, goatish voice:

> He who sanctifies the Sabbath properly,
> He who observes it unprofaned,
> Will have a great reward . . .[11]

"Sing along, go ahead," said Dvoyra, nudging Klobukova, although she herself did not understand a single word of her husband's Hebrew song. Varvara Stepanovna opened her mouth and sang with an expression of timidity and reverence. For a minute or two, a wondrous cacophony filled the room. Then the old man's voice climbed somewhere very high and, halting suddenly, he started to laugh.

"We don't have a conductor, that's why," he explained.

They rose late from the table—it was after nine. Varvara Stepanovna felt both tired and almost intoxicated from all these new and unexpected impressions. She was pleased, amused, and also a bit melancholy. She thought of her own family, of her longing to see them, and of her recent despair. "Dear, dear," she thought, looking at the shortish Dvoyra, so wishing to pour tenderness upon her, to hug and kiss her.

VI

Georgette put out the candles, wished her employers good night, and retired.

Dvoyra lay in bed, stretching with pleasure. It was quiet. The dense white curtains swallowed the moonlight, and a transparent, pale green dusk permeated the room. "Well? What do you say to this whole business?" she asked in a half-whisper.

Shapiro sat on an ottoman by the window. Light fell on him from behind; his expressive, sorrowful face was covered in thick shadow. "All sorts of encounters happen," he replied vaguely, "so this one had to happen too."

"Such a remarkable person," Dvoyra put in, speaking with passion but without raising her voice. "So gentle, so polite. Just like our own child, I swear!"

"She must be well educated," Shapiro said. "You know, they torment us, but their young people, when they're well educated, they're so good, so good, there are none better in the whole world."

"So modest, so tender!"

"Remember, in Krivaya Balka, Vasyl Ivanovich, the priest's son . . . he was later exiled to Siberia?"

"When she saw Dunechka's corsets, the ones embroidered in silk and lace, she

---

11. "He who sanctifies"—the opening of the first of the melodies traditionally sung at the Sabbath meal.

sighed with awe," Dvoyra recalled, dreamily staring at the ceiling. "That's okay. It's good for her to know."

Shapiro didn't reply. He sat, his hands resting on his knees, his head tilted to the side. Several minutes passed in silence. At the lycée across the street, the clock tolled the eleventh hour, slowly, with long pauses. The final beat was especially long and sad, as if sighing after the somber place of its birth even while slipping from the narrow and suffocating clock tower and flying up toward the bright moon and the free sky . . .

"You know, Dvoyrenu, what I'm thinking right now?" Shapiro lifted his head.

"What?"

"This is what I'm thinking: Suppose back then, you and I had suffered through everything and never left Krivaya Balka. Then, say, for instance, our grandchildren, or even our great-grandchildren—would they have been able to live there safely, like human beings?"

Startled, Dvoyra stirred in bed. "Oh, that old tune!" she said in vexation.

Shapiro didn't reply. "Sure, it's old," he acknowledged after a pause. "Old is right." He continued to sit without moving, his head tilted toward his left shoulder.

"In front of the little house where our heder stood, there was always a swampy patch," he spoke again, unhurriedly, smiling a quiet, clumsy, pained smile. "And whenever it rained, a sort of pond would form there, and the boys used to go wading. They would roll up their trousers to the groin and roam around in it. Me, too. And my grandmother would drag me out and beat me. I would weep, and my grandmother would weep, and she would give me a cookie. I had scrofula on my legs, and it got inflamed when I waded in that water. I wonder if the little house is still there, and that swamp."

"Please, go to bed already," Dvoyra whispered with irritation. "Sleep!"

Shapiro didn't move. Something knocked against the ceiling. Upstairs, in Dunechka's room, Varvara Stepanovna was throwing off her boots.

"Fifty years we lived and worked there," the old man went on sorrowfully. "Our fathers, grandfathers, great-grandfathers are all buried there . . . and four of our children."

Dvoyra turned noisily to the wall. "So what do you want? Why all this now? Now he's going to drag it out and drag it out. Go to bed, I'm telling you!" Strangled tears could be heard in her trembling voice.

Shapiro sighed loudly. "If a time came . . . if only for our grandchildren, our great-grandchildren," he muttered.

Dvoyra no longer responded. "They'll get hit on the head with a log," her heart cried out. But she suppressed the words and lay without moving, with the blanket pulled over her head.

Shapiro looked over at his wife. He wanted to say more, but he took pity. Quietly he got up and went out into the yard. There, near the cellar, in a broad band of shadow, stood a large planter with a short, stocky boxwood tree. The French are fond of these shrubs, which are in leaf throughout the year and provide green branches for decorating headstones. The little tree had been watered earlier in the evening, and now, under the bright rays of the moon, the green drops on its dark branches sparkled like fireflies.

Shapiro sat on the edge of the wooden planter and turned his face to the sky. With his lone eye he gazed mournfully at the clear, docile moon pouring its light on this alien Chaumont as well as on that distant, sorrowful country where they had taken out his eye, where his dear ones were buried, a country to which he felt such a solid, such a sacred claim. He gazed, and the same old, old tune sounded in his sad heart: if only for our grandchildren, if only for our great-grandchildren, if only one day . . .

1902

Translated from the Russian by Maxim D. Shrayer

SEMYON YUSHKEVICH

Semyon Yushkevich (1868–1927), fiction writer and playwright, grew up in Odessa in an affluent family of Russianized Jews. Odessa's multiethnic population remained as a background in Yushkevich's literary imagination throughout his life, and assimilated urbanized Jews were his characters of choice and figures of verisimilitude. Yushkevich attended a Jewish government school and later a gymnasium, which he did not complete. He left home after marrying at seventeen and supported himself by working as a pharmacist's assistant and contributing prose to *The Odessa Sheet* (*Odesskii listok*). From 1893 to 1902 Yushkevich lived in Paris, graduating from the medical faculty of the Sorbonne. In 1897 Yushkevich's story "The Tailor. From Jewish Daily Life" appeared in the *narodnik* journal *Russian Wealth* (*Russkoe Bogatstvo*); some critics consider the publication of this story to be the start of a new period in Jewish-Russian literature. The most famous—or infamous—Jewish-Russian author of the prerevolutionary period, Yushkevich is credited with making the Jewish question a piece of the thematic repertoire of mainstream Russian prose and drama in the 1900s–1910s.

Written in 1895, the short novel *Disintegration* appeared in *Sunrise* (*Voskhod*) in 1902 and made Yushkevich famous; his 1904 collection of stories sold a record 6,000 copies in one year. In the 1900s–1910s, Yushkevich published numerous works of fiction, including the short novels *Ita Gaine* (1901), *Our Sisters* (1903), *The Jews* (1904), and *Street* (1908, published 1911), and the three-volume satirical novel *Leon Drei* (1908–19). The Jewish literary historian Sergey (Israel) Zinberg (1873–1943) labeled Yushkevich the "assimilated chronicler of the disintegration" of the traditional Jewish petit-bourgeois family. While the products of this "disintegration "—the Jewish haute bourgeoisie and working class—sometimes interacted in Yushkevich's works in a rehearsed quasi-Marxist dialectic, in the best works history's footlights paled when compared to the blazing and often physical individuality of his characters. Yushkevich focused unabashedly on the urban extremities of abject poverty, crime, and prostitution. While less charismatically portrayed, Yushkevich's Jewish criminals anticipate the legendary Odessan gangsters of Isaac Babel (in vol. 1). Yushkevich described his characters' sexuality and bodies with naturalistic and at times vulgar openness. His obsession with eroticism and carnality signaled a covertly modernistic orientation and reflected his aesthetic allegiance with such fashionable non-Russian authors of his age such as the Austrian Jews, Hugo von Hofmannsthal and Arthur Schnitzler, and the Pole Stanisław Przybyszewski, all three of whom were popular in turn-of-the-century Russia. In his artistic imperative to push forward the chaste boundaries of

Russian literature, Yushkevich anticipated the later works of his great contemporary and friend Ivan Bunin (1870–1953).

Through the writer Nikolay Teleshov, Yushkevich entered the "Wednesday" circle of neorealist writers and became affiliated with Maxim Gorky's Znanie publishing house; in 1903 through 1938, Znanie released the first five volumes of Yushkevich's eight-volume *Collected Works*. After the Kishinev Pogrom (1903), Yushkevich moved to Berlin and turned to playwriting. He wrote a total of fifteen dramas and comedies, which were staged by major theaters in Moscow and St. Petersburg and in the Russian provinces. His plays included *In the City* (1905), *The King* (1905, cf. Babel's eponymous story of 1921), *Hunger* (1906, cf. the title of Knut Hamsun's 1890 novel), *Miserere* (1909, staged by the Moscow Art Theater), *Comedy of Marriage* (1909), *Mendel Spivak* (1914), and others.

Jewish readers took pride in Yushkevich's achievement but also voiced anxiety about some of the aspects of his works. In an article in *The Jewish Encyclopedia* published in Russian in 1906–13, Zinberg spoke of Yushkevich's "anti-artistic works" such as *In the City* and *Leon Drei*. Some felt that by airing dirty Jewish laundry Yushkevich gave ammunition to antisemites. Russian critics praised his "courage" and "honesty," albeit not always out of their love for Jews. Uneven and perhaps at times lacking in artistic taste and refinement, the talented Yushkevich did not appear either self-conscious or apologetic about his treatment of Jewish characters.

Yushkevich emigrated in 1920. In 1921 he went to the United States, where his works appeared in print in American Yiddish periodicals and in book form, and his plays were staged in Yiddish translation. Yushkevich remained prolific, publishing several books and contributing to Russian émigré periodicals. In 1924 he settled in Paris, where he died in 1927.

Dedicated to Gorky as a gesture acknowledging both a literary affinity and Gorky's numerous philosemitic statements, Yushkevich's famous novel *The Jews* (1903, published 1904) originally appeared, as Ruth Rischin demonstrated in her monumental study of 1993, in the Znanie (Knowledge) *Miscellany 2* (1904), with many censorial omissions.

The novel showcases the strength as well as the limitations of Yushkevich's literary gift. Compared to David Aizman's account of a pogrom in "The Bloody Deluge" (1908), which is harrowing in its controlled presentation, Yushkevich's graphic, shocking portrayal of anti-Jewish violence seems less than nuanced, even if in places it does reach the explosive intensity of Bialik's *The City of Slaughter* (1903). But just how much room is there for nuance and understatement when one writes of the enraged victimizers mutilating and raping their powerless and defenseless victims?

From *The Jews**

CHAPTER 12

The pogrom began . . .

On Sunday, the sixth of April, precisely at two o'clock in the afternoon, bands of rabble, drunken and enraged, with a group of youths in the vanguard, let forth the whistles and catcalls that were to stifle within them the final remnants of compassion for others and of an understanding of their own actions. The sounds of rocks shattering glass were the first noises to break the bar of tension and terror of the moment. This was the initiating communication of an incitement to violence, a secret, mighty, persuasive, and commanding language . . . And the truly menacing, the horrific cries of "Kill the Yids!" carried throughout the city.

The pogrom began . . .

Surrounded by a festive crowd of onlookers and directed by invisible instigators, the violators burst into the first Jewish hovels they came upon, and the lament and howl of people disoriented by terror filled the streets with all manner of human moans. And this lamentation, like an oath of weakness, sounded as a signal, and so the pogrom began to rage . . .

Like those crazed by hatred, like those retaliating for long years of felt grievances, the violators ran into the homes of the poor, where blinded by rage, by joy, by excitation, they threw themselves on domestic possessions. . . . They battered down doors, smashed windows, broke apart furniture, threw dishes to the floor, tore open pillows and scattered the feathers, and after seizing everything that they could carry away— whether money or dresses—they dashed on amidst the approving crowd. They dashed like demons in their tattered clothing, frightful, carrying within them a thirst for destruction, for the eradication of those in whom they saw the unclean ones, the enemy, whom they now considered to be truly guilty for their own miserable lives. Some drunk and others sober, with faces breathing malice and conquest, they already seemed to sense that they held in their hands the dream of a good life, calm and secure, that would reign once they annihilated the Jews. They forgot about the amity in which they had lived with the Jews; they forgot about their own oppressive existence, about the ones who truly were guilty of imposing the yoke under which they lived. They saw only the enemy that was pointed out to them: the Jew, the Jews. And feeling only a hatred toward the Jews, inculcated in them since childhood, and also a pitiless rage, they ignored their own unfortunate lives side by side with the Jews, they barbarically, fiendishly destroyed everything that fell into their hands as if the last day of the world had come and no other would ever be. They spared nothing, and neither pleas nor cries touched them. With each hour this madness of destruction escalated, and now the violators perseveringly

---

* The text has been slightly abridged.

stayed inside the houses of the Jews and with crowbars and axes unhurriedly chopped up, crushed, and destroyed the piteous goods of their unfortunate victims . . .

The pogrom raged, the pogrom spread . . . With astonishing speed, like a flame in a storm, the frightful news swept throughout the city, and the Jews, abandoning their dwellings, with cries and wringing of hands, embracing and making their farewells, tried to save their own lives. They hid in cellars or among Christians, if the latter accepted them, in attics, in outhouses, on rooftops, in stables; submissive as always, not daring to think about resistance, they ran out onto the streets . . . And a heavy, tormenting anger beat in their hearts at the thought of this outrageous injustice that was being visited upon an innocent people . . . Living walls, silent and submissive! By means of them, the current evil validated itself, and this evil presently gave them up to the people's anger in order to assuage their thirst for real vengeance, so terrible, so justifiable. Who could protect the Jews when they had been sacrificed in advance? And the city presented an astonishing aspect: given over to the rule of mindless violators, it was left without rule, and all that happened in it happened as if it had been sundered from the life of the rest of the country. The book of human law lay at its feet, and a drunken, maniacal populace trampled on it with disdain.

The pogrom continued . . . It grew, spread, enveloping new layers of the city, and like a heaven-sent misfortune, resembling an ever more rapidly swinging chain, it beat in every direction, creating calamity among the population. The fiendishness of the violators intensified, and the joy of victory over a defenseless enemy soon attracted the crowd. In threatening handfuls, like Cossack chieftains, well-dressed people ran, bustled about, motioned, directed the violators, whipping up their anger to an even higher pitch. Feathers and down hung in the air and then fell to the ground, covering the city streets with a mask of innocence . . . Everywhere piles of belongings and furniture that had been tossed out of windows and doors were lying about, some heavy and cumbersome, others light, and a well-dressed crowd of rapacious men, women, and children, without repugnance or horror, with the thirst of cowardly robbers, sorted through them, hid things under their clothes and left, innocently blinking their eyes and shaking their heads . . .

The moans and wails carried throughout the city . . . But the hunting rage did not abate, and the more completely the violators felt themselves to be masters of the situation and the more piteously the Jews begged to be spared, the more the anger of the violators increased. It was as if until this moment they had been deceived but only now ripened and clearly saw who their enemy was. The Jews prayed, the Jews wailed in fear, the Jews ran away—they were culpable—and those who were fleeing had to be caught and killed, the submissive had to be tortured, tormented, and beaten . . . Wild rumors spread, passed from mouth to mouth, confusing minds, and the mayhem intensified. And what was most odd in this massive attack was the sense that it seemed to be directed by some kind of conscious will; not a single instance of indecision had been observed among the violators, and no gratuitous moves had been made. Everything took place as if it had been orchestrated . . . From night to morning—and this was later noted—the gates of all Christian homes had been marked with a cross, while icons and cruciforms had been placed in windows; the holy images, as if in mockery, served as pointers for the violators, showing them where they should not and where they should plunder and kill. And there was something truly frightful and inhuman in this conspiracy of conscious will and elemental force . . .

The bands rushed about amidst the din and encouragement of bystanders, and so long as the moans of those being tortured and killed did not resound, the pogrom resembled a created nightmare. But with the first killing, the last sluice-gates seemed to have been thrown open, inundating the city with a bloody wrath in bloody waves. No one had ever heard such mad prayers, such cries of pain and terror; no one had ever seen such refined means of torture to which the defenseless victims were subjected. Inflamed by the instigators, by a previously unknown wild freedom, by popular approval, the violators went haywire with their victory. The wildest plans of vengeance were born in a flash, and the entire horror of the barbarism that resides in a person burst to the surface. The Jews tried to save themselves, but they were found everywhere. They were hunted on city streets with howls, with roars, with outcries. They were pushed from dray carts, from horse-drawn trains. They were stopped at train stations or captured outside train cars, dragged out of churches, seized in churches, and immediately beaten, murdered, fleeced pitilessly, without regard for gender or age. Nothing could soften the instincts of the violators, and this time the entire catechism of torment had to be exhausted. They burst into houses, sought out the Jews in cellars and in attics, they killed, defiled, raped young girls, beat them, or ripped open their bellies, or cut off their breasts, or strangled their babies, and when they ran off they left behind a pile of unconscious bodies or corpses. They bashed in heads with clubs, crowbars, or axes; men who resisted had their tongues torn out, their hands sawed off, their eyes gouged out, or their noses or heads pinned with nails . . .

The slaughter began earlier in the outskirts than in the city. Nakhman and Natan, surrounded by Meita and Feiga, still did not believe what was happening. The gates of their house were locked; the men were walking around in the courtyard, and although they were pale and scowling and the women were wringing their hands and mumbling, still for some reason it seemed that the threat would pass them by. Old Sima and Charna hid under their beds, Mikhele stayed close to his mother, and Blyumochka, standing at the window, kept asking:

"What are those cries, Mother Charna, why are they crying in the yard?"

And Charna would reply, "They're crying because the city is burning, Blyumochka, hush! . . ."

"I'm frightened, Nakhman," resounded Meita's voice. "Let's run away from here."

"There are many men in the courtyard," Nakhman persisted in his determination to stay. From the moment the pogrom began, he became somehow disoriented. His replies were not to the point, he was lost in thought, he paced the room incessantly, while a great sorrow was growing in his soul. It was as if that enormous something that had been kindled inside of him and that had blinded him suddenly began to flicker out, to be destroyed, and because it had flamed up for nothing, because it had beckoned and now was going out, his eagerness for life was being extinguished along with it. A pogrom? Indeed, would the ground hold beneath his feet? Where was the great dream [. . .] about the coming equality of all peoples? Where was the truth that just yesterday had been so palpable? Where was the belief that the Jews and Christians were brothers? They had been slaves of one life, of one suffering, but something enormous divided them, and it was turning out that the stronger slaves were attacking the weaker . . . And each time the torment of spiritual upset possessed him, he would run over to Meita and feverishly ask her, "Do you still believe in it, Meita, do you, at least, still believe?"

But Meita, forlorn and frightened, replied with a question:

"Why are they killing us, Nakhman?"

Only Natan remained calm. He did not pray, he did not ask questions, but in each word, in each glance thrown to Feiga, as ever, lay the force of his conviction.

"You aren't afraid, Feiga," he said, not letting go of her hand. "Tell me that you're not afraid . . ."

But on the second day, it began. Around 10 o'clock in the morning, the sounds of the first blows against the gates rang out.

"They're here," cried someone in a strained voice . . .

Screams were heard. Suddenly the gates were broken apart, with a groan they were thrown onto the ground, and a crowd of forty or so people with the cry "Kill the Yids!" burst into the courtyard. Their leader was the carpenter, a man of forty or so years, with a curly beard and a flat nose. He ran in front in peculiar, ungainly little jumps, and the red shirt he was wearing waved like a banner of blood lust. Behind him came a mob armed with crowbars, bludgeons, and axes, and their threatening shrieks "Kill the Yids!" sounded like striking cymbals . . . Wailing, cries, and entreaties went round immediately. The man in the red shirt stopped, barked some commands, gasped, and completely unexpectedly bludgeoned the head of a Jew cutting across his path. The fall and cry of the Jew at once turned into a signal to plunder and slaughter. The pogromists scattered among the flats, and right away came the ugly sound of glass, furniture, doorframes, and doors being broken. Men, women, and children ran through the courtyard trying to save their lives. They threw themselves on their knees before the pogromists coming toward them, beseeching them. They were beaten, then they got up and flew to the side wall in order to jump into the houses of strangers, but they were pursued, beaten on the head, wounded . . . The howls and shrieks became unbearable. In a single moment the spacious courtyard was transformed into a field of infamous battle.

The great moment of suffering was nearing. Natan and Feiga managed to hide in the cellar, but Nakhman, Meita, Blyumochka, and Charna had not been able to hide on account of the little girl, and so they returned to their own flat and bolted the door. Sima all the while remained under the bed protected by Mikhele.

At the window appeared the face of the red-shirted carpenter, peering into the room for a long time.

"Oho, lads, so many Yids!" echoed his raucous voice. "Lean on the door!"

Out of fear, Charna crawled under the bed and imploringly called to the children, "Hide, my children, hide, my darlings, Blyumochka come to me!"

A strong blow with the crowbar shook the door . . . The face of the carpenter appeared at the window again, and now the glowering gaze and the graying mustache splayed against the glass presented a terrifying image.

"Break down the door!" he commanded, having espied Meita.

Blyumochka crawled under the bed. She lay next to Charna and embraced her, and all her movements and prayers were so quiet that it would have been impossible to guess whether she was preparing to suffer or simply going through meaningless motions. Meita, pressing herself to Nakhman and as if foreseeing her own fate, quietly moaned.

"Oh, Nakhman. Oh, my Nakhman!"

Suddenly a handful of voices filled the room. Now the door yielded to the pressure, and eight men in torn shirts burst into the foyer. An inhuman cry was heard, and it fell into the choir of those who had been tortured in the yard. It was Mikhele who shouted. Like a small dog he did not leave the bed under which Sima was lying, whispering tender words to her and not daring to start crying so as not to frighten her. Upon seeing the hefty pogromist wagging a threatening finger at him, he shouted wildly, and immediately Sima's gray head appeared from under the bed. The pogromist, wielding a piece of iron, breathed heavily and looked at the head of the old woman. His nostrils began to quiver. Then he turned his glance to Mikhele, who was shouting with his mouth open, suddenly drew in his breath, frowned awkwardly, took aim straight at the center of his forehead, and with all his might, as if lashing a whip, struck him with the piece of iron. The old woman turned her head with her cheek upward and started piteously wailing. Clutching at the air with his hands, blood pouring from his head, Mikhele soundlessly toppled over.

"Help!" wailed Sima, and with difficulty and torment she began to crawl out from under the bed. "They killed my little boy, my little boy!"

The pogromist seized the old woman by the hair, and wrapping her gray tresses in his hand, he pulled her toward him and yelled in a thick, oily voice, yanking her hair, "Give me money, you maggot, give me money!" She whimpered in fright, while he pounded her face and her back with his fists.

In the second room, two men were smashing everything that fell into their hands, another two were gathering up all the valuables they could find, while a youngish pogromist pulled Blyumochka out by the legs and, not heeding her shrieks, carried her into the next room, while Nakhman, using the legs of a stool, was defending himself against the last two men, and, in a hoarse, half-crazed voice, he roared:

"Do not touch the girl!"

But the flat-nosed carpenter in the red shirt had already overpowered Meita, who in vain tossed and yelled in the strong hands of the pogromist while Nakhman was being dragged out of the room.

"Nice little Jew girl," the carpenter's ragged voice could be heard, and to Nakhman it seemed that they were tearing off his skin. "Oho, so you bite, do you? Shut up, scourge of mainkind!! That's right, lie still and don't kick!"

"Nakhman, oh my Nakhman!" he could hear her piteous shriek . . .

Nakhman dashed toward her and drew the two robbers after him, not feeling the blows they were now inflicting upon him. And when he reached the threshold of the door, wounded, beaten, his own blood pouring from his face, and saw what was happening there, with a hurried, small cry, choking on his sobs, he wailed:

"Meita, I'll be right there, Meita . . . I'll help you!"

The pogromists threw themselves at him, and seeing how they were beating him, she cried, "Nakhman, oh, my Nakhman!"

She lay on the floor, naked to the waist, in only the sleeves from her blouse—her blouse had been ripped off of her. Her face, piteous and disfigured, was blue from the bruises, but the carpenter, sitting next to her, struck her when she fought back and gradually overpowered her . . . Nakhman stopped, sensing again what he had experienced in the first moment when the violators burst in, that somehow something had gone out in him, that he had been twirled around, had turned into a mouse, a cow, a bear, and that his head was now filled with darkness. And suddenly he noticed the old woman on all fours. She crawled like a big dog whose legs had been broken, with imploring eyes, howling or calling out. She crawled from the bed straight to the man in the red shirt and, when she reached him, raised herself on her knees and standing behind his back prayed to him loudly, louder, and then quietly, more quietly, humbly:

"Don't touch my girl, don't you dare touch her . . . She's honorable, she's a virgin, she's good . . . Don't touch my girl, she's little. I beg of you, I implore you . . . Here I am, I can take it all, please, I ask you, I implore you . . ."

And she beat her hands against her head, licked Meita's dear braids, which lay spread on the ground, kissed the carpenter on the back of his head, his back, his hands. But with malice he pushed her off with his fists. Meita extended her arms to Nakhman, to her mother, but she had no strength to utter a word. One of the violators could no longer stand Charna's supplications, and he struck her on the head with his club. She fell silent.

Nakhman was already shivering and writhing . . . Blood rushed to his head, something began to jump before his eyes, perhaps a bear, or a little bird, or a fly, and suddenly, throwing off the violators, all covered in the blood flowing from his nose and his head, he ran over to the carpenter who had overpowered Meita and suddenly sank his teeth into his hairy arm and immediately raised his face with a bloodied mouth. A long, hoarse howl sounded . . .

The pogromists became confused. But then someone figured out what had happened and snuck up behind Nakhman and cleaved his skull. In the next room old Sima was lying unconscious from the blow to her head. The youngish lad had already overpowered Blyumochka. Agitated by her cries and her moans "Mama, Mama!" he raped her and then at once silenced her with a club . . . Now Meita was alone in the room with the carpenter . . . She lay immobile, exhausted and tormented by the impure caresses. It was not Meita who lay there but something that had been humiliated to the last degree, a miserable creature with a dark swollen face, with tooth marks on her shoulders, on her hands, on her breast, bare and bloody. She lay unmoving and indifferent; and both this poor body, insulted and spat upon, and this poor soul, insulted and spat upon, prayed for death . . .

The pogromist got up. He looked at the girl's body and spat upon it. Then slowly turning from her, as if asking himself what else to do . . . With a strange, lost glance, he looked at the room in which all had been destroyed, the murdered Nakhman, the bludgeoned Charna, and not hurrying began to pull a knife from the back of his high boot. As if drunk, he went up to Meita and got down on his knees as if preparing to pray, and turning the blade sharply toward her breast, with a gesture as if he wanted to free himself from something, he plunged it into her body from the blade to the handle. Her cry and the movement of her hands, as if for an embrace, touched him, and he stabbed the body again, on the other side, twisted it, pulled it out, and he stabbed again and for a long time stared at the black and red blood that ran down her stomach. And again he rose, having heard at the door the call of his fellow-murderers, who were already on their way out of the courtyard, and again he dropped to his knees, entirely in the power of this fresh body, which still demanded something from him. The high bare breast of the girl caught his eye, and he pressed himself to it passionately, not understanding what was happening to him.

And, as if breaking some chains, he rose and ran to his accomplices . . .

The pogrom continued to rage . . . The pogrom did not quiet down; it did not want to quiet down, and the whole day bloody rain poured on the ground of the accursed city. The patrols walked along the streets picking up bodies and dispatching them to the cemetery, to the morgue. And there in a row lay the innocent victims of a created slaughter, of invented hatred . . .

[. . .] Impotent warriors, nursed in slavery, in fear, in suffering—with what shameful submission they gave up their lives. Who could defend them?

Night was falling . . . The windows of destroyed houses and apartments peered out like eyes without eyeholes. Filled with an alien suffering, lulled by the subsiding growls of the thugs, the accursed city was falling asleep sweetly and peacefully. And only in cellars and ditches, on the field beyond the city the Jews did not sleep but moaned and cried over their dear martyrs; they cried over their murdered fathers, mothers, brothers, and sisters, and the blind night echoed them with all of its sorrows . . . And the moans did not die down: a holy, bloody rain poured down on the earth.

It poured down innocently . . .

1903

Translated from the Russian by Ruth Rischin

DMITRI TSENZOR

Dmitri Tsenzor (1877–1947), poet and satirist, was born in Vilna Province to the family of a poor Jewish tradesman. He entered literature in the mid-1890s with a last name, literally "censor," that made him easy prey for satirical poets. Wits penned epigrams, while the real tsarist censors suspected that Tsenzor's name was a nom de plume at their expense. Tsenzor graduated from the Odessa Art College in 1903 and entered the St. Petersburg Academy of Fine Arts. While in Odessa, he participated in the activities of the Literary-Artistic Society and got to know Vladimir Jabotinsky (in vol. 1), Korney Chukovsky, Leonid Grossman, and the publisher of *Odessa News* (*Odesskie novosti*) Yakov Natanson. In 1908 Tsenzor graduated from the Faculty of Philology of St. Petersburg University. At the university he was a member of the "Circle of the Young" along with Sofia Dubnova-Erlich (in vol. 1), Aleksandr Gidoni, Modest Gofman, Sergey Gorodetsky, Vladimir Pyast, and others.

During the 1905–7 revolution, Tsenzor contributed to satirical magazines and revolutionary papers. His "Soldier's Song" (1906) illustrates his militant verses from that time: "Be tempered, my will, like a rock,/Wait for the command, ready your rifle./With my own hands I'll avenge/The people's blood!" Later Tsenzor withdrew from revolutionary activity. His first collection, *The Old Ghetto*, appeared in St. Petersburg in 1907, followed by *The Wings of Icarus* (1908) and *Legends of the Quotidian* (1913). Tsenzor was a known figure on the Silver Age scene and participated in literary collections alongside the literary luminaries of the time, including Anna Akhmatova, Aleksandr Blok, Nikolay Gumilyov, and Osip Mandelshtam (in vol. 1). The poet Innokenty Annensky (1856–1909) characterized Tsenzor's poetry in the following manner: "Dm. Tsenzor increasingly expresses our vague, smoky, and long-accumulated irritation." "Dmitri Tsenzor is a creation of one of the latest formations in Petersburg bohemian circles, the one that, in turn, had been created by the 1905 revolution," the great poet Aleksandr Blok (1880–1921) summed up Tsenzor's orientation. In the same review, Blok said it best: "[. . .] At times he sings like a bird, although worse than a bird; it is apparent that he sings naturally, without forcing himself to sing [. . .] simple vistas of city life are his strongest feature [. . .]." Both an heir to the 1880s (see Semyon Nadson in vol. 1) and a brainchild of Russian symbolism, Tsenzor was among the pallbearers at Blok's funeral in Petrograd in 1921.

During the Soviet period, Tsenzor mainly published satirical and children's verse. In 1924, in the story "An Incident in the Provinces," the famous satirical writer Mikhail Zoshchenko (1895–1958; see Igfail Metter in vol. 2) immortalized the "lyrical poet Dmitri Tsenzor" as one of the participants of a failed literary tour to the countryside: "And poet Dmitri Tsenzor said dreamily, 'The people need pure art. [. . .] They will start bringing us warm loaves of bread, flowers, boiled eggs. . . . We won't charge them money. Why in the devil's name do we need money if one can't buy anything with it these days [. . .]?'" In the 1920s, Tsenzor composed lyrics for operettas performed in Russian, including Johann Strauss's *Die Fledermaus* (1874) and Emmerich Kálmán's *Gräfin Maritza* (1924). He joined the Communist Party and glorified the Bolshevik Revolution in such pedestrian poems as "Partisans": "And he—the city worker—/As if rising for an attack/Waves to his comrades:/'Let us die, like communists!'" In 1940 his *Poems, 1903–1938* appeared in Leningrad to mark the "Thirty-fifth anniversary of [the poet's] literary work." Dmitri Tsenzor lived through World War II and died in 1947.

Jewish themes are manifest in Tsenzor's first collection, *The Old Ghetto* (1907), a cycle of twenty-eight numbered poems. A conflation of symbolist aesthetics, radical spirit, and the civic pathos inherited from the verse of the 1880s makes the book an unusual specimen of Jewish-Russian literature. Tsenzor portrays Jewish life as miserable, stifling, and depressing. Their lives replete with longing, the Jews of Tsenzor's "old ghetto" are "homeless and defenseless," their children are "ragged and pale," and their synagogue is "decrepit." Vestiges of traditional Judaic life emerge in part 7 of the book-cycle, where the poet speaks tenderly of the Sabbath as the traditional "bride of Adonai." "Born to slaves" like the poet himself, the "poor children of the sorrowful ghetto!" (part 22) are called upon to seek "dawns of freedom, lands of merriment." Venturing to "ignite" their souls with a "thirst for a fight, with indignation and wrath," the poet recalls the Maccabees and later pledges to "die for freedom" with his people. Is this revolution as a Jewish liberation from "slavery"?

In *Poems, 1903–1938* (1940), Tsenzor introduced a number of changes in the early poems, in some instances improving upon them, in others adjusting them in keeping with the official Soviet ideology. Translations of both poems below deliberately follow the 1940 versions.

The Old Ghetto[1]

Now dusk has settled in. The empty streets are stern
And secretive. They dream a wilderness of days.
A Jew hurries along the alley in a daze,
Grown weary from his cares and workaday concerns.

I roam beside the synagogue's decrepit western wall
And hear the doleful chanting, muffled like a moan . . .
Here earnest, melancholy faces fret and frown;
From every side they stare—tormented, helpless, frail.

It seems the lonely ghosts of a dark and bloody year,
Emergent from the shadows, querulously weep,
As, languishing in tatters, beggars drift to sleep.

This night drones on like a delirium, austere
And haunting . . . The old ghetto! My own blind fate, my grief!
I'm stifling, gasping . . . I need the open air . . .

1903; 1940

---

1. The sonnet titled "The Old Ghetto" in the 1940 volume is in fact part 1 of Tsenzor's first
collection, and a number of lines in the earlier version read quite differently, notably (in a
literal translation) lines 3–4: "And only sometimes, stirring murky sleep/A Jew hurries along
[the streets]—the child of earthly anxiety"; lines 12–14: "And the old ghetto whispers to me,
falling asleep: 'Take my children . . . They need the free world . . . /They are stifled, stifled here
. . . Their wicked lot is dark . . .'"

Father

My father, old and weak-willed bumbler,
Accustomed to intimidate
Your family, what unhappy bugbears
Did you set loose upon my fate!

I recall how mother murmured meekly,
Her squinting eyes, her questioning stare,
When your open hand would tangle briefly
In a gray-brown ringlet of her hair.

I recall your drunken, grumbling ravings,
Our hunger, cold, the children's tears.
But your sad soul's poisoned depravation
I have forgiven now for years.

A prophet's gaze, a cripple's body,
A creased and furrowed balding pate,
Moist, red-ringed eyelids, listless nodding,
Labors and shame, a dreary grave . . .

Now, father, when you've died, forsaken
By all your family, lost, alone—
I've come to understand your crazy
Anger, the anguish in your bones.

Yes, now your alcoholic weeping,
And your wrinkled, flaccid skin still cling
In my bitter memory more deeply
Than birch trees from a boyhood spring.

At last, your pathetic image dances
Before me in a strange, new light,
Now that my own turn fast advances
To endure old age—that senseless blight.

1914; 1940

Translated from the Russian by Alyssa Dinega Gillespie

VLADIMIR JABOTINSKY

Vladimir (Ze´ev) **Jabotinsky** (1880–1940), writer and Zionist leader, was born to an affluent Jewish family in Odessa. In 1898 Jabotinsky was expelled from a gymnasium and soon went abroad, pursuing the study of law at the University of Berne and later the University of Rome. He became a published author at sixteen. In 1898–1901, under the pen name Altalena (*swings* in Italian), he published regular "Italian Letters" in the *Odessa News* (*Odesskie novosti*). As a newspaperman, he learned from the celebrated Russian fueilletonist Vlas Doroshevich (1864–1922). After Jabotinsky returned to Odessa in 1901, his dramas *Blood* and *So Be It* were staged at the Odessa City Theater. A number of his books were published in Odessa in the 1900s.

Jabotinsky's first Zionist poem, "City of Peace," appeared in 1899 in *Sunrise* (*Voskhod*). The Kishinev Pogrom (April 1903) truly changed his life. Jabotinsky joined Jewish self-defense, formalized in the wake of the Kishinev Pogrom, and became an active Zionist. In August 1903, Jabotinsky attended the Sixth Zionist Congress in Basel, where he heard Theodor Herzl speak. Jabotinsky moved to St. Petersburg in 1903 and wrote for both the Jewish-Russian and the mainstream Russian press. A fabulous speaker, he lectured in 1905–07, traveling across the Pale. In 1910 his play *Alien Land* premiered in St. Petersburg, calling on Jewish-Russian youth to abandon the revolutionary movement and devote themselves to serving Jewish national goals.

Jabotinsky first visited Palestine in 1908. He left for the front in 1914 as a correspondent of *The Russian Gazette* (*Russkaia gazeta*), remaining a Russian journalist until 1917. That year, in Alexandria, he met Joseph Trumpeldor and poured his energies into the newly created Jewish legion, going through a sergeant's training and later taking a commission. Following the dismantling of the Jewish legion, Jabotinsky organized the first regular units of Jewish self-defense (*Haganah*) in Jerusalem. During the 1920 Passover pogrom by an Arab mob, he tried to break into the Old City with a unit. Sentenced to fifteen years of hard labor by the British Mandatory Government, Jabotinsky was released under international pressure. He became a member of the Zionist Executive in 1921 but resigned in 1923 over profound political and strategic differences.

As part of his publishing activities, Jabotinsky prepared the first Hebrew-language atlas of the world. In 1922–34 he stood at the helm of the émigré Jewish-Russian periodical *Dawn* (*Rassvet*), which appeared in Berlin and later in Paris. Jabotinsky contributed essays on Jewish subjects in several languages to a number of periodicals and published the novels *Samson* (1927) and *Five* (1936; English translation 2005), a collection of stories, and a volume of poetry in Russian. After *Dawn* ceased to exist in 1935, Jabotinsky stopped writing in Russian; he wrote his autobiography in Hebrew. As an adult, Jabotinsky, whom Michael Stanislawski called "the most cosmopolitan Zionist leader," had an excellent working command of seven languages besides Russian.

Jabotinsky headed the Jewish military-nationalist youth movement Betar from its creation in 1923 (see Y. Margolin's prose in vol. 1). He established the Union of Zionists-Revisionists (Hatzohar) in 1925 and the New Zionist Organization (NZO) in 1935. The principal political goals of the NZO were to press for free immigration to and the establishment of a Jewish state. Banned by the British in 1930 from entering Palestine, Jabotinsky settled in London in 1936; he organized and became the commander of the Irgun Tzvai Leumi (IZL), the military branch of his tripartite movement. Jabotinsky and his organizations were instrumental in delivering the British Mandate of Palestine to tens of thousands of Jews on the eve of the Shoah.

In February 1940 Jabotinsky left for the United States to create a Jewish army to fight the Nazis on the side of the Allies. He suffered a heart attack on 4 August 1940 and died at a Betar camp in upstate New York. He had requested in his will that he be buried in Israel, and in 1964 the remains of Jabotinsky and his wife Jeanne were reburied on Mount Herzl in Jerusalem.

A number of Jabotinsky's Russian oratorical political poems, including Gonta's monologues in the play *Foreign Land* (1907; published 1922) and "In Memory of Herzl" (1904), belong to the best in this genre. Also remarkable are some of his translations of Hayyim Nahman Bialik, especially *Tale of the Pogrom* [*The City of Slaughter*], and some of his love lyrics. (First published in St. Petersburg in 1911, Jabotinsky's translation of Bialik's *Songs and Poems* had gone through six editions by the time of its 1922 publication in Berlin.) "In Memory of Herzl" appeared in the St. Petersburg monthly *Jewish Life* (*Evreiskaia zhizn'*) in June 1904 and later in *Dr. Herzl* (1905), a slender volume consisting of the poem and two essays. In the original publications it bore the title "Hesped," which refers in Hebrew to the mitzvah of eulogizing the deceased and to the traditional funeral oration.

A volume of Jabotinsky's selected feuilletons appeared in St. Petersburg in 1913 (third, corrected, edition in Berlin in 1922); another collection, *Causeries*, came out in Paris in 1930. Unapologetic about their Jewish-centric political agenda, Jabotinsky's feuilletons present today's reader with gems of intellectually witty and brilliantly feisty literary prose.

In 1926 Jabotinsky wrote in the New York's Yiddish paper *The Morning Journal* (*Der morgn jurnal*): "For most of us Russia has long since become foreign [. . .]. But the Russian language [. . .] has sentenced us to a lifelong bond with a people and a country whose destiny concerns us no more than last year's snow." Compare Jabotinsky's sobering comments with the remarks of the émigré writer Mikhail Osorgin on the occasion of Jabotinsky's fiftieth birthday (1930): "I congratulate the Jewish people that they have such an activist and such a writer. But this does not prevent me from being most sincerely angry that Jewish national affairs have stolen Jabotinsky from Russian literature. . . ."

In Memory of Herzl[1]

He did not fade, like Moses long ago
right at the margin of the promised land;
he did not shepherd to the motherland
her children longing for her far-off song.
He burned himself and gave his whole life
and didn't "forget you, O Jerusalem,"[2]
but fell too soon and in the desert died,
and on the finest day to our dear Palestine
we shall conduct the tribune's ashes home.

I've understood the riddle of the phrase
that Bar-Hanina[3] relates in Aggadah:
that buried in the silent desert are
not just the house of craven runaways,
the lowly line, onto whose hearts and backs
Egyptian whips once seared a burning brand,
but next to them, amid the voiceless tracts,
the mighty ones lie buried in the tracks—
their hearts of steel, their bodies copper strands.

And yes, I've grasped the sage's ancient writ:
we've left our bones throughout the world's reaches,
not forty years, but forty jubilees—
we've wandered endlessly across the desert;
and not a single slave who fed on scourges
we've buried in the arid alien land:
he was a titan who had granite shoulders,
an eagle he was, with eagle-eyed insurgence,
an eagle's sorrow on his noble forehead.

And he was proud and lofty and fearless,
his call would rumble forth like metal stakes,

---

1. Herzl, Theodor (1860–1904)—born in Budapest and educated in Vienna, founder of modern political Zionism, journalist and publicist, author of *The Jewish State* (*Judenstaat*, 1897) and other works; presided over six Zionist congresses (1897–1903). After the formation of Israel, Herzl's remains were moved from Vienna to Israel, where he was reburied on Mount Herzl in Jerusalem in 1949, fifty-two years after the meeting of the First Zionist Congress.

2. Paraphrase of Psalm 137 ("By the rivers of Babylon . . ."): "If I forget you, O Jerusalem, let my right hand wither . . ." (Psalm 137:5).

3. Jabotinsky most likely is referring to Bar Hanina (Hanina [Hinena] Bar Papa), the fourth-century Palestinian *amora* (a special title given to Jewish scholars in Palestine and Babylonia).

his call went out: no matter what it takes!
and led us all ahead and to the east,
and sang amazingly of light-filled life
in a far country—free, majestic, ours.
He slipped away just when his purpose thrived,
the thunder crashed, the song of his life died—
but we shall finish his song in Eretz.[4]

Let us rot beneath a yoke of pain,
let whirlwinds mutilate the holy Torah,
let our sons become nocturnal robbers
and our daughters enter dens of shame,
let us become instructors of smut and vice
at that black hour, on that worst of days
when we forget your song and all your ways
and so disgrace the one who died for us.

Your voice was just like manna from the clouds,
without it we are bowed with grief and hunger:
you dropped your all-commanding hammer,
but hammers we will lift—a hundred thousand—
and grief will fade beneath their crashing clamor,
our hunger die amid all their uproar
of triumphs in the land where we belong.
We'll gnaw the granite cliffs to lay our roads,
we'll crawl just when our legs cannot endure,
but, *chai Ha Shem*,[5] we'll finish his whole song.

Thus long ago our father Israel
came near the threshold of his native home,
but God himself stood waiting in the road
and wrestled him, but Jacob still prevailed.
Like leaves, a storm has tossed us through the world,
but we are your descendents, you who grappled
with God, and we shall win against all odds.
And if the road is guarded by God's sword
we still shall move ahead and wrestle.

---

4. From *Eretz Israel* (Heb.) = Land of Israel.
5. *Chai Ha Shem* (Heb.) = I swear by God; literally, I swear by the Name.

Sleep, our eagle, sleep, our regal tribune,
the day will come—you'll hear our celebration,
the squeak of carts, the footsteps of our nation,
the flap of banners, and our ringing tune.
And on this day from Ber Sheva to Dan
a grateful nation will acclaim its savior,
and singing songs of our independence
our maidens will perform a circle dance
before your crypt in our beloved Zion.

1904

Translated from the Russian by Jaime Goodrich and Maxim D. Shrayer

Vladimir Jabotinsky, "Pamiati Gertslia." English translation copyright © by Jaime Goodrich and Maxim D. Shrayer. Introduction and notes copyright © by Maxim D. Shrayer.

An Exchange of Compliments
A Conversation

It was nothing but a conversation, a discussion, a *causerie*. I didn't participate; I was sitting off to the side and listening, and therefore I am not responsible for the arguments or the conclusions. The topic considered by the discussants came from Stolypin's sensational article about the "inferior race."[6] There were two speakers: one a Russian, the other a Jew. They were sitting quietly, drinking their tea, and tenderly considering whose race was inferior.

"In my opinion," said the Jew, "there is no such thing as an inferior or superior race. Each race has its own characteristics, its particular aptitudes, and I am convinced that if it were possible to find an absolute standard and precisely evaluate the inborn qualities of each race, in general it would turn out that they are all more or less equal."

"How could that be? The Eskimos and the Hellenes are equal?"

"I think so. Put the Eskimos in ancient Greece, and they undoubtedly would have given the world their gifts. Not the same ones as the Greeks, because every nation is different, but gifts nonetheless, and quite possibly equal in value to those

---

6. Most likely Aleksandr Stolypin, brother of the Russian statesman Pyotr Stolypin. A. Stolypin was an author and a journalist, who in the early 1900s edited the newspaper *St. Petersburg News* (*Sankt-Peterburgskie vedomosti*) and later became one of the principal editors of the newspaper *New Time* (*Novoe vremia*).

of the Hellenes. Of course it is not in our power to prove this; I'm simply passing on my convictions, but I have to say that these convictions are deeply held. I don't believe that there are superior and inferior races. All of them, in their own ways, are equally worthy."

"How odd to hear this from the mouth of a Jew. You are the ones who historically saw yourselves as the chosen people . . ."

"Yes, yes, I know that argument. I'll carry it even further: after the destruction of the Second Temple by Titus, what distressed Jewish sages the most was the thought that God had delivered them into the hands of an '*uma shafala*,' literally an inferior nation. You understand, in their eyes the Romans, the marvelous Romans of the imperial age, who had, in addition to their own culture, absorbed the refinement of Hellenism, were nonetheless an inferior race. But this proves only one thing: that those sages were blind. And in the same way, all the modern theories about inferior races are the product of blindness."

"No, I can't agree with that. Of course, Stolypin went too far; this can be explained by his personal sorrows, which are indeed blinding. You have to understand and forgive. But there is no reason to go too far in the other direction. To say that all races are equal is a paradox. I can cite the Negroes, who live in America side by side with the whites and are nonetheless not equal to them. Or the Turks, who built Istanbul in the same place that the Aryans had created Byzantium, and so on. But I consider your general premise, that all races are equal, to be so paradoxical that I won't even bother to refute it. You won't find five men among your coreligionists— especially among your coreligionists—who would agree with you. For that reason, let us put this general question to the side. We were talking about the Jewish race. I repeat, Stolypin went too far. I won't say that I am in complete agreement with Chamberlain, although he is very erudite and a very insightful thinker. Nor am I in complete agreement with your own Weininger,[7] although he presents many striking, thoughtful arguments in support of the notion that the Jewish race is, so to speak, defective. Then I've read a thing or two from your side—Hertz,[8] who in general rejects the concept of race, and the new writer Zollschan,[9] who thinks that the Jewish race is outstanding. But the main thing that interests me is life, and my general sense of this issue, the result of my reading and my observations of life, is the following. You, undoubtedly, constitute a race with certain serious inborn spiri-

---

7. Weininger, Otto (1880–1903)—Austrian philosopher of Jewish origin, author of *Sex and Character*; baptized in 1902, he committed suicide in 1903.

8. Hertz, Joseph Herman (1872–1946)—rabbi, author of English-language commentaries on the Pentateuch and the anthology *A Book of Jewish Thought*; appointed Chief Rabbi of the British Empire in 1913.

9. Zollschan, Ignaz (1877–1948)—Austrian social scientist of Jewish origin, author of the book *The Problem of Race (with a Theoretical Formulation of the Jewish Question)*. A Russian translation of Zollschan's German-language book appeared in Moscow in 1914.

tual defects. (You understand, I am not talking about exceptional cases—there are some very honorable Jews, I myself know some model individuals from your community; though these exceptions can be explained by an accidental mix of blood, and they are not in any case our subject, as you understand.)"

"I understand, I understand, don't restrain yourself, we're used to it."

"So here is my general sense: your race is unquestionably defective. A sound race, in my opinion, is one that is both original and harmoniously well rounded. You are neither. You never had and never will have an original culture. It has been shown that both your monotheism and your Sabbath were borrowed; in respect to these ideas you played the role of popularizers, or even, if you will allow me, of traveling salesmen. That is a role for which, indeed, the Jewish race is eminently predisposed. On the other hand, the Jewish soul is incapable of many higher perceptions. Your range of perceptions is extraordinarily narrow and has no chromatic shades; this explains why even under the best of circumstances, when you were independent, you produced no plastic art. To build his Temple, Solomon had to import talent from abroad. In your Bible, even in the Song of Songs, there isn't, as I understand, a single word for color or tint. David is said to be ruddy, and Shulamith calls herself swarthy, but the colors of nature, the sky, the sea, leaves—all this you ignore, as though it didn't exist, as though it is unnecessary and uninteresting for the dry, calculating, single-minded Jewish spirit. Compare this with Homer, with his *rhododactylos Eos*—his rosy-fingered dawn!"

"I beg your pardon, but what does race have to do with this? That same race eventually produced Israëls and Levitan.[10] . . . And almost all of your, excuse me, Russian sculpture comes from the same source: Antokolsky, Gintsburg, Aronson.[11] It's simply that in their ancient period Jews could not develop a visual art because their religion forbids them to depict that which was 'in the sky above and on the earth below.'"

"No, that is not an argument. Religious beliefs do not explain national character; they themselves have to be explained by it. A people with artistic gifts would never have adopted an antiartistic religion. But you must not interrupt me. I have more to say: even the biblical ethics that you take such pride in are somehow dry and calculating; not only are they not chivalrous, they're almost ignoble. Every ruling has a clear practical reward, the Lord God's promise to pay cash: a land flowing with milk and honey, the prolongation of your days on earth. . . . The Bible knows nothing of higher

---

10. Israëls, Jozef (1824–1911)—prominent Dutch painter; several of his major works dealt with Jewish subjects. Levitan, Isaak (1860–1900)—major Russian landscape painter and member of the Itinerant movement; Jewish themes do not figure in Levitan's works.

11. Antokolsky, Mark (1843–1902)—great Russian sculptor; grandfather of the poet Pavel Antokolsky (in vol. 1). Taking many of his subjects from Russian and world history, he devoted a number of works to Jewish themes. Gintsburg, Yakov (1859–1839)—sculptor, student of Antokolsky. Aronson, Boris (1862–1980)—painter and set designer; left Russia in 1922 and later emigrated to the United States where he enjoyed a successful career as a designer for Broadway and Yiddish Theater.

moral stimuli—not the idea of perfection, not fusion with the divine, not life after death. Consider just this fact: a people whose holy scripture contains not a single word about what will happen to man after death! Compare this to the Aryans, whose entire religion began with the cult of the 'forefathers.' Here we have compelling proof of the complete absence of anything that doesn't have an immediate practical goal. Beyond the practical necessities of communal life you evinced no imaginative power, not even any thought. You were simply uninterested. Doesn't all this give me the right to deny the breadth of the Jewish soul? How can that soul be equal to the soul of the Aryan, which is multifaceted, chivalrous, romantic, harmonious? Of course, I don't mean to offend . . ."

"I understand, I understand. Feel free."

"No, I've finished. I'd only like to add that it's impossible not to find support for this view in real life. I don't want to go on about this at length, but still you must agree that if everyone, everywhere, and always has hated and despised the same race, then you can't just explain it away by saying that people are scoundrels. The reasons for the enmity change, along with the accusations directed against the Jews, but enmity and contempt are eternal. Has it really never entered your own minds that there must be in you something unacceptable or insufferable, if in all times and places you keep running into the same situation? Merely consider the list of eminent people who couldn't stand Jews. It's incredible whom you'll find there: Cicero, Juvenal and Tacitus, Giordano Bruno and Luther, Shakespeare, Wagner, Dühring, Hartmann, and in essence Renan as well; Pushkin, Gogol, Shevchenko, Dostoevsky, Turgenev . . . And this is hardly a tenth of the complete list. Finally, this is what I will say to you. You Jews have not spent a great deal of time with Russians, even with Russian Judeophiles. But I live among them, and I know what they say about you when you're not around. You, gentlemen, have no idea of the number of your enemies even among your friends. Perhaps this is not 'enmity' in the true sense of the word, and it's not even contempt, just a certain irresistible sense of *an inferior being, an inferior race.* Everyone knows it, and if some Milyukov or even Plekhanov[12] tried to argue that he had no such sense, I wouldn't believe him. And when the same feeling is shared by everyone, then this feeling constitutes the truth."

"Have you finished?"

"I have. I await your objections."

"I have no intention of objecting."

"How is that?"

"I don't. Though I may draw your attention to a few minor details that have stayed in my mind. For example, about life after death. The Bible, indeed, doesn't

---

12. Milyukov, Pavel (1859–1943)—major Russian politician of the 1900s and 1910s and of the émigré 1920s and 1930s; a co-founder of the Constitutional-Democratic (Kadet) Party. Plekhanov, Georgy (1856–1918)—major leader of the Russian Social-Democratic movement and Marxist theoretician.

mention it. But it's nonetheless completely clear that the ancient Hebrews held such beliefs. In Ein-Dor, Saul calls up the shade of the prophet Samuel: Samuel *rises up* and asks Why did you *trouble* me? For anyone who understands the history of culture it is clear that a legend like this and expressions like these—in general, the whole idea of calling up the dead—can arise only where there is faith that a dead person continues to live beyond the grave. Consider other biblical expressions, such as the sentence 'Abraham was united with his people,' in other words, died. Or the care with which Abraham seeks a place to bury Sarah? Any sociologist will tell you that these are the obvious marks of a people that believes in life after death. The Bible has not preserved a straightforward exposition of these beliefs, but you must not forget that almost all the literature of the ancient Hebrews has been lost and that the Bible is only a fragment of what once existed. In the Book of Esther, the name of God is not mentioned once. If only this book had remained, you would try to argue that the Hebrews did not know the idea of God. And now, about colors and art in general. First of all, in addition to the ruddy David and the swarthy Shulamith, the Bible has trees 'turning green' and 'red' lentil stew and 'blue' thread. Second, the pictures of nature in the 'Song of Songs' are by the richness of their visual impressions much fuller than Homer with his rosy-fingered dawn. Third, why do you insist on the absence of plastic arts while forgetting the high level of music among the ancient Hebrews? The Book of Psalms is full of music, even to a fault: wherever you turn, there is music and singing. It remains arguable whether plastic or tonal art is the more expressive. And as for foreign architects, for the longest time the greatest Russian cathedrals were built by foreigners, yet you don't deny yourselves artistic souls. But these are just details. In essence I have no intention of arguing with you."

"So you agree with me?"

"No, this simply means that one can't argue over taste. From your words only one thing is clear: you don't like us. This is a matter of aesthetics. There can be no objective criteria. You deem that to await a reward in the afterlife constitutes ethics of a high order, and I deem the opposite. You deem that the teaching regarding fusion with the divine is higher than the teaching that from time to time we are obliged to forgive debt and that when harvesting grain we are obliged to leave the corner of the field untouched, for the poor. I contend that these simple rules contain a lot more truth—and not simply earthly truth but divine truth, truth fusing with the divine. You deem that borrowing cultural elements from Babylon makes us traveling salesmen, and I deem that everything created in the world is built on borrowed elements and that a nation able at the very dawn of its existence to gather these bits of gold and make them into an eternal temple—that nation is a creative nation *par excellence* among all nations of the earth. In short, it's a matter of taste. I'm not denying the existence of race, and I'm not arguing against the idea that there is an Aryan principle and a Jewish principle and that these are different in content. I simply consider it absurd to try to compare them—to determine which is 'superior' and which 'inferior.' I think that looked at objectively both are equal and equally necessary to humanity. And evaluations in general can only come from preexisting enmity. Shall we try an experiment?"

"What kind?"

"I will try to analyze a few key moments from the Russian past. I'll follow your method: I'll pick whatever standard appeals to me and apply it to events from Ilovaysky's History,[13] and we'll see what happens. Are you interested?"

"Go ahead. A compliment for a compliment."

"Precisely. Let's see what standard we will judge by. In your view, the standard for a superior race is creativity and multifacetedness. I could argue this point also: Did the Russian tribe give the world even one new and significant contribution to science, religion, philosophy, law, technology, or art? But we'll put that aside. The fact is that I am proposing a different criterion for the superior race: self-consciousness. In some-one of superior breeding, be that a scholar among savages or an aristocrat among plebians, there always abides an unshakable, uncontrollable sense of his own value. Its external manifestation is called by different names, most often pride. This is the quality that makes King Lear in rags nonetheless a king: he is *conscious* of himself as king; he cannot separate himself from this consciousness. This sense of one's own aristocratic nature is the first and primary sign of an aristocratic nature. Of course, sometimes a parvenu can masquerade as an aristocrat, while on the other hand even among Bushmen there is the belief that the rest of humanity is beneath them. But it's enough for a pretender to come face to face with a real nobleman, and a crack will open in his consciousness: he'll get confused, he'll choose the wrong tone, and he will sense his inferiority. The same thing will happen to a Bushman when he meets a white man: the white man will end up impressing him. Both are conscious of their superiority, but the white man's consciousness will remain intact, while the Bushman's will falter and atrophy, and the white man will prevail not only by force of arms but also morally. Therefore, as the mark of a superior race we can consider only that consciousness of one's own superiority that has withstood long periods of serious conflict and hasn't faltered."

"Now I see where you are headed. If for three thousand years Jews have believed in their superiority, then—"

"—No. We're not talking about Jews but about Russians, about you. I only explain what I understand by the word 'self-consciousness' and why I consider its presence to be the primary mark of a superior race (if, of course, we allow that there exist superior and inferior races). The superior race must possess self-consciousness above all; its essence is an unvanquishable pride, expressed not, of course, in arrogance but in its persistent ability to withstand and in its respect for the values of its own spirit. For

---

13. Ilovaysky, Dmitry (1832–1920)—prominent Russian historian, author, among other works, of the five-volume *History of Russia* (1876–1905).

such a race, the very idea of subordinating oneself and one's soul to an alien principle must be inconceivable. Now let us take Ilovaysky and use that standard to judge your Russian history."

"Let's take a look."

"At the dawn of this history we find the invitation to the Varangians. A remarkable fact. You will tell me that it's not a fact but a fable. Of course that's not the way it happened: probably, the Varangian Vikings simply seized power at some point, and later the dim memory of this event was transformed into a legend. But a legend, after all, is the product of a nation's creative spirit, and the national soul is revealed in it. So even if the Russian people cannot be held accountable for the real 'invitation to the Varangians,' the legend is their responsibility. The idea that forms the basis of this legend was, apparently, completely acceptable to the Russian national self-consciousness; otherwise the legend never would have retained it. And what is this idea? That the rulers of the Russian land got together and decided to subordinate themselves to a ruler from abroad. Not just anybody, not simple peasants; it was the warlords who got together, and they didn't find sufficient pride in themselves to find another solution to their dilemma. Apparently, the nation that created this legend, that chose *this way* to explain the fact of foreign domination, saw it as natural: apparently, this nation was not shocked by the thought that their own forbears were unable to govern themselves and that the only means of bringing order was to import a boss from abroad. To understand the real essence of this legend, compare it to the Jewish legend about what happened at the dawn of Jewish history. At the dawn of Jewish history, Israel escapes from a foreign king and descends through the desert to conquer for itself the Promised Land. Doesn't it seem to you that these two legends reflect two different types of national psychology?"

"No, it doesn't. However, I'm not arguing, I'm listening."

"Let's turn some more pages in your history. Let me draw your attention to the page where we read about the entire people under Prince Vladimir choosing a new faith. They are standing up to their necks in water and taking on a new faith. At this moment they shout to the statue of Perun,[14] which had been thrown into the water on the prince's orders, 'Come out of the water, god!' That is, they still saw Perun as a god who could swim to shore. I understand that a people changes its faith when the old one has shaken free of its foundations. But when the old faith is still rather intact, when it cries 'Come out of the water, god!' from out of the depths of the national soul—at that very moment, for the entire people to get into the water en masse and accept a new faith speaks clearly of one thing: the absence of self-consciousness, the absence of pride in one's internal possessions. There was no sense that I cannot be forced to take on anything that does not have roots in my conscience. If there are such things as superior and inferior races, then a superior race does not act in this fashion."

---

14. Perun—god of thunder and lightning, one of the most important figures in the pantheon of East Slavic pagan gods; Perun resembles the Teutonic Thor.

"One comment: Ilovaysky brings in a proverb explaining why it was necessary to get into the water: 'Dobrynya baptized by the sword, and Putyata by fire.'"[15] "I don't doubt it. Allow me only to remind you for purposes of comparison that we Jews were baptized by fire and by the sword; and in our case it wasn't just a proverb— our history of two thousand years is full of it. Yet neither Putyata nor Dobrynya could do anything with us. Apparently we are a nation that can't be dealt with by means of a big stick. But I am digressing; let us return to Ilovaysky. Before us is the Tartar Yoke. This is one of the strangest political phenomena ever recorded. It has almost no equivalent. When the Romans conquered a country, they left a garrison behind and settled it with either Roman or Latin colonies; in one form or another, this was an occupation. Here we have something completely different. After inflicting terrible destruction, the Tartars went back to their hordes; in essence, they evacuated Rus, keeping control not by a genuine force but by their threatening visage from afar. Doesn't it seem to you that for this to happen it was necessary to have some kind of special . . . talent in subordination? Of course the destruction had been terrible; the memory of that lesson could not be smoothed over, and yet obstinate, stiff-necked characters exist who quickly forget the bloodiest lessons and fight until their arms are cut off. And characters exist whose nature is milder. Let us compare once again, as a parallel, the attitude of Jews toward the foreign domination of Palestine. As long as a handful of Jews remained in the Holy Land, the country did not submit. Nor were Bar Giora[16] and Bar Kokhba[17] fighting with a horde of nomads; they were fighting with the great Rome! The Tatars gave apanage Rus complete autonomy, and they put up with it and paid tribute. The Romans were forced to draw a plough through Jerusalem, raze the flowering cities of the Galilee, destroy and exile the Jewish population down to nearly the last man, and only then did Israel submit. Titus's bloodbath was also a terrible 'lesson,' but seventy years later Bar-Kokhba had already managed to forget it. Apparently, not all races possess the happy ability to remember their 'lessons' so well that it was enough to 'learn' a single lesson once and submission was guaranteed for two hundred years. There are races that cannot be subdued, and races that ask for subjugation. Which are 'superior'?"

"It's a matter of taste, as you yourself said. But I'm listening—go on."

"No, I confess, I'm tired of it. We are not as interested in your history as you antisemites are in ours. Though I might point out just one small detail relating to the same page in Ilovaysky—about the Tatar Yoke. There we learn that your princes went to submit to the Golden Horde and got down on their knees before the khan. I'm not

---

15. Dobrynya and Putyata were both military commanders, dispatched from Kiev by Grand Prince Vladimir to baptize Novgorod. Ilovaysky cites an ancient saying, describing the violent christening of the citizens of Novgorod, most of whom at the time were pagans, in the autumn of 989. (In Russian: *"Dobrynya [krestil] mechom, Putyata ognem."*)

16. Bar Giora, Simon (ca. 50–70 C.E.)—a leader of the Jewish war against Rome, 66–70 C.E. After the fall of Jerusalem to the forces of Titus in 70 C.E., Bar Giora was executed.

17. Bar Kokhba—see Ilya Selvinsky's wreath of sonnets "Bar Kokhba" in vol. 1.

criticizing; it was very wise and patriotic of them. But here is a parallel for you, from the novel *Quo Vadis?* by Sienkiewicz.[18] Various people come to see Nero and get on their knees before him; only two rabbis do not bend their knees, and Nero makes his peace with this since he apparently understands that he can't do anything about it: Jews don't get on their knees. So, in a word, there are races and there are races, and which of them are 'superior' is hard to say."

"You know how I'm going to respond to this? You are more of a Russophobe than I am an antisemite."

"I refute this absolutely. For me all nations are equal and equally good. Of course I have the greatest love for my own nation, but I don't think it is 'superior.' But if you start making judgments, everything depends on the standard you use to judge. And in that case I'll insist on my own standard: the superior race is the one that is unyielding, the one that can be annihilated but not taught a lesson, the one that never, not even in subjugation, gives up its inner independence. Our history begins with the concept of a 'stiff-necked people'—and now, after so many centuries, we are still struggling and still fighting; we haven't given up. We are an unvanquishable race, now and for all eternity, and I know no aristocracy superior to that."

"Hmm," said the Russian. "Yes, you're right, it's a matter of taste. And I . . . I prefer my own."

1911

Translated from the Russian by Alice Nakhimovsky

Vladimir Jabotinsky, "Obmen komplimentov." English translation copyright © by Alice Nakhimovsky. Introduction and notes copyright © by Maxim D. Shrayer.

---

18. Sienkiewicz, Henryk (1846–1916)—major Polish author, winner of the 1905 Nobel Prize in Literature; *Quo Vadis?* (1896; the Latin title of the novel means "where are you going?") is Sienkiewicz's famous historical novel set in Rome during the rule of Nero and dramatizing the love between a Roman officer and a Christian woman.

LEYB JAFFE

Leyb (Lev) **Jaffe** (1878–1948), poet, translator, and Zionist author and activist, was born in Grodno, a Russian provincial capital in Belarus. One of the oldest Jewish communities of the former Greater Lithuania, Grodno had 27,343 Jews out of 39,826 residents in 1887. A Zionist hub, Grodno was a stronghold of Bundism and a center of Jewish printing. Jaffe's grandfather, Rabbi Mordecai Gimpel Jaffe, traced his origins back to Rabbi Mordecai Jaffe of Prague (1530–1612), the compiler of the treatise *Apparel* (*Levush*).

In 1891–92 Jaffe studied at the famous Volozhin Yeshiva, and in 1897–1901 he read philosophy at Heidelberg, Freiburg, and Leipzig. Jaffe participated in the Zionist movement from the late 1880s, initially under the influence of his brother, Bezalel Jaffe (1868–1925). In 1890 Jaffe cofounded a branch of Hovevei Zion (Lovers of Zion) in Grodno. He reported for Russian newspapers at the first three Zionist congresses (1897, 1898, and 1899) in Basel. He gained prominence in the democratic faction at the Fifth Zionist Congress (1901, Basel) and at the sixth (1903, Basel) spoke against the "Uganda Scheme." In 1904–5, Jaffe spent six months in Eretz Israel. At the 1906 conference of Russian Zionists in Helsingfors (Helsinki), he was elected a member of the Central Committee from Vilna, where he lived in 1906–9, carrying out editorial tasks in the Jewish press at *The Jewish People* (*Die Yiddishe folk*) and *The Word* (*Ha-Olam*). At the Eighth Zionist Congress (1908, The Hague), he was elected to the Executive Committee and remained in this office until 1911. During World War I Jaffe played a key role in the Jewish Society for Assistance to War Refugees. In 1915–17 he coedited the Zionist Russian-language newspaper *Jewish Life* (*Evreiskaia zhizn'*) in Moscow.

In 1919 Jaffe moved from Moscow to Vilna, serving as president of the Zionist Organization of Lithuania; in 1920 he moved permanently to Eretz Israel and in 1921–22 served as editor of the Hebrew daily *The Land* (*Ha-Aretz*) until the newspaper moved from Jerusalem to Tel Aviv. A notable Zionist author in Hebrew, Yiddish, and Russian, Jaffe signed his essays and articles with the pen name Dreamer. Jaffe's missions on behalf of Jewish organizations took him to South Africa, Great Britain, North America, Latin America, Poland, and the Baltic states. During a visit to the United States in 1942, he pushed for a greater effort to save European Jewry; the War Refugee Board was finally created in January 1944. Jaffe died from an Arab terrorist bomb explosion in Jerusalem on 11 March 1948.

Jaffe created a trilingual body of Russian, Yiddish, and Hebrew verse, some of which, such as his lyrics on the death of Theodor Herzl, "With Woe We Choke and with Tears" ("Fun troyer dershtikt un fun trern"), were famous. His Yiddish poems were collected in *Sounds of a Native Home* (*Heimats-Klangen*); Warsaw, 1925). Jaffe edited the Yiddish anthology *Songs for the People* (Odessa, 1908; reprinted Vilna, 1919) and also translated Russian poets into Hebrew.

In the late 1890s and early 1900s, Jaffe's Russian poetry and his translations of Hebrew poetry (J.L. Gordon, M.Z. Mane, and others) appeared in Jewish-Russian periodicals *Dawn* (*Rassret*), *Sunrise* (*Voskhod*), *Books of Sunrise* (*Knizhki voskhoda*) and collections *Messenger of Zion* (Kharkov, 1897); *Jewish Melodies: A Collection of Poems* (Moscow, 1901). Bearing an epigraph from Jaffe, *Jewish Motifs: A Collection of Zionist Poems* (Grodno, 1900) included six of his poems next to ten by Simon Frug in vol. 1. In his early Palestinophilic verse, Jaffe leaned on the cultural and ideological experience of Frug, the first Jewish-Russian "national" poet. Yet Jaffe's early poems, such as, "My Heart's in the Orient (On a Motif of Judah Halevy)" (1898), following the tradition of the Zionides, already exhibited Jaffe's superior command of Russian versification. Jaffe's first Russian-language collection of poetry and translations, *The Forthcoming*, appeared in his native Grodno. Only scant references appear to Jaffe's second collection, *City of Lovchen* (Moscow, 1916), apparently printed in a miniscule run during World War I and unnoticed by the general public.

Jaffe's principal contribution to Russian culture was that of a facilitator of dialogue among Russian and Jewish authors and thinkers. In 1917–18 he stood at the helm of the Moscow-based publishing house Safrut (the Hebrew term refers to the Laws of Sanctified Writing or simply to literature). He took advantage of a unique historical moment in 1917–18: the Russian public was overcome with revolutionary fervor, and the Jewish community was enlivened by the promises of the Balfour Declaration (November 1917). Zionist aspirations temporarily resonated with the utopian Christian ideals of Russian religious thinkers. As Brian Horowitz observed, "During the short period after the destruction of tsarism, but before the formation of the new Soviet state, intellectuals in Russia could engage in activities and form dialogues that later would seem contradictory."

Jaffe's first initiative was the anthology *By the Rivers of Babylon: National Jewish Lyrics in World Poetry* (Moscow, 1917), which expanded the contents of the 1900 *Jewish Motifs* to include Jewish-Russian poets, nineteenth-century Russian and western Biblical verse, and translations of Hebrew poetry, and opened its pages to Russian Silver Age writers such as Ivan Bunin and Dmitry Merezhkovsky.

Jaffe's activities as a conduit between Jewish and Russian authors and intellectuals culminated in the publication, in 1918 in Moscow, of *The Jewish Anthology: A Collection of Young Jewish Poetry* (reprinted in Berlin in 1922 by S.D. Zaltsman, whose press specialized in Jewish-Russian works), which he coedited in close, almost daily collaboration with Vladislav Khodasevich (vol. 1; Jaffe's later reminiscences about working with Khodasevich in 1916–17 appeared in Hebrew in his *Writings, Letters, and Diaries* [Jerusalem, 1964]). The prominent critic and philosopher Mikhail Gershenzon wrote a preface to the anthology (in vol. 1). In his editor's introduction, Jaffe counterbalanced Gershenzon's view by arguing that, as Brian Horowitz suggested, "inspiration did not originate from the liberation from Jewish life but rather emerged from a deepening and transformation of it. The Jewish artist found his strength by embracing the Jewish national movement and identifying himself fully as a Jew." The landmark anthology featured fifteen Modern Hebrew poets (see details in vol. 1 under M. Gershenzon). Several translators who were authors in their own right knew Hebrew; among them were Samuil Marshak, Elisheva, Vladimir Jabotinsky (all in vol. 1), and others. The translators who did not know Hebrew relied on Jaffe's literal translations with notes on versification. The translators included such prominent Russian symbolist poets as Jurgis Baltrušaitis, Valery Bryusov, Vyacheslav Ivanov, and Fyodor Sologub, and the anthology represented a high point of Jewish-Russian cultural synthesis.

Jaffe's efforts also resulted in the publication, in 1917–18, of three Safrut collections. Sections of the first and third volumes, later reprinted as a single book (Berlin, 1922), had a broader cultural appeal and featured contributions by Jewish-Russian authors (S. An-sky, Samuil Marshak, Andrey Sobol [all in vol. 1]) and Russian Silver Age writers, as well as translations of works by Hayyim Nachman Bialik, Saul Tchernichovsky, Martin Buber, and other Jewish authors. The second volume, dedicated to the twentieth anniversary of the First Zionist Congress, had a Zionist political focus and showcased writings by Max Nordau, Efim Chlenov, Yosef Klausner, and others.

Jaffe's departure for Vilna in 1919 and for Eretz Israel in 1920 removed him from the Russian cultural scene, while Zionist political duties took precedence over his literary ambitions. Jaffe's Russian poetry and translations were collected in *Lights at the Heights* (compare the virtually identical title of a 1923 Berlin volume by Evgeny Shklyar [in vol. 1]) and published in 1938 in Riga. Featured in *Lights at the Heights*, both poems selected below had originally appeared in Jewish-Russian publications in the 1900s. Addressing the Jewish-Russian writers' dual experience of culture and identity, the first poem speaks directly to the focus of this anthology. Published in the collection *Young Judea* (Yalta, 1906), the second poem reflects an impression of the poet's first visit to Eretz Israel.

In an Alien Tongue

In an alien, alien language I sing
My severe and monotonous foreign refrains,
And I dress all my sorrow and hope in the swing
Of an alien song as if shackled in chains.

Can a song in an alien language expand
With the power and freedom to soar on the wing?
Can it bloom in a desert of waterless sand
With the color of hope and sheer joy when you sing?

Every note of my tune makes you dull like a gong
Or a chain that is clanging somewhere in the gloom,
And in sorrow and darkness I've watered my song
Like a flower that struggled to grow in a tomb.

Oh, what torments could make a more miserable sound
Than your song, with its burden of love, has become,
To aspire to heights and yet flail on the ground,
To be powerless, speechless, and utterly dumb,

And to fashion your hopes in an alien tongue
In the frigid embrace of a foreign wasteland
And exhaust all your strength and the passions you've sung
To the waterless, barren, insatiable sand?

1900s

Off the Corfu Coast
(From *Travel Notes*)

When we got back aboard ship late,
The rusty anchors rattled on.
The sea began to ululate
Eerily at the break of dawn.

Then suddenly a wave of sound
Came rushing toward us, strong and loud:

With all their battered trunks around,
Faithful Jews gathered in a crowd.

They made, dressed in their Sabbath best,
The deck their temple at sunrise,
And rays of quiet joy and rest
Were shining from their faded eyes.

They'd braved huge waves along the way
Through fearful gales to come ashore,
And now to greet the Sabbath day
These voyagers sang the Psalms once more.

Over the sea their ancient song
Rose up to the most distant star
With the linked voices of the throng:
"*Lecha dodi likrath kalah!*"[1]

We sailed on farther, into night.
The sea swells surged past with a hiss.
The sky's blue curtain came alight
And dropped stars into its abyss.

Behind, the coastline fell away.
A fading distant light was spent,
Extinguished by the Milky Way.
We sailed on toward the Orient.

The feeble candlelight was gone,
And tremulous darkness spread afar,
But in my heart the song throbbed on:
"*Lecha dodi likrath kalah!*"

1905–6

Translated from the Russian by J.B. Sisson and Maxim D. Shrayer

---

1. "Come, my beloved one, toward the bride"—verse of a hymn celebrating the Sabbath [L.Ja.].

SASHA CHERNY

Sasha Cherny (1880–1932) is the pen name of Aleksandr Glikberg, arguably the most celebrated Russian satirical poet of the pre-Revolutionary era. Born to a pharmacist's family in Odessa, Cherny was baptized at the age of ten in order to bypass the *numerus clausus*. In 1895 he ran away from home to St. Petersburg, and the following year, after he was expelled from a gymnasium in St. Petersburg for poor grades, his parents disowned him. Cherny was taken in by the family of K. Roshe, a civil servant in Zhitomir, a provincial capital in Volhynia. In Zhitomir, due to a conflict with the headmaster, Cherny was later expelled from a local gymnasium, without the right to enter a university. After serving in the military in 1900–1902, Cherny worked as a customs officer in Bessarabia. Living in Germany in 1906–7, he audited courses at Heidelberg University.

In 1904 Cherny debuted as a feuilletonist in the Zhitomir newspaper *Volhynian Messenger* (*Volynskii vestnik*). In 1905 his poem "Gibberish" appeared in the satirical magazine *The Viewer* (*Zritel'*) under the pen name Sasha Cherny, and his first collection of poems, *Sundry Motives* (or *Sundry Tunes*), came out the following year. Cherny himself later scorned the volume and considered the next one, *Satires* (1910), to be his true entrance into literature; it was followed in 1911 by *Satires and Lyrics*. Each volume subsequently went through five editions, with revised versions reprinted in Berlin in the 1920s. In 1908 Cherny joined the staff and quickly became the leading poet of the weekly magazine *Satyricon*, gaining a vast audience, national fame, and the admiration of many writers. The great Russian poet Vladimir Mayakovsky (1893–1930) readily acknowledged Cherny's influence. Cherny left *Satyricon* in 1911 to become an "unemployed humorist" and freelance contributor to such periodicals as *Contemporary World* (*Sovremennyi mir*) and *Sun of Russia* (*Solntse Rossii*) as well as newspapers in Kiev and Odessa. He also translated the works of the great Jewish-German poet Heinrich Heine and others from the German. Cherny's next collection, *The Living Alphabet*, was published in 1914 and included the long poem *Noah*. Cherny's lyrical poetry is suffused with existential pessimism.

During World War I, Cherny was called into active duty and served in military hospitals. In 1918 he made his way from Pskov to Vilna, then to Kovno, and eventually to Berlin, becoming an émigré. Settling in Charlottenburg, a suburb where many Russians lived at the time, Cherny was active in Russian émigré publishing, which in the 1920s had its main center in Weimar Berlin. He headed the literary department of the review *Firebird* (*Zhar-Ptitsa*) and edited the émigré "Children's Library 'Word.'"

His collection *Thirst*, more lyrical than satirical, was published in 1923. Soon after emigrating, Cherny slightly altered his pen name to A. Cherny. His satirical poems became staunchly anti-Bolshevik. In 1924 he moved to Paris and in 1927 became a regular contributor to the leading Russian daily *The Latest News (Poslednie novosti)*. Still, in exile Cherny's artistic talons did not twitch nearly as much as they had in Russia, especially as compared to those of the other famous émigré satirists Nadezhda Teffi (1876–1952) and Don Aminado (1888–1957, in vol. 1).

Cherny's first collection of children's verse, *Knock-Knock!* had appeared in 1913, and in emigration he devoted much energy to writing for children, producing about twenty books for young émigré readers. Soon after moving to La Favière in Provence in 1932, Cherny died of a heart attack while helping to extinguish a fire. His *Soldier's Tales* appeared posthumously in 1933. In an obituary published in Berlin in *The Rudder (Rul')*, Vladimir Nabokov thanked Cherny for having shown him kindness when he was starting out as a poet in the early 1920s. More importantly, Nabokov pointed out a salient feature of Cherny's poetics: "It seems there is not a poem by [Cherny] where one would not find at least one zoological epithet [. . .]. A little animal in the corner of the poem is Sasha Cherny's trademark [. . .]."

Cherny's best satirical poems are unforgettable: irresistibly hilarious, biting, and politically poignant. They mock things laughable and worthy of derision, from corrupt and stupid politicians to provincial Russian philistines trying hard to be Europeans. Cherny's redoubled attitude to Jewishness was rather typical of assimilated and some converted Jews of his age: while embarrassed by "shtetl Jews," he was hypersensitive to even the most minute hints at antisemitism. His two best-known Jewish poems appeared in 1909 in the special "Jewish" issue of *Satyricon*; the second, "Judeophobes," was signed "Heine from Zhitomir," Cherny's alternative pseudonym, which alone said so much. Cherny had translated the works of the Jewish-Austrian humorist Moritz (Moses) Saphir (1795–1858) into Russian, including his story "Judeophobe," which may have informed the second poem included in this selection.

The Jewish Question

There are four Jewish questions, not one:
Among gentleman cardsharps and whores of the pen,
Among monsters whose hearts are harder than leather,
Among half-starved police spies with the souls of bellwethers
An axe is the answer, again and again:

"Thump those Jews to a pulp! They suck people's blood!
Who got Russia beaten? Why, it was the Yids!
We'll grind up their bones into stinking manure.
They're vermin! They're Judases! Killers! They're dogs!"
Black facts, not my fancy, be sure.

For others, fine ladies and toffs,
It's all such rib-tickling stuff:
Policemen are baddies, but a Jew is quite good
Provided his fat nose is hooked.
"Hi Moshe, hi Abe! The lads with pig's ears!"[1]
Yes, that's what they're waiting to hear.
Earlocks and box-pleated jackets,
Anecdotes to send you crackers.

"On the way—I came by train—
I saw a funny Jew again,
Saying his prayers next to the door.
The carriage jolted—to the floor
From off the rack, via his nut,
Fell his filthy case—and what
Was it made of? Just imagine: PIG SKIN!"

For others again,
Those deserving the name of men,
The question's settled once and for all:
There *is* no "Jew" or "Finn," or "Negro" or "Greek,"[2]
But only men. That's it.

---

1. A form of mocking the Jews was to fold the corner of a jacket flap to resemble a pig's ear and thus to allude to the Judaic prohibition against eating pork.
2. Likely an allusion to Galatians 3:28: "There is no such thing as Jew nor Greek, slave and free man, male and female; for you are all one person in Christ Jesus."

Such people deserving the name of men
Sense and will always sense
The most burning shame at those who pour
Life-blood in the dirt, on the forest floor,
To the sound of mad-dog guffaws.

And the Jewish question for Jews?
Such defeat, damnation, and inner pain:
Forgive me if I refuse
To touch on *that* with my sullied pen.

1909

Judeophobes

Roll up, roll up for the latest excursion
Round the *cloaca maxima* of chewed-over lies!
"Jewboys and Jewgirls. Earlocks and onion.
Good people, save Russia! Sharpen your knives!"

Donning surgical gloves and gripping my nostrils—
The stench of that puke is too much to bear—
I politely request you might stop being hostile
And answer this question—it's pointless, but clear:

I see very well you're as pure as the driven
January snow, and as wise as the grave:
So could you please tell me why six in a dozen
Jew-haters are scoundrels, and six have no brains?[3]

1909

Translated from the Russian by Catriona Kelly

---

3. The last two lines of the original literally read, "So why is it that in a hundred Judeophobes/ Fifty are scoundrels, fifty are asses?" The "hundred" may be an allusion to the antisemitic Black Hundreds.

OSSIP DYMOW

Ossip Dymow (1878–1959), humorist, fiction writer, and playwright, was born Yosef Perelman in Bialystok, Grodno Province (now Poland), to a father who was a minor civil servant, originally from Germany. In 1897–1902, Dymow studied at the St. Petersburg Institute of Forestry. He started writing and publishing as a teenager, contributing fueilletons and humoresques to smaller newspapers. His autobiographical story "Silhouettes" won a prize in 1901 awarded by *The Stock Exchange News* (*Birzhevye vedomosti*). Dymow became a regular contributor to the paper, publishing over one thousand pieces between 1901 and 1917. He also contributed to other newspapers, using an additional nom de plume, Cain, when signing feuilletons in *Rus'*. In St. Petersburg Dymow met a number of littérateurs, including the symbolists Ivan Konevskoy and Aleksandr Dobrolyubov. He was close to the influential Jewish-Russian critic Akim Volynsky (1865–1926), who was one of his champions; he also befriended the Yiddish novelist Sholem Asch (1880–1957), whose play *God of Vengeance* he translated into Russian.

Dymow's lifelong relationship with the stage began in 1899–1900, while he worked at the magazine *Theater and Art* (*Teatr i iskusstvo*), whose editor, Aleksandr Kugel (1864–1928), had an impact on his aesthetics. In 1903 his play *Voice of Blood* was unsuccessfully staged by the Maly Theater in St. Petersburg. In 1908 Max Reinhardt (1873–1943), a powerful expressionist director and theater owner of the time, staged Dymow's drama *Nju. Tragedy of Every Day* (*Nju Eine Alltagstragödie*) in German translation at his Kleines Theater Berlin. Following the success of Dymow's play in Berlin, it appeared on numerous European stages, as Dymow himself was spending months at a time in Berlin and Vienna. A total of thirty of his plays appeared on stage and/or in print in Russia. Two of Dymow's pre-Revolutionary plays, *Hear, O Israel!* (1907) and *Eternal Wanderer* (1913), dealt with pogroms and Jewish suffering.

Dymow's debut collection of stories, *The Sun Circle*, was published in 1905 to favorable reviews. Critics indicated the influences of both Maurice Maeterlinck and Anton Chekhov. In the period following the October 1905 Manifesto, when Russia's satirical periodicals experienced rapid growth, Dymow became one of St. Petersburg's most visible writers. He was closely affiliated with the magazines *Signals* (*Signaly*) and *Hellish Mail* (*D'iavol' skaia pochta*), contributed to leading literary journals such as *The Golden Fleece* (*Zolotoe runo*), and worked with the principal theaters. Dymow's second collection of stories, *The Earth Is Blooming* (1908), structured like a musical symphony, was unfavorably received. The late 1900s saw a decline in Dymow's repu-

168

tation in Russia; by the mid-1910s many writers and critics associated his name with eclecticism, dandyism, and fashionable themes borrowed from Western coevals. Reviewing Dymow's collection *The Girl's Crime* (1917), Vladislav Khodasevich (in vol. 1) wrote of its "Pinkertonian spirit" and "semiliterary language."

In 1913 the theater impresario Boris Tomashevsky (1868–1939) invited Dymow to New York, where he spent the rest of his life, becoming an American citizen in 1926. In the 1920s he wrote a number of plays in both Russian and Yiddish, among the most successful of which were *The World in Flames* (*Die velt in flamen, 1917*), *Slaves of the Peoples* (*Shklafn fun folk, 1918*), *When the Messiah Comes* (*Ven Mesiakh kumt, 1924*), as well as the earlier *Hear, O Israel* (*Shema Israel*), now rendered in Yiddish. Two of Dymow's plays were produced in English on Broadway: *Nju*, which premiered at the Bandbox Theater in 1917, and *Bronx Express*, which premiered at the Astor Theater in 1922. *Bronx Express* dramatized the immigrants' conflict of values: the new country versus the old country. Dymow also co-wrote screenplays for several films, including *Rasputin* (Germany, 1932), *Sins of Man* (United States, 1936), and *Overture to Glory* (United States, 1940).

In the 1920s–30s, Dymow was a regular contributor to *Russian Voice* (*Russkii golos*), one of America's leading Russian-language papers of the time. He subsequently wrote mainly in Yiddish. His memoirs, *What I Remember* (*Vos ikh gedenk*), appeared in two volumes in 1943–45. Dymow died in New York in 1959.

Historians of Russian letters credit Dymow with being one of the founding fathers of the modern political feuilleton. As a feuilletonist and humorist, Ossip Dymow was phenomenally popular and had hundreds of provincial imitators across Russia. Dymow the writer of prose was at his best in miniature stories and sketches: elegant, witty, with perfectly intoned dialogue. Dymow selected the fueilleton-story "The Guardian Press" for his collection *Merry Sadness: Humorous Stories* (1911), and it is included here as an example of his Jewish laughter through tears.

The Guardian Press

Once upon a time there lived the guardian press and the Jew.

The guardian press concerned itself with state business. The Jew minded his own business.

Whether it was a long or a short time later, one day a messenger came to the Jew and the Jew said to him, "*Shalom aleikhem.* Peace be with you."

The messenger from the guardian press lowered his eyes and responded, "This be what be wanted. Themselves be waitin.' Cause a certain matter has turned up. There be need to justify it. The editorship be waitin.'"

The Jew put on his black long-skirted frock coat, the very one in which he had been married twelve years before and which he only wore on the Sabbath and religious holidays.

His wife Sura saw him to the gate.

"My husband has gone away on important state business," she proudly informed the neighbors.

An hour later the Jew came back.

"It needs mending," he said to his wife summarily, pointing to the long-skirted holiday frock coat, "here, look, and here, and the sleeve as well, and the collar, and the buttons, and the lining a bit. The lining only a bit."

Sura set about the sewing and thought, "What strange state business if a frock coat gets so damaged by it."

And she sighed. Because twelve years before he had been married in that very frock coat.

After that the messenger took to coming often and gradually stopped lowering his eyes. He was a very able fellow, quick on the uptake, and was already being groomed for transfer to the ranks of journalists.

And the Jew also stopped saying, "Peace be with you. *Shalom aleikhem.*"

Because what sort of peace was it if they damaged his clothes like that?

"This be what themselves want," the messenger began.

The Jew sighed, obediently rose from his seat and asked, "Yes, what?"

"The peasantry starving. Poor harvest. And ice damage. There be need to justify it."

The Jew left with the messenger and returned toward evening. Sura spent all night applying compresses and Goulard water to him.

"I don't understand," groaned the Jew, "why . . . hey, careful please! . . . why the peasantry should cease to starve if . . . ouch! . . . if they've yanked out half my beard in that front-page editorial."

"The beard will grow back," Sura replied philosophically. "What's a beard? And what's a front-page editorial?"

Then the Jew got sick of being all ears, waiting and trying to catch the messenger's footfalls, and he subscribed to a liberal newspaper.

The liberal newspaper was at that time small and gray; its whole appearance seemed to say: "Let me breathe. I only want to breathe."

The Jew did the reading, and his wife and children—the children were already growing up—listened:

"The *zemstvo*,"[1] declaimed the Jew in a quiet voice.

"*Oy!*" responded Sura.

"An electricity supply line in St. Petersburg . . ."

"*Oy! Oy!*" shrieked Sura.

"The introduction of judicial regulations in the provinces of Siberia."

"*Oy, veyz mir!*" groaned Sura, wringing her hands. "Prepare yourselves, children."

And indeed, the messenger arrived after lunch with an invitation for a front-page editorial or a feuilleton . . .

All the men left and Sura ran to the pharmacy for gauze and bandages.

"Mama," said her eldest son, a law student, that evening. "Mama! Times are changing for the better! Everything is getting better. Soon it will be perfectly fine."

"Your whole uniform's torn," replied Sura, "and it was sewn just last year . . ."

"Well that's from the proposed electricity supply line in St. Petersburg, but there was nothing for the introduction of judicial regulations in the provinces of Siberia! Nothing!"

"But it was sewn last year. I remember," rejoined Sura.

"You don't understand anything. You're a materialist," replied the law student. "Surely you see that our legal position is improving?"

And he clutched his swollen left eye.

One day they opened the paper and read, "War is declared!"

They all turned pale and the old man said, "There'll be a pogrom, there'll be killing."

"Killing of whom?" asked the middle son; he was training to be a doctor. "The Japanese?"

"No," answered his father.

"The Russians?"

"Again no."

"Then killing of whom?"

"Us."

They were all silent for a while. Because war is a serious matter.

"But isn't it possible to be exempt from military service?" Sura asked, putting her oar in timidly. "'If we don't stint on the money, then . . .'"

---

1. *Zemstvo* (from the Russian *zemlia*, "land")—the name of a district or provincial assembly established in Russia during the reforms of 1864 and given partial autonomy in such issues as social welfare.

The old man raised his arms toward the ceiling and intoned prayerfully, "I thank You, our Lord God, that You did not create me as a woman. It is indeed possible to be exempt from military service, the more so as Moses limps and Jacob is almost blind in his left eye. But how are you going to get exempt from the important obligation of serving the business of state renewal? How are you . . . He's coming."

It was the messenger. He congratulated everyone on the war and took them with him.

Then the spirit of patriotism spread like wildfire, and the Jew groaned.[2] Folk songs were sung in the streets—he groaned. Urgent troop transports waited at stations for three weeks at a time—he moaned. Two Japanese torpedo boats were sunk—he groaned; the *Petropavlovsk* was lost—he moaned. Stessel received a medal, the frosts came on, talk began about the patriarchate, mass meetings were being called. There came a wafting of social democracy, "people became shadows," Stessel was accused of treason, the fleet was lost at Tsushima, they started marching with tricolors[3]—and he still groaned and moaned . . . Sura was constantly running to the pharmacy. The law student said, "Better times are already on the way. Our legal position is improving. What? I'm on my way. . . . Right now. Let me just postpone the exam until the autumn. Well, all right then, I'll go even without. How impatient the press has grown!"

Once late in the evening, when they had already gone to bed, someone rang loudly at the door.

"Telegram!" said Sura. "Perhaps they want you to travel to the provinces . . ."

"Are there really so few of us there?"

"Not few but possibly no longer enough now . . ."

It was the messenger again, still the same old messenger, who by this time was shaking hands with them, feeling quite at home in their house, and often even borrowing money from the Jew.

"Congratulations," he said. "They intend to establish a Duma."[4]

"A Duma?" The Jew turned pale and shouted into the bedroom, "Children, do you hear?"

"To make life easier, the why and wherefore of it. Or else they'll pocket the people's money and that's that. Some joke. So themselves be wanting you."

"All right, we'll come in the morning."

"You be asked for pronto. 'Cause it be an important matter. Workers unite, as the

---

2. Dymow is referring in this paragraph to events during the Russo-Japanese War (1904–5). Major-General A.M. Stessel was the commandant of Port Arthur, which was surrendered in December 1904. The *Petropavlovsk*, the legendary Russian flagship, struck a Japanese mine and sank during the defense of the Port Arthur harbor. In a decisive battle in the Tsushima Straits located between Japan and Korea, the Japanese fleet met the squadron of Russia's Baltic Fleet under the command of Admiral Z.P. Rozhdestvensky and nearly destroyed it.

3. Russia's tricolor "St. Andrew's" flag.

4. Established by the October 1905 Manifesto and defined by the Fundamental Laws (May 1906), the First State Duma was dissolved after two stormy months of deliberations.

sayin' goes. Just what we need, I don't think. And I, by the way, have also dashed off a feuilleton."

The Jew sighed and handed him a three-ruble note—for bringing the good news.

"What sort of Duma?' asked the law student. "Deliberative or legislative?"

"I don't know."

"A legislative one would be best."

"A legislative one would be more painful," his father remarked didactically.

"It may be more painful, but they don't need a deliberative one . . ."

This time, though, "themselves" were not waiting, and they came in person. They had terrifying faces. The tinkle of breaking glass could be heard.

They buried their old father on Friday and very quickly, because the Sabbath was already coming and it was time to pray and thank God—who did not create us as women—for the legislative Duma . . .

1900s

Translated from the Russian by Brian Cooper

S. AN-SKY

S. An-sky (1863–1920), prose writer, playwright, and folklorist, was born Shloyme (Solomon) Rapoport in Chashniki, in Vitebsk Province (presently in Belarus) and received an Orthodox Jewish education in the family of an affluent broker. He learned to read and write in Russian between the ages of sixteen and seventeen and became interested in the ideas of the Haskalah. An autodidact, he studied rigorously while also learning bookbinding and blacksmithing. In 1881 An-sky wrote his first Russian story, "History of One Family," which was published in *Sunrise* (*Voskhod*) in 1884.

In the early 1880s, An-sky was taken with the ideology of the Russian populist-revolutionary movement and resided among Russian peasants, teaching their children and working at coal and salt mines. Upon the advice of Gleb Uspensky (1843–1902), a leading representative of *narodnik* literature, An-sky moved to St. Petersburg and adopted a pen name derived from the name of his mother, Hanna (Anna). An-sky's *Sketches of Popular Literature* appeared serially in *Russian Wealth* (*Russkoe bogatstvo.*) and as a separate edition in 1894. From a sociological perspective, his collection *The People and the Book* (Moscow, 1913–14) remains illuminating to this day.

In 1892 An-sky left Russia and in 1894 settled in Paris after a brief stay in Germany and Switzerland. In Paris he became personal secretary to Pyotr Lavrov (1823–1900), a philosopher and a prominent figure of the international socialist movement living in permanent exile. In Paris, An-sky composed in Russian stories of traditional Jewish life in the Pale. His sketches memorialized the aspirations of the Haskalah-minded Jewish youth of the 1870s. Until 1904 he mainly wrote in Russian but then transitioned partially to Yiddish. In Yiddish he composed the one-act play *Father and Son* and the long poem *Ashmedai*. In 1905 An-sky took advantage of the October 1905 Manifesto and returned to Russia, where he joined the Socialist-Revolutionary Party (SR). He contributed to periodicals, both *narodnik* (*Russian Wealth*) and Jewish-Russian (*Sunrise*), published a collection of Russian-language stories in 1905, and wrote, notably, the lyrics for the Bund anthem "Di Shvue" (The Oath).

In the late 1900s An-sky developed a strong interest in Jewish folklore and Hasidic legends. This interest led to his ethnographic research and publications and to the gradual creation of his world-renowned play *The Dybbuk*. In 1911–14, An-sky headed the Jewish Ethnographic Expedition, funded by Baron Horace Günzburg, collecting oral materials in Volhynia and Podolia. During World War I, An-sky organized relief committees for Jewish refugees, and in 1917 he was elected to the All-Russia Constitutional Assembly as a deputy from the Socialist-Revolutionary Party.

The archeology of An-sky's famous play originally titled *Tsvishn tsvei veltn* (Between Two Worlds) is ponderous. He began it in Russian around 1911. In 1916 an excerpt from Act 1 appeared in Russian in the Moscow Zionist newspaper *Jewish Life* (*Evreiskaia Zhizh'*), then sought to have it staged at the Moscow Art Theater by Konstantin Stanislavsky, who made valuable suggestions but passed on it, and then by Dovid Herman's Vilna Theater, where it was also rejected. Hayyim Nahman Bialik translated it from Yiddish into Hebrew, and it appeared in *The Epoch* (*Ha-Tkufa*, vol. 1, 1918). While relocating to Vilna in 1919, An-sky lost the original Yiddish text and had to retranslate the play from Bialik's Hebrew, introducing changes. In Vilna Ansky founded a Jewish ethnographic society. He moved from Vilna to Warsaw, where he died in 1920. The second Yiddish version of *The Dybbuk*—a palimpsest of the Russian, first Yiddish, and Bialik's Hebrew versions—was staged by the Vilna troupe only a month after An-sky's death. In 1922 the visionary director Evgeny Vakhtangov (1883–1922), a Russified Armenian who did not know Hebrew but identified with An-sky's play, gloriously staged *The Dybbuk* in Hebrew at the Habimah Theater in Moscow. A posthumous fifteen-volume edition of Ansky's *Collected Works* appeared in Yiddish in 1920–25. Inspired by Jewish folklore and the modernist theater of Henrik Ibsen, Anton Chekhov, and Maurice Maeterlinck, *The Dybbuk* remains a prominent part of the world theatrical repertoire.

Dated "Minsk, 1910," An-sky's story "The Book" differs from the earlier stories of the Pale for which he is well known, such as "In a Jewish Family" (1900) and "Mendel the Turk" (1902). Of particular interest here is the setting: Königsberg, the capital city of East Prussia, Immanuel Kant's city and an early center of the Haskalah. Here in Königsberg, the Hebrew monthly *The Gatherer* (*Ha-Meassef*) was founded in 1783, spreading its influence not only across central Europe but also eastward, into the Russian Empire.

An-sky's autobiographical storyteller is both an observer of and a witness to the "fruits of Enlightenment." Himself an acculturated Russian Jew, he is anxious about the survival of Jewish identity in the face of both external and internal assimilation. Coming from An-sky, the student of popular readership and reading, the story's title is doubly significant. While Jewish culture, broadly conceived, is one of the sources of Jewish endurance, a different source—an indispensable one—is reaffirmed at the end of An-sky's story.

The Book

A few years ago I had occasion to be in Königsberg.[1] I went there on business, thinking it would just be for a few days, but as it turned out I had to stay there much longer. It was sad to be in an unfamiliar town, without acquaintances, without my usual routine, and in extremely uncertain circumstances. In addition, it was autumn, rainy and slushy. To escape the oppressive loneliness, I often sat all evening in a big, noisy, brightly lit café, looking through newspapers, writing letters, and spending hours watching some skillful billiard players at their game.

One evening I sat at a small table in that café and read a Yiddish newspaper that had come in the mail that day along with my letters. Lost in my reading, I sensed rather than noticed that someone was right next to me. I lifted my head and saw that a man who had been sitting at the next table over a mug of beer was leaning close and peering at my paper. He was about thirty, a typical Prussian, fleshy, with a short fat neck, an angular face, a shaven blunt chin, slightly glassy eyes, and an arrogant, self-important expression. Not at all disturbed by my startled, questioning look, he pointed his short fat finger at the paper and asked hoarsely, "What kind of newspaper is that?"

"An antisemite. He wants to start a fight," went through my mind. But I answered him in a dry, calm tone, "It's a Jewish newspaper."

"I see it's a Jewish paper," he answered, not at all confused by my tone. "I'm asking what the title is. I've read the first three letters, but I don't know the rest." He jabbed his finger at the title.

I was very surprised. Could he really be a Jew? I looked at him again carefully. I saw nothing Jewish either in his features or in the expression of his eyes.

"How do you know Jewish letters?"

"I learned them as a child. I even read well then, but now I've forgotten," he answered coolly.

"You're a Jew?"

"No . . . My father's Jewish, but I'm a freethinker and . . . a German!" he added meaningfully, thrusting out his chest.

In order to prolong our conversation, I threw out a phrase: "One can be a freethinker and remain a Jew."

He leaned against the cushion of his seat and chuckled in a self-satisfied way. "Ha, ha! I've heard that already . . . It's an old tune! . . . I see you're from Russia? Everything is barbaric in Russia, and the Jews are barbarians, too. They don't understand what *Vaterland* is."

---

1. Königsberg, formerly the capital city of East Prussia; a part of Prussia and Germany until the end of World War II; presently Kaliningrad, capital of Kaliningrad Province of the Russian Federation.

The arrogant, self-important tone with which he pronounced these words was so unpleasant that I decided to cut our conversation short and buried my head in the newspaper. However, my neighbor paid no attention and spoke up again, "Do you know someone in Russia, in Petersburg, named Alekseev or Eliseev? I think he's a count. He has a big stud farm. Last year he sent two horses here, Naddai and Igor, to compete at the races. He hoped to win first prize, but he failed."

"You like horse racing?"

"I'm a jockey!" he answered proudly. "I've won prizes seventeen times. Twice I took first prize, and I've never let a foreigner outrun my horse. Germans always have to be ahead!" he concluded with some feeling.

I became intrigued by this horsey German patriot, and I began to ask him about who he was. He willingly told me that his father had come to Königsberg from Poland about forty years ago. The old man was still alive, worked as a broker at the exchange, and had remained a pious Jew to this day, going to synagogue, observing all the rituals, and often sitting over religious books until late at night. He read German books but only those about Jewish religious matters.

"What's his attitude about the fact that you don't consider yourself a Jew?" I asked.

He burst out laughing. "What kind of attitude could he have? He used to scold me, but now he's calmed down and keeps quiet . . . And what's wrong with me? After all, I haven't converted. My two sisters, you see, both converted. One married a traveling salesman and the other a civil servant. And he didn't break off relations with them either. He visits them sometimes. But he doesn't like to talk to them or to me. He's always quiet, or he sits with his books . . . After the second daughter converted, though, he decided to go back home to Poland . . ."

My interlocutor either clicked his heels in some special way or made some kind of sound with his lips and then told the waiter to bring him another mug of beer.

I imagined the father of this freethinking jockey, an old Jew coming from some small Jewish town, living his whole life in a strange land, losing all his children here, and now returning, alone and foreign, to his home country—and I began to feel sorry for this unknown old man.

The jockey sat for a while, leaning back with his legs stretched out, slowly drinking his beer. Clearly, he somehow grasped my mood and, putting the mug down, said briskly, "You know what? You should come over and meet my father. He'll be awfully happy to speak with someone from his country! Whenever he meets a Jew from Russia, he sits with him, sometimes for whole evenings, and talks about metaphysical subjects. It's true! Really, you should come! And it will be interesting for you to talk with him. He's a clever old fellow."

Seeing that I was wavering, he added, "You should come over to my place—I live with my father—and I'll introduce you!"

I agreed.

The next evening, I arrived promptly. My new acquaintance met me, brought me into a big, well-furnished room, and introduced me to his father. "Here, father, is the man I spoke of yesterday."

And he went out.

A short, very stooped, but seemingly still strong old man with a small gray beard and a weary, thoughtful, patient gaze arose from the desk and came toward me. He held out his hand, asked me to sit down, and sat down across from me.

"You're from our parts? Have you come here for long?" He began to ask the usual questions, looking at me coldly and distrustfully.

I satisfied his curiosity.

"My son told me that you'd like to look at Jewish books. I have rather a lot of them." (He pointed toward a big bookcase full of books). "But except for me, there's no one in the house to use them," he added with a sad smile.

"I admit that I'm more interested in a live Jew than in books," I answered. "I don't know a soul here."

"And I know half the city, but I also rarely encounter a live Jew," he answered with the same sad smile.

I went up to the bookcase and began to look at the books. Along with the thick volumes of the Talmud and other religious books, I noticed some German books on Judaism.

"What do you do?" my host asked.

"I'm a writer," I answered and turned back to the desk, sensing that my answer would provoke a whole series of questions.

"A writer? What do you write about?"

"A lot of things. Mostly issues that affect Jews."

"What do you write? What do you argue in your writings?" the old man continued his questioning calmly and persistently, a note of distrust in his voice.

"It's hard to say briefly. In general, I argue that it's important to stay Jewish."

The old man was not satisfied with this answer. His eyes expressed even more distrust, and he asked again, "To stay Jewish? . . . Su-u-ure! . . . And how do you argue that? And what do you call 'staying Jewish'?"

The old man's endless interrogation and his distrustful tone began to annoy me, and I decided to give him my *profession de foi* once and for all. Everything that Jewishness once depended on—religion, the Torah, the Talmud—has fallen away, is lost. So here we representatives of the new Jewry are trying to create something new, aside from religion, to bring the people together and unify them. That's what we write about.

The old man listened to me very carefully. But as soon as he got my basic idea, he raised his wide-open eyes, where I saw a severe protest and barely restrained indignation. "You think the old fence has been destroyed?" he said in a dry, hostile tone. "Don't worry, it's still strong, and we don't need a new one!"

"But look at what's happening around us, not just here, but in Russia as well!" I couldn't help exclaiming.

"And what's happening?"

"What do you mean, what? The religion has fallen away completely, Jewish schools are empty, yeshivas are closing, nobody studies the Talmud."

The old man's face froze with its stern expression. Looking fixedly into the distance like a sleepwalker, he said coldly and calmly, "That doesn't mean anything!"

"But what else do you need?" I continued. "Jews are forgetting their native language, they're forgetting that they're Jews, they're denying their own people, they're converting . . ."

I broke off, remembering that my words touched at the most painful spot in the life of an old man whose children had converted. But he didn't even pay attention to that and continued as persistently as before.

"Tha-a-at doesn't mean anything!"

"So what in your opinion would mean something?"

The old man stood up, silently went to the bookcase, took out a German book, returned to me, and, pointing at the title, spoke slowly and very deliberately, "Read this! Do you see? Here it says, *'Zurück zum Talmud.'* Do you understand? *Zurück zum Talmud,*"[2] he drew the words out. "Read this book, and you'll see that the old fence is not yet destroyed. Jews *must* return to the Talmud—it can't be otherwise!"

I looked at the old man silently and could not decide what I was seeing: an old madman who can't see or understand what is happening around him, or a sage who, through blatant facts, through generations, through his own tragedy, has looked into the future . . .

1910

Translated from the Russian by Gabriella Safran

---

2. *Zurück zum Talmud* (Ger.) = Back to the Talmud.

ILYA EHRENBURG

Ilya Ehrenburg (1891–1967), fiction writer, poet, and journalist, was born in Kiev to a family of Jewish-Russian intelligentsia. His father, an engineer, moved the family to Moscow in 1894. Ehrenburg later studied in Moscow's First Gymnasium. In 1908 Ehrenburg was arrested for his involvement with Bolshevik activities and spent almost a year in Moscow jails. In December 1908 his father arranged for him to travel abroad, and Ehrenburg spent the next eight years as an expatriate, soon distancing himself from Bolshevik activities. In the 1910s Ehrenburg forged connections with members of the artistic avant-garde, including a lifelong friendship with Pablo Picasso. He started out as a poet in 1910, publishing six collections in the pre-1917 period. His first story, "In November," appeared in 1911. Richly equipped to absorb artistic innovations from the air of culture, Ehrenburg treated style as a means and not an end of expression. Formal aspects of writing served to underscore Ehrenburg's principal métier: a polemicist and a witness to his torrid times.

During World War I, Ehrenburg served as European correspondent for *Morning of Russia* (*Utro Rossii*) and *The Stock Exchange News* (*Birzhevye vedomosti*) and wrote about the war in *Verses about the Eves* (1916). Following the February 1917 Revolution, Ehrenburg returned to Russia. He did not accept the Bolshevik coup and moved to Kiev, where he witnessed civil-war violence, including a Jewish pogrom. Ehrenburg's poetry of the time echoed the anti-Bolshevik sentiments of his articles. In Kiev Ehrenburg met and married Lyubov Kozintseva, who would remain his wife despite Ehrenburg's extramarital affairs.

In 1921 Ehrenburg was allowed to travel abroad with a Soviet passport. He headed for Paris but was not permitted to stay. At the Belgian resort of La Panne he composed his first (and best) novel, *The Extraordinary Adventures of Julio Jurenito and His Disciples* (published in Berlin in 1922; excerpt in vol. 1); the Jewish theme played a significant role in the novel. Ehrenburg spent the next two years in Berlin (see excerpt from Viktor Shklovsky's *Zoo* in vol. 1) before moving to Paris in 1924. Between 1921 and 1927, he published seven novels, several of them interspersing European and Russian (Soviet) settings and characters. Ehrenburg also published collections of essays, poems, and stories, including *The Thirteen Pipes* (1923). In the opinion of Shimon Markish, Ehrenburg's novella "Shifscard" from the collection *Six Novellas about Easy Endings* (1922) was the worker's "first Jewish prose." Ehrenburg's 1927 novel *The Stormy Life of Lazik Roitshvanets* was not reprinted in the USSR until 1989 as it flew in the face of the Soviet rhetoric on the Jewish question.

Stalin's rise to absolute power in the late 1920s signaled a change in Ehrenburg's orientation. In 1932 he became a special correspondent of *Izvestia*. Making a prominent appearance at the First Congress of Soviet Writers in 1934 and drawing on the impressions of a perfunctory tour of Soviet industrial sites, Ehrenburg concocted *The Second Day of Creation*, a production and construction novel praised by Stalin. In the mid-1930s Ehrenburg increasingly turned his energies to writing and lobbying against Fascism and Nazism. He reported on the events of the Spanish Civil War from the trenches of the Loyalists. He visited the USSR briefly in 1936 but went back to Paris and waited out the Great Purges. Following the defeat of the Loyalists in 1939 and the Soviet–Nazi pact, Ehrenburg continued to dispatch to Moscow vitriolic articles that did not get printed while he remained an *Izvestia* correspondent. In July 1940 Ehrenburg was evacuated from Paris to Moscow with the Soviet embassy staff.

Right after Nazi Germany invaded the Soviet Union, Ehrenburg became staff war correspondent for *Red Star* (*Krasnaia zvezda*), the Soviet army's central newspaper. He wrote daily articles during World War II. Ehrenburg's impact on the morale of the Soviet troops was paramount. Largely responsible, along with the writer Aleksey Tolstoy, for the "Kill the German" wartime rhetoric, Ehrenburg sensed, despite his own internationalism, that the Soviet people needed a visceral anti-Nazi message. His writings were personally targeted by Adolf Hitler and Joseph Goebbels in their speeches. In 1942 Ehrenburg's novel *The Fall of Paris* was published and awarded a Stalin Prize in literature.

From the very beginning, Ehrenburg wrote more openly about the Shoah than any Soviet writer of his official status and magnitude. One of his wartime projects, *The Red Book*, memorializing Jewish heroism in battle, was derailed. The second was *The Black Book*, documenting Nazi atrocities against the Jews. Ehrenburg led this collective project in 1943–44 under the auspices of the Jewish Antifascist Committee (JAC), working closely with a team of Soviet writers that included, of the authors featured in volume 1 of this anthology, Margarita Aliger, Pavel Antokolsky, Vassily Grossman, Vera Inber, Veniamin Kaverin, Vladimir Lidin, Lev Ozerov, and Viktor Shklovsky. Toward the end of the war, Ehrenburg had a falling-out with the JAC (several interpretations of his conduct have been advanced), resigning as head of *The Black Book* project, and Vassily Grossman (in vols. 1 and 2) took over. *The Black Book* was scheduled to appear in the USSR in 1947, with Ehrenburg and Grossman listed as co-editors. Its publication was banned, and a reconstructed text appeared in Israel only in 1980 (English translation, *The Black Book*, 1981; *The Complete Black Book of Russian Jewry*, 2002). Ehrenburg's novel *The Storm* described the murder of Soviet Jews at Babi Yar and the destruction of European Jewry. It was awarded a Stalin Prize in 1948.

The end of World War II and the late 1940s constituted the peak of Ehrenburg's favor with Stalin. He was sent on official foreign missions as a propagandist for the Soviet state. His tour of the United States and Canada in 1946 and a second trip to the United States in 1948 produced starkly negative and distortional essays in the spirit of cold-war Soviet rhetoric. Despite the raging "anticosmopolitan" (read: antisemitic) campaign of 1948–53, Ehrenburg was unharmed, although at the time he constantly feared arrest. On the occasion of Stalin's seventieth birthday, Ehrenburg published in *Pravda* an embarrassing dithyramb. In 1949 he was one of the few Jews elected to the Supreme Soviet, and in 1953 he was awarded a Stalin Peace Prize.

Soon after Stalin's death in 1953, accustomed as he was to recognizing the winds of history, Ehrenburg quickly wrote and published the novel *The Thaw* (1954), which lent its title to the period of de-Stalinization and temporarily expanded artistic freedom in the middle to late 1950s. *The Thaw* gave impetus to greater anti-Stalinist works and placed Ehrenburg in the camp of liberalizers. One of the main characters, Vera Sherer, is a Jewish doctor; both the Doctors' Plot and the Shoah were depicted. From 1960 until his death in 1967, Ehrenburg worked on his great memoir, *People, Years, Life*. Even in its expurgated published form, it amounted to a large window onto fifty years of western modernist culture and played a major role in the aesthetic education of the postwar generations.

Helen Segall wrote that Ehrenburg "felt a strong obligation to his fellow Jews to make the world aware of what had befallen them during the Holocaust." A man of "tangled loyalties" (the title phrase of Joshua Rubenstein's 1996 biography of Ehrenburg), a survivalist by profession but never a conformist by conviction, Ehrenburg was a unique creation of his personal predilections, Jewish history, and Soviet ideology. Ten million copies of his books were published in the USSR in thirty languages. While not the most talented of the Jewish-Russian writers of the twentieth century, Ehrenburg was the most visible and audible champion of the Jewish cause.

Ehrenburg wrote poetry his whole life and also translated French and Spanish poets into Russian. As was the case with other prominent prose writers who also write poetry, such as Vladimir Nabokov, Ehrenburg treated his poems as public diaries or sketchbooks filled with studies for future fiction. Formally diverse and lacking a signature intonation, some of Ehrenburg's poems are very accomplished, especially his lyrical poems of soul-searching.

In 1911 Ehrenburg went through a phase of fascination with Catholic medieval mysticism and with the poetry of Francis Jammes (1868–1938). He planned to enter a Benedictine monastery but had a crisis and changed his mind. The two poems here anthologized appeared, respectively, in Ehrenburg's early collections *I Live* (1911) and *Dandelions* (1912) and reflect the poet's strained identity. They bring to mind the words of Morris Feitelzohn in Isaac Bashevis Singer's novel *Shosha* (1974; in English, 1978): "I love Jews even though I cannot stand them." (See also an excerpt from Ehrenburg's *Julio Jurenito* and wartime poems and essays in vol. 1.)

To the Jewish Nation

You trace your roots to Abraham, Jewish nation,
O nation once both powerful and grand.
You staunchly tilled your fields for generations,
Year in, year out you labored on the land.
You were a youthful and a cheerful people
While dwelling in your native, cultivated fields,
In palm tents shimmering with dew so sweetly,
You sprawled across the fertile hills and dales.
But not contented with the lot you'd chosen,
You quit your pastures and ancestral homes
To wander destitute through foreign regions,
Becoming strangers, slaves in lands unknown.

Now, everywhere abased and hunted,
Beneath your heavy load of shame,
Just tolerated, you roam all countries,
O nation impotent and lame.
So many exiles you have weathered,
Bonfires and prisons, such disgrace,
That like a pestilence you're dreaded,
And you're avoided like the plague.
Pitiful and wretched strangers,
You prize all nations but your own;
Revering the Hebrew God no longer,
You don't recall your native tongue.
You tend no more the fields and furrows,
Or guard your gentle flocks of sheep.
In shabby shops you now are merchants
Cringing fearfully with greed.
Old, blind, ill-fated, all your kinsmen
Born long ago upon the land
Are dying with each passing instant
In cities' unrelenting cramp.
Deprived of fields, in stifling basements,
Confined by strong walls all your lives,
Engendering freakish aberrations
With your degenerating wives,

O Jews, you're slaves to all the nations,
Pariahs among all the tribes!

Here no one needs you: you're alien and hunted,
So gather your debilitated brood,
Return now to Jerusalem, your native country,
Where you knew blessed rapture in your youth.
Behold again the pastures you abandoned,
In barren furrows wield the rusty plow.
And maybe there beneath the olive branches
You'll finally rest from years of fret and woe.
And if you must die soon, then do not perish
Here, in these foreign fields, far from your roots,
But there, where dawn was radiant and lavish,
Where you knew blessed rapture in your youth.

                                                        1911

                              *   *   *

Jews, I haven't strength to live with you.
So, hating you, I keep my distance,
And when amid my long and dismal
Meanderings I come to you,
Each time your steadfastness, your patience,
And your extraordinary fate—
The fate of wanderers, of slaves—
Arouse in me a cold amazement.
But I am poisoned with Jewish blood,
And somewhere in the dusky desert
Of my desultory soul, I cherish
For you a son's reluctant love.
And in the hour of grief, of rue,
I know and feel that I'm a Jew.

                                                        1912

Translated from the Russian by Alyssa Dinega Gillespie

VLADISLAV KHODASEVICH

Vladislav Khodasevich (1886–1939), poet, critic, and translator, was the son of an impoverished Lithuanian-Polish nobleman. Khodesevich's mother was the daughter of Yakov Brafman, convert to Russian Orthodoxy and author of the nefarious *Book of the Kahal* (1869); she was born Jewish but brought up Catholic by a zealous Polish-Catholic family. Born in Moscow, Khodasevich studied at Moscow's Third Classical Gymnasium and attended lectures at Moscow University in 1904–5 without taking a degree. In 1905 his poems appeared in print, and his first collection, *Youth*, came out in 1908 as Khodasevich began to translate from Polish and French and work as an editor.

Khodasevich's second collection, *The Happy Little House*, was published in 1914. Sickly from birth, in 1916 Khodasevich developed tuberculosis of the spine, and for the rest of his life he was plagued by poor health. In late 1916 Khodasevich befriended Leyb Jaffe (in vol. 1) and worked with him on *The Jewish Anthology: A Collection of Young Jewish Poetry* (the first two editions appeared in Moscow in 1918, the third edition in Berlin in 1922). Jaffe and Khodasevich coedited the volume, and each translated some of the poems. Jaffe selected the Hebrew poems while Khodasevich did the editing of the Russian translations. The prominent critic Mikhail Gershenzon, a friend of Khodasevich's, wrote the preface (see text in vol. 1).

Khodasevich's third collection, *By Way of Grain*, appeared in Moscow in 1920 and was reprinted in Petrograd in 1922. Khodasevich left Russia in June 1922 in the company of the young Russian poet Nina Berberova (1901–1993); in emigration Berberova developed into a prominent prose writer. His fourth collection, *The Heavy Lyre*, was published in Moscow in 1922 and reprinted in 1923 in Berlin. Khodasevich published *From the Jewish Poets* in 1922, also in Berlin, taking his translations of six Hebrew poets from *The Jewish Anthology*: two by David Frischmann (1861–1922), four by Saul Tchernichovsky (1875–1943), two by Yaakov Fichman (1881–1958), one by Zalman Shneour (1887–1959), two by David Shimonovitz (Shimoni, 1886–1956), and one by Avraham Ben Yitzhak (1883–1950). He removed a poem by Judah Katzenelson (1847–1917) but supplemented the selection with a poem by Hayyim Nahman Bialik (1873–1934) and an additional one by Tchernichovsky ("Dumplings")—a gem of the new Hebrew poetry and of literary translation.

After wandering around Europe in 1924–25, Khodasevich and his common-law wife Berberova settled in Paris. Although he was a leading émigré critic and major poet, Khodasevich did not have an easy time making a living. His *Collected Poetry* (Paris, 1927) included poems from *By Grain's Way* and *The Heavy Lyre* and, as its last section, Khodasevich's fifth collection, *European Night*, which gathered his émigré verses. After 1927 Khodasevich only wrote about fifteen poems. In 1932 Berberova left Khodasevich, and in 1933 he married Olga Margolina (he had been married twice in Russia). In 1939 *Necropolis*, a volume of his literary memoirs, was published in Brussels. Khodasevich died in Paris the same year. His wife, Olga, perished in a Nazi concentration camp in 1942. As Donald Rayfield remarked, "[Khodasevich's] death [. . .] spared him from the Nazi extermination camp."

Khodasevich gained his own voice in the 1910s after shaking his symbolist affinities. To quote John Malmstad, "In poem after poem between 1916 and 1920 Khodasevich clarified his vision in a language resistant to subjective overstatement and capable of dealing with a world of actualities." Starting from his third collection, *By Way of the Grain* (1920), Khodasevich's best poems derived their intonation from a distillation of the lyrical impulse that is buttressed by dissonant prosaic details and often framed by irony and even absurdity. Few Russian poets have been able to strike chords of confessionalism and ruthless introspection—and communicate a sense of a poet's physical and metaphysical alienation—with the doomful clairvoyance that marks Khodasevich's best love poems.

Manifest in Khodasevich's biography, Jewish questions occasionally pulsated in his poetry. His principal contribution to Jewish letters was as a translator of Hebrew poets into Russian and as a critic who wrote profoundly about Jewish literature (Tchernichovsky, whom he favored, Bialik, and Semyon Yushkevich [in vol. 1]). To a believer in the mutually mirroring relationship between life and art, the two early poems that follow may signal an identification with a Jewish mother that expands the boundaries of both Gospel narratives and Old Testament history. (See also Khodasevich's poems in the section "Emigrations: 1917–1967" in vol. 1.)

Evening

Ruddy Mars climbs high above the agave,
But the peaceful shop lights of this port—
Genoa, once mysterious and savvy—
Seem to us to shine more brightly forth.

The mountains' coastal spurs grow dimmer,
Dust, sea, and wine exude a mingled smell.
On the road a straggling donkey lingers,
We hear his hasty steps, his plashing bell . . .

Was it not on such a night, the starry
Heavens curing to a deeper blue,
On such a donkey's back that Mary
Bid teeming Bethlehem adieu?

Hoof beats clattered, now hesitant, now frequent,
Joseph lagged behind, all swathed in sand . . .
What did the ragged Jewess want with Egypt,
Strangers' sheep, a strange and hostile land?

A mother weeps. The child beneath her mantle
Seeks her breast with sleepy lips,
Under rustling palms the donkeys amble,
Whilst distant starlight guides the fugitives.

1913

Rachel's Tears[*]

A salute to our vile evening planet!
Puddles, banisters, windows glisten.
Through the downpour I wanly straggle,
Shoulders sodden, and hat brim dripping.
Now we all have been rendered homeless,
Made to wander through all the ages,
And the desolate rain sings hopeless
Songs of Rachel's tears so ancient.

Let our progeny, proudly loving,
Fashion legends about their forebears—
In our hearts each new day is governed
By our sins and blood, by our horror.
Woe to us, that our blessed Maker
Willed us live in this grievous era:
On an old woman's cheekbones rankle
Signs of Rachel's tears so searing.

I esteem neither honor nor glory,
If last week she was sent a package
That held shreds of a uniform, gory
Bits of fabric, congealing tatters.
Ah, in light of our ponderous burden
Though we pound out the very freshest
Tunes—one single refrain is worthy:
Strains of Rachel's tears so wretched!

1916

Translated from the Russian by Alyssa Dinega Gillespie

Vladislav Khodasevich, "Vecher" and "Slezy Rakhili." English translation copyright © by
Alyssa Dinega Gillespie. Introduction and notes copyright © by Maxim D. Shrayer.

---

[*] Compare Jeremiah 31:15: "Thus said the Lord:/A cry is heard in Ramah—/Wailing, bitter
weeping—/Rachel weeping for her children./She refuses to be comforted/For her children,
who are gone"; later quoted in Matthew 2:17–18.

RAHEL

Rahel (pseudonym of Rakhel [Raya] Bluwstein, 1890–1931), poet and translator, was born in Saratov, in the Lower Volga region and raised in Poltava, Ukraine. Having a weak chest from childhood, she spent time in the Crimea undergoing treatment. She started writing Russian poetry in her teens and after secondary school studied painting in Kiev. In 1909, partly under the influence of her brother, the Zionist activist Yakov Bluwstein-Sela, Rahel moved to Eretz Israel with her sister Shoshanna and settled in Rehobot. She decided to limit speaking Russian to one hour per day while studying Hebrew; she joined the *halutzim* (pioneers) and worked in olive groves. In 1911, while training at a young women's farm at Lake Kinneret, she met Aaron David Gordon (1856–1922), Zionist author and thinker and champion of Jewish agrarianism; Gordon made a great impact on Rahel. In 1913 she was sent to France to study agronomy at the University of Toulouse. While in Europe, she continued to compose verses in Russian and also took drawing lessons in Rome. After graduating from the university, Rahel went back to Russia to visit her family. Since World War I and Russian citizenship prevented her from returning to Eretz Israel, then still part of the Ottoman Empire, she worked with Jewish refugee children in Berdyansk and her native Saratov, and later lived in Baku, Sukhumi, and Odessa. In Odessa she contributed her translations from Hebrew as well as occasional essays to Jewish-Russian periodicals.

In 1919, Rahel sailed from Odessa back to Eretz Israel and settled in Dgania on Lake Kinneret. One of her first Hebrew poems, signed "Rahel" and dedicated to A.D. Gordon, appeared in 1920 in the periodical *Siloam* (*Ha-Shiloah*). During World War I Rahel had been infected with tuberculosis, and she soon became too ill to work as an agronomist and was forced to leave the agricultural colony of Dgania. She moved to Jerusalem and worked as a teacher. Rahel spent her last years relocating from one place to another, and at tuberculosis sanatoria. She died in 1931 at Hadassa Hospital in Tel Aviv.

The first modern Hebrew woman poet and one of the first twentieth-century Hebrew poets to write in a conversational if not colloquial style (among female Hebrew poets from Russia, also Elisheva in vol. 1), Rahel owed her success to two main factors. On the one hand, she drew her poetic language from the evolving Hebrew she had learned while immersed in the vibrant environment of the *halutzim* (with the Sephardic norm as its foundation) and from the Hebrew of the Bible; such fusion created a potential for both mundane everyday diction and lofty rhetorical flights. On the other hand, students of Hebrew poetry indicate the influence of the Russian modernist poetic movements of acmeism (especially Anna Akhmatova) and later imaginism (especially Sergey Esenin).

One might say Rahel wrote Russian verses in Hebrew. Short, lyrical and tuneful, many of Rahel's poems deal with memory and remembrance. Coined in a new Hebrew idiom, broadly popular still today for their seemingly uncomplicated nostalgic quality, Rahel's poems do not yield facilely to translation; in this sense her poems may be compared to those of Russia's beloved poet Sergey Esenin (1895–1925). A number of her Hebrew poems have been set to music and are widely performed. Rahel was also an important translator of Russian and French poetry into Hebrew.

In her lifetime, two Hebrew collections appeared: *Safiah* (Aftergrowth, 1927) and *Mi-neged* (From the Opposite Side, 1930). A third one, *Nevo* (Mount Nevo) came out posthumously in 1932, and a volume in Yiddish translation, *Rohls lider* (Songs of Rahel), appeared in Winnipeg the same year. Collected in *Shirat Rahel* (Songs of Rahel, 1935), Rahel's poetry has gone through numerous editions, most recently in 2001.

Although never published as a separate collection, over thirty of Rahel's Russian poems from 1915–18 have appeared in Hebrew editions of her work and in Russian-language anthologies of Hebrew poetry. In 1963 Russian translations of two of her Hebrew poems appeared in the anthology *Poets of Israel*, published in Moscow and edited by Boris Slutsky (in vol. 2). The most extensive selection of Rahel's Russian poems appeared in *Lekha ve-alekha* (For You and about You), edited by Binyamin Hachlili (Tel Aviv, 1987).

Rahel's Russian poems are mainly intriguing as miniature stages on which she rehearsed in Russian what she would later perform with much greater power in her adopted Hebrew. Although in some poems Rahel made recuperative stops in Russian romantic verse, she was mainly a feeble daughter of the Silver Age. Notes and motifs of four major Silver Age poets are present in her Russian verses: Aleksandr Blok (1880–1921), as in the two poems selected here, Anna Akhmatova (1889–1966), Mikhail Kuzmin (1872–1936), and Igor Severyanin (1887–1941).

* * *

I love all temples—my own and others',
Places that breathe the breath of God.
They are equally close to me—the golden cupolas,
The pared down dais of the synagogue.

They are equally close to me—vengeful Jahweh
And the all-forgiving glance of Christ.
I love the grace-granting language of prayer,
I love everything that's "highest."

1916

Tablets of the Past and Chains of the Past

To leave the past. To break its tablets,
Stamp its chains in the rich dust,
To dispatch a fleet of my finest ships
To far-off, undiscovered places.

And if I knew there was no return to the dead,
Having wounded my soul with losses,
I wouldn't look back on the past with remorse
And the memories wouldn't be sacred.

1916

Translated from the Russian by Larissa Szporluk

SAMUIL MARSHAK

Samuil (Samuel) **Marshak** (1887–1964), poet, children's author, and translator, was born in Voronezh in 1887. His father worked at soap-making factories as a foreman. The philanthropist and scholar Baron David Günzburg (1857–1910) took an interest in the gifted Jewish youth and in 1902 introduced him to the influential critic Vladimir Stasov (1824–1906). Stasov was impressed by Marshak's "masterful command of *our* language" (italics added), helped arrange his transfer to a gymnasium in St. Petersburg, and served as his mentor.

Marshak's poems first appeared in 1904, in the St. Petersburg monthly *Jewish Life* (*Evreiskaia zhizn'*). While in Yalta in 1906 he became active in the illegal Poalei Zion movement and helped organize its branch and distribute *The Jewish Workers' Chronicle* (*Evreiskaia rabochaia khronika*), publishing his Russian translation of "Di shvue" (The Oath) by S. An-sky (in vol. 1). In the middle to late 1900s, Marshak created a body of Zionist verse, some of which appeared in periodicals and collectives such as *Young Judea* (*Molodaia Iudeia,* Yalta) but never in a separate book. Marshak and his Soviet students and censors later obliterated their existence. His Zionist connections, including those with Poalei Zion ("Workers of Zion") activist Ber Borochov (1881–1917), continued into the early 1910s. In 1908 Marshak became a contributor to *Satyricon* (see Sasha Cherny in vol. 1) and in the 1910s published satirical verses and sketches in provincial and central newspapers. In 1911 Marshak and the poet Yakov Godin (1887–1954) journeyed to Palestine and Syria. In 1912, unable to enter a university in Russia, Marshak went to England and Ireland. While in England he studied at the University of London, traveled, and worked on translations of English poets, including Shakespeare, Blake, Robert Burns, Coleridge, and Wordsworth, and English folk ballads.

Marshak and his wife worked with Jewish refugee children in Voronezh after returning to Russia in 1914. The death of Marshak's young daughter the following year directed him toward children's literature. In 1917 Marshak moved to Ekaterinodar (now Krasnodar), where he headed the province's section of orphanages. His first book, *Satires and Epigrams*, appeared in 1919 in Ekaterinodar under the penname Dr. Friken. After the Reds captured Ekaterinodar, Marshak co-organized the first Soviet children's theater with Elena Vasilieva (Cherubina de Gabriak, 1887–1928) and co-wrote plays, collected in *Theater for Children* (Krasnodar, 1922; later reprinted).

Marshak moved to Petrograd in 1922 to join the new Theater for Young Spectators. In 1925 he became head of the children's literature section of the State Publishing House in Leningrad. In the 1920s to early 1930s he also edited several children's magazines. Many of Marshak's books for children became classics, including *Kids in the Cage* (1923), *Fire* (1923), *Story of the Silly Little Mouse* (1923), *Baggage* (1926), *So Absentminded* (1930), and others. In 1930, when Marshak became the butt of ideological criticism, Maxim Gorky declared him the "founder of our children's literature." When the Children's State Publishing House was established on Gorky's initiative, Marshak became its editor-in-chief. He worked in this capacity until 1937, when a number of his staff were purged; to escape a possible arrest, Marshak fled to Moscow.

Marshak's popular anti-Nazi feuilletons in verse appeared during World War II, along with cartoons by Kukryniksy (the collective composite pen name of three artists), in *Pravda* and military papers. Marshak's translations were gathered in several volumes, and his later verses were published in *Collected Lyrics* (1962). His greatest achievement as a translator was his renderings of Shakespeare's sonnets. Marshak also translated from the Yiddish, including the work of Itsik Fefer, Shmuel Halkin, Dovid Hofshtein, and Leyb Kvitko. In his latter years he continued to write occasional Jewish poems, which were not published in the USSR. In 1961 Marshak published *At the Beginning of Life*, a tender memoir featuring scenes of a childhood and hinting at an Orthodox Jewish life. A beloved Soviet children's author, Marshak died in Moscow in 1964.

Although never published as a separate collection, Marshak's verse of the 1900s–1910s presents the Jewish historian with arguably the most accomplished body of Zionist verse written at the time in Russian. The thematic repertoire of Marshak's Jewish poetry encompasses not only his inspirational verses about young Zionists but also Biblical legends and dramatic historical events, such as the Spanish Inquisition. His translations of Hayyim Nahman Bialik, Zalman Shneur, and David Shimonovich (Shimoni), which appeared in *Young Judea* (Yalta, 1906), *The Jewish Anthology* (Moscow, 1918; see V. Khodasevich, L. Jaffe, and M. Gershenzon in vol. 1), and other Jewish-Russian publications of the late 1900s–1910s, are linked to his early poetry both thematically and formally.

Marshak was a talented if unadventurous poet in the classical vein. The powerful Zionist energy of his early poems was clad in the perfectly starched shirts of his classical prosody. The five-part poem *Palestine* (1916) apparently appeared in the Moscow Zionist weekly *Jewish Life* in 1916 and was later included in the landmark collection *By the Rivers of Babylon: National Jewish Lyrics in World Poetry* (1917), edited by Leyb Jaffe (in vol. 1).

Palestine

1.

Now when my eyes grow dark from grieving
I conjure up our fathers' lands:
The stormy sea's expanse where weaving
Boats full of oarsmen's rhythmic hands

Tilt on the crest, then finely diving
Speed on toward town, the lazy hum,
The ringing shouts of vendors' striving,
The coffeehouse where those who come

Will find a game, a hookah ready
Beneath low vaults and cool, bare walls,
Where nearby, dusty, slow but steady,
A caravan of camels crawls.

The Bedouin who walks behind them,
Dark skinned, free, and dignified,
Need make no gesture to align them;
Their straight procession warms his pride.

Unbothered by the flow of gritty
Life, the uproar of the town,
Now near the gates of the Holy City
He lets his camels hunker down.

And now, beneath a peaceful wonder,
An olive grove's discovered shade,
His camels sleep, their legs bent under,
Till the morning call must be obeyed.

Long ages past Jacob's descendants
Took to their mournful exiles' ways,
But still the nomads' independence
Preserves the charm of far-off days.

They move like dreams of past devotion
That modern city dwellers scan;
You cannot watch without emotion
Their slender, filing caravan.

2.

How strange that in the cyclic flowing
Of peoples, centuries, events,
The past's not washed away, that, growing
Upon our country's soil, the sense

Of names survives, of sacred places.
In a poor village of fellahin
Called Anotot, in this oasis,
The prophet lived who learned to keen

The fate of Israel's exiled nation . . .
Eyeing the speechless stones around,
I sought what tied my pained sensation
So closely to this rugged ground.

It was not forbears' graves, the gashes
That mark the sites of their last retreat,
But Jeremiah, born from ashes,
Standing there in the village street.

The *Lamentations*, slow and swelling
As father read on the Ninth of Ab,[1]
Sound near an Arab's modest dwelling;
From Prophet's holy lips they throb.

3.

I trail the caravan: the cunning
Bells are ringing, singing, the sand
Emits a sound that's low and running
As if gold ocean moved on land.

---

1. The Ninth of Ab (*Tisha b'Av*), the ninth day of the Jewish month of Ab (corresponds to July–August), is a day of mourning and fasting for Jews. It memorializes several mournful events in Jewish history: the burning of the city of Jerusalem by King Nebuchadnezzar of Babylon, the destruction of the Temple in Jerusalem in 70 C.E. by Emperor Titus's forces, and others. The same five activities prohibited on Yom Kippur are prohibited on the Ninth of Ab: eating and drinking, bathing, anointing, wearing (leather) shoes, and engaging in sexual relations.

My midday hour I spent by dreaming
Through spineless ecstasies of heat,
But I recall a cool spring streaming
And rustling leaves; that hour was sweet.

The spring runs out from nearby boulders,
Innocent as in paradise;
Whoever drinks with bending shoulders
Will gaze upon reflected eyes.

The Bedouins' way through once granted,
An Eastern girl, dark-skinned and slight,
Stands at the spring, her jug down-slanted.
She's gorgeous in the blazing light.

And still more sudden, one sees showing
Beyond the fences' green confines
A fragrant lemon grove and glowing
Clusters of grapes on arbor vines.

O Happy land! Longing, privation,
I'm ready still to bear the load
For one such hour of meditation,
Of perfect peace along the road.

When will you come through torments' welter,
Nomads across the world's wide span,
Home to the welling source, the shelter,
As did this swaying caravan?

                        4.

But those today who have come questing,
Who did return to their promised land,
Have found, not long-awaited resting,
But fates in struggle never planned.

Belligerent and wily neighbors
Disturbed their dreams of peaceful life;
Their years of stubborn, honest labors
Were stained with bloody civil strife.

And as they sowed the desert, sinking
Their blessed, healing stands of trees
Fever crept in, unnoticed, slinking,
Killing their youth by slow degrees.

Yet now in the desert one oasis
After another rises fast,
The fighting spirit at their basis
Uncrushable from first to last.

There the guards, on foot or mounted,
Throughout the watches of the night
Preserve the vineyards times uncounted,
Alert in the dark's unnerving spite.

The sky rains stars on those who listen,
Thick as the leaves that autumn scrapes,
Mild drops of condensation glisten
On bunches of the blue-black grapes,

And out beyond the fence, where cooling
Sands stretch endlessly away,
The sly night jackals, weeping, drooling,
In fits of fear and longing, bay.

5.

We lived in crowded camps, in tenting.
A ring of hills ran all around;
Great tangles of dry bushes, venting,
Smoked and burned on the scorching ground.

My old comrade, upon arrival,
Picked out on nearby slopes in haze
A wretched village's survival—
Zorah of Samson's infant days.

Now here's where we need Samson's service;
From dawn till nearly round the clock,
We're chasing scorpions and serpents,
Burning the brush and hauling rock.

How patiently the crew is thronging
To build the valley's well today.
The scream of a donkey made with longing
Disturbs the silence, dies away.

But now night breezes waft and hover;
Large wreaths of sunset roses blaze;
A flock of goats, quick to recover,
Runs easily downslope to graze.

Moonrise comes brighter than expected;
Each constellation claims its place;
With curtains of our tent rejected
We gaze upon the night sky's face.

As if a bubbling spring's insistence
Were caught in song upon the air,
Our Arab watchman in the distance
Intones his verse of nighttime prayer.

He stands there white in moonlight, glowing,
As in the realm of nearing dreams
The spell of droning prayer is growing
Along with the orb's increasing beams.

The night's mysterious candescence
Floats my soul till it drinks its fill.
A luminous angelic presence
Alights upon the selfsame hill

On which he stood when times were other,
When angels visited the earth,
And told to Samson's humble mother
The good news of his coming birth.

1916

Translated from the Russian by Andrew Von Hendy and Maxim D. Shrayer

SOFIA PARNOK

Sofia Parnok (1885–1933), the "Russian Sappho," was born to an educated Jewish family in Taganrog, Anton Cheknov's birthplace. Parnok's father ran a pharmacy, and her mother was a physician. Parnok's mother died in 1891 soon after giving birth to twins, both of whom became writers: Valentin Parnakh (1891–1951; in vol. 1) and Elizaveta Tarakhovskaya (1891–1968). The family name was spelled "Parnokh," but Sofia Parnok and her brother both spelled it slightly differently, Sofia electing the more Slavic-sounding "Parnok." The Parnokh children received no Jewish religious upbringing but were given a solid European education.

Parnok attended the Taganrog Empress Maria Gymnasium and studied piano in 1904–06 at the St. Petersburg Conservatory and the Geneva Conservatory of Music. She later studied law at the Bestuzhev Higher Academy (Kursy) for Women at St. Petersburg University. Her first poems, sustained by symbolist aesthetics, were published in 1906. Parnok's first long-term relationship, with Nadezhda Polyakova, lasted from 1902 to 1907. She married the playwright Vladimir Volkenshtein (1881–1974) in a Jewish ceremony in 1907, but they divorced two years later; in a letter to her friend Mikhail Gnessin (1883–1957), the founder of the Society for Jewish Music, Parnok later acknowledged, "I have never, unfortunately, been in love with a man." In 1913 Parnok converted to Russian Orthodoxy, perhaps believing, as some others among the Jewish-Russian artistic intelligentsia have believed, that conversion would accord her greater harmony with Russian culture—without a disavowal of her Jewish self.

A poet outside literary movements, in the 1910s Parnok participated in the literary life of St. Petersburg. An affair with the great poet Marina Tsvetaeva (1892–1941) entranced Parnok in 1914–16; Tsvetaeva dedicated to her the cycle "Girlfriend" (1915). Prior to 1917, Parnok's poetry appeared in *European Messenger* (*Vestnik Evropy*), *Russian Thought* (*Russkaia mysl'*), and other periodicals. Parnok's first collection, *Poems* (St. Petersburg, 1916), displayed her fine mastery of versification. Parnok published perceptive criticism and reviews under the pen name Andrey Polyanin as a staff critic for *Northern Notes* (*Severnye zapiski*) in 1913–17.

Parnok lived in the Crimean town of Sudak in 1917–21 with her second major partner, actress Lyudmila Erarskaya (1890–1964). Having fallen under the spell of the ancient lesbian poet in 1914, Parnok consumedly read—and rewrote—Sappho. Her Sapphic stylizations appeared in her collection *Roses of Pieria* (Moscow–Petrograd, 1922). Parnok settled in Moscow in 1922. She became a member of the "Lyrical Circle"—an informal literary group whose members included Vladislav Khodasevich (in vol. 1), Leonid Grossman (see Leonid Tsypkin in vol. 2), and Vladimir Lidin (in vol. 1); the members of this group emphasized literary clarity and harmony.

Parnok had an increasingly difficult time making a living and publishing. In the 1920s she managed to publish three collections with small print runs: *The Vine* (1923), *Music* (1928), and *In a Half-Whisper* (1928). In 1926–28 Parnok poured her energies into the publishing cooperative "The Knot" (Uzel). The premier scholar of Parnok, Diana Lewis Burgin, described Parnok's Soviet years as a "double poetic isolation"; Parnok was alienated from the Soviet literary environment both as an apolitical poet and as a lesbian writing lesbian lyrics. To support herself, Parnok worked for publishing houses translating Henri Barbusse, Marcel Proust, Romain Rolland, and others from the French. After 1928 she was unable to publish poetry. In 1929 she completed the libretto for the opera *Almast* by Aleksandr Spendiarov (1871–1928). Based on an Armenian legend shaped by the Armenian classic Ovanes Tumanyan (1869–1923), *Almast* premiered in 1930.

Starting in 1925, Parnok lived with the mathematician Olga Tsuberbiller (1885–1975). In her late poetry, Parnok shed her ornamental richness of diction and prosody for the sake of conversational lyrical simplicity couched in undexterous meters. Her love for the physicist Nina Vedeneeva (1882–1955) precipitated *Ursa Minor* (1932) and *The Useless Good* (1932–33), two cycles of startling lyrics. Parnok died of a heart attack outside Moscow in 1933. Her first *Collected Works* appeared in the United States in 1979, edited by Sofia Polyakova. Parnok editions and scholarship on Parnok finally appeared in Russia in the post-Soviet period.

As early as 1903, in the poem "To the Jews," Parnok expressed faith in the renascence of the Jewish nation. A number of Parnok's poems drew from the stories of the Old and New Testaments. In her poetry Parnok continued to ask controversial, and occasionally Judaic, questions even after her conversion to Russian Orthodoxy.

All three poems chosen here were written between 1913 and 1922 and gathered in "Green Notebook," gifted by Parnok to her friend, the writer Evgeniya Gertsyk (1878–1944). "My anguish does the Lord not heed . . ." and "Not for safekeeping for awhile . . ." appeared in the group collection *Lyrical Circle* (Moscow, 1922); Parnok included "My anguish does the Lord not heed . . ." in her third collection, *The Vine* (1923).

* * *

My anguish does the Lord not heed,
And does not gladden me with coldness,
My tired flesh He does not lead
From out a fevered, flaming vortex,

And people still drink up my lips,
Undrunk yet their last drops of fever.
Like age-old mead, my blood is thick,—
Oh, sultry servitude! My Egypt! . . .

But still I dream, a light-blue current
Flows upward from the hollow deep
And I ascend,—and all alone—
I'm standing face to face with Thee.

1913–1922

Hagar

So Hagar sits in obloquy
And gushing piteously
The spring pours out a threnody
Beer-lahai-roi.[1]

Yon lands belong to Abraham,
But this expanse—to none:
In front of her, the wilderness
To Shur itself does run.

Despair, despair instinctual!
In her Egyptian eyes,
Disconsolate, elongated,
A nascent teardrop cries.

---

1. *Beer-lahai-roi* (Heb.) is usually translated as "the well/source of the Living One Who sees me"; see Gen. 16, esp. 16:13–16, where the Angel of the Lord speaks to Hagar near a drinking source on the road to Shur: "And [Hagar] called the Lord who spoke to her, 'You Are El-roi,' by which she meant, 'Have I not gone on seeing after He saw me!' Therefore the well was called Beer-lahai-roi; it is between Kadesh and Bered.—Hagar bore a son to Abram, and Abram gave the son that Hagar bore him the name Ishmael. Abram was eighty-six years old when Hagar bore Ishmael to Abram."

The frigid torrent's shimmering,
A dagger's cutting edge,—
O, terrifying, childless,
O, dread proprietress!

"Hagar!"—And her countenance
Dark-skinned did drain of blood.
She looks,—her eyebrows lifted at
The angel of the Lord . . .

1913–1922

* * *

Not for safekeeping for awhile,—
For the altar, not donation,—
For the fire, the fire, its oblation
Rapt Israel brought in times gone by!

And pleasing to the Lords's own nostrils
Was smoke from sacrificial fires,
Because a consecrated offering
In truth cannot be taken back . . .

You, pastors of the flocks of Christ,
Merchants of patristic bearing!
What is your gift? A simple price:
Deposit and withdrawal banking!

And Israel, your ancient torch
Shall shine above the world again,
The cross atop the church is stained
And God is not inside that church!

1913–1922

Translated from the Russian by Diana L. Burgin

Sofia Parnok, "Ne vnial toske moei Gospod' . . . ," "Agar," and "Ne na khranen'ie do pory. . . ." English translation copyright © by Diana L. Burgin. Introduction and note copyright © by Maxim D. Shrayer.

❋ Revolution and ❋ Betrayal 1917–1939

Russia was the last major European country to grant its Jews equal rights and freedoms. One of the great accomplishments of the February 1917 Revolution was the 20 March 1917 ukase "Abolition of Restrictions Based on Religion and Nationality": "All the laws and statutes are abolished, whether in effect throughout all Russia or in its various parts, which establish—on the basis of the adherence of citizens of Russia to a particular religious denomination or sect or by reasons of nationality—any restrictions. . . ."[1] For the Jews of the former Russian Empire, this meant abolition of the Pale of Settlement and of official discrimination at all levels of society, including *numerus clausus* at institutions of learning. For Jews worldwide, November 1917 brought not only the Bolshevik Revolution but also the Balfour Declaration, which made the Zionist dream of a Jewish state in Israel a foreseeable possibility. In the years following the 1917 revolutions, as the social and cultural life of European Russia stabilized after the end of the civil war, Jewish-Russian artists expressed their sense of liberation by shaping the early Soviet cultural landscape. At the same time, the official campaign against Judaism and traditional Jewish life proceeded at a fast clip.

The 1920s and early 1930s were the most fascinating and turbulent time in the history of Jewish-Russian culture; indeed, these years saw an eruption of Jewish-Russian creativity. Anti-Jewish restrictions had been temporarily removed both de jure and de facto. Thousands of Jews born in the 1890s–1900s poured into the Russian cultural mainstream. They came from Yiddish-speaking and Yiddish- and Russian-speaking bilingual households of the former Pale, as well as from the already thoroughly Russianized Jewish families of such large urban centers as Kiev, Odessa, or Kharkov. While the former Pale gave early Soviet culture the majority of

---

1. See *The Russian Provisional Government*, ed. R. Paul Browder and Alexander F. Kerensky, vol. 1, 211–12 (Stanford: Stanford University Press, 1961).

its Jewish writers, all areas of the former Russian Empire where Jews had been allowed to live, including the Urals and Siberia, contributed their young and initially enthusiastic Jewish authors (e.g., Iosif Utkin [1903–1944]). So many remarkable literary Jewish-Russian figures burst onto the Soviet literary scene in the early Soviet decades that it has been impossible to do them all justice even in an anthology of this scope and ambition.

The 1920s were also a time of openness in the discussion of antisemitism and Jewish identity by Soviet authors writing in Russian and Yiddish. Some of the most penetrating fictional treatments of the parallel dynamics of swift Soviet assimilation of the Jews and the persistence of popular antisemitism appeared in the 1920s. Of the authors in this anthology, Andrey Sobol (1888–1926) and Mikhail Kozakov (1897–1954) readily come to mind in this connection. Writing with astounding linguistic power, often in a language that was not that of their parents, Jews made countless and peerless contributions to the Russian poetry, prose, and drama of the 1920s and 1930s. Jewish-Russian writers were represented in every corner of the early Soviet literary scene. They included Lev Lunts (1901–1924), Veniamin Kaverin (1902–1989), and Elizaveta Polonskaya (1890–1969), members of the Serapion Brothers group. Among these Jewish-Russian writers were inveterate avant-gardist poets, such as the imagist Matvey Royzman (1896–1973) and the jazz-poet Valentin Parnakh (1891–1951). They also counted among their ranks the most gifted literary representative of the Russian formalist movement, author and theorist Viktor Shklovsky (1891–1984). The writers featured in this anthology betoken much of the political and aesthetic spectrum of the literary groups of the Soviet 1920s: the constructivists Ilya Selvinsky (1899–1968), Vera Inber (1890–1972), and Eduard Bagritsky (1895–1934); Semyon Kirsanov (1906–1972) from the Left Front of Art (LEF); Yury Libedinsky (1898–1959) from the Russian Association of Proletarian Writers (RAPP); and others. Some of the best Jewish-Russian writers of the early Soviet decades, including one of the strongest Jewish-Russian geniuses, Isaac Babel, came from Odessa and the Black Sea area and collectively formed, in the eyes of their readers and critics, the so-called South-Western School (Victor Shklovsky's expression). Jewish-Russian literature gave the early Soviet readers their most beloved satirical writers, the Odessans Ilya Ilf (1897–1937) and his (questionably) non-Jewish coauthor Evgeny Petrov (1903–1942). By the early 1930s, after the relatively independent literary and artistic groups of the 1920s had been suppressed and dismantled, Jewish-Russian writers keenly participated in the formation of the Union of Soviet Writers and the institutionalization of Soviet literature.

The First Congress of Soviet Writers convened in Moscow in 1934. The statistics of its officially published stenographic report are revealing.[2] Of the 597 Soviet delegates, 201 were Russians and 113, about 19 percent, were Jews. While Jews made up only about 1.8 percent of the country's population, Jewish delegates outnumbered

---

2. See Yehuda Slutsky, "Jews at the First Congress of Soviet Writers," *Soviet Jewish Affairs* 2.2 (1972): 61–70.

Georgians (28), Ukrainians (25), Armenians (19), Tatars (19), Belorussians (17), and so forth. There were 57 Jews in the Moscow delegation (second after 91 Russians) and 11 Jews in the Leningrad organization (second after 30 Russians). Twenty-four Yiddish writers were delegates at the congress (holding the fourth place after Russian-, Ukrainian-, and Georgian-language writers), but the vast majority (about 70 percent) of all the Jewish delegates were writing in Russian, and only a few of the Jewish delegates were writing in other languages, such as Ukrainian or Belorussian, or in more than one language.[3] Of the more than 130 writers featured in this anthology, 18 were delegates at the 1934 congress, 13 of whom are included in this section.

One of the most telling aspects of these statistics for the story and history of Jewish-Russian literature was that Jews from the former Pale, whether or not they physically migrated to Russia from where they had grown up, were almost exclusively (im)migrating to Russian literature, although they might have been linguistically equipped to become Ukrainian or Belorussian authors. This movement was to have been expected, so powerful was the draw of the expanses of Russian literary culture. Only a small minority of Jews from the former Pale born in the 1890s–1900s, such as Leonid Pervomaisky (1908–1973), became Jewish-Ukrainian writers, that is, Jews writing in Ukrainian as opposed to Jewish-Russian or Yiddish writers from Ukraine. And even fewer followed the earlier example of the older Zmitrok Biadulia (Samuil Plavnik, 1886–1941) and joined the ranks of the Jewish-Belorussian *pismenniki* during the early Soviet decades.

Writing about Isaac Babel and the early Soviet decades, Shimon Markish proposed that the works by Jews "represent the first in time . . . and the most significant other-national branch [*inonatsional'naia vetv'*] in Russian-language Soviet literature." While the report and activities of the First Congress of Soviet Writers made very obvious the omnipresence of Jews in Soviet literature, neither the congress nor Soviet literary criticism, more generally, acknowledged the existence of a bicultural Jewish-Russian literature as such. The only "Jewish" (*evreiskaia*) literature that fit the mold of the Soviet policy on nationality and of national cultures was Yiddish literature, at the time still enjoying the official green light. Yet one should be mindful of the fact that, despite the significant presence of Jewish delegates and of Yiddish writers, the First Congress of Soviet Writers did not feature a separate speech about or presentation on Jewish literature. As Vladimir Khazan pointed out in 1996, "the Jewish theme was being tendentiously provincialized, shifted to the peripheral spaces of Soviet culture." The congress also made clear that an unspoken taboo on Jewish topics was already in place in Soviet Russian letters. The Israeli-Russian critic Khazan has argued that as early as the 1930s this resistance to the presentation of the Jewish experience in Russian literature stemmed from "the official Soviet political line, based on the idea that the 'Jewish question' does not exist, as it has been completely and finally

3. See "Prilozhenie 5" in *Pervyi vsesoiuznyi s"ezd sovetskikh pisatelei. 1934. Steno graficheskii otchet*, 697–708 (Moscow: Khudozhestvennaia literatura, 1934).

resolved in the Soviet Union." (In the famous satirical novel *The Golden Calf* (1931) by Ilya Ilf and Evgeny Petrov (excerpt in vol. 1), a Soviet journalist tells an American Jewish activist visiting the USSR, "We no longer have this question." "How can there be no Jewish question? . . . But aren't there Jewish people in Russia?" the American presses on. "There are Jews, but no question," the propagandizing journalist replies.)

It was the position of Shimon Markish that Jewish-Russian literature "was suffocated and ceased to exist on the eve of World War II. . . . Babel's literary generation . . . turned out to be the last one; after it was a desert." The quality and volume of the material gathered in the last section of volume 1 and in volume 2 of this anthology does not empirically support Markish's view. What is tragically true is that the Jewish-Russian periodicals and editions had disappeared in the USSR by the early 1930s, not to be resuscitated until the late 1980s. The Jewish-Russian samizdat of the 1970s–80s is another story, to be discussed in the introduction to the section "Late Soviet Empire: 1964–1991." As Dmitry Elyashevich put it, Jewish-Russian print culture in the 1920s "for a short time agonized in the ugly forms of OZET [acronym for the Society for the Settlement of Jewish Toilers on Land] publications, becoming an ersatz of the same sort as was the politics of 'Birobidzhanism.'" Continuing into the 1930s, the propaganda publications of the "Jews on the land" movement and the Birobidzhan project produced little of literary value in Russian a notable exception being, *Jews on the Land* (1929) by Viktor Fink (1888–1973), featured in the pages to follow.

In the 1930s, a group of lesser writers (e.g., Lev Fridland, David Khait, Lina Neiman, Leon Ostrover, Lev Vaisenberg) treated Jewish themes within the prescribed guidelines of the Soviet—and Stalinist—rhetoric on Jewish history and identity. (Margarita Aliger's poem "To a Jewish Girl," written in connection with the annexation of eastern Poland after the Soviet–Nazi Pact of 1939 and featured in the section "War and Terror: 1939–1953," well illustrates such ideologically faithful Jewish-Russian works.) The selection of materials for the section on the early Soviet decades has been especially challenging. I have not included, for instance, the artistically wanting but historically and ideologically fascinating novella *The Nose*, its title recalling Nikolai Gogol's famous St. Petersburg tale, by the Warsaw-born author and Communist activist Bruno Yasensky (Polish spelling Jasieński, born Wiktor Bruno Zysman, 1901–1938). In 1929 Yasensky made his way from western Europe to the USSR and soon transitioned from Polish to Russian. Serialized in *Izvestia* in 1936, Yasensky's *The Nose* employed Gogolian phantasmagorical realism to expose the absurdity of Nazi racial anthropology. I have also left out such nationally renowned authors for young readers as Lev Kassil (1905–1970) and Ruvim Fraerman (1891–1972), who entered the literary scene in the 1920s and early 1930s.

Despite the various degrees of revolutionary and Soviet enthusiasm among many Jewish-Russian authors in the 1920s and early 1930s, by the late 1930s echoes of a growing anxiety over the future of Jewishness in the USSR began to register in the works of Jewish-Russian writers (in this anthology, see Eduard Bagritsky's *February*,

Elizaveta Polonskaya's "Encounter," and the poems by Arkady Shteynberg [1907–1984]). Alarming was not only the rise in popular antisemitism, still discussed in the Soviet press and vociferously opposed by the Bolshevik Party, but also the realization that the Soviet rhetoric on Jewishness was, perhaps, more harmful to the survival of Jewish identity than the tsarist-era policies. And yet, until the early 1930s, Babel, Bagritsky, Ehrenburg, and many other writers who had been born in the 1890s and 1900s and experienced the horrors of anti-Jewish violence during the 1903–05 pogroms and the civil war felt that Bolshevism was still a better alternative for the three million Soviet Jews. The seizure of power by the Nazis in Germany in 1933 brought the anxiety of many Jewish-Russian writers to a new level as they now faced the reality of Europe's Jews being collectively placed by history between Stalin and Hitler.

LEONID KANNEGISER

Leonid Kannegiser (1896–1918), the poet who earned a place in history by assassinating a major Bolshevik official, was born in St. Petersburg to an affluent Jewish family. His father, Akim (Joakim) Kannegiser, a brilliant engineer, was granted hereditary nobility (a great exception for a Russian Jew who was not a convert to Christianity) and in 1907 became chairman of the board of Nikolaevsky Shipyards in St. Petersburg. Because of his father's prominent position, Kannegiser grew up in an exceptionally privileged social environment that few Jews enjoyed at the time. Tsarist generals mingled with radicals and artists in the Kannegisers' St. Petersburg house; several writers, notably Georgy Ivanov and Marina Tsvetaeva, later reminisced about the Kannegisers' salon. In 1915–17, Kannegiser studied at the Petrograd Polytechnic Institute, where he was an active member of an organization of Jewish students. Kannegiser participated in literary events and readings and had several poems published in *Northern Notes* (*Severnye zapiski*) and *Russian Thought* (*Russkaia mysl'*). He aligned himself most closely with poets of the acmeist movement.

After the February 1917 Revolution, which Kannegiser welcomed, he entered the Mikhailovsky Artillery Officers' Cadet School and soon became chairman of the Union of Socialist Cadets. While not initially hostile to the October Revolution, Kannegiser's view of the new Bolshevik regime turned negative after the signing of the peace treaty of Brest-Litovsk in March 1918. In the summer of 1918, a group of cadets and officers from Kannegiser's circle was arrested by the Cheka and executed; among them was Viktor Pereltsveig, an officer and Kannegiser's intimate friend. On the morning of 30 August 1918, Kannegiser entered No. 6, Palace Square, where the offices of the Interior Department of the Northern Commune and the Petrograd Cheka were located. The Northern Commune incorporated Petrograd and the vast surrounding regions, and its interior minister was Mikhail (Moisey) Uritsky (1873–1918); Uritsky doubled as chairman of the Petrograd Cheka. When Uritsky arrived in the office, Kannegiser pulled out a gun and shot him. He fled but was arrested and charged with Uritsky's murder. The official published account of the investigation indicated that after his arrest Kannegiser admitted he killed Uritsky not by order of a party or organization but on his own, to avenge the execution of his friend Pereltsveig by the Bolsheviks.

The best-known account of Kannegiser's life and a version of the assassination story were offered in "The Assassination of Uritsky" (1923) by the émigré Mark Aldanov (in vol. 1). In the past two decades, Aldanov's heroic-romantic version was questioned by historians and journalists. Conspiracy theorists are tickled by the fact that on the same day, 30 August 1918, Lenin was wounded by gunshots outside the Mikhelson Factory in Moscow. The person charged with the assassination attempt was Fanny Kaplan (1890–1918), a Socialist-Revolutionary who had served a sentence of hard labor for her revolutionary work in the tsarist years and was half blind. Kaplan allegedly stated that she wanted to kill Lenin for his "betrayal of the revolution." Like Kannegiser, Kaplan was Jewish, and both were executed on the same day, 3 September 1918. Suggestions have been made that Kannegiser was set up by forces within the Bolshevik regime that were trying to get rid of Uritsky. Others have suggested that both the murder of Uritsky and the attempt on Lenin's life were orchestrated to give the Bolshevik regime the justification to unleash the Red Terror in early September 1918.

In his *Book of Life*, the great Jewish historian Simon Dubnow (1860–1941) characterized Kannegiser's assassination of Uritsky as a "heroic deed." Émigré anti-Bolsheviks and Jewish apologists alike have capitalized on Kannegiser's story to stress that not all Jews were pro-Bolshevik and that Kannegiser's loyalties to Russia— and to justice—outweighed his Jewish national self-interest. At the same time, one still hears today from the ultranationalist Russians that the murder of one Jew (Uritsky) by another (Kannegiser) did not stop "the Jewish Cheka" from "murdering" thousands of Russians.

Both poems chosen for this anthology appeared in the memorial volume *Leonid Kannegiser* (Paris, 1928). In addition to a selection of the poet's verses, the volume contained essays by émigrés Mark Aldanov, Georgy Ivanov (1894–1958), and Georgy Adamovich (1894–1972).

Initially a poet of acmeist orientation, Kannegiser also composed stylizations with elements of peasant folklore under the impact of his friendship with Sergey Esenin. Thematically, his poems fall into two groups: religious and political. While no direct evidence points to Kannegiser's conversion to Christianity, his religious poems feature Catholic ("Poems about St. Francis,"1915), Russian Orthodox ("Yaroslavl," 1916; "Snowy Church," 1918), and Judaic motifs. "A Jewish Wedding" (1916) possibly refers to the wedding of Kannegiser's brother Sergey, who committed suicide in 1917.

By passing the 20 March 1917 ukase "The Abolition of Restrictions Based on Religion and Nationality," the Provisional Government abolished all forms of legal inequality for Jews in Russia. One of Kannegiser's last poems, "Regimental Inspection" (1917), registers an enthusiasm shared by educated assimilated Jews in the first months of the February 1917 Revolution.

A Jewish Wedding

Seven melting candles are burning,
With another held in His hand,
While an organ surges with yearning
For the ancient Jewish homeland.

Oh, the rabbi, stern with deep feeling,
Raised his hand, the ring, to rejoice,
To the drowsy synagogue ceiling,
Like a soaring falcon, his voice.

Adonai! Adonai! Dread power!
Do you hear that keen wailing whine?
Under scythes, the rose, softest flower
Of Your gardens in Palestine.

1916

Regimental Inspection

The sun makes their bayonets glisten—
Foot soldiers. Don Cossacks in force
Beyond, at attention to listen:
Kerensky astride a white horse.[1]

His eyes are fatigued with endeavor.
Long silence in corps upon corps.
His voice, to remember forever,
Of Russia, of freedom, of war.

Fire, iron—the heart alchemizes,
The spirit—green oak against threats,
And the eagle, *Marseillaise*, arises
Aloft from our silver cornets.

---

1. Kerensky, Alexander (1881–1970)— Russian political leader in the 1900s and 1910s; in the short-lived Provisional Government (1917) he was, in turn, minister of justice, minister of war, and later both prime minister and supreme commander of the Russian army.

To arms! And the demons will cower.
As darkness descends over all,
Archangels of limitless power
Will envy our cavalier fall.

If rasping my racking death rattle,
O Mother, O land I love best,
If after defeat in some battle,
In agony, shot in the chest,

Near death, with a dream of pure pleasure
In bliss at that entrance and source,
With Russia and freedom, I'll treasure
Kerensky astride a white horse.

1917

Translated from the Russian by J.B. Sisson and Maxim D. Shrayer

MIKHAIL GERSHENZON

Mikhail (Meilikh) **Gershenzon** (1869–1925), literary historian, philosopher, and essayist, was born in Kishinev, Bessarabia (now Moldova). His father, a merchant, gave him a traditional Jewish upbringing. After graduating from a private gymnasium in 1887, Gershenzon spent two years studying in Berlin. In 1889 he received special permission to enter Moscow University (Jewish access was restricted by the *numerus clausus*), graduating in 1894 from the Faculty of History and Philology. Gershenzon's paper on Aristotle and Plutarch received a gold medal in 1893 and was published in 1895.

An unconverted Jew, Gershenzon was unable to obtain an academic post and earned a living as a writer and journalist. In the 1900s he undertook monumental research on the literary culture of Moscow, on Decembrism, and on Russian westernizers. Gershenzon's books include *A.I. Herzen's Social-Political Views* (1906), *The History of Young Russia* (1908), and *Griboedov's Moscow* (1914). His further investigations concerned the broader contexts of Russian nineteenth-century political thought, including the Slavophiles (especially Ivan Kireevsky and Yury Samarin) and Pyotr Chaadaev (his 1908 book *P.Ya. Chaadaev. Life and Thought*). In the late 1900s–1910s, Gershenzon enjoyed the reputation of a chronicler of the Moscow intelligentsia. Aleksandr Pushkin was for Gershenzon an ideal embodiment of a cultural synthesis of the national and the universal, and Gershenzon read the poet's life and work through the prism of his own beliefs about one's personal quest for the transcendent, one's place in history, and one's duty before society. His studies were collected in *Essays on Pushkin* (1926).

Organized on Gershenzon's initiative and published with his introduction, the collection *Landmarks* (Moscow, 1909) became a major event in Russia's cultural life. Besides Gershenzon, whose essay was titled "Creative Self-Consciousness," the contributors included religious philosophers Nikolay Berdyaev, Sergey Bulgakov, and Semyon Frank, legal theorist Bogdan Kistyakovsky, economist and politician Pyotr Struve, and politician and author Aleksandr Izgoev (Aron Lande); three of the seven contributors were of Jewish background. Affected by liberal and Marxist thought as well as a resurgence of Russian religious philosophy, the contributors to *Landmarks* explored the intellectual landscape of the Russian intelligentsia after the failed 1905 Revolution, seeking to define a new agenda—ethical, religious, and philosophical—for Russia's vision of its future.

Gershenzon published several essays on Jewish culture and history and on Judaism.

They include "The People Tried by Fire" (1916; early version 1915) and "Yoke and Genius" (1916, about Hayyim Nahman Bialik). The main theme of his book-essay *Key of Faith* (1922) is man's struggle with God and modern man's relationship with the Bible. His most important work on a Jewish subject, *Destinies of the Jewish People* (Petrograd–Berlin, 1922), betrays his universalist vision of Jewish history and culture but also his rejection of political Zionism, which he did not consider—or perhaps did not have sufficient Jewish historical training to consider—a solution for Jewish liberation and spiritual renewal.

In March 1917 Gershenzon became one the founders of the All-Russia Union of Writers and its first chairman. He remained in Russia after the Bolshevik Revolution and worked in educational and cultural institutions. Gershenzon's books of the time included *The Poet's Vision* (1919), *The Dream and Thought of I.S. Turgenev* (1919), *The Wisdom of Pushkin* (1919), and others. In 1920 Gershenzon spent time at a sanatorium outside Moscow, sharing a room with the symbolist poet and philosopher Vyacheslav Ivanov (1866–1949). Ivanov initiated an epistolary exchange on subjects of mutual interest, including issues of faith and immortality. Published in Petrograd in 1921 as *A Correspondence from Two Corners*, this major polemical work ends in discord and mutual disappointment, notably when it comes to Gershenzon's and Ivanov's views of Jewish history (see the general introduction). Gershenzon died in Moscow in 1925. Writing in *The Menorah Journal* in 1926, Valentin Parnakh (in vol. 1) thus characterized Gershenzon: "He has the spirit of a learned rabbi in love with the beauty of the poetry of the Gentiles."

In addition to his 1916 polemical essay about Bialik (whom he met in 1917 through Leyb Jaffe), Gershenzon as the critic of Jewish literature is best remembered for the introduction he wrote to *The Jewish Anthology: A Collection of New Jewish Poetry*, coedited by Leyb Jaffe (in vol. 1) and Vladislav Khodasevich (in vol. 1) and originally published in Moscow in 1918. The anthology showcased Russian translations of Hebrew poetry by fifteen authors: I.L. Peretz (1852–1915; wrote in both Yiddish and Hebrew), David Frischmann (1861–1922), H.N. Bialik (1873–1934), Saul Tchernichovsky (1875–1943), Yaakov Cahan (1881–1960), Yaakov Fichman (1881–1958), Zalman Shneour (1887–1959), David Shimonovitz (Shimoni, 1886–1956), Jacob Steinberg (1887–1947), Judah Kantzenelson (1847–1917), Avraham Ben Yitshak (1883–1950), Yehuda Karni (1884–1994), Eliahu Meitus (1892–1977), Avigdor Hameiri (Feuerstein, 1890–1970), and Rotblat Shoul (Shoul Rotblat, 1893–1914). Echoing *Destinies of the Jewish People*—and exhibiting some of the insurmountable contradictions and cultural complexes of Gershenzon's own life and thought—the preface communicated a spirited enthusiasm about a Hebrew cultural renascence.

The Jewish Anthology
A Collection of New Hebrew Poetry

Preface

The best works of the new Hebrew lyric poetry are gathered in this book, but the translation of poetry is a melancholy business. In the original each of them shines with the colors of the rainbow, sparkles with innumerable rays of light; translation inevitably extinguishes most of the rays and replaces many with others. This is why there is no point in speaking here about the artistic contents of the collection. May whatever has survived, through retelling, of the originals' living inspiration penetrate immediately into the soul of the reader. I will only speak of that which even in translation reaches the reader completely, although it does lose much of its luster: of the psychological contents of these texts.

Just as if a fresh sapling has risen from an old mossy root, just as if an old heart has started pulsing with new freedom and ecstasy—such is the miracle of the renaissance, the renewal, the liberation that I see in the writings of the young Jewish poets. What has happened with Jewry in the past fifteen years? Its external position has not improved one bit: still the same dispersion, the same animosity from all around, the same abject poverty of the masses. Nothing has changed from without, but something very important has changed within the Jewish soul—and Jewish poetry unequivocally bears testimony to it. It speaks not only about the spirit of ten or fifteen poets; it speaks in clear sounds of what has vaguely taken shape in the national consciousness. That a procession of poets moves along a new path is a true sign that behind them, having dispatched them with a secret motion of will, walks all of Jewry. What is this new path? Where are the poets heading?

Until recently, Jewish poetry had only complained and remembered, and both modes spoke equally of hopelessness. Jewish poetry insisted that the past had been beautiful and the present was unbearable, but the past had ended and vanished forever, and one had better not look to the future: ahead lay an endless continuation of the woeful present. At times that poetry would rise, through complaint and remembrance, to an overwhelming power—earlier, not in recent centuries—but still, this was the poetry of old-age frailty. And old age also expressed itself in its obsession with its own troubles, in its inability to soar above the earthly lot and the people's sorrow. That poetry was anchored to Jewry, to the Jewry forever frozen in time.

And suddenly—the Jewish Muse has been rendered unrecognizable. It would be arrogant to suggest that thought is capable of divining the dark motions of the people's spirit, in which secret forces act according to irretrievable laws. Even more so than does an individual, an entire nation experiences events that are impossible to foresee or observe but are only possible to verify through their external expressions. It is to such a spiritual event that the new Hebrew poetry bears testimony. It is doubly different from the old poetry. It is no less national than the old one but in a different and more profound way. The old one spoke of nothing but Jewishness, like a patient who ceaselessly talks of his illness; the new one draws inspiration from everything to which one's heart responds with rapturous beating. These young poets love like young men from all different countries, and their songs of love ring freely; open before them is the life of nature, and they portray it lovingly; they contemplate life, humanity, God, and the inescapable memory of Jewish woes no longer weighs on them like a heavy burden. And this is why, when they turn to its subject—for one can never forget the Jewish woes—how novel are their words about Jewry! They are individuals, perfectly free individuals, and a free man is proud and clear. Tchernichovsky *cannot* wallow in powerless complaints; Shneour *cannot* mournfully reminisce about past greatness. Now and then the past complaints and recollections can still be heard in this book, but the dominant tone is different: a sense of national selfhood, tranquil with some and proud—like an echo of the past—with others; and a free, although passionate, discussion of the plight of Jewry, of the irredeemable guilt of nations, and of Jewry's obligation to build its own destiny.

I do not know what happened to Jewry, but I can only testify that in this book Jewry is like a leper who is just as entirely leprous as before but has suddenly lifted his face, and everybody can now see that his spirit is clear and pure, in his spirit he has vanquished his disease. For centuries Jewry lived not only in a material ghetto; external slavery also made the Jew a spiritual slave, shackled to the incessant thoughts of his plight. *Being carefree*—a most precious blessing of mortals, a source of spiritual freedom, a spring of grandeur and beauty—this is what history has stolen from Jewry, and with it, it has taken everything. I think of Tchernichovsky's poetry as a miracle: there is not even a trace of that leaden-heavy, insurmountable anxiety of the Jews. There is a truly healthy Jew: he is carefree and stands in the forest examining life unhurriedly; sensitive to outside noises, he also listens to his inner self; yes, he is in no hurry. I cannot find the words to express what I see as a great promise, an assurance of a bright future, in this spiritual freedom of the self-liberated Jewish poets. To be a free Jew does not mean to cease being Jewish. Quite the contrary: only a free Jew can be filled with the Jewish element so as to sustain the fullness of the flourishing human spirit. I see Bialik as the antecedent of this Pleiades. He was the first not to complain, not to whine; he detested whiners. He called Jewry to courageous self-determination, but he was still almost entirely preoccupied with a Jewish agenda; he was not yet destined to enter the open expanses of human freedom. His gift is endlessly mightier than the others, but they have gone further.

1917

Translated from the Russian by Maxim D. Shrayer

Mikhail Gershenzon, "Predislovie," in *Evreiskaia antologiia: Sbornik molodoi evreiskoi poezii*, ed. V.F. Khodasevich and L.B. Iaffe, 1st ed. (Moscow, [1918]). English translation and introduction copyright © by Maxim D. Shrayer.

ELISHEVA

Elisheva (1888–1949), poet, novelist, translator, and critic, was born Elizaveta Zhirkova in Spassk-Ryazansky, Ryazan Province, to a Russian Orthodox father and a Catholic mother of Anglo-Irish stock. Her mother died when Elisheva was three, and the girl went to live with relatives in Moscow. At the women's gymnasium she befriended a Jewish classmate and through her was exposed to Judaic traditions. The gifted Elisheva taught herself Yiddish after developing a passionate affinity for Jewish history and culture. She was taken with the Zionist movement, finding its ideals spiritually uplifting. During World War I Elisheva lived in Ryazan, working with Jewish refugees.

In 1916 Elisheva signed up for a two-year course of Hebrew offered in Moscow at the Society for Lovers of the Hebrew Language. She chose the pen name E. Lisheva, an anagrammatic rendition of the Hebrew equivalent of Elizaveta. The choice of pen name also highlighted a self-inscription of the young Hebrew-loving Russian poet into the Biblical tradition: Elisheva, the daughter of Aminodav, was Aaron's wife and Moses's sister-in-law. After switching to Hebrew in 1921, signed her work Elisheva.

Elisheva's first book, translations from the Yiddish of Shmuel Yakov Imber (1889–1942), appeared in 1916 as *In the Jewish Country*. Her Moscow publisher, Shimon Bikhovsky, was a Zionist and an enthusiast of Jewish literature. Two of Elisheva's collections of Russian poetry appeared under Bikhovsky's imprints: *Secret Songs* in late 1918 and *Minutes* in 1919. In 1916–20, Elisheva translated from Hebrew the works of Judah Steinberg, Gershon Schoffmann, Joseph Hayyim Brenner, Uri Nissan Gnessin, and others, as well as the Yiddish poetry of Hersh-Dovid Nomberg and Anokhi (Z.Y. Aronson). She contributed translations to *The Jewish Anthology* (1918), edited by L. Jaffe and V. Khodasevich (both in vol. 1; see M. Gershenzon's vol. 1). "I am a Jew in my heart and soul," Elisheva wrote to a Jewish correspondent in 1919. A Christian and a Jew, in 1920 Elisheva and Shimon Bikhovsky were married in a civil ceremony.

Elisheva's first Hebrew poem was published in the magazine *Epoch* (or *Age*, *Ha-Tekufah*) in 1921. Her poems and stories appeared in Hebrew periodicals in the British Mandate of Palestine, Europe, and America: *Young Worker* (*Ha-Po'el Ha-Tza'ir*), *The Mask* (*Ha-Toren*), and others. In 1925, when Elisheva and her husband and daughter immigrated to Palestine, she was a well-known Hebrew author. Contemporaries, including the literary historian Joseph Klausner (1874–1958), admired her lyricism and "pure Hebrew." In Palestine Elisheva's husband set up the publishing house Tomer (Date Palm) and released a number of her books, including the poetry collections *A Small Chalice* (1926) and *Rhymes* (can also be *Rosary* [Haruzim], 1928; cf. the title of Anna Akhmatova's collection of 1914), *Stories* (Sipurim, 1927), and the novel *Back Alleys* (Simtaot, 1929). Elisheva's essays on the great Russian poet Aleksandr Blok appeared as a separate book in 1929. In 1930 a collection of articles about Elisheva came out in Yiddish in Tel Aviv.

Bikhovsky took his wife on another reading tour when their income from publishing shrank by the early 1930s. He died in Kishinev in 1932, and Elisheva and her daughter returned to Palestine. She had an increasingly hard time surviving as a writer; she translated from English and later, unable to find other work, washed people's clothes. She died in 1949 in near isolation and was buried near Lake Kinneret, next to the grave of Rahel (in vol. 1).

A volume of Elisheva's selected poems appeared in Israel in 1970 after a hiatus. *Secret Songs* and *Back Alleys* were reprinted in 1972 and 1977, respectively, and Russian translations of Elisheva's Hebrew poetry were published in Israel. In 1991, in his study of Hebrew female authors, Dan Miron characterized Elisheva's poetry as epigonic, sentimental, awash with clichés. In 1999 Zoya Kopelman attributed the "secret of [Elisheva's] success" to a synergy of factors: freedom from Biblical diction, facile use of the Sephardic—not the Ashkenazic—norm, the novelty of a female Hebrew poet in the 1920s, and Elisheva's cooption of the heritage of Russian lyrical poetry. In 2002 a volume of her selected stories appeared in Tel Aviv, summoning a new era for the contested legacy of "Ruth from the banks of the Volga."

Elisheva left about two hundred Russian poems, only some of which appeared in her two Russian collections. Oscillating between the aesthetics of mid–nineteenth century Russian verse and the poetry of the Silver Age (Anna Akhmatova, Aleksandr Blok, Sergey Gorodetsky, and Fyodor Sologub), they parse a lyrical diary of a Russian woman destined to become a Jewish writer and to make aliyah. Both poems selected here appeared in *Secret Songs* (1919), where seven out of eight texts address Jewish and Zionist topics. As an epigraph to the book, Elisheva used the famous response of the Moabite woman Ruth to her Jewish mother-in-law, Naomi: "Do not urge me to leave you, to turn back and not follow you. For wherever you go, I will go; wherever you lodge, I will lodge; your people shall be my people, and your God my God" (Ruth 1:16).

Eretz Israel

The land of Israel . . . through darkness and tears,
Through the abstract of time, in shame and blood,
Those words sounded out as in reverie,
They burned with the hushed flame of love.

And like a holy distant vision,
In tearful prayer, you arose, Zion,
In the vastness of sorrow, the black of abandon,
Faraway, faraway . . . unattainable, a dream.

But the hour has come! With the invincible strength
Of a single will, power, labor,
Your people were summoned back from the grave,
And the chain of exile fell forever.

The deserted land rose again, alive again—
In gardens and in fields, life and toil go on,
And again, in the glorious past as then,
The star of David shines in the heavens.

Land of Israel, land of the Lord!
We've fulfilled our holy promise:
Not "next year"—no, today, Lord,
In your fields we hail your blossoming.

1919

* * *

I won't light a candle at the Sabbath hour;
At twilight, pensive and clear,
I won't celebrate with joyful prayer
That quiet, lovely queen's arrival.
On the night when the world greets spring,
I won't conjure with ancient words
Those, who as slaves, journeyed
And gained a free land at the finish.
And the one to whom my soul belongs—

Before God and the world, my chosen one—
My hand won't sanctify his love
With a vow or a silver ring . . .

What difference does it make? In the shift
Of years, these rites thin like smoke;
Our children won't keep them going;
But there's another inextinguishable light . . .
In the evening, I light stars, not candles,
In the transparent heavens, far-off;
I greet the coming of my heart's Sabbath,
And my soul prays without language.
All that I dare not call blessed,
In the radiance of a dream, means more,
And more indestructible than a nuptial
Ring is the ring of my soul—beloved.

I'm not afraid of endless wandering.
I won't make it to the foot of the sacred place;
I'll bury my soul on the way, in the wilderness—
But I loved the stars above it that were listening.

1919

Translated from the Russian by Larissa Szporluk

VALENTIN PARNAKH

Valentin Parnakh (1891–1951), poet, translator, critic, and choreographer, was born in Taganrog on the Sea of Azov. Parnakh's mother died while delivering Parnakh and his twin sister, the writer Elizaveta Tarakhovskaya; their elder sister, Sofia Parnok, was a poet and critic (for details of their childhood, see Sofia Parnok in vol. 1). Parnakh attended St. Petersburg University while also training in music under Mikhail F. Gnessin and in theater under Vsevolod Meyerhold. Parnakh's early poems, composed under the spell of acmeism, appeared in 1913–14. Initially signing his work Parnokh, as in his birth papers, he opted for Parnakh, which in Russian evokes Parnassus. Parnakh's choice was also influenced by a name in Numbers 34:25: "From the Zebulunite tribe: a chieftain, Elizaphan son of Parnach." (Abroad Parnakh spelled his name Valentine Parnach or Parnac.) Impressions of a 1913–14 trip to the Middle East awoke an interest in Judaic subjects, which already figured in his first collection, *Samum* (1919).

While living in Paris in 1914–22, Parnakh befriended Ilya Ehrenburg (vol. 1), Guillaume Apollinaire, Max Jacob, and other writers and artists. Performances by African-American jazz bands in Paris in 1919 astonished Parnakh, and his biographer, Evgeny Arenzon, identified 1919 as a turning point. A synthesist, Parnakh sought to translate the music and movement of jazz into poetry and choreography. Soaking up dadaism, cubo-futurism, and early surrealism, Parnakh began to give recitals combining his verse, pantomime, and dance. A 1919 French-language poetry collection was followed in 1920 by the bilingual *Wordshift/Mot-dinamo* (Slovosdvig/Mot-dinamo). In 1921 Parnakh cofounded in Paris the Chamber of Poets (*Palata Poetov*), a group of "younger" Russian poets that included Aleksandr Ginger (1897–1965), later the husband of the poet Anna Prismanova (vol. 1).

In August 1922, *Izvestia* reported Parnakh's return to Moscow: "In the near future Parnakh will demonstrate his work in the field of eccentric dance. . . ." Parnakh brought a collection of jazz instruments and scores of music with him from Paris. He lectured and wrote about jazz, ragtime, and Negro music and taught choreography. Parnakh worked in Vsevolod Meyerhold's theater in 1922–24 and in 1923 created what was apparently the first jazz band in the USSR.

Despite an affinity for the aesthetics of the Left Front of the Arts, Parnakh felt like an outsider in Moscow's literary world. At the end of 1925, after financing the publication of his selected poems *Introduction to Dances*, Parnakh went back to Paris. He lived in France with a Soviet passport until the end of 1931, contributing essays in Russian, French, and English to various publications, including émigré publications, in Europe, as well as to publications in the USSR and the United States. Parnakh's polemical essay "Habimah and Theater in Hebrew," published in the French magazine *Europe* in 1926, analyzed Evgeny Vakhtangov's 1922 production of S. An-sky's *The Dybbuk* (see vol. 1). "Quite a few Russian socialists," Parnakh wrote, "some of them Jewish, had the stupidity to decide that Hebrew is a 'bourgeois language' because it is used in religious rites and 'the Jewish masses do not speak it.'" The American *Menorah Journal* printed Parnakh's letter "In the Russian World" in 1926. An early treatment of Jewish-Russian literature in English, it discussed Mikhail Gerzhenzon, Boris Pasternak, Osip Mandelstam, Pavel Antokolsky (all in vol. 1), and Boris Lapin (1905–41).

A collection of Parnakh's essays on dance appeared in Paris in 1932. The same publisher had planned to publish his book *Inquisition*, a labor of extensive research with translations from Spanish, Portuguese, and Hebrew. The book did not appear in France, and in 1932 Parnakh returned to Moscow. Marriage and family demanded earnings, so Parnakh began to translate for a living. Parnakh's greatest contribution, a reworked version of *Inquisition*, appeared in 1934 in Russian as *Spanish and Portuguese Poets, Victims of Inquisitions: Poems, Scenes from Comedies, Descriptions of Autos-da-fé, Protocols, Prosecution Speeches, Verdicts*. Virtually unknown to Hispanists and Luso-Brazilianists outside Russia, Parnakh's *Spanish and Portuguese Poets* deserves greater attention and recognition.

Parnakh survived the Great Purge and during World War II was evacuated to Chistopol in Tatarstan. He had an increasingly difficult time earning a living and died in Moscow in 1951. Parnakh's strongly worded memoir, *Pension Mobert*, still unpublished, offers important discussions of antisemitism.

The critic Igor Loshchilov observed that Parnakh achieved "the unique, 'syncopated' sound of verse" through the frequent use of monosyllabic words. Parnakh's use of this device was just one aspect of his densely textured and sometimes excessively choreographed poems, which conflated futurist and constructivist verbal experimentation with structural transpositions of cubo-futurist and expressionist art and jazz-like orchestration. All three poems in this selection appeared in Parnakh's 1922 Parisian collection, *The Acrobat Climbs* (*Karabkaetsia akrobat*), featuring a portrait of Parnakh by Picasso; the numerous anagrams (*arab* [Arab], *brat* [brother], *rab* [slave], *rak* [cancer and crawfish], and so forth) and the various palindromized and alliterative combinations (e.g., *kar–rak*) embedded in the Russian title underscore the poems' verbal kinetics. Parnakh treated topics in contemporary Jewish-Russian history (pogroms) and Biblical and Jewish history (false messianism) in a manner that has few parallels in modern Russian poetry.

* * *

Leviticus 26:19

"I will make your heaven as iron,
I will make your earth as brass!"
The underground train severed through the tunnels,
Aeroplane-dance like the lightning's revenge!
Iron-brass music
Be mute!

Enormous drill that's been turned upside down,
Eiffel Tower is narrowly knashing.
An embolism of iron veins and spew.
Mere suit of mail, just flatness and jagged notches.
A pair of cymbals steadily bangs.
Although if we're imprisoned here, and ruined,
The sentence can hardly bring us joy.
Rag propellers and Pentateuch!
We'll prospect for pleasure, flaming sinners—we.
The Bible's threat! In my heart I'm not circumcised.
Not with words do I speak; I beat like brass,
I'm crashing down sounds, chattering like iron,
I'm ready for a good time and getting high!

1919

From the Lord's words to Moses on Mount Sinai (Leviticus 26:18–20): "And if, for all that, you do not obey Me, I will go on to discipline you sevenfold for your sins, and I will break your proud glory. I will make your skies like iron and your earth like copper, so that your strength shall be spent to no purpose. Your land shall not yield its produce, nor shall the trees of the land yield their fruit."

Deportees
(1914–1917)

By invoice and side by side!
Lie Jews in cattle-car fetidity,
After a routine mass homicide,
Palms of Solomon, here's your fertility!

Dim grows the gaze and the memory of obsequies.
Blockade of prison-train transports.
"During a railhalt of deportees
Don't go out on the platforms!"

Alternation of upchuck
From a laying-in–praying-in building.
Amidst swamp muck
An ark of pogrom-meat filling.

1919

Sabbetaians[1]
(Excerpt)

Impassioned Africa of cymbals,
We wait. Sabbetai! Kabbala and strife.
Deafening calls of creeds and prayers
Have bowed over bodies in solemn rites.

---

1. Sabbetaians—followers of the false messiah Sabbetai Tzvi (1626–1676), who was purportedly moved to action by news of the massive anti-Jewish violence perpetrated by Bohdan Khmelnytsky's troops in 1648–49. Undated, the poem was signed "Paris–Seville"; Parnakh had visited Spain and later published an essay, "Spain in Our Day," in the Soviet magazine, *Little Flame* (*Ogonek*).

The haydamaks' mugs mock and cackle
Carousing in putrid Khmelnytsky's time.
Pogrom. In the Ukrainian cloaca
Pupils and souls are magnified.

The lord of orgies has taught you elation!
From the death-pangs
Of rasping paroxysms the words raided
The dirges' jewbilation!

Dance of psalms and ecstasies,
And turbans' mourning, the gathering weaves!

"With feasting, finally, break your fast!
A sudden dance shall be your manna,
You are deemed worthy of this hosanna!
May the new dance's rule of the world last.
Transmute the funeral hymn to gladness.
For Israel—King Sabbetai long-awaited."

[1919–22]

Translated from the Russian by Diana L. Burgin

Valentin Parnakh, "Nebo vashe sdelaiu, kak zhelezo. . . ," "Vyslannye (1914–1917)," and "Sabbateiantsy (otryvok)." English translation copyright © by Diana L. Burgin. Introduction and notes copyright © by Maxim D. Shrayer.

ILYA SELVINSKY

Ilya Selvinsky (1899–1968), poet, dramatist, memoirist, and essayist, was born in Simferopol, where his family suffered during the 1905 Simferopol pogrom. The grandson of a Crimean Karaite (*krymchak*), Selvinsky grew up in Evpatoriya in the family of a furrier merchant. In 1919 Selvinsky graduated from a gymnasium in Evpatoriya, spending his summers as a vagabond and trying his hand at different trades, including sailing, fishing, and acting in an itinerant theater. A man of great physical prowess, the young Selvinsky also worked as a longshoreman and circus wrestler.

Selvinsky published his first poem in 1915 and in the 1920s experimented with the use of Yiddishisms and thieves' lingo in Russian verse. He is credited with innovations in Russian versification, including the proliferation of *taktovik*, a Russian nonclassical meter. Extensive travel and turbulent adventures fueled Selvinsky's longer narrative works and cycles, "loadified" (term used by the Russian constructivists) with local color.

Selvinsky first joined the anarchist troops in the Russian civil war but later fought on the side of the Reds. In 1919 he entered the medical faculty of Taurida University. He moved to Moscow in 1921 and studied law at Moscow University, graduating in 1922. From 1924 until its dismantlement in 1930, Selvinsky was the leader of the Literary Center of Constructivists (LTsK), an early Soviet modernist group, and edited several landmark anthologies by constructivist authors (e.g., *The State Plan of Literature*). In the late 1920s, the LTsK counted among its members the poets Eduard Bagritsky (in vol. 1), Vera Inber (in vol. 1), and Vladimir Lugovskoy, critic Kornely Zelinsky, prose writer Evgeny Gabrilovich (in vol. 2), and others. In the middle to late 1920s, after the publication of *Records*, *The Lay of Ulyalaev* (1924, published 1927) and the narrative poem *Notes of a Poet* (1927, with a cover by El Lissitsky), Selvinsky achieved fame and acclaim. In 1929, his tragedy *Army 2 Commander* was staged by Vsevolod Meyerhold. In 1930, trying to redeem himself after the dismantlement of the independent literary groups, Selvinsky composed the opportunistic poem "From Palestine to Birobidzhan"(1930, published 1933; on Birobidzhan, see Viktor Fink in vol. 1).

During World War II, Selvinsky served as a battalion commissar, joined the Communist Party in 1941, and was decorated for valor. In "I Saw It!" (1942), he depicted the aftermath of the mass execution of Jews outside the Crimean village of Bagerovo. One of the first Soviet poets to write extensively about the Shoah, Selvinsky treated the topic of the mass extermination of Soviet Jews in two other works of 1942: "Kerch" and "A Reply to Goebbels."

Through a combination of personal bravery and political navigation, Selvinsky weathered the storms of Stalinism and was a major literary figure of the post-Stalinist years. He remained a proud Jew during the most antisemitic of the Soviet years and despite direct official ostracism. Selvinsky's major early Jewish works include "Anecdotes about the Karaite Philosopher Babakai-Sudduk" (1931), "Motke Malechhamovess [Motke the Angel of Death]" (1926), and *The Lay of Ulyalaev.* "Portrait of My Mother" (1933) contains a constructivist bitter comment about Jewish-Soviet assimilation: "Henceforth her son's face will remain defiled/Like the Judaic Jerusalem,/Having suddenly become a Christian holy site." Selvinsky's long poem *Kandava* (1945) unfolds around a nightmare in which he imagines himself and his wife "somewhere in Auschwitz or Maidanek." Shortly before his death, Selvinsky published the autobiographical novel *O My Youth* (1966), where Jewish themes figured prominently.

Ilya Selvinsky was a poetic virtuoso of high caliber. His uneclipsed literary records (cf. the title of his 1926 collection, *Records*) include the epic poem *The Lay of Ulyalaev* and the novel in verse *Fur Trade* (1928).

Bar Kokhba (1920, published 1924) occupies a special place among Selvinsky's Jewish works. While Selvinsky was probably influenced by the widely performed Yiddish drama *Bar Kokhba* (1887) by Abraham Goldfaden (1840–1908), as well as by Vladimir Jabotinsky's "In Memory of Herzl" (in vol. 1), the formal sophistication of the twenty-year-old poet's wreath of sonnets is astonishing. Literally, it is a wreath laid in memory of the Jewish zealot; figuratively, it is a form that textually embodies might, power, resistance, and strength of conviction. One could well imagine Selvinsky's art in "Bar Kokhba" as sculpting words. Bar Kokhba, the leader of the second Jewish revolt against Rome (132–35 C.E.), was for Selvinsky a symbol of Jewish resistance and spiritual endurance. Against the backdrop of a growing campaign against traditional Jewish life and Judaism in the Soviet Union, Selvinsky's "Bar Kokhba" remained a powerful monument to Jewish—and Judaic—survival.

Scholars learned from the Dead Sea Scrolls that Bar Kokhba's name was Simon ben Kosibah. Rabbi Akiba ben Joseph, who approved of the uprising, regarded him as a messiah; Rabbi Akiba used wordplay to change the name to the Aramaic *bar Kokhba,* "the son of a star." Rabbi Akiba was the intellectual leader of the movement and Bar Kokhba its military and political leader during the second revolt (coins minted during the year of his power bear the title "Simon, Prince of Israel"). Emperor Hadrian's attempt to build a Graeco-Roman city (Aelia Capitolina) on the site of Jerusalem and a shrine to Jupiter on the ruins of the Temple is usually considered a major impetus for the Jewish revolt. The revolt was eventually put down by Sextus Julius Severus, Hadrian's best general, recalled from Britain—Severus razed Jerusalem.

Bar Kokhba

1.

And he was huge, his whole frame filled with might,
As if Leviathan's own nursling splendid.
His wary bowels rumbled in despite,

Within him sinews intertwined upended,
His bushy shoulders' solid slabs extended
Aglow, like a rich fish stew, with a lustrous light.

He dwelt within the realm of trees and boulders.
He spied the eagle's weighted pennons winging.
And to his face the reddish smoke was clinging
That from the ringlets of his ram's fleece smolders.

But sorrow sits, like waves, upon his brow,
A scorpion, he is gorged with poison now.
He waits. The land grows colder every hour.
The desert demons heed him from their bower.

2.

The desert demons heed him from their bower.
He's thrust Asmodeus[1] down to the dust,
The mountain pards and lions all entrust
Themselves to his commands without a glower.

But now his tongue tastes pungently so sour,
But still he sleeps on wormwood's feathered flowers,
But he recalls the drums, the thunder's gust,
Beneath the condor's rallying wing thrust.

---

1. Asmodeus (Heb. *Ashmedai*)—prince of darkness in Biblical mythology. These notes by
Maxim D. Shrayer and Jaime Goodrich supplement and/or supercede some of the notes provided by Selvinsky himself in the original text.

He waits and counts the signs of firs portending,
A promised *melekh*,[2] still he waits unbending,
An arrow raised upon his forehead brave,
Much better a fanatic than a slave.

And down below are groans and anguish dour.
And so his people bend to Latin power.

3.

And so his people bend to Latin power,
For iron Rome has crushed them with its yoke.
Jerusalem, laid waste by Rome's fell stroke,
Since Caesar now sends dicta to devour,

Must give Capitolina's[3] pagans dower:
Its ancient temple, sacrificial smoke,
And sacred flame, which secret urns embower.
Is it not time Eloheynu[4] awoke?

The gaols have cankered all the prophet's vigor;
Amid gems, viands, princes by birthright
To Caesar lift their goblets every night;

The tetrarchs hold their gracious courts with rigor,
While 'neath the lash their tribesmen's wounds grow bigger,
Now with the yoke of screechers proud bedight.

4.

Now with the yoke of screechers proud bedight,
One sesterce[5] makes Bar Kokhba just a servant;
Gall fills the goblet of his breast so fervent,
A ball constricts his throat. Is the time right?

---

2. *Melekh* (Heb.) = here "king."
3. Capitolina—according to Emperor Publius Aelius Hadrian's orders, Jerusalem was to be renamed Aelia Capitolina after his family name.
4. Eloheinu—one of the names of God in Judaism; compare *Adonai Eloheinu* (Heb.) = the Lord our God.
5. Sesterce—a small silver coin in ancient Rome.

The mills gnawed grain, the haystacks moved about,
The potters splashed around hot clay in measure,
While Rome in epicurean displeasure
A hippopotamian whip lashed out.

But he could suffer all. And so, stouthearted,
He gave his ribs soon as the flaying started
So that his soul endured his kin's travail.

He knew the joy beasts feel in every hour
Once he'd inhaled rebellion's catching gale.
He bellowed to his tribe from his watchtower.

5.

He bellowed to his tribe from his watchtower,
And saying thus unto his nation, spake:[6]
"Beware, Yehudi! This jet black daybreak
Foretells that war on cliffs and vales will flower.

Aflame as if a tree unburnt for sake[7]
Of faith, I won't desert our sacred bower—
Against these fattened swine I'll lead the fight,

So grave dust on the goyim we'll be pouring.
Now flock, you eagles clamoring and soaring.
Sh'ma Israel![8] Now the final hour's in sight!

So let it be fulfilled, the proclamation
That blazoned this: down from the mountain's height
A leader will arise to free the nation.
Let there be singing in the arrows' flight.

6.

Let there be singing in the arrows' flight.
I sayest: let the fence collapse, my heeders!

---

6. Compare: "The Lord spoke to Moses, saying" (Leviticus 18:1).

7. The Russian literally refers to a "fig tree," but compare Exodus 3:3.1: "And Moses said, 'I will turn aside and see this great sight, why the bush is not burnt.'"

8. *Shema Israel!* (Heb.) = Hear, O Israel!

Now neither God, nor Caesar, nor your leaders
Will save you—shepherds! plowmen!—from your plight.

This blaze of riots and rebellions lingers,
All you who have an ear, within your fingers!"

The hour arrived. And then towns through the nation,
And then all husbands, elders, stripling boys,
Their brothers, grandsons, maidens with persuasion
All whet their swords, new honed by trees' abrasion,

On Rome, on those who for a portal's ploys
Betrayed their homeland and their hovel's joys,
On those who hide their sons in fear and cower.
Now let the breath of khamsin[9] cease to shower!

7.

Now let the breath of khamsin cease to shower!
So ponderous and rank, it casts a pall
Just like a cloud upon a dank nightfall,
And yet its strength no man can overpower.

Above an ebon synagogue, silt scoured,
As if a smoky fleece, this strength now sprawls.
Within the smoke the image of Cain towered,
And men called it the moon, fools one and all.

And then Bar Kokhba galloped up well dight
With horsehair plumes in helm, red mail of metal.
He cast his eyes about, and then unsettled

His sword obsidian from sheath, and cried
"Hey-Dod![10] Attack the swine with all your mettle!"
The Roman yoke, burnt ash, fell down aright.

8.

The Roman yoke, burnt ash, fell down aright.
But skyward, for a hundred week duration,

9. Khamsin (of Arabic origin)—a hot southerly wind that blows in the spring.
10. "*Hey-Dod!*" (Heb.) = a war cry of the ancient Hebrews.

Austere Cain, grinning in the new moon's light,
Cast over sand his blank eye socket's sight.

The one-eyed rabbi, in the devastation,
Would thrust himself among the thickest fray,
His form poured into fiery mail's array,
Made tight by spurs and tail-like horn's fixation.

And setting gainst his groin his own spear butt,
With utmost strength he punctured bodies, faces.
Until flesh turns to smoke, the iron razes,
And then Bar Kokhba's drunk with battle glut.

The crater boiled and boiled as it dilated.
The holy emperor saw, eyes fixated.

9.

The holy emperor saw, eyes fixated
Upon the whirlwind clouding his crown's ray.
The whole stage shook as senators orated:

"*Romani, ave!*"[11] Zion flaunts our sway.
To rush by horses I saw them elated . . . [12]
Enough now—we've disputed and debated.

So Maccabees and Gideon prompt us,
Hyrcanus, Yannai, Aristobulus,[13]
And other torsos of past statuary.
We'll seize them in our iron grip, though wary."

And Publius Aelius Hadrian,
Their caesar, pleased by such a proposition,
Now waved his hand: "Send legions on a mission
Out to the devilish Judean land."

---

11. "Romani, ave!" (Lat.) = "Romans, hail!"
12. Here Selvinsky is deliberately imitating two grammatical Latin constructions. The ablative of instrument, replicated with "by horses," indicates the means by which an action is done. In indirect speech, Latin uses the accusative with an infinitive, a construction duplicated by "to rush."
13. Names of some of the ancient Jewish leaders and kings who opposed foreign (Roman) domination.

10.

Out to the devilish Judean land,
At Ostia they boarded vessels teeming—
The Roman sailors went with copper gleaming,
Went Gauls, Etruscans, and a host Alan,

From Noricum, Caria, troops were streaming,
In snowy pard skins Cimbri well beseeming,
A Horde of Basques, Scythians, and Corfians
And handfuls of majolican Parthians.

And praetor[14] Julius, called Severus,
The chief commander of these savage races,
Surveyed barbarians, their lupine faces,

Reserves, and cavalrymen and spoke thus:
"We're talents—they are carats,[15] scarcely weighted."
And glossy arms rang out and resonated.

11.

And glossy arms rang out and resonated;
To pour the earth in a red globe they planned.

(At Beth-Ter fortress, on Judean land,
Lucilia dwelt in a hut and waited.
Her tongue, more sour than pomegranate, sated.
Lunettes of flesh divine, her breasts are grand.

He came to her, the warrior celebrated.
His eagle's beak with sweet words overran,
Once from his close-fit helmet liberated
His cheeks with purpled bruises were serrated.

His love, she's lissome as a pine tree's span.
Her love's a brother, a snow tiger rated.)

---

14. Praetor—a Roman magistrate who often commanded branches of the army.
15. Carat—ancient measure of weight or money used by Syrians, Greeks, and Romans;
1 talent equals 70 pounds and 100,000 carats.

Like locusts into fire, the hordes now ran.
From east to sunset. Thousands unabated.

12.

From east to sunset. Thousands unabated.
The helmets glistening, the armament.
And now their catapults the fray foment
With blazing tow and tar-soaked cotton freighted.

Beset by arrows, infantry, like brambles,
All shields, as if a beetle bronze now crept.
At flank, the camel cavalry forth swept
Like swimming thunder. To the gates they scramble!

Pawns, queens, and bishops of each class and clan.
Their ancient pyrrhic dance[16] with iron ringing,
The soldiers' armor charged with sparks outspringing.

Through crimson smoke, the feathered arrows winging
Would dart in the embrasures near at hand;
Above the fort, fog turned a bloody band.

13.

Above the fort, fog turned a bloody band.
"Bar Kokhba? Where's the rabbi now?" fear shouted,
"With one swift blow from him, they'd soon be routed!"

Their chief, Bar Kokhba, with his love at hand,
Had lost his mind in winsome joy's embraces,
Much like a lion red the jungle traces.

Then "rabbi," like a spear, came to his hearing . . .
He found his wits, tore out the windowpane.
He heard the rush of Gauls, Celts, Arabs nearing,
The neighing of his faithful horse in vain.

---

16. Pyrrhic dance—the war dance of the ancient Greeks, performed while wearing armor.

Bronze on his shoulders—in a minute's time—
The girl won't let him don his belt meantime.
He turned to her: then agates, lips placated . . .
A shaggy giant, he was immolated.

14.

A shaggy giant, he was immolated,
Pierced by a feathered knife in duskiness.
But as his fitful deathbed throes abated
With one hand's grasp he bared his girlfriend's breast.

That night a quadriga,[17] with Roman streamers,
Lucilia rides to the camp of screamers,
Up to the tent below whose silken span

The praetor Julius, a toga wearing,
Before the soldiers greets his wife, so daring
In this ideally executed plan.

The matron's ears were deaf to all that night . . .
She dreamt about the musk scent of her lover,
The tawny fur, his tousled chest's thick cover—
And he was huge, his whole frame filled with might.

15.

And he was huge, his whole frame filled with might,
The desert demons heed him from their bower,
And so his people bend to Latin power,
Now with the yoke of screechers proud bedight.

He bellowed to his tribe from his watchtower
Let there be singing in the arrows' flight!
Now let the breath of khamsin cease to shower!
The Roman yoke, burnt ash, fell down aright.

---

17. Quadriga—chariot drawn by four horses harnessed abreast.

The holy emperor saw, eyes fixated
Out to the devilish Judean land.
And glossy arms rang out and resonated.

From east to sunset. Thousands unabated.
Above the fort, fog turned a bloody band.
A shaggy giant, he was immolated.

1920

Translated from the Russian by Jaime Goodrich and Maxim D. Shrayer

OSIP MANDELSTAM

Osip Mandelstam (1891–1938), poet, prose writer, and translator, was born in Warsaw and grew up in and around St. Petersburg in a secularized middle-class Jewish family, receiving no systematic Jewish upbringing. Mandelstam studied at the private Tenishev School from 1900 to 1907, lived in Paris attending lectures at the Sorbonne during 1907–8, and studied in Heidelberg in 1909–10. In 1911 he was baptized at a Methodist Church in Vyborg. No longer subject to *numerus clausus*, he entered St. Petersburg University, where until 1915 he read Old French without taking a degree. Mandelstam's first, civic poems were composed in 1907 under the spell of Semyon Nadson (in vol. 1). He debuted as a poet in 1910 in the review *Apollo* (*Apollon*) and in 1912 joined the acmeists, developing a lifelong friendship with Anna Akhmatova. His manifesto "Morning of Acmeism" dates to 1913, and his first collection, *Stone*, was printed in that same year (second edition 1916; third edition 1923).

Mandelstam's attitude to the Revolution was contradictory. Initially enlivened by the revolutionary events, he regarded the destruction of the Russian monarchy as historically justified. At the same time, Mandelstam abhorred bloodshed and reportedly responded to the 1918 assassination of Mikhail (Moisey) Uritsky by Leonid Kannegiser (See vol. 1) with the words "Who appointed him judge?" In 1917–18 Mandelstam worked on the staff of the Socialist-Revolutionary newspaper *Banner of Labor* (*Znamia truda*). He moved south in 1919 and lived in Kiev, the Crimea, and Georgia. It was in May of that year that he met Nadezhda Khazina, who would become his wife. With the assistance of Ilya Ehrenburg (in vol. 1), Mandelstam returned to Russia in the fall of 1920. In 1922 his second collection, *Tristia*, appeared in Berlin (second edition 1923).

Mandelstam published twenty books of translations, including the prose of Franz Werfel and Arthur Schnitzler. In the 1920s he turned to prose, writing (semi)autobiographical nonfiction and fiction. In 1928, Mandelstam's publishing difficulties mounting, *Poems*—his last collection—was helped into print by Nikolay Bukharin. A 1928 scandal, resulting from false charges of plagiarism, was conveniently used to ostracize Mandelstam. A feuilleton by the odious critic and journalist David Zaslavsky (1880–1965) was printed in Moscow's *Literary Gazette* (*Literaturnaia gazeta*) on 7 May 1929; in 1958 the Jewish-born Zaslavsky was one of Boris Pasternak's official detractors (Pasternak in vol. 1). A letter in support of Mandelstam appeared there on 13 May 1929, signed by Leopold Averbakh, Eduard Bagritsky (in vol. 1), Aleksandr Fadeev, Mikhail Kozakov (in vol. 1), Leonid Leonov, Yury Olesha, Boris Pasternak, Boris Pilnyak, and others, a total of sixteen writers representing different parts of the Soviet literary spectrum. Mandelstam traveled to the Caucasus to escape the nerve-wrecking scandal, but the publication of his politically uncommitted prose about Armenia bred further controversy in 1933.

Mandelstam's growing dissent exploded in November 1933 in his anti-Stalinist poem "We live without feeling our country beneath ourselves . . ." (see Nadezhda Mandelstam's memoir in vol. 1). After his arrest in May 1934, Mandelstam was exiled for three years to Cherdyn in the northern Urals. After attempting to take his life, he was allowed to settle in Voronezh, where *The Voronezh Notebooks* were composed. The Voronezh exile lasted until May 1937, when, hoping to rectify his position, Mandelstam composed a Stalinist panegyric. It did not help him. Unlike such contemporaries as Pasternak or Ehrenburg, Mandelstam was remarkably unsuccessful in his tortured attempts to collaborate with the regime. For instance, while conveying an anti-Fascist message, the poem "Rome" (1937, in the *Third Voronezh Notebook*) was far too complex and riddled with nonformulaic Mandelstamian questions about art, power, and religion to fulfill an ideological commission. Evoking motifs from both the Old Testament (David, Moses) and the New Testament (the birth of Jesus in Bethlehem: "the gates are opened before Herod"), Mandelstam denounced the poem's new Herod, the "dictator-degenerate" Mussolini and his Fascists ("Italianate blackshirts"). The poem first appeared in New York in 1961 and not until 1967 in the Soviet Union. Mandelstam was rearrested several months after his return from the Voronezh exile and sentenced to five years of labor camps. He is believed to have died in December 1938 in a transit camp near Vladivostok in a state of mental distress. Mandelstam's widow, Nadezhda Mandelstam (in vol. 2), preserved his legacy and memorialized his life.

Mandelstam's posthumous rehabilitation began in 1956. His return to Soviet print was perilous, and an incomplete and expurgated edition of his poetry appeared—in the Poet's Library series in Moscow—only in 1973, edited by the literary scholar Nikolay Khardzhiev. However, his texts circulated widely in the underground. In 1995, a comprehensive edition of Osip Mandelstam's poetry, edited by the Estonian-born Russian poet Arvo Mets, finally came out in St. Petersburg in the New Poet's Library. Still, Mandelstam's impact on postwar Russian poetry was tremendous. In the West, the first postwar collection of Mandelstam's verse appeared in 1955, followed by extensive efforts to publish his heritage, efforts that culminated in a four-volume Russian-language academic edition (1967–81). Outside Russia, Osip Mandelstam is perhaps the best-known twentieth-century Russian poet.

A handful of Mandelstam's poems, including the three included here, address Jewish and Judaic questions. An impressive number of his prose works, among them *The Noise of Time* (1925), *Theodosia* (1925), "Kievan Sketches" (1926), *Egyptian Stamp* (1927), and *Fourth Prose* (1928–30), discuss Jewish topics and showcase Jewish fictionalized characters (most brilliantly in *Egyptian Stamp*, set in 1917 Petrograd; the protagonist of this short novel was partly based on Valentin Parnakh [in vol. 1]) as well as real-life Jews such as mathematician Veniamin Kagan.

Multiple incongruities characterize Mandelstam's self-awareness as a Jew and as a Jewish writer. Mandelstam's career exhibits a Judaic–Christian dynamic that is far more complex than what the poet's Jewish and Christian apologists would like to believe. Those who speak of his rejection of Orthodox Judaism probably overstate the case for Mandelstam's knowledge of the Judaic traditions. At the same time, even Russian ultranationalist critics fail to agree on Mandelstam's place in their Judeophobic fantasies of Russian culture. In the 1970s, Pyotr Palievsky reportedly spoke of Mandelstam as a "kikeish boil on the pure body of [Fyodor] Tyutchev's poetry." In the 1990s, Stanislav Kunyaev sermonized in print that "it is impossible to chase Mandelstam back into 'Judaic chaos' [. . .] he has irreversibly entered the wide Russian expanses."

The apostasy of the twenty-year-old Mandelstam, however low-key or even opportunistic, was only part of his emblematic story. Over the years his self-awareness as a Christian changed as his interests ran the gamut from Catholic universalism, to Russian Orthodoxy, to a Hellenic-Christian outlook. Christian references are prominent in his poetry and prose of the early and middle periods. To suggest that Christianity was largely a cultural category for Mandelstam is to do the poet's sensibility an injustice. During the earlier part of Mandelstam's career, Hellenism ousted Judaism as a spiritual and ethical foundation for his version of Christian civilization. Furthermore, Mandelstam's response, in his prose of the mid-1920s, to contemporary un(der)assimilated Jews was predominantly that of embarrassment. Reproduced below, "Judaic Chaos" (from the memoir *The Noise of Time*) illustrates what Maurice Friedberg described as Mandelstam's "painfully neurotic self-hating awareness of his Jewish antecedents." Not surprisingly, Mandelstam was receptive neither to Zionism nor to the early Soviet rhetorics on the Jewish question.

Mandelstam made his most positive discursive statements about Jewish culture in 1926, notably in his essay about the great Jewish actor Shloyme (Solomon) Mikhoels (1890–1948). Due in large measure to Mandelstam's misfortunes of the late 1920s, the years 1929–30 were marked by a reassessment of Jewishness. (Mandelstam reportedly likened his ostracism to the Dreyfus affair.) Critics cite chapter 12 of *Fourth Prose* as evidence that Mandelstam had re-embraced his Judaic roots: "The profession of a writer, as it has evolved in Europe and especially in Russia, is incompatible with the honorable title of a Judean, of which I am proud. My blood, burdened by the heritage of shepherds, patriarchs, and kings, rebels against the thievish gypsiness of the tribe of writers." Earlier in the same text Mandelstam spoke about the charges of plagiarism that had been brought against him by Arkady Gornfeld (a Jew and a respected littérateur who had been used to instigate the scandal) and the scandal itself, which David Zaslavsky (a Jew who was a scoundrel and vilified Mandelstam in print) had spun into the public's eye: "At a certain year of my life, adult men from the tribe that I detest with all my heart and soul and to which I do not want to and will not belong intended to perform upon me collectively a repulsive and vile ritual. The name of this ritual is literary circumcision or dishonorment, which is performed according to the custom and calendar needs of the tribe of writers, while the victim is selected by the choice of the elders." Elsewhere in *Fourth Prose* Mandelstam described the House of Writers as a building with "twelve lit Judas's windows" and his ostracism as a "ringing of [thirty] silver coins." One can only speculate what precisely the hurt and hunted Mandelstam had in mind, but it is doubtful that his stance in *Fourth Prose* is that of a proud Jew embracing his roots.

Seeking spiritual nourishment not in Judaism but in the more accessible Christianity, some members of the Jewish-Russian intelligentsia in the Soviet 1960s–1980s identified with Osip Mandelstam. What makes the Jewish-born Mandelstam unique and worthy of admiration and further study is not his relationship to either Christianity or Judaism, which was symptomatic of his time and milieu, but his peerless poetic genius.

* * *

Slip back into your mother, Leah,
Into the lap where life's begun.
This yellow dusk is your idea,
Instead of Ilion's midday sun.[1]

No one will blame you for transgressing.
Safe in the silent midnight dark,
Head on his chest, their blood coalescing,
May daughter join her patriarch.[2]

You can expect tremendous changes
Fulfilled through you, since you've been caught
In currents destiny arranges.
You're Leah, not Helen, thought not

Because blood flows so thick when royal.
No, but you're bound to love a Jew
And, as you grow completely loyal,
Vanish in him. God be with you.

1920

---

1. Ilion is one of the names of Troy; Helen, hero of Homer's *Iliad*, was the indirect cause of the Trojan War.
2. In her second memoir, *Hope Abandoned* (1972), Nadezhda Mandelstam suggested that Mandelstam had her in mind in writing the poem: "Our relationship had sharply heightened his awareness of belonging to Jewry. . . . He perceived the Jews as one family—hence the theme of incest. . . . Once at night, thinking of me, he suddenly realized that it was me who would lie with him at night, like Lot's daughters" (N. Mandelstam was referring to the episode in Gen. 19:30–35).

* * *

One Alexander Herzovich,
A Jewish pianist,
Played Schubert songs with perfect pitch,
Clear as an amethyst.

From dawn to dusk he would perform
The pure immortal art
Of one sonata, light and warm
And splendidly by heart.

What, Alexander Herzovich?
Dark is the street below?
Dear Alexander Schmerzovich,
So what! On with the show!

That beautiful Italian girl
On snowy afternoons
Brings out her little sled for a whirl
To your Schubertian tunes.

When we hear music sweetly played,
We don't mind death's sour notes,
And afterward we're not afraid,
Hung like crow-feather coats.

This, Alexander Herzovich,
Began long, long ago.
Dear Alexander Scherzovich,
So what! On with the show![3]

1931

---

3. An individual by the name of Aleksandr Gertsevich was a neighbor of O. Mandelstam's
brother, Aleksandr Mandelstam. *Herz* (Germ.) = heart; *schermz* (Germ.) = pain; *serdtse* (*Russ.*) =
heart; *scherzo* (Ital.) = musical form, from the Italian "joke."

* * *

Say, desert geometer, shaper
Of Arabic sand into form,
Can lines that you scribble on paper
Be stronger than wind in a storm?

To me his convulsions don't matter—
Judaic upheaval and strife.
He charters a life out of chatter
And laps up the chatter of life.

1933

Translated from the Russian by Maxim D. Shrayer and J.B. Sisson

Osip Mandelstam, "Vernis' v smesitel'noe lono. . . ," "Zhil Aleksandr Gertsevich, evreiskii muzykant . . . ," and "Skazhi mne, chertezhnik pustyni." English translation copyright © by Maxim D. Shrayer and J.B. Sisson. Introduction and notes copyright © by Maxim D. Shrayer.

From *The Noise of Time*
Judaic Chaos

Once, a foreign character came to visit, a spinster in her forties in a crimson bonnet and with a sharp chin and dark vicious eyes. Claiming to hail from the small town of Shavli,[4] she demanded we find her a husband in Petersburg. She stayed a week before we managed to send her on her way. Every so often wandering writers would turn up: bearded men in long coats, Talmudic philosophers, peddlers of their own printed quotations and aphorisms. They would leave signed copies behind and complain of persecution by mean wives. Once or twice in my life I was taken to a synagogue as though to a concert, following lengthy preparations, all but buying tickets from scalpers; and I would return in a heavy fog from all that I had seen and heard there. In Petersburg there is a Jewish quarter: it begins just beyond the Mariinsky Theater, where the scalpers freeze, behind the prison angel left over from the Lithuanian Castle that burnt down in the time of the Revolution. Scattered throughout market streets

---

4. Shavli is the Russian name of Šiauliai, a district capital in northern Lithuania, also known as Schaulen in German and Shavel or Shavl in Yiddish; Mandelstam mistakenly (or condescendingly) refers to Šiauliai as *mestechko* ("small town," "shtetl"); in 1902 it had a Jewish population of about 9,900 out of a total of about 17,000.

were Jewish signs with a bull and cow, women with marriage wigs peering out from beneath headscarves, and worldly child-adoring old men mincing in their floor-length caftans. The synagogue, with its conical hats and onion spheres, is lost among the wretched buildings like a luxuriant, alien, exotic fig tree. Velvet berets with pompons, tired attendants and choristers, menorah clusters, tall velvet headdresses. The Jewish vessel, with its balcony full of ringing altos, with a choir of overwhelming children's voices, is gliding full sail, split by some ancient tempest into male and female halves. Lost in the women's balcony, I sneaked around like a thief, concealing myself behind the beams. The cantor, like mighty Samson, brought down the leonine building—the velvet headdresses responded, and the wondrous equilibrium of vowels and consonants, in clearly enunciated words, communicated an unvanquishable force to the chanting. But what an insult—the rabbi's banal, albeit literate, speech. What vulgarity when he pronounces "His Majesty the Emperor," how vapid is everything he says! And suddenly two gentlemen in top hats, splendidly dressed, gleaming with affluence, approach the heavy book with the elegant gestures of high society, leaving the circle to perform in our place, on behalf of everyone, something honorable and most important. "Who is he?"—"Baron Günzburg." "And he?"—"Varshavsky."[5]

As a child I absolutely never heard Yiddish, only later on did I get my fill of that crooning, ever surprised and disillusioned, questioning speech with its sharp accents on the semitones. The speech of the father and the speech of the mother—doesn't our language feed all its life on the confluence of the two? Do they not form its character? Mother's speech is clear and shrill, not the slightest foreign additive, with its somewhat widened and overly open vowels—grand literary Russian. Her vocabulary is meager and compressed, her phrases repetitive, but this is a language in which there is something rooted and confident. Mother loved to talk and enjoyed the stems and sounds of proper Russian speech, impoverished slightly by the way the intelligentsia used it. Was she not the first of our kin to obtain pure and clear Russian sounds? Father had no language at all; it was hotchpotch, tongue twisting, and languagelessness. The Russian of a Polish Jew? No. The speech of a German Jew? Not that either. Perhaps a particular Kurland accent? I've never heard one like his. A totally detached, invented language, a weave of words, the embellished and tangled talk of an autodidact, where ordinary words interlace with the obsolete, philosophical terms of Herder, Leibnitz, and Spinoza, the wondrous syntax of a Talmudic scholar, artificial, often incomplete locutions—anything but a language, be it Russian or German.

In essence, my father would transport me to a completely unfamiliar epoch, to surroundings that were remote but in no way Jewish. If you like, it was the purest

---

5. Günzburg, Baron Horace (1833–1909)—banker, diplomat, philanthropist, and major spokesman for the Jewish-Russian community; Varshavsky, Mark S. (1853–1897)—attorney, prominent Jewish-Russian public figure and author, and nephew of the railroad builder and philanthropist Abram Varshavsky (1821–1888); M.S. Varshavsky was close to Baron Günzburg and shared in his efforts on behalf of Russian Jewry.

eighteenth or even seventeenth century of an enlightened ghetto somewhere in Hamburg. Religious interests had been completely scratched out and dissolved. Enlightenment philosophy was transformed into intricate Talmudic pantheism. Somewhere in the vicinity Spinoza is breeding his spiders in a jar. There is a general anticipation of Rousseau and his natural man. All is detached, intricate, and schematic to the outer limits of possibility. A fourteen-year-old boy, raised to be a rabbi and forbidden secular books, runs away to Berlin, finds himself in a Talmudic academy alongside equally stubborn, brainy youths from backwater small towns, who regard themselves as geniuses; instead of the Talmud, he reads Schiller and, note, reads it as though it had just come out. After sticking with it for some time before falling out of this strange university, he dives back into the boiling world of the 1870s, where he learns about the conspiratorial dairy stand on Karavannaya Street from which a mine was planted under Alexander [II], and he preaches the philosophical ideals of the eighteenth century to flaccid and bemused clientele in a glove shop and a leather factory.

When they were taking me to the city of Riga, to my Riga grandfather and grandmother, I resisted and nearly wept. It seemed to me they were taking me to the homeland of my father's unfathomable philosophy. We set out with an artillery of boxes and baskets with padlocks, our bulging, cumbersome household belongings. Winter clothes were sprinkled with the coarse salt of naphthalene. Armchairs stood like white horses in the horse-blankets of their covers. The preparations for the trip to the Riga coast depressed me. At the time I collected nails: the most peculiar collector's fancy. I would run my fingers through my piles of nails like the miserly knight,[6] rejoicing as my prickly treasure trove grew. Now they took my nails and used them for packaging.

The trip was disquieting. At night in Derpt,[7] some *Vereins*[8] stormed our dimly lit train car, singing their loud Estonian songs; they were returning from a big song festival. The Estonians pounded and endeavored to break through the door. It was very frightening.

Grandfather was a blue-eyed old man in a yarmulke covering half his forehead, with prominent, rather solemn features, of the sort very esteemed Jews sometimes possess. He smiled, happily greeting us—he wanted to be affectionate but didn't know how—his thick brows lifted. He wanted to take me into his arms; I was on the verge of tears. My kindly grandmother, with a black wig over her gray hair, in a housecoat with yellowish flowers, shuffled with tiny steps across the squeaky hardwood floors and continuously tried to treat me to something or other.

She would ask, "Hungry? Hungry?"—the only Russian word she knew. But I didn't like the spiced old people's delicacies, their bitter almond taste. My par-

---

6. Reference to the title of Aleksandr Pushkin's "little tragedy" *The Miserly Knight* (Skupoi rytsar', 1830).

7. Derpt (Germ. Dorpat; orig. Russ. Yuriev)—German name of present-day Tartu, the location of Estonia's oldest university.

8. Mandelstam uses the German word *Verein* (organization, society, association), probably in reference to members of a society or union of ethnic Estonians, perhaps a student brotherhood.

ents went out to town. My disappointed grandpa and sad and frantic grandmother try striking up a conversation, then frown like old ruffled birds. I tried to explain that I wanted my mother, but they didn't understand. Then I used my fingers on the table to depict my desire to leave, making a walking motion with my middle finger and pointer.

Suddenly grandfather drew a black-and-yellow silk shawl from the drawer of a commode, put it over my shoulders, and made me repeat after him words made up of unfamiliar noise; dissatisfied with my mumbling, he became angry and shook his head with disapproval. I felt suffocated and afraid. I don't remember how my mother came to my rescue.

Father would often refer to grandfather's honesty as a spiritual virtue. For a Jew, honesty is wisdom and almost sanctity. The further back in the generation of these somber, blue-eyed old men, the more honest and serious they were. Great-grandfather Benjamin once said, "I'm through with my business and trade—I need no more money." He had exactly enough to last him until the day he died. He did not leave a kopeck.

The Riga coast might as well be an entire country. It's famous for its viscous, incredibly fine and pure yellow sand (only an hourglass had such sand!) and for the fenestrated little walkways, one or two boards wide, spanning the twenty-verst resort Sahara.

No other resort can compare with the vacationland of the Riga coast. The walkways, flowerbeds, palisades, and glass spheres form a never-ending settlement, all on the kind of yellow stone-ground flour of the canary-tinted sand that children play with.

In their backyards, the Latvians dry and string out flounder, a one-eyed, bony fish, flat as a wide palm. Children crying, piano scales, countless dentists' moaning patients, the clang of dishes in small resort *table d'hôte*, singers' trills, and peddlers' cries never wane in the labyrinth of kitchen gardens, bakeries, and barbed wire; and along horseshoe rails on a sand foundation, as far as the eye can see, run toy trains filled with fare dodgers who jump aboard while the trains are moving, from the meticulous German Bilderlingshof to the overcrowded Jewish Dubbeln, which smells of diapers. Through the sparse pine groves wander traveling musicians—two pretzel-shaped trumpets, a clarinet, and a trombone—and, emitting their unforgiving brass out-of-tune notes, are cast out at every stop, here and there regaling listeners with the cavalry march of the lovely Karolina.

The whole territory was owned by a monocled baron by the name of Firks. He had partitioned his land into "clean of Jews" and "not clean." On the clean land sat the German students, ironing little tables with their beer mugs. On the Judaic land, diapers were hanging and scales gagged their way up and down. In Majorenhof, on the German side, there was music—a symphony orchestra in a garden shell, Strauss's "Death and Transfiguration." Elderly fraus with flushed cheeks, in fresh mourning, found comfort there.

In Dubbeln, where the Jews were, the orchestra gagged on Tchaikovsky's "Pathétique." And one could hear the two stringed nests calling to each other. It was at that time that I fell in love with Tchaikovsky, with a sickly nervous tension reminiscent of the desire of Dostoevsky's Netochka Nezvanova[9] to hear a violin concerto playing behind a flame of silk curtains. I would glean the broad, smooth, purely violin phrases in Tchaikovsky from behind a barbed-wire fence, and more than once I would tear my clothes and scratch my hands while trying to sneak up to the orchestra shell. I would fish fragments of strong violin music from the wild gramophone of the resort cacophony. I don't remember how this awe for the symphony orchestra grew in me, but I think I correctly understood Tchaikovsky, sensing in him a particular feeling for the concertesque.

How convincing they sounded, these violin voices, softened by Italian lack of will but still Russian, in this dirty Jewish cloaca! What a thread extended from those first squalid performances to the silk fire of the Assembly of Noble Deputies and the puny Scriabin, who might be squished any minute by the still mute semicircle of singers and the violin forest of "Prometheus" surrounding him from all sides, over which, like a shield, hangs the sound receiver, a strange glass apparatus.

1925

Translated from the Russian by Amelia Glaser and Alexander Zeyliger

---

9. Netochka Nezvanova—protagonist of Fyodor Dostoevsky's short novel of the same name (1849).

VLADIMIR LIDIN

Vladimir Lidin (1894–1979), fiction writer and memoirist, was born Vladimir Gomberg in Moscow to a Russianized family; his father ran an export business. Lidin attended the Larazev Institute of Eastern Languages and graduated in 1915 from the Law Faculty of Moscow University. A disciple of the Russian neorealists (see David Aizman in vol. 1) and of Guy de Maupassant, Lidin published his first stories in 1908 and began to contribute stories to popular magazines and newspapers in 1912. Lidin's first collection, published in Moscow in 1916, was nihilistically titled *Tryn-trava* (an expression that means "nothing matters") and conjured up disoriented characters from the ranks of the bourgeoisie and the intelligentsia. The stories were free of specifically Jewish concerns and points of view. This first collection was followed by *Black Horses* (also 1916) and *Flooding Waters* (1917). An influence of the ornamentalism of Aleksey Remizov (1877–1957) on the style of Lidin's early prose was especially manifest in his longer prose works of the 1920s.

During World War I, Lidin fought on the eastern front and later joined the Red Army, serving in eastern Siberia. The experience informed the stories gathered in *Daily Humdrum* and *Tales of Many Days* (both 1923). In the early 1920s Lidin was a member of the Moscow Literary group "Lyrical Circle" (see Sofia Parnok in vol. 1). The New Economic Policy (NEP) gave Lidin's fiction a new subject. Lidin was among the most visible Soviet authors in the 1920s, publishing about twenty books of fiction, travelogue, and essays, including the story collection *Son of Man* (1927; two editions). Elliot Paul, coeditor of *transition* in 1926–28 with Eugene Jolas, published Lidin in the magazine and wrote there about him in August 1927: "Some of the American writers may even learn from Lidin, or at least be stimulated by him [. . .]. His attitude is much like that expressed by Gertrude Stein in 'Composition as Explanation,' that 'everything being the same, everything is naturally different.'" Lidin's novel *The Apostate* made a big splash, appearing in English in 1931 (American edition, *The Price of Life*, in 1932) and in other European languages.

In the 1930s Lidin pared down his style and straightened out his message. After a trip to the Far East, he produced *Grand or Pacific* (1932) about the creation of hunting and fishing collectives—a novel of "social command." In 1936 it appeared in Yiddish as *Groyser oder Shtiler*. Lidin was a military reporter for *Izvestia* in 1941–42; his essays on the first year of the Nazi invasion were gathered in *Winter of 1941*. Owing to Stalin's displeasure with one of Lidin's reportages, the writer was demoted to an editorial position on the staff of a regional military newspaper. A gap in Lidin's publications during 1943–46 reflects his having fallen into disfavor; *Exile*, Lidin's novel about the first two years of the Nazi invasion, did not appear until 1947. His conformist works of the late 1940s and 1950s included the novel *Two Lives*. In the post-Stalinist years, Lidin published the literary memoir *People and Meetings* (1957) and held positions of some prominence in the apparatus of the Union of Soviet Writers, living and actively publishing to the ripe age of eighty-five. Lidin's three-volume *Works* (1973–74) did not do justice to his best writings from the 1920s. His unpublished notebooks of the 1970s were included in the post-Soviet volume *The Four Seasons* (1991).

Vladimir Lidin devoted one early story, "Jewish Luck" (June 1922), to the destinies of Russian Jews during the Revolution and the civil war. The sentiment, although not the style, of "Jewish Luck" parallels some of Isaac Babel's stories in *Red Cavalry* (see Babel in vol. 1). The story first appeared in Lidin's 1923 collection *Daily Humdrum* and was included in his *Stories of the Year 1920* (1925) and his six-volume *Collected Works* (1928–30), never again to be reprinted in Lidin's numerous Soviet editions or even in the 1991 volume of his stories and essays edited by his daughter. In his fiction, Lidin revisited Jewish themes and topics only once after "Jewish Luck," drawing a less than flattering portrait of a Jewish black marketeer in *The Apostate*.

Lidin contributed a piece on the annihilation of the Jewish population of Talnoe in Ukraine to *The Black Book*; the book never appeared in the USSR (see Ilya Ehrenburg and Vassily Grossman in vol. 1). A memorial essay about Mikhail Gershenzon (vol. 1) was included in Lidin's 1927 volume *Routes and Versts* and reprinted in 1930. Lidin did not include it in his postwar memoir *People and Meetings*, where other Jewish writers and artists had speaking parts, including Sholem Asch, Emmanuil Kazakevich (vol. 2), Shloyme Mikhoels, Joseph Roth, and Stefan Zweig. As he revised and enlarged the memoir (1961, 1965, 1974), the cast of Jewish characters moderately expanded.

Jewish Luck

In winter the shaggy sky scatters puffy, fluffy lamb's wool; in summer it blooms like forget-me-nots. Beyond that puffy, woolly sky, beyond that radiant, forget-me-not sky—in spring and in summer, in fall and in winter—is the Great One, Adonai. Under the sky, seven floors down, under a dark staircase, is Aaron Pinkhus. All children are equally pleasing to their father, and Aaron Pinkhus is equally dear to His Father's heart, but can the Lord keep up with all his sons, and what does he know about Aaron Pinkhus? For seventy-seven years now, Pinkhus has been praising His name; and for thirty-three years, he has been living under the staircase, seven floors down, under the engineers, under the dentists, under the lawyers, singers, and shopkeepers.

The shaggy sky, still bearing its winter frown, hangs low, its drooping belly clings to the upper floors: the dentists are still sleeping and the singer is curled up under his pink blanket when Pinkhus begins his day. What awaits an impoverished Jew, and what does the whitish day hold out to him? Yet he is already praying at the window, his brown prayer book in his hand, and he is thanking his Father for his long life, for his Father's generosity, for the radiant glory of His name. Each man is going about his earthly business, and so let the dentists, the lawyers, and the shopkeepers continue to sleep on peacefully; all in good time the machine will sing out as its needle drills through someone's aching tooth, the lawyer will run off clutching his briefcase, the singer in his canvas jacket will whine away at the piano, and the shopkeeper will open up for business. And even though the lawyer is not rushing to court in his formal frock coat, and even though the shopkeeper has no business, nevertheless the lawyer rushes off at the usual hour with his overstuffed briefcase, and the sealed packages of goods continue to lie in the shops, and people's chipped teeth continue to hurt.

And though fame has come and poverty has gone, and the colonel from the fifth floor is walking around in a derby shiny from years of wear, and though red flags are licking the ashen sky in the October wind—at the appointed hour Pinkhus whispers as before in his corner, and his gray eyes look up with Jewish sorrow from the cherished lines of his prayer book, look out over the brownish windowpanes of the basement, look out at the great expanse man has created, at the great will man has shown, at his daily toil. And so what if all people are not equal and if there are poor Jews who have nothing—will not they all be laid out at the appointed time with their feet to the east, and will not the rabbi strew the sacred soil of Israel on their purplish eyelids? It is all the same to the Lord how a Jew travels on his last journey, whether he is borne in a black hearse adorned with a six-pointed star or whether his wife takes him in a shroud in the janitor's sleigh.

Fate drives people from start to finish: they lie in unheated railroad cars, they hang from roofs, they pile themselves up side by side at railroad stations; and through the railroad cars, from car to car, and through lice-infested stations filled with soldiers' ragged clothes, walks the Dark Lady, typhus. The train, dirty as a hog, tosses out many of them: they crawl away from the station with bags and sacks. They lie on steps and nibble stale bread clutched in their hands, while a strange, starving, and empty city looms foggily ahead. But a poor Jew is always a wanderer, and he is used to his wanderings. He arrived at the big city barely an hour ago, and he has already found other Jews; and after another day has passed, he is setting up his business and rushing across streets, his hands in his pockets, a bowler hat cocked back on his head; and after three more days, many people already know him and greet him. There are a lot of things that can be done if you just stand all day at the train station: give directions to someone, how to get somewhere; watch over someone else's things. He stands on the steps of the station in a peaked cap, with white *peyes*, with Abraham's staff: what's thrust into his hand is what he lives by. Day after day, he gathers potato peelings on the upper floors, and in the evening he sits in the unheated basement—and whispers. Today he carried a suitcase for a druggist from out of town, and though on Sabbath eve he is not sitting at a table covered with a white tablecloth, and though there is no silver candlestick, nevertheless the Lord hears both the prayer of the rich man at his heavily laden table and the prayer of the pauper from that corner of the basement.

For what does a man know of his fate? For seventy-seven years he lives on this earth and knows nothing of the morrow. And for the thousandth time Pinkhus whispers the ancient prayer, knowing nothing of the dentist Yakov Abramovich, whom, together with his son Aronchik, the black train is taking on an interminable ride from places where people are starving, where no one goes to the dentist, to a big city. On and on goes the train through the night and stands for days on end at wet stations, roars, and crawls on. It is carrying people, flour, and lice. And Yakov Abramovich is sitting at the dark door, looking at the dark fields woven with golden clusters of locomotive sparks—and he is thinking. What is the dentist thinking about at night in the dark railroad car, among the sacks, lice, people, next to a case on which his five-year-old son Aronchik is sleeping and which contains the neatly arranged instruments of his trade. He thinks about how he will lay them out in a bright room in the big city, how his first visitor will enter, and then another; the fame of his precise and skillful work will spread, he'll write down appointments in a yellow book, and his son Aronchik will eat not just a crust of black bread and wheat gruel, for he'll cook him white rice and thickly smear butter on warm wheat bread. And the Almighty Adonai does not sleep; He listens to the prayers from the damp cellar and from the railroad car as it is pulled along the night rails and ties together into one knot the fate of two Jews, so that they may both remember His name, fear His wrath, and praise His wisdom.

Man lives his life; and although somewhere, beyond the gates of each city, lie white markers on flat graves, he gives little thought to his hour of death and bustles about, toils, and rushes off somewhere. And little did the dentist Yakov Abramovich think that he was not taking his son to a big noisy city where he would feed him well but that he was taking him to that quiet silent boundary where there is sleep, silence, and peace. His son Aronchik, who with his curls and lively eyes looked like him, gazed cheerfully through the doors of the railroad car at the endless fields flying by. But the longer they rode and the more fields they left behind, the more bored was Aronchik, and when the train finally ended its journey and the city rose up in the fog and the rain, Aronchik was lying silently and looking past it all with his sad hazel eyes that seemed to hide an adult soul.

And nothing happened the way Yakov Abramovich had thought it would: there was no big bright room where he could lay out his instruments and begin earning his daily bread, and there was no big noisy city where no one could come to naught and where even the poorest man went to the dentist. Instead, there was an alien, damp, shuttered city; people rushed by with their burdens, and though many had a cheek bound up, but no one went to the dentist. And there was a department where Yakov Abramovich stood in line and where a frenzied individual in a soldier's jacket shouted to everyone that he had no rooms and that he could not deal with everyone at once; and Yakov Abramovich, without a document for a room, wandered together with all the others from there to the train station, to track number seven, the holding track, where in the darkness of the railroad car lay feverish Aronchik. And for the first time in his entire life Yakov Abramovich did not offer up the evening prayer but lay face down and stayed that way, sleepless, his mind blank. Engines hooted on the tracks, pulled at the car, dragged it down the track switches and pushed it again, and the morning that descended onto the wet tracks was boundless, washed down by a sticky dawn. Once again from early morning on Yakov Abramovich went along the empty tracks to the department where people stood downcast and no one believed in a miracle, and again in the evening he hastened back to his mobile residence with a warm *pirozhok* for his son Aronchik; but the boy only blinked his bright eyes and did not eat the *pirozhok*.

And that evening, when Yakov Abramovich went to the station seeking a doctor, people, help, he saw a fellow Jew, an old Jew, who looked like his father, and he approached him seeking help. People seemed just like ants: they crawled toward each other, wiggled their whiskers—and Pinkhus has already dived into the familiar darkness of the empty square, he has gone to find a doctor and brought back with him an ear specialist whom fate had long ago taught how to treat any and all illnesses.

But what does it matter to the Lord, who sets the limit to the fates of all living beings—what does it matter to him that Pinkhus is rushing about in desperation that morning to find medicine. And so that morning He calls to a brown-eyed dark angel and orders him to descend to earth, to receive the soul of the child Aaron the son of Yakov, to put an end to his five years of wandering. In the morning, when the engine is pulling the railroad car for the eighth time and taking it down track eleven, the angel seeks out freight car No. 1724 on track eleven—an urgent return—and takes curly-haired Aronchik with him into a spacious room. The dentist Yakov Abramovich is still sleeping and so is the homeless pharmacist's apprentice, who has come from starving places to the big city to study and to earn his daily bread.

Morning has already dawned, and the dentist has prostrated himself with a moan before his son. The locomotives toot, the trains roll on—he lies there unmoving, having lost faith in his Father. And that morning there comes to him old Pinkhus, whom for seventy-eight years now the Wise One has been forcing to live out a life of toil, to praise His Name, and to reaffirm his faith in Him.

"Great is Adonai, and wise are his deeds," he says, "and a man should not grieve for his son. A man must go on living and working—and give his son over unto the earth. But while a man may know how expensive it is to live, he does not know how expensive it is to die. Everyone needs to eat, and the poor cantor has little children who are asking for bread, and the coachman and the horses who pull the hearse need to eat; for it is all the same to the Lord how the son will come to his final resting place: whether in a black hearse or whether for a small payment Pinkhus will carefully carry him all the way to the cemetery, where he will give him over unto the earth in accordance with the proper rites.

I ask you, how could a parent allow his child to be carried in a sack like a blind kitten? And I ask you: What is a parent to do when he has neither lodging nor money and when he's already being expelled from his mobile home on track eleven and all he has are instruments for the care of teeth, those teeth which no one bothers about? And then everything is clear to the Lord, and it is clear to curly-haired white Aronchik; where and why the old Jew is carrying him on his back in a sack, trudging from street to street, wheezing and whispering prayers. But though Pinkhus is whispering a prayer and walking with a firm stride along a familiar route on wide noisy streets, does he know that in the sack he's carrying not someone else's cold little boy but his own bitter Jewish luck?

People are hurrying about their business, and each one has his own cares. And no one stops to look at how a policeman comes up to the aged Jew with a sack and feels the sack. And the policeman is already blowing his whistle, and a crowd is gathering around, and a woman is waving her umbrella, saying that in her house there's a boy who's missing . . .

Does it take a lot for an eighty-year-old man to follow after Aronchik into his Father's bosom: a rock to the temple or a kick between the shoulder blades? But the Wise One protects his elderly son. And so he's already being led away under guard, and the crowd is being dispersed, and has not the man with a close-cropped haircut and a policeman's whistle who is leading him away been sent to earth by a radiant angel?

Days pass. Time flows like a stream of sand and the sand brings new worries, respite, and toil. The dentist Yakov Abramovich has already been given the white permission slip with which he has moved into a room and is heating the stove, and the first visitor has already come to see him and has thanked him for extracting a tooth. Thirty mornings Pinkhus has already whispered his prayers in a dark corner of his new home, where behind an iron grille the day pours down dully and people sit on the planks and swear at each other and languish at the windows and the Father's prodigal children play at four-leaf clover—thieves, rogues, swindlers. But each morning he carefully performs his ritual among them, and on the thirty-first morning he is taken across the city to be put on trial.

He walks along with the others, lands in puddles, and passersby turn to have a look: where are they taking that aged Jew and for what misdeed? But he pays no attention to them, and how can he expect any happiness in life when in the eighth decade of an honest life he's being put on trial like a swindler. The judges and a crowd of people are all sitting on benches around him, and they are all watching how mournfully he stands on his weak legs, how close his weak dying voice is to his eternal, old, and blessed Father.

The judges want to know a lot of things: how he lived and where he was carrying the boy from, and why he was carrying him in a sack like a kitten. And Pinkhus answers all the questions: how he lived in dire poverty for seventy years, and how little money the dentist with no patients had, and how he carried the dentist's son for a small payment—for who knows what kinds of jobs the Lord may send a poor man. And the judges ask a lot of questions of other people, and when they have found out everything from everyone, they write everything down and go off to decide their earthly fates. But can earthly judges be frightening to a Jew when his eyelids are already trembling from the weight of the holy earth that is coming ever closer and his drooping eyes see the great open space far above the roofs and people? He sits and whispers—and the Lord sends down to earth a third angel, who puts on a green army jacket and jackboots, goes to the table, and together with the other judges reads what is on a white sheet of paper. He reads out that the Jew Pinkhus lived for seventy years in dire poverty and did that deed because of that poverty, and that he had hauled a thousand sacks with loads. That they held flour and salt and rich fabrics, and that these sacks were for people's enormous vanity; and the one thousand first sack that he had carried was the sack with dead Aronchik, and that dead Aronchik was his Jewish luck: from now on he would have a roof over his head and bread and would live out the rest of his days in a house where all the old men have a hot meal on weekdays and on holidays.

For how can a traveler know where he will be able to drink his fill of water, and how can a poor Jew know in which sack he bears his bitter good luck on his bent shoulders?

1922

Translated from the Russian by Lynn Visson

LEV LUNTS

Lev Lunts (1901–1924), fiction writer, playwright, critic, and translator, was born in St. Petersburg to an affluent family and received a Jewish education in his childhood. He studied at Petrograd University in 1918–1922, staying on to do graduate work and to teach Spanish and French (Lunts knew eight or nine languages). Both Maxim Gorky and Evgeny Zamyatin were taken with his literary talent, and Lunts's essays, stories, and plays made him a celebrity in the early 1920s.

Lunts became the guiding spirit behind the Serapion Brothers literary group in 1920–21. Active until 1929, the group included the prose writers Konstantin Fedin (1892–1977), Vsevolod Ivanov (1895–1963), Mikhail Zoshchenko (1895–1958), Nikolay Nikitin (1897–1963), Mikhail Slonimsky (1897–1972), and Veniamin Kaverin (1902–1989; in vol. 1); the poets Elizaveta Polonskaya (1890–1969; in vol. 1) and Nikolay Tikhonov (1896–1979); and the critic Ilya Gruzdev (1892–1960). The poet Vladimir Posner (1905–1992) and the writer and critic Viktor Shklovsky (1893–1984; in vol. 1) were initially close to the group, as was the playwright Evgeny Shvarts (1896–1958). Lunts proposed the group's name after E.T.A. Hoffmann's collection *The Serapion Brethren* (1819–21). Hoffmann's hermit Serapion and his brothers became an allegorical model of literary salvation. The Serapions used coded names: Lunts's was "Brother Buffoon"; Kaverin's, "Brother Alchemist"; and so forth. In addition to camaraderie, humanistic values, and a penchant for fantasy, the Serapions shared a commitment to narrative fiction. Lunts's manifesto, "Why We Are Serapion Brothers," appeared in 1921. "It is high time to say that a non-Communist short story can be mediocre, but it can also be a work of genius," he stated. "And we do not care with whom [meaning "on whose side"] Blok the poet, the author of *The Twelve* [1918 epic poem about the Revolution] was, or Bunin the writer, the author of 'The Gentleman from San Francisco' [1915 novella about the death of a wealthy American on Capri. [. . .] We are with hermit Serapion. [. . .] We write not for propaganda." Lunts responded to the barrage of official Marxist criticism in the essay "On Criticism and Ideology." He spelled out his orientation in the second manifesto, "Go West," published in 1923 in Gorky's Berlin-based magazine *Conversation* (*Beseda*).

Living at the Petrograd House of the Arts in harsh conditions with his health deteriorating, Lunts remained prolific, writing short stories ("Native Land," "In the Desert," "Reference No. 37"). The Moscow-based Habimah Theater (see S. An-sky in vol. 1) asked Lunts to join its staff (he was unable) and commissioned from him a translation of *Saul* from the Italian of Vittorio Alfieri (1749–1803; Lunts completed it in 1923).

Lunts's first play, *Outside the Law* (1920), was accepted for production in Petrograd in 1923 but was banned. It was published in 1923 in *Conversation* and staged in several European cities. Luigi Pirandello thought it "the best play to come out of Russia in recent years." Lunts's other dramatic works include the one-act absurdist play *Here Come the Monkeys* (1920; published 1923), *Bertran de Born* (1922; published 1923), and the dystopian *City of Truth* (1923; published 1924).

In 1921 Lunts's family emigrated to Germany; Lunts joined his parents in June 1923. He died in Hamburg in 1924, probably of a congenital heart condition that resulted in a brain embolism. Inscriptions in Russian, German, and Hebrew on his gravestone pay tribute to his Russian and Western literary selves and his Jewish soul. In the words of Gary Kern, "fate spared Lunts from compromises but also kept his imaginative works from their intended public."

Wiping Lunts's name out of literary history, Soviet officialdom never forgave him his declarations. Launching the postwar campaign against "cosmopolitanism" in 1946 and vilifying Mikhail Zoshchenko, Andrey Zhdanov remembered the Serapion Brothers and cited Lunts's "preaching of rancid apoliticism [. . .]." Lunts's works circulated in the 1970s in Soviet samizdat, including in the underground magazine *Jews in the USSR* (*Evrei v SSSR*). Although collections of his works have appeared in the West, both in Russian and in translation, his literary return to Russia has been slow: a volume of Lunts's works, edited by the Israeli-Russian critic Mikhail Weinstein, finally came out in St. Petersburg in 1994.

In her notebook, Elizaveta Polonskaya wrote about Lunts's death: "He was the best of the Jewish boys who came to Russian literature" (see Polonskaya's "Shop of Splendors," written in commemoration of Lev Lunts, in vol. 1). More Jewish than his Jewish-Russian literary peers raised in Russianized families, Lunts expressed doubts about being a Jew in Russian literature. In 1922, Lunts wrote but never sent a letter to Maxim Gorky: "But I am a Jew, convinced, faithful, and I rejoice at that [. . .]. But I am a Russian Jew, and Russia is my native land, and I love Russia more than any other country. How can I reconcile these things?"

Two of Lunts's best stories draw parallels between Jewish life in ancient times and in Soviet Russia. "In the Desert" (1923) focused on the return of Jews from Egyptian bondage; composer Sergey Slonimsky, the son of Lunts's friend Mikhail Slonimsky, likened the story's "unique expressionism" to that of Arnold Schoenberg's *Moses and Aaron* (1932; 1957). Dated 1922 and included below, "Native Land" was published in Moscow in *The Jewish Almanac* (1923). To quote Efraim Sicher's commentary on Lunts's story, "Petrograd is decadent Babylon, and it is to ancient Babylon—the Jews' first exile, where they prayed to the West (the direction of Jerusalem) and where they

forgot their fathers' names—that [Lunts] dream travels dressed in his ancient He-
brew-Yiddish name Yehuda[h]–Leib, together with Binyamin ([Benjamin]–Veniamin–
Kaverin), who, like the other Serapion Brothers, also turns to the West." The dedication
to Veniamin Kaverin, who came from a much more assimilated family than Lunts,
hinted at the Jewish questions that galvanized the two young Jewish-Russian writers.
Both published in 1923, Kaverin's two early Jewish stories, "The Purple Palimpsest"
and "Shields (and Candles)" (in vol. 1), represent Kaverin's entries in his interrupted
dialogue with Lunts.

Native Land

To V. Kaverin

I.

"You do not know yourself, Venya,"[1] I said. "Just take a look at yourself."

A mirror. And in the mirror, a tall man with a powerful face. Black locks lash about
his stern forehead, and savage, deep, desertic eyes shine passionately under his calm,
clear brows.
"Venya, you do not see yourself. Thus you came out of Egypt to Canaan, remember? You lapped water from the Cheron, like this, with your belly on the ground,
thirstily and quickly. And remember how you overtook the hated one when he caught

---

1. "Venya" (Venia) is a common affectionate diminutive of Venyamin (Veniamin), the first
name of the writer V. Kaverin, to whom L. Lunts dedicated the story. Venyamin is the Russian
equivalent of the biblical name "Benjamin," youngest son of Jacob by Rachel, born on the road
between Bethel and Bethlehem. The smallest of the Jewish tribes at the time of the Exodus
from Egypt, the Benjaminites later gave the Jews their first king, Saul. Having formed a close
alliance at the rule of King David, the tribes of Benjamin and Judah formed the body of the
Jewish nation after the return from Babylonian captivity (see Ezra 1).
    "Lyova" is a common affectionate diminutive of Lev (literally: lion), Lunts's first name.
The latter explains the story's (ironically tragic) identification of the modern character of the
Russian Jew Lyova with the ancient Judean Yehudah (Judah). In Genesis 49:8–10, Jacob be-
stows this blessing upon Judah: "You, O Judah, your brothers shall praise/Your hand shall be
on the nape of your foes;/Your father's sons shall bow low to you./Judah is a lion's whelp;/On
prey, my son, have you grown,/He crouches, lies down like a lion,/Like the king of beasts—
who dare rouse him?/The scepter shall not depart from Judah,/Nor the ruler's staff from between his feet;/So that tribute shall come to him/And the homage of people be his." Commentators
commonly interpret Jacob's blessing of Judah to mean that he is destined to rule over the
Jewish people (lion as the king of animals) and to have the courage of a lion in fighting the
enemies of the Jews. At the end of the Torah, Moses "lion-blesses" two tribes: Gad (Deut.
33:20) and Dan (Deut. 33:22).

his hair in the foliage and hung over the ground? You killed him, and you screamed, and he screamed, and the cedar screamed . . ."

"Silly guy," answered Venya. "Why do you pester me? I don't like Jews. They're dirty . . ."

"Sure, Venya. But in every Jew, even in you, there exists—how can I put it?—an ancient prophet. Have you read the Bible? Look, I know what is in me, I have a high forehead . . . but then, I am small and puny, my nose peers down at my lip. Lev they call me—or Yehudah—but where is the lion in me? I want to, but I cannot squeeze it out of myself; I cannot summon forth what is austere and beautiful. . . . Pathos, Venya. But you can, you have the face of a prophet."

"Leave me alone, Lyova, please. I don't want to be a Jew."

On a summer evening in Petersburg, my friend and I are sharing homebrew. In the next room my father, an old Polish Jew, bald, with gray beard and peyes, prays to the east; and his soul mourns that his only son, the last scion of the ancient line, drinks homebrew on the holy eve of the Sabbath.[2] And the old Jew sees the blue sky of Palestine, where he has never been, but which *he has seen, now sees, and will always see*. And I, not believing in God, I also mourn. For I want to, but I cannot see the distant Jordan and the blue sky, because I love the city in which I was born and the language I speak—a foreign language.

"Venya," I say, "do you hear my father? Six days a week he trades, deceives and grumbles. But on the seventh day he sees Saul, who threw himself on his own sword. You too can see, you should see, in you there is rapture and frenzy—and cruelty, Venya."

"I'm coarse and hardened," he answers. "I don't like Jews. Why was I born a Jew? Still, you are right. I am foreign to myself. I cannot find myself."

II.

"Well, I am going to help you," I said. "Let's go, Venya."

Behind the wall my father stopped praying. They sat down at the table: father, mother, sister. They did not call me, for three years they had not called me; I lived like a Philistine in their home. Their home stood under an eternally blue sky, surrounded by vineyards, on a Bethlehem[3] mountain. But my home faced Zabalkansky Prospekt[4]—straight, foreign, but beautiful. And my sky was dirty, dusty, and cold.

The Revolution: empty streets. A white evening. The street swims along like a railway track, receding in the distance. Streetcar posts fly by like a flock of birds.

---

2. The writer's father, Natan Lunts, originally from Lithuania and a pharmacist by training, was an educated man with a strong flair for European languages and literatures. Not a traditional Orthodox Jew in his adulthood, he did honor Judaic rituals and raised his children to do the same.

3. The city of Bethlehem (*Bet Laham* in Hebrew) stands within the boundaries of the territory assigned to the tribe of Judah; see Joshua 15, esp. 15:20–63.

4. Zabalkansky Prospekt—old name of a street in St. Petersburg, renamed Mezhdunarodny Prospekt in 1922 and renamed Moskovsky Prospekt in 1956.

"Venya, when I look at this city it seems to me that I've seen it before: it was hot, straight and monstrous. And it was there we met; you were the same, only in different, strange clothing. You're laughing at me . . ."

But he is not laughing. On Obukhovsky Bridge, he is black and savage, he stands up taller, stretching his hands out over the river. His gray cloak flies up behind his shoulders, and his desertic, passionate eyes see.

"Yes!" he shouts, his voice singing like a violin string, long and powerfully. "I remember. We sailed on a boat together. It was round as a ball. And we poled it with boat hooks. It was hot . . ."

"It was hot!" I answer with a shout. We exchange frenzied looks, standing taller, feverish, and we recognize each other. Then suddenly we bend down humbly and laugh.

"What an odd one you are," says Venya. "Even I couldn't hold out. Such nonsense."

A white summer evening. The choral synagogue stands surrounded by dry stone houses. We go up the broad steps, and the puny custodian, an old shammes, comes out toward us. He says: "Ach, so it's you again? Not today. Today is Sabbath."

This is directed at me. It is not the first time I have come to him. And it is not the first time I have turned my back on him in disgust.

Looking aside, I thrust some money into his hand, and he slips away like a mouse, leading us noiselessly through an entryway into a gigantic sleeping hall.

Venya, bored, walks along and looks lazily about. But I take small, mincing steps, lowering my eyes.

"This vay," says the shammes.

A barely noticeable door screeches open, and we are seized by the bitter cold. Slippery stairs lead downward. The lamp flickers. And the door closes behind us.

"Listen!"

Far below—a rumbling.

"I have been here three times already, Venya. I was afraid . . . but with you I am not afraid.

"I also am not afraid," he says. "But I don't want to go. I don't want to."

He says, "I don't want to," and heads down the slippery stairs. "I don't want to," he says and keeps going.

The descent is long and stifling. And the further we go, the louder grows the rumbling. The lamp flickers as before.

The stairs end. A wall. Behind the wall sounds a loud, heavy rumble, the roar of wheels and the cracking of whips. And the lamp goes out.

"Lev," says Venyamin, "come on!"

"There's a wall here, Venyamin. I've been here many times. There is no exit."

And again in the dark his voice sings out like a violin string, long and powerfully.

"Yehudah! Here! I know the way!"

The stone door heaved open, and the blazing gold of the sun struck us furiously in the face.

1.

The first thing Yehudah remembered: The street, straight as the royal way. The heavy, sleepy sun dazzles the great city, and a white transparent dust floats over Yehudah. Yehudah—a boy in a dirty flaxen mantle and a dirty tunic—sits on the roadway and swallows the dust. A chariot flies by. The powerful horses, spread out like a fan, run snorting and tossing their stupid snouts in the sky. Toward them speeds another chariot, and with a dusty rattle the two chariots cross in the narrow street, maintaining their firm pace. Yehudah sits between them, and the sonorous Lydian whips whistle over his head.

The first thing Yehudah loved: The great city, the straight and precipitant streets, straight, precise angles and the huge, quiet houses. In Babylon was Yehudah born. He was short and fast, and his spirit was weak, like that of a senseless but cunning bird. He had no father, no mother, no grandfather, no friend; and no one knew his family or tribe, but he was a Judean.

Yehudah knew: far to the west, beyond the desert, lay a beautiful land, from which came his mother, whom he did not know, and his father, whom he did not remember. Yehudah saw his tribesmen praying to the west, praying to the mysterious and terrifying Yahweh to return them to the land of their ancestors. But Yehudah did not pray. For he lived in the street, and he loved the white, translucent dust of the city in which he was born, Babylon.

2.

But when the wind blew from the west the transparent dust turned yellow and stung the eyes. Then Yehudah arose and ran until the wind abated. Like a wild Nysaean horse, he flew along the straight streets. Babylonians lay on the ground, basking in the sun and swallowing the dust. Yehudah jumped over them, outstripping the chariots, and his red Judean hair fluttered in the wind like the mane of a lion. The wind blew from the west, across the desert, from the land of his father, whom he did not know, and his mother, whom he did not remember. And the yellow dust of the desert lifted Yehudah and swept him through Babylon like a grain of sand.

Babylon spread out over the Euphrates with straight streets and straight intersections. Straight as sunbeams at noon, the streets dropped to the river, proceeding in under the high embankments, tearing through the brass gates and descending in steps to the river. Like a stone from a sling, Yehudah ran beneath the gates, plunged into the rapid river and swam. The river was mottled with boats, and more than once boat hooks struck the Judean, and more than once they called to him coarsely and painfully loud. But Yehudah neither heard nor saw. After crossing the river, he ran up the steps and flew on, not stopping to shake the cold, bright drops from his mantle, pursued by the western wind.

He was weak and sickly, but when the wind blew from the desert he ran from sunrise to sunset to sunrise—faster than the angars,[5] footmen of the king. He ran past the old palace on the right bank and under the bright new palace on the mountain. Eight times he circled the temple of Bel Marduk, eight times according to the number of towers standing one on another. Four times he circled the mound of Babil, where the mysterious gardens hung in four stories, high over the city. The guards beat him with the blunt ends of the lances, and the archers drew a thick bowstring to see if an arrow would overtake him. The arrow did overtake him. But Yehudah, tireless as the yellow wind blowing from the desert, ran on and on through the city.

Around the city crept Nilitti-Bel, the great wall. It looked out on all four sides of the earth, and all four sides were equal in handbreadths. A hundred gates cut into the wall, and at the hundred gates the Bactrian trumpets trumpeted at sunset. The rampart was as wide as a street, and there was a street on the rampart. Toward evening Yehudah climbed the western wall and ran along its edge, looking out into the desert from where the wind blew. And when the wind abated and the dust again became white and transparent, the Judean lay down on the wall and looked to the west where there lay a mysterious, beautiful, foreign land.

3.

And when the wind blew from the swamps a damp stench crept into Babylon. Then the people went inside, and the horses, slowing down, lowered their heads. And then despair floated into Yehudah's soul. He got up and walked solemnly across the bridge to the right bank, where the Judeans lived in low, gloomy houses. He walked along heavily, swaying like a youth returning from a woman's bed for the first time. And coming up to his fellow tribesmen, he listened avidly to the ringing and cruel words of a prophet who told of a marvelous distant land. But Yehudah did not believe the prophet, and despair grew in his soul.

And it came to pass that once as he heard the prophet his gaze fell on the youth standing afar. He was a tall youth with a powerful face. Black locks lashed about his stern forehead, and savage, deep, desertic eyes shone passionately under his calm, clear brows. Yehudah recognized the youth but could not recall where he had seen him. And incomprehensible words spoke in his soul. He saw a gray, unfamiliar, cold sky, and a cold wind whistled in his ears.

And the youth looked at Yehudah and recognized him. His stern forehead tensed painfully, his eyes looked deeply: they saw a gray, unfamiliar cold sky.

Yehudah went up to him and asked: "Who are you, boy?"

And the youth answered: "I'm Benjamin, but my father's name I do not know. And who are you, boy?"

---

5. The word *angar* is apparently of Persian origin and entered modern European languages via the Greek *aggaros* (king's courier or messenger); its main imprint in English is the word "angariate" ("mounted courier") and its derivations.

And Yehudah answered: "I'm Yehudah, a Judean, but my father's name I do not know." Then Benjamin said, "I have a longing, Yehudah. I'm a stranger in Babylon. Where is my native land?"

And Yehudah repeated: "Where is my native land?"

And both fell silent. They breathed quickly and lightly, and incomprehensible words arose from their souls. Then suddenly Yehudah noticed that on the youth's left arm, just below the shoulder, there were three white spots like the marks of an ulcer in the form of a triangle. And the two youths cried out in a strange foreign tongue.

And Benjamin said: "I know you."

And Yehudah said: "I know you."

For a long time they stood looking in confusion. But then the prophet shouted that deliverance was at hand, that Yahweh was coming with the forces of Koresh,[6] king of Persia, to return the Judeans to the promised land.

4.

The first thing that Benjamin recalled: the dark and strange itch on his left arm beneath the shoulder. On the left arm beneath the shoulder were the white porous spots. They itched like a salted wound. Benjamin fell to the ground like a wounded Epirusan dog, rubbed his arm in the sand, tore at it with his fingernails and kissed the spots with his burning lips, pushing back the skin with his right hand. But the pain did not abate. And only when the northern wind blew from the swamps did Benjamin arise and breathe in the cold, and with cold—peace.

The first thing Benjamin loved: a hot and consuming hatred. Eman the goldsmith, who was called his adopted father, found him as a baby in Babylon. Benjamin was very handsome, and Eman loved him as his own son, but Benjamin hated him and left him. And Benjamin went to Amasai the Levite and left Amasai the Levite. He changed many homes and fathers, for everywhere the blessings of Yahweh lay upon the home of his master, and upon his deeds, and upon his family. But Benjamin left. He had the soul of a beast, wise, silent and hating. He hated Babylon, the city in which he was born, and the beautiful land from which came his father, and where there once lived the father of his father, and the father of the god Yahweh, mysterious and foreign.

5.

And the years flowed on like the waters of the Euphrates plunging into the Erythraean Sea. New days rolled behind the old, Yehudah grew, a beard grew on his face and love grew in his heart for Rimat the Babylonian girl, daughter of Ramut the engraver. Rimat was small and dark and uncomely, but she had blue eyes like a northern slave girl. Yet Yehudah was poor and naked. He had the soul of a bird and he lived like a

---

6. Koresh—the Hebrew transliteration of Cyrus (559–529 B.C.E.), the Persian king who permitted the Jews previously held captive in Babylon to return to Judah in 538 B.C.E.

bird: senselessly and clearly. But when a beard grew on his face and love grew in his heart, he arose and went through the city seeking work. But he found none.

Every day Yehudah met Benjamin, and he shivered with fear and joy, seeing the gray, cold, native sky, which he did not recognize. The two youths looked long at each other and parted without a word.

But once Benjamin came up to Yehudah and said: "Yehudah, you are hungry."

And Yehudah said: "I am hungry."

And Benjamin said: "Come with me. I know a boat which has no boatmen."

And Yehudah asked: "Where shall we take it?"

And Benjamin answered: "To Ur."

And Yehudah said: "So be it."

6.

From Babylon to Ur they floated skins of Chiosian wine, Maltese fabrics, Cyprian copper, and Chalcedonian bronze artifacts. Thus was it done: the vessel was made of Armenian willows joined together and covered by skin: it was round and deep and filled with straw. Yehudah and Benjamin poled it downstream with long boat hooks. The wares lay on the straw, and an ass stood on the wares. And when they came to Ur, they sold the wares, the vessel and the straw, but the skin they removed and packed on the ass. Then they returned along the bank to Babylon, for the Euphrates was rapid, and no man could master its current.

More than once the youths coursed the Euphrates from Babylon to Ur, and more than once they measured the road from Ur to Babylon. Their old master Abiel had already died, and now they bought and sold the wares and the boats by themselves. Yehudah now had three changes of clothes and a pair of low Boeotian shoes. The girls began to look at him. And once while returning from Ur they were met on the road by some women. And Yehudah said: "I love you, girl." And she answered: "All right." And she lay down in the sand. But Benjamin stood off and looked to the west. There in the west were sesame fields lined with canals, fig orchards and the yellow desert beyond, but beyond the desert lay a beautiful and unknown land, from which came Benjamin's father, and where there once lived the father of his father.

And Yehudah began to love Benjamin, and Benjamin began to love Yehudah. But they loved each other in silence. Several times they made the journey without saying a word to each other. But once, as they neared the brass gates of Babylon, the western wind arose from the desert, stirred up Yehudah's spirit, and Yehudah exclaimed: "Is my native land not there?" His hand pointed to the west. And Benjamin exclaimed: "No!" And again he exclaimed: "No! I hate you, Yahweh, cruel and malicious one. Our sins lie upon your head, and your crimes lie upon your heart." And Benjamin fell to the ground, and his body was seized with writhings, and foam sprayed from his mouth. And he exclaimed: "Thus says Yahweh, who created you, O Jacob! Fear not: for I have redeemed you, you are mine. When you pass through the waters, I will be with you; and through the rivers, they shall not overflow you. For I am Yahweh, your God, the Holy One of Israel!

"I will bring you seed from the east, and gather you from the west; I will say to the north, Give up; and to the south, Keep not back: bring my sons from afar, and my daughters from the ends of the earth. I am Yahweh, your Holy One, the creator of Israel, your King."[7]

And Yehudah understood that the spirit of Yahweh had descended upon Benjamin, and he prostrated himself. But off in the distance, beyond the dust, he perceived the great wall, the eighth tower of the temple of Bel Marduk, and the hanging gardens on the mound of Babil; and he recalled the straight streets and the white, transparent dust, and said: "I do not believe!"

And on the following day Benjamin the prophet arose, took his knife and stripped the skin from his left arm beneath the shoulder. But when the wound healed and the new skin grew out, once again there showed the three white spots in the form of a triangle.

7.

And it came to pass that Yahweh took Koresh king of Persia by the hand to subdue the nations before him, and he loosed the loins of kings to open the gates before him. He went before Koresh and smoothed out the mountains, broke the gates of brass and cut in sunder the bars of iron.

Then Koresh king of Persia diverted the waters of the Euphrates into a lake; and when the star Tishtrya arose, he set out for Babylon along the dry bed. There he slew the king of Babylon and all those close to him. The king's treasures he took for himself, but the wives he distributed among his soldiers.

And that very night, when the Tishtrya arose, Bai-baiul, the bird of love, sang in Yehudah's heart. For Ramut the engraver was on the wall defending the city from its enemies, and Rimat his daughter let down a thick cord from her window. Yehudah climbed up the cord, and on that great night he knew Rimat and he knew happiness.

But in the morning, Habiz, a Persian, came to tell Rimat that he had killed her father and that henceforth she would be his slave.

8.

Thus says Yahweh through the lips of Benjamin the prophet:

"Fear not, O Jacob, my servant, whom I have chosen. For I will pour water upon that which thirsts and streams upon that which has dried up, I will pour my spirit upon

---

7. Here and below, Lunts presents a compressed and freely retold rendition of Isaiah 43–44, which the translator rendered more or less literally, although in keeping with the diction of the King James Bible.

your seed and my blessing upon your offspring; and they will spring up as among the grass, as willows at the watercourses. Remember these things, O Jacob and Israel, for you are my slaves. I will blot out, as a fog, your transgressions, and, as a cloud, your sins. Rejoice, O ye heavens, for Yahweh says this; shout for joy, ye depths of the earth; break forth into singing, ye mountains and forests. Thus says Yahweh, your redeemer and he that formed you from the womb. I am Yahweh, who made all things, who stretched forth the heavens alone, who spread abroad the earth by myself, who destroyed the tokens of liars and revealed the madness of diviners, who turned wise men backwards and made their knowledge foolish; who says to Jerusalem, You shall be inhabited; and to the cities of Judah, You shall be rebuilt; who says to the deep, Be dry; who says of Koresh, He is my slave."

And alone from all the crowd of Judeans, Yehudah spoke: "I do not believe!"

And Benjamin the prophet said: "Be accursed!"

9.

Along Aibur-shabu the processional way, across the canal Lilil-Khegalla, across the bridge to the Western Gate—crept the Judeans. The neighing of horses and the lowing of mules, the shouting of singers and the ringing of Judean harps and cymbals: all these glorified Yahweh and Koresh king of Persia. The horsemen in high hats held the crowd with whips. And all of them together were forty-three thousand six hundred people; from Bethlehem, Netophah, Azmaveth, Kiriath, Shaaraim, and other places. All were going to the land from which came their fathers, and where once there lived the fathers of the fathers. They went in tribes, in families, with wives, with children, with cattle, with utensils. And Sheshbazzar the son of Jehoiakim led them. And so they went out of Babylon.

Babylon spread out over the Euphrates with straight streets and straight intersections. Straight as sunbeams at noon, the streets were flying, and under the cruel, sleepy sun, the huge, quiet houses were burning. A white, transparent dust arose over Babylon.

Around Babylon crept Nilitti-Bel, the great wall. On its western side by the large gates lay Yehudah. And when the sons of all the tribes walked by, a congregation of men who did not know the names of their fathers came out onto the road. Ahead of them went Benjamin the prophet. He was straight and tall, and he looked to the west. And Yehudah shouted to him: "Benjamin!" And Benjamin answered: "Be accursed! One day you will come to me and tear off your clothes and sprinkle your head with ashes and say, 'Take me with you!' But you shall be repaid for your deeds, and for a traitor there is no forgiveness. Be accursed!"

And it was evening. The wind blew from the swamps. Then Yehudah arose and went to Habiz the Persian, saying: "Give me your slave Rimat for a wife." And Habiz asked him: "What will you give me in return?" And Yehudah said: "Myself!" And they shaved off his beard, and he bowed down to Ormuzd, and so he became a slave of the Persian and married the slave girl Rimat.

10.

On the fourth day Yehudah the slave went out in the street and lay down in the middle, as once he had lain as a boy. And he inhaled the white transparent dust of his native city, breathing quickly, deeply, and joyfully. Passersby stepped over him, chariots flew past him, cracking Lydian whips over his head.

But it came to pass when the sun stood in the west that a yellow wind arose from the desert. And the wind lifted up Yehudah. And Rimat the Babylonian girl asked him: "Where are you going?" But he did not answer.

And the wind bore Yehudah toward the western gates, toward the road which led through Circesium and Riblah to Jerusalem. It was hot, and Yehudah ran snorting like a horse, tireless as a horse, or an *angar*, footman of the king. The road was firm and sonorous, and Yehudah ran. His body was torn and bleeding, his head hung heavily on his shoulders, and he ran. He breathed loudly and with hissing, striking his heels soundlessly on the firm road; he ran during the day and he ran at night. Blood flooded his eyes, foam covered his body, his soul grew weak, but the western wind blew as before, and he ran.

On the third day toward evening he saw the Judeans away in the distance. He shouted and stretched his arms out to them, and he kept on shouting and stretching his arms, but he could not catch up with them. Then he fell on the ground and crawled along the road like a snake. His body was torn and bleeding, his soul was dripping with blood, and he crawled. The sun went down and came up again, and came up again; dust arose in the distance, the Judeans were walking to their native land, and Yehudah crawled. Behind Yehudah a bloody track crawled on the road. The wind blew from the west as before.

On the sixth day he reached the Judeans. Behind the others walked men who did not know the names of their fathers, and Benjamin the prophet was leading them. And when they stopped to rest beside a wrecked wayside house, Yehudah crawled up to them.

And Benjamin said: "He has betrayed his people and shaved off his beard. Kill him, Judeans!" And Yehudah said: "Brother!" But Benjamin answered: "You are not my brother." Then Yehudah got up. His knees were bent, his body was dripping with blood, his arms were covered with blood, but on his left arm beneath the shoulder there showed three white spots in the form of a triangle. Blood spurted from his mouth, and together with the blood he spit out unfamiliar words, foreign and cold. And the slave grabbed Benjamin by the left arm, and the Judeans saw the three white spots beneath the shoulder in the form of a triangle. And the prophet trembled and screamed in a foreign, sonorous tongue, thrusting his left arm out to Zaccai, a soldier, and saying: "Cut it off!" And Zaccai the soldier severed his left arm from the collarbone, and the arm fell onto the ground. And the Judeans saw the three white spots on the arm, just like the marks of a sore.

With his right hand Benjamin lifted it up and threw it at Yehudah. Yehudah fell, and the Judeans stoned him. The stones landed loudly and deliberately, collecting in a great heap.

Without a sound the door heaved closed, and a gray gloom peered silently at me. But the gold of a desertic, sleepy sun lingered in my eyes.

"Venyamin!" I cried. "Take me with you Venyamin!"

A steady rumble answered me from behind the wall, like stones falling on stones. And suddenly a voice rang out, long and powerfully, like a violin string: "Be accursed!"

And the clatter of numberless feet. I pressed against the damp wall, scratching it frantically. My wounded body, covered with blood, cried out in pain. The clatter died out in the distance. Then there was silence.

"Venyamin!" I cried. "Brother! Why have you left me?"

And again silence.

Minutes, perhaps days passed. I do not know how long I remained standing there: unmoving, without thought, in pain. And I do not know why suddenly I hunched over and went up the stairway. The ascent was difficult and stifling. My torn feet slipped, my knees touched the stairs and suddenly I stumbled. At that moment the lamp flickered, and I saw on the step before me my clothes, Venyamin's clothes and Venyamin's left arm. Blood, still warm was oozing from the shoulder, and standing out whitely and triumphantly in the form of a triangle were three *pock marks:* the eternal stamp of sapient Europe.

III.

I went out in the street. My beloved old pea jacket, my beloved old pants covered a ragged tunic and ragged body. I was no longer in pain; the clothing stopped up my wounds like a plaster. Only a golden, hot sun still roamed in my eyes.

A store. In the window, a mirror. And in the mirror, a little man, bald, with a narrow forehead and moist, cunning eyes; he is dirty and abominable. It is I. I recognize myself. And I understood: everything beautiful and ancient in me, my high forehead and enraptured eyes, everything remained there on the road which runs through Circesium and Riblah to Jerusalem. The Judeans are walking along that road to their native land; Sheshbazzar the son of Jehoiakim leads them, and behind them walks Benjamin the one-armed prophet.

Petersburg spread out over the Neva with straight streets and straight intersections. The streets precipitant as sunbeams and the huge, quiet houses. And over Petersburg lay a gray, cold sky: a native but foreign sky.

1922

Translated from the Russian by Gary Kern

VENIAMIN KAVERIN

Veniamin Kaverin (1902–1989), fiction writer, playwright, and memoirist, was born to an assimilated Jewish family and grew up in Pskov, a provincial capital southwest of St. Petersburg, where his father, a military musician, was stationed. Their family name was Zilber, and Kaverin later became the writer's Russian pseudonym. At the age of sixteen, Kaverin left Pskov to finish a gymnasium in Moscow. In 1920 he transferred from Moscow University to Petrograd University. The literary theorist and writer Yury Tynyanov (1894–1943) became his mentor; Kaverin later married Tynyanov's sister. Giving up poetry, Kaverin turned to prose as he trained with the people who redefined literary and cultural studies in the name of formalism—Tynyanov and Boris Eikhenbaum (1886–1959). After graduating from Petrograd University in 1924, Kaverin stayed on to do graduate work.

In 1920 Kaverin joined a group of writers formalized in 1921 and called the Serapion Brothers (see Lev Lunts and Elizaveta Polonskaya in vol. 1). His first published story appeared in a 1922 Serapion collective volume. Kaverin belonged to the western wing of the group, as reflected in his published statement of 1922: "Of the Russian writers, I love [E.T.A.] Hoffmann and [R.L.] Stevenson above all else." Kaverin's debut collection *Masters and Apprentices* (1923) contained his most experimental fiction. His novel *The End of the Gang* (1926) marked a shift from un-Russian realms toward contemporary life. Kaverin's novel *The Troublemaker, or Evenings at Vasilievsky Island* (1929) dealt with academic and literary politics; his professors and colleagues, including the Serapion "Brother Troublemaker" Viktor Shklovsky (vol. 1), served as the prototypes for this novel.

Kaverin's "Speech not Given on the Eighth Anniversary of the Order of the Serapion Brothers" (1929)—unpublished at the time but preserved—underscored the disintegration of the group. His novel *Artist Unknown* (1931), a defense of artistic freedom from collectivist and utilitarian aesthetics, was attacked as "a battle call of bourgeois restorationism." This attack pushed Kaverin toward the salutary formula of his next four decades: masterfully crafted novels that satisfied official ideological demands while also leaving room for the eternal ethical dilemmas of art and science. The novel that propelled Kaverin toward national fame, official acclaim, and prosperity was *Two Captains* (1938–44), awarded the Stalin Prize in 1946. A hit with both adolescents and adults, a romantic-heroic adventure tale with a double plot, *Two Captains* underwent over fifty editions in Russian alone.

Kaverin served as a war correspondent in 1941–45, reporting from several fronts.

Among his wartime books were *House on the Hill* (1941), *Leningrad. August 1941* (1942), and *We Became Different* (1943). Kaverin wrote about Israel Fisanovich (1914–1944), the heroic Jewish submarine officer, for the Jewish Antifascist Committee (JAC); his essays about Fisanovich appeared as a book in Yiddish. With the poet Pavel Antokolsky (in vol. 1), Kaverin coauthored "Sobibor Uprising" for the Ehrenburg–Grossman derailed *Black Book* (see inroductions to Ilya Ehrenburg and Vassily Grossman in vol. 1); in 1945 they managed to publish the essay in the magazine *Banner (Znamia)*.

Kaverin's trilogy *Open Book* (1949–56) fictionalized the careers of Zinaida Ermoleva (1898–1974) and her husband, Kaverin's brother Lev Zilber (1894–1966), both major microbiologists. Ermoleva headed the group that created Soviet penicillin in 1942; Alexander Fleming's discovery and Howard Walter Florey's laboratory production of penicillin had preceded Ermoleva's. The novel's subject was advantageous as Soviet science was under great pressure to make advances "independently" of the West.

Searches and Hopes, the third part of *Open Book*, depicted the darkest years for Soviet biological sciences and appeared only after Stalin's death, bridging Kaverin's middle and latter periods. Kaverin's anti-Stalinist works included *Piece of Glass* (1960) and *Seven Pairs of the Unclean* (1962). A leading Soviet author of the liberal camp, Kaverin, who remained prolific, was more restrained in his published works than in his support of dissident writers. One of Kaverin's best novels, *A Two-Hour Walk* (1979), elegantly dissected a scientist's moral undoing. The memoir *Illuminated Windows* (1970–75) was Kaverin's compromise with the Brezhnevite reality. Kaverin finished *Epilogue* in 1979; the last in a series of memoirs, it was written for the desk drawer. It was published in Moscow in 1989, the year of Kaverin's death, summing up his life of limited artistic cooperation with—and measured resistance to—Soviet ideology.

Jewish characters appeared in many of Kaverin's works, but Jewish topics were confined to his early works, including *Masters and Apprentices* (1923) and the novel *The End of the Gang* (1925). Still, in his later works Kaverin made the point of manifesting Jewishness, sometimes unexpectedly, as in the scene of a Jewish funeral in siege-stricken Leningrad (*Two Captains*).

The collection *Masters and Apprentices* showcased two of Kaverin's most Jewish stories, "Shields (and Candles)" and "A Purple Palimpsest" (both 1922); they were never reprinted after 1930. In "A Purple Palimpsest" (not included in this anthology), Diaspora in Western Europe represents the top layer of history's parchment, beneath which one can glean Jewish life in ancient Israel. In "Shields (and Candles)," which is found below, young Kaverin allegorically describes the place Jews held in European history. Kaverin's stories share their metahistorical exploration of the Jewish past with the early fiction of Lev Lunts (in vol. 1).

Shields (and Candles)

The game isn't worth the candle.
—A well-known [Russian] saying

I.

All three preserved silence or spoke briefly.

The cobbler's workroom—small, square, with a little oblong window looking out on a yard—was lit by a candle. The candle burned and crackled. Shadows crept behind it, and in its light three faces appeared in sharp outline: the first with a low brow and a heavy chin, the second redbearded and blunt, and the third the face of Birheim the cobbler.

They were playing.

The jack of diamonds was expending his worthless fate in an unequal squabble with the queen and king of clubs. The hearts calmly followed the course of the battle.

"There's the shadow," said Birheim. "There's the shadow of your head, carpenter."

The carpenter glanced at the cards, smiled in his beard and spoke:

"Keep your mind on the game, Birheim."

"There is no sorrow in the world," said Birheim again. "Carpenter, do you agree with me? There is no sorrow in the world."

"Maybe so," answered the carpenter. "I'm discarding the jack of spades, what do you say to that?"

And so the game continued. But late that night, after a fixed period of time had elapsed, Birheim arose, removed the decree from the table drawer and said:

"Lay down your cards."

And he threw his own down on the table.

The mute lowered his hands and cautiously unclasped them, but the carpenter only glanced at Birheim expectantly.

"Silence," repeated Birheim. Then he placed a tabouret on the table and sat down on it, stretching out his long and bony legs.

The mute removed the snuff from the candle, walked off and leaned against the wall, crossing his arms.

Birheim read:

---

1. Landsknecht (from Germ. *Land* = "land, country, state" and *Knecht* = "servant, helper, slave")—a wagering card game for two or more players, wherein one player acts as a dealer/banker, covers all the bets, and usually remains a dealer throughout the entire game. The game is believed to date back to the sixteenth century.

The decree of Landsknecht,[1] the ancient game invented in Germany.

We, the game of Landsknecht, bearing in mind both honor and faith, hereby inform our faithful servants: preserve our merits.

By edict of the king and the heretics, We, Landsknecht, are henceforth outlawed on penalty of death. Our servants are beset by unexampled persecutions. Many have paid with their lives for opposing this edict.

Yielding to the protracted prayers of Our faithful subjects and wishing to safeguard the life of Our people, We direct:

To change the symbols and names of the suits in the deck: hearts are shields, diamonds—banners, spades—lances, and clubs—swords.[2]

"So then," said Birheim, "listen, both of you, mute and carpenter."

"Someone's knocking," answered the carpenter. "Birheim, can you hear?"

In order that the new suits be fixed in the hearts of Our subjects, We deem it appropriate to institute and effect a game on the night of Saturday, month of August, year of 17—, using the new suits. But since the masters, as yet unaware of Our edict, were unable to print the aforesaid, the carpenter, mute and Birheim will serve as the suits for Our game.

"You are lances," said Birheim to the carpenter, "I am swords and the mute is banners, the merry suit."

"Listen," said the carpenter, "someone's knocking. Do you hear it? Or are your deaf, Birheim?"

"Someone's knocking," answered Birheim, "but in the edict there is no fourth person for hearts. The game cannot take place; there are only three of us, carpenter."

He continued reading:

At the conclusion of the game to notify us how the game was effected and in what way it ended.

Proclaimed in the year 17—, month of August, on the 7th day.

Signed on the original in His Majesty's own hand:

Landsknecht

---

2. The substitution is based on the French national symbols of card suits, which became international and were adopted in Russia: hearts (*coeur*); diamonds (*carreau*); spades (*pike*); clubs (*trefle*); in the Russian language, the terms for the four suits are *chervi* (hearts); *bubny* (diamonds); *piki* or *vini* (spades); and *trefy* or *kresti* (clubs). The mysterious substitution in the "decree of Landsknecht" possibly takes into account the German suit symbols: *Herz* (hearts); *Schellen* (bells, corresponds to diamonds); *Grun* or *Blatt* (green or leaf, corresponds to spades); and *Eichel* (acorn, corresponds to clubs); as well as the Italian and Spanish decks, where the suits are cups, coins, swords, and clubs, and the cups are sometimes drawn like chalices or candle holders.

"Birheim, you have been mad from the day of your birth," laughed the carpenter. "But I will obey the edict."

"Quiet," answered Birheim, "we lack the fourth suit."

"Night will pass quickly and we will fail to enact the king's edict."

The mute moaned indistinctly. His eyes blazed, while he himself, firmly clasping both elbows, shook from the terrible strain.

"An awl will serve as a sword," said Birheim, "needles as lances, scraps of leather as banners. But where will we get the shields?"

"When did you write that decree?" asked the carpenter. "Haven't I spent the whole day with you?"

The skin on Birheim's forehead gathered into creases and his eyebrows rose up toward his knotted hair.

"Someone's knocking," said the carpenter again, "I'll open the door."

He took a knife from the table and held it near the candle.

The light slid along the sparkling blade, formed a point and disappeared behind the folds of clothing.

The carpenter went to the door.

"Who knocks?" he asked, raising his hand to the bolt.

No one answered.

"Silence," said Birheim and tossed back his head, baring to the light a chin overgrown with coarse stubble.

The carpenter ran the tip of his finer along the blade and began to unfasten the bolt. The door flung open.

The flame of the candle tossed to the left, to the right, and again to the left.

The wind coursed through the room, and the mute, freeing his firmly clinched arms, breathed deeply and noisily.

A man stepped slowly through the door. The carpenter closed it and refastened the bolt.

"Who here is Birheim the cobbler?" asked the man. "The Jew Birheim, damn his soul!"

"His Majesty, the King," announced Birheim. "Landsknecht, I see. The fourth suit is shields."

He pursed his lips slyly and raised a finger to his brow.

"The Jew Birheim," repeated the soldier, sitting down at the table. "Hell's spawn. Are you Birheim, you with the red beard?"

The carpenter remained silent.

"We will enact the king's edict," screamed Birheim, and laughed: "Four suits: swords, lances, banners, shields—and the heretics will not touch us."

"He abducted my sister," said the soldier wearily. "Which one of you is Birheim, speak up."

The mute walked up close to him and raised his hands to the level of his shoulders. But then as if fearing something, he pressed his lips tightly and hurried back.

"Sister?" said Birheim, trying to recollect. "Your sister, Landsknecht? My memory has been rather vague of late."

"The Jew Birheim abducted her," repeated the soldier. "And stop calling me by that blasted name. I must kill him and return my sister to our home. Our home is burned down and destroyed."

"The devils dance on its ruins," said the carpenter sympathetically. "You're too late to return."

"Night fell long ago," observed Birheim. "Time to start the game."

His hands flicked away the cards and they landed on the table in a disordered heap.

The mute removed a bundle of candles from his pocket and began to light them slowly, one by one.

The workroom splintered into sharp angles under Birheim's unwavering gaze.

He lifted his eyelids with his fingers and looked around smiling: the window grating had weaved itself solidly into iron fingers and the gloomy night had fused into one mass behind the window.

"Where is my sister?" repeated the soldier. "I cannot find her anywhere."

"Birheim is anxious," said Birheim, placing his hand over his heart. "It is time to begin the game."

"Let us begin," prompted the carpenter, and the mute nodded in approval.

And they began.

II.

"May I have your attention," said Birheim, raising his hand. "May I have your attention. *Ching tsze tung*[3] says that our game was created in 1120 and that its origin is divine."

"I do not remember," answered the carpenter, "are the diamonds banners, or the clubs? The decree was vague on that point. And if I am lances, why don't you give me a shoe needle?"

"I will give you a needle," said Birheim, "and the mute a scrap of leather."

He separated the four suits from a deck of colored cards and threw one suit before each player. The black fell to the carpenter and Birheim; the mute and the soldier got red.

"Landsknecht, Your Majesty," said Birheim, "pick up your cards, you are delaying the game."

The soldier stood up and rattled his weapons. Instantly the mute's eyes blackened and his eyelids slightly flared. The carpenter fingered the knife in his pocket.

"Just a minute," said the soldier hoarsely and wearily, "I do not wish anyone ill. The Jew Birheim abducted my sister. I wish only to kill him. Nothing more."

"This may be so," replied Birheim, "but you are delaying the game. Please begin, Your Majesty."

---

3. *Ching tsze tung* (1678)—Chinese encyclopedic dictionary compiled by Eul Koung; historians of playing cards often cite this dictionary's entry on the origins and history of the game.

The soldier sat down and moved the candle to the center of the table.

The jack of lances and the ten and ace of banners were dealt to Birheim.

He threw down the ace and gathered in the low cards. The soldier calmly discarded the queen of shields.

Landsknecht, the king of banners, was still far away.

"Your beret is crumpled," said the queen of clubs to the jack, "and your face reveals expectation."

"Silence," rustled the jack, bending over in the hands of the soldier. "The people are in a peculiar mood today. The hands of that one sitting at the end of the table are trembling."

"Trembling?" repeated the queen derisively. "They are exchanging some frayed pieces of paper, and the hands of the one who is losing them are beginning to tremble."

"The hands of the hook-nosed man are trembling," answered the jack. "But don't you love it when they play with those round pieces of yellow and white? They ring gloriously when they fall and it's so pleasant to cover them with jacks' clothing."

"Their minutes are centuries to us," rustled the king of spades. "The senate must be convened; we will perish this night."

"That cannot be done until a new game begins," responded the jack. "Your Majesty, we will take every measure to safeguard your precious life. Take care, Your Majesty, not to scratch the dotted line on the uneven surface of the table."

"Seven years ago you left her a marvelous maiden," said Birheim. "But now you have not found her and you have not even found your own home."

"Home is burned down," answered the soldier. "Enough said about that. I recall with perfect clarity that her tresses were fair."

"The sister of His Majesty, King-Landsknecht, cannot disappear without a trace," said Birheim again. "You need only intensify your search and you will find her. But you have forgotten her face."

"Birheim killed the maiden," said the carpenter, beginning to tremble, but the mute squeezed his arm firmly and he fell silent.

"In the course of seven years I have forgotten her face," said the soldier. "Nothing wrong with that. But why do you keep calling me by the name of a king?"

And he threw down the ace of shields. The carpenter and the mute threw down low cards, Birheim—the jack of banners.

The first hand was coming to an end. The candles had burned down half-way and long streams of bright wax had poured down from the flames.

Landsknecht, the king of banners, a fair-headed man in a blue beret with a scepter in his hands, lay on top of the deck. The crossed insignia of the game, the sign of Landsknecht, had been cut by Birheim into blue ribbon which was strung across his shoulder. He fell to the soldier, who noisily pushed away the tabouret and stood up.

"Landsknecht?" said Birheim, glancing at the soldier's cards. "His Majesty, the King. Just look, carpenter, how pale his face is."

"Noble senate and loyal subjects," said the soldier, standing up to full height and raising his hand, "we have summoned you here today in order to discuss in the most sagacious manner the many difficulties which we have encountered at the very source of our lofty responsibilities."

"Madness, madness," screamed the carpenter, covering his face with his hands. "Birheim killed the maiden. Why play on any further?"

The soldier rose up from behind the table and waved his hands furiously.

"Play!"

They played.

III.

"In the name of our King-Landsknecht," announced the king of clubs, when all the kings had gathered in the center of the deck, "I declare this session of the senate open. The following questions require deliberation: First, an attack on His Imperial Majesty by those persons commonly termed the people."

All present startled and reached for their swords.

"Second," continued the king of clubs, "the replacement of our sacred suits by others. And third, the threat to the whole happy family of our subjects presented by the distressing condition of those persons who direct our fate."

"The people are our fate," grumbled the king of spades with contempt, "and we are the fate of the people. Who can make sense out of it?"

"I request a guard at the doors of the senate," he said loudly. "A crowd is rumbling at the windows. The fires on the squares have gone out."

"As regards the first question, it behooves me to state the following," said the third king, raising his scepter: "From whom came the information of the assassination attempt? In my domain all is quiet."

"The information came to us from the province of diamonds," answered the king of clubs. "During the last hand the mood of the people became unusually alarming."

"I have every basis," declared the king of hearts, arising from his place and holding high his scepter, "to confirm the aforesaid information. Our firm decision, taken in a recent session of the senate—"

"—I beg your forgiveness, Your Majesty," interrupted the king of clubs, "the guard has snapped to attention. It appears that the king is approaching the senate chamber."

The doors flung open and Landsknecht entered, jangling his weapons. His face twitched with a fierce spasm, his lips trembled.

"Who among you is Birheim the cobbler?" he screamed, going up to the table and casting his weary eyes about. "Home is burned down. My sister has vanished."

The kings glanced around in confusion.

"Your Majesty is ill," prompted the king of clubs, bowing low and blanching, "the events of recent days have taken a heavy toll on Your Majesty's health."

"Nonsense," answered King-Landsknecht, breathing heavily and attempting to draw his sword, "disloyalty pursues me, death snaps at my heels."

"He's falling, my God, he's falling," screamed the king of clubs, extending his arms. Night passed and the quick rays of dawn rushed in through the chinks of the windows.

"It seems to me," said the soldier, after the second hand had ended, "that games of chance were outlawed by an edict of the king. I will play no more."

"One more hand," answered Birheim. "Landsknecht, pick up your cards, we will continue the game."

"No," said the soldier again. "I will play no more. Night has passed. I came here to kill Birheim."

"You will kill him at the end of the game," insisted Birheim. "I beg you to pick up your cards."

"Nonsense," said the soldier, arising. "You see that morning has come, it's time to snuff the candles."

The mute pushed from the tabouret and stood up. Then he began to snuff the candles.

"He is executing the king's order," laughed the carpenter. "His Majesty gives orders."

"I will not play," repeated the soldier, breathing heavily and drawing the shiny steel of a cutlass from its scabbard. "You have a hooked nose. Are you Birheim, tell the truth?"

"Indeed I am," said Birheim, "you are not mistaken. But look at your shadow. Does it not seem to be falling?"

All the candles but one had gone out. And this last one rested in the hands of the mute.

He walked slowly from one man to the next. Coming up to Birheim, he stopped and peered into his eyes.

"The maiden was killed by me," said Birheim. "Night has passed, the candles have gone out, it is time to end the game."

And all three threw themselves on the soldier. He tried to lean forward and swing the cutlass but suddenly fell and lay still.

"We shall continue the game without the fourth suit," said Birheim. "We shall enact the king's edict."

And he wrapped a white rag around the teeth marks on his hands and outlined the soldier's profile with an awl on the edge of the table.

1922

Translated from the Russian by Gary Kern

Veniamin Kaverin, "Shchity (i svechi)." English translation reprinted by permission of Ardis Publishers. English translation copyright © by Ardis Publishers. Introduction and notes copyright © by Maxim D. Shrayer.

ILYA EHRENBURG

See Ehrenburg's early poems and the introductory essay (pp. 180-82) in the section "On the Eve: 1902–1903" in vol. 1 and Ehrenburg's wartime poems and essays in the section, "War and Terror: 1939–1953" in vol. 1. The complete title of Ilya Ehrenburg's novel excerpted below is *The Extraordinary Adventures of Julio Jurenito and His Disciples: Monsieur Delet, Karl Schmidt, Mr. Cool, Aleksey Tishin, Ercole Bambucci, Ilya Ehrenburg, and Aysha the Negro, in Days of Peace, War, and Revolution, in Paris, Mexico, Rome, Senegal, Kineshma, Moscow, and Other Places, as well as Diverse Opinions of the TEACHER about Pipes, about Death, about Love, about Freedom, about the Game of Chess, about the Tribe of Judah, about Constructivism, and about Numerous Other Matters.*

The prototype of the novel's charismatic protagonist was the great Mexican muralist Diego Rivera (1886–1957), whom Ehrenburg befriended in Paris. Oddly enough, despite a controversial episode of Jurenito's visit with Lenin in the Kremlin, Lenin and Boris Kamenev (1883–1936), a major Bolshevik leader, both liked the book. Originally published in Berlin in 1922, *Julio Jurenito* was reprinted in the USSR in 1927–28 and subsequently included there in Ehrenburg's collected editions. Jurenito, an anarchist, seeks to bring the world to the brink of self-destruction so as to summon a better new world. Jurenito dies under banal circumstances, his prospects unfulfilled. In the novel told by Jurenito's "disciple" Ehrenburg, Jewish questions keep popping up, and the chapter included here famously presents Ehrenburg's vision of Jewish history and his prophesy of the Shoah. The prophesy is crowned by a replaying of the famous Grand Inquisitor "poem" from Dostoevsky's *The Brothers Karamazov*, where structurally Ehrenburg assigns himself the place of Christ and Jurenito, that of the Grand Inquisitor.

From *The Extraordinary Adventures of Julio Jurenito and His Disciples*

Chapter XI
The Teacher's Prophecy Concerning the Destinies of the Tribe of Judah

On a lovely April evening, we forgathered once again in the Teacher's Paris studio on the seventh floor of one of the new buildings in the Grenelle quarter. We stood for a long time by the large windows, admiring the beloved city with its unique, insubstantial, unreal twilight. Schmidt, too, was with us, but I tried in vain to convey to him the beauty of the dove-gray houses, the stony groves of the Gothic churches, the leaden reflections in the slow Seine, the chestnut trees in flower, the first lights in the distance, and the touching song of a hoarse-voiced old man with his barrel organ underneath the window. Schmidt said that all this was excellent for a museum but that he had detested museums from childhood; one thing that did enchant him was the Eiffel Tower, so light, so slender, swaying in the wind like a reed, the indomitable iron bride to another age silhouetted against the tender blue of an April night.

Amid such peaceful talk we awaited the Teacher, who was dining with some important military supplier. He soon came in and, after putting away in a small safe a pile of documents that had been thrust untidily into his pockets, said to us cheerfully:

"Tonight I've done good work. Things are looking up. Now we can rest and chat for a while. But first, before I forget, I must draw up the text of the invitations, and you, Alexey Spiridonovich, will take them tomorrow to the Union Printing Works."

Five minutes later he showed us the following:

To Take Place Shortly
Solemn Performances
of the Destruction of the Tribe of Judah
in Budapest, Kiev, Jaffa, Algiers
and many other places.
The program will include, apart from the traditional pogroms—a public favorite—
a series of historical reconstructions in the spirit of the age, such as burning of Jews,
burying same alive, sprinkling of fields with Jewish blood, as well as modern methods
of "evacuation," "removal of suspicious elements," and so on and so forth.
This invitation is extended to
cardinals, bishops, archimandrites, British lords, Roman noblemen, Russian liberals,
French journalists, members of the Hohenzollern family, Greeks regardless of profession
or trade, and all others wishing to attend.
Time and place to be announced later.
Entrance free.

"Teacher!" Alexey Spiridonovich cried in horror. "This is unthinkable! The twentieth century and such vile doings! How can I deliver such a notice to the Union—I who have read Merezhkovsky!"[1]

"You are wrong to think that the two are incompatible. Very soon, in two years' time perhaps, or in five years, you will be convinced of the contrary. The twentieth century will turn out to be a very jolly and frivolous age, without any moral prejudices whatsoever; and the readers of Merezhkovsky will be the most enthusiastic audience at the performances. The diseases of mankind, don't you see, are not the measles of infancy but old, deep-seated attacks of gout, and certain habits have been formed in the course of time concerning their cure. You don't break a habit in your later years.

"When, in ancient Egypt, the Nile went on strike and drought set in, the wise men would remember the existence of the Jews, who would be summoned and slaughtered to the accompaniment of prayer; and the earth would be sprinkled with fresh Jewish blood: 'May famine pass us by!' Naturally this could not replace either rain or the Nile in flood, but nevertheless it gave some satisfaction. Even at that time, it is true, there were some cautious people of humane views who said that killing a few Jews wouldn't do any harm, of course, but sprinkling the earth with their blood was a bad idea because this blood was poisonous and would produce thistles instead of wheat.

"In Spain, whenever there was an epidemic—of the plague or the common cold—the Holy Fathers would solemnly proclaim forgiveness for the 'enemies of Christ and mankind' and, shedding profuse tears (not, however, profuse enough to put out the pyres), would burn a couple of thousand Jews. 'May the pestilence pass us by!' The humanists, fearing the high temperature of the fire and ash that the wind wafted everywhere, would whisper guardedly in each other's ears—lest they be overheard by some stray Inquisitor—'Wouldn't it be better just to starve them to death?' . . .

"In Southern Italy, during the earthquakes people would at first run away to the north, then come back cautiously, one by one, to see whether Mother Earth was still shaking. The Jews would also run away—in fact before anyone else—and also come home—later than anyone. Naturally, the earth shook either because they—the Jews—had wanted it or because it—the earth—had not wanted the Jews. In either case it was advisable to take representatives of the tribe and bury them alive, which was done

---

1. Merezhkovsky, Dmitry (1865–1941)—Russian writer and Christian religious philosopher, major representative of the symbolist movement; emigrated in 1919 with his wife, the writer Zinaida Gippius (1869–1945), and spent most of his émigré years in Paris. In the mid-to-late 1930s, Merezhkovsky's anti-Bolshevism (conjoined with his religious and political antisemitism and a degree of opportunism) pushed him to express enthusiasm for European Fascism and pay homage to Mussolini. To Ehrenburg's Aleksey Spiridonovich, the Merezhkovsky of the early 1920s embodies a Russian modern cultural prophet of Christian love. Unlike his character, Ehrenburg displays unerring intuition regarding the trajectory of Merezhkovsky's career.

with all speed. What did the progressive folk say? Oh, yes: they were very much afraid that the buried Jews would make the earth shake still more.

"There, my friends, is a short excursion into history. And since humanity is to experience both famine and pestilence, as well as a goodly amount of earth shaking, I am merely looking ahead in a commonsense way by having these invitations printed in advance."

"But Teacher," Alexey Spiridonovich retorted, "aren't the Jews men like ourselves?" (During Jurenito's "excursion," he had sighed loud and long and wiped his eyes with his handkerchief but moved to a place fairly far from my side, just in case.)

"Of course not! Are a football and a bomb one and the same thing? Do you think the tree and the axe can be brothers? You can love the Jews or hate them, you can regard them with dread as fire-raisers or with hope as saviors, but their blood is not yours, nor is their cause your cause. You don't understand? You refuse to believe? Very well, I'll try to make it clear to you. The night is calm and cool; let us amuse ourselves with a rather childish game over a glass of Vouvray. Tell me, my friends, if you were asked to keep just one word from the whole of human language—namely 'yes' or 'no'—and discard the rest—which would you choose? Let us begin with the oldest. You, Mr. Cool?"

"Of course I'd choose 'yes': the affirmation and the basis. I don't like 'no'; it's immoral and criminal. Even when a workman I've just sacked entreats me to take him back to work I do not say to him that harsh and bitter word, 'no'; I say 'wait a while, my friend; you'll be rewarded for your sufferings in the next world.' When I show my dollars, everyone says 'yes' to me. Destroy any words you like, but leave the dollars and the little word 'yes,' and I'll undertake to cure humanity of all its ills."

"I'd say that both 'yes' and 'no' were extremes," said Monsieur Delet, "whereas I like moderation in all things: the golden mean, you know. But still, if the choice must be faced, I'll say 'yes.' 'Yes' is joy, élan, what else? Everything! Madame, your poor husband is dead. A fourth-class funeral, *n'est-ce pas?* Yes! Garçon, a Dubonnet! Yes! Zizi, are you ready? Yes, yes!"

Alexey Spiridonovich, still shaken by what had gone before, could not collect his thoughts, made mooing noises, jumped up several times, sat down again, and finally yelled: "Yes! I believe, O Lord! Communion! The sacred 'yes,' the 'yes' of Turgenev's pure young girls! O, Liza! Come, sweet dove!"

Schmidt, who found the whole game completely ridiculous, declared briefly and in a businesslike manner that the dictionary should really be revised with a view to expunging certain unnecessary, archaic words such as "spirit," "sacred," "angel," and so forth; "yes" and "no," however, must be retained, being serious words. Last night, if he had had to make a choice, he would have chosen "yes" as a word having an organizing function, something like a good river.

"Yes! *Si!*" replied Ercole. "On all pleasant occasions in life they say 'yes'; you only hear 'no' when you're being thrown out on your ear."

Aysha, too, preferred "yes." When he begged Krupto (the latest god) to be kind,

Krupto said "yes." When he asked the Teacher for two sous to spend on chocolate, the Teacher said "yes" and gave him the money.

"Why aren't you saying anything?" the Teacher asked me. I had not replied earlier, afraid of vexing him and my friends.

"Teacher, I cannot deceive you. I would keep 'no.' Candidly speaking, I'm always rather pleased when something goes wrong or breaks down. I'm very fond of Mr. Cool, but it would give me pleasure if he were suddenly to lose all his dollars; yes, simply lose them like a button, down to the last one. Or if Monsieur Delet's clients mixed up all the categories. Imagine what would happen if the man with a class-sixteen burial—three years' tenure, you remember—suddenly got up and cried, 'Bring out your scented handkerchiefs, I want the luxury class!' When the purest young girl who has been running round this dirty world picking up the hem of her skirt, making a great to-do of her virginity, meets a resolute tramp in a little wood outside the town, that's not bad either. Or when the waiter slips and drops a bottle of Dubonnet: I love that. Of course it's as my great-great-grandfather, that clever fellow Solomon, said, 'There is a time to gather stones and a time to cast them aside.' But I'm a simple man, I've got only one face, not two. No doubt someone'll have to gather them, maybe Schmidt. As for me, believe me I'm not trying to be original if I say in all conscience: destroy 'yes,' destroy everything in the world, and then 'no' will remain of its own accord."

While I was speaking, all my friends who had been sitting next to me on the sofa moved into the opposite corner. I was left by myself. The Teacher addressed Alexey Spiridonovich:

"Now you see that I was right. A natural division has taken place. Our Jew is left alone. You can destroy all the ghettoes, wipe away all the Pales of Settlement, dig up all the frontiers, but there's nothing to fill those ten feet that separate you from him. All of us are Robinson Crusoes, or convicts if you prefer; the rest is a matter of personality. One man will tame a spider, study Sanskrit, and lovingly sweep the floor of his cell. Another will bang his head against the wall: crack! a bump; another crack! and another bump; and so on. What will prove stronger: the wall or his head? The Greeks came along and looked around—the place could have been more comfortable to live in, it's true; without disease, or death, or suffering, something like Olympus. But it couldn't be helped; this was where they had to live. And so, to keep their spirits up, they decided to proclaim every discomfort, including death (you couldn't abolish the discomforts anyway), as the greatest boon. The Jews came along and crack! it's the head against the wall at once. 'Why is this place the way it is?' You have two men, why shouldn't they be equal? But no, Jacob finds favor, Esau's out in the cold. And so it begins: the undermining of heaven and earth, of Jehovah and the kings, of Babylon and Rome. The ragged beggars who spend their nights on the steps of the temple work away, concocting a new religion of justice and poverty, as though mixing an explosive in a cauldron. Now just watch unconquerable Rome go flying head over heels! The poor, ignorant, dull-witted sectarians come out against the beautiful order and wisdom of the ancient world. Rome trembles. The Jew Paul has conquered Marcus Aurelius. Yet ordinary people, who prefer a cozy little house to dynamite, begin to settle down in the new faith, making the bare hut homely and pleasant. Christianity is no longer a well-beating machine, it has become a new fortress. Terrible, naked, destructive justice has been replaced by human, comfortable, india-rubber mercy. Rome—the world—has withstood the onslaught. But seeing this, the tribe of Judah repudiated its child and started undermining once again. At this moment there's undoubtedly someone in Melbourne sitting alone, sapping away, not in deed but in thought. Again they're mixing something in cauldrons, again they're preparing a new faith, a new truth. Forty years ago the gardens of Versailles shivered with the first access of fever, just like the gardens of Hadrian long ago. Rome prides itself on its wisdom, the Senecas write their books, the brave cohorts stand ready. It trembles again, 'Rome the unconquerable!'

"Israel has borne a new child. You will behold its wild eyes, red hair, and little hands that are as strong as steel. Having given birth, Israel is ready to die. A heroic gesture: 'there are no more nations, I am no more, but we are.' Oh, naïve, incorrigible sectarians! They'll take your child, wash it, dress it, and it'll become exactly like Schmidt. Once more they will say 'justice,' but they'll replace it by expediency. Once more you'll go away to hate and wait, beat your head against the wall, and moan 'how long?'

"I will tell you: until the day of your madness and theirs, until the day of infancy, a distant day. Meanwhile the tribe will be drenched once more in the blood of parturition in the squares of Europe, giving birth to another child that will betray it.

"But how should I not love that spade in the thousand-year-old hand? It digs the graves, but does it not turn up the soil of the fields too? It will be shed, the blood of Judah, the invited guests will applaud, but (remember the whispers of long ago?) the blood will only make the earth still more poisonous. The world's great medicine!"

And the Teacher came up to me and kissed me on the forehead.

1922

Translated from the Russian by Anna Bostock in collaboration with Yvonne Kapp

Ilya Ehrenburg, *Neobychainye pokhozhdeniia Khulio Khurenito i ego uchenikov.* . . . Introduction and notes copyright © by Maxim D. Shrayer.

ANDREY SOBOL

Andrey Sobol (1888–1926), fiction writer, playwright, memoirist, and translator, was born Israel Sobel; he Russianized his name to Yuly Sobol. The pen name Andrey Sobol, which in English would be Andrew Sable, was probably fashioned after Andrey Bely's (Andrew White in English). Left without means after the death of Sobol's father, Sobol's mother moved the family from Saratov on the Volga to Shavli (Šiauliai, Lithuania), where Sobol studied at a government Jewish school. At fourteen he left home for a life of wonderings. In Perm he joined a Zionist socialist group and composed verses in the manner of Simon Frug (in vol. 1), publishing some. In response to the Kishinev pogrom (1903), Sobol wrote militant poems, kindred in message to Hayyim Nahman Bialik's *The City of Slaughter*. (Sobol would publish a powerful essay on Bialik in 1916 in the Moscow-based Zionist newspaper *Jewish Life* [*Evreiskaia zhizn'*].) Sobol joined the Socialist-Revolutionary (SR) Party in 1904 and was arrested in 1906. He served part of his four-year sentence of hard labor at the construction site of the Amur Railroad. (In the 1920s, Sobol depicted his convict's experience in memoir and drama.) Penal servitude interrupted his creative work.

Sobol escaped from Siberian exile to Europe in 1909. A prosaist of life's shifty gray, he contributed fiction to Russian periodicals in the 1910s. The novel *Dust*, published in 1915 in *Russian Thought* (*Russkaia mysl'*), was a landmark in Sobol's early prose. Featuring Jewish SR terrorists, the novel argued that even within the revolutionary movement Jews felt alienated. Sobol also created heroic images of Jews in contrast to the doubly estranged Jewish intellectuals. Of special interest is his story "The Gentle Current" (1918) about Jews in Siberia.

Sobol returned to Russia illegally in 1915 and reported from the Caucasian front under an assumed name. Five books by Sobol appeared in 1916–17. In the late 1910s and early 1920s, Sobol contributed to Jewish-Russian publications, among them *Collection Safrut* 1 (1918) edited by Leyb Jaffe (vol. 1), and coedited the volume *Jewish World*, published in Moscow in 1918. Sobol enthusiastically received the February 1917 Revolution and served as an army commissar of the Provisional Government. The Bolshevik coup had a sobering effect on him, however, and he spent the civil war in the south. Unwilling either to support Bolshevism or to oppose it, he was in turn arrested by the Whites and the Reds, and as a prisoner of the Odessa Cheka in 1921, he barely escaped execution. In 1922 Sobol returned to Moscow and, in 1923, published an open letter admitting his political "errors."

Responding to the chaos and violence of the revolutionary years, Sobol embraced an expressionist style. Characteristic of Sobol's narrative aesthetics of that time is the short novel whose Russian title, *Bred* (1917–19), means delirium, gibberish, and nonsense. In the 1920s Sobol published a number of books. Two different editions of his *Collected Works* appeared, respectively, in 1926–27 (four volumes) and in 1928 (three volumes). Some critics cite the short autobiographical novel *Salon Car* (1922) as Sobol's best work.

In spite of the negative reception of Sobol's work by party-minded critics deeming him a "right-wing fellow traveler," Sobol enjoyed popularity. In several questionnaires of the mid-1920s, readers identified Sobol as their favorite prose writer, alongside the beloved poet Sergey Esenin (1895–1925). Sobol's success did not stop the onset of depression as he continued to defend artists' autonomy from official control. Sobol shot himself in the center of Moscow in 1926. In his suicide letter, Sobol wrote, "My entire life is a story about things turning out in the opposite way. A real story. And I'm ending it fittingly."

The Lethean waters of Stalinism rushed Sobol's name into oblivion. No works by him were reprinted until 1989, but contemporaries conjured up Sobol's image in their memoiristic fiction. In *The Golden Rose* (1955), Konstantin Paustovsky described a 1921 encounter with Sobol in Odessa. Valentin Kataev (his brother, Evgeny Petrov, in vol. 1) mockingly portrayed Sobol, disguised as Serafim Los, in the short novel *Werther Has Been Written* (published in 1980). Two volumes of Sobol's prose appeared in 2001–2 in Moscow.

In her 2002 dissertation on Sobol, Diana Gantseva suggested that in depicting Jewish characters Sobol created a "drama of a personality with a split [. . .] consciousness." Throughout his career, Sobol highlighted the liminality of Jewish characters while pondering the limits of assimilation (his 1916 novella "Inadvertently" scorned apostasy).

Among Sobol's greatest Jewish work was "When Cherries Blossom" (published in 1925), which dialogues with Isaac Babel's *Red Cavalry* (see vol. 1). The novella's bespectacled "Yid," who introduces himself as Marat (after Jean-Paul Marat), wins in a confrontation with the chieftain Dzyuba, who evokes the anarchist leader Nestor Makhno (1888–1934).

Sobol included "The Count" in his *Book of Little Stories, 1922–25* (1925), where two other stories, "The Cellar" and "Pogrom," offered haunting footage of Jews caught in the Revolution's meat grinder.

The Count

His fingers burning, raising himself up only to fall down again, Lipman crawled toward the fence that remained unscathed—to seek shelter.

If only for a moment, for just one brief moment, to reach that patch of land where it was damp and cool, where the suffocating black smoke does not blind the eyes.

And on that patch of earth—of his earth—to die, to fall asleep.

There was shooting in the distance . . .

Or is all the earth reduced to fiery coals? Or is all the earth breathing fire?

And through all the days and nights—endless nights and endless days—without cease, without abatement, without respite, will these smashed and scorched human mouths moan, scream, and wail?

And will today be yesterday? And tomorrow, today?

The synagogue still smoldered.

Meanwhile, to the left a new fiery whirlwind had leapt up, and Lipman with his clouded eyes still managed to make out that it was Monozon's house that was burning, that the wind was gusting to the right and that he should crawl not to the fence but to the well.

And—on all fours, on all fours, his palms against the flaming earth, his knees against cinders, his face turned slightly toward the sky, silent and shut tight (thus the eternal circle closes over a man's tiny life)—Lipman started to crawl along the fence.

And at the end of it—where the fence adjoins the post office—he saw around the bend the top row of lighted windows and close by, right by his ear, spurs jingled—one, two, three.

And when the last pair of spurs—maybe the fifth—stumbled against his leg and, after stumbling, immediately became still, he only had time to reflect that he was not to lie upon the damp cool earth.

Is all the earth reduced to burning coals?

Is all the earth to end in fire?

The shot at so close a range did not even flash.

A chuckle—and a young voice, slightly hoarse from the night air.

"You're lucky, Romka. How many does that make today?"

"I'm not counting. Nine, I think. But it's all crap—they're all old geezers. Give me some young ones, some Bolsheviks. Don't bother to check, he's a goner. I don't miss."

The spurs began to jingle again, as they set off to catch up with those who'd gone on ahead.

Behind the well, hunched up, Shaya nudged Gdalevich:

"Another one. Did you hear? Did you hear?"

"Quiet," wheezed Gdalevich. "I'm counting. Quiet. I know the count. Quiet." And he lay face down in the puddle.

And the dark water, screened from the treacherous, terrible flashes of light by the shell of the well, washed his cracked, swollen lips and the bloody scar on his forehead. And the dark water lightened the pain.

But his eyes, swollen tight, it could not pacify—and they will remember everything, and they will register everything, and they will take everything with them, within them.

Rivers flow, they merge together, they wash their banks, they know a quiet, even current, they know the murmur of a rolling wave, but the dark water of the puddle by the well will never flow anywhere, and it will preserve the blood spilled in the night and return it to the earth: from the earth it came—into the earth the blood will be restored.

And the swollen eyes know: this blood must not be forgiven.

And the eyes bend toward the puddle—and the heart drinks the smell of blood, and the heart will not return this smell, will not give it back to the earth, for all the old commands and the old laws are dead, they lie, and the earth, the old cheat, lies too.

For the earth does not wish to keep the great count.

"Quiet. I know the count. Quiet. I'm counting."

They will carry away everything with them, those eyes, which have become determined, penetrating.

Everything: the horses' distinct clatter, and the unit commander's moustache, and the cart loaded with smashed boxes of tobacco, and the children's toys on the steps of the house, and next to the toys a slate with some scribbling, and a lit cigarette stuck in the dead teacher's mouth. Everything: the carriage with the woman dressed in a seal-skin coat and an officer's cap over her blond curls—the cap jauntily perched, her ringed fingers holding the reins tight, and the red-haired little girl with her naked, bloody legs spread wide apart, and the waltz from *Pupsik*[1] in the plundered house to the accompaniment of gunshots, the tread and clatter of horses' hooves, a woman's screams, and the crackle of burning roofs.

"Quiet . . . Quiet. I know the count."

Shaya merged with the well, Gdalevich with the earth.

He felt his way in the direction of where the shot had just sounded—blindly, with his stomach in the puddles, toward the broken glass, his chin level with the filth, dung, and his restive eyes turned toward the fresh fire.

With his hand he groped for the body; hugging the ground even more tightly, he dragged the corpse, and, without getting up, he labored to turn the dead man's head toward him.

The roof of Monozon's house collapsed, a wild and fiery rocket slashed the sky; in the light the slain man bared his teeth.

---

1. *Pupsik*—Russian title of *Püppchen* (1912), an operetta by German composer and conductor Jean Gilbert (pseudonym of Max Winterfeld, 1879–1942). The operetta was reworked for the Russian stage in 1914–15. (Trans.)

"Lipman," Gdalevich said, upon returning to the well. "That's the seventeenth today." And, like Shaya, he merged with the well.

Flashing crimson for a moment, the bloody puddle again became dark—the earth reclaimed that which it had given up.

The cavalrymen departed from Monozon's house, the horses' rumps shining in the light.

They were moving the tables in the postmaster's apartment. Olympiada Petrovna was ransacking the drawers of her dresser: the napkins had disappeared somewhere; Semyon Grigorievich had just brought some six dozen, but nobody knew where they'd gone to.

She was panicking, flinging things around, until she found them. But she found only three dozen. Where were the rest—all of the household goods seem to get lost little by little, and the Monozons were known for their linens.

Semyon Grigorievich trailed behind and begged that he be allowed to count them again, perhaps a mistake had been made.

Meanwhile, on the staircase, spurs were already ringing; the good officers had arrived for the banquet.

In nervous haste, Anichka primped her curls with a pencil stub.

Three or four houses down from the post office, Mendel Shmerts said distinctly, for the last time:

"I gave a thousand. There's nothing left," and he closed his eyes: the gray eyebrows met, as if they had drawn the final line.

"Give him a treat," Valitsky nodded to Yevtushenko.

Without a word Yevtushenko methodically struck a match, lit the cigar, took a long pull, coughed a few times, then took another puff.

And when the circle of the tip had grown wider and turned red, Yevtushenko pinched the cigar between two fingers and bent down toward Shmerts.

Valitsky raised his hand.

"Well, are you going to cough it up? One . . . two . . . three . . ."

The old man was silent.

Tearing open the collar of Shmerts's shirt, Yevtushenko thrust the cigar into Shmerts's hairy gray chest.

The smell of singed hair filled the room.

The bed creaked under Shmerts, his legs, bound with ropes, jerked and fell still again; the gray brows met even more tightly. Valitsky, holding his saber, stooped down toward the old man:

"Will you talk, you shit? Damn you, you tight-fisted bastard! You going to talk?"

Yevtushenko stooped down as well, but he had trouble keeping his balance and started to sway; the cigar slipped from his fingers and fell on the exposed body.

The cigar lay there and smoldered. Bluish smoke wafted over the old man's face, toward his eyebrows.

"I'll give it to you, I'll give it to you," shouted Basya from the doorway; she was trying to get up, but her crooked fingers kept slipping down the door jamb. "I know. I'll give it to you."

"She's lying," Yevtushenko muttered without turning around. "She's the maid."
"No. No," Basya choked. "His very own sister. *Oy . . . oy*, his sister."
"Maid," Yevtushenko repeated.
"Sister," her mouth spat out its bloody drool.
"Maid. The dirty whore's lying. She's wearing an apron . . . Plain as day."
The cigar smoldered.

The clatter of horses' hooves—Valitsky glanced out the window: in the purple light horses with sacks thrown across their saddles glided by; the ends of the saddlecloths fluttered.

"Hey! Hey!" barked Valitsky, leaning out the window.

The men on horseback did not stop.

Valitsky darted down the stairs with his saber, boots, and a balalaika thrown over his shoulder clattering behind him.

Yevtushenko unsteadily hurried after him, after crushing the old woman Basya by stamping on her legs.

"Stop! Hey!" Valitsky hollered, as he jumped into the stirrups.

"Ho-ho!" answered the cheerful fading voices. The strings of a balalaika twanged; Yevtushenko tumbled down the stairs; from afar the beams of Monozon's house crackled.

The fire crept on in all directions, embers shot up in the sky like flares and sparks, like stars; both embers and sparks vanished in the darkened half of the small town. While on the illumined side a cross burst forth, sharp and bright, from the church, as crimson as though bathed in blood from top to bottom.

The cigar smoldered; the torn white shirt did not stir beneath the ropes. The old woman lay stretched out on the floor, writhing and bellowing.

Behind the well there is darkness and mud.

In the mud and darkness are two figures: maybe people or perhaps shadows, begotten of the night, the flames, the smoke, and the blood.

"Quiet, Shaya. Quiet. I know the count."

They crawl—from night into night, from fire into fire, from smoke into smoke. They crawl, holding their breath. But when they come to the house with the illumined windows, their fingers and mouths dig into the earth: figures could be glimpsed in the illumined windows.

Service jackets and uniforms rushed past, curved sabers dragged behind, and the piano jangled with spirit: the good officers, having finished their dinner, were dancing.

1922–23

Translated from the Russian by Natalia Ermolaev, Sergey Levchin, Ronald Meyer,
Jonathan Platt, and Timothy Williams

VIKTOR SHKLOVSKY

Viktor Shklovsky (1893–1984), literary theorist, critic, fiction writer, memoirist, and screenwriter, was born in St. Petersburg. Shklovsky's Jewish father converted when he was a student and married Shklovsky's mother, who was half-Russian and half–German-Latvian.

Shklovsky studied philology at St. Petersburg University and sculpture at Leonid Shervud's studio. During World War I, he was a noncommissioned officer in an armored-car unit, and after the war, in 1917–18, he was active in the right wing of the Socialist-Revolutionary (SR) Party. After announcing that he was ceasing political work, Shklovsky returned to Petrograd and in 1920 was elected professor of the Russian Institute of Art History. In 1922, after the extent of his previous involvement in the SR anti-Bolshevik underground was disclosed in a book by the former head of the SR military faction, Shklovsky fled abroad through Finland. In 1922–23, he stayed in Berlin.

The year 1914 marked the publication of two slim books by Shklovsky—the first two of many to appear over his seven prolific decades. Shklovsky's *Resurrection of the Word* (1914) was instrumental in pulling together a group of young theorists collectively bent on replacing the traditional notions of creativity, textuality, and literary dynamics that were prevalent at the time with radically new approaches. In 1916 the group called itself OPOYAZ, the Russian abbreviation for Society for the Study of Poetic Language. Fondled by the winds of neo-Kantianism wafting in from Germany and inspired by the literary experiments of the Russian futurists, Shklovsky and his colleagues laid the foundation of Russian formalism in 1916–21. Influential and stimulating to this day, this movement constitutes an indispensable part of university courses on literary theory. Among the principal formalists were Yury Tynyanov (1894–1943) and Boris Eikhenbaum (1888–1959). A Jewish background was dominant among the members of the formalist movement; in the 1970s–90s, the ultranationalist Russian critics, Vadim Kozhinov most vociferously, charged them with promoting allegedly alien and destructive ideas about (Russian) culture.

One of Shklovsky's most influential essays, "Art as Device" (1917), postulated that new styles and forms came into existence not to express new contents but to oust previous ones. It also introduced the powerful concept of estrangement. Shklovsky published a number of books blending theory and philosophy of culture with criticism of contemporary works and analyses of such iconic texts as Cervantes' *Don Quixote* and Sterne's *Tristram Shandy*. They included *The Articulation of the Plot* (1921), *On the Theory of Prose* (1925, expanded edition 1929, where his major early essays were gathered), *The Hamburg Reckoning* (1928), *Pro and Contra. Notes on Dostoevsky* (1957), *Artistic Prose. Thoughts and Analyses* (1959), *The Bow-String: On the Incompatibility of the Compatible* (1970), and others. In the post-Stalinist years, Shklovsky repackaged his formalist works in revised and expanded volumes, such as the 1985 edition of *On the Theory of Prose*. As a theorist, Shklovsky was increasingly self-referential, writing about himself reading and writing. As a literary historian, he coined a number of seminal formulations, including the term "South-Western school" (1933) after the title of Eduard Bagritsky's collection *South-West* (1928); Shklovsky used it in reference to the constellation of writers, originally from Odessa and the Black Sea area, who entered the mainstream in the 1920s (Isaac Babel, Eduard Bagritsky, both in vol. 1, and Yury Olesha, and others). Lev Tolstoy preoccupied Shklovsky, from "Art as Device" (1917) to the monograph *Material and Style in Tolstoy's Novel "War and Peace"* (1928) to his 1963 Tolstoy biography.

To return to Shklovsky's years abroad: in Berlin he completed his two best works, both of which were published in 1923. Shklovsky's *Sentimental Journey. Memoirs. 1917–1922* took its title from Laurence Sterne's antinovel *A Sentimental Journey Through France and Italy* (1768). Shklovsky's epistolary novel *Zoo, or Letters Not about Love, or the New Héloïse* negotiated the terms of his "surrender" and return to Soviet Russia. Letter twenty-nine, the last in the first edition, was titled "Declaration to the All-Russian Central Executive Committee." "I cannot live in Berlin," Shklovsky wrote. "I am bound by my entire way of life [. . .] to the Russia of today. I am able to work only for her" (trans. Richard Sheldon).

In 1923 Shklovsky returned to Soviet Russia. He continued to write memoiristic nonfiction; *The Third Factory* (1926) and *Daily Work* (1930) subtly chronicled the evaporation of artistic freedom. In 1930 Shklovsky published in *Literary Gazette* (*Literaturnaia gazeta*) the article "Monument to a Scientific Error," both "scientific" and "error" referring to formalism. (In the late 1930s and early 1950s, the term "formalist" acquired more and more ominous tones in official Soviet lingo.) Shklovsky's literary "professionalization" in the USSR followed several directions. He turned to the safety of historical belles-lettres, churning out a number of books; in 1958, some were gathered in the hefty *Historical Tales and Stories*. Having previously made a contribution to film theory (for example, his 1923 *Literature and Cinematography*), Shklovsky now produced film criticism and screenplays. In the 1920s he wrote screenplays for prominent Soviet directors, among them *By the Law* (1926, screenplay with director Lev Kuleshov), *Traitor* (1926, director Abram Room, screenplay with Lev Nikulin), and *Meshchanskaya, 3* (1927, screenplay with director Room, *Bed and Sofa* in English). Shklovsky's work in cinema continued through the 1960s.

Feeling doubly vulnerable because of his SR and formalist past, Shklovsky felt the need to prove his loyalty by taking part in such notorious cultural events as a team of thirty-six who coauthored, in 1934, a volume about the construction of the White Sea–Baltic Sea Canal (the Belomor Canal), built by prison labor. The volume featured, of the writers in this anthology, Evgeny Gabrilovich (vol. 2), Vera Inber (vol. 1), and

Mikhail Kozakov (vol. 1). During World War II, Shklovsky lived first in Almaty, Kazakstan doing film work, then in Moscow reporting for periodicals.

A skillful survivalist, Shklovsky never shunned magazine and newspaper "daily" work. Such article titles as "The Time of Maturity—Communism" (1961, about German Titov's flight into space) captured the absurdity of Shklovsky's Soviet literary life while subverting his formalist tenets. Shklovsky privately helped many victims of Stalinism and Soviet totalitarianism, earning the gratitude of such a harsh judge as Nadezhda Mandelstam (vol. 2; see chapter about Shklovsky in her *Hope against Hope*). The apogee of Shklovsky's *sui generis* prose, both shrewd and lyrical, transcending boundaries of genres and forms, was the publication in 1964 of *Once Upon a Time*, which included *Zoo, About Mayakovsky*, and tales about Isaac Babel, Sergey Eisenstein, Yury Tynyanov, and others. About Babel—but also about himself—Shklovsky wrote in *Once Upon a Time*: "I saw him for the last time at Yasnaya Polyana [Lev Tolstoy's estate in Tula Province, now a museum]. [. . .] Babel walked forlornly, calmly, talking about cinema; he looked very tired, calmly describing and unable to tie together, to complete that which he already understood. [. . .] We strolled together on soft green grass; a river that was not wide shot blue in front of us; it was like a line drawn in blue pencil in an accounting book, so as to write under that line the word 'thus.' We were not old at the time; the year 1937 had begun."

One of the most metafictional of Soviet authors, endowed with artistic gifts comparable to Vladimir Nabokov's, Shklovsky might have achieved so much more if he had stayed in Berlin—as he knew better than anyone else.

Given Shklovsky's origin and sensibility, his Jewish half expressed itself mainly in reflections on antisemitism, presented from the sidelines and with doubly ironic distancing, as in *Sentimental Journey*, as well as in Shklovsky's memoirs of Jewish cultural figures.

In his review of Aleksandr Granovsky's 1925 film *Jewish Happiness* (*Yiddishe Glikn*), based on Sholem Aleichem's writings, Shklovsky wrote skeptically of Zionism. In 1926, on the commission of OZET (the Society for the Settlement of Jewish Toilers on Land), he cowrote with Vladimir Mayakovsky the screenplay for Abram Room's 1927 documentary *Jew on the Land* (see also Viktor Fink's *Jews on the Land* [1929] in vol. 1). Ever the master of subtlety, Shklovsky managed to signal his Jewish interests in rather unexpected places. For example, one of his tales about Peter the Great, published in 1941, was titled "Jester Lacosta" and portrayed one of the several Sephardic Jews at the czar's court (see David Markish in vol. 2). Shklovsky contributed an essay on the Nazi atrocities in Kislovodsk to the derailed Ehrenburg–Grossman *Black Book* (see Ehrenburg and Grossman in vol. 1).

Selected below are three letters from Shklovsky's great novel *Zoo* (1923). Disguised as "Alya," the novel's romantic heroine was Elsa Triolet (1896–1970), then a young Russian writer of Jewish descent living abroad. Shklovsky included six of Triolet's own letters in the text of *Zoo*. In 1928 Triolet married the French writer and left-wing activist Louis Aragon; later she became a prominent French author, explicitly addressing Jewish subjects in her novel *Le Rendez-vous des étrangers* (1956). While writing about Ilya Ehrenburg, Shklovsky coined one of his enduring aphorisms, "Pavel Savlovich" (literally, Paul the son of Saul), thus mapping the extreme boundaries of a Jewish-Russian identity. *Lekhaim* (*To Life*), a post-Soviet Jewish magazine published in Moscow, features a column about Jewish-Russian writers that is titled "Pavel Savlovich."

From *Zoo, or, Letters Not about Love*
Letter Seven

About Grzhebin on canvas, about Grzhebin in the flesh. Since the letter is written in a penitent mood, the trademark of the Grzhebin Publishing House is affixed. Here too are several fleeting remarks about Jewry and about the attitude of the Jews toward Russia.

What to write about! My whole life is a letter to you.

We meet less and less often. I've come to understand so many simple words: yearn, perish, burn, but "yearn" (with the pronoun "I") is the most comprehensible word.

Writing about love is forbidden, so I'll write about Zinovy Grzhebin, the publisher.[1] That ought to be sufficiently remote.

In Yury Annenkov's portrait of Zinovy Isaevich Grzhebin, the face is a soft pink color and looks downright delectable.

In real life, Grzhebin is pastier.

In the portrait, the face is very fleshy; to be more precise, it resembles intestines bulging with food. In real life, Grzhebin is more tight and firm; he might well be compared to a blimp of the semirigid type. When I was not yet thirty and did not yet

---

1. Greatly indebted to Richard Sheldon's notes accompanying his English translation of Shklovsky's *Zoo*, the editor assumes all responsibility for the information provided below.
    An artist and well-known editor and publisher, Zinovy Grzhebin (1877–1929) ran several major literary and arts publishing houses, including Shipovnik (Sweetbriar) and Panteon (Pantheon); *Sweetbriar* was also the name of the series of collections and annuals that Grzhebin published in Russia. In 1920 he left Russia and soon settled in Berlin. Taking advantage of the economic situation in Germany at the time and hoping to distribute his Russian-language books outside the émigré communities, mainly in Soviet Russia, he started a large and highly ambitious publishing venture. By 1926, Grzhebin's publishing ventures had completely failed.

know loneliness and did not know that the Spree is narrower than the Neva and did not sit in the Pension Marzahn, whose landlady did not permit me to sing at night while I worked, and did not tremble at the sound of a telephone—when life had not yet slammed the door to Russia shut on my fingers, when I thought that I could break history on my knee, when I loved to run after streetcars . . .

"When a poem was best of all
Better even than a well-aimed ball"—
(something like that)
. . . I disliked Grzhebin immensely. I was then twenty-seven and twenty-eight and twenty-nine.

I thought Grzhebin cruel and rigid for having gulped down so much Russian literature.

Now, when I know that the Spree is thirty times narrower than the Neva, when I too am thirty, when I wait for the telephone to ring—though I've been told not to expect a call—when life has slammed the door on my fingers and history is too busy even to write letters, when I ride on streetcars without wanting to capsize them, when my feet lack the unseeing boots they once wore and I no longer know how to launch an offensive . . .

. . . now I know that Grzhebin is a valuable product. I don't want to ruin Grzhebin's credit rating, but I fervently believe that my book won't be read in a single bank.

Therefore, I declare that Grzhebin is no businessman, nor is he stuffed either with the Russian literature gulped down by him or with dollars.

But, Alya, don't you know who Grzhebin is? Grzhebin's a publisher; he published *Sweetbriar*, he ran the publishing house Pantheon, and now he seems to have the most important publishing house in Berlin.

In Russia, between 1918 and 1920, Grzhebin was buying manuscripts hysterically. It was a disease—like nymphomania.

He was not publishing books then. And I frequently called on him in my unseeing boots, and I shouted in a voice thirty times louder than any other voice in Berlin. And in the evening I drank tea at his place.

Don't think that I've grown thirty times narrower.

It's just that everything has changed.

I hereby give the following testimony: Grzhebin is no businessman.

Grzhebin is a Soviet-type bourgeois, complete with delirium and frenzy.

Now he publishes, publishes, publishes! The books come running, one after another; they want to run away to Russia but are denied entry.

They all bear the trademark ZINOVY GRZHEBIN.

Two hundred, three hundred, four hundred—soon there may be a thousand titles. The books pile on top of each other; pyramids are created and torrents, but they flow into Russia drop by drop.

Yet here in the middle of nowhere, in Berlin, this Soviet bourgeois raves on an international scale and continues to publish new books.

Books as such. Books for their own sake. Books to assert the name of his publishing house.

This is a passion for property, a passion for collecting around his name the greatest possible quantity of things. This incredible Soviet bourgeois responds to Soviet ration cards and numbers by throwing all his energy into the creation of a multitude of things that bear his name.

"Let them deny my books entry into Russia," says he—like a rejected suitor who ruins himself buying flowers to turn the room of his unresponsive beloved into a flower shop and who admires this absurdity.

An absurdity quite beautiful and persuasive. So Grzhebin, spurned by his beloved Russia and feeling that he has a right to live, keeps publishing, publishing, publishing.

Don't be surprised, Alya. We are all capable of raving—those of us who really live.

When you sell Grzhebin manuscripts, he drives a hard bargain, but more out of propriety than greed.

He wants to demonstrate to himself that he and his business are real.

Grzhebin's contracts are pseudo-real and, in that sense, relevant to the sphere of electrification in Russia.

Russia dislikes Jews.

All the same, though, Jews like Grzhebin are a good remedy for high fever.

It's nice to see Grzhebin, with his appetite for the creation of things, in idle, skeptical Russian Berlin.

[. . .]

Letter Twelve

Written, it would seem, in response to a comment apparently made by telephone, since the dossier contains nothing in writing along these lines; the comment had to do with table manners. Also contained in the letter is a denial of the assertion that pants absolutely must be creased. The letter is liberally garnished with Biblical parallels.

So help me, Alya, pants don't have to be creased!
  Pants are worn to thwart the cold.
  Ask the Serapions.[2]
  As for hunching over one's food, maybe that ought to be avoided.
  You complain about our table manners.

---

2. On the Serapion Brothers, see introductions to Lev Lunts, Veniamin Kaverin, and Elizaveta Polonskaya (all in vol. 1).

We hunch down over our plates to minimize the transportation problem.

We will no doubt continue to surprise you—and you us.

A great deal surprises me about this country, where pants have to be creased in front. Poor people put their pants under the mattress overnight.

In Russian literature, this method is well known; it's used—in Kuprin—by professional beggars of noble origin.

This whole European way of life provokes me!

Just as Levin was provoked (*Anna Karenina*) when he noticed how preserves were being made in his house—not his way, but the way it had always been done in Kitty's family.

When Judge Gideon was gathering a guerrilla band for an attack on the Philistines, he first of all sent home all the family men.[3]

Then the Angel of the Lord commanded him to lead all the remaining warriors to the river and to take into battle only those who drank water from the palms of their hands, and not those who hunched over the water and lapped it like dogs.[4]

Are we, by any chance, bad warriors?

Well, when everything collapses—and that will be soon—we will leave two by two, with our rifles on our shoulders, with cartridges in the pockets of our pants (not creased); we will leave, firing at the cavalry from behind fences; we will head back to Russia, perhaps to the Urals, there to build a New Troy.

But it is preferable not to hunch over one's plate.

Terrible is the judgment of Gideon the judge! What if he refuses to take us into his army!

The Bible repeats itself in curious ways.

Once the Jews defeated the Philistines, who fled, fleeing two by two, to seek safety on the other side of the river.

The Jews set out patrols at the crossing.

On that occasion, it was difficult to distinguish a Philistine from a Jew: both were, in all likelihood, naked.

The patrol would ask those coming across, "Say the word '*shibboleth*.'"

But the Philistines couldn't say "sh"; they said "*sibboleth*."[5]

Then they were killed.

In the Ukraine, I once ran across a Jewish boy. He couldn't look at corn without trembling.

---

3. See Judges 7, where, in assembling his army against the Midians, Gideon reduces his large force to three hundred men and wins.

4. Paraphrase of Judges 7:5–7.

5. See Judges 12:5–6, where the Gileadites conduct a pronunciation test to identify the Ephraimites. *Shibboleth* (ancient Heb.) = ear of corn.

He told me this:

When the killing was going on in the Ukraine, it was frequently necessary to check whether the person being killed was a Jew.

They would tell him, "Say '*kukuruza*.'"

The Jew would say "*kukuruzha*."[6]

He was killed.

Letter Twenty-Five

About spring, the Prager Diele, Ehrenburg, and pipes. About time, which passes, and lips, which renew themselves—about a certain heart that is being worn to a frazzle while the lips in question are merely losing their paint. About my heart.

It's already forty-five degrees outside. My fall coat has become a spring coat. Winter is passing, and, come what may, I won't be forced to endure a winter like this again.

Let's believe in our return home. Spring is coming, Alya. You told me once that spring makes you feel as if you've lost or forgotten something and you can't remember what.

When it was spring in Petersburg, I used to walk along the quays in a black cape. There the nights are white and the sun rises while the bridges are still drawn. I used to find many things on the quays. But you will find nothing; all you know is that something has been lost. The quays in Berlin are different. They're nice, too. It's nice to follow the canals to the workers' districts.

There, in some places, the canals widen into quiet harbors and cranes hover over the water. Like trees.

There, at the Hallesches Tor,[7] out beyond the place where you live, stands the round tower of the gasworks, just like those at home on the Obvodny Canal. When I was eighteen, I used to walk my girlfriend to those towers every day. Very beautiful are

---

6. *Kukuruza* (Russ.) = corn; Shklovsky relates a well-known historical anecdote, versions of which continued to circulate throughout the Soviet period. In the anecdote, people were asked to pronounce words such as *kukuruza* in order to identify Jews by their Yiddish ("Jewish") accent, especially audible in words containing the Russian *r* and *z*; see also Semyon Kirsanov's "R" in volume 1 and Eduard Shulman in volume 2.

7. Hallesches Tor—an area in the Kreutzberg section of Berlin known for its very busy traffic with street and canal transportation, long-distance trains, and an elevated railway built there in 1902. The cemetery at Hallesches Tor is a major cultural site in West Berlin; the writers E.T.A. Hoffmann and Adelbert von Chamisso are buried there.

the canals—even when the high platform of the elevated train runs along their bank.
I am already beginning to remember what I've lost.

Thank God it's spring!

The little tables in the Prager Diele[8] will be carried outdoors, and Ilya Ehrenburg
will see the sky.

Ilya Ehrenburg promenades in Berlin as he promenaded in Paris and in other
cities full of émigrés—always bent over, as if looking on the ground for something
he's lost.

However, that's an incorrect simile. His body is not bent at the waist: only his head
is bent, his back curved. Gray coat, leather cap. Head quite young. He has three
professions: (1) smoking a pipe; (2) being a skeptic, sitting in a café, and publishing
Object; (3) writing *Julio Jurenito*.[9]

Later in time than *Julio Jurenito* is the book called *Trust D.E.* Rays emanate from
Ehrenburg; these rays bear various names; their distinctive feature is that they all
smoke a pipe.

These rays fill the Prager Diele.

In one corner of the Prager Diele sits the master himself, demonstrating the art of
smoking a pipe, of writing novels, and of taking the world and his ice cream with a
dose of skepticism.

Nature has endowed Ehrenburg lavishly—he has a passport.

He lives abroad with this passport. And thousands of visas.

I have no idea how good a writer Ilya Ehrenburg is.

His old stuff isn't any good.

But *Julio Jurenito* gives one pause. It is an extremely journalistic affair—a feuilleton
with a plot, stylized character types, and the old Ehrenburg himself, garnished with a
prayer; the old poetry functions as a stylized character.

The novel develops along the lines of Voltaire's *Candide*—though with a less var-
iegated plot.

Candide has a nice circular plot: while people look for Cunégonde, she is sleeping
with everybody and aging. The hero winds up with an old woman, who reminisces
about the tender skin of her Bulgarian captain.

This plot—more accurately, this critical orientation on the idea that "time passes"
and betrayals take place—was already being processed by Boccaccio. There the be-

8. Prager Diele—café where Berlin's Russian writers and intellectuals liked to congregate
in the 1920s.

9. About Ilya Ehrenburg, in vol. 1. In 1922 Ehrenburg and the artist El Lissitsky (1890–
1941) published three issues of the international constructivist trilingual magazine *Vesch'* (*Object*). *Trust D.E.: A History of the Demise of Europe* is the title of Ehrenburg's novel, published
in Berlin in 1923, a year after the publication of *Julio Jurenito* (1922), by A. Vishnyak's Gelikon,
which in 1923 brought out Shklovsky's *Zoo*. Part of the print run of Gelikon's books was
distributed in Soviet Russia.

trothed woman passes from hand to hand and finally winds up with her husband, assuring him of her virginity.[10]

The discoveries she made during her travels were not limited to hands. This novella ends with the famous phrase about how lips are not diminished but only renewed by kisses.

But never mind, I will soon remember what I've forgotten. Ehrenburg has his own brand of irony; there is nothing Elizabethan about his short stories and novels. The good thing about him is that he chooses not to continue the traditions of "great" Russian Literature; he prefers to write "bad stuff."

I used to be angry with Ehrenburg because, in transforming himself from a Jewish Catholic or Slavophile into a European constructivist, he failed to forget the past. Saul failed to become Paul.[11] He remains Paul, son of Saul, and he publishes *Animal Warmth*.[12]

He is more, though, than just a journalist adept at organizing other people's ideas into a novel: he comes close to being an artist—one who feels the contradiction between the old humanistic culture and the new world now being built by the machine.

Of all these contradictions, the most painful to me is that, while the lips in question are busy renewing themselves, the heart is being worn to a frazzle; and with it go the forgotten things, undetected.

1923

Translated from the Russian by Richard Sheldon

---

10. The reference is to the seventh story of the second day in *The Decameron* by Giovanni Boccaccio (1313–1375).

11. Shklovsky is here alluding to 1913–15, when Ehrenburg, under the influence of French mystic authors Francis Jammes and Léon Bloy and his friendship with Max Jacob, was on the verge of conversion to Catholicism and planned to enter a Benedictine monastery. Ehrenburg then went through a spiritual crisis and changed his mind.

12. *Animal Warmth* (*Zverinoe Teplo*, 1923) is the title of Ehrenburg's volume of poetry, published in Berlin by the same publisher (Gelikon) that also published Shklovsky's *Zoo* and the first edition of Ehrenburg's *Julio Jurenito*.

MATVEY ROYZMAN

Matvey Royzman (1896–1973), poet, fiction writer, and translator, was born in Moscow to a traditional family of a Jewish tradesman. The principal source of Royzman's understanding of Judaism was his grandfather, a former *kantonist* and "Nicholas's recruit" (see John D. Klier's outline in vol. 1). As a teenager, Royzman participated in many amateur theater productions; in 1916–18 he appeared on stage in Moscow's drama studios. He entered the Law Faculty of Moscow University in 1916.

Serving as a translator in a Red Army office, Royzman debuted as a poet in 1918. In the late 1910s and early 1920s, he worked on the staff of several newspapers and magazines in Moscow. In 1920 he aligned himself with the imaginists (*imaginisty*), a postsymbolist movement whose members included Sergey Esenin, Ryurik Ivnev, Anatoly Mariengof, and others. The imaginists were completely independent of the imagists in Anglo-American poetry, the name entering Russian from the Italian *immagine*. Visible on the Moscow literary scene in the 1920s, Royzman directed the publishing house of the All-Russian Union of Poets. He contributed to the collections *Horse Garden* and *Imaginists*, and other publications of the imaginists. Jointly with the group's leading theoretician Vadim Shershenevich, Royzman published two volumes of poetry, *Red Alcohol* (1921) and *With This We Repent* (1922). His first solo collection, *The Wine of Hebron* (1923), included several long poems divided into shorter, numbered parts: Kol Nidre (included below), *Passover* (in Russian, the same word, *Paskha*, refers to both Passover and Easter), *The Garden*, and *The New Year* (referring to Rosh Hashanah, the Jewish New Year). The arrangement of texts in *The Wine of Hebron* corresponds to the Jewish calendar. Royzman's second collection, *The Palm Tree* (1925), showcased his shorter poems of 1922–23, the lyrical cycle "Sabbath" among them. Weaving Biblical and Talmudic motifs into a fabric of metaphorically colorful and exuberantly rhymed modernist verse, poems in *The Wine of Hebron* and *The Palm Tree* amounted to one of the strongest manifestations of Jewish-Russian poetry. In addition to original verse, Royzman also published translations from the Yiddish and Belorussian poets. In the late 1920s, Royzman put together a volume of Yiddish poets in translation, which was never published.

The mid-1920s marked Royzman's double shift: to prose, and to safer ideological pastures. Set during the years of the New Economic Policy (NEP), Royzman's first novel, *Minus Six* (1928; second, corrected, edition 1930), tendentiously "exposed" the Jewish bourgeoisie. Having jumped on the self-hating wagon carrying Jewish writers around the Soviet antireligious racetrack, Royzman portrayed the Jewish private entrepreneurs as unethical and hypocritical. The novel's inferred authorial worldview stood in grave contrast to the proud, self-consciously Judaic self of Royzman's earlier poetry. Essays and sketches in two collections of nonfiction, *Good Acquaintances* and *Gold Hands* (both 1931), presented Jewish life in the Soviet Union according to the prescribed Soviet rhetoric on the Jewish question. In his second novel, *These Landlords* (1932), about Jewish settlements in the Crimea, Royzman signaled an outgrowth of popular antisemitism in the lower echelons of Soviet bureaucrats. He was criticized for "nationalism" and never again attempted anything even mildly controversial. Formulaically depicting Jews and Belorussians working side by side in a small town near the Polish border, the novel *Frontier* (1935) was the last of Royzman's published works to treat Jewish topics.

Royzman worked as an editor at a film studio in Moscow in the 1930s. He discovered a thematic niche, detective-adventure tales about Soviet law-enforcement organs and spies. His first book on the subject, *Friends Risking Their Lives* (1943), was followed by *Wolf* (1956), *Berlin Azure* (1961), and others. Toward the end of his life Royzman turned to the genre of memoirs. His last book, *Everything I Remember about Esenin*, appeared shortly before Royzman's death in Moscow in 1973. Unlike the poetry of his friend, the famous Russian poet Sergey Esenin, who killed himself in 1925, Royzman's poetry was unavailable in print and remembered by few.

Royzman's collection *The Wine of Hebron* (1923), where Kol Nidre appeared, was quite unique for its fusion of the avant-garde poetics with Judaic motifs. Blazingly metaphoric, Royzman's language, in Kol Nidre and other poems, celebrated the ecstasy of being alive after the millennia of Diaspora, alive and astride in several cultures. As a Jewish participant of the Russian Imaginist movement writing and publishing in the Soviet 1920s, Royzman deserves more attention by students of Jewish culture.

Kol Nidre[1]

1

Ashes on my hair
After centuries flaming,
In my heart the seeds of prayer,
In Your hand a sling,
Sent out on the prophets' path
In the footsteps of their wrath.

Neither for Romanovs' song
Nor the *Marseillaise* do I care,
Someone else's wrong,
If to mimic snowy air
Feathers spilled and floated
From the pillows of my sky?

And the sunset is a bloated
Belly slashed and wrenched awry,
Blood, intestines over brick,
Over crosses, over roofs,
Where the headlong wind will scream,
Fling its arms, and kick:
"*Oy, el malei rahamim!*"[2]

You will, if you listen,
Hear the distant gravestones,
Executioner's blocks,
Whispering as witnesses
Of the murdered children.

Israel, arise!
Blow your burnished golden horn

---

1. Kol Nidre—the solemn public breaking of all commandments (vows) read at the beginning of the evening service of Yom Kippur. The first two words of the prayer, *kol nidre*, mean "All commandments." Here and hereafter the commentary draws on Royzman's own notes to the text as well as the commentary by Eduard Shneiderman in his splendid anthology *Poetyimazhinisty* (St. Petersburg, 1997).

2. *El malei rahamim*—opening of the traditional Jewish mourning prayer: "God, filled with mercy!"

So that dusk creeps into town
Like the weevils in the corn,
Eating deeply down
In the greedy killers' eyes.

2

O Reb Yeshua, great-grandfather of my grief,
Adamantine bolt in Israel's door,
O forefather, whipped for your belief
And wounded while besieging Turks in the war,
The wine of your memory, my brave,
Is more fragrant and far stronger,
And may this elegy grace your grave
Like falling leaves of myrrh.

True to Savaof, firstborn son,
I'm imbued with Torah learning.
Does the fathers' bloodline run
Through the stanzas of my yearning?

Aren't I in the book[3] since I,
On a Yom Kippur abroad,
Exiled, was the first to cry
Vengeance on their pogrom squad?

Was not my shell of heartache
Circumcised[4] for Him, so I've
Been reflected in fate's lake,
And my rooster is white, alive,
As a sacrifice of joy
For my brother and my God.

Land! Now in the name of Adonai
Cities and groves are overawed,
And by my spell let that horde submerge
In our slaughtered people's blood,

---

3. Book of Life, see Daniel 12.
4. Cf. Jeremiah 9:24–25: "Lo, days are coming—declares the Lord—when I will take note of everyone circumcised in the foreskin [. . .]. For all those nations are uncircumcised, but all the House of Israel are uncircumcised of heart."

And on the crimson waters of that flood
My white heart will surge
Out of the wound like an ark.

3

Ah, my Tishrei, Tishrei,[5]
Wandering and wearing out your shoes,
You should stride more quietly
Along the city avenues.

Here the sun will never clip those
Curls of almonds, delicately gray,
With shining scissors of gold,
Nor has a groggy lily ever tolled
Its gentle bell to sway
To the rhythm of whispering meadows.

Here olives are never meant
To shed onto the dry sand
Their black embossed earrings, nor
Will a grapevine ever pour
Its fragrant autumnal scent
Into the goblets of a forestland.

Here only lindens overfill
Themselves with so much blood
Aortas of leaves burst and spill,
And onion domes are whipped by an ill
Wind that's pouring evening ashes
On coppery bald spots.

Ah, sempiternal Tishrei,
Savaof summoned me to say,
Would I light the candles of our ancestry
In the Old Testament way?

---

5. Tishrei—seventh month of the Biblical year, first month of the civic year; corresponds
to September.

4

Oh, my star, well may you stare
In the lap of the ancient East:
I'll reply the cruel nightmare
And its visions have increased.

Seven withered ears of wheat
Have devoured the seven full ears.[6]

So, North, rend your clothes.
Sackcloth, South, for evermore.
Soon your world will decompose,
Sifted through revengeful sieves,
All your people fugitives
Scourged with internecine war.

Drought will give the fields a shave
And manure instead of dates,
Urine, not the finest wines,

Spades to dig a grave,
And a wind that mutilates
Flags like branches off dead pines.

Grass throughout this land will hiss,
Rustling with funereal words
Of the pogroms' prejudice,
In a dirge to birds.

So the naked earth
Opens jaws of iron wide.
Some man in a pitch-black womb
Lies like grapes crushed in a winepress,
Blind and bloody eyed,
In the city's rubble tomb
Buried deep, skull smashed.

---

6. Cf. the dream of the Pharaoh in Gen. 41:20–30: "Immediately ahead are seven years of great abundance in the land of Egypt. Immediately ahead are seven years of famine, and all the abundance in the land of Egypt will be forgotten. . . ."

5

And in the windows of the synagogue here
The spreading branches of a palm tree
Are glowing crimson in the sunset.

And here a gray rabbi,
The oak of Bassan,[7] won't falter in fear
In the cherished *Shmoine Esrei*.[8]

Borukh, Ato, Adonai![9]

O Yahveh's Marranos most true,
I stand in your bonfire's flame,
And I, ever trampled anew,
Renounce every promise and claim.

And seven times sprinkling away
The blood from my fervent heart thus,
Like Aaron, my keen Kol Nidre
I give as an offering for us.

Shema, Isroel!

On the Torah these bells
Tremble like a fallow deer.
Held as by a knifepoint spell,
Congregants chant pure and clear.

This is David's rising shield
Like the true new moon tonight,
And of all the fast has healed,
Freed, the shofar sings delight.

---

7. The oaks that grew in the Bassan area on the east coast of Jordan; mentioned in the Bible as particularly sturdy.
8. *Shmoine Esrei*—eighteen praises, liturgical prayer.
9. *Borukh, Ato, Adonoi*—"Blessed Be You, Lord."

This is Savaof lifting high
Faithful souls above the land,
This the dove that gives her sigh
Gently in His blessed hand.

Shema, Isroel,
Adonai Eloheinu
Adonai Ehod.[10]

1923

Translated from the Russian by J.B. Sisson and Maxim D. Shrayer

---

10. "Hear, o Israel, the Lord Our God, the Lord is One."

ISAAC BABEL

Isaac Babel (1894–1940), fiction writer, playwright, essayist, and screenwriter, was born to a Jewish mercantile family in Odessa and grew up in Nikolaev and Odessa. Babel's last name, an Ashkenazic corruption of Bavel, embodies the Diaspora and its greatest text, the Babylonian Talmud. At home Babel received private instruction in Hebrew and Jewish law. He attended the Nicholas I Commercial School in 1905–11 and then studied at the Kiev Commercial Institute in 1911–15. Babel wrote his first stories in French at the age of fifteen. His first published story, "Old Shloyme," about the suicide of an old Jewish man faced with his family's conversion, appeared in 1913 in Kiev. After arriving in St. Petersburg in 1915, Babel was encouraged by Maxim Gorky. Two of Babel's stories were published in Gorky's *Chronicle* (*Letopis'*), earning Babel a charge of pornography. Babel published short sketches in 1916–17 under the pen name Bab-El (Hebrew for "Gates of God"), promising the arrival of an "Odessan Maupassant."

In the fall of 1917, after serving on the Romanian front, Babel returned to Petrograd and worked for the Cheka (earliest incarnation of the Soviet secret police), using his knowledge of languages. His first nonfictional reflections on the new Bolshevik state appeared in 1918 in Gorky's paper *New Life* (*Novaia zhizn'*), which was soon shut down. These reflections anticipated some of the controversial aspects of his *Red Cavalry*. While endorsing the Revolution and repudiating tsarism, Babel questioned the use of terror and violence and the destruction of the old culture. Refracted through the Jewish consciousness, the confrontation of the old and the new took the shape of a clash between a traditional Judaic mentality, both constricted to and preserved by the Pale, and the revolutionary rhetoric of Jewish liberation.

In the spring of 1920, during the Polish campaign, he was attached to the First Red Cavalry Army as a correspondent. Under the assumed Russian name Kirill Lyutov, literally Cyril the Ferocious, Babel traveled with the troops, contributing to the newspaper *Red Cavalryman* (*Krasnoarmeets*). He kept a diary (part of which has survived), graphically recording the antisemitic violence of Semyon Budyonny's Red Cavalry units. Babel returned to Odessa in November 1920 to recuperate from typhus. Fictionally transmogrified, the war events found their way into the stories of his *Red Cavalry*, which were published in the periodicals of Moscow, Leningrad, and Odessa in 1923–26 to become a cornerstone of Babel's reputation. From the very beginning, Babel's great success was laced with controversy. In 1924, General (later Marshal) Semyon Budyonny rancorously attacked Babel in the magazine *October* (*Oktiabr'*). Titled in Russian "Babism Babelia," a play on the Russian word *baba* ("peasant woman" or pejorative "woman"), Budyonny's title might be translated as "Babel's Babism" and interpreted as the "womanish hysteria of babbling Babel." The first edition of *Red Cavalry* came out in 1926 in Moscow; by 1933 it had gone through eight editions.

In 1921–23, Babel wrote and published four pieces from the cycle of "Odessa Stories": "The King," "How It Was Done in Odessa," "Father," and "Lyubka Kazak." The stories mythologized Benya Krik, a gangster whose fictitious name, in vintage Babelesque fashion, encodes Judaic and Slavic meaning: "Ben Zion the Scream." Babel's fascination with the Odessan underworld betrayed a fantasy of "strong" self-empowered Jews who would feel adequate to Gentiles in every way. In "How It Was Done in Odessa one reads": "You can spend the night with a Russian woman, and the Russian woman will be satisfied with you. You are twenty-five years old. If heaven and earth had rings attached to them, you would seize hold of those rings and pull heaven down to earth. . . . And that is why [Benya Krik] is the King, while you are nothing" (trans. David McDuff). Babel composed two other stories with the subtitle "from Odessan stories," and all six constitute a strand of his fiction. Additionally, Babel used gangster material as the basis of the screenplay *Benya Krik* (1926) and a stage play *Sunset* (1928), which Sergey Eisenstein called "the best . . . post-October play in terms of the mastery of drama."

The third distinct unit in the corpus of Babel's short fiction (about eighty altogether) is composed of the "autobiographical" childhood stories. Spanning fifteen years of Babel's writing and set in Nikolaev and Odessa, they feature an autobiographical protagonist-narrator, aged nine to fourteen. Babel composed the first, "Childhood. At Grandmother's," in 1915. The most famous of the childhood cycle, "The Story of My Dovecote," was dated 1925. Babel referred to these stories as his "cherished labor," returning to his childhood in 1929–30 and hoping to have a book ready in 1939. Finally, there are Babel's stories unconnected to cycles. They include such metafictional masterpieces as "Guy de Maupassant" (1920–22; published 1932), a favorite of American creative writing workshops, and "Line and Color" (1923), Babel's manifesto about art and ideology with a glimpse of Trotsky's speech.

Odessa constitutes an overarching text in Babel's life and art, figuring prominently not only in his fiction and drama but also in his discursive writings. Babel identified with a group of writers from Odessa and the Black Sea coast, most of them Jewish, who poured onto the literary scene in the late 1910s–early 1920s. Termed the South-Western school by Viktor Shklovsky (in vol. 1), the constellation included Eduard Bagritsky (in vol. 1), Ilya Ilf and Evgeny Petrov (in vol. 1), Valentin Kataev, Yury Olesha, Zinaida Shishova (Brukhnova), Konstantin Paustovsky, and others. In a preface to a 1925 collection by Odessan writers that never appeared, what Babel wrote of his friend's vibrancy and *joie de vivre* fully applied to his own writings: "Bagritsky is full of purple moisture like a watermelon that in the remote days of our youth he and I would break open against the bollards of Pratique Harbor [in Odessa]."

By 1925 most of the South-Westerners had migrated to Moscow, which became Babel's home literary base. Evgenia Gronshtein, whom Babel had married in 1919, moved abroad in 1925. For over a year, in 1927–28, Babel stayed abroad. His daughter Nathalie, who later edited his publications in the West, was born in Paris in 1929. Babel once again joined his family in 1932, returning to Russia alone the following year. In 1935 Babel made his last visit abroad, attending the Anti-Fascist International Congress of Writers for Peace in Paris. His peregrinations, and especially the fact that he returned when he could have stayed abroad, puzzle his students. In 1934 Babel started a second family in Moscow with the engineer Antonina Pirozhkova, who bore Babel a daughter, Lidia, in 1937.

Babel's work in the cinema began in the late 1920s, when he did the Yiddish subtitles for a movie based on Sholem Aleichem's *Wandering Stars*. In 1936, he and Sergey Eisenstein coauthored the screenplay for *Bezhin Meadow*; the film was banned and destroyed. Babel also wrote another stage play, *Maria* (1935), inferior to *Sunset*. Babel published a small number of new stories in the 1930s, as his previous ones were reprinted in various collections. "The Trial," the last short story published in Babel's lifetime, appeared in 1938. Although at the First Congress of Soviet Writers Babel referred to himself as a "master of silence," he never stopped writing. After visiting areas of so-called "total collectivization" of agriculture in 1930–31, Babel worked on a novel under the provisional title *Velikaya Krinitsa* (fictionalized name of Velikaya Staritsa, a village outside Kiev). The manuscript apparently disappeared after Babel's arrest in 1939. Only one chapter, "Gapa Guzhva," was published in 1931; another chapter, "Kolyvushka," survived and appeared in 1963 in New York.

In 1969 A New York–based émigré journal published a fragment from another unfinished work, "The Jewess," in which a widow leaves a decaying small town to live in Moscow with her son, a Red Army commander. Like this story, several other works published in the 1930s placed the theological and ideological gaps between Jewish parents and their Sovietized children at center stage. Babel's gentle authorial humor helped surmount the courtroom confrontation in "Karl-Yankel" (1931), in which a Jewish infant, circumcised by his grandmother against his father's will, receives a hyphenated name, after *Karl* Marx and *Jacob* the Patriarch. More problematic is the message of "The Journey," an autobiographical, if fictionalized, story Babel published in 1932. Dated 1920–30, it sets the protagonist's service at the Cheka, portrayed as a joyful camaraderie, against the virulent antisemitic violence that he encounters en route from the Pale to Petrograd. As usual, the difficulty with Babel is to ascertain the degree of fictionalization as well as the extent of his romantic-ironic authorial detachment. He was also contemplating an entire novel about the *chekisty*.

Babel, who had had ties to former NKVD chief Nikolay Ezhov (1894–1940) and other officers of the Soviet secret police, was arrested in Peredelkino on 15 May 1939. A number of unfinished works apparently disappeared after the arrest. (The fate of Babel's confiscated papers continues to fuel the imaginations of scholars and writers alike; as Carol J. Avins demonstrated in 2003, the protagonist of *Vast Emotions and Imperfect Thoughts*, a 1988 novel by the Brazilian writer Rubem Fonseca, is obsessed with the prospect of possessing a Babel manuscript stolen from Soviet archives.) Babel was executed in Moscow on 27 January 1940 on charges of espionage and conspiracy. During the Thaw, Ilya Ehrenburg (in vol. 1) steered Babel's works back to print and wrote an introduction to the 1957 Soviet edition of Babel's *Selected Works*. Only a few book editions of Babel's works had appeared in the USSR by 1990, when a two-volume edition was prepared there by his widow Antonina Pirozhkova. It came out in 1991–92.

The first English translation of *Red Cavalry* appeared in 1929. Furnished with Lionel Trilling's introduction, Walter Morrison's 1955 translation of *Collected Stories* made Babel a household name in Anglo-American letters. Maurice Friedberg, Shimon Markish, and Efraim Sicher wrote poignantly in the 1970s–90s about the "Jewishness" of Babel. His popularity with the Anglo-American reader is likely to continue now that *The Complete Works of Isaac Babel* (2002), edited by Nathalie Babel and introduced by Cynthia Ozick, are available in English—even though these new translations do not do justice to Babel's genius.

The Odessan Jew Isaac Babel was an incomparable master and manipulator of the Russian language. His short stories are structured and textured like highly self-conscious poetic texts; a single object, reference, or trope often builds up and unfolds into a narrative entanglement. In "The Story of My Dovecote," the dove, both a shared universal (also Judeo-Christian) symbol of peace, hope, and renewal (e.g., Noah's dove) and a specifically Christian symbol (the Holy Spirit), becomes an instrument of antisemitic violence. In "First Love," the patronymic of the Russian woman, Galina Apollonovna, signals connections with both Greek mythology and Nietzschean thought. Babel was in some ways an embodiment of the rich heritage of both classic Yiddish storytelling (S.Y. Abramovich and Sholem Aleichem, both of whom he translated) and Hassidic folklore. His texts sparkle with subtle Hebrew and Yiddish verbal play.

A grand European belletrist, Babel is also one whose works concentrated most profoundly on the parameters of the Jewish experience: violence and antisemitism; Jewish–Christian relations; Jews and the Revolution; and recastings of the Jewish identity. A witness to the destruction of the Pale in the areas that had fallen under Soviet control, Babel recounted the uprooting of communal Jewish life, in both rural and urban settings. His humor, ranging from the hilariously hysterical (reciting Julius Ceasar in the story "In the Basement") to the lyrically perverse (earned love lessons from a prostitute in "My First Honorarium"), teeters on the brink of tears. Babel wrote some of the greatest tales about the psycho-sexual, ideological, linguistic, and religious trauma of the Jewish youths who discover "that world" and seek an "escape."

Until the seventh, expanded edition of *Red Cavalry*, where the story "Argamak" was added to uplift the tone of the ending, "The Rebbe's Son" (1924); was the book's final story. Both the title of Babel's story and the last name of its young Jewish protagonist reveal Babel's dialogue with one of the most famous tales by the Hassidic leader Rabbi Nahman of Bratslav (1772–1811), recorded by his disciple Rabbi Nathan Sternharz.

Composed in 1930 and published in 1931, "Awakening" belongs to the cycle of Babel's "autobiographical" stories.

The Rebbe's Son

. . . Do you remember Zhitomir,[1] Vasily? Do you remember the Teterev, Vasily, and that night when the Sabbath, the young Sabbath stole along the sunset, crushing the stars with her little red heel?

The thin horn of the moon was bathing its arrows in the dark water of the Teterev. Absurd Gedali, the founder of the Fourth International, had taken us to the home of Rebbe Motale Bratslavsky[2] for evening prayers. Absurd Gedali was waving the cockerel feathers of his top hat in the red smoke of the evening. The predatory eyes of candles blinked in the Rebbe's room. Inclined over prayer-books, broad-shouldered Jews were groaning hollowly, and the old buffoon of the Chernobyl *tsadikkim* was jingling the copper coins in his tattered pocket . . .

. . . Do you remember that night, Vasily? . . . Outside the window horses neighed and Cossacks shouted. The desert of war yawned outside the window, and Rebbe Motale Bratslavsky, clutching his prayer shawl in his worn fingers, prayed by the east wall. Then the veil of the Ark was drawn back, and in the funereal light of the candles we saw the scrolls of the Torah, wrapped in coverings of purple velvet and blue silk, and, hanging above the Torah, the lifeless, submissive, handsome face of Ilya, the Rebbe's son, the last prince of the dynasty . . .

And then, Vasily, the day before yesterday, the regiments of the Twelfth Army opened the front at Kovel.[3] In the town the scornful cannonade of the vanquishers thundered. Our troops wavered and got mixed up together. The Politotdel[4] train began to creep away along the dead spine of the fields. [. . .] The typhus-ridden muzhik horde rolled in front of itself its customary hump of a soldier's death. It jumped on to the footboards of our train and fell off, knocked down by blows from rifle-butts. It puffed, scrabbled, flew forward and said nothing. And at the twelfth verst, when I had run out of potatoes, I chucked a pile of Trotsky's leaflets at them. But only one of them stretched out a dirty, dead hand for a leaflet. And I recognized Ilya, the son of the Zhitomir Rebbe. I recognized him immediately, Vasily. And so painful was it to see a prince who had lost his trousers, broken in

---

1. Zhitomir—provincial capital in north-central Ukraine, on the river Teterev; center of Jewish Hebrew book printing in nineteenth-century Russia; site of a 1905 pogrom; in 1897, about 31,000 Jews lived in Zhitomir, or 47 percent of the population.

2. The name Bratslavsky is derived from Bratslav, town in Ukraine that became a major center of Hassidism after the famous tzaddik Nahman of Bratslav (1772–1811) settled there in 1802 and lived there until 1810.

3. Kovel—town in western Ukraine, forty-three miles west of Lutsk, the capital of Volhyn Province; in 1897, about 8,500 Jews resided in Kovel, or 48 percent of the population.

4. Standard abbreviation of *politicheskii otdel*, literally "political department," in Red Army units.

tow by a soldier's knapsack, that, breaking the regulations, [we] hauled him into our carriage. His bare knees, as clumsy as an old woman's, bumped against the rusty iron of the steps; two plump-breasted girl typists in sailor's jackets dragged the long, shy body of the dying man along the floor. We put him down in a corner of the editorial office, on the floor. Cossacks in wide red oriental trousers adjusted his fallen clothes. The girls, having placed on the floor the bandy legs of simple cows, coldly observed his sexual parts, the wilted, curly virility of a Semite worn to a shadow. While I, who had seen him on one of my nights of stray wandering, began to pack the scattered belongings of the Red Army soldier Bratslavsky into a trunk.

Here everything was dumped together—the warrants of the agitator and the commemorative booklets of the Jewish poet. Portraits of Lenin and Maimonides lay side by side. [The nodulous iron of Lenin's skull] and the tarnished silk of the portraits of Maimonides. A strand of female hair had been placed in a book of the resolutions of the Sixth Party Congress, and in the margins of communist leaflets swarmed crooked lines of Ancient Hebrew verse. In a sad and meager rain they fell on me—pages of the Song of Songs and revolver cartridges. The sad rain of sunset bathed my hair, and I said to the youth, who was dying in the corner on a torn mattress:

"Four months ago, on a Friday evening, Gedali, the junk dealer, brought me to your father, Rebbe Motale, but you were not in the Party then, Bratslavsky . . ."

"I was in the Party then," the boy replied, scratching his chest and writhing in fever, 'but I couldn't leave my mother . . .'

"And now, Ilya?"

"In a revolution a mother is a minor episode," he whispered. "My letter came up, the letter B, and the organization sent me away to the front . . ."

"And you ended up in Kovel, Ilya?"

"I ended up in Kovel," he shouted in despair. "The kulak rabble opened the front. I took over a scratch regiment, but it was too late. I didn't have enough artillery . . ."

He died before we got to Rovno.[5] He died, the last prince, among poems, phylacteries and foot-bindings. We buried him at a forgotten station. And I—who am barely able to accommodate the storms of my imagination within my ancient body—I received my brother's last breath.

1924

---

5. Rovno—provincial capital in western Ukraine; in 1897 about 14,000 Jews, or 56 percent of the total population, were living there.

Awakening

All the people of our circle—brokers, shopkeepers, bank and steamship office employees—taught their children music. Our fathers, seeing no chance of success for themselves, devised a lottery. They established it on the bones of little children. Odessa was seized by this madness worse than other towns. For decades our town put *Wunderkinder* on the concert platforms of the world. From Odessa came Mischa Elman, Zimbalist, Gabrilowitsch; Jascha Heifetz began among us.[6]

When a boy was four or five, his mother took the tiny, puny creature to Mr. Zagursky. Zagursky[7] ran a *Wunderkind* factory, a factory of Jewish dwarfs in lace collars and patent-leather shoes. He sought them out in the slums of the Moldavanka, in the evil-smelling courtyards of the Old Market. Zagursky gave them a first push in the right direction, and then the children were sent to Professor Auer in St Petersburg. In the souls of these starvelings with blue, swollen heads dwelt the mighty power of harmony. They became renowned virtuosi. And so my father decided to hold his own with Heifetz and Mischa Elman. Though I had passed *Wunderkind* age—I was in my fourteenth year—my short stature and puny physique made it possible for me to be mistaken for an eight-year-old. In this lay all their hopes.

I was taken to see Zagursky. Out of respect for my grandfather he agreed to charge a ruble a lesson—a low fee. My grandfather Levi-Itskhok was the laughing stock of the town, and its adornment. He stalked about the streets in his top hat and ragged boots resolving doubts on the obscurest of matters. He was asked what a gobelin was, why the Jacobins betrayed Robespierre, how artificial silk was made, what a Caesarean section was. My grandfather was able to answer these questions. Out of respect for his learning and madness, Zagursky charged us a ruble a lesson. Also, he spent time on me because he feared Grandfather, for there was no point in spending time on me. The sounds crawled out of my violin like iron filings. I myself was cut to the heart by those sounds, but Father kept up the pace. At home there was no talk of anything but Mischa Elman, who had been exempted from military service by the tzar himself; Zimbalist, according to my father's information, had been presented to the king of England and had played at Buckingham Palace; Gabrilowitsch's parents bought two

---

6. Elman, Mischa (1891–1967), born in Kiev and raised in Odessa; Zimbalist, Efrem (1889–1985), born in Rostov on Don; Heifetz, Jascha (1901–1987), born in Vilna (Vilnius)—Russian-American violinists. Elman, Zimbalist, and Heifetz studied in St. Petersburg with Leopold Auer. Gabrilowitsch, Ossip (1978–1936)—Russian-American pianist, born in St. Petersburg of Odessan ancestry.

7. Fictitious name; Zagursky's prototype was P.S. Stolyarsky (1871–1944), violinist and violin teacher in Odessa; Stolyarsky was a student of Leopold Auer (1845–1930), violinist and conductor, a professor of the St. Petersburg Conservatory of Music.

houses in St. Petersburg. *Wunderkinder* brought their parents wealth. My father could have reconciled himself to poverty, but he needed fame.

"It's impossible," people who had dined at our expense said, to stir up gossip, "it's impossible that the grandson of such a man . . ."

But my thoughts were elsewhere. During my violin practice I placed on my music stand books by Turgenev or Dumas and, scraping out heaven only knows what, devoured page after page. By day I told tall stories to the neighbors' urchins, by night I transferred them on to paper. Writing was a hereditary occupation in our family. Levi-Itskhok, whose mind became touched as he approached old age, had spent the whole of his life writing [a short novel titled] *Man with No Head*. I took after him.

Three times a week, laden with violin case and music, I trailed off to Witte Street, formerly Dvoryanskaya Street, to Zagursky's. There, along the walls, waiting their turn, sat Jewish women, hysterically aflame. They pressed to their weak knees violins that were larger than those [boys] who were to play at Buckingham Palace.

The door of the inner sanctum would open. From Zagursky's study, reeling, emerged large-headed, freckled children with thin necks like the stalks of flowers and a paroxysmic flush upon their cheeks. The door would bang shut, having swallowed the next dwarf. On the other side of the wall the teacher in bow tie and red curls, with weedy legs, exerted himself to the utmost, sang, conducted. The director of a monstrous lottery, he was inspired, peopling the Moldavanka and the black cul-de-sacs of the Old Market with the ghosts of pizzicato and cantilena. This chant was later brought to a devilish height of brilliance by old Professor Auer . . .

In this sect I had no place. A dwarf, as they were, I discerned a different kind of inspiration in the voices of my ancestors.

I found the first step difficult. One day I left the house loaded up with case, violin, music, and twelve rubles in cash—payment for a month's tuition. I walked along Nezhinskaya Street. In order to reach Zagursky's I should have turned into Dvoryanskaya, but instead I went up Tiraspolskaya and found myself at the port. The time of my lesson flew by in Pratique Harbor. Thus did my liberation begin. Zagursky's waiting room saw me no more. My schoolmate Nemanov and I got into the habit of going aboard the steamship *Kensington* to see a certain old seaman, Mr. Trottyburn by name. Nemanov was a year younger than I but had since the age of eight engaged in the most intricate commerce one could imagine. He was a genius at commercial deals and always delivered what he promised. Now he is a millionaire in New York, the director of General Motors, a company as powerful as Ford. Nemanov dragged me along with him because I obeyed him without a word. From Mr. Trottyburn he bought smuggled tobacco pipes. These pipes were carved in Lincoln by the old seaman's brother.

"Gentlemen," Mr. Trottyburn would say to us, "mark my words, children must be made by one's own hand . . . To smoke a factory-made pipe is like putting an enema tube in your mouth. Do you know who Benvenuto Cellini was? . . . He was a master.

My brother in Lincoln could tell you a thing or two about him. My brother doesn't get in anybody's way. He's just convinced that children must be made by one's own hand, and not by somebody else's. . . . We cannot but agree with him, gentlemen . . ."

Nemanov sold Trottyburn's pipes to bank managers, foreign consuls, wealthy Greeks. He made a 100 percent profit.

The pipes of the Lincoln master breathed poetry. Into each one of them had been inserted an idea, a drop of eternity. In their mouthpieces gleamed a yellow eye, their cases were lined with satin. I tried to imagine the life in Old England of Matthew Trottyburn, the last master of the pipe, resisting change.

"We cannot but agree with him, gentlemen, that children must be made by one's own hand . . ."

The heavy waves by the sea wall distanced me further and further from our house, which was steeped in the smell of onions and Jewish destiny. From Pratique Harbor I moved on to the breakwater. There, on a stretch of the sand bar, the boys from Primorskaya Street spent their days. From morning to night they did not pull on their trousers; they dived under the barges, stole coconuts for dinner, and awaited the time when the steamers full of watermelons would drift slowly in from Kherson and Kamenka, and those watermelons could be split open on the moorings of the port.

It became my dream to learn to swim. I was ashamed to confess to these bronzed boys that, born in Odessa, I had not seen the sea until the age of ten, and at fourteen did not know how to swim.

How late I had to learn the essential things! In my childhood, nailed to the Gemara,[8] I led the life of a sage, and when I was grown older began to climb trees.

The ability to swim proved to be beyond my reach. The fear of water that had haunted all my ancestors—Spanish rabbis and Frankfurt money changers—pulled me to the bottom. The water would not support me. Exhausted, saturated with salt water, I would return shoreward to my violin and music. I was attached to the instruments of my crime and dragged them about with me. The struggle of the rabbis with the sea continued until pity was shown me by the water god of those parts, the proofreader of the *Odessa News*, Yefim Nikitich Smolich. Within this man's athletic breast dwelt compassion for Jewish children. He lorded it over throngs of rachitic starvelings. Nikitich gathered them in the bedbug-infested rooms of the Moldavanka, took them to the sea, dug in the sand with them, did gymnastics with them, dived with them, taught them songs, and, getting thoroughly fried in the vertical rays of the sun, told them stories about fish and animals. To grown-ups Nikitich would explain that he was a natural philosopher. Nikitich's stories made the Jewish children die with laughter; they squealed and fawned upon him like puppies. The sun besprinkled them with creeping freckles, freckles the color of lizards.

---

8. Gemara—integral component of the Talmud, both a commentary on and a supplement to the Mishnah.

The old man had watched my single-handed combat with the waves out of the corner of his eye without saying anything. Having seen that there was no hope and that I was never going to learn to swim, he included me among the tenants of his heart. It was always with us here, his merry heart, it never put on any airs, was never mean, never troubled. With his copper shoulders, with his head of a gladiator grown old, with his bandy, bronzed legs he lay among us behind the breakwater, among the last dregs of a tribe that did not know how to die, like the ruler of these watermeloned, kerosened waters. I loved that man as only a boy who is sick with hysteria and headaches can love an athlete. I never left his side and tried to oblige him.

He said to me: "Don't you worry . . . Strengthen your nerves. The swimming will come by itself . . . What do you mean, the water won't support you? . . . Why shouldn't it?"

When he saw how I was reaching out to him, Nikitich made an exception for me alone of all his disciples, invited me as a guest to his clean, spacious attic covered in mats, showed me his dogs, hedgehog, tortoise, and pigeons. In exchange for these riches I brought him a tragedy of my own composition.

"I *thought* you scribbled," said Nikitich, "you have that kind of a look . . . [Most of the time you don't] look anywhere else. . . ."

He read my writings through, shrugged one shoulder, ran his hand through his abrupt gray curls, walked to and fro about the attic.

"I suppose," he articulated in a drawl, falling silent after each word, "that within you there is a spark of the divine . . ."

We went down to the street. The old man stopped, banged his stick forcefully against the pavement, and fixed his eyes on me.

"What is it you lack? . . . Your youth is no problem, it will pass with the years . . . What you lack is a feeling for nature."

With his stick he pointed out to me a tree that had a reddish trunk and a low crown. "What kind of tree is that?"

I did not know.

"What's growing on this bush?"

I did not know that, either. He and I walked through the small square on Aleksandrovsky Prospekt. The old man poked his stick at every tree; he clutched me by the shoulder whenever a bird flew past and made me listen to the different calls.

"What kind of bird is that singing?"

I was unable to reply. The names of trees and birds, their division into species, the places birds fly to, which direction the sun rises in, when the dew is heaviest—all that was unknown to me.

"And you presume to write? . . . A man who does not live in nature as a [rock] or an animal lives in it will never write two worthwhile lines in all his life. . . . Your landscapes are like descriptions of stage scenery. The devil take me, what have your parents been thinking of for fourteen years?"

"What have they been thinking of? Protested promissory notes, the private residences of Mischa Elman." I said nothing of this to Nikitich, I kept quiet.

Back home, at dinner, I did not touch my food. It would not go down. "A feeling for nature," I thought. "My God, why did I never think of that before? Where am I going to find someone who can explain the calls of the birds and the names of the trees to me? What do I know about them? I might be able to recognize lilacs, when they're in bloom, anyway, lilacs and acacias. There are lilacs and acacias on Deribasovskaya and Grecheskaya Streets."

While we were having dinner Father told a new story about Jascha Heifetz. Near Robin's he had encountered Mendelson, Jascha's uncle. The boy, it turned out, was getting eight hundred rubles a performance. Work out how much that made at a rate of fifteen concerts a month.

I worked it out; it came to twelve thousand a month. Doing the multiplication and carrying four in my head, I looked out of the window. Across the cement yard, in a gently billowing cloak and cape, with reddish ringlets showing from under his soft hat, leaning on his cane, stalked Mr. Zagursky, my music teacher. It could not be said that he had noted my absence before time. More than three months had already passed since my violin had sunk down to the sand off the breakwater.

Zagursky was coming up to the front door. I rushed to the back door—it had been boarded up the day before to keep out thieves. There was no salvation. I locked myself in the lavatory. Half an hour later the family had gathered outside the door. The women were crying. Bobka, my aunt, was rubbing a fat shoulder against the door and going off into fits of sobs. Father said nothing. Then he began to speak more quietly and distinctly than he had ever spoken in his life.

"I am an officer," said my father. "I have an estate. I ride out hunting. The muzhiks pay me rent. I have put my son in the Cadet Corps. I have no reason to worry about my son. . . ."

He fell silent. The women breathed heavily through their noses. Then a terrible blow fell upon the lavatory door. Father was beating against it with his whole body, he was hurling himself against it in a run.

"I am an officer," he howled, "I ride out hunting . . . I'll kill him . . . His number's up . . ."

The hook sprang off the door, but there was still the bolt, held by a single nail. The women, squealing, rushed across the floor and seized Father by the legs; out of his mind, he tore himself loose. In the nick of time Father's old mother arrived.

"My child," she said to him in Yiddish, "our grief is great. It has no bounds. Only blood was lacking in our house. I do not want to see blood in our house . . ."

Father began to groan. I heard his shuffling, retreating footsteps. The bolt hung by a final nail.

I sat in my fortress until nighttime. When everyone had gone to bed, Aunt Bobka took me to Grandmother's. We had a long way to go. The moonlight froze on unknown bushes, on trees that had no name. An invisible bird gave a peep and was silent—perhaps it had fallen asleep. What kind of bird was it? What was its name? Is there dew in the evening? Where is the constellation of the Great Bear situated? In what direction does the sun rise?

We walked along Pochtovaya Street. Bobka held me tightly by the hand, so that I should not run away. She was right. I was thinking of escape.

1931

Translated from the Russian by David McDuff

Isaac Babel, "Syn rabbi" and "Probuzhdenie." English translations from *Collected Stories by Isaac Babel*, translated by David McDuff. Reprinted by permission of The Penguin Group (UK). English translation © by David McDuff. Introduction and notes copyright © by Maxim D. Shrayer.

IOSIF UTKIN

Iosif Utkin (1903–1944), poet and translator, was born in Khingan, Manchuria (presently Khingansk, Khabarovsk Region of the Russian Federation), where his father worked for the Chinese Eastern Railroad. Utkin grew up in Irkutsk, a provincial capital with the largest Jewish community in Siberia at the time (about 8,500 at the time of his birth). Expelled from public school, he changed several jobs, including a stint as a poolroom attendant in Irkutsk's Grand Hotel, where his knowledge of things Jewish was enriched by contacts with Jewish businessmen and members of the underworld.

In 1920 Utkin joined the Red Army as a volunteer, serving on the Far Eastern front. After returning to Irkutsk in 1922, he reported for *Power of Labor* (*Vlast' truda*), where his first poems appeared. A Komsomol activist, in 1924 Utkin was sent on a *putyovka* (roughly "official placement directive") to study at the Moscow Institute of Journalism. In Moscow he became associated with a group of "Komsomol poets," including Aleksandr Bezymensky, Mikhail Svetlov, Vissarion Sayanov, and Aleksandr Zharov; all of the above, except Zharov, were Jewish. In this city Utkin completed the long poem *The Tale of Red-Headed Motele, Mr. Inspector, Rabbi Isaiah, and Commissar Blokh*. Printed in 1925 in the review *Young Guard* (*Molodaia gvardiia*), the poem made Utkin famous for having provided the most ambitious if politically opportunistic treatment of Jewish topics in Soviet Russian-language poetry of the time. (Eduard Bagritsky [in vol. 1] wrote and published *The Lay of Opanas* in 1926.) *The Tale* received a jubilant endorsement by Anatoly Lunacharsky, the people's commissar of enlightenment, and was immediately translated into Yiddish by Moses Michl Kitai (1886–1938). Book editions followed, including one illustrated by Natan Altman (1889–1970). Eight songs from the poem (opus 44, 1926–29) were set for voice and piano by Mikhail Gnesin (1883–1957).

In 1927 Utkin's collection *First Book* was published. His soulful song-lyric poems about the civil war, friendship, and love went through many editions. Readers commonly knew by heart such poems of his as "The Guitar," "Song about a Mother," "A Song" ("In the Carpathians,/in the Carpathians . . ."), and "A Komsomol Song" ("The lad was gunned down in Irkutsk . . ."). In his capacity as poetry editor at the State Publishing House of Literature in the 1930s, Utkin mentored younger poets and translators and edited anthologies, including *Young Moscow* (1937, with Pavel Antokolsky, in vol. 1). He was the editor of the two-volume *Collected Works* of Eduard Bagritsky, but its publication derailed after the first volume. In 1938–40, Utkin had his share of difficulties, in part because he had been married to the daughter of Soviet official

Khristian Rakovsky, who was executed after the March 1938 show trial of the "Anti-Soviet Bloc of Rights and Trotskyites."

Utkin volunteered for military duty right after the Nazi invasion and was seriously wounded in the fall of 1941. He returned to the front as a correspondent. His wartime poems appeared in *I Saw It Myself* (1942). While flying back from the front lines in 1944, Utkin died in an airplane crash. His works remained in print in the 1950s–80s.

Occasional Jewish references surfaced in Utkin's shorter poems. In "Friend from Sungari" (1925) a "yellow-skinned Chinese man/and a pale-skinned Hebrew [*iudei*]" fight side-by-side for the Revolution.

A brief summary hardly does justice to Utkin's only notable contribution to Jewish-Russian literature, the satirical poem *The Tale of Red-Headed Motele* (1925). Much of its sociolinguistic charm—Utkin's use of Yiddishisms and a recreation of the Jewish "flavor"—is inescapably lost in translation. Set in Kishinev, Bialik's "city of slaughter," the poem focuses on the career of a poor tailor, Motele, who returns home as Commissar Blokh, a Soviet authority figure, following the Revolution. Two patriarchal figures betoken the Jewish tzarist past: police inspector Bobrov and Rabbi Isaiah. Having previously enforced the anti-Jewish restrictions, the former inspector winds up working as a clerk under Commissar Blokh. The rabbi, too, undergoes a transformation, offering the commissar his daughter Riva as a bride. The poem schematizes daily Jewish life in the Pale—a life that Utkin never experienced. It ends with a hymn to the "free" homeland.

Utkin composed *The Tale* during the years of a ferocious campaign against Judaism and traditional Jewish life, delivering to the Soviet propaganda machine exactly what it needed. Not surprisingly, Utkin's poem was a hit with the Jews of Utkin's generation who had made a transition from the Pale to large Russian cities in the late 1910s–early 1920s, receiving higher education, rapidly assimilating, and hopeful about Jewish prospects in the USSR. Derivative as compared to the best in the 1920s Russian poetry, Utkin's poem delivered an omnibus package to the middlebrow Soviet reader. Particularly representative of Utkin's ideological accomplishment is "The Second Miracle." It focuses on a refusal by Hayyim Bais to allow his son's circumcision. Spelled in Russian as "Bèz," with the back rather than the front "e," the Jew's last name literally means "without" (i.e., without the ancient Judaic heritage) while reflecting a Jewish accent. Utkin's unambiguous rhetoric on the Jewish question stands in stark contrast to a doubly ironic treatment of the same anecdote in Isaac Babel's story "Karl-Yankel" (1931; see introduction to Babel in vol. 1).

From *The Tale of Red-Headed Motele,*
Mr. Inspector, Rabbi Isaiah, and
Commissar Blokh

Chapter 2: Miracles of Kishinev

THE SECOND MIRACLE

Each and every one, thank god,
No matter what yardstick you use—
His own road,
His own path must choose.
And thus
Alone,
Step by step,
Through slush and snow,
Venturing,
People walk their own
Paths across the century.

To walk through life happily is rare.
Not for many folks
Life's a bowl of compote:
Some break their legs,
Others come out
Unscathed.
So there!

. . . .

The wind mumbles prayers,
Echoing the rabbi's grief.
The rabbi prays
By the Torah,
The rabbi divines
By the Torah.
Touching the rusty threads
Of his discolored

Talles:
—When will it all end?
Just how much longer?

Shadows of candles
Grow stronger,
And taller,
Riding across the ceiling
Of the rabbi's den
Like a funeral procession
Through the mournful town.

—This is true punishment!
Have you heard yet?
Hayyim Bais
Has refused
To allow his son's bris.
What a shame!

The first case in Kishinev!
Would you believe him, the bastard,
He said,
"Esteemed rabbi,
Enough blood!!!"

. . . .

Many paths, many roads,
As many as eyes!
Going from us
To god,
And from god
To us.

1925

Translated from the Russian by Maxim D. Shrayer

Iosif Utkin, *Povest' o ryzhem Motele, gospodine inspektore, ravvine Isaie i komissare Blokh.* English translation, and introduction copyright © by Maxim D. Shrayer.

ELIZAVETA POLONSKAYA

Elizaveta Polonskaya (1890–1969), poet, translator, and children's author, was born Elizaveta Movshenzon in Warsaw, in the assimilated family of a Jewish-Russian engineer; she subsequently took the last name of her husband, Lev Polonsky. Living in Łódź until 1905, Polonskaya learned both Polish and Yiddish. After a 1905 pogrom, her family fled to Berlin, later moving to St. Petersburg. Taking part in the revolutionary movement, Polonskaya fell under police surveillance. In 1907 she went to France, where she studied medicine at the Sorbonne. Polonskaya served with the Russian Red Cross during World War I and continued practicing medicine after the Bolshevik Revolution, working in various Soviet healthcare institutions until 1931.

Leslie J. Dorfman, Polonskaya's biographer, wrote of her literary pedigree: "Having passed through Symbolism and Acmeism, she returned to her own particular brand of civic verse, written in a rhetorical, often biblical style sometimes described as masculine, yet with a distinctly feminine point of view." A participant of the legendary literary studio at the World Literature publishing house, in 1921 Polonskaya became the only "sister" of the literary group that called itself the Serapion Brothers (see Lev Lunts and Veniamin Kaverin in vol. 1). Her early poetry was gathered in *Omens* (1921) and *Under Stone Rain, 1921–1923* (1923). Among Polonskaya's controversial poems of the early 1920s was "Carmen" (1924), in which a Russian Bolshevik woman was portrayed as both a zealous revolutionary and a passionate and sexual female. *A Trip to the Urals*, Polonskaya's 1927 volume of essays, already signaled the ideological compromise that she and most of her fellow travelers probed in the mid-to-late 1920s. Polonskaya's collection *Stubborn Calendar*, featuring some of her best lyrical and epic verses from the 1920s, appeared in 1929. Polonskaya published a dozen children's books in the 1920s and 1930s.

In 1931 Polonskaya gave up medicine for the next ten years, earning a living solely as a writer. She traveled as a reporter for *Leningrad Truth* (*Leningradskaia pravda*), earning the kind of mileage that filled the pages of her next four books. The volume of essays *People of the Soviet Working Days* (1934) was followed by three poetry collections: *Years. Selected Poems* (1935), *New Poems, 1932–1936* (1937), and *Times of Courage* (1940), including many unremarkable verses tired of their own formal and ideological concessions. Her "Song of Youth" (1936) ended with the lines "Long live Stalin!/Long live May!" During World War II, Polonskaya served as a front-line military doctor. Some of her wartime poems were gathered in *The Kama Notebook* (1945) and her prose in *On Our Own Shoulders* (1948).

Polonskaya published virtually no original verse in 1946–56, the shadow of

Zhdanovshchin (the postwar onslaught of reaction known by this name after Andrey Zhdanov) and the "anticosmopolitan" campaign, hanging low over her shoulders. She concentrated on translations and in the 1950s served as the head of the Translators Section of the Leningrad branch of the Union of Soviet Writers. Polonskaya included few of her early poems in *Selected Poems* (1966). Her contorted introduction pledged allegiance to the "spirit of her people" (here she meant "Soviet people") and to "the wide road of October." And yet, the mere remembrance of her poetry mentor Nikolay Gumilyov and her Serapion brother Lev Lunts, both forbidden in the USSR, said more about Polonskaya's past and her poetry than most of the verses in the volume. Toward the end of her life, Polonskaya worked on *Encounters*, a memoir of the 1920s and 1930s, which she left unfinished. Polonskaya died in Leningrad in 1969, a survivor and circumspect witness whose "rebellious" early poetry (L. Dorfman's expression) was almost unknown to the postwar generations of Russian poets.

Jewish and Judaic motifs are visible in Polonskaya's early poems, including "February 1" and "Shylock," both in *Omens*. Russian and Christian readers cringed at her poem "I cannot stand the infant Jesus . . . ," also included in *Omens*, where the poet unapologetically identified with the Jewish God of the Old Testament and called Jesus of Nazareth a "forger." While exhibiting ample Judaic pride, Polonskaya's declarative poem betrayed insensitivity to the beliefs of the Christians. Polonskaya's early Jewish poems were never reprinted in her subsequent Soviet editions.

Polonskaya included the intriguing poem "To a Friend" (1932) in *New Poems* (1937). Referring to both herself and the "friend," presumably a western Jew, as having "inherited" "the Arian word" and a "Judaic childhood," and alluding to Nazism, she offered to show the "friend" "her home and her country." Was this a thinly veiled invitation addressed to Jewish Socialists and Communists in the West? Polonskaya translated the anti-Nazi poets Johannes R. Becher and Eric Weinert, who found themselves in the USSR in the 1930s. Also included in *New Poems* was "'Gold Rain'" (1936), an embarrassing piece of Birobidzhan propaganda. Occasional echoes of the Shoah were heard in Polonskaya's writings.

An early version of "Shop of Splendors" was published in 1925 in the magazine *Leningrad*. The full text, to which the present lines 1–10 and 16–32 had been added, appeared in Polonskaya's collection *The Stubborn Calendar* (1929). In Polonskaya's last free-spirited collection, the poem memorialized much more than the prematurely dead Lev Lunts (in vol. 1). For Polonskaya, Lunts, and their literary brothers and sisters, the departing 1920s had been the "shop of splendors." "Encounter," Polonskaya's second poem included below, also appeared in *The Stubborn Calendar*. Reprinted in *Years. Selected Poems* (1935), this poem deserves special attention for the clarity and courage with which it articulated the impossibility of assimilation.

Shop of Splendors
In Memory of Lev Lunts

Yes. It's already been five years
That we've stood behind this counter
Hanging around, dealing. Should we
Cash out early? The shoppers can wait.
Let's count the goods. Work's over.

Now that the lock on remembrance is off,
Let's pull out from the bottom
What our memories have guarded,
Kept stuffed in secret corners—
Audacity, brazenness, a grin.

Though if words go for nothing now,
Call us what you will—
Though life is for sale and death is for sale—
The head is not negotiable,
And the heart's no take-out.

"For wind, against stiffness."
It's singing to us, this verse.
A commander of armies, now you lead
A complex formation of simple things.

And suddenly another friend:
"I know battle. I was there.
The bullets and the banners speak
All too cleverly for the enemy.
But for those dumb with words,
You fix them like a donkey—
A thorn in the big soft ass."

And a third friend responds:
"It's not enough to see.
The pen and word must redo
Everything from scratch—
The taste of a small town, a station's smoke,
The humungous game of war."

Yes, we the living speak this way.
But there, in an alien land,
Under a blanket of earth,
My last friend lies in a final dream.
He cherished the letters' gentle link
Like the link of life itself.
And he was buried hastily
After the Jewish rite.

But he loved a hearty laugh,
Good company, verse sung aloud,
And he was nicer than anyone here,
A wise great friend, a dear pal,
And it terrifies me, in this fifth year,
That he's not in a distant land, nor in a vault,
But was simply cleared out, final sale,
Here, in this shop of splendors.

1925–29

Encounter

Morning flew by in the usual way,
Up and down streets, it raced,
Unwinding the spring of an ongoing watch
That the night would wind up again.

A coat was fastened over the chest
With a clasp and a little chain,
Then a voice from the gut: "*tayer yiddish kind*,
Give to a beggar, Jewish daughter."

From under her rags she studies me
With a tender, cunning old face,
A sentinel's eye and a hookish nose,
And a black wig, parted smooth.

An ancient, yellowish hand
Grabs my sleeve, and the words
Of a language I don't comprehend
Sound out, seizing my heart.

And there I stop, I cannot go on,
Though I know—I shouldn't, I shouldn't,
And drop a small coin in her open palm
And lift a thirsty heart to her face.

"Old woman, how did you, half-blind,
Pick me out among these strangers?
After all, your muttering is odd to me,
After all, I'm like them, the same as those—
Dull, alien, strange."

"Daughter, dear, there are things about us
That no one can mistake.
Our girls have the saddest eyes,
And a slow, languorous walk.

And they don't laugh like the others—
Openly in their simplicity—
But beam behind clouds as the moon does,
Their sadness alive in their smiles.

Even if you lose your faith and kin,
A yid iz immer a yid![1]
And thus my blood sings in your veins,"
She says in her alien tongue.

That morning flew by in the usual way,
Up and down streets, it raced,
Unwinding the spring of an ongoing watch
That the night would wind up again.

1927

Translated from the Russian by Larissa Szporluk

---

1. Polonskaya's (imperfectly fictional?) old Jewish lady living in Moscow uses a Germanism, *immer* (always), in place of a Yiddish equivalent.

YURY LIBEDINSKY

Yury Libedinsky (1898–1959), fiction writer and critic, was born in Odessa to a doctor's family and grew up in the southern Ural region, in Miass, a factory town, and in Chelyabinsk. In 1910, there were about 850 Jews out of Chelyabinsk's total population of about 63,000; the Jewish population spiked during World War I, due to an influx of refugees. In preparation for his bar mitzvah, Libedinsky briefly studied Hebrew and the Torah.

By the time of his graduation from Realschule in 1918, Libedinsky had read works by Marx, Engels, Plekhanov, and Lenin, which had forged his worldview. He fought in the civil war and became a Bolshevik in 1920. After serving in the political department of the Chelyabinsk Military Authority, Libedinsky was transferred to Moscow in 1921 and completed his first novel, *A Week*. Published in 1922, it soon appeared in English (1923); the Yiddish translation, by the poet Aaron Kushnirov (1890–1949), came out in 1925. Libedinsky's prose betrayed the influence of symbolism (Andrey Bely) and the neorealists (Leonid Andreev, Ivan Bunin). Committed though he was to Bolshevism, Libedinsky honestly depicted the hostility of the rural population toward the Revolution.

Demobilized in 1923, Libedinsky worked in a Moscow factory. He cofounded the "October" faction of the All-Russia Association of Proletarian Writers (VAPP), many of whose leading members were Jewish: Leopold Averbakh, G. Lelevich (Labory Kalmanzon), Semyon Rodov. Libedinsky's next novel, *Tomorrow,* portrayed Bolsheviks confronting the New Economic Policy (NEP). In their distrust of the peasants, skepticism of the NEP, and emphasis on "permanent revolution," *A Week* and *Tomorrow* reflected the ideas of Leon Trotsky, who lost the battle for leadership to Stalin after Lenin's death in 1924.

VAPP changed its name to RAPP (Russian Association of Proletarian Writers) in 1928 as it vied for dominance. Libedinsky, one of RAPP's main polemicists, authored two books of theory: *The General Tasks of Proletarian Literature* and *For the RAPP Theater Platform* (both 1931). Published in 1930, Libedinsky's *The Birth of a Hero* was to be the poster novel for RAPP literature. However, RAPP was dismantled in 1932, and *The Birth of a Hero* was attacked in *Pravda* on Stalin's initiative. Libedinsky deemed his RAPP years an "error" and distanced himself from Leopold Averbakh, who persisted in his defense of the platform. Arrested in 1937, Averbakh perished in the Great Purge.

In 1934, the critic Ivan Vinogradov identified Libedinsky's novel *Tomorrow* with Trotskyism, and Libedinsky was expelled from the Party in 1938 for being a

"Trotskyite." Withdrawn from the libraries along with Libedinsky's early works, *A Week* and *The Commissars* were reprinted in "revised" form only in 1955. With the help of his friend Aleksandr Fadeev (1901–1956), a major functionary of the Union of Soviet Writers, Libedinsky was reinstated in the Party in 1939. (Fadeev headed the union from 1946 to 1954; Libedinsky was with him on the eve of his suicide.)

The Caucasus, where Libedinsky traveled extensively in the 1930s, became the setting of his trilogy *Mountains and People* (1947), about socialist change in Kabardino-Balkaria; the first part, *Batash and Batay*, appeared in 1939–41. In 1941 Libedinsky volunteered for the People's Defense Troops and later worked in the army newspaper *Red Warrior* (*Krasnyi voin*). He fell into disfavor again during the "anticosmopolitan" campaign; no books of his fiction appeared between 1947 and 1954. He adapted the Osetin Nartic legends, producing books for adults and children. During the post-Stalinist years, Libedinsky published formulaic works of fiction and self-censored reminiscences. His timorously anti-Stalinist short novel *Family Matters* (1962) described a family of Moscow intelligentsia during Stalin's last weeks.

Initially owing to his Marxist convictions and later because he feared repressions, Libedinsky minimized the place of Jewish questions in his life and writings. (The sketch "The Road from the Shtetl" in the 1933 collection *Stories of My Comrades* stands as a notable exception and deserves attention.) Yet, owing to the hyperrealist authenticity of Libedinsky's novels of the 1920s, Jewish Bolsheviks received prominent speaking parts.

Libedinsky's major novel *The Commissars* (1925) is set in a provincial military district after the end of the civil war, and the excerpt below comes from the opening. The physically frail Iosif Mindlov and the stern and unswerving Efim Rozov constitute two halves of a composite image, which anticipates the Jewish protagonist of another famous early Soviet novel, *The Rout* (1927), by Libedinsky's friend Aleksandr Fadeev, who was not Jewish. What unites Libedinsky's commissars and Fadeev's resilient Red Army commander Osip Levinson is a limited figuration of their Jewishness, restricted to names and phenotypical characteristics, conflated with their fierce loyalty to the Revolution. Whether or not such exemplary images of Jewish Communist knights planted new seeds of popular resentment and antisemitism remains an open question. They most certainly gave ammunition to various perpetrators of the Judeophobic myth of the "Jewish Revolution."

From *The Commissars*

CHAPTER 1

The garrisons and separate units of our expansive district were scattered among the mountain factories, where machine life barely lingers, and among the little towns scattered across the trackless steppe where isolated district party committees toil without the support of workers.

The civil war had thundered past, and the military commissars, lads tempered by their army experience . . .

"They're bored, Efim! That's the whole problem."

"Worse than that, Comrade Vlasov! Lots of them are demoralized."

"That's what I'm saying. You can chalk it all up to boredom. To take an example, marrying a merchant's wife or a priest's daughter . . . Lots of the men are drunks. . . . And others have set up housekeeping and lost the proletarian spirit. In a word— there's none of that old fire in the belly anymore."

"With the shift to peaceful forms of agitprop work, most of our political staff are unable to cope. They lack the knowledge. Take Vasiliev, an intelligent man, a metal worker from Moscow. He writes that it's hard to work with his regiment. Yet at the front he'd been a brigade commissar. Or take that old man . . . Shalavin, the brigade commander of the Seventh Workers' . . ."

"Yes, he wrote me, too. We have to come up with something."

Vlasov, commander of the military district, reached that conclusion after an hour-long conversation with his deputy, head of the district political department, Efim Rozov, face to face in the high-windowed, white-walled office.

They had both lapsed into silence. Vlasov stroked his wide beard, which covered two orders of the Red Banner pinned to his chest; he started painstakingly rolling a cigarette with his thick, peasant fingers.

Rozov had the slender, nimble fingers of a clockmaker. First he adjusted his glasses; then he stroked his sparse hair with a widow's peak intruding onto his high yellow forehead; then he quickly leafed through the reports as if seeking a decision in them.

The civil war had thundered past. Its whirlwind had run its course in the Crimea and at the Polish border; it had run its course in Siberia, ceased to howl in Kronshtadt, and seemingly settled down. Was this perhaps the calm before a new, mightier storm?

Vlasov and Rozov had both been contemplating the situation, and, each in his own way, as their line of work suggested, had understood the threat and prepared to mount a fight. And vigilantly, too, the whole party heeded to the soundless movement produced by the class forces of the vast country as they closely followed reports and accounts. Now the idea was to take all these commissars, whom they knew from the war, and look them over as if they were an old weapon: have they begun to rust, have cracks appeared, have they gotten chipped? And once more to temper, to sharpen them for some battle that may or may not take place?

"Summon the whole gang here . . . As if to some sort of congress. And we'll probe and ponder . . . I hate to say it, as they are all fine lads, but it's just that they're bored, the sons of bitches. Who wouldn't be? I'm bored, too," he added, sort of surprised as if he hadn't exactly expected such words from himself. And his blue eyes gleamed brightly and cunningly. "The only way I keep my sanity is by hunting."

Rozov, the head of the political department, heard these last words and began rubbing his brow and wincing: he hadn't approved the hunting diversions, and the commander knew about that. Rozov began rubbing his brow and then froze for a second. Then he slammed the palm of his hand against the table.

"So," he said, "we need to create a retraining program. We'll gather political staff from the whole region. Some we'll order to come; others can choose whether or not to come. First, everyone will be under military discipline; second, there'll be a broad program of study, both political and general; three, everyone will be under observation."

The commander screwed up his eyes. The stogie went out and stuck to his lower lip. Rozov watched him triumphantly and adjusted his glasses.

"That may be true, Efim, but we need to check what's where and why and see what it all adds up to . . . We need someone in charge who would be able to handle these people, handle them responsibly, someone who knows his way around. Someone who could give lectures . . ."

"Nothing doing! That's up to the party committee of the province. General education subjects will suffice for the hungry intelligentsia. You won't have any trouble finding a specialist for military training, but tracking down the right person to run this thing and finding political instructors will be a bit harder . . ." He pondered for a minute, and paper once again began to rustle under his quick, excited fingers. The commander was waiting. He had known Efim for a long time, so he knew better than to hinder his organizational inspiration with exhortations and questions, when, completely unexpectedly, the right combinations—people, jobs, institutions—would lightly and freely be born in his high square head.

"Whom shall we put in charge?" Efim repeated slowly. "Arefiev? Where do you propose to dispatch him?"

"Arefiev? I want to send him to the Academy of General Headquarters . . . He'll make a strong commanding officer . . . Only . . ."

"Well, that's not a bad idea. A former tsarist army officer—he could set up the military training [. . .].

"All the same, don't forget he's a former Menshevik . . ."

"Then maybe he needs a deputy who's a dyed-in-the-wool Bolshevik. Who?"

"Mindlov, Iosif, the chief political officer of N-sk Province."

"He's sick . . . I told him to submit a report. He arrived here yesterday."

"Well, well . . . We'd better find someone else. I'm summoning Arefiev. He'll be here tomorrow and assume the new position the day after tomorrow. Next week, say, on Tuesday, the sessions will begin, all right?" said Rozov as he got up. "Or earlier?" The commander didn't reply. The wind was moving the curtains at the window. From there, creeping under the town's colorful roofs, came the faint smell of pine needles burning in the distance.

Rozov was not a local man, so he didn't understand that smell, dry and light as the pine smell of last year's summer, because in his childhood he had never gathered, year after year, wild strawberries that had been infused by the sun on top of a rich, resinous snow crust. He had never wandered around lithe lakes, nor had he served in Red guerrilla units in Admiral Kolchak's rear. The civil war had taken him from Russia's southern seaside provinces and thrown him here, and therefore he wasn't like the slow-moving local people. Small and skinny, he turned quickly and sharply, but with no extra motion, like a pocket knife in the hands of a man skilled at carving.

"The forests are burning early this year," said Vlasov, pressing Efim's hand. "Looks like there won't be a harvest. If only . . ."

"So tomorrow I'll send the papers for your signature."

"All right. So long."

The commander sat there for a long time, with his face turned to the window. He kept puffing at his cigarette and squinting at the blue mountains that surrounded the multi-colored stone carpet of the town on all sides. The commander thought back to a time two years before, when he was in the rear of the Whites and drop by drop was mustering workers into his division—a time when he didn't have enough rifles or cartridges and absolutely no artillery. Had they told him he would be sitting here in the commander's chair in the key town of the region and the war would be finished—why, he would have considered that as the supreme victory of the Revolution. And now they've achieved a supreme victory, but new dangers have arisen—and such great ones! And, shaking his head, he reflected on the cruel uprising of the peasants, which they had just extinguished, the smoking charred logs of unrest still smoldering there in the Cossack villages that girded the windswept steppes to the southeast.

Tanya spoke briefly, all at once, and then she grew silent.

Efim felt that she was waiting for his words and, mainly, his joy. This would have fortified her in the decision that she had made. But he had washed his hands and was drying them meticulously, as if he were engaged in something very important, and was evidently delaying his reply. And since the answer was not immediately forthcoming, Tanya became sad, her eyes lost their luster, the corners of her mouth turned down. She began to droop and sat down on the bed.

"Tanyusha, first of all, this will tear you away from any kind of social life; second . . . You yourself think about it. I . . . I fear for your life . . . and . . . I'm afraid to be left alone. And I have to say plainly that you won't be such a comrade to me as you have been up to now, right?" He sat down next to her, embraced her broad shoulders, and looked into her face, with its high forehead and slightly downturned lips, and into her long, prominent eyes. And she said, brushing his ear with her lips:

"Efim, think like a Communist. Actually, if we Communists don't have any children, what then? Who will take our places? I'll raise him into a true Communist . . . What is it, Efim?"

She looked at him with bewilderment; he turned the other way, and she saw the unbearable, dry smirk she knew so well.

"Why the hypocrisy? Why don't you just say it: I want to be a mother. It's instinct. Instead you use Communist principles as a cover-up. Why don't you go work in the orphanage? They're in such bad shape there. You could bring up Communists there."

She blushed furiously, but her blue gaze never wavered. There was nothing more to say, but something fundamental, wordless told her she was right. And since he failed to understand that she was right, she had nothing more to say.

"Fine, Efim, let's see what happens . . . By the way, you know, Iosif Mindlov was here. He's very sick."

Rozov turned around and looked out the window.

"We're all sick," he said in a muffled voice.

"Yes, well, yes . . . certainly . . . But, you know, his face twitches so badly. Then, too, he's afraid to stay in his room by himself, and he has lost a lot of weight. And his wife is already in a sanatorium, and he wants to go see her."

Efim moved away from the window; right now he looked especially pale to her.

"Yes and you, Efim, don't look well. Why do you stay up so late? Go to bed! Go to bed!"

She went up to him; next to him she seemed tall and full-bodied, as if she were his mother. She put him to bed and brought him a mug of milk. And watching him drink small gulps and seeing how the milk set off his pale lips, so familiar and so dear to her, she told him about her Red Army school.

And then he told her about the things that had piled up during his day. As always, after eight to ten hours of separation, they would immediately tell each other what they'd been doing and share their thoughts about each other's work, asking advice of one another. The work never left them, powerfully transforming itself into leisure.

"The director of the retraining program will be Arefiev. You remember, he came to see me in my railroad car; he was commissar of the division, a really tall fellow with military bearing."

"Yes, I remember. A former officer . . . But I don't like him much. There's something aristocratic about him. He's sure to interfere in the work with the masses."

"We won't find anyone better. He has a powerful will. Plus he's strong in Marxist theory. And commands authority. And we've appointed as his deputy . . . he suddenly caught his breath as if he had swallowed something bitter, "and his deputy will be Mindlov."

Efim grew silent. Tanya remembered that just a few seconds before his face had struck her as especially pale and his voice had seemed muffled. She didn't speak.

"You realize, Tanya, don't you, just how short-handed we are," he said hoarsely. "I went through the whole list of political officers in the region—not a single suitable soul. Plus this furious demobilization."

"But he's really sick," Tanya said quietly. "Efim, if you had seen how his face twitches."

Efim carefully extricated himself from Tanya's arm and walked over to the table. He suppressed his irritation with her easily and customarily.

This custom had been developed when he was still a boy learning the clock business in the big workshop of a southern city. Rozov would be sitting hunched over a little table, gathering little wheels, gold screws, and miniscule springs, tiny even through a magnifying glass. Blue circles formed under his eyes from the stress. His well-trained slender fingers trembled from stress. He would remember that this little clock will be set in a gold ring or a broach or a necklace—and it is for that he was ruining his eyes—and he would feel like losing his temper, gnashing his teeth, and hurling this golden trifle into the fire of the stove.

No, no. Easy does it. There's a book called *The Erfurt Program.* In Petrograd there's a newspaper called *Pravda.* It doesn't always come on time, but it does reach these parts. The good old mole keeps doing his work, and everything will happen in its own time.

In March 1917, Rozov entered the workshop, surveyed the scene for the last time, looked at his stool and at the master craftsmen, who were hunched over their jobs. He got the money he had coming to him and returned no more.

But the patient and careful skills of a clockmaker had eaten into him for his whole life and stood him in good stead in the struggle and in his work.

Tanya was dozing. Her eyes half-closed, she looked in the direction of the desk, over which Rozov's back was stubbornly hunched. She thought about his sternness. It was no accident that he had a reputation in the region for being a bureaucrat, and here she was, already justifying his ways. She knew that the mainspring of his strong-willed striving toward the future—*toward communism*—was so strongly screwed into him that he broke his own life just as pitilessly as he broke the lives of others. . . . Actually, he was sick, too. He had a nasty cough, and he didn't sleep nights, but he never complained about his health to her, and he continued his work. She no longer reasoned about it; she felt only tenderness for him.

"Efim," Tanya called quietly. "Come over here."

He came. She kissed him on his hard, cold forehead and on his lips. He embraced her soft, warm shoulders. She whispered something to him with a face that was artful, but invisible in the darkness:

"So what're you asking—do I have the right to want a child? But it's not right to ask that question. Tell me, please, do you have the right to want me? Actually, if it weren't for you, I wouldn't want a child. True?"

Efim usually felt like Tanya's superior in his understanding of life, and she silently submitted to his guidance. But at times she flared up with such simple and warm thoughts that under their impact, as under the light of the sun after a cold night, she brought radiance and warmth to life in a new way and showed her own unseen sides. But these new sides always scared Efim. They kept him from acting. Mighty reason once again got the upper hand. The colors that had unexpectedly burst forth disappeared, and once again an exact, detailed plan was put in place. That's what was happening now.

"Nothing but silliness," he said with a grin, whereupon he stroked her fine, dry hair and went back to work.

Iosif Mindlov walked the ancient, winding lanes. The spring morning sun stroked his black, fluffy hair with its warm palm and kindled rainbow flashes in his cracked pince-nez.

Iosif Mindlov felt good because in two or three weeks Liya's warm palm would be stroking his face. So many times has that warm palm passed over his forehead and cheeks on its way to his throat that all its movements could be predicted like the melody of a familiar and simple, joyful song. Mindlov smiles tenderly and even murmurs to himself. The lanes are deserted, the little houses have small myopic windows, the lilac bushes are green, and acacia trees line the fences. His footsteps ring out as he walks along the wooden sidewalks.

The doctor had said that he would need a furlough for four months. That was too much. With that much time, you could, heaven forbid, miss the world revolution. What did that doctor know anyway? And such questions: "What exactly are your duties?"

Duties—you're kidding! Duties? That was the least of it. Eight hours in the political department—nothing at all. The duties would seem to be few. But is it really duty that forces a man to sit through all the meetings? Is it really duty that forces a man to every corner of the province in order to inspect the political school over and over again? Is it really duty that forces a man to hand over hours of sleep to Marx?

So in his pocket are two slips of paper. On one, behind the official stamp, Mindlov's six ailments, a long list of medicines, and, in fierce Latin, justification of the dire need for a four-month convalescence in the Crimea.

As he handed Mindlov that slip of paper, the doctor weightily said:

"If you don't go immediately, you'll find yourself—well, in two weeks or so—in an insane asylum. I'm astonished that you've been able to hang on this long. That's number one. And you will die of tuberculosis and anemia—that's number two."

He had to live; he wanted to live.

That is why the second slip of paper was a report addressed to the head of the regional political department requesting a two-month furlough. Two months would be plenty. After all, Liya would be at his side—the best medicine. Without a doubt the report was an empty formality. They knew in the region that if Mindlov was requesting a furlough, things were bad. Besides, the chief political officer was Efim, his friend and comrade from the anti-Denikin underground.

There was the white building of the Regional Political Administration. The familiar mural, the familiar slogan, the familiar grounds. In the office, a meeting with the chief political officer. Rozov saw Mindlov at the door, and it seemed that Rozov wanted to turn away; but then, without looking in his direction, he quickly nodded at him and continued speaking.

Mindlov sat down a short distance away on the couch and listened. It was apparently a meeting of the division heads.

Carefully, detail by detail, Efim criticized the work of the information department. Mindlov knew that the work of the information department was poor. He himself had cursed more than once the stupidly organized and incomprehensible system of bookkeeping that scared the life out of the commanding officers. It was necessary to simplify. Efim was right.

All the same, it was strange that when Mindlov entered, Rozov had sharply, brusquely turned away from the door. Maybe this was because of what he was saying when Iosif came in? But he barely acknowledged him. Mindlov had imagined this meeting differently.

Should he first tell Rozov about his ailment and then hand him his report? No. According to the rules, the report is to be handed over immediately. How long would this meeting last? . . .

"Here, read it over. This should cover everything. The political department has been liquidated and . . . For two months."

Rozov read and, without looking up from the desk, he began to pore over the papers. His lips had begun to quiver ever so slightly, as had the lids of his lowered eyes. He found and handed a sheet of paper to Iosif.

"Read what it says at the end," he said.

Now his face froze; his eyes looked calmly through Iosif exactly as if he weren't seeing him.

"What's this?"

Mindlov felt a chill run through his knees and shoulders.

"Look at the end."

"Comrade Mindlov, Iosif, has been appointed commander of the educational-political department and deputy." Mindlov mechanically rose to his feet and reread the entire document.

"Take your report back, Iosif. I'd rather not write a resolution of rejection on it. Besides, you're the only one suitable for the appointment."

Rozov's voice was muffled and indistinct; once again his eyelids and lips began to quiver.

What a tormented face. But to take the report back meant to recognize that it could never be presented.

"You surely know, Efim, that if I submit such a report, I know what I'm doing."

"There's nothing . . . else . . . I can do. Take back your report, Iosif, I'm asking you."

"Comrade Rozov, I demand an official resolution concerning my report! Official!" Rozov repeated Mindlov's final word, and it rose between them like a glass wall. Rozov reread the report, and his face inexorably froze. He shifted his gaze, glittering, cruel, and cold, like the gaze of a hawk, from the letters of the report to Iosif's eyes.

"Officially? Do you think I don't have the guts?"

Spattering the report with tiny drops of red ink, he wrote REJECTED. The tip of the pen shattered on the signature.

"Tomorrow, Comrade Mindlov, report for duty."

Mindlov stood transfixed for a moment or two. He felt that all the wires fastening their lives together had snapped; what remained was only the hurtful, nagging pain. With fingers beginning to sweat, he picked up the report and walked out of the office.

1925

Translated from the Russian by Richard Sheldon

VERA INBER

Vera Inber (1890–1972), poet, prose writer, translator, and playwright, was born in Odessa. Her father, Moisey Shpentser, operated the Methesis publishing house, and her mother ran a school for Jewish girls. Leon Trotsky (1879–1940), her father's cousin, had been raised in their home; this connection later haunted Inber. Inber took the last name of her first husband, with whom she had a daughter, the writer Zhanna Gauzner (1912–1962).

After graduating from a gymnasium, Inber entered Odessa's Higher Women's Courses but soon left for Europe, spending four years there. From her early poems, Inber's writing was marked by what the Moscow critic Inna Rodnyanskaya identified as "stylish, sober irony" and by elegance of form. In 1914 Inber's first collection, *Melancholy Wine*, appeared in Paris in Russian. Critics pointed out the influence of Anna Akhmatova (1889–1966) on Inber's lyrical personae. Acmeist—and symbolist—influences aside, Inber's early poems testified to her authentic poetic sensibility. *Bitter Delight* (Petrograd, 1917) and *Wasteful Words* (Odessa, 1922) signaled a developing interest in description and landscape and a growth of narrativism.

In 1922 Inber moved to Moscow. After joining the Literary Center of Constructivists (LTsK; see Ilya Selvinsky in vol. 1), she incorporated into her verses the constructivist emphasis on the "semantic dominant." Political and industrial themes entered Inber's writing in the mid-1920s. Her *Goal and Path* (1924) contained a poem dedicated to Trotsky, as well as verses about Lenin's funeral. To the constructivist collective *The State Plan of Literature* (1925), Inber contributed the long poem *Black Coal*; she also contributed to *Business* (1929), the third and final LTsK collective. Inber's poems of 1924–26 were gathered in *To the Son I Don't Have* (1927). Although Inber is commonly remembered as a poet, her greatest achievement was not in poetry but in fiction. Collections of her stories included *Nightingale and Rose* (1925), *Stories* (1926), *Catcher of Comets* (1927), and others. *Place under the Sun* (1928), her autobiographical "lyrical chronicle," enjoyed success. The 1920s were Inber's most prolific decade, as evidenced by her six-volume *Collected Works* (1928–30).

Shifting gears, Inber wrote with romantic enthusiasm about socialist construction (e.g., her 1932 *Poems*). She participated in the 1935 collective volume about the Belomor Canal (see also Mikhail Kozakov and Viktor Shklovsky in vol. 1; Evgeny Gabrilovich in vol. 2). Safely Soviet, Inber's 1935 collection *Lane of My Name* preserved nuggets of talent, as did her long poems *Travel Diary* (1939, a Stalinist overture about Georgia) and *Ovid* (1941).

Staying in Leningrad during the nine-hundred-day Nazi siege, Inber wrote about the city and its defenders. She worked at the Soviet Information Bureau and joined the Communist Party in 1943. Inber's wartime books included *The Soul of Leningrad: Poems 1941–42* (1942) and *Diary: Almost Three Years* (1946; English: *Leningrad Diary*). Her famous long poem *The Pulkovo Meridian* (1942) received the Stalin Prize in 1946; a Hebrew version soon appeared in Israel, translated by Avraham Shlonsky (1900–1973), founder of the symbolist school in Hebrew poetry. To the derailed *Black Book* (see Ilya Ehrenburg and Vasily Grossman in vol. 1), Inber contributed a section on the Nazi and Romanian atrocities in her native Odessa.

After the war, Inber continued to publish poetry (e.g., *April: Poems about Lenin* [1960]) and essays about writing. She held positions of prominence in the Union of Soviet Writers, behaving ignobly during the Pasternak affair (1958; see Boris Pasternak in vol. 1). Inber's four-volume *Works*, both censored and self-censored, came out in 1965–66.

Jewish characters and themes took center stage in Inber's stories of the 1920s. Endurance of antisemitism was the subject of "Garlic in the Suitcase" (1926; title story of Inber's 1927 collection), and memories of pogroms informed "Parallel and Essential" (1929). Four Jewish stories stand out: "Nightingale and Rose" (1924; text below; title story of a 1925 collection), "Hayim Egudovich's Liver" (1924), "Exceptions Do Occur" (1925; title story of a 1927 collection), and "Equation with One Unknown" (1926; title story of a 1926 collection). With representatives of the South-Western school, Inber's prose shared a sensation of being blissfully alive in language. While Inber's stories of the 1920s may remind today's readers of Isaac Babel's irony and of Yury Olesha's crystalline keenness, they were original and deserve to be read anew.

Set during the NEP (New Economic Policy), Inber's "Nightingale and Rose" appeared in the Moscow magazine *Searchlight* (*Prozhektor*) in 1925. In addition to the prominence of the motif in classical Persian poetry (Hafiz, Rudaki, Saadi) and its imitations by Aleksandr Pushkin, Afanasy Fet (in vol. 1), and other nineteenth-century Russian poets, the title brings to mind Oscar Wilde's "The Nightingale and the Rose" (1891).

The story's Russian title is "Solovey i Roza." "Solovey" (literally "nightingale"), both the name of the bird and the last name of the Jewish tailor, is familiar to readers from Sholem Aleichem's novel *Yossele Solovey* (1889). "Roza" (literally "rose") is both the name of the flower and the first name of Nightingale's wife.

The Nightingale and the Rose

1

Here's my recipe for spring: fresh, sharp leaf-buds, with sun poured over them, left to open slowly on an old black poplar (breathe the scent in deeply—could anything be more wonderful?). Then have a slender new moon rise above the whipped-cream clouds: it looks vast, far larger than the roundest full one. Just at that moment, stir in a heavy warm rain, falling slowly, no more than a drop a minute. The bundle of small, round, dark-blue domes over the little centuries-old church in Uspensky Lane[1] will start shining, reflecting the starlight. And in the herb-scented churchyard, the sound of kisses will ring out: one long note and two short ones. And there you have it: city springtime in the 1920s.

Spiced by accordion music from a basement bakery and the roar of distant trams like surf on a seashore, spring like that goes down a treat. The problem is, once you've swallowed it, it's hard to digest, and you get heartburn.

Southern countries have their own kinds of spring, much more imposingly luxuriant: real classical springs, with roses and nightingales. But there are roses and nightingales in this town, too, if you know where to look for them. And the nightingales sound just as yearning under a pallid northern sky, and the thorns on the rose are just as sharp. It's the classic recipe for spring.

If you know where to look, you can find a nightingale in Uspensky Lane as well. See the house opposite the church with the dark-blue onion domes, the one with the bakery in the basement, where the accordion music comes from in the evenings. On the ground floor is Emmanuel Nightingale's tailoring workshop, "Orders taken for military uniforms and gentlemen's suits. Repairs also carried out."

Nightingale the tailor is put together this way: long skinny legs, stooped shoulders, balding gingery hair, and bright blue eyes with a slightly absent look in them. You won't often see a Jew from Minsk with eyes that bright blue color, but if it happens, you can be sure they'll have exactly that other-worldly expression. They're the eyes of someone who's still afloat in Noah's Ark, who's still looking down on the earth from the height of Mount Ararat.

People ordering suits from tailor Nightingale who didn't know the man very well sometimes took fright when they saw his eyes. This bodes no good, they'd think, you can tell what kind of suit you'll get here: the lines down the sides of your trousers will be skewed, your jacket lapels will be as wide as the runners on a car, and the collar will be jibbing you in the neck like no one's business.

But only people who didn't know tailor Nightingale well thought that.

---

1. Uspensky Lane = literally "Assumption" Lane.

The man was transfigured by his work. His eyes narrowing like a snake charmer's, chalk held fast in his hand, pins in his mouth, and a tape measure around his neck, he'd get going on his magic. And the cross-grained cloth would submit to his creative powers, the swirling chaos of suiting turn into a smooth linear flow.

As he worked, tailor Nightingale, undaunted by his mouthful of pins, would sing select passages of the Song of Songs, set to tunes of his own devising. His favorite place was Shulamith's fragrant verse: "Sustain me with raisin cakes, refresh me with apples, for I am faint with love."[2] And, hearing his rising descant, the tailor's wife Rose (every Nightingale must have his Rose, as you see) would say to five-year-old Izzie, a born hooligan if ever there was one:

"Izzie, put the hammer down, for heaven's sake! Do you hear me? You know perfectly well your father's singing 'I am faint with love.' He must be working on the sleeves then. He needs quiet."

"Don't wannoo," Izzie would say, driving yet another nail into the croup of his long-suffering toy horse.

Rose the tailor's wife was full-blown and had plenty of thorns. She loved Nightingale and was violently jealous of all the other flowers in the world. And especially the baker's wife, Klavdiya Makarovna, who was as circular and plump as a fresh currant bun, with a deep dimple on her chin like the cicatrix of a dropped-out raisin.

"Why does that hussy Klavdiya always look at you in that funny way, out of the corner of her eyes?" she would say, as they lay down together on their big goosefeather bed. "Why does she look at me in that funny way too? She's got something on her conscience, Emmanuel. Mannie, Mannie, I can tell you like her really."

"Rosie my dear," Nightingale would object from under the big puffy comforter. "How could you even think such a thing?"

"Well then. And so what was you saying to her this morning, while you was ironing that gray weskit, eh?"

"Rosie, I didn't say nothing to her, she just said to me it looked like the cold would be lasting into May, Rosie."

"Well then, the cold would be lasting would it, Emmanuel. So what did you say to her then, Emmanuel?"

"I said to her, Rosie, just that same way, dead cold—and how could you suppose anything else, for heaven's sake? I said to her, and even little Izzie could hear what I was saying, it was that loud . . . Rosie, my honeybunch, move up a little, will you? I can't hardly breathe. That's it, my sweetheart . . ."

And Rose would hide her thorns and turn, fragrant with love, toward her Nightingale. An hour or two. Afterward, Rose would sleep gently, but Nightingale would lie awake. In the corner of the bedroom, which also served as the workshop, stood a wooden dummy, almost always with an unfinished jacket hanging on it. With a

---

2. See Song of Songs 2:5.

crafty wink of its top button, the jacket would start a telepathic conversation with Nightingale:

"What, mate," the jacket would say, "not sleeping again? It's high time you was getting some rest. There's lots to do tomorrow. I dropped you a heavy hint yesterday when you was doing the fitting: those darts aren't in the right place."

"Never mind the darts," Nightingale would answer, with a thoughtful flash of his bright blue eyes. "Never mind them, I say. It's my heart that's not in the right place."

"What do you mean?" the jacket would ask, the top of its pocket dropping open in surprise. "What do you mean? Hang on, I've got to hear this . . . Rose and you . . ."

"My Rose, Rosalia Abramovna, and me, we're just fine together! And little Izzie's a wonderful boy; there his is, sleeping in his cot now, still as a thimble. But what does Shulamith say about all that, eh? 'Upon my couch at night I sought the one I love—I sought him, but found him not.'"[3]

"I don't get this," the jacket would say, wrinkling its lapel. "Emmanuel, you shock me. Do you really mean to say family life don't make you happy?"

"Shut your face, you no-good lounge lizard," Nightingale would snap, annoyed. "You double-breasted scoundrel, you. You're trying to push me into saying something I'll regret. I can see straight through you. You've got white stab-stitching all over you, you have, and a cheap shiny lining."

And turning his back on the jacket, Nightingale would fall sound asleep.

2

One snowy morning, there was a ring at the door.

"That'll be someone to collect the uniform jacket you made for that shady type Well-Yessabut," Rose says. (This wasn't, of course, the man's surname. It was just that this client had the habit of starting every sentence with the phrase "Well, yes sir, but. . . ," a habit that for some reason made Rose think he must be suspicious.)

"That'll be someone to collect Well-Yessabut's jacket," said Rose. "Got it ready, have you, Mannie?"

"Yes, Rosie," said Nightingale, "but the problem is that it might be someone to pick up the trousers I was supposed to make over for Leybovich before New Year's. I haven't quite got round to those yet, you see."

A second ring interrupted these thoughts.

Rose opened the door with its covering of oilcloth and felt, and stepped back in silence. On the doorstep, dressed in a snow-covered fur coat, stood a beautiful woman, asking for tailor Nightingale.

"He's right here," said Rose, "but first tell me what exactly you want. Have you come for Leybovich's trousers?" She looked suspiciously at the woman's fur coat and long eyelashes.

---

3. See Song of Songs 3:1.

"No, I've got nothing to do with Leybovich. I'm here on my own account. I want to order a suit. A suit with a uniform jacket and riding breeches."

"You? For yourself?"

"I do. For myself."

"'Sustain me with raisin cakes, refresh me with apples,'" Nightingale whispered with shaking lips and took hold of the tape measure around his neck to stop himself from keeling right over.

"Some Well-Yessabut," Rose thought, looking at the woman's felt bootees. "This is a real Well-Yessabut."

Well-Yessabut sits herself down on the holey wicker chair that Izzie generally used as a stable for his wooden horse. Well-Yessabut flutters her eyelashes at Nightingale and repeats that she needs a uniform jacket and breeches, made in blue cheviot (and here she hands over the cheviot) to wear in a play, that she's an actress, and that she got citizen Nightingale's name as a nightingale whose work's good quality and well priced. And that she'd like a fitting right now, if he can manage, as she's in a tearing hurry.

She's in a tearing hurry, yes. She rips off her fur coat. Underneath she's got long dangly earrings on and a necklace of green stones. She goes and stands in front of the mirror and lets Nightingale measure her arms, her shoulders, her knees—whatever he says he needs to. And Rose, silent and fuming, thorns bristling, takes down the measurements.

"Waist, twenty-four, Rose, my dear," says Nightingale. "Your waist is so supple," he adds, turning to Well-Yessabut, "that I really don't know how I'm going to fit it properly."

Rose gives a meaningful cough, and Nightingale nearly swallows a pin.

"Bust, thirty-six, Rosie, dear," says Nightingale very faintly.

Rose notes this down in silence. Not a peep out of her, but her silence is so oppressive that Izzie starts bawling his eyes out and wailing that his toy horse just bit him.

Well-Yessabut gets back into her fur, makes an appointment for her fitting, and, having dipped her eyelashes in the blue radiance of Nightingale's eyes, vanishes into the snow.

"'Thou has ravished my heart with one of thine eyes, with one chain of thy neck,'"[4] Nightingale sings to himself soundlessly, as he marks up the blue cheviot with chalk. "Bust, thirty-six. And her eyelashes must be a full quarter-inch long. Staggering." And although the blue cheviot is cheap, coarse stuff, his shears fly over it, twittering gently, like swifts.

The suit is finished: Rose takes it off to the address the client gave. The suit is finished, delivered, and forgotten. While it was being measured and made, a cloud hung over the Nightingale house like a lead weight. Rose faded and drooped; she was so desperate she even made friends with Klavdiya, the baker's wife. Izzie got hardly any attention and managed to pick up scabies somewhere. But Nightingale's blue eyes shone so fiercely that when he went into the district housing office to pay his rent for January, they forgot to charge him for heat and light.

And the suit is delivered and forgotten . . .

---

4. See Song of Songs 4:9.

3

Six months have gone by. It's spring in Uspensky Lane.

Tailor Nightingale, worn out by his long working day and the heady mood of spring, sits at the window in the falling light, listening to the kisses in the churchyard: one long one and two short. A beautiful plump cloud covers the western sky. But it's not going to rain: or not more than a warm drop or two, one every minute. The new sickle moon is slender. His heart is so full it hurts. And Nightingale says to Rose:

"Rosie, dear, suppose we go to the pictures?"

The Electric Wonder cinema house is crammed with loving couples. The lights go down. Whispers go through the rows like breezes. The lovers sit hand in hand, cheek to cheek, watching the adventures on the screen. They gallop wildly along with the heroes, plunge into foaming waterfalls, bring nests of criminals to book. The thin air of spring pours in through the singing ventilators. And a fireman in the back row feels uneasy, sensing all the smoldering conflagrations around him.

The movie showing today in the Electric Wonder is *The Deluge in Mine No. 17B*. The lights go down. A wedge of light strikes the screen. The action flies along. An evil-doer has planned a dreadful accident. He has bored a hole into the mineshaft, and soon water will pour in to flood the shaft. But the wicked plot has been discovered. And now, crawling over strange airy bridges and walkways, along a spider's web of scaffolding, hanging in the air itself, scrambles the woman who is going to avert disaster.

Squashed up as tightly as autumn swallows on telegraph wires, the lovers freeze, hearing a loud cry:

"My breeches, my breeches! Hey, hang on, hang on . . ."

Mine No. 17B vanishes from the screen. The lights go up, and a policeman looms menacingly over the man with bright blue eyes.

"Emmanuel," Rose whispers, "you've disgraced me now for good and all."

"Beg pardon," a trembling Nightingale says to the policeman. "Beg pardon. I didn't mean it that way at all . . . But they really are my breeches, you see. I made them. The ones on the rescuer in Mine No. 17B. And when I saw them hanging in the air like that, I kind of took fright. Seeing her so high up, taking such risks . . . I even thought the side seams might give way."

"It wasn't the side seams you were worried about, Emmanuel," Rose sobs. "You were worried about that wretched woman. Pity she didn't break her neck, I say. Ought to be ashamed of yourself, and you a family man!"

Rose has cried herself to sleep. But Nightingale, stung by love, can't sleep at all. For the first time in his life, he leaves the family nest at night and flutters off into the streets.

It's midnight outside, but people are up and about spring, is so short. There's a scattering of stars over the central square. Emmanuel Nightingale makes his way there by back lanes, hardly realizing where he's going.

He's seen the woman with the quarter-inch-long eyelashes only twice. The first time was when she brought round the blue cheviot, the second when he did the second fitting. And now he's seen her again, in the air, hair streaming above the mineshaft, collar unbuttoned, eyelashes wide.

Nightingale walks into the night alone. There are two people ahead of him. They're walking hand in hand, cheek to cheek, in loving harmony, like one being not two, but there are two of them all the same, and they're happy. Nightingale, slowly coming to himself after the flood in the mineshaft, is able to look and listen again. A dark woman— a Gypsy, maybe—is selling flowers.

"Buy some nice flowers," she accosts the couple walking ahead of Nightingale. "Buy a lovely rose for your beauty," she says to the young man, "buy it for your airy beloved."

But it's Nightingale who buys one, in delirium, in electric wonder, bewitched by the woman from the mineshaft, the one hanging in the air. He buys it for his beauty, for his airy beloved. He buys her a red rose without thorns, a beautiful night-dark rose of love. He takes it to the address she gave. He gives it to the janitor and tells him to give it to so-and-so without delay. There's a note attached to the rose. "I saw you yesterday evening in that movie. My name doesn't matter, but I'll never forget you."

Afterward he feels weak and shaky, as though he'd been carrying a steam iron, not a rose. His mouth goes dry; it longs for moisture, it is feverishly hot. And on Sadovaya Street, Nightingale walks up to the first Mosselprom[5] kiosk he sees and whispers softly through scorched lips:

"I beg of you, refresh me with apples, for I am faint with love."

1925

Translated from the Russian by Catriona Kelly

---

5. Mosselprom—abbreviation for Moscow Association of Establishments for Processing Products of the Agricultural Industry; Mosselprom kiosks sold soda water by the glass. Since Sadovaya Street means "Garden Street," there is additional play on the word "apples" in the last line.

MARK TARLOVSKY

Mark Tarlovsky (1902–1952), poet and translator, whose last name originates from the town of Tarlow, is not to be confused with the Russian poet and translator Arseny Tarkovsky (1907–1989). Tarlovsky was born and grew up in Elizavetgrad (now Kirovohrad, Ukraine). Tarlovsky's father, a printer, moved his family to Odessa in 1916. Tarlovsky attended Moscow University in 1921–24, graduating in Russian philology; his first poems appeared in Moscow. As a young poet, Tarlovsky enjoyed the patronage of Eduard Bagritsky (in vol. 1).

Published in Moscow in 1928, Tarlovsky's fascinating first collection, *Ironic Garden,* was intended as a record setter. It would have been an even greater achievement had it not been for the almost simultaneous publications by Tarlovsky's illustrious contemporaries, including Bagritsky (*South-West,* 1927) and Osip Mandelstam (*Poems,* 1928 in vol. 1). *Ironic Garden* was immediately targeted by the raging proletarian critics. Charges of "formalism" and of cultivating pre-Revolutionary literary traditions were leveled in the press. Already shaken by the negative reception of *Ironic Garden,* Tarlovsky was broken by the banning by censors of his second collection, *Carrier Pigeon,* set in galleys in 1929.

Trying to second-guess his censors, Tarlovsky rewrote about thirty poems from *Carrier Pigeon,* ruining most of them, and added new ones. Now titled *Boomerang,* the collection appeared in 1931 to hostile reviews. Tarlovsky's last collection, *Birth of a Motherland* (1935), marked his public surrender and included a poem celebrating the demolition of the Cathedral of Christ the Savior in 1931, to make room for a swimming pool (the cathedral was built anew in the 1990s). In the words of Tarlovsky's post-Soviet champion Vadim Perelmuter, the collection "was unworthy of [Tarlovsky's] gift."

In the 1930s Tarlovsky applied himself to translation. His virtuosic poetic craftsmanship enabled him to translate with ease and make a living. A standard Soviet practice, these "translations" were poetic renditions of literal translations prepared by linguists, often showcasing the poet-translator's mastery at the expense of the original. Tarlovsky was known for his translations of the major Kazakh poet-singer (*akyn*) Zhambul Zhabaev (1846–1945). In 1952, less than a year before Stalin's death, Tarlovsky had a fatal stroke on Gorky Street outside the famous Eliseev food store.

In 1978, after working in Tarlovsky's archive, the Moscow translator and poet Evgeny Vitkovsky published Tarlovsky's two-volume works in samizdat form, a typewritten run of twelve copies. Preserved for posterity, Tarlovsky's poetry has been slowly returning to readers in the post-Soviet years. Tarlovsky left a memoir in verse, *The Merry Stranger,* whose protagonist was Bagritsky. He also immortalized Bagritsky in several poems that bear his mentor's influence: "Style 'à la Brasse'" (1928), "Game" (1932), "Iron" (1933), and others.

In 1929, following the fiasco with *Carrier Pigeon*, Tarlovsky composed but never published a "Draft of a Literary Manifesto" (1929). "We are transitioners [*perekhodniki*; the word can also mean 'conduits']," Tarlovsky wrote. "We are not fellow travelers walking side by side with the proletariat, parallel to it [. . .]. Our path is zigzagging because we want to know what is taking place on either side of the road. This is why we have to cross the path of the proletariat and also many other paths [. . .]." The meanderings of Tarlovsky's "transition," in the early 1920s, from the Odessan Jewish-Russian aspirant to the ambitious Moscow poet, found their embodiment in "Our Path" (1927), subtitled "A Chronicle" and included in *Ironic Garden*.

"Our Path" chronicled the migration to Moscow of the writers of the South-Western school, many of them Jewish. Although the word Jew appears nowhere in the text, Tarlovsky planted telltale signs, such as a reference to Simon Petlyura (1879–1926). Supreme commander of the army—and president of the directory—of the Ukrainian National Republic, Petlyura fought against the Bolshevik takeover. While Petlyura himself was not an antisemite and took some measures to halt antisemitic violence, he failed to prevent it. Some of the worst pogroms were perpetrated by detachments of Petlyura's army. In Tarlovsky's historical imagination, Petlyura's name was associated with violence against the Jewish population during the civil war. Tarlovsky may also have known that in 1926 Petlyura was assassinated in Paris by Sholem Schwartzbard, who was tried for murder but acquitted in 1927.

Tarlovsky's—and his fellow Odessans'—love affair with Moscow finds expression in other poems, including "Moscow" (1928), where the city is portrayed as a pagan, Asiatic woman, with whom the poet is wed by Moscow's "ringlike drives." The "gangsters" in Tarlovsky's opening stanza hint at Isaac Babel's "Odessa" stories (Babel in vol. 1). The poem articulates, with Babelesque humor and irony, the predicament of Tarlovsky and his confreres who, having left Odessa for Moscow in the early 1920s, found themselves willing captives in the streets and corridors of Soviet culture.

This Path
A Chronicle

Down south in Odessa
The gangsters abound,
Along with my girlfriends
Though I'm not around.

Forgotten the fog there,
The coolest teen craze,
Ineffable dreaming
Of lost glorious days

And rowdy, rambunctious,
Uproarious nights—
Misfortunes, offenses,
And wild drunken fights.

The parks and the boulevards,
The city's romance,
Those goons of Petlyura's
In wide swagger pants,

But I knew the grandeur,
The order "Attack!"
A bull's final effort
With no turning back.

He charged at a gallop
From sea into years,
Odessa barbarian
With bull's neck and ears.

And well I remember
He burst into flame,
The label of Epoch
That branded his name.

The coarse voice was sickly,
The train station cried,
The hunger of others
Became my true guide.

Delirious with Moscow,
I left home behind
And took to the highroad
For what I could find.

Three nights through a windstorm
And deep in a fen,
I sniffed their campfire:
Makhno and his men.[1]

Fatigued beyond reason,
Collapsed in a heap,
I thought of the train tracks
That rushed into sleep.

Due north into darkness,
The train made me doze
And dream about blizzards,
Hallucinate foes.

The steppe of my childhood
Sent eagles ahead,
Those eager Ukrainians
Parading in red.

In seizures of nightmares
The road swirled with mists.
The white winter whirlwind
Went whistling through fists.

---

1. Makhno, Nestor (1889–1934)—commander of an anarchist army during the civil war. Makhno's army, which counted a number of Jewish anarchists among its commanders and fighters, sided with the Reds against the Whites but was later forcefully disbanded by the Red Army, Makhno himself fleeing to exile in 1921. Tarlovsky subtly highlights an opposition between the artists' anarchic allegiances and their subsequent service to the Soviet regime.

And like a snow mastiff,
A bitch killing prey,
The train, a blind ruffian,
Was ripping its way.

But that cup was taken
And tossed off for this:
The trek was forgotten
In Moscow—what bliss!

A Soviet New York City!
To work boundlessly—
The Kremlin, the Forum,
The Capitol free!

The circle is closing,
The job is all done,
So now Moscow's boring,
The south is more fun.

Imperious Ukrainians
Salute going by.
Above the red outfits
Their eagles fly high.

We're dressed up in feathers,
Pink fluff. Where are you,
Oh, Motherland, really?
Which one of the two?

From south to the northland
And back, I'm afraid,
They'll stretch their machinery
Of mutual aid.

And I, fellow traveler,
Obedient and bland,
Both northern and southern,
Have no motherland.

So marry a southerner,
Marry her soon,
And go for a sleigh ride
On your honeymoon.

Embrace her on frost heaves,
Hold tight as you go,
With hints of acacia
Caught up in the snow,

And, flying home frozen,
Enclose in your care
The wild rose you've chosen
From your meadows there.

1927

Translated from the Russian by Maxim D. Shrayer and J.B. Sisson

MIKHAIL KOZAKOV

Mikhail Kozakov (1897–1954), fiction writer, playwright, and essayist, was born in Poltava Province, in the town of Romodan. Kozakov studied at Kiev University while participating in revolutionary activities. During the civil war, he held posts in the Bolshevik executive in Lubny, Ukraine. Heading an evacuation echelon in August 1919, Kozakov ended up in Kazan, continuing his studies there. In 1922 he graduated in law from Petrograd University.

Kozakov's first collection of stories, *Parrot's Happiness*, appeared in 1924. His stories and short novels went through a number of editions in the 1920s and 1930s, never to be reprinted afterward in the Soviet Union. Some of his best-known tales, including *Burgher Adamenko* and *Brute and a Half* (both 1927), were set during the NEP and dissected the lives of Russian lower-middle-class urban dwellers. His short novel *Abram Nashatyr, Innkeeper* offered a Jewish-Soviet narrative of fratricide. While creating negative portrayals of Jewish NEPmen (businessmen who were active during the years of the New Economic Policy), Kozakov also wrote powerful tales about antisemitism and the limits of assimilation. They included *The Tale of the Dwarf Max* (1926) and culminated in the short novel *A Man Is Brought to His Knees* (1928; excerpt below).

A four-volume edition of Kozakov's works appeared in 1929–31. In the 1930s Kozakov held important editorial positions. He was married to the literary editor Zoya Nikitina, who was not Jewish. Their son, the actor Mikhail Kozakov, was born in 1934, the year Kozakov participated in the ill-famed collective volume about the White Sea Canal. Arrested in 1937, Nikitina was released three years later. According to the memoirs of the writer's son, in 1940 Stalin deemed Kozakov's play *When I'm Alone* "harmful, pacifist." In the political context that followed the signing of the Soviet–Nazi Nonaggression Pact (23 August 1939), Kozakov's play and two others, Valentin Kataev's *Little House* and Anatoly Glebov's *All the Way Out*, were banned as "ideologically harmful and anti-artistic" by a 14 September 1940 Decree of the Party Central Committee. Kozakov's earlier play, *The Chekists*, glorifying the early Soviet secret police did not save him from a virtual ban on publications of prose, lasting until 1945.

To make a living, Kozakov wrote plays, including *Darya* (1942) and *The Nightingale Sings* (1943), and he coauthored several, among them *Island of Great Hopes*, with Anatoly Mariengof, a former imaginist poet (see Matvey Royzman in vol. 1) who was ostracized in the late 1940s. Ill and marginalized, Kozakov died in Moscow in December 1954. From 1929 until not long before his death, Kozakov labored on an epic novel about the Revolution. Its first four books appeared between 1929 and 1939 under the title *Nine Points*. The entire work was published posthumously in 1956, now titled *The Collapse of the Empire*; one of its plotlines featured a Jewish family.

"Mercilessness of vision," Shimon Markish wrote, "ranks [Kozakov] together with Isaac Babel." An articulation of the most "damning" questions distinguishes Kozakov's short novel *A Man Is Brought to His Knees*, completed in 1928 in Leningrad and published several times in 1930–32.

Popular antisemitism grew rapidly in the late Soviet 1920s. *Pravda* ran an editorial on 19 February 1929 titled "Attention to the Struggle against Antisemitism." The chairman of the presidium of the Central Executive Committee (TsIK), Mikhail Kalinin, spoke out against antisemitism. Books such as Mikhail Gorev's *Against Antisemites* (1928) and Yury Larin's *Jews and Antisemitism in the USSR* (1929) appeared. Of particular interest is *The Unvanquished Enemy: A Collection of Literary Works against Antisemitism* (1930), edited by the critic Vladimir Veshnev and composed of works by Jewish and non-Jewish authors of the late imperial years (S. An-sky, Vladimir Korolenko, Semyon Yushkevich, all in vol. 1) and the early Soviet period (Isaac Babel, Eduard Bagritsky, also in vol. 1, Aleksandr Fadeev, Aleksandr Serafimovich, and others). In his introduction, Emelyan Yaroslavsky (pseudonym of Miney Gubelman), head of the notorious League of the Militant Godless and Stalin's would-be official biographer, quoted Lenin's "Anti-Jewish Pogroms" (1919). In spite of the Marxist-Leninist introduction claiming that antisemitism would disappear in the classless Soviet Union, *The Unvanquished Enemy* conveyed a stringent sense of antisemitism's stride across Russian history.

In *A Man Is Brought to His Knees*, set in the Soviet 1920s, the visceral antisemitism of the caretaker Nikita is set against the anxieties of Miron Rubanovsky, who is married to a non-Jewish woman. Overtly presenting the confrontation in ethnic and cultural terms, Kozakov subtly links antisemitic words and actions to their religious roots. In the final chapter, which follows below, the brute Nikita displaces violence onto the Jews' cat, whose death evokes a pogrom and a crucifixion. Voznesensky, a Russian "friend" of Rubanovsky's, divides Jews into "kikes" and "proud Hebrews." Voznesensky's last name likely betrays his origins in the clergy and points to the Russian word for the Ascension (*Voznesenie*), thus casting a morbidly ironic shadow on Christian antisemitism and its Soviet tentacles.

From *A Man Is Brought to His Knees*

Chapter 11. Thirty Pieces of Silver

This is the final chapter of our story.

And just as the tailor Elya Rubanovsky would not have given his customer a suit that he had sewn without making it just right, so the author must stitch together his story along the seam of his ideas, iron out its thematic fabric, pull out the threads of the plot that were left sticking out and only then, supplying the story with its maker's mark, his signature, offer it to his readers.

This is about the craft of writing. But an artist is not a tailor or a cutter but rather a whimsical, secretive creator of his own thoughts and images.

So grows a tree filled with sap that bears its ripening fruit in plain view but conceals from prying eyes the tangled twists of its fruit-nurturing roots: they are secreted in the earth's vaults. And one and the same tree bears bitter fruit and fruit that is sugary sweet. Ask a gardener—and he will tell you the same thing.

Thus with heartfelt sadness will we pluck the fruit of sorrow and quiet grief and give it to just such a quiet and doleful person as Elya the tailor, a "refugee" from a little Jewish town on the western border.

The tailor did not leave his room all evening, remaining alone with his thoughts.

Meanwhile, on the other side of the apartment in [his son] Miron's room, after an hour of the usual insignificant small talk, an unguarded conversation was born, the inception of which went unnoticed, through the love of these two people, who on parting had kissed instead of hitting each other.

"My dear," Voznesensky said softly, but with fervor and ardor, and the words, quivering, fell to his listener's ears like a tender nursing swallow to its nest. "My de-ear! Why do you give yourself as an example? You are a member of the intelligentsia, a Russian by culture, educated by a Russian university, Russian literature, and so forth . . . You are a splendid example of the noble Jew, an ancient Hebrew. Yes! Yes! You are a Russian *Kulturtraeger*, you are a renegade. You do not belong to the ranks of Jewish officialdom, Party members or not, that 'stand by the throne in greedy throng. . . .'[1] But you may blamelessly suffer because of them all."

"How's that?" Miron smiled faintly, having grown tired of arguing.

---

1. A slightly altered line of M. Yu. Lermontov's famous poem "Death of the Poet" ("Smert' poeta," 1837), written on the occasion of Aleksandr Pushkin's death following a mortal injury he received in a duel.

"That's precisely the misfortune, my dear-est. Yes, yes . . . Does anybody—the masses, embittered savages—know you as do I, Nadezhda Ivanovna, and a dozen of your friends? . . . Nobody does. And if something were to happen . . . well, you understand! And I and all of us very likely would be powerless—I'll say it without beating around the bush—to save your neck. And that is a horror, a misfortune. You and a thousand like you will be smeared, perhaps destroyed by those whom I (you know my convictions—all my life I have fought against bigotry), whom I, forgive me, Miron, can only refer to as kikes. There are kikes and then there are proud Hebrews."

"Nonsense! There are classes, there is culture and stupidity, there is work and environment . . ."

Nikolay Filippovich [Voznesensky] obstinately shook his head in response.

"That's not true. And what about the historical evidence of the ages? The Jews do not change, which is all the worse for them. Of course, you're the only one I can say this to: you are my friend, I love you, and you won't take my words the wrong way. My brother is a research chemist, a professor in Leningrad. He once advanced a clever idea. It's amusing! He called Jewry a catalyst. You don't know what that is? That's what substances are called that accelerate the process of a chemical reaction. My de-ear, you see, I'm sharing some popular science with you today. A very small number of these same catalysts are capable of causing a reaction among an immeasurably large number of substances. It's a remarkable thing, Miron! And what's more, you see: as a consequence of the presence of this same catalyst, the formation of all sorts of intermediary compounds takes place. But then they quickly disintegrate—in the *opposite* direction."

"But why does that happen?" Rubanovsky had become interested, having already forgotten the main subject of the argument.

"Who the devil knows, Miron! Most probably everything depends on a certain temperature. Yes, yes, I remember: that's what it is. Here's an interesting example: in the presence of, say, manganese peroxide one can obtain oxygen from potassium chloride . . . or from something else altogether, the devil only knows! And here's the most interesting thing, Miron: while facilitating all sorts of chemical manipulations and accelerating the action of this same chemical energy, the catalyst, itself does not *change or dissolve*—isn't that something? This, you know, is truly an amusing analogy for the Jews. That's it precisely—they don't dissolve! Oh, the world today has known and knows so many of these catalysts! And nevertheless everything disintegrates—remember—in the *opposite* direction . . . of Russian Russia. This combination of words seems strange to you . . .

"Miron, Mirosha! Why are you playing at being gloomy?" Voznesensky, disconcerted, had adopted a jocular tone. "Well, you can go to hell . . . really. Do you for some reason find this conversation unpleasant? After all, you were the one who started it. The vileness at the factory astonished you so that you've spoken of nothing else now for several days. Knock it off! In the end, it's nothing more than the trivialities of life. And life . . . life is such a big . . . wonderful thing. What doesn't it have! Treat me to some *kvas*,[2] Mirosha . . . Do you have some?"

And neither of them returned again to the interrupted conversation, because now they had become aware of the fragrant warm night beyond the window flung wide open, because from somewhere nearby came a human song just as warm and simple, and in the distance, from the direction of the station, the whistle of an approaching train fell on the hushed city, and some female voice in the neighboring garden laughed, but in a muffled sort of way, as she gave herself up to her beloved; because out of somebody's briefcase they took out and put on the table a new novel, and the maid had brought the glasses and *kvas*.

And they drank the cold, yeasty *kvas*, lamented the quality of Russian corks, because it had rotted and broken into small pieces; they feasted their eyes on the June starry night without affectation; and not knowing how better to sing its praises, they both sang the same popular love song; they remembered that the chairman of the trust was leaving for Moscow on the night train to deliver a report on expanding one of the factories, that they both had drawn up the agreement for leasing from the Regional Department of Communal Property a building their trust needed; they expressed joking misgivings in regard to the dress of the unknown woman who had taken cover in the garden with her lover, because it had just rained recently and the grass would make green stains; they criticized and praised the novel they had just read.

And—they said goodbye. And as always (such was the way of Nikolay Filippovich Voznesensky, a gentle and warm-hearted person) they embraced, their cheeks touching.

"And life . . . is such a big, wonderful thing."

Well-worn, understandable words that were also mysterious in their simplicity.

Ordinary, simple, measured—like the earth.

But put your ear to the ground and you will hear the noise of the bubbling blood, the wellspring of life.

And in the noise make out the siren's call and groaning, and the maternal entreaty of love, the frenzied gnashing of hate, the cheerful song of friendship. And each of these sisters gives a person the fruit it bears—his passions—as he comes into this life.

One should write about them: human passions that are simple in their mysteriousness.

And among these we have chosen for our story small and bitter fruits: dread and meekness.

They were not to be found in the woman who loved him, who was a friend, who reproved human weakness—they were not to be found in Nadezhda, Mironov's wife.

She said to him simply, reproachfully:

"I heard your entire conversation through the door. It's insulting, humiliating. In your presence he uttered the words of savage hoodlums—and you kept silent. The chauvinism of the Russian intelligentsia that suffers from . . . a nervous disorder."

"What are you talking about, my dear?"

---

2. *Kvas* (*kvass*)—popular Russian soft drink made from malt.

"Yes, a nervous disorder. The so-called 'universally Russian' dislike for people of your nation—or, for example, of a Turk for a Greek—this is some sort of mental, nervous illness—and nothing more. He chose his example from chemistry, and I'll give you one from medicine. You have the sensation all the time that something (precisely *something*—and you don't know what!) is stuck in your throat, but really there's nothing there. It seems that this very same thing that is 'stuck' is preventing you from eating and drinking, but you chew and swallow your food—and your stomach digests it just fine. Why did you keep silent?"

"I didn't keep silent. I argued—didn't you hear? . . ."

He looked at his wife with a radiant, joyous smile.

"You were trying to vindicate yourself more than raising objections. The devil knows what you were thinking. My God, you reminded me of a baptized Jew who was concealing his origins. No respect at all for yourself, for your work . . . for the work of hundreds of thousands of your own people. They now are members of the same intelligentsia, they are the same workers and peasants working the land like all the rest. And you . . . you . . ."

"What about me?" his eyes looked at her guiltily and gratefully.

"Show you a 'little icon' from some stupid 'Russian' or 'Slavic' tradition, and you are brought to your knees . . . Oh, you say, how wonderful, magnificent, original! . . ."

And a day later he heard from her lips, after caresses and words of comfort, something sullen and cold:

"You struck in the direction of least resistance, but in principle—of course, not with your fist!—you should have led your attack in the other direction."

. . . .

The manuscript was already finished. The author invited his friend over and began to read it to him. When he reached this place, his friend, who had been listening carefully, unexpectedly got up from the sofa, walked over to the table, and covered the manuscript with his hand.

"Give it some thought," he said vexatiously and sullenly. "Give it some thought before you pen down all sorts of verbs here. It's a matter of great responsibility, brother. Of course, you can do whatever you like with your little moralizer Voznesensky, but don't you dare treat your friend like that. I won't allow it! You've slandered me; I'm not at all like that. And later on—it's all lies! Lies! You gave my words, my gentle words, to Voznesensky, and you've attributed his words to me. Change it! Can you really say that I am a bigot?!"

He was very likely right on this last point. The author loved his friend and accordingly left out everything that he might find unpleasant when the friend resumed his reading of the story.

That's why there are so many ellipses points here.

. . . .

The story about hate, meekness, and indignation ends like this:

A day later and Tsukki still had not returned to the house from which she had escaped. Toward evening the inhabitants of the house saw the caretaker Nikita drunk and cursing fiercely. But what astonished the inhabitants was that the next morning he was drinking again.

He walked over to the Rubanovskys' open kitchen window, imperiously beckoned Darya over to him with his index finger (for some reason his hand was bandaged with a calico rag), and, when the maid had leaned out the window, he said quietly, taking his time:

"Listen here . . . Your *khatsale*[3] has gone missing. Do you hear me? Tell the mistress that Nikita the caretaker says that he promises to bring another cat. And as far as the other one goes . . . the little Jew cat—some citizen not known' round here has done some mischief. Do you hear me? Tell them that Nikita the caretaker saw it with his own eyes. There. And don't go calling out to Our Lord and crossing yourself on account of the vile little thing!" he shouted threateningly at the flustered servant. "Tell the mistress. And that's that . . ."

But the tailor was the first to return home, and the woman, after shedding pure tears of grief, told him everything.

"Quiet . . . sh," whispered the gray-haired, sallow Elya in a halting, prayerful voice. "Let him tell us just where we can find our *katse* . . . kitty, poor kitty," he repeated twice in Russian. Go and ask him to come here."

And several minutes later he was following Nikita to the end of the overgrown garden, toward the dilapidated fence of the neighboring property.

The caretaker walked slowly, almost unwillingly; he stopped three times to stack up on the side of the path, for some reason now, the twigs he had picked up along the way, and to brush off a spider web and a worm from a tree. He remained silent the whole time, and only as he walked up to the fence did he smirk sullenly, without looking at his companion.

"Ahem. . . ! Your little Jewess . . . is hanging over there. A fly is circling near her, but birds won't peck at it—they don't care for the smell."

Elya looked at the corner of the fence and with a flinch immediately turned away, instinctively covering his face with his hand.

A string was tied to Tsukki's tail, the other end of the string was tied to a crosspiece of the fence. The cat was hanging upside down. Her skull was smashed in, and thick coagulated blood had covered her face with its bared teeth and had matted her fluffy chest.

Elya was breathing heavily. The caretaker was looking at him sideways with unconcealed curiosity and satisfaction:

---

3. This is the way Nikita pronounces the Yiddish *katsele* (little cat, kitten), perhaps to mock the sounds of Yiddish.

"Who could have done it . . . huh? She used to bite, the little thing, like she was rabid!" Nikita suddenly blurted out against his will, and he hid his bandaged hand behind his back just as unwittingly.

Elya noticed this and looked up. He met Nikita's glance.

The caretaker's green eye, as if in defense, narrowed to a sliver, almost completely covering itself with the freckled eyelid; it looked from under the lid like a wily but cowardly little beast. The beast did not know whether it should jump away or bide his time, because he could not see the eyes of his opponent: Elya was standing sideways to him, and the glass in his spectacles reflected the sun.

Thus a minute died in silence.

"Caretaker," Elya said sadly and quietly, "you killed my cat. I know it; I see it by your heavy eyes. You are a monster, caretaker, I will not say more than that."

He turned to go, but stopped.

"Take her down from that . . . gallows. Take her down and immediately bury her in the ground."

Nikita said nothing in response.

"Caretaker, did you hear me?" gray-haired Elya said even more forlornly and quietly. "Take her down and bury her. And you will receive from me thirty kopecks for the job. Thirty pieces of silver. . . ," he sighed. "Here, take it."

"Okay. I'll do it . . ."

And two identical coins fell into the caretaker's palm. Then he walked over to the fence and untied the string.

In the evening he was drunk once again.

"On Sa-a-a-tur-day, on a rai-ny-y day. . . ," he sang loudly in his box of a room, swinging his cane to the beat.

But when he saw Miron Rubanovsky in the doorway he stopped his singing and—even though he was drunk—looked at the person who entered obligingly but with his guard up.

"Good day to you, sir, comrade Rubanovsky!" broadly delivering the soldier's greeting to an officer.

"You barbarian!" Miron shouted in reply. [. . .] "How dare you, you *pogromshchik*?!"

"What are you shouting for . . . I don't answer to you."

"Barbarian! Scoundrel! Monster. . . ," the words fell crashing down, like heavy, resonant objects that had fallen from a high altitude. "I know everything . . . the maid, my wife told me."

"Your papa did it out of spite. . . ," the cunning Nikita said sullenly, not knowing how to defend himself. "Would I really? . . ."

"You're lying! Father is a weak man, a rabbit . . . he's afraid of everything. He's brought to his knees by anything at all. But I . . ."

He ran right over to the recoiling caretaker and firmly grasped him by the front of his shirt.

"Let me go, you kike!" the drunkard shouted in warning and began hurling insults. Miron did not even remember what had fallen from the other's lips. He only sensed right away that he had been hit hard on his shoulder and neck, his pince-nez was bobbing up and down and fell onto the floor from being struck, and his whole body was in pain. Then he grabbed the cane from the caretaker's drunken hands, took a swing, and it fell hard onto something solid that made a muffled sound in response but that immediately recoiled.

To keep from falling down along with Nikita, he unclenched the fist that clutched at the calico shirt.

The caretaker was lying on the floor and quietly moaning. His cheekbone and cheek were cut and bleeding heavily.

"You are an animal, and you make others behave like animals," Miron said in a weak, faltering voice. "Really, Nikita, is this the way to behave . . . Well, get up . . . and show me where you're hurt . . ."

He left, but several minutes later the maid brought Nikita a bandage, iodine, and some hot water.

Thus this story about hate, meekness, and indignation ends.

But others may continue the story wherever they find some white space in this book.

. . . Let whoever wants to collect together everything thrown out here from the author's notebook, though he may not remember even the first and last names assigned here, or the eyes, profession, or age of each of them, let him, if he was listening, remember only the character's *word* or his *action* and, having done so, let him create his own story in his own way.

But the *idea* will recognize itself here.

1928

Translated from the Russian by Ronald Meyer

VIKTOR FINK

Viktor Fink (1888–1973), fiction writer, essayist, and memoirist, was born and grew up in Odessa in a family of Jewish-Russian intelligentsia. In 1906 Fink entered the Law Faculty of Novorossiysk University in Odessa. After moving to Paris in 1909, Fink studied law at the Sorbonne. During World War I he fought in the French Foreign Legion. He returned to Russia after the February 1917 Revolution.

Fink's first book, *Buzya Lipak*, appeared in 1927, followed by *Jaurès* (1928), a short book about the famous French socialist, the defender of Alfred Dreyfus. Fink became well known for his nonfiction after the release of *Jews on the Land* (1929; excerpt below) and *Jews in the Taiga* (1930; second, expanded edition, 1932). His best-known fiction, *Foreign Legion*, appeared in 1935. A novel-length cycle of thirteen novellas set during World War I and narrated by a Russian legionnaire fighting for France, *Foreign Legion* has been compared, generously, to the war tales of Guy de Maupassant and Alphonse Daudet. Unsparing and unsentimental, Fink's tale of service sometimes resorts to humor and lyrical characterization.

The 1930s were the peak of Fink's official prominence. In 1937 he lived in Paris, contributing to Soviet periodicals, and was a member of the Soviet delegation at the Second International Congress for the Defense of Culture in Spain. In the late 1930s Fink turned to the subject of Moldavian (Moldovan) history. His short novel *Death of the World*, set in a Moldavian village, appeared in 1938–39. The theme found further treatment in Fink's formulaic novel *Moldavian Rhapsody* (1966), spanning 1917–1944 to end with the defeat of the Romanian fascists. During World War II, Fink worked in the French branch of Moscow Radio world service. His *In France. Writer's Sketches* appeared in 1942, and his novel *The Fate of Henry Lambert* came out in 1948, when the anticosmopolitan campaign was gaining full speed. After having rebounded from a hiatus in publications in the late 1940s–early 1950s, Fink saw *Foreign Legion* and *Moldavian Rhapsody* reprinted several times in the 1950s–early 1960s.

From the Thaw until his death in Moscow in 1973, Fink enjoyed the status of "one of the oldest Soviet writers." First published in 1960, Fink's *Literary Memoirs* went through several editions—a pale, tame peer of Ilya Ehrenburg's *People. Years. Life* (see vol. 1). Some chapters were set abroad (Paris, Spain) and focused on meetings with left-wing European intellectuals and writers (e.g., Romain Rolland), yet Fink did succeed in planting occasional Jewish references, in safe contexts, such as mentioning the word "antisemitism" in a discussion of the Dreyfus Affair; evoking the Shoah in connection with the death of Jean-Richard Bloc's family members; recall-

361

ing Isaac Babel's love for Jewish cuisine in the 1930s; including the "Jewish poet from Haifa Isaac Ioffe [Jechok Joffe]" in a list of writers who perished in the Spanish Civil War; identifying the Jewish origins of Grigory Iolos and Mikhail Gertsenshtein, members of the Duma assassinated by "monarchists"; and so forth. At the same time, Fink avoided even the most hushed references to his research for *Jews in the Taiga* as he described a 1929 expedition to the Far East. In 1967, Fink's memoir appeared in German under the unduly sensationalist title *Zwischen Paris und Moskau* (Between Paris and Moscow).

Owing to tsarist-era restrictions, by 1917 only 2 percent of the Jewish population was engaged in agriculture. Among the chief concerns of the Jewish Section (*Evsektsiya*) of the Bolshevik Party was to battle massive Jewish poverty. In 1919, the Jewish Section helped organize the first Jewish agricultural cooperatives in Belorussia and Lithuania, and, starting with 1924, it poured its energy into placing Jews in industry and in agriculture. The elemental drive of Jews on the land was already under way, the Jewish agricultural population increasing from about 53,000 in 1917 to about 76,000 in 1923. In August 1924, KOMZET (KOMERD in Yiddish), the Committee for the Settlement of Jewish Toilers on Land, was founded under the auspices of the Council of Nationalities of the TsIK (Central Executive Committee). Led by Pyotr Smidovich, KOMZET was in charge of the "Jews on the land" program. In 1924 new Jewish settlements were founded in the Ukraine, where by the late 1920s three Jewish national districts operated: Kalinindorf, Novozlatopol, and Stalindorf. By 1925, the number of Jewish peasants had grown to about 100,000. While the state provided concessions to the settlers, a large part of the aid came from abroad, from the American Joint Distribution Committee (which incorporated Agro-Joint to distribute assistance), ORT, the Jewish Colonization Association, and other agencies.

To abet KOMZET, the Society for the Settlement of Jewish Toilers on Land (OZET) was created in 1925 and was headed by Yury Larin. It was a citizens' organization, but leaders of the Jewish Section in effect controlled it starting in 1926. OZET assisted with the logistics of creating Jewish agricultural colonies and concentrated on fundraising and propaganda work. Enlisting the support of the Jewish intelligentsia, OZET engineered such appeals for help as the 1926 declaration "To the Jews of the World," whose signatories included Soviet Yiddish writers Shmuel Halkin, Dovid Hofshteyn, Itsik Fefer, and others. OZET had branches in the Soviet republics and regions, and groups of support abroad. At the First Congress of OZET in 1926, Mikhail Kalinin, tutelary head of the Soviet state and champion of the "Jews on the land" program, spoke strongly against Jewish assimilation (the so-called "Kalinin Declaration"), lending temporary support to the previously rejected idea of a Jewish national enclave (or enclaves) in the USSR. The late 1920s marked the height of OZET propaganda and cultural-education work, which included publications in a number of languages. In 1927 Abram Room directed the documentary *Jew on the Land*, based on a screenplay that OZET commissioned from Vladimir Mayakovsky and Viktor Shklovsky (in vol. 1).

By the mid-1920s, a grander program of Jewish settlement was introduced, targeting the north and northeastern parts of the Crimea, with vacant lands and difficult conditions for agriculture; in 1930 the Freidorf Jewish national district was established there. Some settlement work proceeded in Belorussia, in Smolensk Province, Russia, and in Uzbekistan and the Caucasus. In 1928 KOMZET introduced its five-year plan, forecasting the number of peasant Jews to increase from 100,000 to 250,000 in 1933, and eventually to one-half million. In 1936 there were about 200,000 "Jews on the land" in the USSR, and it is estimated that there were still about 100,000 Soviet peasant Jews on the eve of the Nazi invasion in 1941. The program of Jewish agricultural settlement was never realized on a scale as ambitious as declared. The collectivization of Soviet agriculture harmed and in many cases devastated Jewish agricultural colonies. Be that as it may, the "Jews on the land" program did produce, if temporarily, some impressive results. The shortcomings of the program hardly justify a comparison to the Birobidzhan fiasco.

Jewish agricultural colonies in the Ukraine and Crimea represented efforts to battle some real socioeconomic problems of the Jewish population. At the same time, in the 1920s the prospects of solving the Jewish question in the USSR through the "Jews on the land" program—and especially through the Birobidzhan project—offered the Soviet leadership a politically advantageous alternative to Zionism. The plan for the creation of a Jewish enclave in the Far East, in the Amur River basin near the Soviet–Manchurian border, was put forth in 1927. The first 654 settlers-pioneers arrived in Birobidzhan in the spring of 1928 to find themselves in severe climactic conditions, surrounded by the taiga (boreal forest), with insufficient logistical and equipment support. The population grew slowly, many Jewish settlers returning after temporary stays. In 1930, a Jewish national district was incorporated with 2,672 Jews out of the Birobidzhan area's total population of 38,000. By 1934 the Jewish population of the Birobidzhan area was a little over 8,000 instead of the projected 50,000. Yet the Soviet leadership pushed on with its plan, making the area a Jewish Autonomous Province in 1934. While the Birobidzhan project initially stirred enthusiasm among Soviet Jews, it existed primarily as an ideological tool of the Soviet leadership, attracting support and even enlisting settlers among Jewish Communists abroad. (According to Soviet data for 1959, 14,289 Jews, or about 9 percent of the total population, were living in the Birobidzhan area, and fewer than 2,000 people called Yiddish their native language.) Both KOMZET and OZET were liquidated in 1938, and many of their leaders were purged.

* * *

The propagandistic, socioeconomic, and educational literature that emerged from the "Jews on the land" and Birobidzhan projects was significant. Several books and brochures with virtually the same title were published including Fyodor Veitkov and B. Polishchuk's *Jews on the Land* (Moscow, 1930) and I. Geller's *Jew on the Land* (Smolensk, 1930). A number of Jewish-Russian littérateurs wrote about Jewish peasants and Birobidzhan, among them Iosif Kleinman, Semyon Bytovoy (Kogan) (1931 collection *Roads. On Jewish Collective Farms of the Crimea*), and others. Matvey Royzman (in vol. 1) devoted the novel *These Landlords* (1932) to Jewish settlements in the Crimea.

Most extensive and stimulating from a literary point of view was Viktor Fink's dilogy *Jews on the Land* (1929) and *Jews in the Taiga* (1930; 1932); two sections of *Jews on the Land* follow below. Derivative editions and brochures, such as *On the Way from Egypt* (1929), *Jews in the Field* (1930), and *The Taiga Region* (1931), were issued. *The Taiga Region* appeared in Yiddish translation in Kharkov (*A kant a taygisher*, 1932) and in Warsaw (*In Biro-Bidzshaner tayges*).

Critics in the 1930s noted Fink's skill at rendering with precision and humor the minutiae of life in Crimean and Belorussian agricultural settlements and in Birobidzhan. While Fink's ideological position is in line with that of the Party circa late 1920, his sketches are particularly interesting where they capture an intertwining of old traditions and new, of religion and technology, of ancient Hebrew and Soviet-infused Yiddish. In addition to prose efforts, Fink devoted a play, *New Motherland* (1933), to the collectivization of Jews in Birobidzhan. It was criticized for its lack of the "typical" and the "epochal."

In the December 1938 issue of *Red Virgin Soil* (*Krasnaia nov'*), Fink published the essay "The Jewish Question." Probably rushed to print, the essay makes reference to the events of Kristallnacht (November 1938). Fink described a recent visit to the Stalindorf Jewish national district in the Ukraine, situated between Dnepropetrovsk and Krivoy Rog. Fink slapped together truths about the persecution of Jews in tsarist Russia and Nazi Germany, half-truths about life on the Jewish collective farms and communities in Stalindorf, and lies about the "solving of the Jewish question" in the USSR. Reading Fink's ideological commission is a painful experience for a number of reasons, and less so because of the loyalism with which Fink pounded the chords of Marxist-Leninist rhetoric on the Jewish question and established Stalin, the People's Commissar of Nationalities in 1918, as the founder of the first Jewish agricultural colonies in the Soviet Republic. Despite—or perhaps because of—its glorification of Jewish life in Stalindorf, Fink's essay reads today like a eulogy for the Jewish national districts in Ukraine and Crimea. Devastated by World War II and the Shoah, some Jewish settlements were taken over by non-Jewish neighbors; the Soviet authorities liquidated Jewish national districts soon after the victory over the Nazis.

From *Jews on the Land*

3. The Preachers

Hand-written posters appeared in the neighborhood of the synagogue to the effect that on Friday evening a preacher would be making a presentation. The program: (1) on the divinity of Lenin (the word "divinity" had been scratched out and replaced by the word "greatness"); (2) on the significance of the Sabbath; and so forth.

"Actually, this very expression 'and so forth' is the most important part of the sermon, because the first two points are only the introduction," said my host to me. "Go see what he has to say."

Onto the pulpit strode an emaciated man with a fiery gaze. Clearing his throat and swaying as if he were intoning a prayer, he began in a singsong voice to relate a parable.

"Listen, Jews, to the story of what happened, *oy*, happened to me . . . Once I had a horse, yes, a horse! It was a sickly nag, a sickly nag for sure, which I was disgusted to ha-a-a-arness! It was blind, and its ribs showed to such an extent that the harness wouldn't stay in place on them, *oy*, just wouldn't stay in place! And poverty reigned in my house from the fact that my nag was weak, and no matter how much I rode her, I had a hard time earning any money with her for the Sabbath.

"Then came market day. Yes, market day did come, and I traded my nag for a steed. The steed was beautiful and smooth. Smooth he was and beautiful, and his eyes were sighted, and my soul rejoiced when I looked at him! I thought—this marks the beginning of a new life for me, fast and easy.

"But, *oy oy oy oy oy oy*, Jews! *Oy oy oy oy oy*! Hardly had I handed over my nag and taken possession of the reins pulled by my new steed when I saw, *oy*, Jews, what did I see?

"I saw that my steed was colicky and lame. I could not ride him a single step! . . . So there I sat, exclaiming: 'Why did this have to happen to me? I would have been better off keeping my old nag. She at least had the use of her legs. What use to me is this gorgeous beast everyone admires? What use to me is this beauty if I cannot ride him?'"

That's it, the whole parable. The audience consisted entirely of small tradesmen. Their wretched lives under the tsars had been like the feeble nag, so they had traded it for the steed of the Revolution. And their "souls rejoiced."

But then it all ended when private enterprise was eliminated.

"So what use to me is this beauty if I cannot ride him!"

There are other good parables—for example, the parable about the ladder:

"I entered a courtyard overshadowed by an enormous new building. And I see, *oy*, what do I see: I see a ladder lying there among the trash.

"And having seen me, it called out:

'Man! Man! See how wretched is my fate! You see this marvelous building? Know, then, that I took part in its construction. I stood upright. The builders went up me and down me; they carried materials up me, and I served as a support for many activities. But now that the building is completed, I have been thrown into a trash heap, and no one so much as looks in my direction—oy, in my direction no one so much as looks!'

"And I answered it:

'Ladder! Ladder!' I answered it, 'don't lose hope! No building on earth is permanent. The time will come when this building, too, will collapse and you will once again be needed and they will pull you out of the trash! Oy, out of the trash will they pull you, and you will once again stand upright . . .'"

In this case, too, the dots will not be put over the *i*'s with too much precision. But that doesn't matter. The audience consists of people for whom the concept of class has been drowned in the concept of nationality. The audience believes that it has actually taken part in the Revolution. Hasn't this small town produced revolutionaries? And now that the building is completed, it turns out that trade has been taken over by the co-ops, while they, the audience, are lying in the garbage, being trampled by the tax assessor . . .

Of course, the sermon from the pulpit of the synagogue is not always constructed so wittily. Sometimes it's hysterically coarse.

In Mogilev, on the day of the Jewish New Year, the blast produced by the shammes from a ram's horn was barely sounded when the preacher bellowed:

"Jewish women! It is better to lead your children to slaughter than to hand them over to the Young Pioneers."

Sometimes the sermon is insultingly naïve and obtuse. The town of Orsha found a smart fellow:

"Jews!" he proclaimed. "I will explain to you, Jews, why there's such a decline in trade. In the old days a Jew sat day and night poring over the holy books in search of virtue and wisdom. This irritated Satan the tempter, so he sent to the Jew some Christians in order to lure him away from the holy books on the pretext of trade. And the Jew traded. And now Satan saw that the Jew, on his own, no longer pored over the holy books; that he, on his own, had fallen away from the faith of his fathers; that he, on his own, no longer sought virtue and wisdom. What else did Satan need? He was satisfied! There was no longer any need to tempt Jews. Therefore he no longer dispatched Christians to the Jew under the pretext of trade."

But the audience cleverly distinguishes between professional wailers and subtle political propagandists. It demonstrates a clear preference for worldly motifs. They demand of the cantor at the synagogue—the *hazan*—that after the service he provide songs on secular topics born of anonymous folk creation during the years of the Revolution. Here we find both satire aimed at old-style Jews, and a sharp comment or two for the Jewish commissar, and complaints about life's hardships, sometimes directed at the hope for a better future, sometimes frittered away in endless grief.

A certain *magid*[1] of the erstwhile merchants wandered through Belorussia. He at one time had possessed a second-class license, but that document had vanished by the time an armful of subpoenas arrived from the tax collector. The merchant didn't give a good goddamn about anything, so he went off "to burn the hearts of men with the word."[2] He was a strapping burly fellow about thirty years of age, with a well-oiled tongue. In the old days, that tongue had helped him speculate in textiles; now he speculated in the thirst of those former merchants to hear a word of sympathy . . .

His speeches were witty and laced with humor. Those same parables about the horse and the ladder he would deliver without hysterical lamentations—as cheerfully and playfully as he had once sold the "best calico in the world." He would invariably end as follows:

"Jews! Keep in mind that there are three possibilities, Jews!"

After a pause came an enumeration:

"It can happen that everything is fine. Kopeck chases kopeck, and ruble chases ruble. Then the Jew has no need of a preacher. Or it can happen the other way around—that everything is bad, and you've lost all hope. Then kopeck is in no hurry to chase kopeck, and ruble simply lies in place, and it's not clear just what place that is. In that case, too, the Jew has no need of a preacher. Yet there is a third possibility—the one in which the Jew does need a preacher. For example, the preacher hasn't a half-kopeck to his name; he isn't reimbursed for his board and room; he hasn't had a bite to eat or a drop to drink. He needs the Jews to remember that the support paid to the wise man is pleasing to God. So I ask you: have you thought to collect several rubles for the *magid*, or haven't you? . . ."

[. . .]

7. The New Culture

The Revolution put forward powerful weapons against small-town squalor. Let's put aside for now the Jewish schools, the Jewish workers' organizations, the Jewish athletic societies. Take the recognition of Yiddish as an official state language! . . . How hard is it to penetrate the soul of a Jew who finds himself at a railroad station? Only a few years ago, he would have slid through the railroad station in order not to be noticed by a policeman, a stationmaster, even a switchman or a porter. Now all the station names are written in Russian, Belorussian, and Yiddish, and a Jew feels in this an unprecedented recognition of the fact that he is not a stranger but a real citizen just like everybody else.

---

1. *Magid* (Heb., Yiddish) = preacher; used in Poland and Ukraine in reference to a popular, charismatic preacher.
2. In Russian, "*Glagolom zhech' serdtsa liudeï*" is the last line of Pushkin's famous poem "The Prophet" (1826), based in part on Isaiah 6.

Or take, for example, the Jewish courtroom! . . . The judge, the members of the jury, the clerk, the parties to the lawsuit, the witnesses, the lawyers—they all speak Yiddish. Court records, summonses, court orders—all of it is written in Yiddish. It seems to me that there's not a single Jew whose heart doesn't stop, if only for a minute, when he sees with his own eyes a Jewish courtroom. For Jews, especially for the Jewish poor who hang around courtrooms, having a legal proceeding in their own language is not just a question of convenience. These days all Jews speak Russian, so Jews could be tried in a Russian court. Even, I must confess, the participants in the pleadings, unbeknownst to themselves, lapsed into the sort of Yiddish in which the indictment is called "der indictment" and the subpoena is called "die subpoena."

"The malice smells mit denunciation!" was said, for example, by a Jewish defense attorney.

But the very existence of a Jewish courtroom, even with the occasional "die subpoena," encourages in the Jewish masses an awareness of their legal and civic value, which is precisely those elements of the Jewish national psychology that various governments always tried in vain to destroy by every possible means.

A Jew who can come to a Jewish courtroom clearly feels his value as a human being and his significance as a citizen, and this is enormous for him, and new.

The Institute of Belorussian Culture in Minsk has a Jewish section. Several young researchers sit there pouring over their books with the same fanaticism that their fathers and grandfathers displayed in poring over the Talmud. Bit by bit, brick by brick, letter by letter, they collect the scholarship pertaining to Jewish culture.

Working in the Jewish section are the following groups: (1) a historical commission, which has already succeeded in collecting extremely interesting new data on the history of world Jewry; (2) a literary commission, which is studying both old and new Jewish literature, elaborating questions of literary form, Jewish theater, and collecting folklore; (3) a linguistics commission, studying questions of Jewish lexicology, composing a Jewish-Belorussian, Belorussian-Jewish dictionary, an academic dictionary, and a linguistic geographic atlas, elaborating questions of orthography and terminology; (4) an economic and demographic commission studying the economy of the small town and the colony.

This is the germ of a future Jewish Academy of Sciences . . .

Someone may say, I suppose, but this isn't such a big deal: people are paid a salary, and they work up a sweat, but who needs it? . . .

But therein lies the whole unexpected crux of the matter. The labor of these young scholars cannot keep up with the demands of a reawakened Jewish culture. *The Proceedings of the Jewish Section* are hefty editions of some 400 to 800 pages. One volume costs five rubles, and the edition is sold out—two thousand copies of each book have been distributed. A vast amount of research on the history of Jewry, on literature, on socioeconomic and cultural-social issues, detailed elaborations of the colossal statistical data on the past and the current life of Jewish towns, on the collection of folklore, on area studies—to all this information gravitate not only assiduous workers but also readers, obviously extremely eager readers, because five rubles to a member of the Jewish intelligentsia is a lot of money.

But if it is necessary to demonstrate the enormous cultural growth of the Jewish masses, its vital creative connection to the institutions of culture , it is worth acquainting oneself with the Letters to the Editor section of *The Proceedings*. It turns out that a rigorous study of culture is going on not only here, in the halls of the research institutions—here it is being systematized—but out there, in the small urban centers and remote little towns.

"We have gotten involved in the collection of folklore," I am told by one of the researchers. "We published an appeal. More than 250 correspondents have responded."

Someone else says, "We began to compile a dictionary. Unpaid volunteers have helped us. We now have 200,000 index cards."

"From where?" I ask. "How did all this happen?"

We were chatting as we sat by a window. My companion made a motion with his hand, pointing toward the street beyond the window. All kinds of folk were darting about—toilers.

"That's where they come from! . . ."

You can already discern the face of the new Jew—the Jew who is passionate about culture. In the turmoil of the historical breakage, his life still unsettled, he struggles against poverty; he overtaxes himself in the artels The Red Baker and The Red Lathe Operator, where he haggles over meat pies or uproots tree stumps on his land allotment. In his struggles, he is already creating his culture and is being drawn to the organizing cultural center.

There you have it—what the Revolution has done with him, the small-town Jew. He flies head over heels out of the demolished small town. The flight is uncomfortable, but the course is true. In the final analysis, he arrives at spiritual liberation and converts his flight into productive labor.

1929

Translated from the Russian by Richard Sheldon

Viktor Fink, *Evrei na zemle*. English translation copyright © by Richard Sheldon. Introduction and notes copyright © by Maxim D. Shrayer.

SEMYON KIRSANOV

Semyon Kirsanov (1906–1972), poet and translator, was born in Odessa to the family of a Jewish tailor. Kirsanov organized the Southern Association of Futurists in 1921, and his first publications appeared in 1922–23 in Odessa's newspapers. In 1924 Kirsanov founded *Yugo-LEF* (Southern Left Front of the Arts, modeled after *LEF* in Moscow). The same year Vladimir Mayakovsky visited Odessa, deciding the young poet's lot. Mayakovsky published two of Kirsanov's poems in *LEF* 3 (1925). After graduating from the Odessa Institute of People's Education in 1925, Kirsanov moved to Moscow. He captured the readers' attention with his robust, verbally inventive, mercurial poems revealing both his natural talent and an apprenticeship with Mayakovsky and Nikolay Aseev (1889–1963). Kirsanov toured the USSR with Mayakovsky in the 1920s, giving readings.

Kirsanov's first collection, *Backsight* (1926), subtitled "rhymed stories," was followed by many more in the 1920s and 1930s among them, *Essays, 1925–26* (1927), *The Last Contemporary* (1930, illustrated by Aleksandr Rodchenko), and *Notebook* (1933). Kirsanov published long poems as separate editions: *My Nameday Poem* (1928), *Conversation with Dmitry Furmanov* (1928), and others.

Following Mayakovsky's death in 1930, Kirsanov carried his teacher's torch. His *Five-Year Plan* (1931) continued Mayakovsky's last long poem, *At the Top of My Voice*, and incorporated bits of Mayakovsky's text. Kirsanov's long poem *Comrade Marx* (1933) dialogued with Mayakovsky's *Vladimir Ilyich Lenin* (1924). Kirsanov lent his talent to the Soviet industrial effort by visiting construction sites, contributing verses to factory newspapers, and authoring "agit-posters" such as "The 14th of October" (1933). His incessant verbal artistry hardly suffered from propagandistic commissions.

The mid-1930s marked a shift toward the lyrical, triggered by the death of Kirsanov's wife, whom he mourned in the stunning *Your Poem* (1937). Among his finest works are the lyrical cycles "A Groan while Sleeping" (1937–39) and "The Last of May" (1940). In 1936 Kirsanov visited Europe with a group of Soviet authors and later published a strong anti-Fascist poem, *War to the Plague!* (1937). Kirsanov spent the war years as a newspaper correspondent at several fronts; his wartime poems were gathered in *Poem for the War* (1945). Creating the poetic persona of a charismatic soldier, Kirsanov chronicled the war in *The Cherished Word of Foma Smyslov* (1942–43), printed as leaflets in millions of copies. He reported on the Nuremberg Trial; he composed the poem *Aleksandr Matrosov* (1946) in the post-mortem voice of the soldier-hero, conflating patriotism and formal estrangement. During the anticosmopolitan campaign Kirsanov scored an official victory with his "production" poem *Makar Mazay* (1951 Stalin Prize).

In the postwar years Kirsanov turned increasingly to philosophical poetry: *The Peak* (1954), *Once Tomorrow* (1962), and *Mirrors* (1967); and the cycles "Footprints in the Sand" (1950) and "The World" (1962). In *Eden* (1945) he treated the creation of the world in biblical terms. During Khrushchev's Thaw, Kirsanov published the anti-Stalinist long poem *Seven Days of the Week,* attacking Soviet bureaucracy; it was deemed "politically immature." The late 1950s and early 1960s witnessed the second peak of Kirsanov's popularity.

Kirsanov's poetry showcased an astonishingly wide spectrum of generic and stylistic modes, from futuristic and expressionistic verse to folkloric poetry (e.g., *The Tale of King Maks-Emelyan,* 1962–64). Separate mention should be made of Kirsanov's enduring interest in poetic science fiction and fantasy, displayed in *Cinderella* (1934), *Poem about a Robot* (1934), *The Dolphiniad* (1971), and other works. Kirsanov also translated modernist left-wing poets, including Louis Aragon, Bertold Brecht, Nazim Hikmet, and Pablo Neruda.

Kirsanov called himself a "circusman of verse," and both admirers and detractors took to heart this *profession de foi.* Diehard Soviet critics charged Kirsanov with "verbal trickery" and "formalism," but the shadow of Mayakovsky guarded Kirsanov. Much of his poetry was spoken in the first person and exhibited brilliant puns and sound orchestration and exceptional compound rhyming. A living legacy of the formal achievements and ideological compromises of the 1920s "Left Art," Kirsanov was a Soviet modernist par excellence.

Kirsanov died in Moscow in 1972 after a battle with larynx cancer. Echoing Mayakovsky's *The Backbone Flute* (1915), Andrey Voznesensky wrote in "Kirsanov's Funeral," "A flute that hadn't cried itself out/ fell into its red case."

Kirsanov never shunned his Jewishness, nor did he deliberately seek out Jewish questions. Published in the collection *The Floor* [literally "the word"] *Is Given to Kirsanov* (1930), "R" vertiginously captures through its wordplay and sound orchestration the travails of a Jewish young man, an aspiring Russian poet, who rolls his *r*'s differently. In using Russian, native speakers of Yiddish and their children would display a characteristically uvular (grunted) *r* instead of the lingual (tongue-trilled) Russian consonant. This would make them targets for taunting, and anecdotes about identifying a Jew by his misrolled *r*'s belonged to the common repertoire of anti-Jewish jokes. In this anthology, two other Jewish writers address the subject of ethnic, cultural, and religious markers of speech: Victor Shklovsky in *Zoo* (in vol. 1) and Eduard Shulman in *Jew Ivanych* (in vol. 2).

R

Trouble
with rolling your *r*'s
    can be painfully torturous.
Everyone
cuts you
    disdainfully.
Me, as a kid
I had problems
    with *r*'s.
Talk about torture—
my larynx
    has scars.
I've had a serious inhibition.
    See, young lovelies
        mock this
        r deficiency.
Rasping *r*'s
    made my throat and neck sick.
So closemouthed,
    I was anorexic.

I'd start a lai:
"O Rus! O Rus!"
But I would say,
"O Ghoose! O Ghoose!"
And here would come,
    alackaday,
a neighbor's loose
    misshapen goose.

Kids would whistle
    and smirk:
"Hey, yellow quitter,
    homework jerk,
        homework jerk,
say
    Rotten corn fritter!"

And not "Officer Carl,"
   I'd croak, "Officegh Caghl."
In some medical books
   I would mull it.
Where, oh, where are you, R?
   I beseech you, dear R.
Can't you reach
   to my rickety gullet?

And an actor
   at the wretched Roc Theater would come,
and he'd splatter my mispronounced *r*'s
   with his curses,
and he made me recite,
   "Rumty-tum, rumty-tum,
rumty-tum, rumty-tum,
   rerehearses!"

Corridor!
   Frame!
      Carborundum!
      Overrun!
Like a pea from its pod,
   that *r* struggled.
Like the seed of a grape trying to grow,
   how it guggled,
till it burst out and glowed in the sun.

Then that letter would roll
   like a lustrous black pearl
from my larynx
   as if I were cured of catarrh.
And I swaggered around
   as if gargling
      with fire,
with that sound, that miraculous
         R!

And three times I exhorted
   Muscovites, everybody,
mouth contorted
   in trumpet-like shapes:
"Up on Mount
   Ararat
      grow
         great
            ruddy
grapes,
   GRAPES,
   GRAPES!"

1929

Translated from the Russian by Maxim D. Shrayer and J.B. Sisson

EDUARD BAGRITSKY

Eduard Bagritsky (1958–1934), poet and translator, was born Eduard Dzyubin (Dzyuban) to an Odessan family where Judaic traditions were respected but the life style was that of the secularized petite bourgeoisie. He began publishing in 1913 using a nom de plume that was derived from *bagrovyi*, the Russian for "crimson," and sounded both decadent and revolutionary. Bagritsky was a contributor to Odessa's literary publications in 1915–17 and lived the life of a bohemian. After the February 1917 Revolution he served briefly in law enforcement for the Provisional Government and joined the Red Army in 1919. He moved to Moscow in 1925 and by the time of his death had achieved wide admiration. A number of books followed his collection *South-West* (1928): *The Lay of Opanas* (1932), *Selected Poems* (1932), *Victors* (1932), *The Last Night* (1932), and others. Bagritsky never shed the skin of an Odessan Jew from Market Street and retained a strong bond with Jewish culture until his death, splendidly translating Yiddish poetry (Itsik Fefer, Perets Markish). Bagritsky was hailed second only to Vladimir Mayakovsky himself in the Soviet literary pantheon and given an official funeral.

Owing to his unique talent, the epoch, and the brevity of his career, Bagritsky cuts a most controversial figure among the Jewish-Russian poets of the Soviet period. Facets of his colorful personality survive in the accounts of his contemporaries: in the story "Idler Eduard" (1925) and later the fictional memoir *My Diamond Crown* (1980), where Bagritsky is called Birdcatcher, by Valentin Kataev, the brother of Evgeny Petrov (with Ilya Ilf in vol. 1); in the memoir-novel in verse *The Merry Stranger* by Mark Tarlovsky (in vol. 1); and others. A former cocaine addict and a fabulous fictionalizer and mystifier, Bagritsky hardly compels his students to rely on his writings as a source of information about his ideology.

In many respects, his career mirrors that of his friend and coeval Isaac Babel (1894–1940; in vol. 1). Bagritsky's short life typifies the destinies of Russia's Jewish artists born in the late 1890s and early 1900s, and his career betokens several emblematic facts for his generation of Jewish-Russian writers: upbringing in a mercantile Jewish family and some exposure to Judaic traditions; cultural Russianization through reading and group literary activities; enthusiastic endorsement of the February Revolution and engagement in the events of the civil war on the side of the Reds; assimilation through marriage to a non-Jewish woman; move from the southwest to Moscow; and a major literary success after the move to the Soviet capital in 1925. Following Bagritsky's premature death, the Soviet ideological machine quickly contrived Bagritsky's legacy into a convenient literary legend. A forbidden subject even at the height of Khrushchev's Thaw, Bagritsky's Jewish themes were engaged head-on only when he became the object of virulent attacks by official critics. Bagritsky was a symbol of the alleged Jewish destruction of Russian culture for the Judeophobic Russian ultranationalists gaining a voice in the Soviet 1970s.

A profusely talented transgressor of boundaries—Jewish, Russian, and Soviet—Bagritsky has influenced several generations of Russian poets, including such major postwar figures as Joseph Brodsky and Evgeny Reyn (both in vol. 2). In spite of the efforts of various critics to pigeon hole him as a "bourgeois nationalist" (Zhdanovites in the late 1940s and early 1950s), a "revolutionary Romantic" (conformist Soviet moderates in the 1960s and 1970s), or a Zionist and Russophobe (Russian ultranationalists in the 1970s and 1980s), Bagritsky's beliefs and loyalties are difficult to negotiate. Bagritsky may have occasionally trumpeted allegiance to the Bolsheviks—consider his opportunistic verses about the Industrial Party trial of 1930—yet his texts cannot be said to provide reliable information about his allegiance to the regime. Bagritsky agonized over the status of his Jewishness during the years of the ferocious campaign against traditional Jewish life. Up until the early 1930s, Bagritsky—like Babel, Ehrenburg, and other Jewish-Soviet writers of his generation—must have believed that Bolshevism was a better alternative than tsarism for the three million Soviet Jews. In 1931, in "Conversation with My Son," Bagritsky wrote both about the virulent pogromists of his childhood and about marching units of "blackshirts" and "black fascist signs" marking the wings of (Italian) fighter planes. (Bagritsky's son, the poet Vsevolod Bagritsky, was killed in World War II.) The severely ill Bagritsky spent his last two years mainly confined to his apartment in the center of Moscow; he died in 1934. In 1936, Isaac Babel said of his deceased friend: "The fame of François Villon from Odessa earned [Bagritsky] love but did not earn trust [. . .] he was a wise man, conjoining a Komsomol member with Ben Akiva" (i.e., Akiva ben Joseph, ca. 40–135 C.E., great Talmudic scholar, Jewish leader, and martyr).

Jewish topics and characters figure prominently in less than a dozen of Bagritsky's works. But in both "Origin" (1926) and his last poem *February* (1933–34; published 1936), Bagritsky produced definitive poetic statements about the making of a Jewish-Russian identity and the boundaries of Jewish-Soviet assimilation. "Origin" is a militant (and self-hating) monologue of a Russian Jew at odds with his familial past and upbringing.

Published posthumously in 1936 and banned for long periods of time in the Soviet Union, *February* is set in Odessa in the 1900s and 1910s. It depicts the traumatic formation of its protagonist's Russian-Jewish self at the time of historical cataclysms. While the main events of *February* unfold in Bagritsky's native city of Odessa between the autumn of 1916 and the autumn of 1917, the first excerpt found below contains a flashback to the protagonist's childhood. The second excerpt takes place in September or October 1916, as is evident from an earlier reference to the Stokhod operation of July–August 1916, in which the protagonist has participated. Tsar Nicholas II abdicated on 15 (2) March 1917. In Odessa, the power of the Provisional Government was established on 25 (12) March 1917. On 17 April 1917, a permanent militia was created by an edict of the Provisional Government. The third excerpt, in which the Jewish protagonist describes his activities as a deputy commissar of the militia, takes place in the spring and summer of 1917 and definitely prior to the Bolshevik coup d'état of 7 November (25 October) 1917. The local soviet assumed power in Odessa only in December 1917, and the Bolshevik takeover as well as the events of the civil war remained outside Bagritsky's historical focus in *February*.

Since its posthumous publication in 1936, *February* remained a thorn in the sinewy side of Clio the Commissar, and the post-Soviet years have not made it less controversial.

Origin

I can't recall the exact night
When I felt the ache of a life to come.
The world rocked and swayed.
A star stumbled on its way,
Splashing into a sky-blue basin.
I tried to grab the star . . . Slipping through my fingers
It darted off, a carp with blazing fins.
Over my cradle rusty Jews
Crossed rusty blades of crooked beards.
And everything was upside down.
And nothing was ever right.
A carp pounded on the window;
A horse chirped; a hawk dropped into my hands;
A tree danced.
And my childhood went forth.
They tried desiccating it with matzos.
They tried deceiving it with candles.
They pushed its nose into the tablets—
Those gates that couldn't be opened.
Jewish peacocks on upholstery.
Jewish cream that always turned sour,
Father's crutch and mother's headscarf—
All muttered at me:
"Scoundrel! Scoundrel!"
And only at night, only on my pillow

Did a beard not split my world in two;
And slowly the water fell,
Like copper pennies from the kitchen faucet.
The water dripped. Descending like a storm cloud
It sharpened the crooked blade of its jet . . .
—Tell me, how could my Jewish disbelief
believe in this ever-flowing world?
They taught me: a roof's a roof.
The chair's hard. The floor dies under your feet,
You must see, comprehend, and hear,
Leaning on this world, as on a counter.
But the watchmaker's precision of a woodworm
Already hollows the beams of my existence.
—Tell me, how could my Jewish disbelief
Believe in this solid world?
Love?
But what about lice-eaten braids;
A jutting collar bone;
Pimples; a mouth, greased with herring,
And a horsey curve of the neck?
Parents?
But aging in the twilight,
Hunchbacked, knotty, and wild
Rusty Jews fling at me
Their stubbly fists.
The door! Fling the door open!
Outside the stars have chewed all the leaves
From their branches,
The moon's crescent smokes in the middle of a puddle.
A rook screams not knowing his kin.
And all that love,
Rushing at me,
And all the self-deprecation
Of my fathers
And all the nebulae
Creating the night,
And all the trees
Tearing through my face—
All this stood in my way,
Wheezing in my chest through my ailing bronchi:
—Pariah! Take your poor belongings,
Your cursedness and rejection!

Run away!
I'm abandoning my old bed:
—Should I leave?
I'm going!
Good riddance!
I don't care!

1930

From *February*
(Three excerpts)

[. . .]
I never loved properly . . .
A little Judaic boy,
I was the only one around
To shiver in the steppe wind at night.

Like a sleepwalker, I walked along tram tracks
To silent summer cottages, where in the underbrush
Of gooseberry or wild blackberry bushes
Grass snakes rustle and vipers hiss,
And in the thickets, where you can't sneak in,
A bird with a scarlet head darts about,
Her song is thin as a pin;
They've nicknamed her "Bull's eye" . . .

How did it happen, that born to a Hebrew,
And circumcised on the seventh day,
I became a fowler—I really don't know!

I loved Brehm better than Mayne Reid![1]
My hands trembled with passion

---

1. Brehm, Alfred Edmund (1829–1884)—world-renowned naturalist. Brehm's books, including *The Animals of the World*; *Bird-Life, Being a History of the Birds*, and others, written in German and translated into many languages, including Russian, were extremely popular among Russian teenagers. Reid, Mayne—a.k.a. Main Rid (1818–1883)—American author. His novels of adventure, including *Adventures among the Indians: or the War Trail and the Hunt of the Wild Horse* (1853); *Afloat in the Forest* (1866); *The Headless Horseman* (1866); and *Chris Rock, a Lover in Chains* (1889), were translated into Russian and enjoyed much popularity—especially *The Headless Horseman*—in both tsarist and Soviet times.

When I opened the book at random—
Birds would leap out at me from chance pages
Looking like letters of foreign alphabets,
Sabers and trumpets, globes and rhombuses.

I imagine the Archer once paused
Above the blackness of our dwelling,
Above the notorious Jewish smoke
Of goose-fat cracklings, above the cramming
Of tedious prayers, bearded faces
In family pictures . . .
[. . .]

                    * * *

I evaded the front: I tried everything . . .
How many crumpled rubles
Escaped from my hands to the clerks'!
I bought my sergeants vodka,
I bribed them with cigarettes and pork fat . . .
From ward to ward,
Coughing in a paroxysm of pleurisy,
I roamed.
                    Puffing and gasping,
Spitting into bottles, drinking medicine,
Standing naked, skinny, unshaven
Under the stethoscopes of all and every doctor . . .

When I was lucky enough by truth
Or lie—who can remember?—
To get a liberty pass,
I would shine my boots,
Straighten my blouse, and sharply
Walk to the boulevard, where an oriole sang
In the treetops, its voice like baked clay,
Where above the sand of the path
A green dress swayed
Like a slender strand of smoke . . .

Again I dragged on behind her,
Dying of love, swearing, stumbling into benches . . .
She would go into a movie theater,

Into the rattling darkness, the tremble
Of green light in a square frame,
Where a woman beside a fireplace
Wrung her alabaster hands,
And a man in a granite vest
Was shooting from a silent revolver . . .

I knew the faces of all her admirers,
I knew their habits, smiles, gestures,
How their steps slowed down, when on purpose,
With chest, hip, or palm,
They would feel through a dainty cover
The anxious tenderness of a girl's skin . . .
[. . .]
The girl had already approached the square,
And in the dark-gray circle of museums
Her dress, flying in the wind,
Looked thinner and greener . . .

I tore myself from the bench
With such effort, as if I had been
Bolted to it.
            And not turning back
Rushed after her toward the square.
All the things I used to read at night—
Sick, hungry, half-dressed—
Birds with non-Russian names,
People from an unknown planet,
A world where they play tennis,
Drink orangeade and kiss women—
All that was now moving before me,
Dressed in a woolen dress,
Flaming with copper locks,
Swinging a striped satchel,
Heels running over cobble-stones . . .

I'll put my hand on her shoulder,
"Look at me!
            I am your misfortune!
I'm dooming you to the torment
Of incredible nightingale passion!
Wait!"

But there, around the corner,
Twenty steps away her dress shows green . . .
I am catching up with her.
          A little farther on
And we shall stride abreast . . .

I salute her like a soldier—his superior,
What shall I tell her? My tongue
Mumbles some nonsense,
          "Will you . . .
Don't run away . . .
          May I
Walk you home? I was in the trenches! . . ."

She is wordless.
          Not even a look
In my direction.
          Her steps
get faster.
          I run beside her, like a beggar,
Bowing respectfully.
          How on earth
Can I be her equal!
          Like a madman
I mumble some ridiculous phrases . . .

And suddenly a halt.
          Silently
She turns her head—I see
Her copper hair, her blue-green eyes
And a purplish vein on her temple,
Pulsating with anger.
"Go away. Now." And her hand
Points to the intersection . . .
          There he is—
Placed to guard the order—
He stands in my way like a kingdom
Of cords, shiny badges, medals,
Squeezed into high boots,
And covered on top by his hat,
Around which whirl in a yellow
And unbearably torturous halo

Doves from the Holy Scriptures,
And clouds, twisted like snails;
Paunchy, beaming with greasy sweat,
A policeman,
        from early morning pumped
With vodka and stuffed with pork fat . . .

                * * *

[. . .]
I stayed in the area . . .
        I worked
As deputy commissar.
        At first
I spent many nights in damp sentry boxes;
I watched the world passing by me,
Alien and dimly lit by crooked streetlamps,
Full of strange and unknown monsters
Oozing from thick fumes . . .

I tried to be ubiquitous . . .
        In a gig
I churned rural roads, searching
For horse thieves.
        Late at night
I rushed out in a motor boat
Into the gulf, curved like a black horn
Around rocks and sand dunes.
I broke into thieves' lodgings,
Reeking of overfried fish.
I appeared, like the angel of death,
With a torchlight and a revolver, surrounded
By four sailors from the battleship . . .
(Still young and happy. Still rosy-cheeked.
Sleepy after a night of reckless fun.
Cocked caps. Unbuttoned pea jackets.
Carbines under their arms. Wind in their eyes.)

My Judaic pride sang,
Like a string stretched to its limit . . .
I would've given much for my forefather
In a long caftan and fox fedora,
From under which fell gray spirals

Of earlocks and clouds of dandruff
Flushing over his square beard,
For that ancestor to recognize his descendant
In this huge fellow, rising, like a tower,
Over flying lights and bayonets,
From a truck, shaking off midnight . . .

1933–34

Translated from the Russian by Maxim D. Shrayer

ILYA ILF AND
EVGENY PETROV

Ilya Ilf (1897–1937) was born Ilya Fainzilberg to a lower-middle-class Odessan Jewish family. Despite pressure from their father, an accountant, to pursue business careers, two of Ilf's three brothers became artists and Ilf, a writer. In Odessa, Ilf worked for the Southern Russian Telegraph Agency, where the poet Vladimir Narbut (1888–1938) employed Odessan writers. Ilf contributed to the Odessan newspaper *Seaman* (*Moriak*) and edited the satirical magazine *Syndetikon*. After migrating to Moscow in 1923, he landed a proofreader's job at *Whistle* (*Gudok*), the railroad workers' newspaper and a hub for members of the South-Western school. In 1925 in Moscow, Ilf, a writer of sketches, essays, and feuilletons, met Evgeny Petrov, a fellow Odessan. Together they became (arguably) the greatest Soviet satirical writers.

Evgeny Petrov (1903–1942), born Evgeny Kataev, was the younger brother of the famous Soviet writer Valentin Kataev (1897–1986). The Kataev brothers enjoyed a sheltered childhood in Odessa. Their father taught at the Women's Diocesan High School; some evidence indicates that their mother, Evgeniya Bachey, was of Crimean Karaite stock, although she was apparently born Russian Orthodox. Not only their Odessan upbringing but also a link to the Karaites, a Judaic sect that rejected the Talmud, may explain the penchant of both Kataev brothers for friendships with and marital and family ties to Jews. Prior to moving to Moscow in 1923, Petrov had a stint at the Odessa Criminal Investigation Department. After running the satirical magazine *Red Pepper* (*Krasnyi perets*), Petrov joined *Whistle* in 1926. In the 1920s he published a number of story collections, including *Accident with a Monkey* (1927).

Ilf and Petrov's collaboration began in 1927 "by accident," as they later stated: "When we started writing together, it turned out that we were a good fit, as they say, complemented each other." After joining forces, Ilf and Petrov continued to publish some work of single authorship. Valentin Kataev apparently gave his brother and Ilf the idea for their debut, the satirical novel *Twelve Chairs* (1928), and intended to be the third author. Set during the NEP, *Twelve Chairs* relates the travails of Ostap Bender, a charismatic rogue identified as the "son of a Turkish subject." Bender had his prototype in Osip (Ostap) Shor (1899–1978), a younger brother of Anatoly Fioletov (pseudonym of Natan Shor, 1894–1918, an Odessan Jewish-Russian poet). Ilf and Petrov's novel appeared serially in the magazine *Thirty Days* (*Tridtsat' dnei*), which Vladimir Narbut edited, and came out in book form in the publishing house Land and Factory, which Narbut had founded. (As Nadezhda Mandelstam [in vol. 2] remarked in *Hope Abandoned*, "Odessan authors ate bread" from Narbut's hands.) In the novel Bender chases after the dispersed chairs from a set of twelve, in one of which a general's widow had hidden her diamonds. Bender's partner, the former nobleman Vorobyaninov, murders him on the eve of possessing the last chair, only to learn that the diamonds had already been discovered and a workers' club built with the funds. To this day *Twelve Chairs* remains a beloved read owing to its hilarious mock-adventure plot coupled with witty language. In Russia, Bender's aphorisms became popular adages (e.g., "key to the apartment where the money is"). Ilf and Petrov popularized the Yiddish-influenced and Yiddish-infused Odessa-speak (compare Babel's Odessa stories; Isaac Babel in vol. 1), while also cleverly underplaying Ostap Bender's Jewishness.

Nikolay Bukharin's endorsement of *Twelve Chairs* might have backfired, and critics attacked it. However, prompted by Stalin's positive response, *Literary Gazette* (*Literaturnaia gazeta*) printed an affirmative assessment in 1929. Taking advantage of the official literary policy, which deemed satire a potent ideological weapon, Ilf and Petrov mocked corrupt officials, lazy bureaucrats, and potboilers in the feuilletonistic cycles *1001 Days, or the New Scheherazade* and *Extraordinary Stories from the Life of the Town of Kolokolamsk*, both signed "Tolstoyevsky." As Alexandra Smith noted, the cycles "were written in the spirit of the Sixteenth Communist Party Conference, which took place in April 1929."

Resurrecting Ostap Bender, the writers completed a sequel, *The Little Golden Calf*, by early 1931. It appeared in *Thirty Days* and was published in book form by émigré houses in Berlin and Riga; the first Soviet book edition was delayed until 1933. Ilf and Petrov coauthored more stories in the early to middle 1930s; their collections included *How Robinson Was Written* (1933). In the 1930s they wrote for the cinema and the stage. With Valentin Kataev, Ilf and Petrov created the show *Under the Dome of the Circus*, basing upon it their script for *Circus* (1936), a musical comedy by Sergey Eisenstein's disciple Grigory Aleksandrov; in the film's conclusion, which portrayed the USSR as an internationalist society free of bigotry, Shloyme Mikhoels sang in Yiddish while holding a child of an African-American man and a white American woman; the biracial child is played by the would-be Russian poet Dzhems (James) Patterson.

In 1935–36, Ilf and Petrov undertook a road tour of the United States. Their book of nonfiction, *One-Storey America* (1936), garnered criticism, mainly for not being hostile enough toward capitalism. (Ilf and Petrov showed enthusiasm for some aspects of American life, including football.) Their last work, "Tonya," appeared in 1937, the year Ilf died of tuberculosis. "Poor Ilf died," Vladimir Nabokov wrote his wife from Paris in 1937. "And, somehow, one visualizes the Siamese twins being separated."

Ilf's quotable *Notebooks, 1925–37* were published in 1939 in expurgated form (a complete edition by Ilf's daughter Aleksandra appeared in 2000). Following Ilf's death, Petrov wrote scripts and the political comedy *Island of Peace* (first staged in 1947). He reported on the Soviet–Finnish war, after joining the Communist Party in

1940, and visited Germany as a *Pravda* correspondent in the spring of 1941. He died in a plane crash while returning to Moscow after reporting on Nazi-besieged Sebastopol.

During the "anticosmopolitan" campaign, after Soviet Writer Publishers reprinted Ilf and Petrov's *Twelve Chairs* and *The Little Golden Calf* in 1948, the secretariat of the Writers' Union issued a resolution deeming the publication a "severe political error" and the two novels about Ostap Bender a "slander of Soviet society." The novels were rehabilitated during the Thaw and later canonized as a model of Soviet satirical literature. A five-volume edition of Ilf and Petrov's works was printed in 1961 in a run of 300,000 copies. Both novels were translated into numerous languages, and their film versions have been produced both in Russia and abroad.

Following perestroika, uncensored editions of the novels appeared, including Yuri Shcheglov's edition of *Twelve Chairs* (1995) and Mikhail Odessky and David Feldman's edition of *The Little Golden Calf* (2000). Ilf and Petrov have remained popular among post-Soviet readers.

In a number of works, both those authored jointly with Petrov and those written solo, Ilf satirically examined Jewish topics. Ilf's story "The Prodigal Son Returns Home" appeared in the mass-produced illustrated magazine *Little Flame (Ogonek)* in 1930. Ilf and Petrov used the same title (from the parable of the prodigal son in Luke 15:11–32) for chapter 17 (part 2) of *The Little Golden Calf.* Free of the tenderness of Ilf's autobiographical voice, echoes of the antireligious campaign in the Soviet Union resurfaced in Ilf and Petrov's novel: "The great schemer [Ostap Bender] did not like Catholic priests. He was equally negative about rabbis, dalai-lamas, Orthodox priests, muezzins, shamans, and other servants of the cult."

The Prodigal Son Returns Home
Ilya Ilf

Sometimes I dream that I'm a rabbi's son.

I'm seized with fear. What can I do about it—I, the son of a servant in one of the most ancient of religious cults?

How did it happen? Surely not all my ancestors were rabbis. Take my great-grandfather. He was a coffin maker. Coffin makers are classified as craftsmen. So without going overboard, I can tell the Purge Commission[1] that I'm the great-grandson of a craftsman.

"All right," the commission will say, "but that's your great-grandfather. What about your father? Whose son are you?"

I'm a rabbi's son.

"He's not a rabbi anymore," I whimper. "He long since cast off his . . ."

What did he cast off? His robes? No, rabbis don't cast off their robes. It's priests who cast off their robes. Then what did he cast off? He cast off something or other, he abdicated, he renounced his bearded ways, with hew and cry he severed his ties with the almighty and refused him entry into the house.

But I can't explain exactly what my father cast off, and my explanations are deemed unsatisfactory. I'm fired.

I walk along the indigo snowy street and whisper to myself:

". . . Comrade Krokhky was completely right, when he . . . Tell me who you are friends with, and I'll tell you who you are . . . The apple doesn't fall far from the tree . . ."

Commission Chairman Krokhky was completely right. I have to stamp it out. Really, it's high time.

I'll go back home, back to my father, the rabbi who cast off something or other. I'll demand an explanation from him. How inconsiderate can you get? Aren't there lots of other professions? He could have become a gravedigger like my grandfather, or in the final analysis he could have made himself into a white-collar proletarian, a bookkeeper. Would it really have been so awful to work at a high desk, sitting on a revolving stool? What made him pick rabbi? And couldn't he see that it was totally unethical to have sons who are rabbi's sons? I'll go back home to see him. We'll have a major conversation.

---

1. Operating at places of employment and study, "purge commissions" in the Soviet 1920s and 1930s sought to identify and weed out members of families who were considered disenfranchised outcasts (*lishentsy*) based on their social background; the outcasts commonly included descendants of the "bourgeoisie" (defined rather loosely) and of clergy.

The prodigal son returns home. The prodigal son in a Tolstoyan peasant shirt and cannibal tie returns to his father. His heels echoing, he runs up the Varenna marble staircase to the fourth floor. In a melancholy voice he mutters:

"I live on the fourth floor, where the staircase ends."

He's pretending. He's not melancholy, he's nervous. The son hasn't seen his father in ten years. He forgets about the impending major conversation and kisses his father on his mustache, which smells of gunpowder and saltpeter.

Father asks anxiously:

"Do you need to wash up? There's the bathroom."

The bathroom is dark, as dark as it was ten years ago when the knocked-out windows were replaced by a piece of plywood. Nothing in father's apartment has changed in a decade.

In the dark I raise my hand overhead. There used to be a shelf there with soap in an enamel dish. My hand meets the shelf and finds the soap.

Shutting my eyes, I can make my way through the whole apartment without stumbling, without bumping into furniture. Memory saves me from colliding with a chair or the little table with the samovar on it. Maneuvering with closed eyes, I can pass into the dining room, take a left, and say:

"I am standing in front of the chest of drawers. It is covered with a linen runner. On it is a mirror, a blue porcelain candlestick, and a photograph of my brother whose schoolmates called him Jumbo. He was a chubby boy, and at that time all chubby boys were called Jumbo. As for the real Jumbo, that was an elephant."[2]

Opening my eyes, I see the chest of drawers, the runner, the candlestick, and the photograph . . .

The apartment is like a ship. The furniture seems riveted into the floor, placed there once and forever. Father stands beside me, stroking his gunpowder mustache.

Why does his mustache smell of gunpowder? Because he's not a captain and not a hero of battle—he's a rabbi, an unethical servant of a cult, and a duplicitous hypocrite to boot. Did he stop believing in god? Not at all. He apparently came home one day, let out a sigh, and said:

"Taxes are killing me. Seventeen rubles a month for electricity. It's robbery."

And he cast off his robe, that is, not a robe but something like that. A simple matter: electricity won out over religion.

But that didn't help me. I remained a rabbi's son. The victory of the light bulb in the toilet over the Almighty did not help me in the slightest.

A father like that should be despised. But I feel that I love him. So what if his mustache smells of saltpeter? Ham also smells of saltpeter, and nobody demands that it lead troops into battle.

---

2. Evgeny Petrov's brother, Valentin Kataev, referred to an actual elephant by that name, a celebrity of one of Odessa's menageries, who went berserk and held the city captive for a whole week before he was shot down.

My father has sixty-year-old amethyst eyelids and a scar on his cheek, an immobile ship's scar.

Shame—I love a rabbi!

The heart of a Soviet citizen, a citizen who believes in the building of socialism, trembles with love for a rabbi, the former instrument of a religious cult. How could this have happened? Comrade Krokhky was right. Apple, apple, tell me who your friends are, and I'll tell you who'll eat you up.

Horror: my father is an apple tree, a rabbi with a leafy beard. I have to renounce him, but I can't. No, there won't be a major conversation, I love my father too much. And I only ask:

"Why, why, did you become a rabbi?"

Father is surprised. He looks at me with tender anxiety and says:

"I never was a rabbi. You dreamed this. I am a bookkeeper, a hero of labor."

And sadly he strokes his gunpowder mustache.

The dream ends with a motorcycle revving up and firing. I wake up, joyful and excited.

How good to be a loving son, how pleasant to love your father if he's a bookkeeper, if he's a white-collar proletarian and not a rabbi.

1930

Translated from the Russian by Alice Nakhimovsky

The title of Ilf and Petrov's second novel hints, diminutively, at the episode in Exodus 32 where the wandering Jews, weary of waiting for Moses, ask Aaron to make them a golden calf to worship. Aaron acquiesces and has an idol made from the molten gold jewelry collected from women and children. Returning from the mount, the wrathful Moses destroys the idol (see also 1 Kings 12 and 2 Chronicles 10 and 11 on Jeroboam and the schism of the Jewish tribes).

The Little Golden Calf depicts a scheme that Ostap Bender and his cohorts mastermind so as to "relieve" the "underground" Soviet millionaire Koreyko of his wealth. Bender's associates include the Jew Panikovsky, whose name suggests "panic"; the name of the profiteer Koreyko signals treyf (non-Kosher), derived as it is from koreyka, Russian for "cured pork." Through a series of road adventures, Bender succeeds in obtaining Koreyko's money but fails to cross the border. After the riches are confiscated by Romanian border guards, Bender is sent back to the USSR.

In addition to featuring major and minor Jewish characters, The Little Golden Calf reflected a moment in Jewish-Soviet history, as it appeared to Ilf and Petrov in 1929–30. While paying lip service to what was at the time the official campaign against antisemitism, Ilf and Petrov restricted the Jewish problem to individual antisemites, anachronisms of the pre-Revolutionary tsarist past. At the same time, the positioning of Hiram Burman, an American newspaper correspondent and a Zionist, in the opening chapter of part three, is meaningful. With a group of newspapermen, Burman takes a "special-charter train" bound for the construction of the Turkestan–Siberia Railroad (Turksib). Completed in 1931 as a major project of the First Five-Year Plan, Turksib ran from the Trans-Caspian Railroad to the Trans-Siberian Railroad, linking Central Asia and Siberia. In 1930 a measly Jewish district was incorporated in Birobidzhan (see introduction to Viktor Fink in vol. 1), the Soviet ideological machine trumpeting to the world the "success" of a Jewish national enclave in the Far East. Both the direction of the connected railroads and Burman's skepticism toward the Soviet rhetoric on the Jewish question prompt a reading of Ilf and Petrov's satire not only along but also against its Soviet grain. In the chapter that follows the one reproduced below, Ostap Bender narrates the "Story of the Wandering Jew," in which the ancient Jew (in Russian, literally "Eternal Yid") meets his death in 1919 at the hands of Simon Petlyura's Ukrainian troops. An Austrian journalist "sells" Bender's "story" to Burman, who prints it in his American newspaper. The inserted "Story of the Wandering Jew" is supposed to betoken the annihilation of traditional Jewish (Judaic) living, which in the Soviet Union has been replaced by a society in which there are Jews but no Jewish question. Still, one detects double irony in Ilf and Petrov's treatment of the Jewish question. In 1930, were Ilf and Petrov laughing about the future of Soviet Jews as they peeked out the window of the train taking them to the Turkestan–Siberian Railroad?

From *The Little Golden Calf*
Ilya Ilf and Evgeny Petrov

PART 3, CHAPTER 26

Passenger of the Special-Charter Train*

A short special-charter train stood in the asphalt bay of the Ryazan Station[3] in Moscow. It had only six cars: a luggage car, which, contrary to the usual, stored not luggage but a supply of food on ice; a restaurant car, from which a chef in white kept peeking out; and a governmental lounge. The other three were couch cars, and their berths, clad in coarse striped covers, were waiting to accommodate a delegation of shock workers,[4] as well as foreign and Soviet correspondents.

The train was headed for the linking of the tracks of the Eastern Railroad.[5]

The trip ahead of them was long. The shock workers were shoving into the car vestibules their travel baskets with little black padlocks dangling on metal rods. The Soviet journalists were dashing about the platform, swinging lacquered plywood cases.

The foreigners kept an eye on the porters who were moving their big leather suitcases, trunks, and hat boxes with the colorful stickers of travel agencies and steamboat companies.

The passengers had already managed to procure copies of the booklet *The Eastern Railroad*, the cover of which depicted a camel sniffing a rail. Copies of the booklet were sold on the spot, off a luggage cart. The author of the book, the journalist Palamidov, had already walked by the cart several times, casting vigilant glances at the buyers. He was considered an expert on the Eastern Railroad and was going there for the third time.

The departure time was nearing, but the parting scene didn't at all resemble the send-off of a regular passenger train. There were no elderly women on the platform, and nobody was sticking a baby out the window so that it could cast one last look at his grandfather. Nor was there a grandfather, whose dim eyes usually reflect a fear of railroad draughts. Needless to say, nobody was kissing. The delegation of shock-workers was accompanied to the train station by trade-union leaders who hadn't yet

---

*The text has been slightly abridged.

3. Presently Kazan Station in Moscow.

4. "Shock worker" is a less than perfect albeit accepted literal translation of the Soviet Russian term *udarnik*. *Udarniki* were initially Soviet overachieving workers who "overfulfilled" their quotas; the term eventually came to designate any Soviet employees who achieved high records of output; they were rewarded by the system and given special privileges.

5. Il'f and Petrov are referring to the Turkestan–Siberia Railroad (Turksib).

worked out the protocol of goodbye kisses. Members of editorial staffs had come to see off their Moscow correspondents, and on such occasions they were used to limiting themselves to handshakes. As to the foreign correspondents, all thirty of them were traveling to the opening of the railroad in full order, with wives and gramophones, so they had no one to see them off. [. . .]

Ukhudshansky,[5] a correspondent of a trade union paper, arrived at the station well before anybody else and was leisurely strolling along the platform. He was carrying with him *The Turkestan Region, Being a Full Geographical Description of Our Fatherland, a Reference and Travel Book for the Russian People*, compiled by Semenov-Tian-Shansky[6] and published in 1903. Now and then he would stop next to a group of departing passengers or ones seeing someone off and say with something of a sarcastic note in his voice, "Departing, ha? Well, well!" or "Staying, ha? Well, well!"

In this manner he walked up to the head of the train, looked at the locomotive for a long time, his own head pulled back, and finally said to the engineer, "Working, ha? Well, well!"

Then the journalist Ukhudshansky went into his compartment, unfolded the most recent issue of his union paper, and surrendered himself to reading his own article titled "Improve the Work of Small Business Commissions" and subtitled "Commissions Are not Being Sufficiently Restructured." The article contained a report on some meeting, and the author's attitude toward the event being described could have been defined by a single phrase, "Convening, ha? Well well!" Ukhudshansky read on until the departure. [. . .]

In the meantime, the train, rushing out of Moscow-in-scaffolding, had already started its deafening song. Its wheels banged, sending hellishly laughing echoes under the bridges, and only after entering the wooded area of country homes did the train settle down a bit and go at high speed. The train was going to make an impressive curve across the globe, traverse several climate zones, travel from the cool of central Russia to the hot desert, leave behind many large and small towns, and beat Moscow time by four hours.

---

5. The humorous last name Ukhudshansky is actually derived from the Russian verb *ukhudshat'*, which means "to make things worse."
6. Il'f and Petrov are referring to *Rossiia polnoe geograficheskoe opisanie nashego otechestva. Nastol'naia i dorozhnaia kniga dlia russkikh liudei*, ed. V.P. Semenov-Tian'-Shan'skii, under the general supervision of P.P. Semenov-Tian'-Shan'skii and V.I. Lamanskii (St. Petersburg, 1899–1913), incomplete; vol. 19 *Turkestanskii krai* (1903). Petr Semenov-Tian-Shansky (1827–1914) was a famous Russian explorer of Central Asia.

Toward evening of the first day, two heralds of the capitalist world made an appearance in the car of the Soviet correspondents: a representative of a free-thinking Austrian paper, Mr. Heinrich, and an American, Mr. Hiram Burman. They came to introduce themselves. Mr. Heinrich wasn't very tall. Mr. Hiram was wearing a trilby. Both spoke rather clean and correct Russian. For some time everybody stood in the corridor silently, curiously looking each other up and down. At first, they talked about the Moscow Art Theater. Heinrich praised the theater, and Mr. Burman evasively remarked that as a Zionist he was mainly interested in the Jewish question in the USSR.

"We no longer have this question," said Palamidov.

"How can there be no Jewish question?" marveled Hiram.

"There just isn't. Doesn't exist."

Mr. Burman was beginning to feel agitated. He had spent his whole life writing articles on the Jewish question for his newspaper, and he would have found it painful to part with the subject.

"But aren't there Jewish people in Russia?" he asked cautiously.

"Sure," replied Palamidov.

"Then the question is there also?"

"No. There are Jews, but no question."

The tension that had accumulated in the corridor of the train car was released by the arrival of Ukhudshansky. He was walking to the washroom with a towel over his neck.

"Talking, ha?" he said, rocking from the quick run of the train. "Well, well!"

By the time he was walking back, clean and energetic, with droplets of water on his temples, the argument had consumed the entire corridor. Soviet journalists had left their compartments, several shock workers had showed up from the next car, and two more foreigners had arrived: an Italian correspondent with a Fascist badge depicting a bundle of lictor's rods and a mace, and a German professor of oriental studies who had been invited to the celebration by the All-Union Society of Cultural Ties. The front line of the argument was very long—from building socialism in the USSR to the men's berets that were becoming fashionable in the West. And on all topics, whatever they were, disagreements arose.

"Arguing, ha? Well, well," said Ukhudshansky, retiring to his compartment.

Only separate exclamations were audible in the overall noise.

"If that's the case," said Mr. Heinrich, pulling the Putilov Factory worker Suvorov[7] by his Russian shirt, "then why is it that you've just been blabbing about it for thirteen years? Why don't you organize the world revolution that you talk so much about? Because you can't? Then stop blabbing!"

---

7. A rather comical juxtaposition of the name of St. Petersburg's largest machine-building factory (Putilov, later renamed Kirov) and the last name of Russia's legendary military commander Field Marshal Aleksandr V. Suvorov (1729–1800).

"We aren't even going to make a revolution for you! You do it yourself!"

"Me? No, I won't be making a revolution."

"Well, then they'll do it without you and won't even ask your permission."

Mr. Hiram Burman stood leaning against the embossed leather partition and list-lessly looking at the arguing sides. The Jewish question had fallen through some discussionary crack at the very beginning of the conversation, and the other topics didn't spark any emotions in his heart. A poet-feuilletonist who used the pen name Gargantua[8] separated himself from the group in which the German professor was making positive remarks about the advantages of Soviet matrimony over the ecclesiastical one. He approached the pensive Hiram and started explaining something to him with great passion. Hiram listened at first but was soon convinced that he couldn't make out a single thing. In the meantime Gargantua kept fixing things in Hiram's outfit, tightening his tie, taking lint off him, buttoning and unbuttoning his coat, and all the while speaking very loudly and even distinctly. But there was some imperceptible defect in his speech that turned his words into mulch. The problem was aggravated by the fact that Gargantua liked to talk and kept asking for confirmation from his interlocutor.

"It's true, isn't it?" he would say, twisting his head, as if he were going to peck some birdfeed with his nice big nose. "It's true, isn't it?

These were the only comprehensible words in all of Gargantua's speech. Everything else blended into a marvelous, convincing rumble. Mr. Burman kept agreeing out of politeness but soon ran off. Everybody kept agreeing with Gargantua, and he considered himself a person capable of convincing anybody of anything.

"See," he said to Palamidov, "you don't know how to talk to people. I persuaded him. I just proved it to him, and he agreed with me that we no longer have any sort of a Jewish question. It's true, isn't it? Isn't it?" [. . .]

The evening conversation was burning out. The clash of the two worlds had ended peaceably. Somehow, a fight didn't result. The coexistence on the charter train of the two systems—capitalist and socialist—would have to continue, willy-nilly, for about a month. The enemy of world revolution, Mr. Heinrich, told an old road-trip joke, after which everyone proceeded to the restaurant car for dinner, walking from one train car to the other over shaking metal shields and squinting from a windy draught. In the restaurant car, however, the two sides sat separately. It was right there, over dinner, that the bride show took place. The "abroad," represented by the world's correspondents of the largest newspapers and telegraph agencies, decorously applied itself to the grain spirits and looked with terrible politeness at the shock workers in

---

8. Protagonist of François Rabelais's *Gargantua et Pantagruel* (1532–64), an enormous man.

jackboots and the Soviet journalists who, after a homey fashion, showed up in slippers, wearing only shirtsleeves and no neckties.

A wide range of people sat in the restaurant car: the provincial Mr. Burman from New York City; a Canadian girl who had arrived from the other side of the ocean only an hour before the departure of the charter train and who for that reason was still discombobulated, twirling her head over a cutlet in a long narrow metal dish; a Japanese diplomat and also another, younger Japanese man; Mr. Heinrich, whose yellow eyes twinkled with a derisive smile; a young English diplomat with the thin waist of a tennis player; a German orientalist, who rather patiently listened to the conductor's account of the existence of a strange animal with two humps on its back; an American economist; a Czech; a Pole; four American journalists, among them a pastor who wrote for the newsletter of the YMCA; and finally a blue-blooded American lady with a Dutch last name from an old pioneer family, who had abandoned a train in Mineralnye Vody[9] and for purposes of self-promotion had spent some time hiding in the station cafeteria (this event raised havoc in the American press, and for three days the papers published articles with such sensational titles as "Girl from Venerable Family in Clutches of Wild Hill Tribesmen of the Caucasus" and "Death or Ransom"); and many, many others. Some of them felt animosity toward anything Soviet, others hoped to figure out—as soon as possible—the enigmatic souls of the Asians, yet others diligently tried to comprehend what was really going on in the land of the Soviets.

The Soviet side made lots of noise at its tables. The shock workers brought food in paper bags and applied themselves to tea with lemon in glass holders made of shiny Krupp metal. The wealthier journalists ordered schnitzels, and one Lavoisian,[10] overcome by a sudden paroxysm of Slavophilia, decided to put on a show in front of the foreigners by ordering sautéed kidneys. He didn't eat the kidneys because he had disliked them since childhood, but he was all puffed up with pride nevertheless and kept casting defiant looks at the foreigners. The Soviet side likewise included different sorts of people. There was a worker from the Sormov Shipyard, voted to go on the trip by a general factory meeting, and a construction worker from the Stalingrad Tractor Factory who ten years earlier had lain in the trenches fighting Vrangel's[11] troops in the very same field where the tractor-building giant now stood; and a textile worker from Serpukhov who was interested in the Eastern Railroad because it was supposed to speed up the delivery of cotton into the textile regions. [. . .]

---

9. Mineral'nye Vody (literally "Mineral Waters")—a resort of curative waters in the Stavropol Region of Russia in the foothills of the North Caucasus.

10. This seemingly Armenian name ("Lavuazian" in exact transliteration) is a pun on the name of Antoine Laurent Lavoisier (1743–1794), one of the founders of modern chemistry.

11. Vrangel, Pyotr (1878–1928)—baron, general, and commander of the Volunteer Army (the White Army) from early 1920 until its defeat and evacuation from the Crimea in November of that year.

Later on, when even Ukhudshansky was already asleep, the car door opened, making audible the unrestrained thunder of the wheels but for a moment, and Ostap Bender entered the empty shining corridor, staring around. He hesitated for a second then sleepily waved his hand and opened the door of the first compartment. Gargantua, Ukhudshansky, and the photographer Menshov were sleeping by the light of a blue night lamp. The fourth berth, an upper one, was empty. The great master plotter didn't give it much thought. Feeling weak in his legs after all his wanderings, irreparable losses, and the two hours he had spent riding on the steps of the train car, Bender climbed up.

From there, a miraculous vision appeared to him: a white-fleshed boiled chicken was lying on the table by the window, its legs stuck in the air like two shafts. [. . .] He picked up the chicken and ate it without bread or salt. He stuck the bones under the hard sackcloth mattress. He fell asleep happy, to the squeaking of the partitions, inhaling the inimitable smell of railway paint.

1931

Translated from the Russian by Margarit Tadevosyan Ordukhanyan
in collaboration with Maxim D. Shrayer

MARK EGART

Mark Egart (1901–1956), fiction and nonfiction writer, was born Mordekhay Boguslavsky in Krivoy Rog, Ukraine; Egart based his pen name on his mother's maiden name, Elgart. His father was a teacher at the town's Jewish elementary school. In 1922 Egart left home with a group of *He-Halutz* (Heb. *The Pioneer*) members. He spent a year in Poland, working and recruiting other *halutzim*.

Egart spent three years in the British Mandate of Palestine, arriving there in 1923. He experienced unemployment and hunger, and conflicts with the Arab population and the British authorities. Disillusionment with the merciless realities of the marketplace and class division among Jews, coupled with the economic crisis of 1926–28 in Palestine, resulted in Egart's decision to return to the USSR. According to the writer's daughter, Frida Egart, the crucial factor was his progressing illness, tuberculosis of the bones.

While living in Moscow in 1928, Egart turned to writing and joined a proletarian-oriented literary group. After traveling with a group of writers to the Altai Mountains in 1930, Egart wrote *The Crossing: Altai Sketches*. Describing collectivization in the Altai region, *The Crossing* appeared in 1932 in the series "New Works of Proletarian Literature"; it came out in English and German in Moscow that same year. In 1932 Egart published his most important literary work, the novel *Scorched Land*, about the struggles of young Jewish settlers in Palestine. Book One was serialized in *October* (*Oktiabr'*), numbers 9–12 (1932), overlapping in one issue with Mikhail Sholokhov's *Quiet Flows the Don*; Egart's entire novel appeared in book form in two separate volumes (book 1 in 1933 and book 2 in 1934). In 1937, the year when a "corrected" version of *Scorched Land* came out in one volume, Egart published the factory novel *Marusya Zhuravleva*. Reprinted in 1948, *Marusya Zhuravleva* was supplemented by an equally formulaic sequel, *Friends* (1950).

In January 1940, Egart published the short novel *Talisman*, about a Soviet careerist, in *Novy mir*. Like *Scorched Land*, *Talisman* was never reprinted after World War II. Despite poor health, Egart served as a fiction editor at Navy Publishing House during the war, and subsequently he worked for many years as head of the Commission for Young Authors at the Soviet Writers' Union. After the war, Egart mainly wrote for adolescents. Some of Egart's works, especially his "adventure tale" *Bay of Mists*, remained in print into the 1980s.

●❖

In addition to *Scorched Land*, Egart addressed the Jewish experience in the tale "Sinner Khet and Righteous Lot," composed for the desk drawer in the summer of 1953. A biblical allegory reminiscent of Lev Lunts's "Native Land" (1922, in vol. 1), it was printed in 1997 in the Russian-American magazine *Messenger* (*Vestnik*).

Told in the agonistic first-person voice, *Scorched Land* followed Egart's autobiographical protagonist, Lazar Dan, from the former Pale to the British Mandate of Palestine. Egart presented Dan's life in his home town in Ukraine, Gnilopol (from the Russian word *gniloi*, "rotten"), as one plagued by poverty and disemboweled by pogroms and one his idealistic *halutz* left behind. In many Soviet literary works (e.g., in this anthology, Yury Libedinsky's *The Commissars* and Iosif Utkin's *The Tale of Red-Headed Motele*), historical logic brought Jewish characters to the Revolution. Egart's Soviet novel is unprecedented for outlining an alternative, if broken, trajectory: to emigration and building a Jewish enclave in Palestine. In the words of Vladimir Khazan, "in *Scorched Land*, it seems, for the first and last time in Soviet literature, was sounded an unhidden sympathy for Zionism, naturally paling in comparison with the novel's overall concept." Part 1 of book 1 opened with an epigraph from Theodor Herzl's *The Jewish State*. Politically advantageous in the early 1930s, the novel's tendentious narrative logic clamored for a Marxist-Leninist conclusion: only in the USSR—and not in Palestine—can the Jewish question be "solved." Book 2 ended with the departure of the Soviet-bound Dan from Tel Aviv and included no scenes of life in the USSR. The coarse texture of Egart's prose captured the prosaics of the daily lives of *halutzim*, the harshness of physical work, the malarial swamps, and the rough-hewn hills of Galilee. The emasculated 1937 edition could not erase all of Egart's admiration for the *halutzim*, although it did its best to obliterate the lyrical-authorial pathos of the Palestinian parts of the novel while making the anti-Zionist narrative argument unambiguously clear. Still, even the revised edition stands in contrast to the schematic, simplistic treatment of the subject by Semyon Gekht (1903–1963). In Gekht's novel *The Steamship Sails to Jaffa and Back* (Moscow, 1936), the protagonist reached Palestine *only* to return to the Soviet Union.

Egart's major novel was deleted from Soviet literary history. But its copies have survived, mainly in libraries outside the USSR, and a section of book 2 follows below. Part 2 of book 2 bears the bitterly ironic title "Song of Songs."

From *Scorched Land*
Book 2, Part 1, Chapters 6–8*

CHAPTER 6

[My father], the *melamed* [Sholom-Gersh], lives on the lake. After praying and reading the day's chapter, he takes a turn around our properties. That's all he does all week, measures with his steps the length of the vineyard and the orange plantation, counts the number of *dunams* and converts them into *desiatina*.[1]

"What can I say, the land here isn't all that good," sighs the *melamed*.

He doesn't understand the collective life and is convinced that all of it is just for show, kind of like when work cattle from different owners are used in the same harness. In the end, each person can be his own master. Let the Bolsheviks pull their tricks. The Jews will manage without tricks.

"A Jew," says Sholom-Gersh, "likes to know what's in his pocket and what's not in his pocket. A Jew can't make it any other way." He strokes his grayish scrawny beard and raises his index finger. The familiar finger of the Jewish small town casuist, yellow with tobacco stains and dirt. "A Jew must . . ."

And in the evening father presides in the barrack, as previously in the *heder* in Gnilopol,[2] and sermonizes. But his listeners are few here: only the patient Nekhama and the kindhearted Niakha, who holds the learned *melamed* in high esteem.

"Jewish businesses in Gnilopol are coming to an end," bemoans father, "and Jewish life is also ending . . . Just think—the shtetl is left without a rabbi, without a *shochet*, without a *heder*, and the synagogue has been turned into a Communist club! Jewish children join the *kasamol*[3] and take off. [. . .] They abnegate their parents, eat *treyf*, and marry Russians. Gnilopol looks like an almshouse—nothing but old people. Everyone is running off to Moscow, as if Moscow was Jerusalem. But if Moscow becomes Jerusalem, that's the end of the Jewish people . . ."

"The end . . . the end," sighs the *melamed*, rocking Zevulan on his knees. His bony fingers that have never handled diapers tuck in the flannel blanket, and the faded eyes with red blood vessels look at me with reproach. Surely, it's better to rock your own grandchild than somebody else's. A Jew without a wife is like a carpenter without a saw. A Jew . . ."

---

*The text has been slightly abridged.

1. *Dunam*—measure of area in the Middle East; 1 *dunam* = 1 square kilometer, or about 0.3 acre; *desiatina* (pl. *desiatiny*)—old Russian measure of area; 1 official desiatina = 2.7 acres.

2. Gnilopol (literally "rotten town") is the ironically fictitious name of the protagonist's home town in Ukraine where his father was a teacher in a Jewish elementary school.

3. *Shochet* = ritual slaughter; *heder* = non-kosher; *kasamol* = a mispronunciation of Komsomol, the Young Communist League.

Binka picks up Zevulan, who is sleeping already, and leaves.

". . . will write to Gnilopol—let them not worry. And to Tovia Senderey he will write: Reb Tovia, you like the Bolshevik bread . . . *Oy*, Reb Tovia, that bread is bitter, take a Jew's word. A Jew must have his own Jewish bread, a Jew must . . ."

Tired from the day's work, Nyakha wants to sleep. He rolls his sleepy little eyes but hesitates to leave. Then finally he takes off. Nekhama also takes off and puts out the light. Father gropes his way back to the tent. I hear his mumbling, "While there's a Jewish God in heaven . . ."

Shortly after his arrival, father went to town to find out if they needed a synagogue beadle there. But Tiberias[4] has its own beadles. Perhaps he should inquire in Tsfat. They have a yeshiva there. There they should find a place for a learned Jew. For a week, father waits for a ride to Tsfat. But Tsfat, the town of the devout, has no place for him either.

Kopl Farfel is angry with me. Why won't I say anything? Nobody is driving out the old man. Let him look after the children, after the cow, if he's so restless.

"It's no joking matter," he instructs my father, "to look after a cow that has nothing to eat and three kids who won't give anyone a moment's rest."

And Binka, outraged by my indifference, hands Zevulan to my father.

"Zevulan always cries when he's with him," she points her finger at Kopl, "but with you he even laughs."

Sholom-Gersh reddens with pleasure, and his little beard juts upward.

"Coochi-coochi," he wrinkles his bristly mouth, "coochi-coochi-coo."

Heavy with milk, our Holland cow slowly climbs up the scorched slopes in search of grass. Suffering from hunger, she pushes her forehead into the prickly fence of the stone pool behind which the feed rustles invitingly; she tears her dressy coat on the thorns, thumps her horns against the stones, and moos threateningly. Women sigh loudly when they hear her hungry mooing. Not trusting my father, they drop their work, crawl between cliffs seeking out the shadowy cool corners where the grass hides, protected from the deadly rays, and then take the precious heaps to the barn. And the next morning the drawn-out mooing comes again from the mountain.

The mooing reminds me of the twenty Egyptian pounds the bank expects us to pay [. . .].

"Why do we need a cow?" I ask Nekhama, who's working with me in the vineyard. "All the same, we won't be able to raise the children here, even with the old nanny from Gnilopol. What? He's my father, so what? . . . And the cow, what is she, my wife? . . ."

Nekhama is silent. [. . .]

Nekhama bends down to the drying vines and submissively waits for me to pick up

---

4. Tiberias—town on the western shore of the Sea of Galilee (Lake Kinneret), near where the protagonists of Edart's novel set up their agricultural commune; Tiberias was founded by Herod Antipas around 18 C.E. and named after the emperor Tiberius.

the sprinkler. Her submissiveness irritates me.

"I'll sell the cow," I scream at Nekhama. "Don't call me the leader again if I don't sell the stupid beast."

In the evening, we came close to a fight. The women wouldn't even let me open my mouth. They called me a monster, a heartless bachelor. Whatever. The cow will have a calf, a calf. . . . Binka called me a "withered fig tree," wrathfully pressing Zevulan to her chest.

"Fine, if I'm a fig tree, let the cow deal with all the debts."

Kopl interfered: why not make some extra money on fish? He's been thinking about it for a while. An entire crew used to fish in Migdal.

"There're more fishermen in town than customers."

"Eh . . . ," Sholom-Gersh draws out in a goat-like voice. "Customers? What about Jews? A Jew must buy from a Jew, a Jew . . ."

"Of course he must," the women say in one voice and immediately fall to proving the merits of Kopl's idea. Binka even suggests selling fried fish—in Tiberias they probably haven't ever tasted a stuffing as delicious as she and Kuntsya make.

Nobody speaks for a few moments. Then the entire bunch of us marches to the vineyard, where an old, cracked boat lies near the fence, abandoned by its last owners. Kopl, Zelig, Binka, and I force the grips of the boat-hooks under the keel and get the boat down to the shore as on rollers. Kopl inspects it and announces that we must caulk the cracks and make paddles, better yet—a sail out of the old tent that's lying around in the shed. Kopl crawls on all fours around the battered boat, and the women look at him with hope. He understands; he is a father himself.

On the road, a group of prisoners who are fixing the bridge by Tsemakh walk by clanking their shackles. The dust rises in a dense white cloud. From down below, it looks like cattle raising the dust and ringing their bells.

"*Haydamaki!*"[5]

A man in a convict's robe stops and looks down. Dust is flailing off him like flour.

"*Haydamaki!*" he yells and limps on, driven by the convoy.

---

5. Derived from the Turkish "*hayda/haydi!*" (go/move!), the Ukrainian exclamation "*Hayda!*" ("Go! Let's go!") gave birth to the noun *haydamak* (plural *haydamaki*). The *haydamaki* were Ukrainian Cossack rebels in eighteenth-century Ukraine during the hostilities between Poland and Russia. Continuing the traditions of the 1648–52 major uprising under the leadership of Bohdan Khmelnytsky and considering Jews to be Polish hirelings and enemies of Ukrainian peasants, the *haydamaki* inflicted violence against the Jewish population of the territories they raided, killing and torturing Jews, desecrating their synagogues, and ravaging their communities. A number of smaller and larger *haydamak* uprisings took place, most notably in 1733–34, 1750, and 1768 (the biggest, led by Maxym Zaliznyak and Ivan Honta). In the Jewish collective memory, the term "*haydamaki*" is associated not with the Ukrainians' striving for independence and freedom but with massive brutality against the Jews in Ukraine. In Egart's novel, Sender Kipnis, a Communist Jewish settler from Ukraine arrested by the occupying British authorities, figuratively refers to anyone he perceives as prone to use brutal force, regardless of their ethnic makeup, as "*haydamaki*."

Only now do we realize that it's Sender Kipnis [. . .]. Kopl looks back uneasily; has Binka seen her brother? Binka's not around—she's somewhere, busy with Zevulan. "I've always said," starts Kopl, calming down, "I've said . . ."
All of a sudden I feel hot.
"Whoever works, works; whoever fights, let him fight like he should," I whisper and look in the direction where the shackle-bearers, hurried by the guards, plod on.
We spent the entire week caulking the boat. The women climbed all over the cliffs in search of moss. Zelig Slushch procured some tar from a construction site in town. We built a mast, made a sail, found a dragnet in Dgania.[6]
Kopl suggested going in from the shore to get a feel for the place first. That was a complete waste of time, because all the fish here had already been scared off, but again the women backed Kopl. They now trusted Kopl more than me.
Our entire commune participated in dropping the dragnet. The women put on leggings and went with us. Even the seven-year-old Khaimka was whining and asking to go with us. And father was giving advice from the shore. Zelig Slushch, as the tallest, and Kopl, as the most knowledgeable, were leading the others, and they went in deeper and deeper, they stumbled and quietly cursed. Kopl was worried that the lanky Zelig would rip the net.
Warmed through by the summer sun, the water babbled through the openings of the net, boiling over with rainbow-colored bubbles. The fidgety Kuntsya tripped, swallowed some water, and started coughing. I yelled at her and told her to go back to shore, but she didn't leave. Kopl started turning in. Everyone quieted down, and, gathering their strength, pulled.
Kopl walked to the shore, and the net dragged behind him. First there appeared Kopl's shoulders, round as a woman's; then, his chest covered in red hair; then, his white boxers. One minute . . . two . . . three. He came onto the shore. Two tenches, like two blinding rays, like two knifes, glistened and fluttered on the hot stones. That was the entire catch.
Embarrassed, Kopl began explaining that for starters even tenches are good, but now even Binka wouldn't listen to him. They made fish-chowder out of the tenches, and at night we went out fishing to the middle of the lake.

CHAPTER 7

The waters of Lake Kinneret gently lap at the decrepit boat. The green transparent waters melodiously babble against its beat-up nose; the oarlocks squeak in unison, and the tall sky languidly lowers its sunset sails. The mountains of Transjordan rise up in the smoke of distant fires. Their purple tails crawl over the faraway pale-blue wadi.[7]

---

6. Dgania—see introduction to Rahel in vol. 1.
7. Wadi (Arabic) = bone-dry; usually a narrow riverbed in the desert that occasionally flash floods at times of heavy rain; equivalent of "arroyo" in the southwestern United States; compare also "ravine" and "canyon."

Kopl hoists the mast made from the grip of a big pitchfork. The tarpaulin sail swells with the wind as it catches up to us from the hills of Galilee. The night paints the lake pale blue and violet. It moves the mountains closer and makes the air transparent and hollow. Somewhere to the right, the horses are stomping across a wooden bridge over the Jordan, the bells of a caravan jingle, and on the left the yellow towers of Tiberias rise out of the water. The resourceful Nyakha lights a fig-tree branch. I steer my way around Tiberias toward Migdal. There must be a suitable place there, in a narrow cove concealed by a cliff. The night sails over Kinneret, the fishermen sail through it, and our song sails along with us.

Early in the morning we return with a full catch and pull in to the shore at the wooden gangway of the town bazaar. A canopy made of ripped canvas sacks blankets the marketplace with latticed shadows, and the sun bursts like golden fountains through the holes. The hot sunbeam reflections chase each other over the wide chests, dive in between barrels filled with olives and figs, between vats steaming with meat and greasy pitas, and flash like rainbows on rugs, abayas, and colorful fabrics.

It's still that early hour when the coffeehouse on the shore is closed, the merchants of [. . .], *sabra*,[8] and grapes are still putting out their tables, and the water carriers are driving the donkeys down the crooked slopes to the lake. The embankment laid out in green tiles is empty, and only the fishermen who've just returned from nighttime fishing are drying and mending their nets.

A tall, hook-nosed fisherman [. . .] is gawking at us. He's munching olives, and his greasy mustache trembles with a threat. Who ever saw *yehudim* bringing fish to the marketplace? Really, there are no sneakier people than the *yehudim*. All strewn with large pockmarks, his olive face glitters with sweat like the olives he's holding in his cupped palm. He makes a loud noise as he spits out the pits, wipes his hands on his wide yellow trousers, and looks back at his mates.

The fishermen are sitting beside their nets—their lace-thin decrepit nets that must be mended daily—staring at their competitors. Dozens of eyes are mockingly examining our catch. Under the stares of the Tiberias fishermen, we sort the catch and put it in buckets. With our buckets, Zelig and I climb the mountain to the new part of town where the Jews live. Kopl and Nyakha stay behind, waiting for the stores to open.

We walk along the old Turkish wall, past the tower where there's now a barber-shop. We stop by the brand new building of the power plant. Zelig indecisively walks around the showy flowerbed in front of the plant and looks in from the back door. He returns in a minute. They don't need fish here—the electricians board at Antebi's. There is meat and fish there, and everything else. But they don't recommend asking Antebi—the Bukharan is stingy [. . .] and buys everything cheap from the Arabs.

Zelig lifts his bucket, and we move on. In one house they buy crucians from us but then return them—in summer, crucian carp may carry tapeworms. At the hospital, in the hospital kitchen, they ask us to supply them meat: "If you could only get fresh meat for the patients, we'd gladly take it. Every day even. But fish . . . Soon the stench will make it impossible to pass through the town."

---

8. *Sabra*—Heb. prickly pear = also known as aloe fruit, native to Northern Galilee.

We looked in on the secretary of Histadrut,[9] the doctor, the teacher at the Jewish school, and finally the owner of the bookshop. But the secretary wasn't home, and his wife turned out to be a vegetarian. The doctor didn't let us past the doorstep, mistaking us for patients. "Tell them to go to the hospital!" he passed word through a servant. "Hope he gets sick himself!" I yelled into the open door. The teacher hadn't gotten paid for three months. Besides, he doesn't like it when young people, young farmers, engage in trade. If you really think about it, if you compare . . . In his time, people found other ways to start out . . . A stooping man in tussah pants and a shirt tied with little blue pompons, had some spare time and didn't mind talking about starting out back in his day.

Only the owner of the bookshop, also the librarian, who loaned books to me, buys three tenches. He'll pay later, better yet, count it toward the subscription fee. True, we owe more, but it's okay, no strangers here—we'll square accounts. The librarian, a sickly looking obese man with a brown beard that looks black on his pale face and glasses with very thick lenses, has a strange last name: Bass. Bass is a member of Histadrut, Ahdut Ha-Avodah, Tarbut,[10] and the society for the support of physical renaissance. He likes saying that he would gladly abandon his business and join our commune. But his family . . . his wife . . . "Never get married," he tells me every time and looks through his thick glasses as through vitrines. "A wife is . . ." He sniffs his fingertips but can never say what a wife is.

Bass left Russia before the war, but he still loves Russian books and Russian newspapers, and he's the only person in town who dares subscribe to *Nakanune*.[11] Bass believes the best writers are Russians and the best literature is Russian. When people ask him for advice on what to read, he tells them with conviction to "read real literature" and shoves them something from his Russian stocks. This time he shows me a book by some Ehrenburg[12] and clicks his tongue with pleasure.

Zelig offers the bookseller a commission if he refers some buyers, in response to which Bass remarks, offended, that his business is books, and "fish . . . fish is for the bazaar." Zelig looks at me, I look at Zelig. We lift our buckets and walk toward the bazaar.

The unsold crucians splash in our buckets. Our damp pants stick to our tired knees. The sun hangs right over our heads.

The hook-nosed Galilean women in wide calico trousers and skirts hiked up to their waists walk toward us with pitchers. Their bracelet-like earrings and the piasters

---

9. Histadrut (Heb.)—acronym for the General Federation of Workers in Israel: trade-union federation of Israel founded in 1920.

10. Ahdut Ha-Avodah (Heb.) = labor unity; Socialist Zionist movement founded in Israel in 1919; in 1930 it was merged with Ha-Po'el Ha-Tzair to form the Mapai Party; Tarbut (Heb.) = culture; interwar Hebrew educational-cultural organization in Eastern Europe, with strongholds in Poland and Lithuania.

11. *Nakanune* (*On the Eve*)—Russian-language weekly published in Berlin in 1922–24; it advocated acceptance of and dialogue with the Soviet state.

12. Ilya Ehrenburg, in vol. 1.

plaited into their braids tinkle to the beat of their steps. Eyebrows purple with dye, fingernails red with henna, little violet stars on their lips. They bare their magnificent teeth and walk by. The water carriers haul their full waterskins. Donkeys bawl, turning their sly little muzzles toward the sun. Fanners, young boys, pull on thin ropes. And the fans, which look like brooms made of cane and palm leaves, drive the flies away from the merchants playing Syrian dominoes.

It's noon already. It's already hot. Arab youths moan in the *medrese*.

When we return to the dock, Nyakha Lyam is sitting in the boat by himself, and Kopl, with half a dozen fish strung on a stick, is walking around the marketplace in search of buyers. He greets us with looks of mockery—he wouldn't have come back with a full bucket. Kopl is beginning to get angry, cursing the Arabs who won't let him past the dock. It's obvious he is looking for someone on whom to take out his vexation. We sit in the full blaze of the sun, sleepy, tired, and silent.

Two fishing boats dock in, then three more, and then still more. They must have gone all the way to Transjordan and are just now returning. Huge nets shake out onto the dock's hot boards fluttering fish shiny with metallic luster. Mountains of shiny fish rise in front of our eyes.

We've been wasting our time, even Nyakha understands that now. But Kopl doesn't want to admit it. He gets into the boat and turns it sideways, so that nobody could moor here. The fishermen look at him and continue unloading. Soon their fish blocks off our boat. Then Kopl starts shoving it off with his feet. The hook-nosed guy [. . .] shakes his fist at Kopl.

"It's our marketplace and our livelihood," yells the hook-nosed guy.

"Lazar," Nyakha bugs me, "what's he doing?" . . . Nyakha looks like he is about to run away. The hook-nosed guy points at Nyakha with his finger and laughs. Kopl picks up an oar. In an instant, a crowd gathers.

"Make them leave! Make them get out of here! . . ."

The boys jump out of the water and cheerfully slap themselves on their wet bellies in anticipation of a fight. The police show up. They fine us for selling fish without a permit and tell us to get lost. Histadrut pays the fine for us—on the condition that we'll work it off later.

Kopl spent the entire day mending the torn net and yelling at the frightened Binka. This was the first time Kopl yelled at his wife, and it was the first time she listened to him. Wrapped to the waist in the net, he looked like someone not mending it but trying to untangle himself from its tight embrace. That evening, Kopl went out fishing again. Nobody wanted to accompany him.

Sender Kipnis, who was transporting pebbles from the shore that day, recognized him from a distance. Ignoring the warnings of the convoy, he limped toward Kopl. Who knows, maybe he wanted to see his sister, and maybe he wanted to learn about his old comrades. But Sender didn't ask about his sister or his friends.

"*Haydamaki!*" Sender yelled out and laughed. He turned around and saw me. "Prospectors!" he laughed even louder. The night was approaching, the prisoners were in a hurry to break camp, and Sender had to run pushing his wheelbarrow. And yet he was still laughing.

But I no longer cared. I looked at my bare, scratched feet, my ripped shirt mended many times over, and glanced at the shore, where my mangy comrades toiled in labor and scarcity. Through the dark night, I looked over at all those who bent their backs on the rough earth of Galilee, Samaria, and Judea, and I couldn't find words of hope for them. I remembered the town, the swaggering and ragged town, where there were many people, many words, and not enough joy, and I was indifferent to that as well. The wind threw splashes of water in my face. A gust of tirelessly humming wind passed over the lake. I turned my back to the wind. Back to the wind and the life of which I expected nothing.

I found Kopl by the little cove overgrown with oleanders that had shed their flowers; both boat and net were missing. The wind lifted his shirt, the waves came up to his knees, and he was throwing stones at someone unknown, struggling against the wind.

I turned around and walked away. "Manure for the land," I whispered. "Manure for the land of Israel . . ."

And maybe because the night was dark, or because now I was completely alone, I kept stopping and looking back. I seemed to have lost my tremulous home in this hapless night.

CHAPTER 8

Summer loomed over the lake like an inextinguishable bonfire. The cliffs would get sizzling hot; tufts of scorched grass shot red and rusty along the slope. The lake, exhausted with heat, lay motionless down below, and yellow scummy foam stirred like a spreading pestilence along the shores. And thousands of mosquitoes and midges buzzed all day and all night.

Our tents now stood at the edge of the water. And still it was stuffy. It was so stuffy that in the middle of the night Binka would wake up and start tearing her nightshirt. I could hear how she tossed under the clingy mosquito net, gasping, like a fish out of water. She would push herself out of the mosquito net in the darkness, lean over the suffocating Zevulan, and look over his sunken face. Unable to bear it, Binka would take the child into her arms and, careful not to wake him, carry him to the shore. She would hold him right over the water until his breathing grew slower and deeper. He would open his tiny mouth, all dried up from the ghastly heat, wake up and cry. He had been crying a lot recently.

Sometimes during these night hours I would approach Binka. With a bandage over my eye (I got a black eye at the Tiberias marketplace), I would roam along the shore and stare at the lake. I just couldn't sleep. I would come up to Binka, and she would cautiously retreat, glancing at the tent where Kopl slept.

She would go back to the tent with the child, and I would remain on the shore, staring at the moon's path that ran from my feet toward Transjordan. The silvery path would escape from me, and I couldn't hold on to it, just as I couldn't hold on to the past. [. . .] My book of exodus hadn't materialized, the Jewish truth hadn't risen up, and the cherished notebook was being used to roll smokes.

I would climb a cliff that looked like a stone embrace. The stone shoulders shuddered, and the stone lips, illuminated by the moon, longed for each other but couldn't connect.

A fat pelican sleeping on the cliff would heavily dart off into the darkness. He would circle over my head, and I tried to drive him away, but he only clanked his scissor-like beak. He knew that I'd tire off and leave and the cliff would be his again.

Woken up, Kopl Farfel would come out of his tent and yell angrily that it was time to sleep. Before us lay the lake, terrible in its taciturn beauty. Speechless and indifferent mountains surrounded us. Kopl would quiet down. He would gaze at the lake as if hoping to see his boat and slowly drag his feet back to the tent. Who knows, maybe he thought of the happiness that he had searched for so long and finally found at these shores. He asked himself: Was he happy? And couldn't find the answer.

And I just laughed.

Little by little, Kopl began to replace me in everything. A notice arrived from the bank, informing us that for every overdue day a fine would accumulate. The prices on wheat in Tiberias still held firm, but in Haifa and Jaffa they fell by 20 percent. There was talk that the government intended to import even more flour from Australia than in the previous year. Cheap flour, cheap bread, is beneficial to everyone. But what are the farmers supposed to do?

On his days off Kopl now went to town to get the news. They didn't promise anything good—prices on flour kept falling, and nobody knew when they would bottom out. Dgania, Kinneret, and Melhamia were managing. They had previous supplies, vegetable gardens, milk farms. They could ride it out. But what could the newcomers do? What were we to do, who had neither vegetable gardens, nor vineyards already turning a profit, nor feed—and the only cow had to be sold to pay off the debts? Binka never got to tend the calf. Moreover, we had to send Nyakha to town to earn money. An old bathhouse attendant had died in Tiberias, and Nyakha once again resumed his old trade.

He earned pretty decent money—the people of Tiberias couldn't praise their [new] bathhouse attendant highly enough. And Nyakha was also happy. And so was my father. He prayed in the town synagogue on the Ninth of Ab, and the rabbi promised to keep him in mind. The *melamed* no longer did anything except dispense advice.

"The land is rough here, of course, but the Jews must endure; the Jews have endured things that are much worse . . ." Sholom-Gersh would take off his yarmulke, glossy from years of wearing, and wipe with a handkerchief the bald spot that reflected the Galilean sky. He would run his fingers through his gray beard and pull out his lip. In his faded pants of faux leather and patched-up discolored *tallit katan*[13] worn over his old Gnilopol suspenders, sitting on a rock by ancient Lake Kinneret, he seemed so lost, so out of place that even the [. . .] sly pelican would click his beak-scissors with surprise and mockery, circling over the head of the learned *melamed*.

"Well," I would say to my father, "well, O wise one, the Cossacks on one side, the *haydamaki* on the other, and on the third . . . on the third . . ." And I would go over to Nekhama's; she dressed my wound and gave me advice about insomnia.

"She's kind," I would say to myself, "it's easy to get along with her." Without noticing it, I got used to visiting Nekhama. Her tent was really clean and cool, maybe because she lived alone. I listened to her stories about what guys used to be like in the past and how things used to be done. And now everyone had been scattered all over the place, and not a word from anyone. Guralnik had turned into a "commie," and Khaya Ber had gone back home to Kholm,[14] and Tsaler, Ben-Tsur, and Shoshana had moved to Tel Yosef. That's how life had turned out . . . Nekhama looked at me, and in her eyes were sadness, exhaustion, and submission to the inevitable fate.

One time I overheard a conversation. ". . . One can never escape what's intended for one," Kuntsya Lyam was saying [. . .] to Binka. "Nekhama is an honest girl . . ." Kuntsya pronounced the word "honest" with that special meaning with which married women who have never known great love and joy try to convince themselves that there is no other, better life than the one they live. I noticed how Kuntsya pursed her pale flat lips and recalled that she didn't approve of Binka's relationship with Kopl, considering it shameful for a wife to go swimming with her husband and kiss after they've had a baby. Binka probably remembered the very same thing, and at the thought that Kuntsya can—and probably does—judge her love, she turned bright red and went back to her place without saying anything.

"Binka," I called, but she didn't hear me. And Kuntsya weightily repeated, "Whatever's meant for a person . . ."

In the course of a few days Nekhama changed radically. She got hold of a light dress. It had probably been lying in some trunk for a long time, awaiting its hour. Nekhama cut off her short thin braids. It was funny and touching to look at her "Bubi Kopf" hairdo, which revealed a sharp helpless dimple on the back of her head; venturing to look younger than her age, the unmarried girl applied powder and tried to cover up her freckles.

But the freckles—huge, brown—mercilessly came back on her flabby cheeks and long desiccated arms. And yet they couldn't bring Nekhama down. Her eyes, which had been muddy-brown and despondent, now shined with the joy of fulfilled hopes,

---

13. *Tallit katan* (Heb.) = small *tallit*; four-cornered garment worn by very observant Jewish men; the shape of a *tallit katan* resembles a poncho.

14. Kholm (Yiddish; Pol. Chełm)—Edart is referring to the town (45 miles east of Lublin in Poland) that historically had a large Jewish population.

the hopes she had mourned on her long virginal nights. And this joy had straightened her skinny back, bent from constant work. Joy filled Nekhama's entire being and made her face almost pretty. A truly genuine love had entered her heart. In her withering days of maidenhood, the poor Nekhama had really fallen in love. And I didn't know what to do.

Nekhama used to work from morning until night, carefully peeled potatoes, washed the dishes, patiently busied herself in the cattle shed or the vineyard. Now, as soon as it got a little dark, she already got dressed up by her cot in front of a broken mirror, as if she was going out.

I stopped visiting her. I would take the road toward Tsemah, but Nekhama invariably found me under the pretense of having to go to the store, or to Dgania, or else as if by accident. As if it was possible to meet by accident on a deserted shore where only very few people lived.

Women already considered us husband and wife. They became even more convinced of this when Nekhama, stopping by to see Binka in the dusk and not finding Kopl there, said that it's not good for a husband to leave his wife alone in the evening— Lazar never leaves her by herself. Nekhama laughed, and Binka felt even in the dark that Nekhama was blushing.

Binka told Batsheva, Batsheva told Zelig, and Zelig told me. "Why is she making this up?" I wondered. I felt sorry for her. And Zelig kept sighing that even Lazar got himself ensnared. [. . .]

"No matter what you say, being a bachelor is better. And why were you so impatient, you should have waited until the fall . . ." With small-town simplicity, Zelig used to think out loud and pour over the minute details of my affairs . . .

In the morning, I went to work. I turned and cultivated the soil in the orange plantation, reattached and reinforced the tents, made a new feeder for the mules, then went with them far into the mountains and found a secluded wadi, from which I brought back two huge bales of grass. And when everything was done, I started carrying water for the plantings. [. . .]

Once I yelled at my father, who decided to instruct little Khaimka in his discipline. The *melamed* sat the boy down before a thick volume, which he had brought from Gnilopol, and rocking to and fro, as in a heder, drew out: "And . . . and . . . what did Rabbi Akiva[15] say . . . ?"

"Listen, sage," I yelled, "wrap up your wares, the market's closed."

That evening, Kopl Farfel came to see me in my tent.

"He's your father," said Kopl. "He's an old man."

"I'm old, too."

---

15. Rabbi Akiva—Akiva ben Joseph, ca. 40–135 C.E., great Talmudic scholar, Jewish leader, and martyr.

"You are going to have children, think about it, Lazar."

"I'm thinking."

"And Nekhama . . ."

"What do you want?"

Kopl left.

Zelig got up from the cot and leaned toward me. In the darkness, I saw his puzzled eyes and his neck overgrown with hair like a goat's. Zelig stared at me for a few minutes.

"Why am I here?" I asked loudly.

Zelig was silent.

"You don't know? . . . I don't know either. What do you all want?" I yelled.

But Zelig didn't want anything. He got scared.

At first, Nekhama took my estrangement as a joke. She continued to strike up light conversation and flirt with me, powder her freckles, and spend hours in front of the little mirror. But the joke had lasted for too long, and the joy was draining out of the girl's face. Like the flowers and grasses losing color and luster on the slopes of the nearby mountains, her short-lived joy was fading away from her face. And Nekhama's face became even yellower, older, and uglier. A morning came when Nekhama put on the old dress with caked balls of manure, rolled her sleeves up to her shoulders, once again parading all her freckles to the world. She now exhibited these big, red freckles as her shame, just as her fallen love was drowned in shame. But now I no longer felt sorry for her. And things went back to how they used to be.

One day after dinner, Nekhama approached me as though she wanted to tell me something. But Nekhama's eyes, counter to her will, counter to what her comrades expected of her, suddenly shone with such power, such anguish, such desperation, such joy appeared in her muddy eyes with thin, whitish eyelashes—and there was more joy than anything else—that I shuddered. But immediately Nekhama's face grew dim. She looked back, met Kuntsya's greedy stare, touched the bare back of her head helplessly and sorrowfully, as if trying to defend herself, and ran out. In the evening she was at work, as usual, then went to sleep, and we never saw her again.

We searched all around, went to Tiberias, Tsemah, and Dgania [. . .] But Nekhama was nowhere to be found. Again, for entire days I roamed around the shore and threw stones into the water. No, I wasn't tormented by remorse. After all, how was it my fault that she's crazy? And what was so special in me that she had to throw herself at me, get a fashionable haircut, and powder her nose?

I examined my reflection in the water and saw a familiar, narrow-chested, gray-eyed fellow, unshaven for quite some time, with eyebrows unevenly grown together, as if clinging to each other, and a swollen right eye. I shrugged my shoulders in bewilderment and so did my double in the water. No, my conscience didn't demand that I answer for it.

On the fourth day, we found Nekhama. I found her, when I went to the stone pool to get water. The water in the pool was transparent, motionless; it looked like a square block of green glass. Only the edges of the block were embroidered by a fluffy fringe of algae and seaweed, and tadpoles darted around it. Nekhama lay on the very bottom, face up and arms spread. She lay so calmly and her body swayed so rhythmically that it looked as if she were breathing.

"Nekhama!" I called out. And hearing my hoarse voice, I suddenly realized that Nekhama was dead.

Everybody gathered around the stone pool. Kopl and Zelig undressed and got in the water. But they couldn't pull out the drowned girl right away. Somehow her hair caught on the rocks, and her feet in thick English boots were pressed against the opposite wall of the reservoir. Binka had to run back down and get scissors. Kopl cut off a braid, and the girl, as if she were still alive, stood up on her heels, and popped her swollen, freckled face out of the water. Her wide mouth was smiling dolefully, and in that smile I once again read Nekhama's desperate last love.

Nekhama was buried the following day, after the necessary formalities, not far from the place where her short-lived happiness had run its course. On the hill, from where the lake, Transjordan, and Hermon[16] could be seen, we interred the girl's body and wrote on the marker: "Nekhama Grille. Died of great love." I made the inscription myself, and nobody objected.

After that, I packed my rucksack and announced that I was leaving. Father had gone over to Tsfat and would probably remain there, the cot could be sold—it's worth money after all, and so farewell.

"Farewell," I said. Nobody responded.

Only Kuntsya—her personality hadn't changed a bit—asked whether I intended to order a *matseva*[17] in Haifa for Nekhama. [. . .] Nyakha, who had come home for the funeral, pulled at his wife's sleeve, but Kuntsya spoke up once again about the *matseva* and about . . . see, Lazar, who'd ever have thought . . . oh, trouble, trouble. Kuntsya blew her nose loudly and went to prepare supper, Binka remembered she had to check on Zevulan, and Kopl took the mules to drink their evening fill. He didn't say a word.

Zelig saw me off. In front of the cliff he said goodbye. He put out his hand and wanted to say something. But he didn't. He just tapped me on the shoulder and turned back.

I walked toward the sunset amid the cold mountains that turned their backs on me. Like the Wandering Jew, I roamed through life and was everywhere a stranger.

1932

Translated from the Russian by Margarit Tadevosyan Ordukhanyan and *Maxim D. Shrayer*

---

16. See footnote to Henri Volohonsky's "The Summit of Hermon," in vol. 2.
17. *Matseva* (Heb.) = sepulchral stone, gravestone.

ARKADY SHTEYNBERG

Arkady Shteynberg (1907–1984), poet and translator, was born to an Odessan Jewish family. His father was a well-known physician, his mother had worked as a physician's assistant. Shteynberg had an Austrian governess. "I grew up in the atmosphere of religious freedom [. . .] There was no religious antagonism toward Christianity in our family," Shteynberg reminisced in 1979. Instructed in Hebrew, he became a bar-mitzvah in 1920. In Odessa he studied at St. Paul Reaschule, where instruction was in German.

In 1921 Shteynberg's family moved to Moscow. He began to write poetry at sixteen. In 1925 Shteynberg entered the VKhUTEMAS (Higher State Artistic and Technical Workshops) in Moscow. Throughout his life Shteynberg considered painting his "second profession." From 1927–28 he lived in Odessa, studying at the Art Institute but never took his art diploma after returning to Moscow. Poetry became his main focus.

Shteynberg's first publications date to 1928–29. He contributed poems to *Literary Gazette* (*Literaturnaia gazeta*), *Novy mir, Red Virgin Soil* (*Krasnaia nov'*), and other periodicals. Published in the *Literary Gazette* in March 1930, his poem "Wolf Hunt" impressed contemporaries, including Osip Mandelstam (in vol. 1) and Vladimir Mayakovsky. In 1930 Shteynberg became close to Eduard Bagritsky (in vol. 1), co-translating Arthur Rimbaud's "Parisian Orgy" (1871). "Bagritsky influenced me greatly," Shteynberg reminisced. "Later, not without difficulty, I freed myself of his influences."

In 1932, *Literary Gazette* deemed a poem by Shteynberg "formalistic." After that verdict he was unable to publish poetry and turned to translation, working for the State Publishing House of Literature, as did his friends the poets Semyon Lipkin (in vol. 2), Maria Petrovykh, and Arseny Tarkovsky, who also could not place their original poetry. Shteynberg translated works by Turkmen, Uzbek, and Ukrainian poets, a Yakut folk epic, and also works by the Montenegrin poet Radule Stijenski, who was living in exile in the USSR. Shteynberg amused his friends by creating a literary mystification: the "Karaite" poet Simkha Baklazhan ["Eggplant"] (cf. Ilya Selvinsky's "Karaite philosopher Babakai-Sudduk"; Selvinsky in vol. 1). Shteynberg spent much time in Tarusa, a town south of Moscow favored by artists and writers, and, by his own admission, lived in denial of what was going on in the country. Much to his surprise, Shteynberg was arrested in 1937. Although the NKVD interrogators could not beat a confession out of him, Shteynberg was charged with "terrorism," sentenced to eight years at labor camps, and sent to the Far East. In 1939 he was returned to Moscow and freed, and the verdict was overturned.

In a 1979 interview (published in 1997), Shteynberg referred to the war as "his happiest years" because he knew that "if we do not win [the war], that would be the end of the world, and, God knows, what else. . . ." Shteynberg volunteered in 1941 and was a major by the end of the war. He served in the army's Seventh Department, whose task was to "demoralize the enemy," and headed a special occupation political unit in Romania in 1944. In October 1944 he was arrested on charges of spying, which were eventually dropped; in 1947 he was sentenced to eight years for "anti-Soviet activity." His term ended in 1952; in 1953 Shteynberg was rehabilitated and returned to Moscow from Komi District.

Shteynberg resumed prolific work as a translator. He was one of the editors of the landmark anthology *The Tarusa Pages* (1961), which included his long poem *Bolkhovskoe* and a large selection of shorter poems. In the decades to follow, Shteynberg remained a "poet without a book," since only a handful of his poems appeared. In the 1960s he wrote what some consider his best work, the long poem *To the Rises.* Shteynberg's collection was accepted for publication but stalled, and he spent sixteen years fighting for it, refusing to surrender to all the demands of the publishing house Soviet Writer. *To the Rises,* a large collection of works by and about Shteynberg, finally came out in 1997, posthumously.

As a teenager, Shteynberg discovered Milton's *Paradise Lost,* which played a "tremendous role in the formation of [his] world vision." He spent eleven years working on a new Russian translation, which was published in 1976.

Both selected poems date to the 1930s but appeared in 1997. It is difficult to imagine their publication either in the Soviet 1930s or even during Khrushchev's Thaw. In "David awoke in an unfamiliar bedroom . . ." (1932), Shteynberg articulated with ruthless tenderness the sense of loss that an assimilating Jew experienced in the early Soviet decades, an emptying sense of becoming Sovietly one with *hoi polloi.* "One night I saw the Black Sea in a dream . . ." (1935) speaks of Shteynberg's nostalgia for Odessa, of which other "South-Westerners," including Isaac Babel and Eduard Bagritsky (both in vol. 1), also wrote in the early 1930s.

* * *

David awoke in an unfamiliar bedroom,
Grabbed his wallet, counted all his cash,
And instantly calmed down;
                    threw up his slender
Arms, like a pair of oars; massaged one shoulder,
Then flexed and stretched his muscles, bending back
Until his spinal column creaked like a lock.
He rubbed his eyes, surveying with a yawn
The woman on the bed who long ago
Had splayed her golden fleece out high and low
And now lay still as death while morning dawned,
But did not sleep . . .
                    Outside the thunder broke,
Then, once it finished swearing, departed.
The lightbulb seemed a bubble made of soap,
Transporting dust and rainbow-spotted sparkles.
The woman stared up at the ceiling's vault,
So high, pristine, without a chink or crevice,
And nigh invisible. It was remote
Like the longed-for *fleur d'orange* she'd once been promised
In girlhood, or like linens stashed away
And stiff with starch until her wedding day.

Meanwhile, David abruptly tired of lounging.
Spite lashed him, whiplike; boredom stung like gnats.
He checked his watch in order to keep countenance
And, muttering "Damn!" he dressed in seconds flat.
Hurry, hurry . . . He stubbed his toe and, shaken,
Knocked down a wineglass while buttoning his shirt;
He gargled with cologne, then, cold and curt,
Mumbled good-bye.
                    Again in him there wakened
Last evening's consciousness of lack, depletion,
Sterility, bereavement, homelessness . . .
He gazed intently at her simple features,
Searching for signs of likeness, trying to guess
Another face's contours . . .

We're all the same: we argue, cause commotion;
Fate flings to us now frost, now flame, then hurls
The useless love of a tipsy office girl
Into our lives, like rain upon the ocean.

                                                    1932

                              * * *

One night I saw the Black Sea in a dream,
As an aging man might see his long-lost mama.
I dreamed it as a mighty river—it seemed
To resemble the Pechora or the Kama.[1]

Along the fertile banks of soil freshly plowed
The water streamed, touching heaven at the margins,
And white and yellow waterlilies crowned
The placid surface of the backwaters and marshes.

But this was after all the sea that sprawled afar,
Compressed between the sloping banks! A brackish
Familiar odor—of iodine, or tar—
Came wafting sharply from it; while sails in patches—

The rags of my impoverished, youthful prime—
Flung forth a stubborn challenge to the evening's wanness
And, navigating waves subdued by time,
Caught wind in so unriverly a manner!

And every sigh and every cresting wave
Embodied my poor heart, long since abandoned;
And whether fresh or salt was all the same,
But this cascading moisture, full of sadness,

---

1. The Pechora—large river originating in the Ural Mountains and flowing mainly north into the Barents Sea; originating in Udmurtia, the Kama is a major tributary of the Volga that enters it beneath the city of Kazan in Tatarstan.

In sooth was seawater—an ancient sea
Returned to distant sources, dark and mottled,
To flow as a giant river in my dream,
Like the birth canal that bore me, half-forgotten.

1935

Translated from the Russian by Alyssa Dinega Gillespie

Arkady Shteynberg, "David prosnulsia . . ." and "Ia videl more Chernoe vo sne. . . ." English translation copyright © by Alyssa Dinega Gillespie. Introduction and notes copyright © by Maxim D. Shrayer.

❋ Emigrations ❋
1917–1967

A distinct feature of this anthology is its coverage of literature by Jewish-Russian émigré authors. This section showcases the works by the émigrés of the so-called first wave, who left Russia during and in the aftermath of the Russian Revolution of 1917 and the civil war of 1918–22. Among the émigrés of the so-called second wave—the exiles who left the Soviet Union during and in the aftermath of World War II, many of them as so-called displaced persons (DPs)—there were not many Jews and even fewer authors of Jewish origin. The works by Jewish-Russian writers of the so-called third wave appear in the section "The Jewish Exodus: 1967–1991."

Up to 15 percent of the émigrés who left Russia following the 1917 Revolution and the civil war must have been Jewish. To translate that into real numbers, as many as 120,000 Jewish-Russian exiles lived in Europe between the two world wars. Not surprisingly, a number of Jewish-Russian authors of the older generation ended up abroad, among them Semyon Yushkevich and Sasha Cherny (both in the section "On the Eve: 1903–1917"), and by and large they did not take too well to the new cultural climate. Several of the authors of the middle generation became leaders of the émigré literary community—in this anthology, Vladislav Khodasevich (1886–1939), Mark Aldanov (1886–1957), and Don-Aminado (1888–1957). The careers of a number of younger Jewish-Russian authors took shape (Anna Prismanova [1892–1960]) or unfolded entirely in exile. For those among them who came from provincial areas of the former Pale, such as Dovid Knut (1900–1955), originally from Bessarabia, becoming a Russian writer abroad was a profoundly self-conscious and multicultural experience. Consider this dimly antisemitic joke of émigré Paris in the 1930s: "Who are those old Jews?" one émigré asks another as they pass a café on Montparnasse. "Oh, those are young Russian poets."

Jews were very visible in the Russian-language émigré press both in some of the cultural capitals of the Russian Diaspora (Berlin, Paris, Riga, and later Shanghai) and in smaller communities with a significant Jewish-Russian readership, such as *The Libava Russian Word* (*Libavskoe russkoe slovo*) in Libava (Liepaja), Latvia. The émigré press was dominated in the interwar period by pre-Revolutionary liberal and left-of-

center politicians (especially Constitutional Democrats and Socialist-Revolutionar-
ies), and some of the leading periodicals had Jewish editors and coeditors. Those
included Iosif Gessen of Berlin's daily *The Rudder* (*Rul'*) and Mark Vishnyak, Ilya
Fondaminsky (Bunakov), and Mikhail Tsetlin (Amari) of the Parisian quarterly *Contemporary Annals* (*Sovremennye zapiski*). *The New Review* (*Novy zhurnal*), a direct
heir of the Parisian *Contemporary Annals*, was founded in New York in 1942 by the
novelist Mark Aldanov and the poet Mikhail Tsetlin (Amari). By contrast, the few
émigré publications that targeted the Jewish readership were mostly inferior from a
literary point of view. S.D. Zaltsman's publishing house, active in Berlin in the 1920s,
was the only prominent firm specializing in Russian-language Jewish books, and
attempts to launch major Jewish-Russian journals were not successful. The weekly
Dawn (*Voskhod* or "Dawn 4," 1922–34), relaunched in Berlin by Vladimir Jabotinsky
and subsequently appearing in Paris, was, perhaps, the only authoritative and lasting
Jewish-Russian periodical of the first wave. Established in Paris in 1939, the excellent annual *Jewish World* (*Evreiskii mir*) moved to New York and published only one
more edition in 1944. (In 1992, a middlebrow Jewish-Russian weekly by the same
name started appearing in New York.)

Unlike their colleagues in the USSR, émigrés were free to practice Judaism and
the Jewish traditions. Yet Jewishness as a topic was understated in the 1920s–1930s
émigré literary mainstream; rather, the cosmopolitan spirit of the Russian intelligentsia reigned supreme in the principal émigré editions. The most important writers
among the exceptions were Dovid Knut, perhaps the "national poet" of the Jewish-
Russian emigration, and the historical novelist Abraham Vysotsky (1883–1949; not
in this anthology).

For the overloaded identities of many of the educated Jewish émigrés in the interwar years (e.g., Russian, Jewish, and German or Russian, Jewish, and French), nur-
turing a Russian self-consciousness seemed a higher priority. (Vladimir Nabokov,
who was married to a Jewish woman and lived in Berlin until 1937, noted this in the
short story "Perfection," where a Jewish-Russian family in Weimar Berlin hires an
ethnic Russian émigré tutor for their son David, who is already thoroughly German-
ized and regards Russian as a useless commodity.) At the same time, some Jewish-
Russian authors withdrew from Russian-language publishing activities. In 1930,
Jabotinsky (see his poetry in the section "On the Eve: 1903–1917") inscribed a book
to the writer and journalist Andrey Sedykh (1902–1994) as follows: "from the late
author." Responding to Sedykh's surprised reaction, Jabotinsky reportedly remarked:
"For Russian literature I am now only a 'late' author." Similarly, in the late 1930s,
Knut devoted himself to Jewish activism in France and to Jewish-French journalism.

Nazism was a rude awakening for many of the émigrés, and by the end of the 1930s
the very map of the Jewish-Russian diaspora had narrowed. World War II and the Shoah
claimed the lives of a number of Jewish-Russian authors (in this anthology, Raisa Blokh
[1899–1943] and Evgeny Shklyar [1894–1942]). Some of the survivors had managed
to escape to America, where they continued their literary activity. In postwar Europe,

only France had a considerable community of Jewish-Russian authors, whereas the center of Jewish-Russian émigré writing had shifted to New York. In addition to *The New Review*, several other first-wave "thick magazines" of literature and culture sprang up in Russian New York in the 1940s. Among them, *Housewarming* (*Novosel'e*, 1942–50), edited by Sofia Pregel (1894–1972) had a manifest interest in Jewish writing. In the 1940s and early 1950s, some of the survivors of the first wave settled in Israel (in this anthology, Dovid Knut and Yuly Margolin [1900–1971]).

The legacy of the first wave of Russian émigré literature was kept alive by some of its last Mohicans, such as Sofia Dubnova-Erlich (1885–1986), into the final decades of the twentieth century. Some of the émigré survivors lived long enough not only to reflect in their works the growth of the state of Israel (Andrey Sedykh) and the successes of the Jewish-American community but, in the 1970s and early 1980s, to pass the baton to writers of the new, predominantly Jewish, third wave of emigration from the USSR (see the section "The Jewish Exodus: 1967–1991").

Introduction copyright © by Maxim D. Shrayer.

VLADISLAV KHODASEVICH

See the introductory essay (pp. 185–86) and Khodasevich's poems in the section "On the Eve: 1902–1917" in vol. 1. In June 1922, Khodasevich left Russia and arrived in Berlin to spend the last seventeen years of his life as a Russian émigré in interwar Europe. The most important Russian émigré poet of the First Wave, Khodasevich was more hopeful than many of his émigré contemporaries about the prospects of Russian literature in exile. Of the two poems in this selection, the first was dated in manuscript "12 February 1917–2 March 1922": Khodasevich started it in Moscow and completed it in Petrograd, four months before his emigration. This liminal poem was included in his fourth collection, *The Heavy Lyre*, which came out in Moscow the year he emigrated; the second edition appeared in Berlin in 1923. The son of a Jewish mother who was raised Catholic (and who raised him Catholic) and a Polish Catholic father, in this major poem Khodasevich articulated his anguished sense of never being completely a native in the pastures of Russian culture.

The second poem in the selection is properly an émigré poem, composed in the German resort of Saarow in 1923. A literary critic and a student of the literary culture of the late eighteenth to the early nineteenth centuries, Khodasevich published two books about Pushkin, *The Poetical Estate of Pushkin* (Moscow, 1925) and *On Pushkin* (Berlin, 1937). While he identified with Pushkin the man and the poet, the identification here might have something to do with the strangeness of Pushkin's origins. Alexander Pushkin (1799–1837), who inherited his phenotypic characteristics from his great-grandfather, I.P. Gannibal, "the Blackamoor of Peter the Great," was his whole life preoccupied with his African and Semitic origins. Abducted at a young age, Pushkin's legendary great-grandfather was an Ethiopian prince, a descendant of the royal dynasty founded by Menelik, the son of the Old Testament King Solomon and the Queen of Sheba.

*   *   *

Not my mother but a Tula peasant woman,
Elena Kuzina, nursed me. It was she
Who hung my swaddlings on the stove for warming,
And made the cross above me to chase away bad dreams.

She knew no fairytales, she didn't sing,
But she always saved for me some special treasure
In her cherished trunk encased in shining tin:
A minty horse or a Vyazma[1] cake of ginger.

She never taught me how to say my prayers[2]
But gave ungrudgingly, without reserve,
That wistful, bitter motherhood of hers
And simply everything that she held dear.

Just once, when I had tumbled from the window
But didn't die (how clearly I recall!),
At the Iberian Madonna she lit a penny candle
For my miraculous salvation from the fall.[3]

And that was how, O Russia, "glorious dominion,"[4]
In pulling at her suffering teats,
I sucked out the excruciating privilege
Of loving thee and cursing thee.

In that honorable exploit, that joy of singing
To which I am a servant all my days,
My teacher is thy wonder-working genius,
My field—thy language, with its magic, lilting ways.

---

1. Vyazma—town in Smolensk Province, Russia, about one hundred fifty miles west of Moscow, famous for its *prianiki* (ginger cakes).
2. The nurse was Russian Orthodox; Khodasevich was raised Catholic.
3. Destroyed in 1929 and restored in the post-Soviet years, the chapel with the famous Iberian Madonna icon stands in Moscow in Red Square.
4. Quote from Aleksandr Pushkin's long poem *Gypsies* (1824): "Thus the destiny of your sons/O Rome, O glorious dominion." Pushkin, Russia's national poet, is the "wonder-working genius" in the next stanza.

And so before thy weaker sons and lieges
At times I still can pride myself, and not in vain,
That this majestic tongue, bequeathed by all the ages,
I guard more lovingly, more jealously than they . . .

The years rush by. The future does not lure me.
The past is burnt away within my soul.
But still a secret joy lives on and reassures me
That I, too, have one refuge from the creeping cold:

It's there, where love for me that never perishes
Is harbored in a heart all gnawed by worms:
She sleeps close to the tsar's Khodynka[5] revelers,
Elena Kuzina, my faithful nurse.

1917; 1922

* * *

In Moscow I was born. I never
Saw smoke rise from a Polish hearth;
My father left to me no treasured
Locket filled with native earth.

Stepson to Russia, and to Poland—
I hardly know what I am to her.
But eight slim volumes—and all my homeland
In them is perfectly preserved.

The rest of you choose exile, suffer,
Or bend your necks beneath the yoke.
But I will cart away my Russia
In a traveling case packed tight with books.

---

5. Reference to the Khodynka Field (*Khodynskoe pole*) in Moscow, where the coronation
of Nicholas II and Alexandra took place on 7 November 1894. The coronation proved a calamity since peasants and workers flooded the Khodynka Field when they did not receive the gifts
of food and trinkets they had been promised. As a result, over 1,300 people died; the police
tried to cover up the disaster, although eventually the new emperor and empress were informed.

You need the homeland's dusty vistas,
But I, wherever I am, can hear
The sacred moorish[6] lips that whisper
Of fabled kingdoms far and near.

1923

Translated from the Russian by Alyssa Dinega Gillespie

Vladislav Khodasevich, "Ne mater'iu, no tul'skoiu krest'iankoi . . ." and "Ia rodilsia v Moskve.
Ia dyma. . . ." English translation copyright © by Alyssa Dinega Gillespie. Introduction and
notes copyright © by Maxim D. Shrayer.

---

6. That is, Pushkin's lips. The "eight slim volumes" in the second stanza refer to the eight-
volume edition of Pushkin's works edited by P. Efremov and published in St. Petersburg in 1903–8.

MARK ALDANOV

Mark Aldanov (1886–1957), novelist and essayist, was born in Kiev to an affluent Jewish family. He graduated in 1910 from the Law and Physics-Mathematics Faculties of Kiev University, moved to Europe and studied at the Collège des Sciences Politiques et Économiques, and then returned to Russia in 1914 to work as an industrial chemist. (Aldanov authored papers on organic chemistry; chemists appeared as characters in his fiction.) He made his literary debut in 1915 with the study *Tolstoy and Rolland*. In 1918 in Petrograd, Aldanov published the essay *Armageddon* about early lessons of the revolution. Being a liberal, Aldanov remained a staunch anti-Bolshevik for the rest of his life.

Aldanov emigrated to Paris in 1919 and became an active contributor to the émigré press. Written in French, his *Lenin* (1919; German translation, 1920; English translation, 1922) was followed by *Two Revolutions* (1921), a comparison of the Russian and French revolutions. Aldanov was equipped to become a French author but remained a Russian émigré writer. Turning to fiction, Aldanov produced sixteen novels and philosophical tales. His subject of choice was political cataclysm. The thinker, a gargoyle on the roof of Notre Dame de Paris sticking his tongue out to the world, embodies Aldanov's discomfort with determinist explanations. Centering on the Napoleonic era, Aldanov's tetralogy *Thinker* included *The Ninth Thermidor* (1923; English 1926); *Saint Helena, Little Island* (1923; English 1924); *The Devil's Bridge* (1925; English 1928); and *Conspiracy* (1927).

Aldanov's second cycle of novels was a trilogy about the Russian Revolution and the émigré community: *The Key* (1930), *The Escape* (1932), and *The Cave* (1934). In 1939 Aldanov published part 1 of *The Beginning of the End* (complete English translation, *The Fifth Seal*, 1943), a novel about the members of a Soviet embassy in a small European country on the eve of World War II. The end of "Russia Abroad" was imminent, so Aldanov and his wife escaped to the United States in 1941.

Aldanov regrouped with Mikhail Tsetlin (1882–1945, pen name Amari) and founded the émigré journal *The New Review* (*Novyi zhurnal*) in New York. In the 1940s and early 1950s, before the *Lolita* explosion, Aldanov was the most successful Russian writer in America. Translations of his books included the story collection *A Night at the Airport* (1949), and he continued to write fiction and political-philosophical nonfiction in Russian, including the novel *Live as You Wish* (1952) and the treatise *A Night at Ulm: The Philosophy of Chance* (1953). In addition, Aldanov played a prominent role in organizing relief aid for émigrés stranded in wartime Europe. "I trust this man more than anyone on this earth," the often cynical Ivan Bunin said of Aldanov. Testifying to Aldanov's distinguished status, chapter 5 of Vladimir Nabokov's *Pnin* (1957) presented a gathering of Russian émigrés in America, "sitting on rustic benches and discussing émigré writers—Bunin, Aldanov, Sirin [Nabokov's own Russian pseudonym]."

America never became Aldanov's true home; he returned to Europe in 1947 and died in Nice in 1957. Aldanov's works were banned in the USSR until 1989, but his six-volume *Works*, edited by Andrey Chernyshev, appeared in Moscow in 1991 (reprinted 1994–96).

Some critics judge Aldanov's novels about contemporary historical events less successful than his Napoleonic tetralogy, while others deem Aldanov's nonfiction altogether superior. Aldanov was a superb plot maker but not a wizard of verbal style and not very compelling as a writer of complex character psychology, perhaps knowing in advance that free will was but an illusion. Yet Aldanov refrained from overt metaphysics, and as C. Nicholas Lee remarked, "the prominent place of philosophical discussion in his novels bears witness that rabbi and *pholosophe* both coexist in his nature." The doubly ironic perception of history in Aldanov's novels offered the post-Soviet reader an antidote to much of the historical pulp fiction that had flourished—and continues to flourish—in Aldanov's former homeland.

Owing to Aldanov's background and his sense of historical verisimilitude, Jews received speaking parts in his works. This is not to say that Aldanov the fictionist was interested in Jewish themes but rather to suggest that Aldanov shared his worldview with his principal Jewish characters, an old Jew interpreting the French Revolution in the tetralogy and a Jewish journalist in the trilogy. One aspect of modern Jewish history preoccupied Aldanov: the Jews' participation in the Revolution. A case in point was his investigation of the life of Evno Azef (1869–1918), head of the Socialist-Revolutionary Combat Organization and agent for the tsarist secret police.

Aldanov's memoir-essay "The Assassination of Uritsky" appeared in 1923 in the Warsaw-based émigré newspaper *For Freedom* (*Za svobodu*) and the leading émigré quarterly *Contemporary Annals* (*Sovremennye zapiski*). The version that follows appeared in *Leonid Kannegiser* (1928), a memorial collection consisting of essays by Aldanov, Georgy Ivanov, and Georgy Adamovich and poems by Kannegiser (in vol. 1).

On 30 August 1918, Kannegiser assassinated Mikhail (Moisey) Uritsky, chief of the Petrograd Cheka and the interior minister of the Northern Commune. Kannegiser was executed by the Bolsheviks. Aldanov was cognizant of the perceived ironies of an assimilated Jewish-Russian author's account of an anti-Bolshevik Jew killing a Bolshevik Jew.

Both yesterday's right-wing émigrés and today's Russian ultranationalists cite "The Assassination of Uritsky" as an objective work by a Jew and an exception to what they regard as the Jews' refusal to deal with their alleged responsibility for the Russian Revolution. This was hardly Aldanov's sole intention.

The Assassination of Uritsky

I.

Socrates. *Or in your opinion was there no merit in those divine men who fought beneath the walls of Troy and the first among them, the fearless son of Thetis? After all, it was to him that the goddess said, "If you take vengeance for Patroclus, inevitable doom awaits you." But he answered her, "I scorn death and despise danger. It is worse for me to live without having avenged my friend."*

Plato [*Apology*, 28, b–d]

The pages that follow have to do with a young man who perished tragically five years ago.[1] I knew him well. As impartially as possible, I have collected information about the man whom he killed. What I write is not history but a source for it. A historian will have materials that I do not. But I have also had materials that he will not have, since he will never have seen either Kannegiser or Uritsky.[2]

For various reasons I am not taking upon myself the task of characterizing Leonid Kannegiser. This is a subject that could tempt a great artist; it may be that some day a Dostoevsky will be found to treat it. Truly Dostoevskian also is the city where Kannegiser lived and died: the terrible St. Petersburg of the 1910s.

I shall say only that the young man who assassinated Uritsky had exceptional natural gifts. A talented poet, he left behind several dozen poems. Six or seven of them—far from the best—were published in *Northern Notes* and *Russian Thought.*[3] He recited many others to me at one time or another.

I do not know just how many "proletarian poets" were spawned by the Bolshevik Revolution—for some reason or other nobody hears about their masterpieces. Here is another, very incomplete list: Gumilyov, one of the most significant talents of the last decade, was executed; nineteen-year-old Prince Palei, in whom a competent judge, A.F. Koni, saw the hope of Russian literature, was executed;[4] Leonid Kannegiser was executed.

---

1. This article was written in 1923. [M.A.] Here and hereafter, Mark Aldanov's notes have been expanded and supplemented by C. Nicholas Lee and Maxim D. Shrayer. Unless noted otherwise, all notes are those of the translator and the editor. Aldanov's text has been slightly abridged. In the English translation, the passages Aldanov quotes from Kannegiser's diaries have been abridged.

2. This, by the way, is not such a disadvantage for the historian. He will at least have full freedom of judgment and evaluation. I do not have *full* freedom. [M.A.]

3. *Severnye zapiski* and *Russkaia mysl'* in the original.

4. He was thrown down a mine shaft for being related to the ruling dynasty—there was no other reason. [M.A.]

But when I speak about the exceptional talents of Uritsky's assassin, I have in mind not only his poetry. His entire nature was unusually gifted. Fate placed him in very favorable circumstances. The son of a famous engineer with a European reputation, he was born to wealth and grew up in a highly cultured milieu, in a house frequented by all St. Petersburg. In his parents' drawing room, imperial ministers rubbed shoulders with German Lopatin[5] and affected young poets met with distinguished generals.

Fortune's favorite, endowed by fate with brilliant gifts, good looks, and a noble character, he was the unhappiest of men.

I was recently given extracts from the diary he left behind. The man who wrote the diary was shot by a firing squad; the same fate also befell the man who safeguarded it in the days following Uritsky's murder.[6] These diary entries, connected with the memory of people who have died, have miraculously survived and made their way abroad.

I recall it was Mikhailovsky who remarked that a diary can be kept only by very solitary people. It would be more accurate to say: only by very solitary or very unhappy people. It can certainly not be said that Marie Bashkirtseff, for example, lived in solitude. But she could not remember a single day in her life without torments. Why? She also asked why:

> Pourquoi, pourquoi dans ton oeuvre céleste
> Tant d'éléments si peu d'accord![7]

I will not speak in detail of Leonid Kannegiser's diary, which is truly remarkable in many respects. He began his diary entries in 1914—the first is dated 29 May. The war found him—in Italy—a sixteen-year-old boy. He passionately wanted to go to the front as a volunteer. His parents did not let him. Like all boys, he was attracted to war by what does not exist in war. But there was also something else.

I quote almost at random several diary entries:

"I have a room, a bed, dinner, money, coffee, and no pity for those who do not. If I am killed in the war, then there will undoubtedly be some higher meaning in it. . . ."

"I interrupted my writing, walked back and forth around my room, reflected, and, I think, for the thousandth time decided: 'I'm going!' Tomorrow morning, perhaps, when I wake up, I'll think: 'What nonsense! Why should I go? We have an enormous

---

5. Lopatin, German (1845–1918)—Russian revolutionary and socialist, close to Karl Marx and Nikolay Chernyshevsky in the 1870s. After 1905 he retired from political life.

6. Incidentally, this diary would have had nothing to offer a Bolshevik investigating commission. It breaks off at the beginning of 1918 and does not touch upon Kannegiser's terrorist activity at all. [M.A.]

7. (Fr.) = "Why, oh why, in your celestial work,/Are there so many elements so little in agreement with each other?" Bashkirtseff, Marie (1860–1884)—Russian author, whose best known work, written in French, is *Le Journal de Marie Bashkirtseff*.

army!' And in the evening I'll change my mind again. Then I'll settle for a compromise: 'It's better to go as a medical orderly.' It's the same thing every day: I hesitate, I try to decide, I despair—and I don't do a thing.

"Others at least work for the good of the wounded. I also went once to the railway station. One wounded man had to be taken into the dressing station. As I watched, his bandage was removed, and I saw on his leg a shrapnel wound half the size of the palm of my hand; I saw his whole blue, mutilated, pitted body, thick drops of blood. A doctor had shaved off the hair around the wound. An army nurse was preparing the dressing. Two students walked quietly out. One came up to me, pale, smiling in embarrassment, and said, 'I can't stand to see it.' The wounded man was groaning. And suddenly he asked plaintively, 'Please be more careful.' I felt a shudder, it didn't seem to be anything, and I continued to look at the wound, but I couldn't stand it. I felt my head spinning, everything went dark before my eyes. I was going to be sick. I was on the point of falling, but I pulled myself together and went out into the fresh air, staggering like a drunk.

"And that could happen to—me. To know that that wound is 'on my leg . . .' And when suddenly, as if in response, an irresistibly glad-sweet feeling rises in my soul: 'I'm in no danger,' then I know, 'I am a scoundrel.'"

"[. . .] I am setting myself no external goals. It is all the same to me whether I am the Pope of Rome or a shoe-shine boy in Calcutta—I don't associate any specific emotional states with these circumstances—but my single goal is to lead my soul to marvelous enlightenment, to inexpressible sweetness. Whether by religion or by heresy—I do not know." [. . .]

I make no commentary on anything. All diaries are somewhat alike. Even Tolstoy and Amiel were not exceptions to this rule. But I am struck by the extracts from Kannegiser's diary, even with their naïveté of style and thought. It would be futile to look for logic in them. The decision to go off to war alternates with the decision to go off to a monastery; pages of pure metaphysics are followed by pages that are terrible to read; enthusiasm for the monuments of Ferrara and for the paintings of [Paolo] Veronese gives way to enthusiasm for the Soviet of Workers' and Soldiers' Deputies.[8] And from every page of the diary you can see raw nerves and hear, "My soul is ripping itself away from my body . . ."[9]

---

8. Kannegiser's enthusiasm clearly predates the October 1917 Bolshevik coup; on the changes in his attitude toward the Bolsheviks, see below.

9. Aldanov is quoting from a poem by the Decembrist Kondraty Ryleev, composed in 1826 in the Fortress of Peter and Paul during the inquest and dedicated to a fellow Decembrist insurrectionist, Prince E.P. Obolenskii. Ryleev and four other Decembrists died on the scaffold, hence the parallel with Kannegiser.

I made his acquaintance in the home of his parents on Saperny Lane and often met him there. He also came around to see me sometimes. I could not fail to see that there was a tragic side to his nature. But nothing in him gave any inkling of a future terrorist.

One characteristic scene, however, has stayed in my memory. It was in the spring of 1918. He and I had been playing chess for a long time. I lived in the house on Nadezhdinskaya Street where the Petropolis bookstore was located. At that time this curious cooperative society of bibliophiles bought up the books of its needy participants, trying not to hurt their feelings, and resold them without profit to members of the cooperative who were in better material circumstances. At that time Petropolis was offering for sale the magnificent old library of Prince Gagarin, which consisted principally of French books of the eighteenth and beginning of the nineteenth centuries. I had made a few purchases there, and the books I had acquired were lying on my desk in my study. My guest began to leaf through them. I started talking about books and hazarded the guess (which I had not verified and based solely on their character) that this library belonged at one time to the same Prince Gagarin who was rumored—groundlessly, it appeared—to have written the anonymous letters that were the cause of Pushkin's death.

The expression on Leonid Akimovich's face changed, and he even dropped a book onto the desk.

"What sort of person would you have to be," he said, turning pale, "to write such a letter—about Pushkin . . ."

And he fell silent. Then suddenly, in a low voice, he began to recite the verses:

> The secret guardian of freedom, the punishing dagger,
> The final arbiter of disgrace and offense,
> For the hands of immortal Nemesis
> The god of Lemnos forged you . . . [10]

In general he was poor at reciting poetry, like all Russian poets, I think (with the exception of I.A. Bunin, an amazing elocutionist): he recited poetry without any expression, in an unnatural monotone, as if to show that no expressiveness or oratorical art could add anything to the beauty of the verses themselves. If I am not mistaken, this style of recitation was introduced by Aleksandr Blok. But this time the young man recited these verses differently from the way he always did—or does it only seem that way to me now?

"Note," said Kannegiser after breaking off the declamation at the first quatrain, "note that Pushkin slipped up here: in this stanza the second line should not have been rhymed with the third. If the third line is put in place of the fourth, the result is much

---

10. Here and hereafter, a literal, unrhymed and mostly unmetered, translation of Pushkin's "The Dagger" (Kinzhal) is provided.

more powerful . . . Pushkin slipped up," he repeated with an ironic smile. "This is the way I would have written it . . ."

And he recited the quatrain in his redaction. His tone was amusing—the ironic smile, of course, was to suggest the presumption of this "correction" of Pushkin. I thought to myself that he was right: that way it really was more powerful.[11]

He was silent for a little and then recited in a completely changed voice the end of "The Dagger":

> O righteous young man, fateful chosen one,
> O Sand, thy life was extinguished on the executioner's block,
> But the holy voice of virtue
> Has remained in the dust of the young man who was executed.
> Thou hast become the eternal shadow of thy Germany,
> Threatening criminal force with disaster—
> And on the solemn grave
> A dagger burns without an inscription.

I see him in front of me at that moment as if it were now. He was sitting in a deep armchair, his head bowed low. His fine sensitive face had completely changed . . . I feel awestruck when I remember those lines of "The Dagger" now—as Uritsky's assassin recited them. Art is a frightening thing! Was Pushkin perhaps one of those responsible for the death of the chief of the Petersburg Extraordinary Commission?

I remember that I called the young man's attention to the rare technical perfection of these amazing lines, to the sobbing sound of the second line ("O Sand"), which consisted of short monosyllables, and to the effect achieved by the sound *a*. Pushkin, although he never studied in a poets' guild, had the ear to grasp all the tricks of contemporary prosody. André Chénier, in an ode that, although not as good as "The Dagger," served as a model for it, used a similar dramatic effect, the sound *ar*:

> Le poign*ar*d, seul esp*oir* de la terre,
> Est ton *ar*me sac*r*ée . . . [12]

---

11. The question of whether Pushkin "slipped up" turns out to be rather complex, however. The fair manuscript copy of Pushkin's "The Dagger" was thought to be lost; the famous poem did not begin to appear in print in Russia until 1876.[. . .] Now, in the first volume of *Voices of the Past* (*Golosa minuvshego*) for 1923, M.A. Tsyavlovsky has for the first time published Pushkin's fair copy. [. . .] In this text the second line rhymes not with the third but with the fourth (just as Kannegiser required), but the third and fourth lines (of the usual redaction) also precede the first two lines: "The god of Lemnos forged you/For the hands of the immortal Nemesis,/The secret guardian of freedom, the punishing dagger,/The final arbiter of disgrace and offense!" [M.A.]

12. (Fr.) = "The dagger, sole hope of the earth, is thy sacred weapon . . ."

But the young man was not listening to me (although he could talk for hours about poetry). He began to question me about Sand.[13] I do not wish to say that I might have begun to suspect something that evening. At the time, probably, nothing had as yet even been planned.

Leonid Kannegiser took no part in politics before the spring of 1918. The February Revolution bowled him over—who wasn't carried away by it for the first two or three weeks or so?

He was the chairman of the Union of Socialist Cadets. I cannot guarantee—however strange this may seem—that he did not also feel some enthusiasm for the ideas of the October Revolution. Lenin made a very strong impression on him on 25 October—I have spoken about this elsewhere.

The events of 1918, the peace treaty of Brest-Litovsk, soon changed Kannegiser's opinions. It is not my task to give an account of his political evolution (I'm not really familiar with that evolution). But in April (or May) 1918 he already hated the Bolsheviks with a burning hatred and took some part in conspiratorial work directed to their overthrow. The death of his friend (Pereltsveig) made him a terrorist. . . .

IV.

Le président du tribunal: *Qui vous a inspireé tant de haine?*
Charlotte Corday: *Je n'avais pas besoin de la haine des autres.*
J'avais assez de la mienne.[14]
Court interrogation of Charlotte Corday

The brief and complex process that rent the soul of Uritsky's assassin in the days preceding the drama is not clear to me. Why did Kannegiser's choice fall on Uritsky? I do not know. His assassination cannot be justified even from the viewpoint of an inveterate advocate of terror.

Kannegiser apparently had no accomplices. The Bolshevik inquest was unable to uncover any despite the extraordinary desire of the authorities to do so. The official document says this about it:

"On being interrogated, Leonid Kannegiser declared that he did not assassinate Uritsky in accordance with the decision of a party or any organization but from personal motives, wishing to avenge the arrests of officers and the military execution of his friend Pereltsveig, whom he had known for about ten years. The interrogation

---

13. Sand, Karl Ludwig (1795–1820)—German nationalist student executed for assassinating reactionary German playwright and Russian official August Friedrich von Kotzebue (1761–1819). Kotzebue was an intermittent Bonapartist, and Sand became a martyr to anti-Napoleonic Europe, but Pushkin and in the poem "The Dagger" him more generally as the assassin of a tyrant who pays for his heroism with his life.

14. (Fr.) = Presiding judge: *Who inspired such hate in you?* Charlotte Corday: *I didn't need the hatred of others. I had enough of my own.*

of prisoners and witnesses to this affair revealed that Pereltsveig's military execution had strongly affected Kannegiser. After this execution by firing squad had been made public, he left home for a few days—where he was at this period could not be established."

The [Bolshevik] inquest admitted that "it was impossible to establish by means of direct evidence that the assassination of Comrade Uritsky was organized by a counterrevolutionary organization." The investigation nonetheless remained of the opinion that such an organization existed—and was inclined, as usual, to suspect "the imperialists of the Entente."[15] The Entente at that time—the summer of 1918—had other things to do. Besides, it is difficult as a matter of general principle to imagine Lloyd George as an instigator of political assassinations. His representative in Russia did not inherit the terrorist views of his predecessor, the famous George Buchanan, the sixteenth-century antimonarchist. As for Clemenceau, although he can hardly be numbered among those opposed to terror on principle, of course he did not busy himself in organizing attempts on the lives of Chekists.

I am inclined to think that the evidence Leonid Kannegiser gave at the inquest corresponds to the truth. He carried out Uritsky's assassination alone. No organization —neither the one whose members he and Pereltsveig had been, nor any other organization of any kind—would have entrusted him with the task of assassinating the chief of the Petrograd Extraordinary Commission. Probably the immediate reason for what he did was indeed the desire to avenge the death of his friend (only this can also explain why he chose Uritsky). The psychological basis for it, on the other hand, was of course very complex. I think the psychological motivation consisted of the noblest and most exalted feelings. A great deal went into it: the ardent love of Russia that filled his diaries; the hatred of those that enslaved her; the feeling of a Jew who wanted his name set off against the names of the Uritskys and Zinovievs[16] before the Russian people and before history; the spirit of self-sacrifice—the same old feeling of "but I haven't been in the war"; the craving for strong, agonizing sensations—he was born to become a Dostoevskian hero; and more than anything else, I think, the thirst for "the all-cleansing fire of suffering"—the feeling conveyed by this reverberating figure of speech was not fabricated by poets.

I repeat, he probably had no accomplices, but he may have had a living model. He admired the personality of G.A. Lopatin, and I believe he made Lopatin an example for himself—it was far from a bad example. Of course Lopatin took no part in their circle: in that last year of his life he was no longer capable of any work. Besides that, in the midst of such conspirators, he would have felt a little the way Achilles felt dressed up as a girl among the daughters of King Lycomedes. But Lopatin, who kept his stormy temperament to the end of his days, did not mince his words when he

---

15. In Soviet circles somebody came up with the absurd theory that, escaping after the assassination, Kannegiser rode his bicycle along Millionnaya Street to the English embassy, where he wanted to find asylum. [M.A.]

16. Zinoviev, Gregory (1883–1936)—major Bolshevik leader, born in Ukraine to a family of Jewish dairy farmers.

talked about the Bolsheviks and the means of doing battle with them. I also remember this from my own conversations with the late Lopatin.

I also know this. On the very same day that Leonid Kannegiser's mother was released from prison, she was informed by telephone from the hospital that German Lopatin was dying and would like to see her. R.L. Kannegiser [Kannegiser's mother] went immediately to the Hospital of Sts. Peter and Paul. Lopatin, fully conscious, told R.L. that he was happy to see her before he died.

"I thought you were angry with me . . ."

"For what?"

"For the death of your son."

"In what way were you guilty of that?"

He kept silent and said nothing more. A few hours later Lopatin died.

He can hardly have had any cause to accuse himself of anything except the passionate words that he could blurt out in conversation with Leonid Kannegiser; he was very fond of the young man.

The same official document contains the following:

"The Extraordinary Commission was unable to establish precisely when the decision to assassinate Comrade Uritsky was made, but Comrade Uritsky himself knew that an attempt on his life was being prepared. He was forewarned repeatedly, and Kannegiser was definitely indicated as the prime suspect, but Comrade Uritsky did not take these warnings seriously enough. He was already well informed about Kannegiser from the intelligence information at his disposal."

This is a truly astonishing assertion. It is totally improbable. If Uritsky was warned about preparations for an attempt on his life, with the name of the terrorist indicated, then it must indeed be assumed that the assassination was the work of some organization and that an agent of the Extraordinary Commission belonged to that organization (or at least had some connection with it). But this contradicts the words quoted earlier from the same summary of the investigation: "it was impossible . . . to establish." Besides that, what grounds could Uritsky have for being skeptical about the warning? And why did he not order Kannegiser to be arrested ahead of time? It was very simple to track him down: he spent most of the day at home, in the apartment of his father, who was well known to all St. Petersburg.

Yet all the same there is something mysterious and sinister in this assertion. Was Uritsky well informed about Kannegiser? . . . I have a strange feeling when I read this part of Mr. Antipov's investigative summary.[17]

---

17. Antipov, Nikolay (1894–1941)—Bolshevik official, who served as the deputy chief and then the chief of the Petrograd Cheka in 1918–19.

Here and above, Aldanov quotes Antipov's "Sketches of the Activities of the Petrograd Extraordinary Commission," published in the Soviet newspaper *Petrograd Pravda* (*Petrogradskaia Pravda*). However, Aldanov does not provide more information about his source. He may be referring to Antipov's report of the Kannegiser investigation printed in *Petrograd Pravda* on 4 January 1919. The editor is indebted to Gleb Morev's research on Kannegiser. Also see editor's introduction to Kannegiser in vol. 1.

This is what I heard not so long ago. Some time before the assassination, Kannegiser said ironically to his friend, "NN, do you know whom I talked to on the phone today?"

"Whom?"

"Uritsky."

And that was all. At that time NN paid no attention to what the young man had said. There were plenty of reasons for St. Petersburg residents to phone the Extraordinary Commission in those days! NN, like the present writer, learned about the assassination of Uritsky while he was away from St. Petersburg, from the newspapers, and he was just as astonished as I. That was when he remembered Kannegiser's enigmatic remark.

There really were plenty of reasons for telephoning Uritsky . . . But all the same this is very strange. It is highly unlikely that—even at that time—the chief of the Extraordinary Commission himself could be summoned to the phone to answer a simple inquiry or to put in a good word for an ordinary citizen of St. Petersburg, completely unknown to anyone. In any case, whoever made the phone call had to give his name. Or did Kannegiser use an assumed name as a cover? In that case, why did Uritsky come to the phone to talk to somebody he didn't know? And why did he need to? And just what was it that his future assassin said to the people's commissar?

I cannot understand—and yet I do not doubt for a minute that what NN told me is true. I do not doubt because I knew Leonid Kannegiser. That was his *style* . . . No, style is not the right word for it. But I feel that independently of what he might be about to do (he was capable of dreaming up much more than that!) he needed this terrible, frightening sensation. Why, after the murder, did Raskolnikov go to *listen to the bell* in Alena Ivanovna's apartment? Why, before the murder, did Charlotte Corday *have a long talk* with Marat? . . .

I had left St. Petersburg even before Pereltsveig was arrested. I saw Kannegiser for the last time in July 1918 in his parents' apartment on Saperny Lane. He was animated and in high spirits. I advised his father to send the young man off to the south somewhere: St. Petersburg was a wretched hole . . .

After the execution of his comrades, which profoundly shook him, Kannegiser no longer stayed at home at night. At that time almost half the city tried to spend the night away from home (for some reason arrests were carried out in the dead of night). His relatives suspected nothing and asked about nothing. He said nothing about himself.

On 16 (29) August (the day before Uritsky's assassination), he came home, as always, toward evening. After dinner he offered to read aloud to his sister—this was their custom. Up to then they had been reading a book by Schnitzler and had not yet finished it. But this time he had come supplied with something else: a one-volume French edition of *The Count of Monte Cristo*, recently acquired from a second-hand bookseller. Despite protests, he began to read from the middle of the book. Was it a coincidence, or had he chosen the pages on purpose? It was the chapter about a political assassination that had been carried out in his youth by an old Bonapartist, the grandfather of one of the female characters in the famous novel.

He read enthusiastically until midnight. Then he took leave of his sister. She was fated to see him yet once more from a distance from the window of her cell on Gorokhovaya Street: he was being led for interrogation under escort.

He spent the night, as always, away from home. But early the next morning he came back to his parents' apartment for tea. At about nine he knocked on the door of his father's room. His father was unwell and was not working. Despite the inappropriate early hour, he proposed a game of chess. His father agreed—he never refused his son anything.

Apparently Leonid Kannegiser connected something else with the outcome of this game: the success of his plan? Success in escaping? An hour before the assassination the young man played for all he was worth and did his best to win. He lost, and this made him extremely upset. Chagrined at his success, his father proposed another game. The young man looked at his watch and refused.

He said goodbye to his father (they never saw each other again) and hurried out of the room. He was wearing the sporty leather double-breasted jacket of military cut that he had worn as a cadet and that I had often seen on him. He left the house, got on a bicycle, and headed off in the direction of Winter Palace Square. In front of the Ministry of Foreign Affairs he stopped: Uritsky, who was also in charge of the Northern Commune's foreign policy, received petitioners in this building.

It was twenty minutes after ten.

V.

Death had not been invited . . .

From an old legend

He went in through the entrance located in the middle of the half of the semicircular Rossi palace that goes from the Arch of the General Staff to Millionnaya Street.[18] Uritsky always came into the ministry from this entrance. How had Kannegiser found this out? Or had he been following the people's commissar during the preceding days? I am also prepared to accept the hypothesis, by the way, that he could have simply asked the first staff member who turned up at what time, by what means, and by what entrance Comrade Uritsky came in. The fascination with the risk that asking such questions involved, the craving for acute sensations—"Will they suspect me? Will they arrest me? I must ask in an offhand way, God keep me from turning pale"— all these impulses were part of his nature, just like the telephone call to Uritsky.

A stairway and the cage of an elevator are located opposite the door into the room where the assassination was carried out, a large room directly overlooking the street.

---

18. Some details of the account in this chapter came to me from an absolutely reliable source connected to Soviet ruling circles, which it is impossible for me to name. [M.A.]

A hard wooden sofa, several chairs, and pegs for wraps that hung along the white-washed walls—those are the furnishings of this room, which stood out because of how miserable it looked in the magnificent ministry palace. In it there was always a hall porter, who had served in this position for about a quarter of a century. This old man, stunned by the new way of doing things, like most of the household servants in the imperial palaces, called Uritsky "Your Exalted Excellency."

"Is Comrade Uritsky in?" Kannegiser asked.

"He has not yet arrived, sir . . ."

He walked over to the window looking out onto the square and sat down on the windowsill. He took off his cap and laid it down next to him. He looked out the window for a long time.

What was he thinking? That it was still not too late to renounce this terrible business—that he could still go back to Saperny Lane, have tea with his sister, make up for the chess game he had lost to his father, or continue reading *The Count of Monte Cristo?* That there were only a few minutes left for him to live, that he would never again see this sun, this square, this Rastrelli palace? That maybe it was time to release the safety catch on his revolver and cock it to "fire"? That the hall porter was squinting in a strange way, that he suspected? His sensations in those minutes could have been rendered by Dostoevsky, whom he so loved . . .

He waited. People passed by on the square. His heart was pounding. Twenty minutes passed like an eternity that was too short. At last, in the distance, he heard the approaching soft, terrible roar that meant *the end.*

The imperial automobile slowed down and stopped at the entrance.

Uritsky had come from his private apartment on Vasilievsky Island.

How many death sentences was he supposed to sign on that fateful day?

Another sentence had been drawn up.

"Death had not been invited."

It appeared without an invitation.

The young man in the double-breasted leather jacket had put his hand into his pocket and was already getting up from the windowsill.

The chief of the Extraordinary Commission came in the door and walked toward the elevator.

The visitor made several quick steps in his direction.

Did their eyes meet? Did Uritsky read: *death?*

A shot rang out. The People's Commissar collapsed without making a sound, killed on the spot. At a distance of six or seven paces, a moving assassin shot a man who was walking briskly. Only the sure hand of an experienced marksman could have aimed the bullet like that—if I am not mistaken, Kannegiser had no idea of how to shoot.

At that time there was nobody nearby.[19]

---

19. The hall porter must have been opening the door to the elevator for "His Exalted Excellency." Uritsky's office was on the third floor. [M.A.]

The assassin rushed for the exit.

If he had put on his cap, placed the revolver into his pocket, and calmly walked to the left, he would probably have easily been able to hide by turning under the arch onto Morskaya Street and mixing in with the crowd on Nevsky Prospekt. The chase did not begin until two or three minutes later. That was plenty of time for him to walk along the square to the arch. But he was unable to walk calmly. Of course he lost his self-control at that point. He must have imagined to himself a thousand times at night the way *it* would happen. But *it* didn't *turn out that way. It* never does *turn out that way.*

Without his cap, which he had left on the windowsill, not letting go of the revolver, he ran out into the street, jumped on his bicycle, and sped off to the right—toward Millionnaya Street.

A minute later an uproar erupted in the room where the historic assassination had taken place. Employees of the People's Commissariat heard the shot on the second floor. Several people ran down the stairs and stopped dumbfounded in front of Uritsky's dead body. Not yet understanding clearly what had happened, they picked the commissar up and carried him over to the wooden sofa by the wall.

The man who was the first to remember about the assassin and rush off in pursuit of him was not an ordinary policeman. He was a peculiar fellow, fanatically devoted to the Revolution, poor, illiterate, selfless—even then already soaked in blood from head to foot. He is a fit subject for a work of literature. He still awaits the author of "Loopy Ears" to portray him.[20] He dashed out into the street shouting. Others ran after him. It was easy to decide which way to go: a young man speeding along on a bicycle, without a cap, with a revolver in his hand, could not remain unnoticed on thinly populated Winter Palace Square.

The automobile flew off in pursuit at terrible speed.

Once he was on his bicycle the assassin apparently recovered his self-control. Eyewitnesses said that he seemed to be zigzagging along the streets—trying to avoid a bullet in his back.

When he heard the rumbling of the speeding automobile behind him, he understood that he was done for. At Number 17 on the left side of the street, very close to the Marble Palace, he braked the bicycle, jumped off, and dashed into the courtyard.

The enormous architectural complex of the English Club, like all the buildings on that side of Millionnaya Street, looks out onto the Neva Embankment.

If the entrance gates in the courtyard had been open, the assassin would still have been able to escape.

Fate was against him:

The gates were closed.

In despair, he ran in through the door in the right half of the building and quickly

---

20. "Loopy Ears" (1916) is a famous short story by Ivan Bunin, whose protagonist is a megalomaniacal murderer.

began to climb the back stairs. On the third floor the door to the apartment of Prince Melikov was open. He dashed into it, ran through the kitchen and several rooms, in front of the stupefied servants in the entrance hall put on somebody else's coat, which he had grabbed from the hall coat rack, opened the outside door, and went down the main staircase.[21] [. . .]

VI.

The villain maintained complete composure. He bragged about his crime, asserting that he had avenged his friends who had perished. The attempts of the law court to force Anckarström to name his accomplices, despite the efforts of the executioners, were unsuccessful. The criminal kept his hellish calm even on the scaffold. He said he was dying for Sweden . . .

During the night after the execution, unknown people secretly penetrated to the place where Anckarström's body was displayed and covered the ignominious remains of the regicide with flowers and laurel leaves. The investigating commission was unsuccessful in bringing the guilty to light.

The Case of the Assassination of King Gustav III[22]

I can add nothing to the epigraph of this chapter . . .

What sustained this youth, this boy, in the inhuman sufferings that fell to his lot? I do not know. I want to understand—and I cannot.

Johan Anckarström's "tempestuous soul" had been tempered by passions and trials. Ravaillac and Damien were firmly convinced that on the other side of the torments of earthly death there awaited them the eternal blessedness that they had purchased at a terrible price. To the scaffold of Karl Sand, erected on a meadow that to this day is called "Karl Sand's Himmelfahrtswiese,"[23] there flocked tens of thou-

---

21. I may be mistaken in the details. The future Lenotre [Théodore Gosselin (1857–1935), French historian who wrote extensively about the French Revolution] of the Russian Revolution will be able with greater accuracy and in greater detail to reconstruct this terrible act of the drama that played itself out in the space of a few minutes on the property of the English Club if he has access not only to the stories I have used but also to the testimony of eyewitnesses that has been collected in the archives of the Extraordinary Commission. What I have said is sufficient to appreciate the remarkable self-control of the twenty-year-old terrorist. [M.A.]

22. King Gustav III of Sweden (1746–1792) was shot at a masked ball in the Stockholm opera house by Captain Jacob Johan Anckarström (1762–1792) as part of an antiroyalist aristocratic conspiracy. Gustav died two weeks later, and a month after that Anckarström was beheaded. The allusion to his "tempestuous soul" may be partly connected with the free rendering of the events in Verdi's opera *Un Ballo in Maschera* (1859), where the character representing Anckarström falsely suspects the king of a liaison with his wife.

23. (Ger.) = "The meadow where Karl Sand ascended to heaven."

sands of people who regarded him as a German national hero and craved the chance to moisten their kerchiefs in the blood of the holy martyr. The Russian terrorists of the tsarist period who died *without an audience* in the courtyard of the Shlisselburg Prison were at least sure that only they, not their wives or their fathers, would suffer for their acts. Leonid Kannegiser did not have even that consolation. He knew that the relatives he tenderly loved had been arrested. From his dealings with the Bolsheviks, he could have expected up to the end that execution awaited his whole family. In actual fact, they were saved. It was a miracle: St. Petersburg in those days was awash with torrents of blood. "Revolutionary terror" had obviously set about terrorizing the population so as to protect its Zinovievs from new attempts on their lives—what was more "expedient" than to shoot the families of political terrorists!

He also realized that he was the target of blind curses from totally innocent people who were being murdered as hostages for what he had done. Instead of Uritsky, it was Boky,[24] ten times worse than his predecessor and chief, who carried out the reprisals.

It is not for me to speak about Leonid Kannegiser's fate. It is recounted in black words in the three-volume "Case of the Assassination of Uritsky." Will that case ever see the light?

He behaved and died like a hero.

His whole short life was spent in search of tormenting sensations. He drained that cup to the dregs, and I do not know another to whom fate gave such a cup. He spent long weeks draining it without the consolation of faith, without the triumph of victory over death before a crowd of many thousands of spectators, without Taras Bulba's "I hear!"[25] Nobody heard. Nobody was listening. Will his grave ever be found? Will Russia erect a monument over it? That probably no longer meant anything to him by the time he had reached the level of estrangement from the world to which he ascended in his last days.

There something else was to be revealed:

> Happy is he who falls down on his head:
> For him, if only for a moment, the world's different . . . [26]

1923

Translated from the Russian by C. Nicholas Lee

Mark Aldanov, "Ubiistvo Uritskogo." English translation and notes copyright © by C. Nicholas Lee. Introduction © by Maxim D. Shrayer.

---

24. Boky, Gleb Ivanovich (1879–1937)—prominent Soviet party official who succeeded Uritsky and worked as the chairman of the Petrograd Cheka and the Union of Communes of the Northern Region until November 1918.

25. Taras Bulba—protagonist of the tale by Nikolay Gogol (1809–1852), which bears its protagonist's name. A Ukrainian Cossack leader, Taras Bulba yells, "I hear" from a crowd of onloookers at his son Ostap's public execution, after Ostap cries out: "Father, where are you? Can you hear me?"

26. The last two lines of a 1922 poem from *The European Night* by Vladislav Khodasevich (in vol. 1).

EVGENY SHKLYAR

Evgeny Shklyar (1894–1942), poet, translator, and essayist, was born to an engineer's family in Druya (Druja), a small town in the Disna District of Vilna Province, presently in Belarus's Vitebsk Province. He later attended a gymnasium in Ekaterinoslav (Dnepropetrovsk) in Ukraine, and studied at Warsaw University, following evacuation to Rostov-on-Don during World War I. Shklyar began to contribute poetry to periodicals in the south of Russia in 1911. After being drafted into the army, Shklyar trained at a cadet school, served at the Caucasus front, and was decorated with a St. George's Cross. Shklyar fought the Reds during the civil war in several armies and edited the SR (Socialist-Revolutionary) newspaper *Free Daghestan* (*Vol'nyi Dagestan*).

Shklyar emigrated to Lithuania in 1919, settling in Kaunas (Kovno) in 1921. He worked at the Kaunas newspaper *Echo* (*Ekho*) and in 1924–25 at the Riga-based *People's Thought* (*Narodnaia mysl'*), as well as serving as the Kaunas correspondent of *Today* (*Segodnia*), a major émigré newspaper based in Riga. The three independent Baltic states, especially Latvia and Lithuania, had an active Russian émigré press and, regularly journeying to Riga and Tallinn, the Kaunes-based Shklyar contributed to Russian periodicals in Latvia, Lithuania, and Estonia, while enjoying a reputation in the émigré world outside the *limitrophes*.

In 1923 Shklyar founded *The Baltic Almanac* (*Baltiiskii al'manakh*), advancing a platform of intercultural exchange across the Baltic region. He edited *The Baltic Almanac* in 1923–28 and published it in 1928–29 and 1937. His other ventures included *The Lithuanian Market* (*Lietuvos rinka/Die litauische Markt*, 1928), *Our Echo* (*Nashe ekho*, 1929–31), *The Lithuanian Courier* (*Litovskii kur'er*, 1932–33), and *The Lithuanian Messenger* (*Litovskii vestnik*, 1935–39). Shklyar lived in Paris in 1926–27, returning to Kaunas in 1928.

Shklyar considered Lithuania his home. He wrote with passion about Lithuanian culture and the Lithuanian countryside. More importantly, along with the prominent symbolist Russian poet turned Lithuanian diplomat Jurgis Baltrušaitis (1873–1944), Shklyar was a conduit between Lithuanian and Russian letters. A principal translator of Lithuanian poets into Russian during the interwar independence, Shklyar translated authors from different generations and movements, including Kazys Binkis, J.A. Herbačiauskas, Liudas Gira, Jonas Maironis, Pranas Morkus Putinas, Teofilis Tilvytis, Petras Vaičiūnas, Vydūnas, and others. In 1927 he published *Lietuva, the Golden Name*, a Russian-language collection about Lithuania, which appeared in Lithuanian translation in 1931.

Shklyar published eight books of Russian poetry: *Cypresses* (Kaunas, 1922), *Caravan* (Berlin, 1923), *Lights on Mountain Tops* (Berlin, 1923), *Evening Steppe* (Berlin, 1923), *The Staff* (Riga, 1925), *Lietuva, the Golden Name* (Paris, 1927), *Elyahu, Gaon of Vilna* (Riga, 1929), and *Poeta in Aeternum* (Riga, 1935), this last collection including dedications to Lithuanian poets and translations.

Writing in *The Lithuanian Voice* on 19 August 1935, the critic Boris Orechkin polemicized with Liudas Gira's view of Shklyar as a "fellow-traveler of contemporary Lithuanian writers and poets." "Evg. Shklyar is both a poet and a citizen," Orechkin observed, invoking the dictum by Nikolay Nekrasov that a poet must be committed to civic duty. "[Shklyar] is both a Russian and a Lithuanian poet, and a Lithuanian citizen," Orechkin continued. "Can there be such a combination and can a Russian poet be Lithuania's troubadour [*sic*] and her loyal son?" Although Orechkin did not mention the third key component of Shklyar's identity, his Jewishness, he alluded, conspicuously, to "arguments of 'racists,'" concluding: "[. . .] Shklyar's ties to the Lithuanian land extend far back. He is a Lithuanian, if not by blood, then at least by birth." In 1928 Shklyar published in *The Baltic Almanac* his Russian translation of the Lithuanian national anthem from the lyrics by Vincas Kudirka (1858–1899): "Lithuania, my homeland, land of heroes!/Let your sons draw strength from the past [. . .]." Evgeny Shklyar perished in a Nazi concentration camp outside Kaunas in 1942.

A covert modernist and not an original talent, Shklyar addressed ancient Judaic motifs and aspects of modern Jewish history. The theme of religious pluralism and interfaith dialogue manifested itself throughout Shklyar's career, as evidenced by "Shield of David, crescent or icon . . ." from *Lights on Mountain Tops* (1923). The second poem in the selection, "Where's Home?" appeared in *The Staff* (1925) as part of the cycle "White and Blue," dedicated to Vladimir (Ze'ev) Jabotinsky (vol. 1).

The nine poems of Shklyar's cycle "Names" (*Cypresses*, 1922) focus on female names that bear religious and cultural significance for Muslim (Persia, Turkey, Azerbaijan, Central Asia), Catholic (Lithuania, Poland), and Orthodox (Georgia) regions and for the Judaic civilization. In Shklyar's collections one also finds poems that stylize or imply a genuinely Christian authorial sensibility. The 1931 poem "At Easter" (*Poeta in Aeternum*, 1935) expresses nostalgia for a Russian Orthodox childhood and makes one wonder about Shklyar's Christian leanings. Yet Shklyar's long poem *Elyahu, Gaon of Vilna* (1929), dedicated to the memory of the poet's mother, Lyubov-Rashel Shklyar-Vilinskaya, glorifies the career of the great Rabbi Elyahu of Vilna (1720–1797), thus testifying to Shklyar's enduring Judaic spirit.

*   *   *

Shield of David, crescent or icon,
In the grip of my prayer I'll implore:
"Russia, dear God, is many nations,
How *can* I not love her the more?"

I shall plead with Him loudly; urgent, ardent,
I shall bow my head to the sand:
"Righteous Lord, will you please save and pardon
Russia, the suffering land!"

1923

Where's Home?

For "home," that cherished word, there's no exchange;
The ways of exile press you down like rocks.
A native corner full of memories, old crocks,
Even straw-roofed peasant huts, or grange
Are dearer than a beauty foreign, strange.
You're almost there, now you see the oxen,
The rows of carts, the yellow fields, the riverside,
And then the sunset: red-hot, molten, overflowing,
A herd of purple huts above the river glowing,
And ripening crops extending far and wide;
You lose yourself, then scream with pain inside
As the last enchanting visions flutter, going.
O how, when your heart is split, will you ever come
To love, not these accustomed days and nights,
Nor springtime Dnieper's rushing, golden light,
But Jericho's noise of time, its ancient hum,
How to compare the steppe to Hebron's desertdom,
Thatched roofs to tops of Bedouin tents pulled tight?
In Judaism fierce, hidden strengths appear
To nurture twice exile's flowers
And deep within the heart's most buried bowers
To pick amongst them and to make it clear
You're going either where all's alien but dear

Or where the majestic past regales the hours.
To you, to you, land of the endless years,
The spirit of Israel again is lit
And nothing shall extinguish ancient writ,
My life is full of promise, full of cheer
When olive-skinned, cavorting children there
Greet me with words of welcome in *ivrit*.

1925

Translated from the Russian by Maxim D. Shrayer and Andrew von Hendy

DOVID KNUT

Dovid Knut (1900–1955), poet, prose writer, and journalist, was born David Fiksman in the Bessarabian town of Orgeev (Orheyev, Orhei) and grew up in Kishinev (now Chişinău, Moldova). Knut's father kept a dry-goods store and supported a large family. Knut attended a government Jewish school and debuted as a poet at age 14 in Kishinev periodicals. In 1918 he edited the magazine *Young Thought* (*Moladaia mysl '*). In adopting his pen name, Dovid Knut followed the Yiddish (Ashkenazic Hebrew) orthoepic norm (Dóvid, not Davíd) and used the maiden name of his mother, Perl Knut. The linguist M.J. Connolly has suggested that the poet chose a word ("knut" = standard Russian and Yiddish for "whip, lash") that in both languages has connotations of oppression and slavery/serfdom.

In 1920 Knut left Kishinev, then in Romania, and settled in France, where he engaged in a wide variety of activities: he studied chemical engineering in Caen; he ran an eatery in the Parisian Latin Quarter in the 1920s and later operated a dyeing shop; and he worked as a tricycle delivery courier in the early 1930s. Additionally, the gregarious Knut stood at the helm of cultural initiatives in émigré Paris. In July 1922, he co-organized the "Exhibition of Thirteen," whose participants included Vladimir Pozner, a former Serapion Brother, and Aleksandr Ginger, the future husband of Anna Prismanova (in vol. 1). In 1925 Knut joined the Union of Young Poets and Writers, and in 1925–27 he coedited the émigré magazine *New Home* (*Novyi dom*).

Knut contributed to a variety of periodicals in Russia Abroad, including the reviews *Will of Russia* (*Volia Rossii*, Prague), *Numbers* (*Chisla*, Paris), *Contemporary Annals* (*Sovremennye zapiski*, Paris), and *Russian Annals* (*Russkie zapiski*, Kharbin) and the newspapers *Latest News* (*Poslednie novosti*) and *Days* (*Dni*), both in Paris. Knut's first and most Jewish book, *Of My Millennia* (1925), published in Paris like all five of his lifetime Russian collections of poetry, was well received for its Biblical intonation and verbal vibrancy. Leading senior critics, including Georgy Adamovich (mentor to younger Parisian poets), Alfred Bem, and Zinaida Gippius, gave Knut high marks, yet one sensed a patronizing encouragement of a "Jewish" poet by some Russian authors. Along with Boris Poplavsky (1903–1935), Knut was a star on the pale horizon of younger Parisian émigré poetry. Vladislav Khodasevich (in vol. 1) remarked in a letter to Mikhail Froman in December 1925: "There are quite a few young and not so young poets here, but I do not see major talents. Better than others is D[o]vid Knut, writing some rather interesting verses very much in the Jewish spirit."

The ruthless Vladimir Nabokov (1899–1977) gave Knut's *Second Book of Poems*

(1928) a somewhat sympathetic review in Berlin's *The Rudder* (*Rul'*), appreciating Knut's "energetic verses," his "slightly overdone Biblical coarseness," and a "healthy thirst for all earthly things." Faulting Knut for abusing overloaded terms such as "bread" or "manliness" and for sloppy rhyming, Nabokov rather correctly identified lapses of taste in Knut's treatment of sexuality and the body. In part 2 of the cycle "The Ark" one finds the line "Where [is] the memory of friendships, [of] beloved legs and breasts!" (Gde—pamiat' druzhb, liubimykh nog i grudei!")—and this is not self-parody.

After the 1929 chapbook *Satyr* came *Paris Nights* (1932; cf. Khodasevich's book-length cycle "European Night"), which some critics consider Knut's best collection. Bearing a bitterly ironic title, Knut's collection *Daily Love* (cf. "daily bread") included his best love lyrics and the long poem *The Journey*. World War II undercut plans for the publication of a volume of Knut's rich stories about Bessarabian Jews, originally printed in periodicals.

Knut and his first wife, Sarra (Sofya) Groboys, the mother of his son Daniel, parted in the early 1930s. His growing interest in Jewish activism—and his transition to Jewish-French journalism—paralleled his rapprochement with Ariadna Scriabin (1905–1944), the daughter of the composer Alexander Scriabin (1872–1915). In April 1934 Knut participated in the evening of the Tel Hai Fund, where Vladimir Jabotinsky (in vol. 1) gave a speech. Knut and Ariadna Scriabin sailed to the British Mandate of Palestine in August 1937, returning in December of the same year. While they were there, in October 1937, *Ha'aretz* published a Knut poem in a Hebrew translation by Avraham Shlonsky (1900–1973). Despite a realistic assessment of the limited literary opportunities in Eretz Israel, Knut was enthusiastic about moving there. On the basis of his visit, he composed the cycle "Foremotherland," weaving its Biblical motifs around King Solomon and Ecclesiastes. Knut completed "Foremotherland" in 1939; apparently, no later Russian poems by him survive.

Knut edited the Jewish-French newspaper *Affirmation* (*L'Affirmation*) from January 1938 to September 1939. He had no illusions about the impending catastrophe and attacked authors and intellectuals who professed antisemitism. His essay about L.-F. Céline's *Bagatelles for a Massacre* (1937) appeared in Hebrew in *Haaretz*. In 1939 Knut and Ariadna Scriabin attended the Twenty-first Zionist Congress in Geneva. In September 1939 Knut was mobilized into the French Army. He and Ariadna officially registered their marriage in March 1940, and she became *giur* in May 1940, taking the name Sara. The Knuts reached Toulouse in June 1940, and at the end of 1941 Knut wrote the pamphlet *What Is to Be Done?* (published 1942) about armed resistance to Nazis and collaborators. In December 1942, with the Gestapo on his trail, Knut escaped to Switzerland. Ariadna gave birth to Yosi, Knut's son, in May 1943. A hero of the French Resistance, she was killed in July 1944, two weeks before the liberation of Toulouse.

Knut returned to Paris in the fall of 1944. He worked at the Centre de Documentation Juive Contemporaire, editing its bulletin (as Dovid Knout) and, from August 1946, the newspaper *The Jewish World* (*Le Monde Juif*). Knut's book *Toward a His-*

tory of Jewish Resistance in France in 1940–1944 (Paris, 1947), the first documentary testimony about the Shoah in France and in some respects a Jewish-French equivalent of Ilya Ehrenburg and Vassily Grossman's *The Black Book* (see Ehrenburg and Grossman in vol.1), was reticent about the prominent role he himself had played in the Jewish Resistance.

Knut translated into French the play *The Hill of Life* by Max Zweig (1892–1992), about the 1920 Arab attack on Tel Hai in Upper Galilee. During production in the summer of 1947, Knut met the actress Virginia (subsequently Leah) Sharovskaya, who became his wife. They traveled to Israel at the end of 1948 and vacationed in Tiberias, returning in January 1949. Knut made further contacts with Israeli poets from Eastern Europe, including Leah Goldberg (1911–1970), as he hoped to have a book published in Hebrew. Some poems appeared in Israeli periodicals, but book plans did not materialize.

Knut's *Selected Poems* appeared in Paris in May 1949. An exit gesture, the Russian-language volume got a lukewarm reception in Europe and a favorable one in the United States. Vladimir Khazan, Knut's biographer and the editor of his two-volume *Collected Works* (Jerusalem, 1997–98), suggested that the Russian Montparnasse was not sympathetic to Knut's Zionist views and no longer regarded him to be a Russian author but rather a Jewish journalist. A 16 February 1939 entry in Zinaida Gippius's diary dispels all illusions: "We took a late walk and ran into Knut with his repulsive wife (the former Scriabina) [. . .]. She converted to kikery [*zhidovstvo*], because Knut became not so much a poet as a militant Israelite. 'His blood be on us and on our children.'" (Gippius is quoting Matthew 27:25.)

In the fall of 1949, the Knuts settled in Tel Aviv with his family. They experienced difficulties finding housing and work and studied Hebrew at an *ulpan* (absorption and immersion center) in Kiryat Motzkin. Leah eventually found work as an actress at the Cameri Theater in Tel Aviv, and in 1951 the Knuts settled in a suburb of Tel Aviv. Knut wrote memorial essays about Russian literature and culture, which appeared in Hebrew translation in *Ha'aretz*. He died of a brain tumor in February 1955.

Knut's verse struck the émigré readers with the vitality and vigorous rhetoric of the lyrical self. Critics noted an emphasis on the Old Testament erotic, on the metaphysics of sex, and on the cultural codes preserved in Jewish Diasporic memory and everyday living. According to Vladimir Khazan, "[. . .] in twentieth-century poetry it is hard to name another poet who perceived his national origin as erotically."

The Israeli-Russian scholar Dmitri Segal observed an intriguing dynamic of Knut's career: starting out as a passionate Judaic poet, by the 1930s Knut wrote less about Jewishness in poetry while moving into Jewish-French journalism and activism. Indeed, Knut's voice lost much of its unique "Jewish" accent as his Russian lyrical poetry of the 1930s (in *Daily Love*) closed ranks with the Parisian émigré mainstream.

Knut was influenced by a number of Russian poets, including Ivan Bunin,

Aleksandr Blok, Anna Akhmatova, Vladislav Khodasevich (in vol. 1), Marina Tsvetaeva, and Sergey Esenin. He dialogically responded to the Soviet modernism of the 1920s (e.g., Nikolay Tikhonov, Nikolay Aseev in *Paris Nights*) and his émigré contemporaries ("Parisian Note" in *Daily Love*); futurism and constructivism left traces in his versification. The uniqueness of Knut's poetry lies in its articulation of Jewish motifs and its Jewish intonation. A number of émigré poets of his generation were born Jewish: Lidia Chervinskaya, Leonid Gansky, Mikhail Gorlin, Lazar Kalberin, Vera Lurie, Boris Zakovich, and others. Yet only a few (in this anthology, Raisa Blokh, Anna Prismanova, Sofia Pregel, and Evgeny Shklyar, all in vol. 1)— and especially as compared to their Soviet coevals—addressed Jewish topics; fewer yet experimented with the texture of Jewishness in their verse. Knut towered over his generation as the most important and self-conscious Jewish-Russian poet of the First Wave, and this position resulted in an inflation of his literary reputation.

The Russian émigré philosopher Georgy Fedotov (1886–1951) wrote: "Dovid Knut is one of the most prominent poets of the Russian Paris, but the Russian form might perhaps be a matter of chance for him. This is his difference from many Jewish poets in Russian culture, of which at least one—Osip Mandelstam—has every chance of becoming a Russian classic. But Knut will not fit in Russian literature. In him sounds the voice of millennia, the voice of Biblical Israel and its limitless love, passion, longing." Knut's earlier poems, where Jewish motifs abound, might be regarded as either Russian poetry marred by slight errors of accentuation and idiom betraying a native speaker of a Jewish-Ukrainian-Bessarabian–flavored Russian or as Russian poetry deliberately spoken in a Jewish "voice." This complex issue goes back to the critical discussions of earlier Jewish-Russian poets (Simon Frug, vol. 1), and students of Jewish writing will inevitably confront it in the years to come.

The following selections represent Knut's most exemplary Jewish poems. Knut included them in *Selected Poems* (1949) and opened *Of My Millennia* (1925) with "I, Dovid-Ari ben Meir. . . ." Praised by G. Adamovich as the best twentieth-century Jewish-Russian poem, "A Kishinev Burial" appeared in *Contemporary Annals* in 1930 under the title "Recollection." In *Parisian Nights* (1932) Knut published it without a title, whereas in *Selected Poems* he added the title "A Kishinev Funeral." In the "Jewish-Russian air" of Knut's Kishinev, the traumatic memories of the 1903 Kishinev Pogrom (and of Jewish poets, Bialik among them, who condemned this "city of slaughter") are mixed with blissful memories of Pushkin, who in 1821–22, during his "Southern exile," had strolled where Knut spent his childhood. Published in émigré periodicals in 1938–39, "Haifa," "Tsfat," and "The Land of Israel" come from Knut's cycle "Foremotherland."

*   *   *

I,
Dovid-Ari ben Meir,
Son-of-Meir-Enlightener-of-Darkness,[1]
Born by the foothills of Ivanos,[2]
In a plenteous land of plenteous hominy,
Of sheep cheese and sharp *caccocavallo*,[3]
In a land of forests and strong-loined bulls,
Of bubbling wines and bronzy breasted women;
Where midst the steppes and ruddy fields of corn
Still roam the smoky fires
Of gypsies making camp;

I,
Dovid-Ari ben Meir,
The boy who soothed the angry Saul with song,
Who gave
The rebel line of Israel
A star's six points as shield;

I,
Dovid-Ari,
Whose sling and stone
Brought bellowing oaths from the dying Goliath—
The one whose steps sent tremors through the hills—
I've come into your camp to learn your songs
But soon, I'll tell you
Mine.

---

1. The editor is indebted to Vladimir Khazan's commentary in his two-volume edition of Dovid Knut's works (Jerusalem, 1997–98). Knut simultaneously offers a literal translation and an interpretation of the Hebrew "ben Meir," which literally means "son of Meir," but the word "Meir" means "he who enlightens/illuminates." Given that later in the poem Knut identifies himself with the future King David soothing King Saul with music and song (cf. I Kings 16) and slaying Goliath (cf. I Kings 17), the name "Ari," which in Hebrew means "lion," should not be overlooked.

2. The Ivanus (Ivanos) is one of the left tributaries of the Reut, a river in Moldova and itself a right tributary of the Dniester; Orgeev, Knut's native town, is located in the Ivanus (Ivanos) valley.

3. *Cacciocavallo* (from the Italian for "horse muzzle")—type of hard cheese; Knut uses a Russian corruption, *kachkaval*.

I see it all:
The deserts of Canaan,
The sands and date trees of parchèd Palestine,
The guttural moan of Arab camel trains,
The cedars of Lebanon, and bored ancient walls
Of my Holy Yerushalaim.

And the awesome hour:
The crack, crumble, and roar of Sinai,
When fire and thunder sundered the Heavens,
And in the cauldron of wrathful clouds
Arose the knotted eye of Adonai-The-Lord
Staring in anger through the haze
At the lost creatures in the sand.

I see it all: the grieving Babylon rivers,
The creaking of carts, the tinkling of cymbals,
The smoke and stench of father's grocery—
Its quince, halvah, garlic, and tobacco sheaves—
Where I guarded from roving Moldavian fingers
The moldy half-moon cakes, fish, dried and salted.

I,
Dovid-Ari ben Meir,
Whose wine has wandered some thousands of years,
Stop now at this crossing in the sands
To sing you, brothers, my song—
My heavy burden of love and longing—

The blessed burden of my millennia.

1925

A Kishinev Burial

It was a dismal evening in Kishinev:
We rounded the bend from Inzov Hill,[4]
Where Pushkin once had lived. A sorry knoll
Where the short, curly-haired clerk had lived—
The celebrated rake and scapegrace—
With those hot, those blackamoor eyes
Set in a swarthy, thick-lipped, lively face.

Beyond dusty, sullen, still Asia Road,
Along the hard walls of the Maternity Home,
They were carrying a dead Jew on a stretcher.
Beneath the unclean funeral cover,
Protruded the bony features
Of this man gnawed to death by life.
Of this man so gnawed to the bone that
Afterward there was nothing left on which
The thin worms of the Jewish cemetery might feed.

Behind the elders carrying the stretcher
Walked a handful of Jews Mané-Katz might paint,[5]
Greenish-yellow and with big sunken eyes.
From their moldering gabardine caftans
Came a compounded odor of holiness and fate,
The Jewish odor of poverty and sweat,
Of moths, salt herring, and fried onion,
Of sacred books, soaked diapers, and synagogues.

---

4. The great Russian poet Aleksandr Pushkin (1799–1837), whose great-grandfather, A.P. Gannibal, godson of Peter the Great, was born an Abyssinian prince, lived in Kishinev in 1821–23, serving under the auspices of the Bessarabian governor, General Ivan N. Inzov, before being transferred to Odessa, where he spent the last year of his so-called "southern exile." Inzov Hill is a neighborhood of Kishinev where General Inzov's house was located; Pushkin stayed there from the spring of 1821 to the spring of 1822. Today the streets and buildings of Knut's native city bear the memories of Pushkin and his era, and a Pushkin Museum still functions in Chişinău (au (formerly Kishinev), now the capital of independent Moldova. Inzov Hill was a place in Knut's Kishinev that one passed on the way to Aziatskaya (Asia) Road, a Jewish area to which Knut's family moved around 1903.

5. Katz, Mané (Mané-Katz, Ohel Emmanuel,1894–1962)—Jewish painter, famous for his portrayal of Jewish life in eastern Europe; born in Russia and settled in the west in 1921. Knut was personally acquainted with the painter.

Great grief gave simple cheer to their hearts,
And they walked with an unheard step,
Submissive, easy, measured, unhurried,
As if they had walked behind the corpse for years,
As if there were no start to their procession,
As if there were no end to it . . . With the step
Of Zion's—of Kishinev's—sages and elders.

Between them and their sad black freight
Walked a woman, and in the dusty falling darkness
We could not see her face.

But how excellent was her high voice!

Under the knocking step, under the faint rustle
Of fallen leaves, of rubbish, 'neath her cough
Flowed another, an as yet inconceivable song.
In it were tears of sweet submission
And eternal devotion to the will of God,
In it was the rapture of humility and fear . . .

O, how excellent was her high voice!

Not of the thin Jew on the stretcher
Bobbing up and down, did she sing but of me,
Of us, of everyone, of vanity, of dust,
Of old age, of grief, of fear,
Of pity, of vanity, of bewilderment,
Of the eyes of dying children . . .

The Jewess walked, almost stumbling,
And each time that the cruel stone
Tossed up the corpse on sticks, she
Threw herself on him with a cry, and her voice
Suddenly broadened, grew strong, resonant,
Solemnly gonged a threat to God,
And it grew livelier from her furious cries.
And the woman threatened with her fists
The One Who Floated in the greenish heaven
Above the dusty trees, above the corpse,
Above the roof of the Maternity Home,
Above the hard, uneven road.

But here, the woman became frightened of herself,
And she beat her breast and froze,
And repented, hysterically and long.
Frightened, she praised God's will,
Shouted frenziedly of forgiveness,
Of faith, humility, of faith,
Started up and huddled to the ground
Under the heaviness of the invisible eyes
That gazed down from the skies sadly and sternly.

. . . .

What had taken place? Evening, quiet, a fence, a star
Heavy dust . . . My poems in *The Courier*.
The trusting gymnasium student, Olya,
A simple rite of Jewish burial,
And a woman from the Book of Genesis.

But I'll never be able to tell in words
What hovered over Asia Road,
Over the lampposts of the city outskirts,
Over the laughter suppressed at back alleys,
Over the boldness of an unknown guitar,
Rocking from where, God only knows—over the baying
Of melancholy, snarling dogs.

. . . That peculiarly Jewish-Russian air . . .
Blessed are those who have ever breathed it.

1929

Haifa

1

Where labors languish, where sloth unwatered grows,
Where desert stones have long discouraged beast,
Once more—a drinking place, a saving cave,
A masculine, geometric refuge.

And the huge piece of writer's paper
Without desiring waits stilly for the vital ink,
The last few tears, the blessed moisture
That is preserved for the dark hour.

The country works: pen, shovel, spade—
And the sweat of the soul, like the sweat of the face, runs salty,
But where seed is sown—the blooms of Ecclesiastes,
Your wise garden, love-sick Solomon.

2

O, poor Carmel! Grave-like cubes
Preserve a hygienic comfort:
The radio box, teeth of gold
Through which bronze-clad souls puke.

The fire and brimstone of European lava,
The cinema, the factory whistle . . .
But above all, but through all, like a bane.
A penetrating, a Scriptural chill.

1938

Tsfat

Mounds of humped reddish mountains,
Lying along the slopes like camels,
The color of infertility, where rarely a greedy glance
Is consoled by a dark green spot.

The autumn caravan of sullen mountains
Tired from aimless journeys,
From the motley monotony of the countries,
From the boredom of clouds, sands, and disasters.

Too long did it carry—both night and day—
The humble chattel of homes and graves,
The millennial burden and trash
Of impotent faith, backbreaking spite . . .

Of houses crowded with terraces,
Secret cubes becoming blue,
Flocks of stones, camels, and donkeys
Braying, tedious and coarse.

And again—the ever-dissolving quiet
That hangs over the Holy Writings, sworn forever,
And through the glassy languor that just sits,
I hear God, bending just now over Tsfat.

1938

The Land of Israel

To Eva Kirshner

I was walking along the shore of Tiberias
And joyously, divinely sullen
(As if my heart was glad and was not glad),
I picked my way among the stones of Capernaum
Where once . . . Listen and just think
In the shade, in the dust of the olive grove.

All the while, the same voice in the universal bar,
Sleepless, international, irrevocable,
On the subject of the unslaked desire of the flesh
And those (For all! For a farthing! Indefatigable!)
Faces off of film ads
On the walls of the City—of Jerusalem.

What's there to tell you about Palestine?
What's there to recall? The unpopulated Sedjera,
The orange cloud of the hot desert wind,
The staid voice of the convert from Astrakhan,
Or the slim insulted back
Of the boy shot while keeping watch?

The haughty camel over the trough,
The mute tzaddiks in *peyes* from Tsfat?
The dry sky unsaturated with eternity
Over the childhood of the world in death's embrace?
And the obliterate numerous slabs
Of the senseless dead men of Josaphat.

Or a young woman named Judith
Who waved her swarthy hand long after I had passed.

1938

Translated from the Russian by Ruth Rischin

DON-AMINADO

Don-Aminado (1888–1957), poet and satirist, was born Aminodav Peysakhovich (Russianized: Aminad Petrovich) Shpolyansky to a lower-middle-class Jewish family in Elizavetgrad, Kherson Province (now Kirovohrad in Ukraine; in 1897 Elizavetgrad had 23,967 Jews out of a total population of 61,488). After graduating from a gymnasium, Don-Aminado entered the law faculty of Novorossiysk University in Odessa and in 1910 qualified for a law degree in Kiev, contributing to southern newspapers during his student years. He moved to Moscow and served as a "sworn advocate in training" in 1912–15 while writing for *Early Morning* (*Rannee utro*). Don-Aminado was drafted in 1914 and was wounded and discharged in 1915.

In 1914–15, Don-Aminado contributed to *The New Satyricon* (*Novyi Satirikon*), a leading satirical magazine. He published poems, parodies, and feuilletons in *Red Laughter* (*Krasnyi smekh*), *Alarm Clock* (*Budil'nik*), and newspapers. As though his Jewish name were not zesty enough, Don-Aminado adopted a pen name of manifold irony, underscoring its bearer's unaristocratic origins while hinting at Don Quixote. Don-Aminado's *Songs of War* appeared in 1914 in Moscow (second edition, 1915); in several poems Don-Aminado warned of a crisis of world culture, adumbrating the motifs of his 1930s poetry. Staged in May 1917, Don-Aminado's satirical play in verse *Spring of 1917* reflected a post–February 1917 liberal optimism. After the Bolshevik takeover, Don-Aminado moved to Kiev, which enjoyed a transiently turbulent cultural life, and contributed to Kievan newspapers. A new journal, *Devil's Peppermill* (*Chertova perechnitsa*), attracted a number of famous satirists, whom (Nadezhda) Teffi (1876–1952) dubbed "whipped [wiped out] cream of society" (*bitye slivki obshchestva*). In January 1920, Don-Aminado left Odessa for Constantinople.

After arriving in Paris in 1920, Don-Aminado published in *The Jewish Tribune* (*Evreiskaia tribuna*) and *Free Thoughts* (*Svobodnye mysli*). He began an association with the main Parisian Russian daily *Latest News* (*Poslednie novosti*) in 1920–21. After a 1921 conflict with its editor, Pavel Milyukov, Don-Aminado published elsewhere for several years (e.g., Riga's *Today* (*Segodnia*). His collection *Smoke without Fatherland* appeared in 1921 in Paris; its title ironized the adage from Aleksandr Griboedov's *Woe from Wit* (1825): "And the smoke of our fatherland to us is sweet and pleasant." Don-Aminado arrived in the United States at the end of 1923 and returned to Paris in April 1924. After reconciling with *Latest News* in 1926, he remained the paper's fixture until its closing in 1940. In April–November 1931, Don-Aminado edited the weekly *Satyricon*, a short-lived Parisian émigré incarnation of the glorious pre-Revolutionary magazine (see Sasha Cherny in vol. 1).

Don-Aminado's books include *Our Little Life: Humorous Stories* (1927), *Having Thrown On the Cape: A Collection of Lyrical Satire* (1928), and others. He edited and translated an anthology of humorous Russian works with Maurice Decobra, *La rire dans le steppe* (1927). Don-Aminado was decorated with a Légion d'Honneur in 1934 for promoting cultural ties between the Russian emigration and France. A 1935 volume, *Untedious Garden*, collected his aphorisms and appeared in French as *Pointes de feu: Recueil de maxims* (1939). "The path to oblivion often lies through the Arch of Triumph," stated one of his aphorisms.

By giving émigré readers humorous, topical, gently nostalgic verse, Don-Aminado remained phenomenally popular throughout the 1920s and 1930s. Friends later stressed that he underutilized his talent, that "in life he was more talented than his feuilletons" (Leonid Zurov). Andrey Sedykh (in vol. 1) wrote that Don-Aminado, along with Teffi and Sasha Cherny, continued "the classical tradition of Russian humor, suffused with humaneness and compassion."

During World War II, Don-Aminado lived in Montpellier and Aix-les-Bains. Devastated by the Shoah, he became a recluse and published little after the war, contributing some feuilletons to New York's *New Russian Word* (*Novoe russkoe slovo*). He included few postwar poems in the volume *In Those Fabulous Years* (Paris, 1951), where the last poem was called "Conclusion": "In the sense of world distances/ The power of ideas is unvanquishable:/From Dachau to Narym/The train goes directly." (Thousands were exiled to Narym in Siberia during the Stalin era.)

Don-Aminado's works have enjoyed a revival after being returned to Russia in the late 1980s, in turn stimulating new scholarship in Russia and the West, including an Italian book by Marco Caratozzolo.

Occasional echoes of pre-Revolutionary Jewish life sound in Don-Aminado's émigré verse: consider the poem "Autumn in the Provinces" from *Having Thrown on the Cape* (1928). In the 1930s Don-Aminado refused to make distinctions between Fascist and Communist dictators. It was becoming difficult to laugh: "The limit of metalloplastics—/An artistic coat of arms/In which, besides the swastika/There's both hammer and sickle" ("Fragments," 1939). Don-Aminado's principled position resonated with Vladimir Nabokov's in *Invitation to a Beheading* (1938).

Don-Aminado's remarkable memoir *Train on the Third Track* appeared in New York in 1954. Originally intended to end in 1945, the memoir stopped short in 1939. About Nabokov, Don-Aminado said, "The appearance of the young writer [Nabokov] stirred passionate debate." In *Pnin* (1957), Nabokov gave Don-Aminado's last name, spelled "Shpolyanski," to a liberal Jewish-Russian politician, whose wife approaches Pnin at a party to remind him of Mira Belochkin's death in Buchenwald.

Autumn in the Provinces

Autumn is a whiff of leather,
Brand-new satchel, brand-new belt,
Your heart beating with the weather,
Cheeks aglow as if they'd melt.
Autumn is a whiff of varnish,
Glowing in the polished halls,
And the talk and jokes and laughter
Resonating off the walls.

On the walls hang old framed portraits
Of a grand bemedaled crew.
Wafting mildly from the garden,
Fresh air turns a faint pale blue.

But the doorman, lame Vasily,
Gives that air a copper shake.
Instantly your heartstrings quiver,
Stopping with a sudden ache.
Who has dressed this mundane planet
In this sheer diaphanous robe?
Who has made it all so splendid
Like a parti-colored globe?
Sad to think that the Etruscans
And their children are long gone,
Not surviving for this morning,
For this lovely autumn dawn.

Autumn is the smell of apples
And a peasant's sheepskin vest,
Cantaloupe fresh from the garden
When a melon's at its best.

Autumn is a quiet noontime.
Water tower. Fireman up there.
And a curious town in Russia
With a farmers' market square.
Autumn evening. Gentle rainfall.
Some mute bulldog trying to bark.

Sodden playbill on a fencepost.
Streetlight flickering in the dark.
Dalsky, famous tragic actor.
Drunken prompter whispering low.
Box of the police detective,
Claret-colored calico.

Not to worry, but the propman
Left the wall-sconce torches lit,
So the shadow of Hamlet's father
Creeps across into the pit,
And the jolly band conductor
Played the intermission wrong:
Now a wild Ukrainian folk dance,
Now a Jewish marching song.

In the capitals' huge theaters
With their jaded sense of fun,
Have you ever seen such pleasure,
So much joy in everyone?

When a foreign, alien autumn
Flashes you a sullen grin,
Just remember all that's happened
That you'll never see again.

1920s

Translated from the Russian by J.B. Sisson and Maxim D. Shrayer

RAISA BLOKH

Raisa Blokh (1899–1943), poet and translator, was born in St. Petersburg to a lawyer's family. Her father, (Noy) Noah Blokh, apparently converted to Christianity pro forma, so as to be able to practice law under pre-Revolutionary anti-Jewish restrictions; her mother apparently did not convert. In the autobiographical poem "Remember, father would stand . . ." (1933; translation below), Blokh would remember her father praying, a *talles* over his head. Blokh majored in medieval studies at Petrograd University and also participated in Mikhail Lozinsky's translation seminar. Blokh was accepted to the Union of Poets in Petrograd in 1920. She was encouraged by her brother, Yakov Blokh, who in 1918 founded an important literary publishing firm, Petropolis.

Blokh moved to Berlin in 1922 with her brother's family and continued her studies. In 1928 she completed a dissertation on Pope Leo IX at the University of Berlin and took a job at a German academic publishing house, working there until the spring of 1933. Her research interests included the female German poet Hrosvit von Gandersheim (ca. 935–ca. 975). Blokh's first poetry collection, *My City*, appeared in Berlin in 1928. Operating in Berlin and later in Brussels, Blokh's brother published her lifetime collections.

In Berlin Blokh was part of an informal poetry seminar ("Circle of Thirty"), whose members included Yury Dzhanumov, Essad-Bey, Evgenia Kannak, Sofia Pregel (in vol. 1), and others which convened at the apartment of its chairman, Mikhail Gorlin (1909–1944). They published three collectives: *Housewarming* (later the title of Sofia Pregel's American-based journal), *The Grove*, and *Dragnet*. The titles inadvertently reflect the contributors' insecurity about their place in Russian letters.

Blokh's junior by ten years, Gorlin emigrated to the west from St. Petersburg with his family in 1918. His farther, a timber merchant, was able to transfer some of his assets abroad. A student of Russian literature, in 1933 Gorlin defended a dissertation, "Gogol and E.T.A. Hoffmann," under the distinguished Slavist Max Vasmer. Gorlin published original German poetry, which exhibited Jewish themes. In 1936 his Russian-language collection *Journeys* appeared in Berlin. The Blokh–Gorlin relationship developed over the years from a platonic friendship to romance and marriage. Together they translated Sergey Esenin and Anna Akhmatova into German and composed children's tales. The poetry of Blokh and Gorlin, who were known as "a pair of doves" in emigration, exhibited signs of cross-fertilization.

The Gorlins left Germany in 1933, settling in Paris, and were married in 1935. Both did some research work at the Sorbonne and Bibliothèque nationale and never felt well adjusted socially in émigré Paris (they were friendly with Vladislav Khodasevich [in vol.1]). Blokh's second collection, *Quietude: Poems, 1928–1934* (Berlin, 1935), was well received. In 1939 Blokh's poems appeared in the volume *Testaments* along with poems by the medievalist Myrrha Lot-Borodine (1882–1957). One of Blokh's poems was made popular by Aleksandr Vertinsky (1889–1957), the acclaimed émigré poet-chansonnnier, who returned to the USSR in 1943. With him Vertinsky brought to the Soviet audience a repertoire that included "Alien Cities," a modified version of Raisa Blokh's nostalgically bitter poem "A snatch of speech came floating on the air . . ." that recalls St. Petersburg's Summer Garden (Letny Sad) and rivers and canals (translation below).

Gorlin was arrested by the Nazis in May 1941; he was subsequently transferred to the Silesian salt mines and died there in 1943. The Gorlins' six-year-old daughter, Dora, died in 1942. Living under an assumed name, Blokh attempted to cross the Swiss border in November 1943 but was returned by the Swiss border guards to the Nazis. Blokh was sent to the Drancy concentration camp and deported to a camp in Germany in 1943. She managed to drop a note from the train car, and that note has survived. The exact circumstances of Blokh's death are unknown. After the war the couple's friends published a volume of their essays, *Literary and Historical Études* (Paris, 1957) and a volume of their *Selected Poems* (1959). Anna Prismanova dedicated her poem "Shine" (in vol. 1) to Raisa Blokh's memory.

All three of the selected poems appeared in Blokh's collection *Quietude* (1935) and in *Selected Poems* of Raisa Blokh and Mikhail Gorlin, posthumously published in Paris by the publishing house Rifma (Rhyme), directed by Sofia Pregel (in vol. 1). The third poem was originally published in the collective volume *Dragnet* (Berlin, 1933).

Reviewing Blokh's *My City* (1928) in the Berlin daily *The Rudder* (Rul'), Vladimir Nabokov wrote, "Thus in the end all this [poetry]—golden, lite, and slightly permeated with [Anna] Akhmatova's cold perfume (something almost unavoidable in women's poetry)—may give the undiscriminating reader the impression of something pleasant, simple, birdlike." Nabokov, who had known both Blokh and Gorlin in Berlin and who left Germany in 1937 with a Jewish wife and son, later regretted the harshness of his review. His remorse might have led him to the discovery of the character of Mira Belochkin, possibly a composite image of Raisa Blokh and Myrrha Lot-Borodine in the novel *Pnin* (1957). Mira's death in Buchenwald gives the novel's non-Jewish protagonist, Timofey Pnin, reasons to live and remember.

* * *

A snatch of speech came floating on the air,
Brought me words I didn't need to hear:
Letny Sad, Fontanka, and Neva.

The words flew by, like swallows on the wing:
Blocked out by foreign towns, with all their din,
And foreign water gurgling through the drains.

I cannot grasp, I cannot hide, or drive
Those words away: I won't recall! I'll live,
Suppress my pain, exist, hang on, survive.

I'll never walk along that riverbank,
Hiding my face in a soft crochet wrap,
My woollen mitt held in my mother's hand.

All this was real, but years and years ago:
The path I walked is covered by thick snow
Which muffles sounds and makes a blank white glow.

1932

* * *

Remember, father would stand,
And pray, hour by hour on end?
Black against white, the fringe
On the shawl that covered his head.

The sun stared in from outside,
Shone brightly, enjoying the scene:
The mud you picked up rolling round
In the street just wouldn't scrub clean.

1933

* * *

How can I find you again, holy names,
And you, letters, dark as ruined temples?
O, how my blood cleaves to you, helpless;
Anxious, it heeds, straining through centuries,
For that call, the same down the ages.

Let me stay with you, like all the legions
Of the unborn, the patient children, repeating
The square-root letters of your testament,
Knowing that the unquenchable light is spreading
And pouring the warmth of millennia into the dusk.

1934

Translated from the Russian by Catriona Kelly

ANNA PRISMANOVA

Anna Prismanova (1892–1960) was born Anna Prisman in Libava, in the Kurland Province (presently Liepaja, Latvia; see Lev Ginzburg in volume 2), a major port of entry and a seaside resort. Prismanova revisited a Baltic childhood in her only Russian short story, "On Guard and on Town Gardens" (English translation by Catriona Kelly). Libava's Jewish community (9,454 out of 64,489 residents in 1897) was composed of German-speaking Prussian Jews, Yiddish-speaking Latvian Jews, and the Jewish-Russian intelligentsia to which Prismanova's parents belonged. Prismanova's father was a dermatologist; Prismanova's mother died at the age of thirty-five, leaving three young daughters. At eighteen Prismanova converted to Russian Orthodoxy and Russified her last name. The family migrated to Moscow in 1918, and in 1920 Prismanova moved to Petrograd and joined the Union of Poets.

As Yury Kolker (in vol. 2) noted, "Prismanova's literary formation followed the worst possible scenario." The thirty-year-old Prismanova arrived in Berlin a literary unknown. In Berlin, in 1923, Prismanova's poems appeared in Andrey Bely's short-lived journal *Epic Journey* (*Epopeia*). With poets Vadim Andreev, Semyon Liberman, and Georgy Venus, and critic Bronislav Sosinsky, Prismanova formed the literary grouplet "4 + 1" and published, in 1923–24, two collections, which received scant notice. A reluctant promoter of her work, Prismanova did not contribute frequently to émigré publications. In 1924 Prismanova moved to Paris. Hardly a "young poet," she joined the Union of Young Writers and Poets. In 1926 she married the poet Aleksandr Ginger (1897–1965). Ginger came from the Russianized Jewish family of a St. Petersburg physician. By the time they met, Ginger had published his first collection, *Pack of the Faithful* (1921), which was followed by four more. They had two children: Basile (b. 1925), a genealogist of French Jewry; and Serge (b. 1928), a social psychologist. The émigrés perceived Prismanova and Ginger as a harmonious but odd couple. Notes of cultural superiority if not prejudice crept into postwar accounts; consider Yury Ivask's 1985 letter to fellow First-Wave poet Valery Pereleshin: "She was a two-dimensional figure—out of Modigliani; he resembled a used-goods dealer from a Gomel flea market." Ginger supported the family as an accountant for a chemical company, and in 1929–32 they were based in Normandy. Prismanova's first collection, *Shadow and Body*, its earliest poems dated 1929, appeared in 1937. In the 1940s Prismanova published three French stories in *Cahiers du Sud*, a major French literary journal.

In Paris during the Nazi occupation, Ginger refused to wear a yellow star and spent part of the war in hiding. Ginger's mother was arrested and died in Auschwitz. Apparently considered to be a Russian, because her papers identified her as Russian Orthodox, Prismanova was not in danger of deportation. She spent part of the war with the children in the Auvergne countryside. As did many émigrés, after the war Prismanova and Ginger considered repatriating to the Soviet Union. Both had left-wing sympathies, more artistic than political, but harbored no illusions about Stalinism.

Prismanova's collection *Twins* appeared in Paris in 1946, followed by *Salt* (1949). In her latter years she worked on the verse tale *Vera* (published in 1960), about the famous revolutionary Vera Figner (1852–1943), who was instrumental in the 1881 assassination of Alexander II.

Prismanova died of a heart condition in 1960. Finding no solace in Judaism after the Shoah, Ginger died a Buddhist in 1965. Returned to Russia in the 1990s, their works were collected in the volume *Misty Link* (Tomsk, 1999).

In the words of Victor Terras, Prismanova created "an intriguing world of absurdist yet plastic images, and illogical yet somehow familiar relationships." Prismanova's poems, altogether under two hundred, display a penchant for paronomasia and a quirkiness of intonation, partly deliberate and partly resulting from infelicities of orthoepy and unidiomatic usage. A narrative flow renders her lyrical, leap-driven poems a distinct intonation, and they shine against the dull lustre of much of the Parisian émigré poetry. According to Petra Couvée, the editor of Prismanova's *Collected Works* (The Hague, 1900), Prismanova was largely "concerned with the poet herself and the creative art of writing." Catriona Kelly observed that "feminine identity is represented by Prismanova as a constant struggle between the earth-bound forces of biology and the spiritual release attainable in mysticism."

All three of the selected poems appeared in *Twins* (Paris, 1946); the first two testify to the subterranean workings of Prismanova's Jewish identity. In "Grandmother," Prismanova glances inwardly at her ancestors' Diasporic experience and centuries of cousinage while also melancholizing her own symbolic death in the Shoah. In "Eyes," an alternative explanation of the grandfather's missing eye hints at the violence of pogromists; this explanation aligns the grandfather's suppressed memory with that of old Shapiro in David Aizman's story "The Countrymen" (in vol. 1). "Shine" appeared in 1939 in *Russian Notes* (*Russkie zapiski*) as the third part of the cycle "Ash." In *Twins*, Prismanova broke up the cycle and added a dedication, commemorating Raisa Blokh (in vol. 1), who died in the Shoah.

Grandmother

Forefathers' blemishes live on in children,
some grand-daughters are sick with aged ills.
Lyubóv, or Love, was what they chose to call her,
my grandmother, and thus they bound my will.

My grandmother, she lived in the town nut-house:
She had long sleeves that tied behind her back.
The photographs of her were yellowed, nut-brown,
And when she died, she willed me her straitjacket.

Like two forked paths that reach one destination
The blood and bone in me track different ways.
My blood goes surging off to you, grandmother,
I'm tethered by my bone, so I can't stray.

Once dark begins to close around my bedposts,
I'm pulled to pieces, every night the same.
I'd think my name might be Lyubóv, except that
I don't remember if I have a name.

late 1930s–early 1940s

Eyes

1.

My grandfather had one eye made of glass.
He lost the real live one during the Turkish
campaign—so, in much later days,
he'd tell his small granddaughter as he nursed her.

Water, mixed to a paste with pounded sand,
saltpeter too, was what the eye was made of.
The scar across his temple had long healed.
The eye stayed on the operating table.

How we extol the courage of those eyes
that gave their sight to save the land they lived in.
The veins inside were battered by the pulse
of life; the blood, though, went on giving.

Phoenician merchants, when the world was young,
made beads of glass among the sand on beaches,
So Russian forefathers could, in good time,
use their glass eyes as playthings to amuse us.

You'll never see tears roll from eyes like these:
they're hard as northern hives, when honey-turbid;
as glassy as the eyes the prophets raised
over the soulful dunes of Egypt's deserts.

2.

Alongside, though, there was another eye,
with veins like three blue stitches by the pupil.
It used it to read, without glasses, books by three
world-famous men, and tell apart three orphans.

That eye gave him protection from the fog,
and let him pick his way round drifts and tussocks
in winter's snows. It helped him place his watch,
pouring the chain from buttonhole to pocket.

An ever-watching eye, an eye not made
by human hand. He fed the doves with challah,
and tears rolled from inside the live eye's lid
as the music box ground out its sour-sweet numbers.

A weather-beaten cheek swelled out below.
His bright blue eye, fixed in that fatal socket,
stared on, noting events and days and hours,
steady and careful as a blind watchmaker's.

late 1930s–early 1940s

Shine

In Memory of Raisa Blokh

Who lets us part the curtains of blind eyes,
who gets us to skirt round the walls of silence
and speak to the deaf? Hearts flap against the glass
and fly around the light, like flies at nightfall.

A reading lamp shines on a wooden desk;
(a spring in desert sands might well be shining
for all I know). No words can help direct;
astronomers no longer count the planets.

It could be things don't turn up when you search;
it could be shine implies some kind of shadow.
Perhaps we're not so much astronomers
as merchants who well know the price of diamonds.

But shafts of light, I'm sure, live on and on:
even a morgue's walls glimmer in the moonshine.
In human souls one thread of silvery ore
catches the light: it's pity mixed with passion.

1938–39; 1946

Translated from the Russian by Catriona Kelly

SOFIA DUBNOVA-ERLICH

Sofia (Sophie) **Dubnova-Erlich** (1885–1986), poet, essayist, translator, and memoirist, was born in Mstislavl (Mogilev Province in what is now Belarus), the oldest daughter of the great Jewish historian Shimon Dubnow (1860–1941). In 1903, she enrolled in the Bestuzhev Higher Academy (*kursy*) for Women in St. Petersburg; in 1904 she was expelled after a student political protest. In Odessa, where Dubnova-Erlich's family was living at the time, she observed, among her father's interlocutors, the philosopher of spiritual Zionism Ahad Ha'am (1856–1927) and the writers Ben-Ami, Semyon Frug (both in vol. 1), Sholem Aleichem, and Hayyim Nahman Bialik. In 1910–11, Dubnova-Erlich studied at the Sorbonne. In 1906 her father became chair of Jewish history at the soon-to-be closed Free University of St. Petersburg, and her parents stayed there until 1921.

Dubnova-Erlich debuted with poems in the Jewish-Russian periodicals *The Futureness* (*Budushchnost'*) and *Sunrise* (*Voskhod*). Her literary activity occurred on a sociocultural orbit, which only partially intersected with her involvement in the Russian Social-Democratic Labor Party (RSDRP) and the Jewish Labor Party (Bund, founded in 1897 in Vilna). Dubnova-Erlich wrote and translated for the newspaper *Jewish World* (*Evreiskii mir*), the Bundist organ *Our Word* (*Nashe slovo*), and other periodicals. Her first collection, *Autumn Reed-Pipe*, appeared in St. Petersburg in 1911, the year she married Henryk (Genrikh) Erlich (1881–1942), one of the leaders of the Bund. They had two sons, Alexander Erlich (1912–1985), subsequently an economics professor at Columbia University, and Victor Erlich (b. 1914), later a Yale University professor and prominent Slavist.

During World War I, Dubnova-Erlich contributed to Maxim Gorky's antimilitarist *Chronicle* (*Letopis'*) and the Bundist daily *Jewish News* (*Evreiskie vesti*). Her poetry chapbook *Mother* appeared in St. Petersburg in 1916 (reprinted in Tel Aviv, 1969). Focusing on the anxieties of motherhood in cataclysmic times, it established a continuous theme of Dubnova-Erlich's poetry. Dubnova-Erlich supported the February Revolution but opposed the Bolshevik takeover. In 1918 the Erlichs moved to Warsaw and spent twenty-two years in Poland, where Dubnova-Erlich contributed to Yiddish and Russian émigré publications. She conducted research in the Bund Archives in Berlin in 1925–26.

The Erlichs fled to eastern Poland in September 1939. Henryk Erlich and fellow Bundist leader Viktor Alter (1890–1941) were detained by Soviet authorities in Brest-Litovsk. Dubnova-Erlich and her family made it to Lithuania. She last saw her father in November 1940 in Vilna; he returned to Riga, refusing to emigrate. In Kovno, Dubnova-Erlich obtained a transit visa to the Dutch Caribbean island of Curaçao, which allowed her to travel to Moscow, then to Vladivostok, Japan, and subsequently Canada. Reaching New York City in 1942, Dubnova-Erlich learned of her father's death in the Riga ghetto in 1941. In 1943 she heard that her husband and Viktor Alter were executed by the NKVD, and it was not until the post-Soviet era that the KGB archives revealed that Henryk Erlich had actually taken his life in a Kuibyshev jail in 1942.

In America, Dubnova-Erlich had a rich career as a contributor to the Russian émigré and Yiddish press. In 1950, her biography, *The Life and Work of S.M. Dubnow*, appeared in Russian in New York (Yiddish translation, 1952; English translation, 1991). Her contributions included the monograph *The Social Aspect of the Magazine "Chronicle"* (New York, 1963) and one of the earliest American overviews, "Jewish Literature in Russian," published in a 1952 volume. Dubnova-Erlich's memoir, *Bread and Matzos*, was partially serialized in the 1980s in the third-wave émigré review *Time and We* (*Vremia i my*). Over her long career, Dubnova-Erlich translated into Russian from Yiddish, Hebrew, German, and English the works of Sholem Asch, Thomas Mann, Kate Boyle, and others. Her translation of David Bergelson's Yiddish novel *When All Is Said and Done* (*Nokh alemen*, 1913) appeared in 1923 in Berlin. Her Russian poetry was collected in *Poems of Various Years* (New York, 1973). The legacy of Dubnova-Erlich found dedicated American students in Carole B. Balin and Kristi A. Groberg.

A committed civil-rights activist, Dubnova-Erlich marched in antiwar protests and prochoice demonstrations. She died at age 100 in New York. Dubnova-Erlich's memoir appeared in 1994 in St. Petersburg, with an introduction by her son Victor Erlich. Despite her losses and peregrinations—and the intricacies of her multicultural identity—Dubnova-Erlich insisted she was a *peterburzhanka*.

Dubnova-Erlikh's finest poems, lyrical and confessional, speak of motherhood and living apart from Russia: "An émigré? No, simply a daughter separated from her mother." Her verse aesthetic was nurtured by her love of Russian symbolist poetry. Notes of social protest align her with such Jewish-Russian poets as Dmitry Tsenzor (in vol. 1).

Dubnova-Erlich's wartime essays made a prominent contribution to Russian literature about the Shoah. The essays chosen below appeared in 1943–44 in the New York–based émigré magazine *Housewarming (Novosel'e)*, edited by Sofia Pregel (in vol. 1). Given Dubnova-Erlich's knowledge of Jewish life in eastern Europe, the factographic precision of her prose, and the timing of the publication of her essays, they were an émigré equivalent of the wartime nonfiction of Vassily Grossman and Ilya Ehrenburg (both in vol. 1).

Two Wartime Essays

Shtetl

The shtetl, lost here among Polish fields and groves, might be called Turek or Przasnysz, Konin or Maków, yet what one remembers is not the name but the old marketplace reeking of tar and dung where a rickety, mud-splattered bus would laboriously grind to a stop. What has stayed in my memory is an old town hall with a blackened clock face, a movie house resembling barracks with crude posters at the entrance, and a herd of coarse small houses with tiny blinking windows, all bunched together.

Getting off the bus onto the square, where left-over patches of straw from market day lay rotting between jagged cobblestones, I would step straight into the seventeenth century. Left behind was the frivolous, lighthearted capital, Warsaw, with the defiant clatter of cavalry spurs and the shrill, drunken screech of jazz trying to drown out the somber grumble of the poverty-stricken outskirts and the threatening rumble of oncoming historical storms. Here, in the provincial backwaters, poverty reigned openly and implacably; it was solid, familiar, passed on from father to son, reeking through and through of stove smoke, yesterday's warmed-up borsch, unaired comforters; a poverty firmly rooted in narrow strips of land among the shops, the synagogue, the heder, and the mikvah. The days passed by inaudibly. Every morning the water carrier would bang with his whip handle on sleepy shutters, and the ice-cold cloudy water slopped into the tubs in dark entryways; people, groaning, would crowd together in the half-darkness, like chickens under a roost. Sura-Dvosya, the shopkeeper, would push aside the creaking bolt and with a serrated knife start slowly cutting a bluish herring into five pieces; and a bow-legged boy, standing on tiptoe, opening his little fist to place his sweaty *grosik*[1] on the counter, would carefully pick up the wrapped package—two pieces of herring, topped by a yellowish half-moon of onion.

Usually I arrived in the shtetl on Fridays, late in the afternoon, when shop bolts were beginning to clank, the pathetic stalls were emptying, and saleswomen, lazily winding down their bickering, would deftly tighten their heavy checked kerchiefs about their waists and disperse homeward. A holiday sadness, treacley thick, would slowly envelop the shtetl. Here and there, half-blind tiny windows warmed with candlelight illuminate the tangled fringes of wash-worn tablecloths and a challah's round golden crust.

I'd rather not end my contemplation of these meager comforts through small, low-set windows: the family's polished brass candlesticks and the timid light flickering through work-worn fingers folded in prayer. But already at the far end of the square

---

1. *Grosik* (Polish; Yiddish: *groshik*)—a small penny.

lights have been turned on over the entry to the volunteer firemen's hall, the place for all meetings and town festivities. Skinny, dark-faced David, carpenter and member of the local Jewish socialist youth association, softly reminds us: it's time . . .

We walk to that gloomy barracks along a narrow, wood-planked sidewalk, misstepping time and again into the mud; it doesn't seem easy to make the transition from this centuries-old life to the world of Maxim Gorky, Romain Rolland, and Soviet literature. The hall, however, is already abuzz like a beehive, and I struggle to make my way between benches made of rough boards to a dusty and squeaky stage. Figures and faces merge, but hot currents flow toward me from the back of the hall, I feel a quickened breathing, and I would like to find true and real words to match my listeners' rapt intensity, impatience, and demands born of the depths of a harsh life. I grope to find words borrowed from those seekers of truth, passionate, impatient, and imbued with the gift of clairvoyance. I feel almost physically how invisible wires touch, how sparks of understanding and acceptance flare up, how the idea that not only social conditions but also man himself must be recast—how this idea turns for all of us into Ariadne's thread in this labyrinthine world. These young women with their berets aslant and these young fellows relegated to the stinking back lots of life because of their patched, worn-out jackets will not be satisfied with just a little: they are resolved to jump from the seventeenth century straight into the twentieth and maybe even the twenty-first . . .

By the glass of cloudy, overly sweet tea on the table, a pile of notes mounts—some poorly written, naïve, and clumsy, others surprisingly well phrased, bold, and concise. All the questions could be reduced to one: how to restructure the world.

My interchange with the audience did not stop when a somber custodian began turning out the lights—we just regrouped to a tighter circle. In an attic space, reached by a narrow winding staircase, wooden tables were covered with crude wrapping paper, and smooth pine needles dropped from aromatic branches that hung from low beams. Excited young voices crisscrossed; suddenly singing flared up in a corner, little tongues of flame leapt up from person to person, and the whole attic was humming and sizzling like dry birch bark set aflame, throwing into the dark, dense night of the shtetl the voices' challenge and yearning . . .

My meeting with the shtetl wasn't over yet. The most important thing is often not expressed or understood directly, face to face. Early in the morning, in the small room of the coaching inn where I had spent the rest of the night behind a wooden partition, there came a timid knocking. It was a watchmaker, with stooped shoulders and the distraught look of someone who lives among variously ticking clocks. He had a hollow cough and reddened eyes; he explained that he had spent a sleepless night thinking about the problem I had touched upon in Romain Rolland: the tragic contradiction between the aims and the methods of revolution. We bravely plunged together into the depths of history, disturbing the shadows of Hugo and Anatole France. But again a knock came on the partition, and Rakhil and Simon, from last night's audience, entered hand in hand. She was thin, quick, beautifully dark, her small head covered with dark curls, tight like the twirling petals of a chrysanthemum; he was rough and alert, all gathered together, as if invisibly protecting her from an impending woe. Rakhil, it turned out, was an artist, had been painting for some years, had tried to get to Łódź to study but didn't have the means. Now she does piecework sewing linen and lives in an unheated room, trying hard to earn enough money for paint.

Again I climb to a dovecote occupied by people and stop on the threshold in astonishment: the walls reverberate and shout in deep-brown hues, changing to crimson, wind rattles the shutters of huts clinging to the ground, the air is heavy with an oncoming storm. Her technique is weak and naive, but the genuine anxiety permeating these images is infectious, a stubborn sense that the world is approaching some sort of decisive boundary . . .

On the square, by the bus, I say goodbye to my new friends. Here are Simon and Rakhil, clear-voiced and rosy-cheeked Hannah, the public-school teacher, and David, the carpenter with the sternly Biblical face of a zealot or martyr. Hannah squeezes my hand meaningfully, "I will write you . . ."

A letter arrived after a few days. Hannah wrote that she was pregnant, the child's father was far away, and difficult days lay ahead for she would have to break with her family and her surroundings but was unafraid of the future and happy to take on the hardships . . . That was early spring, 1939.

That fall sirens began howling like hyenas. Bombs and fires, hunger and famine descended on the rough little dwellings gathered together like a frightened herd. The fearful shtetl wailed and surged out onto the road—carrying prayer books in old stiff covers, children in arms, old things grabbed on the run—some headed for the capital, some further away to the east. A hurricane had dispersed the life that centuries had shaped.

I'm thinking now of those who, in those irretrievable and by now inconceivable times, came close to me, face to face. Hannah's child, I am imagining, may have turned up in the kindergarten of a Kazakhstan kolkhoz; David may have been seized by Gestapo spies at an underground printing press and hung in the market square of some district town; Rakhil and Simon, holding hands as at our meeting, may have mounted the barricades on Miła Street[2] and, watching the German troops advance, poked the muzzles of their guns through the slit between the boards. I'm thinking of all the suffering for which there are no words in human language and of the heroism that we just cannot measure by any measure, cannot put into any epic poem, the heroism of impatient and passionate people whom history has marked for greatness.

And you, shtetl, can it be that you have fallen silent for centuries to come, that your strangled gasp will not arouse this dulled world, a world no longer able to wonder at anything? Are you destined, with your impoverished coziness and your yearnings, your acquiescent prayers and your insolent songs, simply to become a silent tract of land, ploughed by history's bloody course for a new sowing?

1943

---

2. Miła Street—one of the main streets in Warsaw's historic Jewish quarter. Dubnova-Erlich hints at the Warsaw Ghetto Uprising of 1943 for details see Aleksandr Aronov in vol. 2, and below, in the essay "Scorched Hearth."

Scorched Hearth

I have before me a list of the victims of last year's uprising in the Warsaw ghetto—a belated echo from *out there*, from the last circle of the infernal regions.

Human imagination is weak: the monstrous image of thousands of deaths in gas chambers does not make you shiver since the brain cannot accommodate it. But news of the death of a person whom we remember alive, as worried or smiling, suddenly pulls the curtain aside: before us rises what now has turned into a cemetery—that fragment of a vibrant, red-hot life named the Warsaw Jewish quarter.

Untamed, frenzied hate encircled it with walls fated to turn into the walls of a cemetery. In peaceful years too. An invisible border separated this quarter from "Aryan" streets, shabbily genteel, boasting plate-glass showcases, spacious sidewalks, and a "pure" public. This is the way it was from way back: hounded by dull-wittedness, prejudice, and cunning calculation, in the course of hundreds of years Jews huddled close together, settled in warm, tight spots, in stuffy air.

The Jewish quarter was old, somber, crowded, oddly built: as if someone from above had angrily thrown into the backyards of a second-rate European capital a heap of slovenly stone boxes, drilled narrow slots for windows, houses stuffed to bursting with people, so that in the cold of winter as in the swelter of summer they would spill out into dank gateways, onto smooth-worn, bespattered sidewalks, onto jagged cobblestones. And if an inhabitant of the central streets—"Aryan" or Jew—turned up there, he would be stunned by the crush, the bustle, the excited voices and gestures, by the gaudy, cheap Oriental goods crying out from hawkers' trays and stalls.

It was far from idyllic, this motley, hard life. Standing over the ruins, we don't want to insult them by adding a gilded, confectionery veneer. "A pair of twins, inseparably fused," mourned over by a poet,[3] became a solid part of that life: "the satiety of the satiated" was considerable here, reeking of fatty food and overgrown with featherbeds and tasteless heavy furniture; and "the hunger of the hungry" was incredible in its nakedness, an absolute king in dwellings whose windows looked out onto the outhouses; in cellars where people multiplied like rabbits on mattresses that, full of holes, were spread on the floor; around courtyard wells and cesspools and woodsheds, where olive-dark kids with pale gums and skinny bowlegs spent their childhood.

People lived in this stuffy and crowded place without pausing for breath, as if sensing an impending catastrophe. A quicker pulse beat in the municipal and parochial schools, in houses of worship and newspaper editorial offices, in political, professional, and cultural organizations. And everywhere one could hear the guttural Yiddish, loud in squabbles, tender in a heart-rending song. The Jewish quarter was a

---

3. Dubnova is referring to the sixth line of the poem "Esli dusha rodilas' krylatoi . . ." ("If your soul was born winged . . . ," 1918) by the Russian poet Marina Tsvetaeva (1892–1941).

special kingdom, and in the greatest heat of antisemitic bacchanalia the hoodlums of different stripes—"idealistic" volunteers from the intelligentsia or tramps paid for beating up Jews—did not dare plunge into the thick of it: for a long time they remembered how an attempted pogrom was met by some hefty, ruddy-faced Jewish porters.

The most astounding fact was this: through stupefying satiety as much as decimating hunger, through feverishly chasing after huge wealth or pitiful penny earnings, fountains of a genuine spiritual life sprang high. This life was particularly intense at two ends—in the grandfathers who preserved tradition and in their grandchildren who destroyed it impudently. The ecstatic melodies of those who, half saints and half holy fools, called themselves "the dead Hassids" and lived in mystical contact with the spirit of their dead *Rebbe* had something in common with the rebellious songs of the young who were demanding truth and justice for the whole world, from one end to the other.

Himmler's henchmen who stormed Warsaw cut the arteries of the Jewish quarter: drop by drop live blood began running out of it. The "satiety of the satiated" vanished: a greedy belly devoured the remnants of corpulent daily living. The "hunger of the hungry" grew to incredible proportions. But the ghetto did not succumb: squeezed between its stone walls, it boiled more than ever as underground, hot springs of rebellion and faith beat forth. Then the conqueror's crazed anger demanded hecatombs. Dejected, the doomed people marched into the jaws of the apocalyptic beast. The Hassids with their long black robes and high fur hats—those who in the autumn holidays filled the sumptuous country houses of the miracle-working tzaddikim and those who mortified the flesh—in the death trains they sang hymns about the Messiah. The young no longer sang: gritting their teeth, they stored up arms. And when the last martyrs were led out of the ghetto, there remained only the fighters.

* * *

The list of the victims of the revolt contains almost exclusively names of the young. I knew many personally—through study groups, meetings, literary evenings, heart-to-heart talks at the desk in my small study. But how they have all grown over these four years of climbing Golgotha, four years in the ghetto!

Among those who perished is a thirteen-year-old boy. On the eve of the war he was nine. His satchel hung down his back, he played hide-and-seek with his schoolmates in the dark doorway, and his mother used to stuff his pockets with tasty, crisply roasted nuts. How terrifying life must have been in the ghetto, when instead of nuts the boy found bullets in his pockets and had to stand watch in that very doorway where he used to hide behind the yardman's wheelbarrow.

Another familiar name. A young man who graduated from a foreign university and came to Warsaw as an engineer; yet hundreds of people called him simply Abrasha. He was one of the most spirited enthusiasts among young Jewish socialists—and remained that way during the years of underground work. By chance we met many times, and I remember him especially in the setting of a young workers' summer camp nestled among green hills. A cool dewy evening was settling in, from a home-made stove rose smoke of pine branches, and agile young hands gathered needles for the fire. When the dry branches began crackling, Abrasha started singing softly, his face lighting up as if in prayer, pure and stern; something childlike and monk-like came through in his expression. . . . This is the way he must have gone to his death.

Michał Klepfisz, called by the London radio a "pillar of the uprising"—him I remember as a boy and a bully, mop-headed, stubborn, awkward in his movements. The boy grew into a young man, a student, silent and bashful; one felt a controlled power in him, tempered steel. I remember that during the floods in the Tatra Moun-tains that inundated mountain villages, he calmly and bravely saved from the raging elements dozens of peasant children. With the same calm courage, he plunged into the wild elements of the uprising.

The girl in the photograph has tender, motherly eyes and a firm chin. She gradu-ated from public school, from teach-yourself workshops, summer youth camps. In the first months of the war, she declined to leave the ghetto for a calmer Lithuania. Later she wrote her father across the ocean: "You've traveled halfway around the world, seen wonderful things. But if we should ever meet, I'll tell you even more remarkable things." Death caught up with her when she was nineteen.

The people's struggle against the tanks, which had conquered all of Europe, en-dured for a whole month before suffocating in the smoke of the fires. There remain skeletons of houses, dug up roads, a cemetery stillness.

Will these skeletons of houses ever be overgrown with stone and glass, will steps again ring out along the jagged sidewalks? Will fugitives hidden in the dwellings of the Polish poor, and guerilla soldiers in the woods burned by gunpowder, and those whom fate has sent over the ocean, will these come back to their scorched hearths? And how will they come—with tears and curses alone or with a firm resolve to re-build their city, their country, their world?

Now, above the scorched hearth are flocks of crows, a raw April wind, low clouds. But beyond the Wisła in the east there is a distant glow. Soon will come a rumble of victorious arms, sweeping away the enemy's filth. The hour of vengeance is near.

1944

Translated from the Russian by Helen Reeve with Martha Kitchen

SOFIA PREGEL

Sofia Pregel (1894–1972), poet, memoirist, and editor was born in Odessa. Her father, Yuly Pregel, was an oil industrialist, her mother, Roza Glezer, a pianist. In 1917 Pregel was accepted to study voice at St. Petersburg Conservatory, but the Revolution undercut her plans. Emigrating via Constantinople, Pregel arrived in Berlin in 1922. She participated in the activities of Berlin's "Circle of Thirty," which often convened in the apartment of Mikhail Gorlin, Raisa Blokh's (in vol. 1) future husband.

In 1932 Pregel moved to Paris, where her work appeared in leading magazines, including *Numbers* (*Chisla*) and *Contemporary Annals* (*Sovremennye zapiski*). Her first collection, *Conversation with Memory*, came out in 1935, followed in the prewar years by *Sun's Mayhem* (1937) and *Noon* (1939), all published in Paris. At the beginning of World War II, Sofia Pregel moved to the United States. She founded the émigré journal *Housewarming* (*Novosel'e*, taking its name from the 1931 émigré collective she had contributed to in Berlin) in New York in 1942. Pregel edited and supported this journal for eight years. Along with *The New Review* (*Novyi zhurnal*), established by Mark Aldanov (in vol. 1) and Mikhail Tsetlin (Amari) in New York, also in 1942, *Housewarming* filled the void that émigré writers and readers experienced after the closing of the Europe-based first-wave publications in 1939–40. Pregel attracted contributions by prominent émigré authors, among them Ivan Bunin and Aleksey Remizov. Sofia Dubnova-Erlich's essays about the Shoah (in vol. 1) appeared in its pages in 1943–44. In several postwar scandals and controversies, Pregel did not conceal her dismay over the alleged collaborationism by some Russian émigrés. Not begrudging space to her own poetry, Pregel generously published poetry and translations by many émigrés. Her translation of an excerpt from the long poem *Polish Flowers* by the Jewish-Polish poet Julian Tuwim (1894–1953) appeared in *Housewarming* in 1942.

Although Pregel was a United States citizen, she returned to Paris in 1948 and published *Housewarming* there until 1950 (a total of fifty-two issues came out). Her postwar poetry appeared in *The New Review*, *Bridges* (*Mosty*), *Facets* (*Grani*), and other journals. Pregel published three more collections: *Shores* (1953), *Encounter* (1958), and *Spring in Paris* (1966). The émigré critic Marc Slonim (1894–1976) edited her posthumous *Last Poems*, which appeared in Paris in 1973. The émigré opinion makers admired her mainly as a philanthropist, a "directress of émigré poetry" (Georgy Adamovich's language).

Pregel financed the Rifma (Rhyme) publishing house, launched in Paris in 1950. Taking over the press after the death of its founder, Irina Iassen (R. Chekver, 1893–

1957), Pregel made possible the publication of many collections by émigré poets, among them the 1959 *Selected Poems* by Raisa Blokh (in vol. 1) and Mikhail Gorlin.

Although lacking formal sophistication, Pregel's robust, colorful verse suggests an affinity with the early Soviet poets of the South-Western school, hailing from her native Odessa (in vol. 1, Eduard Bagritsky, Mark Tarlovsky, Arkady Shteynberg, and others). Pregel's most compelling poems deal with loss of childhood. Some of her American poems are interesting in seeking parallels between the expanses of American and Russian landscapes. Amusing are Pregel's (perhaps class-conscious) observations of the fabric of suburban life: "A would-be worker digs the soil/A would-be banker chews a blade of grass," (written about American children at play).

In two of her postwar collections, Pregel included poems about the Shoah. In her sixth, *Spring in Paris* (1966), she published "Death Trains" with the epigraph "Auschwitz, Buchenwald, Dachau. . . ." The three poems included below appeared in *Shores* (1953), Pregel's fourth—and first postwar—collection. The last two, "In the Ghetto" and "You Shall Not Forget," offer today's reader a hypothetical key to the kind of Jewish-Soviet poet Pregel might have become had she stayed in Russia instead of emigrating as a young woman.

In her latter years, Pregel worked on a three-volume memoir, *My Childhood*, which appeared posthumously in 1973, its second half edited by the émigré poet Vadim Andreev. As an epigraph, Pregel chose the conclusion of Dovid Knut's "A Kishinev Burial" (in vol. 1): ". . . That peculiarly Jewish-Russian air . . . /Blessed are those who have ever breathed it." The spirit of Pregel's memoir stems from her best collection, *Noon* (1939), with its counterpunctal treatment of the theme of an Edenic childhood. Layering the poetically evoked details of her Odessan pre-Revolutionary childhood with palpably Jewish motifs, Pregel ended her post-Shoah memoir with a hauntingly cinematic superimposition: "At the old Jewish cemetery I read the signs on the gravestone slabs. Here is my great-grandfather, a stern old man. [. . .] People have difficulty making their way between graves. The gravestones have cracked and almost merged into a whole. I walk with everyone else down a narrow, invisible path. And this is not a dream. Childhood's over."

Pharaoh's Daughter

The cloth slopes like a temple pylon,
Sighs rise in a chant of prayer,
Ten tawny-colored wine drops
For the dreadful rage of the Lord.

The candlesticks weigh like anchors,
Eyelashes are beaded and fringed:
Last sun picks out dusk's black letters:
Dark settles on sacred words.

The river in full spate hurtles
Through the gloom, for good or for ill:
The buffaloes' spice-dark cluster
Churns the sand by the watering hole.

Pharoah's daughter goes down to the river,
As her women wait in the shade.
The babe's eyes pierce through papyrus
And meet hers: a bitter delight.

early 1950s

In the Ghetto

Down all the alleys shots and rumors rumbled,
Revolvers stammered, gabbling more than bombs,
And we were walking with small, ragged Núkhim,
A waif, but one the streets had not ground down.

We crossed the verge of night in dawn's sharp silence.
The sun peeped out, then stuck to its hiding place.
Just then, the ghetto exploded into stillness,
Darkness went skidding through the slippery yards.

A dense but edgy rain was slowly falling:
The light had fled, had gone into retreat:
But Núkhim stood his ground on the charred pavement
Shooting things out with foes he couldn't see,

Taking alternate gulps of wind and drizzle,
Drowning the Germans' whistles with his laugh:
After the evening fire has nearly died down
Elbows of kindling keep the blaze alive.

When you're thirteen and brave, and very lively,
It seems good fun to die on barricades.
Or maybe he thought a miracle was likely.
A miracle did happen, as we read.

early 1950s

You Shall Not Forget

The nights of terror in cellars,
Under candles' demented light:
The talk in horrified whispers:
This, killers, you shall not forget.

The premature flashes of russet
Down sedges' unsteady blades:
The swooping rainstorm of bullets
Over sand as blank as goodbyes.

From a shtetl's dreamless slumbers
To the jetty you drove them in herds.
The stones were spattered so cleanly:
The rushes straight and fine-boned.

The time when they snatched their last lungfuls:
A three-minute pause on the bridge.
Watch the pale stars, indifferent
And bleaching as they dive.

The air of dawn is bitter,
Cheeks have a slaty glint.
The first minute of waiting:
Is anything worse than that?

Yes: the minute that's second,
A scalding watershed.
A boy calls, 'Hear, O Israel!'
And raises his bony hands.

But the sky lets out no answer:
It stares down blank as lead.
The bloated German sergeant
Taps his watch to give it a test.

He crooks his lardy finger,
Whistles, and drops his arm:
A school cap flies sharp upwards
And slumps on the salt-gray planks.

Curls and eyelashes flutter to silence.
Heartbeats putter out.
Even the birds stop singing.
The sun's veiled, the Alsatians are dumb.

And the children's faces like wax:
No, killers, you shall not forget.

early 1950s

Translated from the Russian by Catriona Kelly

YULY MARGOLIN

Yuly (Juliusz) **Margolin** (1900–1971), essayist, prose writer, memoirist, and Jewish activist, was born Yehudah Margolin in Pinsk (now in Belarus), which in 1897 had 21,065 Jewish residents out of a general population of 28,068. Russian was spoken at home, but, as Margolin reminisced, "Polish, Lithuanian, and Yiddish flowed around my ears [. . .] Poland was in the orchard and house of Pan Kulesz, Russia in volumes of Gogol—and where was Jewishness? It surrounded me on all sides; it was the background of my existence [. . .]." Having lived in the Russian Empire, Poland, the USSR, and Israel, Margolin wrote his most important works in Russian and regarded himself as an assimilated European Jew who found a path to Zionism.

In 1915 Margolin's family left Pinsk with the flow of refugees from the German-occupied western areas of the Russian Empire; Margolin moved to Ekaterinoslav (now Dnepropetrovsk), where he graduated from a *Realschule* in 1919 and entered a university. In 1921 Margolin left Ekaterinoslav and moved to Berlin, where he studied at the University of Berlin and received a degree in philosophy in 1929. In 1925 he married Eva Spektor; their son was born in 1926. In 1929 Margolin settled in Łódź, continuing to publish on culture and politics in Russian and Polish (in 1926 he had authored a brochure on Zionism in Polish). He aligned himself with the Revisionist Zionism of Vladimir Jabotinsky (in vol. 1). Margolin traveled to Eretz Israel in 1936, and his wife and son settled permanently in Tel Aviv. A Polish citizen, Margolin was in Łódź when World War II began. In September 1939 he fled to Soviet-controlled Pinsk; his attempts to return to the British Mandate of Palestine failed. In June 1940 he was arrested by the NKVD in Pinsk and received a five-year sentence. Margolin was released from a camp in Kotlas in 1945 and exiled to Slavgorod in the Altay. He was finally allowed to return to Poland in 1946 and was reunited with his family in Tel Aviv.

In 1946–47, Margolin wrote in Russian the memoir *A Journey to the Land of Camp Prisoners*, which was released in New York in 1952. The published book text was incomplete (some of the missing sections appeared in émigré periodicals), as were the 1949 French and 1965 German editions. (No English or Hebrew editions have appeared to date. Several previously unpublished sections appeared in the June 1976 issue of *Time and We* [*Vremia i my*], based at the time in Israel.) The French version (as Jules Margoline), *La condition inhumaine; cinq ans dans les camps de concentration soviétiques*, was cotranslated by the Russian émigré writer Nina Berberova and Mina Journot. Visiting the United States with lectures in 1953, Margolin attempted but failed to sell a film script based on his book.

One of the first eye-witness accounts by a Gulag survivor, Margolin's memoir should have received greater recognition but was overshadowed, first, by Elinor Lipper's *Eleven Years in Soviet Prison Camps* (1950) and Margarete Buber-Neumann's *Between Two Dictators* (1948), and later by Soviet Gulag literature (Aleksandr Solzhenitsyn and others). One of the principal factors that distinguished Margolin's book was that its author achieved the double perspective of an outsider looking in and an insider looking out. Moreover, in contrast to the West European communists (E. Lipper and M. Buber-Neumann) who moved to the USSR by choice in the 1930s only to be sentenced to the Gulag, Margolin entertained no illusions about Stalinism. Marked by intellectual honesty, Margolin's memoir did not conceal what he had witnessed, however painful it may have been for him to write about Jewish officers still remaining in the apparatus of the Gulag by the start of World War II . The ending of Margolin's preface reads: "Those sympathetic to the Soviet system suppose that the route of my journey was ill-chosen and led me astray from the famous Soviet paths. I was never a defender of Stalingrad; I never stormed Berlin. If I had been there, would I be writing differently? Perhaps [. . .] Where is the truth of Russia, at the victory parade on Red Square or in the land of Gulag inmates deleted from the atlas of geography? Apparently, one must take these things *all together*, in their entirety and interconnectedness. [. . .] May those who place much hope in the Land of the Soviets also take this 'material' into account and reconcile it, as they can, with their consciences."

In the early 1950s, Margolin sought to convince the Israeli public of a need for strong action to free Jewish prisoners in the Gulag. He spent most of 1954 trying to establish the Israel Association of Former Prisoners of Soviet Labor Camps. His pleas went largely unanswered as Israel was pursuing a rather cautious course toward the USSR. Furthermore, not many in Israel were prepared to accept Margolin's rhetoric, which nearly equated Nazi and Soviet concentration camps.

In February 1950, Margolin testified at the United Nations about slave labor in the USSR. He was a key witness for David Rousset in November–January 1951 at his well-publicized anti-defamation suit against the French communist magazine *Les Lettres Françaises* and its editors (Claude Morgan and Pierre Daix).

Margolin's Russian books included *Israel, Jewish State* (Tel Aviv, 1958, as Aleksandr Galin), *A Tale of Millennia: A Concise Overview of the History of the Jewish People* (Tel Aviv, 1959), and *A Jewish Tale* (1960; excerpt below). Margolin contributed to the Russian press in Europe, the United States, and Israel. Of special interest are his essays about Jewish aspects in the career of Boris Pasternak (vols. 1–2) and his *Book of Life*, serialized in *The New Review* in 1965–66. From the mid-1960s, Margolin was active in the movement for the exodus of Soviet Jews (see the section "The Jewish Exodus: 1967–2001" in vol. 2). Following his death, Margolin's writings were collected in several volumes, but his legacy awaits wider recognition and study.

Two excerpts from Margolin's *A Jewish Tale* (Tel Aviv, 1960) follow below. The protagonist of this *biographie romancée*, Yisrael (Srolik) Epstein (1914–1946), was an activist of Betar, a Zionist youth movement founded in Riga in 1923–24. By the middle of the 1930s, Poland was Betar's main stronghold, its centers spread throughout eastern Europe. The Betarists, followers of Jabotinsky, prepared Jewish youth for life in Eretz-Israel through paramilitary training. After escaping from Poland in 1939, Epstein eventually arrived in Eretz Israel. In 1944, the National Military Organization (*Irgun Zvai Le'umi*), known in English as the Irgun, declared a revolt against the British authorities. In 1946 Epstein came to Italy on an assignment from the general headquarters of the Irgun. Captured as part of widespread arrests mounted by the Italian police under British pressure, he died attempting to escape from an Italian jail on 27 December 1946. He was reburied in Israel as a hero in 1953.

From *A Jewish Tale*

The Exodus from Poland

On 4 September 1939, two bombs fell on a crowded passenger train traveling toward Lwów. The train was swarming with passengers: people were sitting on the bumpers and lying on the roofs of the cars. After the train was hit twice, a bloody mash covered the roadbed. Trains were held up until late at night. A few of the rear cars escaped damage. Srolik, safe and unharmed, walked out of one of the cars and looked around. He was immediately put to work rescuing and pulling out the injured, piling up bodies, preparing a common grave. Above the pit in which several dozen indistinguishable remains had been piled, Srolik said the prayer for the dead, "El Malei Rahamim", adjusted his knapsack and took the first bus to Lwów.

Thus began his Exodus from Poland—that Exodus for which he had been preparing since he was a youth and which was for him only the introduction to a great and joyful event: the return to his homeland. Since childhood Srolik had been used to the thought that he would leave Poland, that his generation was destined to overcome Exile—the long night—after which the dawn of a beautiful new day would arise in the true, not the illusory, homeland.

Srolik knew the old legends, preserved in the Talmud, according to which only a fifth or a tenth of the people who were slaves in Egypt followed Moses to the Promised Land. The rest—the huge majority—could not make up their minds, lacked faith, and were consigned to oblivion by History. It was not for them that punishments were carried out and miracles performed, not for them were the omens and the prophecies. Even remembering them was a sin. And yet, when the day came for him to part with the old world where he had spent his young life and he saw himself on the border separating "the one tenth of the chosen" from the condemned, his whole being was outraged and shaken. This Exodus was like the flight from burning Sodom. It was forbidden to look back, but in that destroyed Sodom remained those who were closest and dearest to him, remained millions of ordinary Jews left to their fate.

The night before, in smoke-wrapped Warsaw strewn with bomb shells, Srolik witnessed the joy brought about by the news that France and England had joined the war against Hitler. The crowd's jubilation knew no bounds, as if victory had already been won. In reality, Poland lost the war on the first day, when the Germans cut through the front as if it were a piece of paper, and their planes took possession of Poland's skies without encountering any resistance. The collapse of a state with a population of thirty-six million happened instantaneously, as if the whole history of independent Poland for the past twenty years had been a dream and now came the terrible awakening. Crowds of refugees streamed toward the east, toward the Soviet border. The army dissolved into individual units without communication or a central command. This lightening-fast defeat was so monstrously incredible that the imagination refused to believe it. It seemed as if the catastrophic situation at the fronts could change any day—as quickly as it had arrived. But it was imperative to act, to do something, while waiting for a miracle.

On the fourth day of the war, Srolik and a few of his comrades left Warsaw. Their first thought was to go to the southwest, to the Romanian border. There, in Siniatin, a group of Betarists was waiting for an illegal departure. Srolik had gone there only a month ago to deliver money for their trip. The money was in a small leather suitcase. Srolik did not part with it, did not let it out of his hands; he put it under his pillow when he slept. Srolik was afraid of that money, as if the suitcase were full of a radioactive substance, and watched over it as if it were the only medicine that could save the life of sick people. He wanted to get rid of those two thousand British pounds as soon as possible; they burned his hands.

Siniatin had remained in his memory as a peaceful out-of-the-way place, a sleepy little town on the wide and quiet river Prut, with cozy little houses surrounded by trees, churches, the high tower of the town hall, and a market full of Ukrainian and Moldavian peasant women. Golden corn was drying on the roofs of the peasant huts. Now the very same Siniatin was far away and unattainable, like the past that was gone forever. Death was keeping watch over all the roads.

A metallic sound rang in his ears; it was impossible to hide from the steel wasps humming above his head. Kovel, Zamość, fires on the horizon . . . and finally Srolik's train was overtaken by a German plane. When the first bomb exploded right on the locomotive, a wild flight began from the rear cars. People threw themselves out of the windows, and they were followed by shouts and groans, by the wheezing of the dying under a rain of machine-gun fire.

Then for a fraction of a second Srolik saw in the cockpit of a low-flying plane the first and last Nazi he was destined to see until the end of the war: a young face without eyes, in enormous goggles, with a straight nose and a wide-open mouth, as if he wanted to swallow the whole bombed-out bloodied train. Srolik remembered that wide-open mouth for a long time. Until late at night he helped bury corpses, blackened mountains of flesh, torn-off legs and arms. He carried stretchers . . . feeling neither tiredness nor fear. Everything around was already alien to him, and his soul was shooting forward to that one place on earth where his presence had meaning.

In Lwów it was the same as in Warsaw: continuous air raids, fires, crowds of refugees rushing about, turning Legion Street into a Gypsy camp. In the Hotel France, where Srolik and his comrades took up residence, they divided up the *Aliyah Bet*[1] funds, returning money to those who had signed up to leave. All day people came to them in despair, in panic, and no one tried to calm them down.

The flood came before they were able to prepare the ark.

In their third-rate hotel, its windows shattered from nearby explosions, the wind blew into the broken windows, the staff had fled; no one cleaned the premises or answered the bells. The Polish state had cracked like a nut in the iron claws of the Hitlerite and Red Armies. Aimless resistance still continued in various locations, and Warsaw still held. But Lwów was occupied by the Red Army on the second day of the Soviet attack.

During those days our refugees from the old world were seized by an attack of insane, hysterical gaiety. They had survived against all odds and had no thought of surrender. They felt like shipwrecked oarsmen on a raft amidst the raging waves and the wreckage of what had once borne a proud name. Srolik and his comrades cavorted like children. One dressed up as Napoleon in close-fitting white breeches and a three-cornered paper hat and paced up and down the room with his hands behind his back to the loud laughter of all, while Srolik pretended to be Fouché, dressing himself in bath sponges and pieces of cloth. On the street, however, instead of Napoleon and Fouché, orders were being issued by Stalin and Beria, about whom Srolik's comrades had only the faintest of notions.[2]

A great manhunt began. On Hitler's side, servile Poles pointed out Jews to the Germans. On the Soviet side, servile Jews pointed out "counterrevolutionaries and Zionist-Fascists." And during those first days, after having recognized Srolik on the street, one of the Jewish Communists called the Soviet authorities. Srolik barely escaped. Fortunately he was interrogated by a non-Jew, and during those first few days the NKVD was not yet functioning normally. But that was the first warning. He had to leave Lwów. But where could he go? The Romanian border was shut with a triple

---

1. *Aliyah Bet* (Heb.) = lit.: "Immigration B"; refers to illegal immigration to the British Mandate of Palestine, in contrast to "Immigration A," legal immigration. The *Aliyah Bet* (clandestine immigration to Palestine movement) began in the 1930s in response to restrictions introduced by the British authorities.

2. Fouché, Joseph (1763–1820)—French Minister of Police under Napoleon; Beria, Lavrenty (1899–1953)—one of Stalin's main henchmen, People's Commissar (Minister) of Internal Affairs of the USSR in 1938–1946.

cordon of troops. But the northern, Lithuanian border still remained open.

In the second half of September, on the very eve of the Day of Atonement, Srolik reached Vilna. In Warsaw he had seen defeat, in Lwów he had seen the arrival of the Red Army in a foreign city, but the sight of Soviet Vilna struck him deeply. Here he experienced a real shock.

His native city, the Jerusalem of Lithuania, the rock of his youth, lay in naked shame, in willing debasement before the enemy. The Nazis did not force anyone to call them "liberators," but here in Vilna Jewish hands set fire to the bureau of the Jewish Revisionist Party in the center of the city; they tore the Star of David from the building that had housed Jewish social organizations and hung a five-pointed star in its place. It was inconceivable how easily the enemies of Zionism triumphed. Many of yesterday's Betarists went to serve in the Soviet law-enforcement organs. Those who looked at him with open malice, which promised no good, behaved as if they magnanimously forgave him yesterday's silliness and now expected him to show some sense—and then his past would be forgotten and forgiven like a child's prank. They were ready to "forgive," not knowing that forgiveness was not in their power, and they themselves were in danger. Then came military intervention, which was supposed to give freedom to "everyone": Poles, Lithuanians, Jews, and Belorussians. But Srolik was afraid to sleep at home. He feared denunciations and arrest. Important Zionist activists had already been arrested; rumor had spread their names. An icy hand stretched out from afar, searching, groping for victims. The Jews of Vilna were luckier than those who fell into German hands: they could consider themselves "liberated," but only on the condition about which the prophet Ezekiel said, "because you clapped your hands and stamped your feet and rejoiced over the land of Israel with such utter scorn."[3]

In less than two months the beneficent Soviet government gifted Vilna and its surroundings to the Lithuanian Republic. Such a present could not be refused, and yet it was difficult to rejoice over it. It was clear that the next step would be the Soviet annexation of the whole Republic of Lithuania along with Vilna.

"*Vallo!*" cried the few inhabitants of Vilna who knew Lithuanian, standing on the sidewalk and meeting the first column of Lithuanian troops to set foot on Mickiewicz Street. "*Vallo!*"

But the Lithuanians looked at the Jewish faces with suspicion. They were not convinced by the Lithuanian patriotism of the Vilna Jews.

From now on, wedged between Hitler's Germany and the Soviet Union, Lithuania became an island of freedom, a haven for refugees, and the longed-for goal of all who dreamed of reaching the west. From here planes flew to Copenhagen, London, and America. The Joint was active here, and certificates arrived from Jerusalem. Here, too, little by little, the leaders of the Betar movement in Poland gathered: Menahem Begin,[2] Nathan Friedman, and Shaib. A Rescue Committee was formed,

---

3. Ezekiel 25:6.

4. Begin, Menahem (1913–1992)—formerly a Betar commander in Poland, Begin arrived in Eretz Israel in 1942 and became chief commander of Irgun. Serving as Israel's sixth prime minister (1977–83), Begin signed the peace treaty with Egypt in 1979. Y. Epstein and Begin had been close associates since their Betar youth in Poland.

headed by Y. Glazman and Dilion, Betarists from Kaunas. When an end was put to the eerie independence of the Baltic states in the summer of 1940, it became clear that the Zionist youths had only a few months to break out of the encirclement. They had to decide on extreme measures, to take a risk.

Time did not wait. Hitler ruled Europe from Narvik to Crete; in the countries he had occupied, the unprecedented murder of the Jewish people had already begun. In the Soviet zone, half a million Jewish refugees were sent to labor camps, and the systematic destruction of everything that centuries of Jewish life had created in the countries of eastern Europe was under way. Meanwhile, in Vilna people were still living a semblance of a "peaceful" life. Letters were sent abroad and received. People worked in Soviet offices, listened to the radio, played cards and chess. During evenings at the Café Lute, one could hear Hanka Ordonówna. The theaters put on Molière and Sardou and performed *Beautiful Elena* and *The Csardas Princess*.[5] The Institute for Jewish Research[6] was destroyed to the sound of Offenbach, and its workers were sent into the depths of Russia. Menahem Begin, the former *"natsiv"*[7] of the former Betar, left with his wife for the outskirts of Vilna—to escape from view—and settled in a wooden hut in the pine forest. There, while waiting for the chance to leave, he kept himself busy reading and diligently studied English. Jabotinsky died.

All cards were muddled, all horizons wrapped in gloom. But belief and will were alive, heart and reason had not been destroyed, and far away like a lighthouse shone the country where "life began all over again."

Once more Srolik tried to reach Romania by the old, familiar road.

During the past few months he had become very taciturn, more so than usual. The expression on his face had frozen, and there was ice in his heart. His father offered him his gold watch and chain for the trip. He also remembered the suitcase full of pounds sterling that he had taken on his last trip to Siniatin. "What's the use? Money never saved anyone," said Srolik. "Gold will kill me. I'll take the case as a memento." Instead of the gold watch Srolik took his father's simple antique wind-up watch. That was the watch he finally took to Palestine. To this day it still ticks in his homeland, where his heart ceased to beat.

This second attempt also ended in failure. During those days masses of people whose sole goal was to get as far away as possible from the nightmare tried to break through closed cordons, and others, who had created that nightmare, did not let them pass. In the burning house the exits were sealed.

---

5. *Csardas Beautiful Elena* (*La belle Hélène*, 1864)—operetta by Jacques Offenbach (1819–1880); *The Csardas Princess* (*Die Csárdásfürstin*, 1915)—operetta by Emmerich (Imre) Kálmán (1882–1953). Both Offenbach and Kálmán were Jewish.

6. Margolin is referring to YIVO, founded in Vilna in 1925; in 1939 YIVO's main activities were transferred to New York, although only parts of its rich holdings survived the war and the Shoah.

7. *Natsiv* (Heb.) = here: leader.

Srolik returned to Vilna. The city was empty. People whom the regime found undesirable were constantly being removed from the city and from all of Lithuania. Tens of thousands disappeared as if they had never been alive, and the rest awaited their turn. Everyone who had foreign citizenship or was under the protection of a foreign power finally left Lithuania. The rest, like garbage under a shovel, waited to see what pile they would be thrown onto. Menahem Begin was found in his forest hideaway, arrested, and sent away. His closest comrades awaited arrest any day. Seven or eight "certificates" giving them the right to enter Palestine were received and immediately given out. Srolik did not take a visa. Nor did Yosif Glazman, who was offered the chance to go instead of Begin, who had been arrested. Srolik decided to go last. Glazman decided to stay and share the common Jewish fate. He later perished at the head of a partisan unit that fought the Nazis in 1942.

When hope for additional visas from abroad had dried up, they began to fabricate false visas on the spot. The Betarists obtained blank forms from the British consulate, which had left Kaunas by that time. They put false statements on the forms that an entrance visa awaited an individual in the British consulate in Istanbul. On the basis of such documents the Soviet authorities issued exit visas to Turkey. Betar had its own people in Soviet offices and in the NKVD. On the false documents master technicians forged seals and stamps indistinguishable from authentic ones. There was no time to spare; the eleventh hour was approaching.

Meanwhile in the Vilna markets hungry citizens exchanged a length of cloth for a sack of potatoes and a pair of boots for a hunk of salt pork. Others—hungry for freedom—exchanged their last possessions for another kind of commodity: visas for Curaçao, Japan, the Dutch Indies. . . . Who knew where Curaçao was?—it didn't matter; the important thing was to leave. Blank forms, seals, stamps—everything was false, and only the will "to be free in one's own country—Jerusalem and Zion" was real, more precious than gold and stronger than steel.

A friend—a former Betarist who had gone to work for the NKVD—got Srolik an exit document: "Don't ask how, just get dollars." Srolik did not have any dollars. The Jewish Agency, The Sohnut, whose representatives still remained in Kaunas, paid for his passport in dollars. In April 1940—it was before Passover—they began to prepare Srolik for departure. His whole family—his father, mother, brother, and sister—equipped him for the trip. They bought a big suitcase. What do you take with you at the hour of Exodus? The memory of sleepless nights, the bitterness and sweetness of secret feelings about which you speak to no one, for which the language has no words? Or the burden of daily cares, which stretch out behind you wherever you go? There is no place for that in a suitcase. Or love and hate, all the experience accumulated by a young soul that has already passed through cruel trials? They would not find all that on Srolik even if they were to strip him naked during baggage check at the border.

During the twenty-five years of his life he had not gathered any possessions; he did not have enough to fill such a large suitcase. He filled it to the top with books. The books that had now become illegal in Soviet Vilna. Srolik was sure that in Moscow, where he was supposed to receive the Turkish visa, he would be detained and sent to Siberia. One would need books in Siberia.

In order not to attract attention, he sent his suitcase ahead to Kaunas and arrived at the station without any baggage, with a ticket that others had bought for him at the ticket window.

No one saw him off.

On the Way

Fear and hope were intertwined in Srolik's heart. He was in a state of acute tension, and it was impossible to say if it was happiness or pain that bound the surface of his heart like ice.

The plane, all impulse and yearning, flew toward the future, but it was an alien plane, full of Soviet civil servants and military men. Srolik found everything unusual and new. Two friends were flying with him. They were literally the last ones to depart: after them none of the Betarists were able to leave Kaunas by that route. A feeling of danger and illegality saturated their whole being. They were silent or spoke in whispers. Enemies were all around them.

It was the beginning of March. Clouds sailed by the portholes; far below stretched the vast plains of Belorussia, covered with snow like a tablecloth embroidered with patterns of dark woods. The motors roared powerfully and evenly. The plane now descended, now gained altitude—and there was no turning back.

Suddenly he heard German speech. How boldly and loudly the Germans spoke in the Soviet plane! Were they Hitlerites? No, Nazi delegates did not need planes from Kaunas to get to Moscow. They had the whole air force of the Third Reich at their disposal and a direct route from Berlin to Moscow. Maybe they were German communists, agents of the Comintern? They had no need to hide like Srolik and his comrades, to keep still or speak Russian so as not to attract attention.

Illegals! On the territory of the Soviet Union all their thoughts, feelings, and plans were illegal, their language was illegal; their place was in a prison or a camp. They were conspirators against their will and refugees by necessity. And unwittingly they felt guilty that they had deviated from the general rule. It's difficult to be an exception from the rule, but it's twice as difficult to hide with the burden of one's illegality. They were guilty of not submitting to the authority of the most intolerant power in the world, which did not acknowledge their right to be named "revolutionaries," just as the Nazis did not acknowledge their right to be called human.

And who in that plane *was* a "revolutionary"? That man over there with a gaunt and mean face, with an enormous leather briefcase? Perhaps the briefcase contained a list of "socially dangerous elements" in Lithuania, and he was carrying it directly into the hands of Lavrenty Pavlovich Beria for his decision? What's more, he was probably a fellow Jew, and from Vilna. At that moment Srolik had to fear him more than anyone else. He tried not to look in his direction.

Kaunas–Minsk–Moscow. The enormous city was invisible in the frosty haze, a heavy snow was falling, and the first lights were coming on in the twilight when Srolik came out of the airplane at Vnukovo Airport. A representative of Intourist with a car was already awaiting his clients: "This way, please!" Soon Srolik felt how important he was in Moscow as a foreign tourist. He was free of all material worries. For twelve dollars a day he was surrounded by care and luxury of which the poor Vilna Betarist had never dreamed. Like a "caliph for an hour" from *A Thousand and One Nights*, he was brought to the palace. He was almost amused by the unreality of this change from a hunted beast to an international guest of the Soviet Republic. Everything was at his disposal.

But this was a Soviet tale, not an Arabian one, and instead of a thousand nights Srolik had only three days.

The Novomoskovskaya Hotel where our three travelers stayed was a first-class establishment for foreigners. On the top floor there was a cabaret where gypsy music rang out at night and swarthy beauties with dark burning eyes and naked shoulders sent smiles to Srolik from the stage to the moan of violins. Who did they think he was? Officers of the Red Army and diplomats had taken the place of the merchant and aristocratic revelers of old Russia. Officers lower than the rank of major were not admitted to the Novomoskovskaya Hotel. Expensive wines, caviar, baskets of grapes, and Crimean apples decorated the tables, while on the streets and squares of the snow-covered capital the gray masses crowded: men in felt boots, women in head scarves, and their poverty stood out all the more against the monumental edifices of the Soviet regime.

In the morning a bus was provided for our travelers, and a Scheherazade from the Intourist office explained Moscow's miracles to them. There are the crenellated walls of the Kremlin and the Sukhareva Tower with its clock. The centuries had not touched them, and the cathedrals stand just as their sixteenth-century masters had built them. . . . But what did Srolik care about Ivan the Great, the Uspensky and Arkhangelsky Cathedrals, or the Cathedral of St. Basil? He would give up all those cathedrals for one stone of the Wailing Wall. And over there are buildings that, upon order of the Soviet authorities, were moved whole with their foundations from one end of the city to another, like children's building blocks. Had Srolik ever heard of whole buildings being transported from place to place? That had never happened in Vilna, but Srolik knows that in the Soviet Union they could move not only houses but whole tribes and the populations of villages and cities from the west to the Far East and from the south to the far north. What does a single house matter? And over there are museums, the agricultural exhibit, and there is the metro, the most luxurious in the world.

Srolik, where have you seen so much marble and so many colored mosaics and precious stones from the Urals and halls glistening with tsarist splendor? Srolik, all that is the people's wealth! Everything was built by workers' hands at Stalin's order, evidently for his own satisfaction, and not only had no one earned anything for it but millions huddled and still huddle to this day in pitiful burrows so that the Moscow metro can amaze foreigners.

But Srolik looks at it all with indifference. The underground is not so much the stations as the tunnels buried in darkness for dozens of kilometers along which the trains run, crowded with ordinary people. They don't show these underground corridors—they ride through them without looking. The stations with marble and gold are the holidays of life, and the dark tunnels, its weekdays, the unembellished truth of the lives of millions. And that wonderful hotel where Srolik and his colleagues are staying is also nothing but a departure point that they have to leave as soon as possible.

One evening Srolik is invited to the theater to see the ballet, the famous Russian ballet. The visit to the theater is included in the city tour program. But on that very evening Srolik is busy. Someone in Vilna asked him to give regards to his relatives in Moscow. Srolik phoned them: "May I speak Yiddish with you? What's best, shall I come to your place or do you prefer to come to my hotel? . . . Yes, that will be better. Come this evening."

An elegant lady in a fur coat and hat appears at the appointed hour. One can come to a restaurant in such a hat without attracting attention. But Srolik takes her to his room, and they begin to converse in a quiet whisper in case a microphone is hidden in the room.

"My father is sick, he couldn't come . . ."

Srolik gives her a present from her family in Vilna, who haven't seen their Moscow relatives for twenty years: a tallith—a prayer shawl. The lady looks with surprise at the small package . . . and suddenly her eyes are teary and her lips tremble. She looks wordlessly into Srolik's face for a long time and asks at last, "What kind of a pin is that on your lapel?"

A Betar pin. Srolik didn't take it off in Moscow.

"It's a menorah—the coat-of-arms of the future Jewish state."

"You believe there will be a Jewish state?"

"We are fighting for a Jewish state."

They got their Turkish visas without any delay. When the French consul in Beirut was asked by telegraph if a visa would be issued for passage to Palestine, he answered briefly, "A visa will be issued." On the basis of this telegram from Beirut the Turkish consul issues transit visas to Turkey. A victory! Srolik and his comrades are ecstatic. On their last day in Moscow they still have time to visit the synagogue. But they don't succeed in speaking with the few worshippers. The old Jews look at the young men with suspicion and keep silent. Srolik with his blue eyes and blond hair looks like a *goy*, anyway. Who knows where those fine young men have been until now, and what tomorrow will hold . . . In the best case, they will leave and forget . . .

By tomorrow they are far away. At midnight they pass through Kiev. The enormous train station is empty, and only on the platform an old Jewish woman in a man's boots and a kerchief sells poppy-seed bagels. When she hears that the young men are going to "Eretz," she says to them, "*Fort gezunterheyt*,"—"Go in good health." The compartment of the morning train to Odessa is full of Jewish students, members of the Komsomol. A heated discussion erupts about Birobidzhan[8] and Zionism. These young people know nothing of what's happening in the world; they know nothing about their people, and one thing is clear: they have as little intention of going to Birobidzhan as they do abroad. A few of them have heard the names of Itzsik Fefer and Perets Markish.

"Do you know who the greatest revolutionary poet in the Soviet Union is?"

"Mayakovsky," answers Srolik.

"No, Perets Markish! Have you read Perets Markish?"

"No," answers Srolik, "I haven't had the chance. Have you?"

"I haven't either." Everyone laughs.

Srolik spent one day in Odessa, the city extolled by Jabotinsky. The city of Ahad Ha-am[9] and Bialik. [. . .] Srolik looked in vain for the "favorite Greek coffee house on the corner of Red Lane," the shades of Marusya and Seryozha, that whole life that had passed and would not return. Odessa was a dead city. A gray anguish, a torpor, lay on its streets. Passengers who were going to board the ship tomorrow gathered in the Hotel London. Someone suggested that they take a walk, cast one last look at the Slavic mainland, say farewell . . . They went out, strolled along the boulevard. They walked as far as the magnificent broad staircase that led down to the port. The sea opened out before them.

A storm was on its way. The wind swept over the shore bending the trees mercilessly; water boiled over the iron parapet of the embankment. Above it the sky turned into a single vast canopy of clouds, milky-yellow at its height and coal-black at the horizon, where it mixed with the plain of the sea. From there, from the faraway waters, came the cavalry attack along the whole front, with unfurled banners and the thunderous roar of foaming monsters standing on their hind legs and tearing their bridles until the wind turned their heads toward their backs and, with all its might, threw them, flattened, their hooves turned over their heads, at the feet of a new attack. The storm unfurled in the windows of the café where the travelers had stopped. It buzzed in their ears and pulsated in their temples.

"By tomorrow it will calm down!" smiled the violinist, dressed in a canary-yellow vest and a velvet jacket. "We'll play for the comrades who are going to the Jewish homeland tomorrow. I, too, was in Haifa once . . . It was a long time ago, in 1920 . . . I remember Haifa: it's this little Arab town . . . and there are palm trees on the shore . . . palm trees . . ."

And a drawn-out melody of the Moldavian steppes and Wallachian lowlands poured

---

8. About Birobidzhan, see introduction to Viktor Fink in vol. 1.

9. Ahad Ha-am—pseudonym of Asher Hirsh Ginsberg (1856–1927), influential Jewish philosopher, essayist, and political thinker, proponent of "spiritual Zionism" (in contrast to Herzl's "political Zionism"); for a number of years, Ahad Ha-am lived and worked in Odessa.

forth. Dying away, trembling for a long time on one mournful note, and then subsiding pensively, rustling like the train of a dress along a flight of stairs. And then immediately afterward an ardent change to a lively dance rhythm, with a twinkling eye and moist smile, with the swell and scream of the violins and an accordion solo containing both the gleam of the setting sun and a shepherd's pipe on a faraway field.

A musician with a bald spot that looked as if it were glued to his temples walked up to Srolik and suddenly began speaking Yiddish.

"I'm old already, I will lay my bones here . . . if only my children live until better times . . ."

"Do you have children?" Srolik asked politely.

But the musician did not answer and became lost in thought. "Music will survive everything!" he said to himself and smiled at Srolik as if they shared a secret.

"Music will indeed survive everything."

And now, on the *Svanetia*, a white Soviet steamship, our travelers set out on the Black Sea.

The ship is so clean it shines. Glass doors lead to the dining room, the parquet floor gleams, and Stalin and Lenin look with a fatherly smile at the one hundred fifty Jews who are going to the land of their ancestors. The smile makes them ill. The day before, the customs officials in the port of Odessa had torn off the soles of Srolik's shoes. Will music really survive? The ship rocks lightly, gulls fly toward it in the fresh March wind . . . The night breathes stars in and out, and on the cot in the cabin, sleep is as deep as in the cradle of one's childhood.

And on the next day—mountains, the gulf, and the city. This is Varna, a Bulgarian port occupied by the Germans. The passengers become agitated. What awaits them? They ask the captain for an explanation. He calms them down. "The order is to get you to Istanbul, and I will take you to Istanbul." Brave captain! It's a good thing the order was not to hand them over to the Germans. Under the protection of the Stalin–Hitler pact, the *Svanetia* safely enters and then leaves Varna. On the deck—a crowd of new passengers—swarthy Turks in pantaloons and fezzes.

The waves shine blue, the sky is brighter, the water warmer . . . and now a pitiful little boat, a vessel sailing the Panamanian flag, appears in the *Svanetia*'s path. It was not for nothing that Srolik and his comrades were involved in illegal *aliyah*: they understood at once what a Panamanian flag on the Black Sea meant. About two hundred meters separate the two boats; they could see the Panamanian passengers spilling out onto the deck to gaze at the *Svanetia*, which was easily catching up to them.

"How about singing 'The Hatikvah'?"[10] proposed Tunkel-Banai. Great idea. All together they sing the old anthem:

---

10. The Hatikvah (Heb. Ha-Tikvah = The Hope)—the anthem of Zionism, the national anthem of the state of Israel.

Our hope still lives—
—one minute passes, and a response is heard from the Panamanian ship:
The hope of ancient years still lives . . .
People wave scarves and hands. Half an hour later the tiny, illegal vessel is lost in the ocean's distance. In two months the passengers of both ships will meet in Atlit, a camp for refugees from Europe.

At noon on the third day, the *Svanetia* approaches Istanbul. A fantastic panorama of mosques as big as mountains surrounded by minaret towers rises from the sea in the distance. White palaces doze above the fairytale beauty of the Bosphorus; the gardens of the Seraglio are reflected in the bright blue expanse. The decisive test approaches. Will the Turks let them get off the ship?

The wanderers look, spellbound, at the unprecedented spectacle. Snow and frost in Moscow, storms and rain in Odessa, and here—the bright southern spring. The city stretches out on both sides of the strait; Skutari is far off on the Asiatic shore. Another world, other people, other skies.

On the embankment of the Galata seaport stand crowds of people waving flags and shouting greetings. Simon Brod, short, bald, and round-faced, walks up the gangplank behind the police. Their good genie, he will smooth everything out, will arrange everything. Most of the new arrivals' documents are not in order; they don't have certificates, but what's to be done with them? You can't send them back. The captain has not received orders to take them back. The police are given vodka, and bribes are distributed as needed. Toward the evening, after a whole day of talks, they are allowed on shore. Some of the arrivals go by train to Mersina; others, including Srolik, are put in the Palace Hotel, right here, two steps from the Golden Horn.

late 1950s

Translated from the Russian by Emily Tall

ANDREY SEDYKH

Andrey Sedykh (1902–1994), prose writer, journalist, and publisher, was born and grew up Yakov Tsvibak in the Crimean town of Feodosiya (Theodossia), where he graduated from the gymnasium. From his father, a newspaperman, Sedykh inherited a flair for detail-oriented journalistic brevity in artistic prose. Sedykh sailed with his parents to Constantinople in 1919, finally settling in Paris. In 1925 he received a university diploma from the École des Sciences Politiques.

Sedykh became a staff writer for the main émigré Parisian daily *The Latest News* (*Poslednie novosti*) in 1922. In the 1920s he covered the French Parliament and also contributed to Riga's *Today* (*Segodnia*) and New York's *The New Russian Word* (*Novoe russkoe slovo*). Sedykh's first book, a collection of sketches titled *Old Paris*, appeared in 1925, followed in 1927 by *Montmartre*, also published in Paris. His third book of nonfiction, *Paris at Night* (1928), appeared with an introduction by one of the greats of pre-Revolutionary neorealism, Aleksandr Kuprin (1870–1938), who would return to the USSR less than a decade later. An entertaining volume, *Paris at Night* includes chapters with such titles as "Boulevards at Night," "Parisian Clochards," "Heroines of Sidewalks," and so forth. Less satisfying from a literary point of view was Sedykh's next book, *Where the Kings Lived: Outskirts of Paris* (1930), aimed at the middle-brow émigré reader.

In 1930, Andrei Sedykh became the writer's literary name, whereas he continued to use Yakov Tsvibak (Jacques Zwibak) for legal and business purposes. His next book, *Where Russia Used to Be* (1931), chronicled a trip to Latvia. In 1932 Sedykh married the actress and singer Evgenia Lipovskaya (Jenny Grey). His 1933 book about the lower depths of Russian emigration, *People Overboard*, earned the admiration of the patriarch of émigré letters Ivan Bunin (1870–1953). After Bunin became the first Russian writer to receive the Nobel Prize in Literature in 1933, he asked Sedykh to be his literary secretary. Sedykh accompanied Bunin to Stockholm for the Nobel ceremony.

Sedykh left France in 1941, arriving in New York City in 1942. He joined America's oldest Russian daily, *The New Russian Word*, founded in 1910. (Sedykh supplemented his income as an insurance salesman.) Initially a staff reporter and city editor, Sedykh rose to the top positions, serving as managing editor in 1960–65. He became co-owner and partner in 1967, and after the death of Mark Weinbaum in 1973 he rose to the position of editor-in-chief and president. A savvy businessman, Sedykh was not the most demanding of editors, valuing journalists' personal loyalty above their professionalism. He presided over momentous changes as his paper's readership shifted from the first- and second-wave émigrés to former Soviet Jews of the third wave, who became its principal audience in the 1970s (See the section "The Jewish Exodus: 1967–2001" in vol. 2). Sedykh was also actively involved in émigré philanthropic endeavors.

In New York, Sedykh published seven more books in Russian, starting with *Road across the Ocean* (1942), a dramatic account of his flight from Europe to the new world. He devoted more attention to fiction, publishing two collections of short stories: *Astronomers from the Bosphorus* (1948, introduction by Ivan Bunin) and *The Crazy Organ-Grinder* (1951, with two sections, "Parisian Stories" and "Crimean Stories.") The 1955 volume *Only about People* included more "Crimean" stories and a section of travel sketches, "Summer in Italy." Some of Sedykh's stories and Spanish sketches appeared in *You've Been Snowed Under, O Russia* (1964). Sedykh gathered a cycle of his stories in *Crimean Stories* in 1977, and in 1980 he combined his Italian and Spanish travelogues in the volume *Roads, Crossroads*.

Sedykh's most important contribution to postwar Russian émigré culture was his memoir, *Distant Ones, Close Ones: Literary Portraits* (1962; reprinted 1979). Having gotten to know many émigré authors, artists, and politicians, Sedykh had much to reminisce about, devoting entire chapters to Mark Aldanov (in vol. 1), Sergey Rachmaninoff, Konstantin Balmont, "Three Humorists" (Don-Aminado, Sasha Cherny [both in vol. 1], and Teffi), Ivan Bunin, and others. *Distant Ones, Close Ones* was reprinted in Moscow in 1995, less than a year after Sedykh's death.

Jewish themes were prominent in Sedykh's Crimean and childhood stories, notably "Purim" and "Wheel of Fortune." The style and flavor—as well as the time of composition—connect his largely autobiographical short fiction with the novel *O, My Youth* (1966) by Ilya Selvinsky (in vol. 1), also a native of Feodosiya and Sedykh's contemporary.

In the 1960s, Sedykh's trips to Israel resulted in two books of nonfiction. The first, *The Promised Land* (excerpt below), appeared in New York in 1962, featuring on its cover a reproduction of "A Jerusalem Hassid" by Mané-Katz (1894–1962). Sedykh's only book to appear in English, it was published by Macmillan in 1967 under the title *This Land of Israel* and enjoyed moderate success among Jewish-American readers. A sequel, *Jerusalem, Joyous Name*, appeared in Russian in 1969.

From *The Promised Land*
"If I Forget You, O Jerusalem . . ."

A person who is going to Jerusalem for the first time is overcome by an intense feeling of excitement.

Just one more hour, just a few more minutes, and the holy and ancient city, which down through the millennia of its existence has been bathed in so much blood and by so many tears, will open up to the traveler. "Jerusalem is the center, the navel of the universe, that is—Judea . . . There shall be salvation in Judea, for it lies in the center of the earth," wrote Chrisanf, the Greek patriarch of Jerusalem, in 1728 in his *History of Palestine*.[1]

I have deliberately selected this quotation because it rather accurately conveys mankind's feelings about Jerusalem, which in some way has always been the center, the "navel" of the earth. For the Jews this is the capital of Judea, ruled over long ago by King David, where the Holy of Holies, the Temple of Solomon, used to stand. For Christians this is the city to which Jesus came to don the crown of thorns, the city of Golgotha and of the resurrection from the dead. It was here, on Mount Zion, that the dormition of the Mother of God took place. For the Muslims, too, Jerusalem is a holy site, for they believe that it is from here that the prophet Mohammed ascended to heaven on his white steed.

Jerusalem is a holy city for the three religions. The mystical bonds of the Jewish people with Jerusalem, however, go deep into the millennia well before either Christ or Mohammed.

The Israelites conquered Jerusalem and King David made the city the capital of Israel some ten centuries before the birth of Christ. And 950 years before Christ's birth, King Solomon's Temple was already towering over the city, a temple unprecedented in its dimensions, glory, and beauty. The temple was sixty cubits[2] long, twenty cubits wide, and thirty cubits in height. Faced with pure gold, the walls were made of hewed stone and edged with Lebanese cypress and cedar. The richest adornments were reserved for the Holy of Holies, the ark, the repository of Moses' stone tablets. How many times was Jerusalem destroyed and consigned to the flames? It was from here that in 587 B.C.E. the Jews were taken into captivity in Babylon. That marked the beginning of Jewish exile and of life in the "diaspora." And it was in the period of the Babylonian captivity that the Jewish tradition of eternal longing for Jerusalem was born, that bitter tears were shed for the destroyed Temple, the punishment of the holy city:

---

1. The complete title of the book is *History and Description of the Holy Land and the Holy City of Jerusalem*; Sedykh is most likely referring to and citing the 1887 Russian-language edition published in St. Petersburg.

2. Cubit—ancient unit of linear measure, from the elbow to the tip of a man's longest finger; although the cubit's length varies with the height of the man who performs the measurements, it is usually converted to 0.46 meter, or 18 inches.

> By the rivers of Babylon,
> there we sat,
> sat and wept,
> as we thought of Zion.
> There on the poplars
> we hung our lyres,
> for our captors asked us there for songs,
> our tormentors, for amusement,
> "Sing us one of the songs of Zion."
> How can we sing a song of the Lord
> on alien soil?
> If I forget you, O Jerusalem,
> let my right hand wither.

This psalm of David became part of the flesh and spirit of the Jewish people for all time. Nebuchadnezzar destroyed the Temple of Solomon. The Romans razed the Second Temple, literally ploughed up the land in Jerusalem, left no stone of the holy site standing. Even the name of Jerusalem no longer existed. In its place stood the pagan city of Aelia Capitolina. First the Greeks, then the Arabs, the Crusaders, the Saracens, the Mamelukes, and the Turks became the masters of Jerusalem. There were periods when no Jews at all remained in Jerusalem—they were forbidden upon pain of death from entering the city. At other times only a handful of Jews gathered to pray at the Wailing Wall. But the longing for lost Zion was never extinguished in their souls. Three times each day the Jews pray for the restoration of the Temple and of the throne of David. And each year, as they finish the Passover prayers, the Jews turn to face the holy city and say, "Next year—in Jerusalem!"

*   *   *

The trip from Tel Aviv to Jerusalem is one and a half hours long. For pilgrims in the past this meant two days of travel through wild and dangerous places, through mountains infested with robbers and bandits. Daniil, the father superior whom I have often cited, complained that on the road to Jerusalem "in said mountains there be a multitude of most vile pagans who are beating Christians in these most fearful wilds." And the mountains of Judea where those vile pagans lived "are made of stone and exceedingly high."

Now these wilds have become gardens. A superb new road winds among the vineyards and planted forests. The broad ledges of the terraced vineyards descend from the rocky mountains, catching rainwater and preventing soil erosion. I was admiring the hills of Judea and the dark pines along the road when my companions suddenly exclaimed, "Look who's riding our way!"

At breakneck speed, a strange being—a Jerusalem Hassid—was flying toward us on a motorcycle. He wore a broad-brimmed hat over a head of luxuriant curls, hair that according to the law must never know the touch of a razor. The folds of his black silk caftan unfurled in the wind, revealing the *taleskoten* underneath—the special garment with black stripes and tasseled fringes at each end, an obligatory part of the dress of an Orthodox Jew. His legs in white stockings stuck out to both sides. It was all so strange—the caftan and the motorcycle, the combination of a medieval ghetto with modern progress, that for quite a while I was in a state of shock. Though I saw thousands of such people later, in Mea Shearim, an Orthodox quarter of Jerusalem, I never really got accustomed to them, for even in the holy city they seemed too great an anachronism.

In some places the road to the Israeli capital runs parallel to the Jordanian border. A great deal here reminds us of the war. Along the edge of the road near Jerusalem lie the carcasses of trucks, haphazardly covered over with rusty iron plating. The trucks are covered with wreaths and ribbons bearing faded inscriptions. These are the remains of the 1948 convoys that tried to break through the Arab blockade to deliver food and ammunition to besieged and starving Jerusalem. Many of the trucks were blown up by Arab artillery, and many were the people who perished here. The wrecks of these trucks have been left along the sides of the road as a monument to those who fell in the battle for Jerusalem.

That struggle began back at the end of 1947, during the period of the British Mandate. The population of the city then numbered 150,000, of whom about two-thirds were Jews and the rest were Arabs. Surrounded by stone walls erected by Sultan Suleiman, the Old City was always in the hands of the Arabs; the inside of the Old City was home to only a few hundred Orthodox Jews. And in this Arab part of Jerusalem are found the major Christian holy sites, the Church of the Holy Sepulcher, and the Jewish holy site, the Wailing Wall, which is all that remains of the Second Jerusalem Temple.

Most of the Jewish population lived in the new part of Jerusalem. This section of the city emerged only at the beginning of the 1840s, when the British philanthropist Sir Moses Montefiore built a new quarter for the Jews beyond the city walls. When Sir Moses first visited Jerusalem in 1827, he found barely 2,000 Jews, all living in abject poverty and horrendous sanitary conditions.

Five years after Montefiore, on 28 October 1832, Lamartine came to Palestine and spent an entire day waiting outside the locked gates of the city. Not a single individual ventured beyond the borders of the plague-ridden city. Finally the gates swung open: the corpses of four Arabs who had died of the plague were taken to the Muslim cemetery beyond the city walls. As Lamartine recounts in his fascinating book *The Holy Land*, "The outskirts of Jerusalem can be described in a few words: mountains without shade, valleys without water, land without greenery. . . . Only rarely does a fig tree or a few grapevines make an appearance; or an occasional group of gray olive trees provide scant shade on the slope of a hill."[3] All this changed drastically quite a long time ago, at least on the Israeli side of Jerusalem, which now is overflowing with lush greenery.

Over the past hundred years, Montefiore's quarter has spread out into a large and beautiful city with wide boulevards and a plethora of synagogues, churches, and monasteries.

* * *

The Arab armies invaded Israel from all sides on 14 May 1948, hoping through a single strike to do away with the young Jewish state. Jerusalem was totally cut off from the entire country. The Arab legion dug into its position in the Old City, where seven hundred Jews were trapped. These mostly elderly, religious people, who had never in their lives held a rifle, found themselves facing a superbly armed and trained Arab military force. Nor was the situation any better in the new Jerusalem, where Arab artillery had begun systematic bombardment from the surrounding heights and was obliterating one quarter after another. During the first three weeks of hostilities, eight thousand shells were fired on Jewish Jerusalem, killing four hundred people and wounding more than a thousand.

So many books have been written on this subject that there is no need to recount here the story of the siege of Jerusalem. Ben Gurion was right in his assessment that the fate of Jerusalem was decisive for the fate of all of Israel. Jerusalem had to be held at any price, and yet, since the Haganah did not have artillery; it was impossible to return Arab fire. The few mortars and homemade Davidkas,[4] machine-guns, and rifles were powerless against the stone walls of the Old City.

Though cut off from the city by the Arabs, the Hadassah Hospital and the university building, the pride of young Israel, were still in Jewish hands. A convoy of doctors trying to get there, however, was nearly totally wiped out. Among the victims was a brilliant Russian doctor, Leonid Dolzhansky, whom I had known in my youth in Paris . . .

The Jews suffered another major setback. The freeing of Jerusalem required the taking at any and all cost of Latrun, which occupied a key position on the road to the city, but all the attacks on Latrun were repelled by the Arab Legion of Glob Pasha, and some of the finest soldiers of the Haganah perished here.

Inside Jerusalem the population was starving. Here is a list of the weekly food rations per inhabitant (I cite from the book *The Faithful City* by the former governor of Jerusalem Dov Joseph:[5] 100 grams of groats, 100 grams of dried peas, 40 grams of

---

3. The complete title of the well-known book by Alphonse de Lamartine (1790–1869) is *Souvenirs, impressions, pensées et paysages pendant un voyage en Orient, 1832–1833: ou, Notes d'un voyageur*. In 1835 it was translated into English as *A Pilgrimage to the Holy Land*.

4. Haganah (Hebrew = the Defense)–principal precursor of the Israel Defense Forces. Davidka (Hebrew slang)—the name of home-constructed mortar artillery equipment used during Israel's War of Independence in 1948.

5. *The Faithful City: The Siege of Jerusalem, 1948* (1960) by Bernard (Dov) Joseph.

cheese, 100 grams of coffee (only for adults), 100 grams of powdered milk (only for children), 50 grams of margarine, and 160 grams—approximately two small pieces—of bread a day. During some weeks even those meager rations were not forthcoming. People scrounged for grass and wild lettuce in the gardens and boiled these "greens," producing something vaguely akin to spinach. The water pipes did not work. The inhabitants got one pail of water a day per family. There was no electricity, and only thirty-seven tin canisters of kerosene remained in the city reserves.

On 28 May, after a two-week long desperate battle for each house, for each inch of earth, the Jews in the Old City surrendered. All of the commanders were shot. Only one hundred seventy machine-gun bullets remained. There was not a single grenade. Three hundred forty-five defenders of the Old City were taken prisoner by the Arabs and sent to Amman. Thirteen hundred women, children, and elderly people were evacuated to New Jerusalem under the supervision of the International Red Cross.

This was the worst blow of the entire campaign for the Jews. Henceforth there was no longer any access to the Old City. The truce agreement with the Arabs required that the Jews be allowed access to the Wailing Wall, but that provision of the agreement was never implemented. In the New City, the fires caused by the bombing continued to burn. The inhabitants were afraid to emerge from cellars into empty streets. With predictable regularity a shell went off every ten minutes while people trembled, waiting and wondering where the next one would land.

Suffering heavy losses, convoys from Tel Aviv on several occasions broke through into the city. Even before the conclusion of the 11 June truce, five hundred workers with enormous difficulty managed to lay down the so-called Burma Road in the mountains. At first this was only a path. Later it was widened and the bulldozers made it into a real road. Avoiding Arab-held positions, each night trucks made their way along this road, delivering nearly one hundred tons of food and medicines.

The year 1949 saw the conclusion of the Israeli–Jordanian agreement, which is still in force today.[6] The Old City remained in Arab hands. New Jerusalem, including Mount Zion, was given to Israel and soon was proclaimed the capital of the Jewish state.

After the end of the war, a well-known American general came to Israel, was shown the location of the front line, and was given an account of the hostilities. After reflecting for a little while, the general remarked, "You were lucky that the Jews who were defending Jerusalem were not professional soldiers and officers. If they had had the slightest notion of military science, you'd have definitely lost the war."

*   *   *

We are standing on the roof of the Franciscan Monastery of Notre Dame, right on the border, looking out over the sweeping panorama of old Jerusalem.

---

6. That is, in 1962, when Sedykh's book came out.

Jordan begins just a few steps away from us. Right in front are the wire entanglements, behind them are some battered houses, and further on are the city streets and Arabs going about their business. A light-blue bus drives by. A woman with a basket on her head goes down the shady side of the street. Children are playing in the wastelands . . . Beyond the medieval fortress walls, beyond the Damascus Gate is a cluster of pinkish-yellow Jerusalem-stone buildings, a jumble of church cupolas, bell towers, and spires, and it's hard to distinguish all of them clearly.

My traveling companion and guide, who was born in Palestine, starts explaining: "Let's start on the left, from Mount Scopus. At the peak is the old Jerusalem University with its marvelous library, and the empty, abandoned Hadassah Hospital. This is Israeli territory, surrounded on all sides by the Arabs. Once every two weeks a convoy of four Israeli policemen is allowed to pass through. They live on Mount Scopus in total isolation, waiting for the next shift to relieve them. As you know, since the use of the building is forbidden, Israel has built a bigger and better university and a new, huge building for Hadassah Hospital in the new part of the city.

"Farther on, to the right and beyond the walls of the Old City is the Rockefeller Museum, which unfortunately ended up in the hands of the Arabs. Now let's imagine we're going through the Damascus Gate. See the huge dome of the mosque? That is a Muslim holy site. Under the dome is the very rock from which Mohammed ascended to heaven. 'In those days,' on the site of the mosque and to its right, between two minarets, was built the Temple of Solomon and, in the labyrinth that we can't see from here, the Wailing Wall. There is something symbolic in the fact that the Wailing Wall ended up in Arab hands. From the time that the State of Israel was reestablished, the Jews have had no reason to lament and weep. Is it not written in the book of the Prophet Isaiah:

> And I will rejoice in Jerusalem,
> And delight in her people.
> Never again shall be heard there
> The sounds of weeping and wailing. (Isaiah 65:19)

"Higher up, where the trees are, is Mount Ilion. On the site of the Ascension stands a Russian Orthodox convent, built about a hundred years ago, with a sixty-four-meter-high bell tower. Along the slope of Mount Ilion, the garden of Gethsemane descends to the Old City . . .

"With binoculars it is easy to see the garden of Gethsemane, in which, prostrating himself, Christ prayed to the Lord that this cup pass from Him. Next to it is the Orthodox seven-domed Cathedral of Saint Mary Magdalene, erected by Emperor Alexander III in memory of his mother, the Empress Maria Aleksandrovna."

"And where is the Church of the Holy Sepulcher?"

"Over there—in the farthest corner of the Old City there are two domes with crosses, one somewhat larger than the other. That is the Church of the Holy Sepulcher, Golgotha, and the burial cave."

I had with me a book by Bishop Methodius, *The Holy Land*, published in 1961 in Paris, containing a great deal of interesting information on the Church of the Holy Sepulcher, Golgotha, erected only three meters above the Valley of the Dead. The bishop points out that the Way of the Cross, where a procession is held every year, is only approximately marked. The traces of Christ's real path can only be found in the remaining underground buildings, erected on the ruins of the former city. I was not able to see any of those, for from Israel only diplomats and members of the United Nations Control Commission are able to cross over to the Arab side. Only once a year, at Christmas, the Jordanian authorities allow several thousand Christian Arabs wishing to make a one-day pilgrimage to Bethlehem to pass through the Mandelbaum Gate.

*   *   *

The windows of my room in the King David Hotel look out onto the walls of the Old City. Sitting at the window, I gazed for hours at the walls of Jerusalem. Behind them stood clumps of stone houses, clusters of narrow streets, cupolas, bell towers—all flooded by bright sunshine enveloping the yellow stones of Jerusalem like molten gold.

Late at night, awakened by the protracted cry of the muezzin calling the faithful to prayer, I got up and again admired the city, now a city of night plunged into transparent moonlight, and recalled the lines by Samuil Marshak:

> And though our fleeting mortal sight
> Blots out the past—'tis all in vain,
> Through eons now, through day and night
> Your hills, Jerusalem, remain![7]

In my opinion, the best view of the Old City is from the roof of the Franciscan Monastery of Notre Dame. This huge building, which dominates the city, is linked to an interesting episode of the Arab–Israeli war of 1948.

On the same day when the British were evacuating Jerusalem, one of the highest-ranking British officers said to the Haganah commanders, "Whoever controls the Monastery of Notre Dame will have Jerusalem."

In all fairness, it should be said that, being a gentleman, he also gave the same warning to the Arabs. The battle for the monastery was fierce, and today its walls still bear the traces of numerous Arab shells. At the worst moment of the siege, when there was no bread, water, or ammunition, the Israeli command received intelligence that

---

7. This is the fourth stanza of Samuil Marshak's poem "Jerusalem" (1918); see Marshak's "Palestine" in vol. 1.

the Arab Legion had begun the assault on Notre Dame.

For strategic reasons it was decided to halt resistance and to evacuate the monastery. This was carried out so successfully that there was no chance to warn the sentry standing guard on the roof, and it never occurred to this forgotten soldier that he had remained as the monastery's sole defender.

As the Arab motorized column approached the gates, the sentry hurled a Molotov cocktail off the roof. He had only three bottles. The first failed to explode, but the second hit its target, and the vehicle burst into flames.

Encountering such determined resistance, and "outnumbered by the enemy," the Arab column retreated. Taking advantage of the situation, the Israelis immediately reoccupied the monastery. When the sentry was informed that for an entire hour he had been the sole defender of the fortress—and had put the enemy column to flight—the poor man fainted from shock and fear.

*   *   *

On my first day in Jerusalem I found myself at the Russian church complex near the five-domed, beautiful Cathedral of the Holy Trinity. The western side was all riddled with bullets, for the Arabs had been shooting at the church from a mountain close by.

Like all Russian Orthodox churches and monasteries in Israel, the cathedral had been given to the jurisdiction of the Moscow Patriarch. It's now locked up. Walking around the building, however, I noticed a small door with an engraved copper plate reading "Russian Religious Mission." I rang. A minute later light footsteps could be heard. A cordial young woman whose Russian was marked by typical Soviet intonations opened the door. I asked if I could have a look at the church.

"Right now there's a farewell prayer service going on in the smaller building, and then the fathers are going to Jaffa to the celebration of the patron saints' day of Peter and Paul. So today that would be hard to arrange."

An old nun looked into the corridor. "Mother," asked the young woman. "May the gentleman stand at the prayer service?"

"Of course," answered the older woman. "This is the Temple of God. There's room for everyone."

There indeed was room in the "smaller" but still spacious—and totally empty—church. In the middle stood a couple, who, I learned, were going to Moscow on vacation, the young woman who had opened the door along with two small children, and I . . . Archimandrite Hermogen conducted the service along with an archdeacon blessed with a magnificently rich bass. In the choir the nuns sang in aging, cracked voices. When a few days later I returned to Jerusalem, I was able to visit the Holy Trinity Cathedral. The cathedral was large, obviously intended for a multitude of pilgrims, with beautiful architecture, but the frescoes were typical and quite undistinguished examples of such late nineteenth-century paintings.

Remembering that I had recently been at the prayer service, the archdeacon was astonished: Was I really from America? Were there really Russians in America? And Russian churches? On finding out that I was a journalist, he became less talkative and handed me over to the care of a cordial nun. Yet, as he was saying goodbye, he asked, "And what religion are you?"

"Jewish," I answered.

"Naturally," responded the archdeacon's velvety bass voice.

The nun showed me the church and the side chapels, remarking that she was from Kiev and had come to Jerusalem several years ago. Here, though, it was quite boring, for there were not many services; there were very few Russian Orthodox people. And with a low bow on parting, she turned the radiant gaze of her bright eyes toward me with a touching request:

"Do come by to see us here. You are always welcome!"

1960s

Translated from the Russian by Lynn Visson

❋ War and Terror ❋
1939–1953

This section showcases exemplary works created by Jewish-Russian writers in the Soviet Union between the outbreak of World War II and Stalin's death. In these works, the Nazi invasion and the Shoah are the main topics. In different ways their authors lamented both Soviet and Jewish losses as they pondered the survival of Jewishness: first in the face of the Nazi threat from without and then of the Stalinist threat from within during the postwar repressions.

The early Soviet decades had been a time of massive migration of Jews from the former Pale to large Soviet cities, where many received university and advanced degrees and joined the widening ranks of the intelligentsia. In 1939, when there were about 3.3 million Jews in the USSR, over 6 percent of the total populations of both Moscow and Leningrad were Jewish (about 250,000 in Moscow and about 200,000 in Leningrad).[1] Following the Molotov–Ribbentrop pact and the annexation of eastern Poland (western Ukraine and western Belarus), the Baltic states, Bessarabia, and northern Bukovina, the total Jewish population of the USSR had reached about 5.3 million by the time of the Nazi invasion in 1941. The losses of Soviet Jews during the Shoah are estimated at 1.5–2.0 million, and the vast majority of the murdered Jewish civilians were living in the Nazi-occupied Soviet territories encompassing the former Pale and the south of Russia (over 50 percent of the Jewish population of Belorussia [Belarus] and over 90 percent of the Jews of Lithuania were murdered by the Nazis and their local accomplices). From a cultural standpoint, this meant a further severance of Jewish roots in the former Pale of Settlement. A large proportion of the Soviet Jews annihilated during the Shoah were the less assimilated Jews still living in small towns, whereas the survivors were more likely to have been living in big Soviet cities that were not occupied during the war and were more likely to have been integrated and Russianized. Moreover, the wartime evacuation

---

1. See Mikhael' Beizer, *Evrei Leningrada, 1917–1939. Natsional'naia zhizn' i sovetizatsiia* (Moscow–Jerusalem: Mosty kul'tury–Gesharim, 1999), 360.

of Jewish civilians fleeing the occupied territories to the remote interior of the USSR (the Urals, Siberia, and Central Asia) placed them in a Soviet melting pot, where Russian was the *lingua franca*.

Even before Hitler's armies invaded the USSR, some Jewish-Russian writers who had already witnessed the suppression of Judaism and of the culture of the small Jewish town (shtetl) and had endured the Soviet assimilationist policies of the 1920s–1930s responded to the looming Nazi threat as a call to action. Boris Yampolsky (1912–1972) composed his short novel *Country Fair* (excerpted in this section of the anthology) in 1940 as a valediction of the Jewish culture of the Pale; the miracle of its publication in book form in 1942 resulted from the temporarily broadened opportunities for Jewish self-expression. Serving as military journalists during the war, Jewish-Russian writers such as Vassily Grossman (1905–1964) became voices of the Soviet people fighting both at the war front and at the home front. The chief voice of anti-Nazi resistance was Ilya Ehrenburg (1891–1967), whose double consciousness, both Soviet and Jewish, was nowhere as explicit as in his wartime speeches and his newspaper articles read and heard by millions and in his mournfully militant lyrics about the Shoah. The wartime surge of Jewish-Soviet patriotism engendered a curious blend of Soviet and Judaic rhetoric in such works as the epic poem *Your Victory* (1945) by Margarita Aliger (1915–1992). A modicum of mourning for the victims of the Shoah was tolerated in wartime and postwar lyrical poetry (see the 1945–46 poems of Lev Ozerov [1914–1996] and Pavel Antokolsky [1896–1978] in this anthology). The brief interlude of Jewish self-expression came to a halt by 1947. *The Black Book: The Ruthless Murder of Jews by the German-Fascist Invaders Throughout the Temporarily Occupied Regions of the Soviet Union and in the Death Camps of Poland During the War of 1941–1945*, edited by Ehrenburg (see introduction to Ehrenburg in the section "On the Eve: 1502–1917" in vol. 1) and Grossman and featuring contributions by a number of authors in this anthology, was scheduled to appear in the USSR in 1947. The ban on its publication sent an ominous warning to the Jewish cultural community.

The years of late Stalinism brought yet another test for the Jewish survivors of the war and the Shoah. During the Party's so-called anticosmopolitan campaign (late 1940s–early 1950s), even the mere fact of having a Jewish name (or having had a Jewish name) made one vulnerable. Just as conversion to Christianity did not safeguard Jews from Nazi race laws (and a number of émigré Jewish-Russian authors who had taken baptism did perish alongside their unconverted brothers and sisters), the absence of any expressed Jewishness in the works of writers of Jewish origin did not mean they would not fall prey to charges of "rootless cosmopolitanism" from the Soviet brownshirts. Writers whose work was overtly Jewish (such as Ilya Selvinsky and Eduard Bagritsky, both in the section "Revolution and Betrayal: 1917–1939") were now condemned for "bourgeois nationalism," some of them posthumously. Few Jewish members of the cultural intelligentsia escaped scrutiny, and the unearthing of real Jewish names behind Slavic pen names became a prominent feature of the "anticosmopolitan" campaign.

In the postwar period, as Maurice Friedberg so passionately stated in 1984, "Soviet Russian literature was to deny the Jews their one specifically Jewish 'aspiration'—to honor their heroes and martyrs." And in fact, it would fall to several non-Jewish authors of the Thaw, notably Yevgeny Yevtushenko (b. 1933) and Anatoly Kuznetsov (1929–1979), to tell the mass Soviet reader parts of the story of the wartime Jewish martyrdom. The de facto taboo on writing about the Shoah and about Jewish heroism and valor at the war front was already evident in the well-publicized case of Yury German (1910–1967) and his novel about a Jewish doctor in the Soviet Navy, *Lieutenant Colonel of the Medical Corps*, which was derailed in 1949. In the late 1940s and early 1950s, another author of Jewish origin, Boris Pasternak (1890–1960), was also writing a novel about a doctor. The Shoah must have further convinced the self-fashioned Christian Pasternak that Jews ought to assimilate completely and without a trace, and he spoke about it through his non-Jewish doctor-protagonist, Dr. Zhivago.

Against the backdrop of mounting troubles at home, the formation of the State of Israel in 1948 gave the persecuted Soviet Jews a boost of self-pride while also soon making them doubly suspect as the alleged agents of world Zionism. The late 1940s and early 1950s were, arguably, the darkest years for Soviet Jewry. This period of Stalinism culminated in the so-called Doctor's Plot and was interrupted by Stalin's own death in 1953. The destruction of Yiddish literary culture, concluding with the execution in 1952 of leading Yiddish authors by Stalin's regime, meant that it was left to Jewish-Russian writers, whether they realized it or not, to carry the torch of Jewish self-awareness into the postwar Soviet decades. In those postwar conditions, the issue of Jewish cultural memory became acutely significant. Both the émigré critic Vera Alexandrova (originally in 1968) and the post-Soviet scholar Aleksandr Kobrinsky (in 1994) have emphasized that, for the second and the later Soviet generations of Jewish-Russian writers, the cultural memory of the past and the traditions of Jewish literature would display themselves with subtlety but would never disappear. In contrast to some of their elders, the post-1917 generations of Jewish-Russian authors experienced little euphoria over the prospects of an harmonious Soviet assimilation and Jewish-Russian fusion.

As the materials gathered in the postwar and late Soviet sections in volume 2 will demonstrate, Jewish-Russian authors born in the late 1910s–early 1920s (the generation of Boris Slutsky [1919–1986]) and in the late 1930s–early 1940s (the generation of Joseph Brodsky [1940–1996]) could never shake the burden of otherness even while attempting to escape the Soviet-prescribed boundaries of their own Jewish selves. Among the historical events that shaped the self-awareness of Soviet Jews in the postwar period, Stalin's maniacal Judeophobia of the 1940s and early 1950s and the persecution of the Jewish intelligentsia left an indelible print in memory. After World War II, for the vast majority of Soviet Jews writing in Russian ceased to be a choice, further complicating what Alice Stone Nakhimovsky so aptly described in 1985, on the example of the still bilingual David Aizman (see the section "First Flowering: 1881–1902"): "By *choosing* [emphasis added] to write in Russian and about Jews, a writer is taking on a tradition that runs counter to the kind of unconscious self-identification that others working in their national literatures take for granted. Working in Russian, he becomes both Russian and Jew; a revisionist, a sympathizer, a self-hater." Over the years of the Thaw and the late Soviet period, degrees and shades of Jewish self-expression—and of Jewish self-suppression—determined many a writer's place not only in the official landscape of Russian Soviet literature but consequently in the underground and in emigration.

BORIS YAMPOLSKY

Boris Yampolsky (1912–1972), fiction writer and essayist, was born in Belaya Tserkov, a center of commerce located about thirty-five miles southwest of Kiev. In the annals of Jewish history, Belaya Tserkov is remembered, among other acts of anti-Jewish violence, for the 1648 massacre by Khmelnytsky's troops. In 1897 there were 18,720 Jews in Belaya Tserkov, that is, 54 percent of the entire population. Yampolsky's father was a miller, and his mother ran a small shop. Yampolsky was exposed to a multilingual stream of languages growing up: Russian, Ukrainian, Yiddish, and Polish. ("Do you know the language?" asked Yampolsky in *Dialogues*, referring to Yiddish. "Only the accent.")

Yampolsky left home in 1927. Trying to obliterate his "petit-bourgeois" origins while pursuing a writer's career, he spent several years in Baku, Azerbaijan, and later in Novokuznetsk (Stalinsk), Central Siberia, writing for local newspapers. Yampolsky's first books were the propagandistic tale *They Treasure Hatred* (Tiflis [Tbilisi]) and the collection *Ingilab. Socialist Construction in Azerbaijan* (Moscow–Leningrad, 1931). After moving to Moscow in the 1930s, he attended the Literary Institute in 1937–41. Published serially in 1941, just months before the Nazi invasion, Yampolsky's first short novel (*povest'*), *Country Fair* (excerpt below), a peerless work of Jewish-Russian literature, was virtually unnoticed. During World War II, Yampolsky was a military correspondent for *Red Star* (*Krasnaia zvezda*) and *Izvestia*; he spent over five months with guerrilla units in Belorussia. His essays and fiction from that time focused on events of the war.

Yampolsky's short novel *The Road of Trials* (1955; Ukrainian translation 1956) contains no Jewish characters or themes to speak of, featuring a Red Army fighter whose unit is trying to break out of the enemy circle near Kiev. Yampolsky turned to the subject of the Shoah in the 1960s in works that could not be published in the USSR, such as the powerful short story "Ten Midgets on One Bed." During the Thaw, Yampolsky published the autobiographical short novel *The Boy from Dove Street* (1959), its title gesturing at Isaac Babel's masterwork of Jewish childhood, "The Story of My Dovecote" (Babel in vol. 1). While the narrative logic of the novel fitfully reflected the Soviet formula of Jewish "liberation" through revolution, Yampolsky managed to depict with poignancy the familial aspects of Jewish communal life (a Passover seder, a *heder*, and so forth) as well as a pogrom witnessed by a Jewish boy. Yampolsky's published fiction of the 1960s included the short novels *Three Springs* (1962) and *Young Man* (1963) and, alongside his stories and vignettes, the short novel *Merry-Go-Round* in his collection *Magic Lantern* (1967). Even in Yampolsky's published—and (self-)censored—stories, readers detected elements of Yiddish folklore and Sholem Aleichem's melancholy humor.

Yampolsky wrote a number of works for the "desk drawer" in the 1960s and 1970s. They included some of his best Jewish short stories: "Twins," "Miracle," and "A Kiev Story." Some of his works circulated in samizdat and appeared abroad in émigré periodicals. Finished in 1971 and published in the Israeli Russian-language magazine *Twenty-two* (*Dvadtsat' dva*) in 1978, Yampolsky's short novel *Gypsy Camp* (1971) memorialized the destroyed Jewish communal life: "There are none and there will never again be in the Ukraine: choral synagogues, heders, brises, engagements under a velvet canopy, gold and diamond weddings, fasting until the first star of the day of atonement, Yom Kippur, and the merry, heady holiday Simchas Torah."

Unmarried and without heirs, suffering from kidney disease and fearful of the confiscation of his manuscripts (as had happened to his friend Vassily Grossman [vols. 1 and 2]), Yampolsky distributed them among his friends. He died in Moscow in 1972. During perestroika, the keepers of Yampolsky's manuscripts made possible the publication of his novel *Arbat, a Classified Street* (1960; published in 1988 in *Banner* [*Znamia*] as *Moscow Street*) and other works of fiction and memoirs in magazines and in book form.

Country Fair appeared in the March 1941 issue of *Red Virgin Soil* (*Krasnaia nov'*); in 1942 it came out in Moscow, in book form in the small run of 5,000 copies, of which not many copies survive. It is Yampolsky's best work and his principal contribution to Jewish-Russian literature.

Set between the Russo-Japanese War and the 1905 Revolution and depicting various social tensions in the Jewish community, the short novel *Country Fair* consists of chapters, each a story in its own right, loosely unified by the quest of a Jewish aunt and her nephew to find the nephew a home and a position. At the end of this tragicomic novel, the Jewish boy ends up where he began: in his native small town.

In this novel about Jewish roots, created amid the tempest of Jewish-Soviet uprootedness, Yampolsky mythologized the small Jewish town (shtetl) as a stronghold of Jewish and Judaic traditions. As Vladimir Prikhodko observed in the 1997 volume of Yampolsky's prose, which he edited: "*Country Fair* laid bare that which [Yampolsky's] tales of the 1940s–early 1960s obfuscated while at the same time revealing: the pathos of origins."

In all of Jewish-Russian literature, there is hardly anything to compare with Yampolsky's (Rabelaisian but also Gogolian) depiction of a Jewish feast, found in the pages to follow. Although Yampolsky's intonation is sharply ironic and grotesquely humorous, his scene of the feast recalls the epic catalog of Jewish names and viands in "The Feast" section of Saul Tchernichovsky's Hebrew-language "Brit Milah: An Idyll from the Life of Jews in Taurida" (1901, which Yampolsky probably knew in Vladislav Khodasevich's Russian translation [see Khodasevich in vol. 1]), thus emphasizing a unity and continuity of Jewish literature across time and languages.

From *Country Fair*

Mr. Dykhes and Others*

The small town resounded with whistling and shouting. The smell of stewing, the smell of frying, the smell of boiling.

Mr. Dykhes had sold all his defective soap to the army.

Musicians, go play! Fifers, go dance! Butchers, cut your meat! Bakers, carry your challahs! Cooks, burn in the fire!—bake and fry! Mr. Dykhes is having a good time.

The Dykhes house stands on the river bank—the tallest, most beautiful one in the whole town, with a white zinc roof that sparkles in the sun like silver. The house has a big gilded balcony, curved windows, and a wide front door as in a synagogue. Over the entrance is emblazoned a lion, as if standing watch over the Dykhes gold.

Every morning, when Mr. Dykhes stepped out onto the gilded balcony in his astrakhan, he looked upon the whole small town as his own property. And there was reason to think so. If you looked straight ahead, you saw a five-story windmill, leased from the Countess Branitsky, a mill famous throughout all of Kiev Province. When people saw bread as white as snow, they all said, Dykhes flour! If you looked to the left, you saw black smoke over the Jerusalem neighborhood—that was Dykhes tar smoking and Dykhes soap boiling. If you looked to the right, you saw in the sky the red plume of the sugar factory. Are the old people trudging to the synagogue? It's thanks to Dykhes. He built the town a golden synagogue. Is a corpse being transported? Once again, it's thanks to Dykhes, the honorary head of the local funeral society.

But today is the county fair—the mother of all fairs. Never before has Mr. Dykhes sold so much soap. And what soap it is! Never before have people bought so much flour, so much sugar, so much tar! Gold was flowing in streams.

In Mr. Dykhes's yard a fragrance of fine cooking filled the air. The carcasses of sheep hung on hooks. Steam coiled around the mountains of hot noodles. Gigantic pies, filled with grated apples, were baking in ovens, and the lame baker was keeping an eye on them. The pastry cook in a pink cap was twisting pretzels with his white hands and sprinkling them with poppy seeds and ground nuts. An old woman covered in down and chicken blood was filling the belly of an enormous goose with nuts, apples, and all sorts of good stuff, continually repeating, "That's how Dykhes likes it!" Several ducks craned their necks to get a better look at the proceedings. It probably seemed to them that the goose had been put to sleep so that

---

*The text has been abridged.

surgery could be performed, so they guffawed, asking when it would be their turn for the operation.

The old cooks stood beside the ovens with their arms akimbo, looking boldly at the fire as if they were challenging the pots and pans to a fist fight as they discussed how much pepper and how much vinegar suits Mr. Dykhes. More than anything else, the young cooks were terribly afraid of using too much salt, or not enough, and they were discussing among themselves various incidents involving too little salt or too much salt. On various bonfires, copper basins were seething with jam. The sweet smoke wafted heavenward. Birds flying over the yard stopped in their tracks.

Meanwhile the yard witnessed the arrival of the merry Jew Kukla in his straw Panama hat—a wedding jester.[1] No matter where you wanted to sit down and have something to eat, Kukla would already be sitting there. No matter where you wanted to drink, Kukla was already standing there with a glass. No matter where music was coming from, Kukla was already running there in his silly Panama hat. And a wedding without Kukla was not a wedding: Who would sing and shout? And a bris without Kukla was not a bris: Who would make a speech to the baby? Who would pour into the baby's mouth its first drop of wine? And the chicken that was eaten without Kukla was not a chicken. What kind of chicken was it anyway if Kukla had not eaten the gizzard? If someone said to him, "Kukla, it's impossible to be cheerful all the time," Kukla would reply, "You're taunted by pride; I'm contorted by laughter. You drink tears and I, vodka. What I see on the bottom of a bottle, a sober person will never see. What I have eaten at funerals, you will not get to eat at a wedding." Kukla swore they had bought out the whole fair, slaughtered a bull, stuffed its guts with kasha, killed a hundred of the fattest geese and a hundred of the meanest tom turkeys. Kukla said, "We'll eat, we'll drink."

Auntie beseeched the cooks to let me soak in the smoke: "What does a Jewish boy need? Aroma."

The musicians entered. In front were the fat-faced trumpeters; behind them came the tall flautist, then the little drummer boy with a drum on his belly which was itself like a drum. They entered and stood in a row, and the drummer hit the drum twice with a drumstick, "Pay attention! See what cheeks they have!" The cooks started to laugh and gave him a lamb's leg, and each of the fat-faced trumpeters got a chicken gizzard and the trumpeters said, "God give you health," upon which they swallowed their gizzards and started to play a ceremonial flourish.

---

1. Yampolsky has given a number of his characters "speaking" last names based on the peculiar and often parodic ways in which Russian/Slavic roots enter Jewish last names. Here's a partial list: *Kukla* (Russ.) = doll; *kolokolchik* (Russ.) = little bell or bluebell; *kukharchik* comes from the Russian root for "cook" and "kitchen"; *piskun* = little squeeler, from the Russian *pisk*; *kanareika* (Russ.) = canary; *kozliak* comes from *kozel* (Russ.) = male goat, and can also mean an edible forest mushroom with a crooked leg; *gul'ka* comes from *gulia* (Russ.) = pigeon, dove, but can also mean "shank bone."

The guests were assembling.

"Hey," shouted the coachman, "get out of the way!"

In a lacquered phaeton sat Mr. and Mrs. Prozumentik and three screaming little Prozumentiks in yellow silk breeches. They stood up and stuck out their tongues at everybody.

Seeing no one and hearing nothing, with a finger on his temple, a member of the bank board of directors walked by with calculations dancing in his head.

Waving their arms, Kolokolchik and Kukharchik came running—two rich Jews with flushed cheeks, trying to prove something to each other along the way. When they reached the front porch, Kolokolchik spat in the direction of Kukharchik: "The conversation is over."

Now there appeared a gentleman known to no one, with a big paunch and a mustache. He carried his paunch like a precious vessel. Although he didn't have a penny to his name, everyone looking at the paunch and the mustache and said that he must have a lot of money. No one had invited him yet, but the sight of that paunch was enough to make doors open wide and, although no one knew him, everyone pretended that they had known him for a long time and went so far as to ask, "How do you feel after the party last night?" Everyone walked around him and looked at him, but if they looked only at his paunch, he would clear his throat, showing so that everyone would know he had a mustache, too, and he would smooth out his mustache and blow on it. Cripples, beggars, and hired mourners crowding around the high front door argued as to how much money he had in his pockets: in the side pocket and in the back, where he kept a red handkerchief. "Have you forgotten the vest pocket?" said a dwarf. Some calculated in rubles, some in kopecks, adding even a *grosh*[2] or two.

Along came Mr. Glyuk in his top hat; skipping along behind him was Tsalyuk in a bowler. Glyuk owned an important business with gold signs, and Tsalyuk avoided looking him in the eye.

Mrs. Ratsele in a gauzy dress, proprietress of an establishment where they drink tea with jam,[3] flew into the room on tiptoe, greeting everyone and smiling at everyone, inviting everyone over to drink tea with jam.

Everyone kept coming and coming: the rich Gonikshtein, and Syusman, and Efraim—all the very best families, and Piskun, who also considered himself a good family; and Madame Puri, a woman with a bony neck and a chin like a shovel; and Madame Turi, with a fat neck and a triple chin—one desiring the death of the other; both Madame in the turban and Madame in a burnoose—and one was ready to tear the other to pieces. This group was now joined by a Jew dressed to the hilt like a padishah; after him ran a boy with a gaping mouth and protruding ears. Suddenly new names were announced:

---

2. *Grosh* (Yiddish; Pol. *grosz*) = penny, small change.
3. Teahouse—a euphemism for bordello.

Vasily Sidorovich Yukilzon and Pavel Ermilovich Yukinton.[4] Absolutely everyone was here: swindlers in beaver hats and girls in crimson chapeaux and dandies in starch. The last to arrive was Madame Kanareyka—last so that everyone could see her arrive. She smiled only at the portrait where Dykhes was depicted in his astrakhan with a gold chain across his belly. She smiled as if no one except the portrait were in the hall, as if everything that stood along the walls consisted of dressers and candleholders. Everyone was bursting with envy: Why hadn't they contrived to be last? Then everyone would now be looking not at Madame Kanareyka but at them, and they, too, would have walked slowly by and would have taken Madame Kanareyka for a candleholder or a dresser. Behind Madame Kanareyka came Monsieur François, mincing along on his slender legs as if he were carrying Madame Kanareyka's train, although her dress had no train: Everyone was whispering, "Monsieur François!" "At whom did Monsieur François smile?" Kozlyak, a dentist in orange trouser cuffs, looked at everyone as if he wanted to pull their teeth. He was dying of envy. He, too, wanted everyone to whisper: "Kozlyak smiled!" or "Kozlyak doffed his hat!" or "Did you notice Kozlyak doffing his hat?"

Everyone rushed to walk past the mirror and to start up a conversation with those who were standing by the mirror, but, having seen themselves in the mirror, only to smile as if it were not themselves but an acquaintance whom they hadn't seen for a long time.

And so people walked back and forth, to and fro, displaying who had a gold tooth, who had a false bust, who had a padded rear end, who had an astonishing wig, who had a belly draped with a gold chain. One individual went by with a drooping mustache; he simply had nothing more to show, and the only people who paid any attention to him were those who had not as yet grown a mustache.

Someone's four scrawny daughters with ribbons in their hair glued themselves to the walls, and their faces said, "Not for anything in the world will we get married!" And they took umbrage at everyone, saying that all anyone could think about was getting married. Here came a pharmacist with the face of a lamb, looking them over, and they smiled—beginning with the first, then the second, then all together: "Is it possible that you don't understand why we have ribbons in our hair?" But he was a lamb, and the last thing he wanted was to offend anyone.

The man with the belly and the mustache kept exercising his bass voice, not allowing anyone to get near him, and around him whirled some smart aleck in velvet pants with an insane need to speak. The smart aleck showed the man with the belly the silver charm bracelet on his waist and the chain on his watch and the crown on his teeth and the half-silver cigarette holder and the patent leather boots, but nothing helped, and, when the man with the belly started fanning his mustache, the smart aleck jumped over to the wall.

---

4. The humor, most likely lost on the Anglo-American reader, consists in the clash of their non-Russian, suggestively Jewish-sounding last names (Yukilzon, Yukinton) and their equally marked Russian, non-Jewish, Christian first names and patronymics; the owners of these names may be Jewish converts and/or former *kantonisty*.

At one end of the hall, Madame Kanareyka was speaking through her nose as she talked to the ladies about something, and the ladies paid no attention to what she was saying, but they did want to know how she talked through her nose, and some even started examining her mouth, wanting to find out how she did it, where she hid her tongue. At the other end of the hall, a lady with a blue feather held forth. Whenever she turned, the feather turned. It was visible from every angle as she turned. It was visible from every angle as it floated over all the ladies, and some started running ahead in order to have a good look.

A matchmaker passed herself off as the baker's wife, and the baker's wife as the wife of the pastry cook, and the wife of the pastry cook as the musician's wife, and the musician's wife herself had no idea what to pass herself off as. And the madam could talk only about kolaches,[5] and the baker's wife asserted that she had seen no kolaches only pretzels, and from the wife of the pastry cook could be heard only "do-re-mi-fa-so!" and the musician's wife kept silent, showing that she knew very well what was best left unsaid.

In the center stood the barber, but with such a mustache and such eyebrows, and he argued so extensively and bolstered his arguments with his index finger: a doctor, there's no other word for it. Any minute he would take out his pen and write a prescription! And when people spoke with him, they seemed to take him for a doctor, and on everybody's face was written, "Please prescribe some medicine for us." But just as soon as he gave them the cold shoulder, they didn't even want to recognize him as a barber but said that he was a dog fancier; and they even jerked their feet to show how one catches dogs.

Everyone was mean, flushed, sulky, just waiting for someone to cross them. And only the pharmacist who resembled a lamb, equipped with his little bowler hat, his cane, and his evening slippers, wandered politely among them, inquiring whether he might have stepped on someone's corn or whether anyone was bothered by the smell of the medicine. The thin ones in the assemblage hissed, the fat ones huffed, and the thin ones who wanted to seem fat puffed up their cheeks and also huffed until they drove him into a corner, hurling after him the sound "Ba-a-a."

Now a new contingent insinuated itself: a noisy shammes in a soiled robe who, more than anything else, was afraid that not everything was clear to everyone, and therefore he explained everything at length; the *melamed*[6] Alef-Beiz, with red *peyes*, saying "Eh!" before each and every word; then a midwife with a bow on her bosom, signaling that today everyone was to refrain from talking to her about midwifery. Also Menka, a quarrelsome Jew who would run errands, spread news, and do favors for everyone. The expression on his face always indicated that he had just arrived with the latest news. There was also a spiteful woman named Shprintsa and one Tsatsel, who went around all the time on tiptoe as if he feared that they would say he was making too much noise. And among them were the three salesmen from Diamant's shop, all the while looking at

---

5. Kolaches—Angliczed spelling of Russian *kalachi*: (pl. of *kalach*) a traditional Slavic wheat bread made into round shapes by braiding dough.
6. Melamel (Heb., Yiddish)—teacher in a Jewish elementary school.

their master, who was in the middle of a discussion, smiling meaningfully in order to show that they knew what was being discussed and that it was extremely important. The oldest of them would pull out his watch with the chain every minute and, with an important expression, would press it to his ear and then look to see what time it was. The two junior salesmen had only chains, which they didn't pull out, but just the same they assumed important expressions whenever the senior salesman looked at his watch.

"Akh," the midwife suddenly said in a dreamy voice, "what I wouldn't give right now for a fine chicken drumstick."

Everyone seemed to light up at the memory alone.

"Do you know what I would like right now?" said Mr. Prozumentik mysteriously, not even looking at the midwife, but turning to Kolokolchik and Kukharchik. "Do you know what would be interesting to eat right now?"

People held their breath, listening closely to find out what Mr. Prozumentik would like to eat right now.

"I would take a goose and would remove the stuffing . . . stuffing . . ."

The midwife looked at him with her eyes bugging out. Diamant's salesmen froze with sweetening on their faces. Menka stood as if he had just arrived with the latest news but didn't know how to tell it.

"Ah, a goose with nuts, that would hit the spot!" confirmed the midwife so that even her bow swelled with pleasure. "And how do you feel about goose with apples? Not bad, eh?"

"Ah, then there's sweet red beans," was heard on all sides.

"Ah, radishes with chicken fat," shouted the shammes in the soiled robe as he began to explain to the assemblage what radishes with chicken fat are.

"Gefilte fish," said others.

"And with horseradish."

"And with sauce, and a nice peppery sauce."

Everyone named his favorite food and sighed over his favorite food. Wishes were running rampant. And only Tsatsel kept walking around on tiptoe, afraid to say what he liked to eat.

"There's nothing better than kishke with kasha," the gentleman with the belly and the mustache suddenly said, and he said it in such a way that no one would have dared to suggest that there was something better than kishke with kasha, which the gentleman with such a belly loved so dearly. "I would open the kishke," he said, demonstrating with two fingers how he would open it and carefully eat the fried skin and then the kasha, only then.

And everyone agreed that only then would one eat the kasha, only later.

"Do you really not know how to eat?" he continued, and they all stretched out their faces, acknowledging that they really didn't know how to eat.

"First of all, you have to try it on one tooth and then, only when all your teeth start to ache, do you try it on them."

"Eh!" *melamed* Alef-Beis suddenly made up his mind to say something, and he was himself terribly frightened by his own "Eh!" but all the same people were all ears: would a Jew say "Eh!" in vain?

"Eh!" repeated Alef-Beis, "if you take it, rub it, pop it into the oven and sear it ever so slightly, a-a-a, then you have it."

"Yeah!" Tsatsel suddenly spoke up.

"And then add a bit of cinnamon," said Alef-Beis with growing excitement, "but you have to know how to add the cinnamon!"

"Yes, of course, the cinnamon," assented the midwife, not even hearing that you had to take it, rub it, pop it into the oven, and sear it ever so slightly in order to achieve the a-a-a.

"But I like parsnips," was suddenly heard from the quarrelsome Jew Menka, but no one paid any attention to his preferences. No one was the least bit interested in the likes and dislikes of such a Jew.

In the midst of all this frenzied commotion, Auntie suddenly sneezed loudly so that everyone could see that we were there, too. But they didn't see us, and, what's more, they didn't want to see us. The lady with the feather sat on her haunches more and more frequently. The wife of the pastry cook still more loudly repeated: "do-re-mi-fa-so." In more of a drawl than usual, the *melamed* said "Eh," indicating that he was about to say something.

But here came Mr. Dykhes, who resembled a pig. In spite of such a mug, about which he must have been aware, he, evidently on purpose, stuck out his nose and lips, which made him look even more like a pig. His face said plainly, "I don't have to look like a human being; you'll have to like me as a pig."

No one seemed to have noticed that Mr. Dykhes looked like a pig. No one smiled; no one cried out, "Scram!" On the contrary, they all had such faces as though they were expecting that he would shout "Scram!" at them. But Mr. Dykhes looked around at everybody and suddenly hiccuped as if to say, "Hello, everybody." And as it happened, they all understood the hiccup to mean "Hello" and started to shout in all directions:

"Good health, Mr. Dykhes. How did you sleep?"

But Mr. Dykhes didn't want to say how he had slept, so he looked around at everyone and once again hiccuped.

Mr. Dykhes always hiccupped. Even on Atonement Day, when Mr. Dykhes had eaten woodcock the night before and then fasted till the first star—even on that day he would suddenly hiccup in the synagogue, and everyone would be distracted from God and would think, "Dykhes hiccupped. What was it that he ate today?" And even Dykhes would blush as if he had in fact eaten something.

How everything had changed! Glyuk, who had just been walking on the parquet like a heron, was now twisted into a pretzel. The man with the mustache carried off his paunch so that the entryway would be wider, and Mr. Prozumentik pushed forward the little Prozumentiks, urging them to smile. Even the Diamant's salesmen stopped looking at their master and looked at Dykhes instead. People didn't mind the fact that Dykhes looked like a pig. It was actually appealing; it was somehow touching. Someone even whispered that the lump under Mr. Dykhes's nose was not a simple lump but a lump of wisdom, and that if that lump had been a little closer to the nape of his neck or—better still—on the top of his head, he would certainly have been a cabinet minister.

When Dykhes looked at the ceiling and said, "Hmm," they all gathered into a circle and discussed what that might mean. What had he wanted to say and how was one to understand that sound? Everyone found ten solutions, with commentaries, and even the commentaries generated commentaries, and that "hmm" was being deciphered to mean a whole long speech.

"You, too, will eat from silver platters," Auntie whispered to me.

She was edging me nearer and nearer to Mr. Dykhes. Mr. Dykhes had so much money that all the self-respecting mamas and papas would bring him their children in fancy little Circassian costumes or in sailor suits with gold anchors or lacy pantaloons, and they would stick out a leg and raise an arm as they recited poetry or sang or sawed away at the violin or solved little problems that Mr. Dykhes proposed. But Mr. Dykhes never made an error of judgment: the child in question would be a cantor or a thief, a first violinist or a water carrier. And if Mr. Dykhes said, "Water carrier," then that was that—and you might as well let him grow a beard, because what kind of water carrier would he be without a beard.

At the moment, a boy was standing in front of Mr. Dykhes with a violin. Around him revolved the mama and the papa, not to mention the grandma and the grandpa! Mama provided advice on how to stick out his leg, Papa showed him how to hold his head, Grandma rubbed the bow with rosin, and Grandpa showed him how to handle the bow. Now the boy took the violin, touched it with the bow as if he were asking it about something, and suddenly began to cry, and the violin also began to cry, and the boy ran over it with his bow: "Cry, cry." And no one knew any longer who was crying, the boy or the violin, and Mama and Papa and Grandpa and Grandma were also crying, and now it was perfectly clear that they didn't know the right way to stick out a leg, to hold your head, to handle a bow; their advice was useless and, if you had asked them, they themselves would have said—useless. Everyone was crying. Only Dykhes didn't bat even an eye. He looked at the boy for a long time and suddenly said, "His tooth is somehow not quite right," and he turned away.

At this point Auntie pushed me right up against Mr. Dykhes and said, "This is a golden boy!"

Mr. Dykhes glanced at me and felt my head in such a way as if he wanted to find out whether it contained brains or straw. And everyone wanted Dykhes to say "Straw." But he said "Brains!" though with a grimace and a qualification: "Brains that still need to be twisted and turned so that they're in the right place."

Mr. Prozumentik pushed forward the oldest Prozumentik so that Dykhes could feel his head and ask without fail the kind of question to which he might give a clever answer. He even advised Dykhes, "Ask him the name of his papa . . ."

Mr. Dykhes picked up a thick Russian book with a velvet binding and silver clasps and, after opening it, began to leaf through it, murmuring all the while, "What a smart book."

Mr. Dykhes stopped at a certain page and put the book before me; it lay there as Mr. Dykhes held it—upside down. But when I looked at his face and wanted to turn the book right side up, Auntie gave me such a pinch that I understood: the book was lying properly; it had always lain that way since people began to read. And so, looking at the upside-down letters, I started to read, and he, smiling, ran his finger over the lines and repeated in a singsong voice what I was reading, and his face reflected such pleasure as if he had authored the book. The letters, like ants, ran in all directions and then came together again, and suddenly one of the letters turned a somersault and flew away and right after it went the other letters. I stopped peering at them and started to think up my own and about my own, but Mr. Dykhes ran his finger over the line and, in a singsong voice, repeated everything that I had thought up. Moreover, he looked around at everyone with a smile. "What a smart book!" And Mr. Prozamentik said that such a boy should never be given such a smart book. It should be given to the little Prozumentiks and then—there is so much intelligence in that book that, when they add their own intelligence, it will come out so intelligent that no one will be able to understand a thing.

"Say ah-ah-ah!" was suddenly heard from Mr. Dykhes as he raised a finger.

"Ah-ah-ah!"

"Ah well, ah well, repeat!" exclaimed Mr. Dykhes, holding a finger that resembled a tuning fork and listening for all he was worth.

"Ah-ah-ah!"

"No, he will never be a singer," declared Mr. Dykhes. "It's actually funny—just imagine him in an opera! Isn't that hilarious?"

And the papas in their bowler hats and the mamas in their lace and the cultured grandmas and the pink grandpas all said, "Of course, hilarious!"

"He's a lazybones," said Mrs. Gulka, who had sprung from God knows where as she pointed her walking stick at me."

"Contagious!" exclaimed Madame Kanareyka.

"A thief!" said "Diamant and Bros."

"What is he good for anyway?" they began to wonder.

"Let him be a ragpicker," piped up a small boy in a sailor's jacket, upon which they all immediately started shouting, what a smart boy, and asking who his papa was.

It was suggested that I be handed over as an apprentice to the dog fancier, or else to the sauna to make birch rods, or to haul buckets, to drive out the flies, to grate horseradish. But Auntie continued to say that I was a singer, and such a singer had never been and never would be.

"When he sang at a wedding, angels in seventh heaven rejoiced," she said. "Don't you want to be in seventh heaven?"

Mr. Dykhes did want to be in seventh heaven. He sat down in a comfortable chair, put one fat leg over the other, took a piece of candy from a nearby vase, hiccupped and started to suck the candy and to listen, now picking his teeth, now wagging his leg—especially during the modulations. And they all sighed: how he feels the singing, what a connoisseur!

There I was singing my heart out while Mr. Dykhes was sucking candy, smacking his lips, and slurping. But suddenly he bowed his head, grew quiet, and even stopped sucking his candy. He didn't move a muscle, he didn't hiccup, and he even bugged out his eyes. Auntie, having folded her arms in emotion, stood and listened and continually looked around to see if they had all folded their arms in emotion.

Suddenly Mr. Dykhes began to shout, "Ai-yai-yai!"

Immediately everyone began to whisper in agitation, "That note was too loud," said some. "On the contrary, too soft," said others.

"Ai-yai-yai!" repeated Mr. Dykhes and, pointing to his heel, began to laugh. It turned out that Mr. Dykhes had a tickle in his heel.

"I was listening and waiting: Would my heel start tickling or wouldn't it," said Dykhes, unusually excited.

And they were already discussing what kind of omen that was and relating to one another various historical anecdotes involving ticklish heels.

Music began to play, gramophones began to belt out their tunes, doors opened, and in came the triumphant cook, carrying a stuffed pike, which was welcomed by the approving whisper of the guests.

"Guests!" said Dykhes in a gruff voice. "Can it be that you is interested by that pike?"

"The pike is already exciting them," said Madame Kanareyka as she looked through her glasses, wishing to see the excitement with her own eyes.

The guests smiled timidly, as if they wanted to say that this might well be improper, and a character flaw, but the pike really did excite them. Dykhes put out his leg and grabbed Madame Kanareyka, who was already standing beside him, knowing that he would now grab someone, and headed toward the pike. And after him came Monsieur François, as if holding the train of Madame Kanareyka, Glyuk and Tsalyuk, Madame Puri and Madame Turi, the lady with the turban and the lady in the burnoose, and the member of the bank board of directors, still holding a finger to his temple.

The din increased as the guests took their seats, smiling at the pike.

"When I sit down at the table," said Mr. Dykhes as he tied his white napkin, "I like everything on the table to be as red as a scraped dog and as fat as a pig." And the tips of his napkin began to move along the edges of his pink face like two pig's ears.

Mr. Dykhes drank some pepper vodka and, turning his head, looked at his guests: "U-u-u, bitter," and then proceeded to eat a honey cake; then he poured some lemon vodka. After he drank it, he also turned his head and, once again, peered at his guests: "Sour," and ate some almonds. At this point he moved the carafe with raspberry vodka toward him and, looking at his guests, gruffly asked, "Well, my guests? I suspect that you want some, too."

The guests started to shake and tremble.

"Fortunately," shouted Mr. Dykhes, drinking a glass of raspberry vodka, and, after eating some giblets, he passed the following judgment: "I love gibblets!"

Fortunately, the guests began to eat, some washing it down with pepper vodka, others with lemon, and still others with raspberry, eating honey cake or almond or giblets, and all the while repeating, "Dykhes has good giblets."

"Hail to him who gave us the happiness of living to see this day," with tears in his eyes exclaimed the gentleman with the belly and the mustache, alluding to God but looking at Dykhes, and while the others drank a glass of pepper, lemon, or raspberry vodka, he drank a shot of each one: the pepper, the lemon, and the raspberry.

They were starting to divide up the fish.

"Mr. Dykhes gets the head, because he is the head!"

"The head for Mr. Dykhes," repeated several voices, and Ratsele smiled at the head of the fish as if hoping that the head would report to Dykhes that Ratsele had smiled at it.

"And Mr. Menka gets the tail, because he is a tail!" trumpeted Kukla in a spiteful voice.

"The tail for Mr. Menka, because he is a tail!" everyone began to shout, exulting in the fact that he was the tail and not they.

"And I get all the rest," said Kukla, "because I love all the rest."

Everyone started to laugh, seizing all the rest as they did so and leaving Kukla the nastiest piece, way up by the tail. And the shammes, who had just explained that the pike is the fish of all fishes, got not a single piece, and *melamed* Alef-Beis, no matter how many times he enunciated "Eh," also got not a single piece, and he looked at his empty plate with his mouth wide open, enunciating "Eh." And Tsatsel, not daring even to sit down at the table, went around on tiptoe, constantly afraid that they might accuse him of hindering people from eating their pike.

Just then the air was filled with shrieks as the hall where people were eating and drinking was invaded by a band of shaggy women from the soap-boiling factory. The guests began to twitch their noses. Some even hiccupped, and Monsieur François promptly began to wave his pink handkerchief, at which point the air began to smell of violets, lily-of-the-valley, and cypress.

"I want to know why they've come," shouted Dykhes. "I ask you, what is the meaning of this? Do I not have locks on my doors? Have I no bouncers? Have I no swine?" shouted Dykhes as he looked with hatred into the red mug of the creature standing on the threshold with a log in its hand. "Am I not allowed the peace and quiet to drink a glass of vodka? And a second glass and a third! . . ."

"Don't shout, Mr. Dykhes," said one of the women. "Let the Jews speak out."

"What's up? Does it smell bad in there?" he asked in such a tone that it was clear that he already knew why they had come.

"It smells of dog fat," said a woman with a child in her arms. "Even the baby already smells of dog fat and so does his bagel." The woman began to cry.

"Well, what do you expect? Perfume would no doubt smell better?" Dykhes asked once again.

"Better, Mr. Dykhes, better," replied the woman as she wiped away her tears.

"Well, if it smelled of perfume, I would go there to sniff the air and so would my guests. Right, guests?"

And the guests started to laugh and said that they certainly would.

"We're coughing up blood, we're exhaling blood," whispered the woman.

But no one was listening to her. The guests were laughing, washing the laughter down with vodka and swallowing the pike and meat with thick smears of mustard, not to mention horseradish and brine. [. . .]

Now Dykhes was shouting, "Anyone who wants a raise should stay away from me. Hush! Go home! Lie down with your stomach on the stove and let our great God give you a raise. What do you want anyway—to tear out my guts?" Suddenly he started roaring and started jumping on a chair. "Sit down, drink, gnash your teeth, tear Dykhes apart."

"Drop dead," shouted the woman, and her baby started to cry. "But we want to eat, too. And we're going to exit through the front door and break open all the doors! . . ."

Mr. Dykhes even jumped in surprise.

"You, the masters, are a bunch of villains," said the woman. "Your glasses are filled not with wine but with our blood. Look at how red and sweet it is. You drink it and still you laugh! Is life sweet for you? Do you think there will always be war and you will always be happy and you will always sleep on soft mattresses?"

"Master," all the women began shouting. "We will burn out your red eyes with sulfuric acid."

"Oy, people," shouted Dykhes. "I no longer have any eyes!"

"Oy, we no longer have any eyes," repeated the guests.

"Who is insulting my guests? Where is my wine? Where is my vodka?" bellowed Dykhes when the women had been driven out.

Out of the cellar, as if from under the ground, the servants rolled a barrel of vodka; it whistled with a whistle; it boiled with boiling water.

Ten cooks, with the grease of the ovens on their faces, carried in on their extended arms big platters of smoking meat, Jewish meat, smothered in fiery sauces—some burning with pepper, others sweetened with raisins.

The geese floated like swans.

"Guests, let's eat, let's drink!" Dykhes blared out like a trumpet.

Throwing back their heads, the guests poured the sauce down their throats and questioned one another: Is it sour or is it sweet? They unexpectedly snagged the wings with near effortlessness, but some, having noticed the gizzard, smoothed out their mustaches and, with their mouths, fished out the gizzard and, after swallowing it, gazed at the host with gratitude.

"Down the hatch, guests!" said Dykhes.

Veal breasts, smoked tongue, patés, meat casseroles, chopped herring with potatoes and onions, meat dishes of all kinds and vegetable dishes of all kinds, some baked on coals, others soaked in steam.

The man with the belly and the mustache, who had been advising people to try it first on one tooth, now wolfed the food down using all his teeth. In his hands he carried a leg of mutton, which he ate with gusto. He had already choked twice.

The neighbors had already pounded on his back with their fists. Having caught his breath, he once again went to work on that leg of mutton. I was looking at him, but he continued to eat, driving me away with his eyes. When he had finished devouring the leg of mutton, he heaved a sigh and went to work on a side of mutton.

The salesmen were sitting politely at the table and, when their employer was looking at them, they, like birds, pecked at the nuts and berries, but when their employer lowered his eyes to his plate, they went to work on the most greasy pieces and packed them first in one cheek, then in the other. If their employer suddenly looked up, they pretended that they were pecking at the nuts and berries. And they had already taken off their bowler hats twice to wipe the sweat from their bald spots.

And the guests were served cold dishes and hot dishes, fish in aspic and stews. When it came to the goose with sweet nuts—what work it was for the jaws, trouble for the belly when they began to crunch against their teeth. The guests could not express enough joy, so they said, "This goose is a goose beyond compare!" And several even shouted, "Thank you, Dykhes, for the goose!"

Then there was noodle kugel with raisins, noodle kugel with honey, noodle kugel with cottage cheese, flour kugel with chicken fat—not to mention honey cakes, egg cakes, and almond cakes, strudels with raisins, strudels with grapes, and strudels with poppy seeds. And they ate every bit of it.

Madame Kanareyka, cautiously nibbling on a burned piece, looked at those of us who were standing in the corner, and she said, "How those beggars want to eat! How they're looking at the table! They would gladly eat us. If, in your opinion, we let them in, would they eat us up?"

Mrs. Prozumentik and Madame Puri and Madame Turi and the lady with the turban and the lady in the burnoose—all those whom Madame Kanareyka had admitted to her presence—replied that yes they would eat us up, and Ratsele in the pink scarf, whom Madame Kanareyka had not admitted to her presence, also said, "Of course, they would eat us up."

The musicians, having hiccupped for the last time, picked up their trumpets, and the guests began to sing, banging the serving dishes. Then a group of guests with deep nasal voices started shouting and loudly sniffling. The women at the door started to scream their heads off. Everything was going around in circles, rushing in all directions, flapping their coat tails, chasing after happiness.

Mr. Glyuk, with his top hat in hand, Madame Kanareyka with the shawl over her head, Madame Puri and Madame Turi, the lady with the turban and the lady in the burnoose were all going around, and the lady with the blue feather did also—when she came galloping up, she was followed closely by the galloping feather. When she took a seat, the feather took a seat, at which time the people outside would say, "She's taken a seat!"

On their heels came Mr. Prozumentik, with his fingers in the armholes of his vest, then the smart aleck in velvet trousers. On their way, Kolokolchik and Kukharchik were offering each other a shipment of baby powder that they had bought up from Dykhes. Ratsele, all puffed out in her gauzy dress but managing a big smile, invited everyone to be her guests for tea and jam. And the lamb with the walking stick was using the stick to depict the condition of his soul. Doffing their bowler hats, the firm of Fayvish and Suskind met the firm of Yukinton and Yukilzon. Suddenly between the firms, materializing out of nowhere, appeared Menka with his informative face and red handkerchief. He proceeded to dance, smiling at one and all, but no one even looked at him. They made a circle around him, raising their arms higher. So Menka stayed by himself, with his red handkerchief and his foolish nose, hiccupping from the sweet vodka and sneezing from the strong tobacco as he ecstatically reported the news, not noticing that he was alone and that everyone had forgotten him and that no one even wanted to look at him.

The matchmaker with a smile was heading toward the baker's wife, but the baker's wife turned away and, with a smile, headed toward the pastry cook's wife, but the pastry cook's wife turned away with a smile and headed for the musician's wife, who turned away but without smiling at anyone, and so it went, round and round.

They bowed to one another and bragged to one another as they went up to one another on heels and moved away from one another on tiptoe, teasing one another, hissing at one another, spinning around in front of one another like a wheel or a top, crawling around on all fours—everyone shouting: a-a-a! The musicians because they were musicians, the insane man because he was insane, Glyuk because he was rich, and Menka because he wanted to do some shouting next to a rich man. Mr. Dykhes stood in the middle, fiery from all that he had eaten and drunk, and only moved his paunch up and down a few times as if saying, "That will do it for me."

ca. 1940

Translated from the Russian by Richard Sheldon

ILYA EHRENBURG

See previous sections for introductory essary (pp. 180–82), Ehrenburg's early poems and an excerpt from *Julio Jurenito*. During World War II, while Ehrenburg worked tirelessly as a journalist and anti-Nazi propagandist, he continued to compose lyrical poetry and also to translate from the French of François Villon, sometimes at night when he was unable to sleep. One of the most remarkable things about Ehrenburg's poems about the Shoah is the very fact of their publication in the Soviet Union, in his collections and in central periodicals (for example, "Rachels, Hayims, and Leahs wander . . ." was published in Ehrenburg's 1941 collection *Loyalty* and "Babi Yar" in January 1945 in the magazine *Novy mir*).

The three wartime essays that follow the poems illustrate Ehrenburg's commitment to writing about Nazi atrocities and Jewish heroism. Prior to its publication in *Izvestia* on 26 August 1941, Ehrenburg read "To the Jews" at a rally of the representatives of Jewish people in Moscow on 24 August 1941. "Jews" originally appeared in *Red Star* (*Krasnaia zvezda*, 1 November 1942), and "The Triumph of Man," in *Pravda* (29 April 1944). In light of everything we know today, it is even more difficult to imagine that in the official Soviet conditions of de-Jewifying the Shoah and silencing the valor of Jewish soldiers, partisans, and ghetto fighters, Ehrenburg succeeded in having his essays printed in the central Soviet periodicals and thus reaching an audience of millions of his fellow Soviet citizens.

* * *

Rachels, Hayims, and Leahs wander
Leperlike, half-alive, cast asunder,
Stones that are deaf and blind torment them,
Old women wander, shoeless, demented,
Roused by the night, young children wander,
Dreams goad them onward, earth does not want them.
Woe! An old wound is unsealed, and I suffer:
Hannah, was the name of my mother.

529

* * *

Because remembrance of Esther's sultry midday
Like a bitter wild orange, like our dreams,
We've kept alive for eons in this frigid
Land, where birds in flight are turned to icy plumes,
Because through us the voice of terror whispers,
Because we've secret dealings with the moon,
Because a winding road snakes in the distance,
And tears are far too salty far too soon,
Because our women's hair is splendid,
Their eyes remote, their chatter oddly sings—
We are no longer. Cold alone is regnant.
The gravel burns, and grasses chafe and sting.

1944

Babi Yar[*]

What use are words, pens, paper, banners,
When on my heart this stone descends,
When, like a convict hauling cannon,
I lug the memory of friends?
I dwelt in cities once, complacent,
And held the living near and dear,
But now their graves in dismal wastelands
I must uncover in despair,
Each pit now, each abyss is known
And every one is now my home.
Sometime I must have lingered, kissing
This woman's cherished arms—and yet
When I still lived among the living,

---

[*]At Babi Yar outside Kiev, about 100,000 people, 90,000 of them Jewish, were massacred in 1941; see footnote to Lev Ozerov's "Babi Yar" (in vol. 1) for more information.

This woman I had never met.
My dearest child! My rosy blushes!
My countless relatives, my own!
From every gorge your summons rushes:
You plead with me, beseech, and moan.
We'll gather all our strength and rise,
Our bones will clatter as we wend—
We'll haunt the towns still left alive,
Where bread and perfumes waft their scent.
Your candles sputter. Flags rip out their seams.
We've come to you. Not we—but the ravines.

1944–45

* * *

To this ghetto people will not come.
People once were somewhere. Here are none.
Somewhere even now the days unfold.
Don't expect an answer—we're alone,
All because you're doomed to such despair,
All because upon you is a star,
All because your father's not the same,
All because the others were unscathed.

1944–46

Translated from the Russian by Alyssa Dinega Gillespie

To the Jews

When I was a child, I witnessed a pogrom against the Jews. It was organized by tsarist police and a small group of vagabonds. But individual Russians hid Jews. I remember how my father brought home a letter by Leo Tolstoy that had been copied onto a slip of paper. Tolstoy lived next door to us. I often used to see him and knew he was a great writer. I was ten years old. My father read "I Cannot Be Silent" out loud; Tolstoy was outraged by pogroms against the Jews. My mother broke out in tears. The Russian people were not guilty of these pogroms. The Jews knew this. I never heard a malicious word from a Jew about the Russian people. And I will never hear one. Having gained their freedom, the Russian people have forgotten the persecution of the Jews as if it were a bad dream. A generation has grown up that does not know even the word "pogrom."

I grew up in a Russian city. My mother tongue is Russian. I am a Russian writer. Like all Russians, I am now defending my homeland. But the Hitlerites have reminded me of something else: my mother's name was Hannah. I am a Jew. I say this with pride. Hitler hates us more than anything. And this adorns us.

I saw Berlin last summer—it is a nest of criminals. I saw the German army in Paris—it is an army of rapists. All of humanity is now waging a struggle against Germany, not for territory but for the right to breathe! Is it necessary to speak about what these "Aryan" swine are doing with the Jews? They are killing children in front of their mothers. They are forcing old people in their agony to behave like buffoons. They are raping young women. They cut, torture, and burn. Belostok, Minsk, Berdichev, and Vinnitsa will remain terrible names. The fewer words the better: we do not need words, we need bullets. They are proud to be swine. They themselves say that Finnish cattle mean more to them than Heine's verses. They insulted the French philosopher Bergson before his death; for these savages he was just a *Jude*. They ordered the books of the late Tuwim to be used in soldiers' latrines.[1] *Jude!* Einstein? *Jude!* Chagall? *Jude!* Can we speak about culture when they rape ten-year-old girls and bury people alive in graves?

My country, the Russian people, the people of Pushkin and Tolstoy, are standing up to the challenge. I am now appealing to the Jews of America as a Russian writer and a Jew. There is no ocean to hide behind. Listen to the sound of weapons around Gomel! Listen to the cries of tormented Russian and Jewish women in Berdichev! Do not block up your ears or close your eyes! The voices of Leah from the Ukraine, Rachel from Minsk, Sarah from Belostok will intrude on your still comfortable

---

1. Tuwim, Julian (1894–1953)—great Polish poet, a Jew who escaped to the United States during World War II and returned to Poland after it ended; Ehrenburg must have been relying on uncorroborated information.

dreams—they are crying over their children who have been torn to pieces. Jews, wild animals are aiming at you! Our place is in the front line. We will not forgive the indifferent. We curse anyone who washes his hands. Help everyone who is fighting this rabid enemy. To the assistance of England! To the assistance of Soviet Russia! Let each and every one do as much as he can. Soon he will be asked: What did you do? He will have to answer to the living. He will have to answer to the dead. He will have to answer to himself.

1941

Translated from the Russian by Joshua Rubenstein

Jews

The Germans tortured young Jewish women and buried elderly Jews alive. Hitler wanted to make a target out of Jews. Jews showed him that a target shoots back. Jews had been scientists and workers, musicians and longshoremen, doctors and farmers. Jews became soldiers. They will not hand over to anyone their right for revenge.

Falkovich was over forty. He was a philologist and had spent his life at a desk. Germans lick their lips over such types: catch and hang them. But that is not what happened here. Falkovich volunteered for the front. Cut off from his unit, he pulled eighteen soldiers together. They confronted an enemy company. Falkovich ordered: "Attack!" Eighteen brave souls captured thirty-five fritzes. The philologist killed eight Germans with his own hands.

A year ago, the Germans approached Moscow. Hayim Dyskin is the son of Crimean farmers. He was studying at the Literary Institute. When the war broke out, Dyskin was seventeen years old. He volunteered for the front. At Mozhaysk he saw German tanks. Dyskin was an artilleryman; he destroyed the lead tank at point-blank range. Several Germans jumped out. Dyskin ordered himself: "Fire at the Fascists!" Injured, he stayed with his weapon. He was wounded a second time. Bleeding profusely, he continued to beat back the attack by himself. Fourteen separate wounds on his body, a gold star on the chest of this hero, five disabled German tanks—this is the story of the seventeen-year-old Hayim.

Perhaps Germans think that Jews don't ski? This winter, Leyzer Papernik destroyed several dozen Germans in the village of Khludnevo. Seriously injured, he fell in the snow. The Germans hurriedly approached. Then Papernik lifted himself up and threw grenades at the Germans. Half-dead, he continued to fight against hundreds of Germans. With the final grenade, he blew himself up.

Perhaps Germans think that Jews are not sailors? Israel Fisanovich is a Hero of the Soviet Union and captain of a Malyutka submarine; he showed the fritzes how a Jew can sink Aryan bandits. The Germans threw three hundred twenty-nine bombs at the submarine, but the boat returned to its base. It sank four German transport ships. The fish rejoiced. But pure-bred German admirals were not too pleased.

Who in Leningrad does not know the heroic exploits of radioman Ruvim Sprintson? He broadcast into the air: "Fire into my position!" For three days, four radiomen were cut off from our troops: a Jew, two Russians, and a Ukrainian. Ruvim Sprintson carried out attacks, killing the enemy with his automatic weapon. The Germans came to understand: it is one thing to torment defenseless old women in Gomel; it is another thing to meet Ruvim Sprintson in battle.

Near Leningrad, Lev Shpayer burned a German tank and destroyed dozens of soldiers. The Germans thought they had the sacred right to disembowel unarmed Jewish women. With a Russian bayonet, Lev Shpayer pierced the greedy bellies of three predators. Shpayer fell in battle. Soldiers wrote a letter to his parents: "To the dear and beloved parents of Lev Shpayer: Your son was a hero at the front. He knew that behind him stood the pride of the Russian people—Leningrad. We will remember Lev—our heroic commander—to the Germans. And we will avenge him."

German tanks attacked at Stalingrad. David Kats was sitting in a trench. He threw a kerosene-filled bottle at the lead tank. The tank caught fire. A second tank wanted to turn. But Kats cried out "Stop this nonsense!" and threw a grenade under the tracks. The tank stopped, but a machine gun still fired away at our men. So Kats stuck his bayonet into the enemy muzzle. Injured, he continued to fight—he was defending Stalingrad after all. Only after he was wounded a second time did David Kats allow himself to be taken to a field hospital. How can we not recall the ancient legend of the giant Goliath and the young David with his sling?

There was a time when the Jews dreamed of the promised land. Now the Jew has a promised land: the front line. There he can take revenge on the Germans for the women, for the elderly, for the children.

The Jews have a great love for Russia. It is a love for its spirit and people, for great ideas and native cities, for a country that has become their savior, and for the soil where their ancestors are buried. "For the Motherland!" screamed the Moscow worker Laizer Papernik, throwing grenades at the Germans. He died with these words, a true son of Russia.

1942

Translated from the Russian by Joshua Rubenstein

The Triumph of a Man

In quiet times the world seems gray to some: black and white, nobility and baseness are covered by the fog of everyday life. We live in terrible times: everything is revealed, everything is checked—on the field of battle, on the rack, at the edge of the grave. The Soviet people have displayed a grandeur of spirit during this time of testing. I want to tell the story of one man. Like many others, it testifies to the victory of one individual over the power of evil.

A few days ago, a fighter from a Lithuanian Jewish partisan unit came to Moscow—this was the Yiddish poet Sutzkever.[2] He brought letters by Maxim Gorky and Romain Rolland—he saved these letters from the Germans. He saved the diary of a servant of Peter the Great, drawings by Repin, a painting by Levitan, a letter by Leo Tolstoy, and many other valuable Russian relics.

I had long heard of Sutzkever's poems. Both a wonderful Austrian novelist[3] and the Polish poet Tuwim used to speak to me about them. This was a time when people could still speak about poetry. Now we are in different times, and first of all I will speak of something else—not about verses but about weapons.

In June 1942, near the town of Novaya Vileyka, a German ammunition train was blown up. Who laid the mines? Prisoners of the Vilnius[4] ghetto. The doomed Jews were fighting. The German train was heading east; the Germans were preparing for another attack. Partisans from the Vilnius ghetto blew up the train. The poet Sutzkever was not thinking about verses at that time. He was thinking about weapons: he was obtaining machine guns.

There were eighty thousand Jews in Vilnius. The Germans did not want to kill them right away: they wanted to take pleasure from their prolonged agony. They set up two ghettos—two camps for the condemned. They stretched out the executions. They killed the doomed Jews for two years, one group after another.

A film actor named Kittel lived in Berlin before the war. He wanted to play villains, but even the less-than-gifted directors of UFA Studios considered Kittel too untalented. He found another calling: he became a famous hangman. He killed tens

---

2. Sutzkever, Avraham (Avrom, b. 1913)—prominent Yiddish poet, born in Lithuania, member of the Young Vilna group. In 1943 Sutzkever managed to escape from the Vilna ghetto and join the partisans. In 1947 he emigrated to Palestine and remained an active Yiddish-language poet in Israel. Sutzkever served as a witness at the Nuremberg Trial. Much of his postwar writings are devoted to World War II and the Shoah.

3. Ehrenburg is apparently referring to Joseph Roth (1894–1939), whom he had known in Paris; Roth came from Galicia and read Polish fluently.

4. Ehrenburg is writing for a Soviet newspaper and is employing standard Soviet Russian terms. Thus, he refers to Vilna as Vilnius, because Vilnius was the Lithuanian name of this city that was used during the Soviet period (and is used in the newly independent Lithuania).

of thousands of inhabitants of Riga. Then he came on a tour to Vilnius. They entrusted him with the "liquidation of the ghetto."

The prisoners were lined up in the morning. They knew that if the order sent them "to the right" they would be sent to work. If the order sent them "to the left" it meant Ponary[5] and death. Each morning they saw the same fork in the road and waited, to the right or to the left. For seven hundred days . . .

"Here are some presents for you," said Kittel. Sutzkever recognized his mother's dress. She had been shot the night before.

They burned people alive. Buried them in graves. Poked out their eyes and wrenched their arms.

On the first day of the war, the poet Sutzkever tried to make his way east. He had a child in his arms, someone else's child, a friend's child. Sutzkever could not abandon the child, and this small burden decided everything—the Germans captured Sutzkever. And Kittel himself killed Sutzkever's small son.

What went on in this world of death, where people awaited execution, where women gave birth knowing that they were giving birth to the condemned, where doctors treated the ill, understanding that execution awaited the ill and the cured and the doctors themselves?

In January 1942, a partisan unit was formed in the ghetto. A forty-year-old Vilnius worker named Wittenberg became its commander.[6] The Germans learned that Wittenberg's spirit was not broken. They came looking for him, but he concealed himself in the underground. Then Kittel announced, "If Wittenberg does not surrender alive, then everyone will be killed tomorrow." Wittenberg knew that in any case the Germans would kill all the doomed Jews, but he wanted the partisans to have enough time to get out to the forest. He said, "It's too bad that I cannot shoot myself." Bidding his friends farewell he went out to give himself up to Kittel. The Germans tortured him, poking out his eyes. He kept silent. Sutzkever had accompanied him to the ghetto's gate; recalling Wittenberg, Sutzkever turned away from me to hide his face.

The partisans found type for an underground Polish newspaper. That was how prisoners of the ghetto helped their Lithuanian and Polish brothers. The ghetto was Soviet territory: the condemned listened secretly to the radio, printed communiqués from the Sovinformburo, and celebrated 1 May, 7 November, and 23 February.[7]

A German arsenal blew up in Burbishek. Two Jews from the ghetto perished. Kittel thought that it was an accident, but it was a military action. The two did not die in vain.

---

5. Ponary (Lith. Paneriai) Woods—located about five miles outside Vilna, where thousands of Jews were executed by Lithuanian Nazi collaborators and *Einsatzkommando* 9.

6. Vitenberg (Wittenberg), Itsik—chief commander of the Vilna Ghetto FPO (acronym for Fareinikte Partizaner Organizatsie, the United Guerilla Organization) from January 1942. Along with Abba Kovner and Yosef Glazman, Wittenberg constituted the resistance group's staff command. He surrendered to the German Security Police and died on 17 July 1943.

7. May 1—International Workers' Day; 7 November—Revolution Day; 23 February—Soviet Army Day—all Soviet national holidays.

Tiktin was sixteen years old. He penetrated a sealed wagon from which he took hand grenades. But he was discovered and wounded when he tried to escape. They let him recover before executing him. "Why did you take the grenades?" Kittel asked. Tiktin answered, "In order to throw them at you. You killed my father and mother."

One time they brought a group of Jews for execution. They threw themselves onto the Germans and strangled seven German soldiers with their bare hands.

Three hundred Jews in the ghetto obtained weapons. The Germans were blowing up houses with dynamite. The daring three hundred broke out of the ghetto and joined Lithuanian partisans. The poet Sutzkever was among them.

Those who were escaping the ghetto got out through the sewers. One went mad . . .

A Lithuanian peasant woman hid Sutzkever. A Lithuanian man had been hanged in that village. A sign on the gallows read, "He was hiding Jews." One German told this Lithuanian woman, "You know what is written there?" She responded, "Yes, I know." Then she saved the poet. The Soviet people know that friendship is not just a word.

"Rosenberg's headquarters" was located in Vilnius. This was an enterprise for plundering valuable books, paintings, and manuscripts. Doctor Miller directed this "headquarters." The Germans brought the Smolensk museum to Vilnius and handed it over to Miller. An institute with the finest collection of Jewish books and manuscripts in Europe was located in Vilnius.[8] Sutzkever thought he himself would perish, but he wanted to preserve cultural monuments. He saved drawings by Repin, fifteenth-and sixteenth-century manuscripts, letters by Tolstoy, Gorky, and the Yiddish writer Sholem Aleichem.

I said that he was thinking of weapons, not verses. But a poet will always remain a poet. He obtained machine guns. He awaited execution. He saw Kittel. And he wrote poems. In the autumn of 1942, he wrote the long poem "Kol Nidre." Its subject recalls an ancient tragedy, but it was taken from the life of the ghetto. The Jews are awaiting execution in the courtyard of the Lukishki Prison. An old man is summoning death. The Germans had killed his wife, four sons, and grandsons. An injured man whose legs are broken is brought out. He wears a Red Army overcoat. This is the man's fifth son; they had not seen each other for twenty years. The father recognized his son. The son did not recognize his father. A German storm trooper arrives. He demands to be treated like a king. The wounded soldier throws a stone at the German. Then the father kills his son in order to save him from torture. This story might seem improbable. But anyone who saw Kittel knows that there was no limit to his baseness, and he who accompanied the worker Wittenberg to his death knows that there was no limit to selflessness.

---

8. Ehrenburg is referring to YIVO (*Yidisher Visnshaftlkher Institut*), founded in Vilna in 1925. In 1939 the institute's main center was transferred to New York, where it continues to function to this day as the YIVO Institute for Jewish Research. At the end of World War II, and again in the 1990s after Lithuania regained independence, parts of the institute's salvaged collections were recovered and added to YIVO's holdings in New York.

The poet Sutzkever, together with other partisans, fought for the freedom of Soviet Lithuania. There were Lithuanians and Russians, Poles and Jews in his unit. They were not saved by words but by love for their Motherland. The poet Sutzkever carried an automatic weapon in his arms, new poems in his head, and Gorky's letters in his heart. Here they are, pages with faded ink. I recognize this well-known handwriting. Gorky wrote about life, about Russia's future, about human strength. This insurgent of the Vilnius ghetto, a poet and a soldier, saved his letters as a banner of humanity and culture.

1944

Translated from the Russian by Joshua Rubenstein

VASSILY GROSSMAN

Vassily Grossman (1905–1964), writer of fiction and nonfiction, was born Iosif Grossman in Berdichev (in Zhitomir Province of Ukraine), once known as "the Jerusalem of Volhynia." According to the 1897 census, 80 percent of the total population of Berdichev (41,617 people) was Jewish; by 1926 the number fell to 30,812 (about 56 percent), remaining about the same until 1939. Grossman came from the Russianized Jewish intelligentsia; his father was a chemical engineer and his mother, a teacher of French. Growing up, Grossman was not exposed either to Yiddish or to Judaic traditions at home. A revolutionary-minded youth, Grossman attended the Kiev Institute of Higher Education and transferred to Moscow University in 1924. After graduating in chemistry in 1929, Grossman worked in the Donbas mining region as a chemical engineer and college instructor. He was diagnosed with tuberculosis and left Donbas in 1932.

Grossman's story "In the Town of Berdichev" appeared in *Literary Gazette* (*Literaturnaia gazeta*) in 1934. This civil war story of a Jewish family harboring a pregnant Russian commissar earned the praise of Maxim Gorky and Isaac Babel (in vol. 1). (Aleksandr Askoldov's 1962 film *The Commissar*, based on Grossman's story, was shelved until 1988.) Encouraging Grossman, Gorky gave him suggestions for revising a short novel about Soviet miners, *Glück Auf!* (1934; third edition 1935). Three collections, *Happiness* (1935), *Four Days* (1936), and *Stories* (1937), established Grossman's reputation as a short fictionist. His first long novel, *Stepan Kolchugin*, about a working-class lad's path to Bolshevism, featured descriptions of small-town Jewish life and an array of Jewish characters. Parts 1–3 of *Stepan Kolchugin* were published in 1937–40; a Stalin Prize nomination was withdrawn after Stalin labeled it a "Menshevik" novel. The war interrupted the writing of *Stepan Kolchugin*, and its four finished parts were not published until 1947 (reprinted in 1951, 1955).

In August 1941, Grossman volunteered for the armed forces, becoming a correspondent for *Red Star* (*Krasnaia zvezda*), the largest newspaper of the Soviet military, and gaining wide acclaim for his reportage and essays. Grossman's novel *The People Is Immortal* (abridged edition 1942; full edition 1943, 1945) chronicled the beginning of the Nazi invasion. Alongside Ilya Ehrenburg (in vol. 1), Konstantin Simonov, and Aleksey Tolstoy, Grossman was one of the principal voices of wartime anti-Nazi journalism, and literary propaganda. A number of his pamphlets, including "The Direction of the Main Strike" (1942), appeared in mass editions. Grossman's thirteen essays about Stalingrad hold a special place. They were originally published in *Red Star*, and several were reprinted in *Pravda*, with the title *Stalingrad: September 1942–January 1943*, and appeared in book editions.

His emergent view of the war as a war of both Soviet and Jewish liberation resulted in a ruthless imperative to tell the world about the Shoah and the Nazi atrocities. As a fictionist, Grossman articulated this double perspective in the story "The Old Teacher" (translation below), which was printed in *Banner* (*Znamia*) in 1943, was included in a slim volume (Magadan, 1944), and was reprinted in two postwar volumes (1958 and 1962). From late 1943 to 1945, Grossman worked with Ehrenburg on *The Black Book: The Ruthless Murder of Jews by German-Fascist Invaders throughout the Temporarily Occupied Regions of the Soviet Union and in the Death Camps of Poland during the War of 1941–45*. In April 1944 Grossman was elected a member of the Jewish Antifascist Committee (JAC); he took over the *Black Book* project after Ehrenburg's resignation. Grossman wrote the preface, sections on "The Murder of Jews in Berdichev" and "Treblinka," and prepared "The History of the Minsk Ghetto" and other sections (Grossman and Ehrenburg were listed as coeditors of *The Black Book*). Set in type in 1946, *The Black Book* was derailed: a partial copy appeared in Bucharest as *Cartea Neagră* in 1947; it was published in Israel in 1980; and a complete text was discovered in Lithuania and printed there in 1993. Grossman also wrote the powerful essay "Ukraine without Jews," published in Yiddish in the Jewish Antifascist Committee's newspaper *Unity* (*Einikait*) in 1943 but not in Russian. Teetering on the brink of the forbidden even during the war, this essay, as well as "The Old Teacher," sought to open the public's eyes onto the Soviet population's collaboration with the Nazis in occupied territories. In 1944 Grossman published in *Banner* the essay "The Hell of Treblinka," the first literary treatment of the Nazi death camps, based on eyewitness accounts. Printed as a pamphlet in 1945, it was distributed at the Nuremberg Trials and included in Grossman's extensive volume *Years of War* (1945; reprinted 1946).

The postwar years put Grossman in confrontation with the regime. His prewar play *If You Believe the Pythagoreans*, not published until 1946, was attacked for its non-Marxist interpretation of history. Grossman had started an epic novel back in 1943 under the working title *Stalingrad*. Accepted for publication as *For a Just Cause*, it ran into difficulties in 1949. Parts 1–3 of the novel went through twelve versions of proofs until finally appearing in *Novy mir* in 1952. Mikhail Bubennov, author of the Stalinist potboiler *White Birch*, savaged Grossman's novel in *Pravda*, unleashing a campaign of antisemitic ostracism. Stalin's death eased the situation; *For a Just Cause* appeared in expurgated form in 1954, and the full text appeared in 1956. In both book editions the subtitle was *Book 1. Life and Fate* (in vol. 2) would form book 2 of Grossman's dilogy.

World War II and the Shoah, followed by the postwar "anticosmopolitan" campaign with its collective vilification of Jews, transformed Grossman. By 1952 he had completed a significant portion of *Life and Fate*—an antitotalitarian novel of Tolstoyan ambitions. By drawing parallels between Stalinism and Hitlerism—and by questioning the trajectory of Soviet history—Grossman went much farther than Vladimir Dudintsev, Aleksandr Solzhenitsyn, and other Soviet authors of the principal anti-Stalinist works that were published during the Thaw.

In 1960 Grossman submitted *Life and Fate* to *Banner*. The journal's editor, Vadim Kozhevnikov, forwarded it to the KGB. In February 1961, the KGB searched Grossman's apartment and "arrested" manuscripts of *Life and Fate*. Grossman appealed to Khrushchev but was received by Mikhail Suslov, the Party ideology secretary, who called *Life and Fate* more "anti-Soviet" than Pasternak's *Doctor Zhivago* (in vol. 1). Grossman was devastated. Two copies of *Life and Fate* did survive, and it appeared in the West in Russian in 1980 and subsequently in translation. Its publication in reform-era Moscow in 1989 created a sensation.

From 1956 until his death, Grossman worked on *Forever Flowing*, an essayistic novel written for the desk drawer and uncompromising in its assessment of Stalinism and Soviet history. A key text predating fictional and discursive works by the 1960s–1970s political dissidents, *Forever Flowing* appeared in Germany in 1970. Of *Forever Flowing* and *Life and Fate*, Grossman's American biographer John Garrard wrote in 1994: "Grossman's two major works constitute a thorough-going indictment of the Soviet Union and at the same time a challenge to Russian readers to face their own responsibility for what happened [. . .] the indictment and challenge were issued by a man enmeshed within the very system he autopsied, a man who in his youth believed in the promise of revolutionary change [. . .]." Grossman died in Moscow of cancer in 1964. A volume of shorter fiction, *Autumn Storm*, came out in Moscow, followed in 1967 by an expurgated version of *Goodness Be to You!* (the Shoah is a central theme of this long essay about Armenia).

Forever Flowing appeared in a number of languages abroad, including in Eastern bloc countries (for example, Poland in 1984). The hiatus in Soviet publications of Grossman ended in 1988. A number of volumes have since appeared in the former USSR, including one of shorter prose, *A Few Sorrowful Days* (1989), and a four-volume *Collected Works* (1994), edited by Grossman's longtime friend Semyon Lipkin (in vol. 2).

In the words of Shimon Markish, who edited *On Jewish Themes* (1985), an anthology of Grossman's writings published in Russian in Israel, "no one had written about [the Shoah and Stalinist antisemitism] with as much poignancy and emotion." Boris Lanin, Grossman's post-Soviet student, stated, "Grossman's main philosophical contribution to Soviet literature is the rehabilitation of the concept of freedom."

Vassily Grossman remains one of the best-known and frequently taught Russian writers outside Russia. Displaying a propensity for epic proportions, Grossman did not possess a golden pen. The power of Grossman's greatest works came from their intellectual honesty, the Promethean thrust of their authorial voice, and their commitment to the overwhelming questions. (Also see excerpt from Grossman's *Life and Fate* in the section "The Thaw: 1953–1964" in vol. 2.)

The Old Teacher*

I.

For the past few years, Boris Isaakovich Rozental only ventured out on warm, mild days. When it rained, when it was very cold, and even when it was foggy, he would feel dizzy. Doctor Vaintraub thought that the dizziness was the result of a constricted flow of oxygen to the brain, and he advised him to take a small glass of milk with fifteen drops of iodine before each meal.

On warm days, Boris Isaakovich would venture out to the courtyard. He wouldn't bring along any philosophical books with him, for the bustle of the children and the laughter and cursing of the women all entertained him. With a pocket volume of Chekhov he would sit on the bench near the well. [. . .] He would enjoy the bench's warm, sun-baked stones, breathe in the smell of onions and sunflower oil, listen to the old-ladies' conversations about their daughters-in-law and sons-in-law, straining his ears to catch the relentless, furious excitement of the boys playing. Sometimes the sheets drying on the clotheslines, heavy with wetness, would flap like sails in the wind, spraying his face with moisture. And then it seemed to him he was young again, a student riding on a sailboat in the sea. He loved books—books didn't wall him off from the rest of life. Life was God. And he would encounter God—a vital, earthly, sinful God—while reading historians and philosophers, while reading the great and minor artists, each of whom, to the best of his ability, glorified, vindicated, accused, and cursed man on this wonderful earth. He sat in the courtyard and heard a child's piercing voice:

"Look! There goes a butterfly—fire!"

"There, I got it! Finish it off with stones!"

Boris Isaakovich was not horrified by this ferociousness. He was familiar with it and had never feared it over the course of his long life of eighty-two years. [. . .]

The women in the neighborhood were always astonished by how this old man, who received but a measly monthly pension of one hundred twelve rubles, who couldn't even afford a kerosene stove and a kettle, could have as guests the director of the

---

*The text has been abridged.

Junior Teachers College and the chief engineer of the sugar factory, or how even a car once arrived with a twice-decorated military officer.

"They're my former students," he would explain. And to the mailman who sometimes brought him two or three letters out of the blue, he would also say, "It's my former students." They remembered him, his former students.

And so he sat in the courtyard on the morning of 5 June 1942. Next to him, on a mattress taken out from the house, sat Lieutenant Viktor Voronenko, his leg amputated above the knee. Voronenko's wife, the young beauty Darya Semenovna, was preparing lunch in the summer kitchen. She was crying as she bent down over the pots, and Voronenko, mockingly scrunching up his pale face, said:

"Why are you crying, Dasha? Look, you'll see, my leg will grow back."

"That's not why I'm crying, just as long as you're alive," said Darya Semenovna, weeping. "It's for a totally different reason."

At one in the afternoon they sounded the air-raid warning: a German plane was approaching. Women, scooping up children, ran into the dirt dugouts, looking back as they ran, concerned about whether petty thieves might sneak up to the groceries left behind on the little tables and stools. [. . .]

The small town winced at the terrible blow. Smoke and dust rose high into the air. Shouts and sobs were heard from the dugouts. Then it grew calm, and the women crawled out from the earth, shook themselves off, straightened their dresses, laughed at one another, cleaning off the dirt and dust from the children, and hurried back to the stoves.

"Oh damn it, the stove's gone out again," said the old ladies and, blowing on the fire, tearing from the smoke, they muttered, "May he come to no good."

Voronenko explained that the Germans had dropped a two-hundred-pound bomb and that the antiaircraft guns had missed by five hundred meters. Old woman Mikhailyuk grumbled:

"The sooner the Germans are gone, the better. Yesterday during the air raid some parasite stole a pot of borscht clean off my stove."

In the courtyard they all knew that her son, Yasha, had run away from the army and was hiding out in the attic, going out only at night. Old woman Mikhailyuk said that if anyone snitched, then the Germans would chop off his head. And the women were scared to report him—the Germans were close by.

Koryako the agronomist hadn't been evacuated with the district agriculture office and even boasted that he would leave with the troops at the very last minute. As soon as they sounded the air-raid warning, he ran into his room—he lived on the first floor—gulped down a glass of home-brewed vodka—the agronomist called it "antibomb"—and then descended into the cellar. After the all-clear signal, Koryako paced around the courtyard and said:

"All the same, our city is an invincible fortress. Big deal, so the Germans have destroyed an old peasant shack!" [. . .]

Doctor Vaintraub dropped in on Boris Isaakovich in the evening. Vaintraub was sixty-eight years old. He was dressed in a summer silk jacket and a Russian shirt that was unbuttoned down to his flabby chest of overgrown gray hair.

"Well, how are things, young fellow?" asked Boris Isaakovich.

But the young fellow was breathing heavily, having just made it up the stairs leading to the second floor, and only panted, pointing at his chest. Then the doctor said:

"It's time to go, they say. The last transport with workers from the sugar factory leaves tomorrow. I reminded the engineer Shevchenko—he's promised to send a cart for you."

"Shevchenko studied with me. He was very good in geometry," said Boris Isaakovich. "He must be asked to pick up the wounded Voronenko from our house— his wife found him five days ago in the hospital. And Vaisman with her baby—her husband was killed, she received official notification."

"I don't know if there'll be room; you know there's a few hundred workers," said Vaintraub, and he suddenly began to speak very fast, pouring out his heavy, hot breath at his friend. "Well, that's it, Boris Isaakovich. A town where literally every dog knows me. Just imagine, 16 June 1901 was the day I arrived here." He grinned. "And here's a coincidence: In this house, in this very house, forty-one years ago I visited my first patient, Mikhailyuk, food poisoning from a fish. Whom haven't I treated here since then—him, and his wife, and his son Yasha with his eternal diarrhea, and Dasha Tkachuk, even before she married Voronenko, and Dasha's father, and Vitya Voronenko. And it's literally the same thing in every house. Ahhh, well! I never thought I'd live to see the day that we would have to flee from here. And I will tell you openly, the closer the departure, the less my resolve. Everything seems to say: I'm staying put. Whatever will happen, will happen."

"As for me, I'm more determined to go," said the teacher. "I know what such a trip in an overcrowded freight car will be like for an eighty-two year old. I don't have any relatives in the Urals. I don't have a kopeck to my name. And what's more," he said, waving his hands, "I know, I'm even certain that I won't last until the Urals. But that's the best way to go. I will die on the filthy floor of a filthy freight car, keeping my sense of human dignity, so as to die in a country where I count as a human being."

"Well, I don't know," said Vaintraub, "because in my opinion, it's not that terrible. After all, we're professional people, you yourself understand, we aren't just the riff-raff you find in the street."

"You're a naïve young man," said Boris Isaakovich.

"I don't know, I don't know," said the doctor. "I keep vacillating. Many patients of mine are trying to convince me to stay . . . But there are those who are unequivocally for going." He abruptly jumped to his feet and cried out:

"What is this? Explain it to me! I came to you so you could explain it to me, Boris Isaakovich! You're a philosopher, a mathematician. You must explain to me, a doctor, what is this? Delirium! How can a civilized European people, having created such medical clinics, having brought forth such luminaries of medical science, become the conduit for such an ultrareactionary medieval darkness? Where does this spiritual infection come from? What is this? Mass psychosis? Mass insanity? Degeneration? Or perhaps it isn't so bad, huh? Are they just laying it on thick?"

From the stairs came the thump of crutches, as Voronenko went up.

"Permission to interrupt, sir?" he asked mockingly.

Vaintraub immediately composed himself and said:

"Ah, Vitya, how're you doing?" He used the informal pronoun *ty* with nearly the entire population of the city, because all of the thirty- and forty-year olds had been his patients when they were children. [. . .]

Voronenko suddenly leaned over toward him, and his face became calm and immobile. Quietly, without rushing, he announced:

"The German tanks have crossed the railroad lines and occupied the village of Malye Nizgurtsy. That's about twenty kilometers to the east."

"Half past six," said the doctor and asked, "This means the transport won't be going?"

"Well, it stands to reason," said the old teacher.

"A little sack," said Voronenko, adding after a moment's thought, "a tied-up sack."

"Well, what can you do," continued Vaintraub. "We'll see—it's in the hands of fate. I'm going home."

Rozental looked at him.

"You know, my whole life I've never liked medicine, but now you're going to give me the one medicine that might help."

"What, what can save you?" Vaintraub quickly asked.

"Poison."

"That will never happen!" shouted Vaintraub. "I will never do it."

"You're a naïve young man," replied Rozental. "Didn't Epicurus teach that a wise man, out of love for life, can kill himself if his sufferings become unbearable? And I love life no less than Epicurus."

He stood to his full height. His hair and face and quivering fingers and thin neck—all had become emaciated and ashened by time, making him seem transparent, light, weightless. And only in his eyes was there an intellect unbound by time.

"No, no!" Vaintraub moved to the door. "You'll just see, somehow things will blow over." And he left.

"Most of all I worry about one thing," the teacher declared, "that the people with whom I have spent my whole life, whom I love, whom I trust, that these people will succumb to a dark, base temptation."

"No, that'll never happen!" said Voronenko. [. . .]

That night Rozental didn't sleep. It seemed as if the sun wouldn't rise on the next morning and darkness would cover the town forever. But the sun did rise at its appointed hour, and the sky became blue and cloudless, and the birds began to sing.

Slowly a German bomber flew by low overhead, as if worn out from a night of insomnia. The antiaircraft guns did not fire, and the town and sky above were now filled with Germans. The house began to stir.

Yasha Mikhailyuk descended from the attic. He strolled around the courtyard. He sat down on the same bench that the old teacher had sat on the day before. He spoke to Dasha Voronenko, who was heating up the stove.

"Well, so, where is he, your defender of the motherland? Did the Reds run off without him?"

And beautiful Dasha smiled a sad smile and said:

"Don't report him, Yasha; after all, he was mobilized, just like everyone else."

After sitting for a long time in the darkness, Yashka Mikhailyuk emerged into the warm sunlight, breathed the morning air, and inspected the scallions in the vegetable garden. He shaved and put on an embroidered shirt.

"Okay," he said lazily, "do you know where I can get something to drink?"

"I'll get some homebrew," Dasha said. "This lady I know has some. Please, Yasha, take pity on him, he's a cripple. Don't squeal on him."

Then the agronomist entered the courtyard, and the women murmured:

"Isn't he something? Just like it was the first day of Easter."

He conferred with Yasha, whispering something into his ear, and the two of them burst out laughing.

They proceeded to the agronomist's place, and there they started drinking. Old woman Mikhailyuk brought them some salt pork and pickled tomatoes. Varvara Andreevna, all of whose five sons were in the Red Army, the most pernicious and sharp-tongued old woman in the courtyard, said to her, "Now you, Mikhailyuk, will be quite the notable lady under the Germans: a husband in a prison camp for political agitation, a deserter son, this house all your own. The Germans are sure to pick you as mayor of the town."

The highway lay five kilometers to the east, so the German troops passed by, ignoring the small town. Only at noon did the motorcyclists, black from the sun, pass through on the main street wearing sidecaps, shorts, and slip-on shoes. Each one wore a watch on his wrist.

The old women, glancing at them, said, "Ah, dear Lord, no shame, no conscience, naked in the main street. The shame knows no bounds!" [. . .]

In the afternoon another two deserters, buddies of Yasha's, arrived at his place. They were all drunk and sang in unison: "Three tank drivers, three happy friends and comrades."[1] In all likelihood they would have sung a German song, but they didn't know one. The agronomist walked around the courtyard and, smiling craftily, asked the women, "Where's our Jews at? There's been no sign of them all day, neither the kids nor the old folks, no one, not a trace of them. And just yesterday they were hauling five-bushel baskets from the market."

But the women shrugged their shoulders and cut short the conversation. The agronomist was surprised. He thought they would have reacted totally differently to such interesting observations.

Then the drunk Yasha decided to clear out his apartment, since up until 1936 the whole lower floor had been occupied by the Mikhailyuk. After they deported his father, Voronenko and his wife took over two rooms, and during the war the town Soviet moved the family of young Lieutenant Vaysman, evacuated from Zhitomir, into the third room.

Yasha's buddies helped him clear out the space. Katya Vaysman and Vitaly Voronenko sat in the courtyard and cried. Old woman Vaysman carried out her dishes, the cooking pots, and as she walked past the crying children said to them in a whisper, "Hush, children, quiet, there's no need to cry." [. . .]

Old woman Mikhailyuk stood, tall, gray-haired, with clear bright eyes, keeping silent the whole time. She looked at the crying children, at her son crashing about, at the old woman Vaysman, at the smiling lieutenant-amputee.

"Mama, why are you standing there like a blushing new bride?" Yasha asked her. Twice she didn't answer him, and on the third time she said:

"Here's the day we've been waiting for."

The evicted sat in silence on their bundles until evening, and when it began to grow dark, the teacher came out and said:

"I beg of you, all of you must come over to my place."

The stone-silent women immediately began to sob.

Taking two small bundles from the ground, the teacher went home. Soon the room was completely piled high with small bundles, pots, and suitcases bound with wire and string. The children fell asleep on the bed, the women on the floor, and Rozental and Voronenko talked in a low voice.

"I've dreamed of many things in my life," Viktor Voronenko said. "I wanted to win the Order of Lenin, I wanted my own motorcycle with a sidecar to take my wife to Donets on the weekends. I was at the front, and I dreamed about seeing my family and bringing my son an Iron Cross and evaporated milk,[2] and now I dream only of one thing: to have some grenades—oh what a blast I would make!"

---

1. "Three Tank Officers" (Tri tankista)—popular song by Daniil and Dmitry Pokrass, lyrics by Boris Laskin; originally written for the motion picture *The Tractor Drivers* (Traktoristy, 1939).

2. Rozental is referring to World War I.

And the teacher said:

"The more you think about life, the less you understand. Soon I will stop thinking, but this will happen when they break my skull. While the German tanks are powerless to prevent me from thinking, I think about peace."

"And what's there to think about," said Voronenko. "Hand grenades, just a little blast, while I'm still alive, to take care of Hitler!"

II.

Koryako the agronomist was waiting for his meeting with the town Kommandant. They said that the Kommandant was an older fellow who knew Russian. Word got around somehow that a long time ago he had studied in a gymnasium in Riga. The agronomist had already been announced to the Kommandant, and so he nervously paced the waiting room, glancing from time to time at the huge portrait of Hitler talking with some children. Hitler was smiling, and the children, extraordinarily well dressed, with serious, intent faces, peered up at him from down below. Koryako was nervous. After all, he had once instituted a plan for collectivization in the area, and what if suddenly someone was to denounce him? He was nervous—for the first time in his life he had to talk with Fascists. [. . .]

From the Kommandant's office came a hoarse, muffled cry, full of torment. [. . .]

[. . .] The door flew open, and into the waiting room ran the police chief, recently arrived from Vinnitsa, and the Kommandant's young, pale adjutant, the one who on market day had led a round-up of the partisans. The adjutant said something loudly in German to the clerk, who leapt up and ran to the telephone. The police chief, seeing Koryako, shouted:

"Quick, quick! Where's the doctor around here? The Kommandant has had a heart attack."

"Well, right there, in the catty-corner building, is the best doctor in town," Koryako showed him through the window. "But, he's—I beg your pardon—Vaintraub. He's a Jew!"

"*Was? Was?*" asked the adjutant in German.

The police chief, already having learned a smattering of German, said in his rough, Russianized German, "*Hier, ein gut doktor, aber er ist yud.*"[3]

The adjutant waved his hands, ran to the door, and Koryako, catching up with him, pointed the way:

"Here, right here, this house here."

Major Werner had had a severe attack of angina. The doctor grasped this immediately, after asking the adjutant a few questions. He ran into the next room, hugged his

---

3. (Ger.) = "Here, a good doctor, but he is a Jew."

wife and daughter goodbye, grabbed a syringe and several ampules of camphor, and followed the young officer out.

"Just a minute . . . After all, I should wear an armband," said Vaintraub.

"It's not necessary, go as you are," replied the adjutant.

As they entered the Kommandant's office, the young officer said to Vaintraub:

"I'm warning you. Our own doctor is on the way. They've sent an automobile for him. He'll check all of your medicines and methods."

Vaintraub, smiling, replied, "Young man, you are dealing with a doctor, but if you don't have confidence in me, I can leave."

"Hurry up, hurry up," shouted the adjutant.

Werner, a thin, gray-haired man, lay on the sofa with a sweaty, pale face. His eyes, filled with mortal anguish, were terrible to look at. Werner slowly uttered:

"Doctor, for the sake of my poor mother and sick wife—they won't make it. . . ," and he held out to Vaintraub his feeble hand with white fingernails. [. . .]

And the doctor saved him.

The sweet sensation of life returned to Werner. The heart vessels, freed of the spasms, pumped blood freely, and his breathing relaxed. When Vaintraub wanted to leave, Werner seized him by the hand.

"No, no. Don't leave. I'm afraid. It might happen again."

With a quiet voice he complained, "A terrible illness. This is my fourth attack of angina. At the moment of the attack I feel the total darkness of imminent death. There is nothing in the world more terrible, darker, more awful than death. What injustice it is that we are mortal! Don't you think so?"

They were alone in the room.

Vaintraub bent down to the Kommandant, and not knowing why, or what possessed him, he said:

"I am a Jew, Major. You are right, death is terrible."

For an instant, their eyes met. And the gray-haired doctor saw confusion in the Kommandant's eyes. The German was dependent on him, he feared another attack of angina, and the old doctor with his calm, confident manner had saved him from death; he stood between him and the terrible darkness that had been so near, so very close, and that dwelt in the major's sclerotic heart vessels.

Soon they heard the sound of the approaching automobile. The adjutant came in and said:

"Sir, the chief doctor from the rehabilitation hospital has arrived. Now we can dismiss this person."

The old doctor left. As he walked past the doctor waiting in the office, with the order of the Iron Cross on his uniform coat, he said, smiling:

"Greetings, colleague. The patient is now completely stable."

The doctor stared at him, motionless and silent.

Vaintraub went home, all the while exclaiming loudly, in a sing-song voice: "There's only one thing I want, that I should meet a patrol and they should execute me in front of the windows, in full view of the Kommandant. That is my only wish. 'Don't go out without an armband, don't go out without an armband.'"

He laughed, waved his hands, and it seemed as if he was drunk.

His wife ran out to meet him.

"So, how was it? Did everything go okay?" she asked.

"Yes, yes. The dear Kommandant's life is completely out of danger," he said with a smile and, entering the room, suddenly collapsed, sobbing, and began to pound his large bald head on the floor. "He was right, the teacher was right," he said. "Cursed be the day I became a doctor."

And so the days went. The agronomist became a block warden. Yasha served in the police. The most beautiful girl in the town, Marusya Varaponova, played piano in the officer's café and became the mistress of the Kommandant's adjutant. Women went to the villages to trade old clothes for wheat, potatoes, and millet. They cursed the German drivers who demanded huge transport charges. The labor bureau sent out hundreds of notices, and young men and women arrived at the station with bundles and rucksacks, piling on to the freight trains. [. . .]

Women, old folks, small children—they all clearly understood what was happening in the country and to what fate the Germans had doomed the people and why they had waged this terrible war. And when one day the old woman Varvara Andreevna approached Rozental in the courtyard and, crying, asked, "What in the world is going on, grandpa?" the old teacher returned to his room and said, "Well, probably in a day or two the Germans will arrange a grand execution for the Jews—the life to which they have doomed Ukraine is too terrible."

"What's that got to do with the Jews?" asked Voronenko.

"Can't you see it? It's elementary," said the teacher. "The Fascists have made all of Europe into one massive prison camp, and in order to keep the prisoners under control, they've built a huge stepladder of oppression. The Dutch live worse than the Danes, the French live worse than the Dutch, the Czechs live worse than the French, even worse off are the Greeks, Serbs, then the Poles, and even lower are the Ukrainians and Russians. They are all rungs on a stepladder of penal servitude. The lower it goes, the greater the amount of blood, sweat, and bondage. Well, on the lowest level of this massive many-storied prison camp is the abyss into which the Fascists have consigned the Jews. Their fate should frighten the entire European prison camp, so that the most terrible fate seems fortunate compared to the fate of the Jews. Well then, it seems to me, the suffering of the Russians and Ukrainians is so great, that the time has come to show that there is a fate still more terrible and horrible. They'll say, 'Don't complain. Be content, proud, happy that you are not Jews!' This is the simple calculus of brutality, not a spontaneous hatred."

III.

In the courtyard where the teacher lived, several changes had taken place over the course of the month. The agronomist had become very full of himself and had put on weight. The women would go to him with requests and homebrew in hand. Every evening the agronomist would get drunk, crank up the gramophone, and sing "My Campfire Burns Bright Through the Fog."[4] Germanisms began to appear in his speech. He would say, "When I come *nach hause* or go to *spazieren*, please do not disturb me with your requests." Yasha Mikhailyuk was rarely at home; he mostly rode around the district, rounding up partisans. Yasha would usually arrive on a peasant cart, carrying with him salt pork, homebrew, and eggs.

His mother, madly devoted to him, would prepare sumptuous dinners. Once, at one of these dinners, a Gestapo *Unteroffizier* arrived, and old woman Mikhailyuk said with scorn to Dasha Voronenko, "You had no idea, you fool. You see now what kind of people come to see us, while you go on living with your one-legged one in a dirty Jew's room."

She could never forgive the beauty Dasha for the fact that in 1936 she had rebuffed her son and married Voronenko. Yasha would mockingly and cryptically say, "Soon there'll be plenty of room for you to live in. I've been to the towns that have been totally cleaned out . . . down to the last one." [. . .]

On this day Doctor Vaintraub went to see the teacher. He held out to the teacher a little vial fastened tight with a stopper made of ground glass.

"Concentrated solution," he said. "My views have changed. In the past few days I've begun to consider this substance a necessary and helpful medication."

The teacher slowly shook his head.

"I'm grateful to you," he declared sadly, "but of late my views have also changed. I've decided to refuse this medicine."

"Why?" said Vaintraub with surprise. "I've had enough. You were right, and I was wrong. I'm not allowed to walk around the main streets, my wife is forbidden from going to the market lest she be shot by a firing squad, and all of us wear this armband. When I go out with her on the street, it's like I have a heavy hoop of burning steel on my arm. You are absolutely correct, it's impossible to live like this. And even hard labor in Germany, it turns out, is too good for us. Have you heard how poor young girls and boys work there? But they're not taking Jewish youth. That means that for the Jewish youth—and for all of us—there's something lying in store that's many

---

4. The first line of the poem "Song of a Gypsy Woman" (Pesn´ tsyganki, 1853) by Yakov Polonskii (1819–1898), which has been set to music by several composers, including Tchaikovsky in an 1886 version. As a popular love song (*romans*), it is commonly known as "Campfire" (Koster).

times worse than this terrible penal servitude. What it will be, I don't know. Why should I wait for it? You're right. I would join the partisans, but with my bronchial asthma it's not feasible."

"And during these terrible weeks, when we haven't seen each other," said the teacher, "I've become an optimist."

"What?" replied Vaintraub, frightened. "An optimist? Forgive me, but it seems you've lost your mind. Do you know what kind of people these are? This morning I went to the office of the Kommandant merely to request that my daughter, who's been beaten, would be released from work for one day—and they threw me out, and it's lucky that they just threw me out."

"I'm not talking about that," said the teacher. "I feared one thing most of all. Even more than I feared it, I was terrified of it. Just the thought of it was enough to fill me with a cold dread. You know—that the Fascist calculation would turn out to be true. [. . .] But they've miscalculated. They've been brewing hatred, and instead they produced sympathy. They wanted to arouse malicious pleasure, to cloud the reason of great peoples. And I've seen it for myself. I myself have experienced it, have seen that the terrible fate of the Jews evokes only a mournful sympathy from the Russians and Ukrainians, that, although they themselves are suffering under the terrible oppression of the German terror, they're ready to help in any way they can. We're forbidden to buy bread or to go the market for milk, and our neighbors take it upon themselves to do our shopping. Dozens of people have come to see me and advised me about the best place to hide and where it was safe. I see sympathy in many people. I also see, of course, indifference. But malice, joy at our ruin, I don't see often—only three or four times in all. The Germans were mistaken. The book-keepers miscalculated. My optimism is triumphant. I never had any illusions. I have known, and I know, the cruelty of life."

"That's all true," said Vaintraub and looked at his watch, "but it's time for me to go: the Jewish day is ending; it's three-thirty . . . We probably won't see each other again." He approached the teacher and said, "Allow me to say goodbye. After all, we've known one another for nearly fifty years. This is not the time for me to teach you." They embraced and kissed. And the women, watching their goodbye, wept.

Many events occurred on that day. The day before Voronenko had procured two F-1 hand grenades from a neighborhood kid. He traded a glass of beans and two glasses of sunflower seeds for the grenades. [. . .]

No one saw how he quietly slipped out of the house, tapping his crutches. He stood for a while on the corner, staring at the house where his wife and son remained, and went off in the direction of the Kommandant's office. He would not see his wife or son again. And the agronomist would not return home. The grenade, tossed by the one-legged lieutenant, fell through the window of the waiting room to the Kommandant's office, where the block wardens were assembled, waiting for new orders. The Kommandant was not there at the time. He was strolling in the orchard; he had been advised to do so by the doctor with the Iron Cross on his uniform coat. Every day a forty-minute stroll along the path in the fruit orchard and a short rest on the small bench.

In the morning a policeman sent the sick Lida Vaysman to remove the corpses of Doctor Vaintraub, his wife, and his daughter, who had taken poison the night before. [. . .]

Only toward evening did Lida Vaysman return home.

She said that the doctor and the doctor's wife turned out to be heavy and that the earth was very hard and rocky, but fortunately the German let her dig a shallow grave. She complained that she broke a heel on the shovel and tore her skirt when she was climbing off the cart, catching it on a nail. She had enough common sense, and perhaps the guile of a deranged person, not to tell Dasha that Viktor Voronenko was hanging on the gate at the town's entrance.

But when Dasha came in she said quietly, matter-of-factly:

"Viktor is hanging there, and he's probably terribly thirsty. His mouth is wide open and his lips are completely parched."

Dasha learned of Viktor's fate from old woman Mikhailyuk before nightfall. She silently retreated into the depths of the courtyard, where there were cucumbers planted, and sat down between two rows. [. . .]

A German soldier who lived in the neighboring courtyard ran to the outhouse, undoing his belt as he went, and on the way back he saw Dasha sitting there and approached the fence. He stood and silently admired her beauty, her white neck, her hair, her breasts. She sensed his stare and thought, why, on top of all this grief, did God punish her with such beauty—after all, it's unthinkable for a beautiful woman to live purely, without sin, in this vile, terrible time.

Then Rozental approached her and said:

"Dasha, you probably want to be left alone. In the meantime I'll fetch the water instead of you. Sit as long as your soul needs. I fed Vitalik some cold millet porridge."

She nodded silently, looked at him, and sobbed. He was perhaps the sole person in town who hadn't changed the whole time, remaining just as he was—considerate, polite, reading his books, inquiring, "I won't bother you, will I?" and saying "bless you" after people sneezed. And this when all of the people had lost the very qualities that she had liked so much—courtesy, tact, compassion. It seemed that only this old man alone out of the whole town would say, "How do you feel?" "You look very pale this morning," "Eat something, after all you've hardly had anything to eat this evening." And the rest of the world lived like this: "Oh, it's a war after all, it's the Germans after all, everything's going up in flames, everything's lost." After all, she had lived this way, too, like the rest of the world—carelessly, without thought of her soul. [. . .]

At dusk Rozental placed a candleholder on the table and took two candles from the shelf. He had been saving them for a long time. Each one of them was wrapped in dark blue paper. He lit both candles. Pulling open a drawer that he had always kept closed, he withdrew some packets of old letters and photographs and, sitting at the table, put on his glasses and read through the letters, the writing on the blue and pink paper faded from the passage of time, and carefully scrutinized the photographs. Old woman Vaysman quietly approached him.

"What will happen to my children?" she said.

She couldn't write. In her whole life she hadn't read a single book; she was an ignorant old woman. And yet instead of book wisdom she had developed powers of observation and a worldly wisdom, even a penetrating intellect of sorts.

"How long will these candles last you?" she asked.

"Two nights, I think," said the teacher.

"Today and tomorrow."

"Yes," he replied, "through tomorrow as well."

"And the day after tomorrow it will be dark."

"I believe the day after tomorrow it will be dark."

She trusted very few people. But Rozental could be trusted, and she trusted him. A strange sorrow seized her heart. She looked for a long time at the face of her sleeping granddaughter and spoke gravely:

"Tell me, what is this child guilty of?"

But Rozental didn't hear her—he was reading the old letters.

That night he sifted through the huge piles of his memories. He recalled hundreds of people from his past, his students and his teachers. He recalled enemies and friends, recalled books, arguments from his student days, recalled a cruel, unfortunate love that he had suffered through sixty years ago but that remained like a cold shadow across the rest of his life. He recalled years of vagrancy and years of work, he recalled how much spiritual searching he had done, from a passionate, frenzied religiosity to a clear, cold atheism. He recalled the heated, fanatical, irreconcilable arguments. All of this had run its course and had been left behind. Of course, his life had been far from happy. He had thought much but done little. For fifty years he was a school-teacher in a boring little town. At one time he had taught children in a Jewish trade school, and then, after the Revolution, he taught algebra and geometry in a secondary school. He should have lived in the capital, written books, published in newspapers, debated with the whole world.

But tonight he didn't regret that life had not given him his due. Tonight for the first time he was indifferent to the people who had long since passed out of his life, and he passionately wanted only one thing, a miracle that he could not comprehend—love. He had never known it. In his early childhood, after the death of his mother, he was raised in his uncle's family, in his youth he tasted the bitterness of female betrayal. All his life he had lived in the world of noble thoughts and rational behavior.

[. . .] He knew this: he was destined to die at a time when life was ruled by the laws of evil, of brute force, from which came unthinkable crimes. These laws affected not only the conquerors but also the vanquished. The great enemies of life were indifference and callousness. And it was these terrible days that fate had chosen for his death.

In the morning it was announced that the Jews who lived in the town were required to report the next day at six o'clock in the morning to the square next to the steam mill. All of them would be relocated to the western regions of occupied Ukraine: there the Reich authorities were establishing a special ghetto. Essential belongings weighing no more than exactly fifteen kilograms could be brought along. Taking food with them was not permitted because all along the route of travel the military command would provide them with dried rations and boiled water.

IV.

All day neighbors came to visit the teacher for advice and to ask him what he thought about the deportation order. The old shoemaker Borukh came by, a jokester and foul-mouthed person, and a great maker of fashionable footwear. Mendel the baker came by, taciturn and philosophical, Leyba the tinsmith came by, the father of nine children, and the broad-shouldered, gray-mustached nail driver Hayim Kulish. They had all heard that in many cities and towns the Germans had already announced these deportations, but not a soul had actually seen a single special train of Jews, nor had anyone encountered such a caravan of Jews along the distant roads, and there had been no word of life in these distant ghettos. They had all heard that the transports of Jews that had left from the towns were not taken to railroad stations, nor transported along the wide highways, and that they were bringing the Jews to places outside the towns where there were ravines and gullies, marshes and old quarries. They had all heard that several days after the departure of the Jews, German soldiers had bartered for honey, sour cream, and eggs at the town market in exchange for women's jackets and children's jumpers and shoes, and that, as they went home from the market, the townspeople had quietly whispered to one another: "A German traded the woolen jumper that our neighbor Sonya was wearing on the morning they led them out of town," "A German traded the sandals that the little boy evacuated from Riga was wearing," "A German wanted three kilos of honey for the suit of our engineer Kugel." They knew, they had guessed, what awaited them. But in their hearts they didn't believe it; to murder a people seemed too terrible. To murder a people. No one could believe this in their hearts.

And old Borukh said:

"How could they murder a person who makes such shoes? They wouldn't be ashamed to send them to Paris for a show."

"They could, they could," said Mendel the baker.

"Well, alright," said Leyba the tinsmith. "Let's say they have no use for my teapots, saucepans, samovar pipes. But you don't murder my nine children because of that."

And the old teacher Rozental kept silent, listening to them and thinking: it was a good thing that he had not taken the poison. He had spent his whole life with these people, and with them he should spend his bitter final hour.

"We should flee into the forests, but there is nowhere to run to," said the nail driver Kulish. "The police follow us, since morning the warden has already come three times to the block. I sent my little boy to my father-in-law's, and the building owner followed him immediately. The owner is a good guy. He told me straight out what the police said to him: 'If even one little kid doesn't arrive at the square, then you'll answer for it with your head, Mr. Landlord.'"

"Well, what do you want," said Mendel the baker. "It's fate. A neighbor lady said to my son, 'You don't look like a Jew at all, run into the woods.' And my boy said to her, 'I want to look like a Jew; wherever they send my dad, I'm going there too.'"

"I have one thing to say," muttered the nail driver. "If it comes, I ain't gonna die like a sheep."

"Well done, Kulish." The old teacher spoke up. "Well done, you've really said it."

That evening Major Werner met with Becker, the Gestapo's representative.

"Once we carry out tomorrow's scheduled operation, we'll be able to relax," said Becker. "I'm worn out by these Jews. Every day there are violations: five ran away—there's information that they joined the partisans; a family took their own lives; three were picked up for going around without armbands; at the market a Jewish woman was identified buying some eggs, despite the absolute ban on being at the market; two were arrested on the Berlinerstrasse, although they knew perfectly well that they're forbidden to walk on the central street; eight people were strolling about the city after four in the afternoon; two girls tried to slip away into the forest during the march to work and were executed. All of this is trivial. I understand that at the front our soldiers are forced to deal with much more serious difficulties, but nerves are nerves. And this is only one day's worth of events, and it's like this every day."

"What's the order of operations?" asked Werner.

Becker rubbed his pince-nez with a chamois cloth.

"The order wasn't determined by us. Of course, in Poland we were in a much stronger position to use forceful methods. And without those, in essence, it's not possible to make do. After all, the question is one of statistical figures with a sizeable number of zeros. Here, of course, we're forced to act under field conditions. And the nearness of the front is a factor. The last order permits us to depart from the regulations and to adapt to local conditions."

"How many soldiers do you need?" asked Werner.

During this conversation Becker was behaving unusually confidently, with much more determination than usual. And while talking to him, Kommandant Werner felt himself grow timid.

"This is how we're arranging it," said Becker. "Two squads—one for execution and one for containment. The execution squad will be fifteen to twenty men, all volunteers. The containment squad, by comparison, needs to be a lower ratio, one soldier to fifteen Jews."

"Why?" asked the Kommandant.

"Experience demonstrates that at the moment when the group sees that their route continues past a railroad or a highway, panic begins, hysterics, and many try to escape. Besides that, recently it's been forbidden to use machine-guns—they have a very low percentage of fatal casualties. There's been an order to shoot with side arms. This slows the work down significantly. It must be stressed that it is highly recommended to keep the number chosen for the execution squad to a minimum—for a thousand Jews a squad of twenty men, no more. Then the operation begins, and those in the containment have their work cut out for them too. You yourself understand that among the Jews there's a fairly large percentage of men."

"How much time does it take?" asked Werner.

"A thousand people with an experienced command—no more than two and a half hours. The most important thing is to assign duties and get the group all ready and assembled. This part of the operation must also be done quickly."

"How many soldiers do you need, though?"

"No less than a hundred," said Becker decisively. He looked out the window and added:

"The weather is very important. I consulted the meteorologist. The first half of tomorrow is supposed to be a windless, sunny day, toward evening there's a chance of rain, but that's of no consequence to us."

"Thus . . . ," said Werner indecisively.

"The procedure is as follows: You'll detach an officer, a member of the Nazi party, of course. He'll put together the execution squad as follows: 'Men, I need several fellows with strong nerves.' That should take place tonight in the barracks. You have to recruit at least thirty, for experience shows that 10 percent always drop out. After that you have an individual talk with each one: 'Are you afraid of blood? Are you capable of handling a lot of nervous stress?' You shouldn't make any more explanations that evening. At the same time, the *Unteroffizieren* should be instructed to compile a list of names for the containment squad by nightfall. They should test their fire arms. The squad assembles in formation in their helmets by five in the morning in front of the field office. The officer acquaints them in detail with the mission and must once again canvass the volunteers. After that each one of them is issued three hundred cartridges. By six they arrive at the square where the Jews have been ordered to report. The order is as follows: the execution squad moves thirty meters in front of the column. Behind the column follow two carts, since there is always some percentage of old people and pregnant or hysterical women who faint along the way." He spoke slowly, so that the major would not miss any details.

"Well then, it's all done; further instructions at the site of operations will be brought to you by my colleagues."

Major Werner looked at Becker and suddenly asked:

"Well, and what about the children?"

Becker coughed involuntarily. The question exceeded the bounds of the official instructions.

"You see," he said sternly and seriously, looking straight into the eyes of the Kommandant, "while they recommend taking them away from their mothers and working with them separately, I prefer not to do this. After all, you understand how difficult it is to remove a child from its mother at such a grievous moment."

When Becker excused himself and left, the Kommandant hailed the adjutant, relayed the instructions in detail, and said under his breath:

"I'm quite glad that that old doctor finished himself off beforehand. I have had pangs of conscience regarding him; whatever you say, he was of great help to me; after all, I don't know whether I would still be alive without his aid before our doctor arrived . . . And the last few days I have felt terrific, and my sleep has been much better, and my stomach, and two people have already said to me that I have more color in my face. Perhaps it's connected to these daily walks in the orchard. Yes, and the air in this little town is superb; they say up until the war there were sanatoriums for pulmonary and heart patients here."

And the skies were blue, and the sun was shining, and the birds sang.

*   *   *

When the column of Jews passed by the railroad and cut back from the highway, heading toward the ravine, the nail driver Hayim Kulish drew some air into his chest and shouted loudly in Yiddish, drowning out the rumble of hundreds of voices:

"*Oy*, people, I've had it!"

With his fist he struck in the temple the soldier walking at his side, knocking him down. He grabbed his hand-held automatic. Not having time to figure out the unfamiliar foreign weapon, he drew back the heavy automatic with a full sweep of his outstretched arms, and just as he used to hit with a sledgehammer, struck the *Unteroffizier* who had come running up from the side in the face. In the ensuing commotion little Katya Vaysman lost her mother and grandmother and clutched the hem of old Rozental's jacket. He picked her up with difficulty, bringing his lips closer to her ears, and said:

"Don't cry, Katya, don't cry."

Holding on to his neck with her hand, she said:

"I am not crying, teacher."

It was difficult for him to hold her, his head was spinning, his ears were ringing, his legs shook from walking so much longer than they were used to and from the painful strain of the past few hours.

The crowd moved back from the ravine, pushing each other. Several fell to the ground and crawled. Rozental soon found himself among the first rows.

Fifteen Jews were led to the ravine. Rozental knew some of them. Silent Mendel the baker, Meerovich the dentist, Apelfeld the kind old rogue of an electrician. His son taught at the Kiev Conservatory, and once upon a time, when he was a young boy, he had taken math lessons with Rozental. Breathing heavily, the old man held the hands of the little girl. The thought of her distracted him.

How can I comfort her, how can I distract her? thought the old man, and a boundless feeling of sorrow enveloped him. Now in his last minute no one comforted him, no one said to him the words he had been longing to hear his whole life, more than all the wisdom of books on great ideas and the problems of man.

The girl turned to him. Her face was calm; it was the pale face of a grown-up filled with merciful compassion. And in the sudden burst of silence, he heard her voice.

"Teacher," she said, "don't look over there, it will be too much for you." And she, like a mother, closed his eyes with the palms of her hands.

*   *   *

The head of the Gestapo had made a mistake. He was not able to rest easy after the execution of the Jews. In the evening they reported to him that a large partisan detachment had appeared near the city. At the head of the detachment was Shevchenko, the chief engineer of the sugar factory. One hundred forty workers from the factory, not having succeeded in leaving with the transport, had joined the partisans under the command of the engineer. That night there had been an explosion at the steam mill that served the German quartermaster corps. At the station the partisans set fire to huge stores of hay collected by the foragers of the Hungarian Cavalry Division. All night the townspeople did not sleep—the wind blew in the direction of the city, and the fire might spread to the houses and sheds. The brick-red, thick, heavy flames fluttered, creeping along; the black smoke obscured the stars and the moon; and the warm cloudless summer sky was filled with thunderstorms and flames.

People stood in their courtyards and watched silently as the huge fire spread. The wind brought the distinct bursts of machine-gun fire and several blasts of hand grenades.

Yasha Mikhailyuk ran home that night without his service cap, bringing neither salt pork nor homebrew with him. Passing by the women who stood silently in the courtyard, Yasha said to Dasha:

"Well, what, was I right? You'll have plenty of room to live now—one mistress in the whole room?"

"Plenty of room," said Dasha, "plenty of room! In one grave they've laid my Viktor and a six-year-old girl and the old teacher. With my tears I mourned the loss of all of them." And she suddenly cried, "Get out! Don't look at me with your filthy eyes! I'll cut you with a blunt knife. I'll hack you to death with my shears!"

Yasha retreated to his room and sat there in silence. And when his mother wanted to begin to lock up the shutters, he said to her:

"The hell with them, don't unlock the door; they're all there, like crazies; they'll burn your eyes out with boiling water."

"Yasha dear," she said, "it would be better if you went into the attic again. Your bed is there, and I'll lock you in."

Like shadows, the soldiers flashed by in the light of the fire. They had been placed on alert, summoned to the Kommandant's office. Old woman Varvara Andreevna stood among the courtyards. Her gray, disheveled hair looked pink by the light of the fire.

"Well?" she shouted. "Did you think you'd win? Did you think you'd scare us? How it burns! I'm not afraid of the Fritzes! You're fighting against old people and children! Oh my dear Dasha, the day will come; we'll burn them all, the cursed ones!"

And the sky turned more and more crimson, glowing. And it seemed to the people standing in the courtyards that in the dark smoky flame burned all that was wicked, inhuman, and vile with which the Germans polluted human souls.

1943

Translated from the Russian by James Loeffler

MARGARITA ALIGER

Margarita Aliger (1915–1992), poet, translator, playwright, and essayist, was born in Odessa. After studying at the Junior College of Chemical Technology in Moscow, she worked at a factory. In 1933 she joined a seminar that the writer Efim Zozulya (1891–1941) ran at *Little Flame* (*Ogonyok*) magazine, where her poems first appeared. Aliger studied at the Literary Institute in 1934–47. The poems of her collections *Year of Birth* (1938) and *Rail Road* (literally "iron road," 1939) glorified Stalin's five-year plans. In 1938–40 Aliger was executive secretary of the Writers' Union Komsomol organization.

After the Nazi invasion, Aliger joined the Air Force newspaper *Stalin's Falcon* (*Stalinskii sokol*), making numerous trips to the front, and in 1942 she became a member of the Communist Party. Aliger was at her most prolific during the war; her volume *In Memory of the Brave* (1942) featured her poetry of the first wartime year. In January 1942 the public learned about the fate of Zoya Kosmodemyanskaya, a Moscow high-school girl who had joined the partisans. Captured by the Nazis while on a mission in November 1941, Kosmodemyanskaya was publicly hanged after having been tortured and raped. Reportedly, her last words were "You won't hang all two hundred million." In her Soviet afterlife, Kosmodemyanskaya became a larger-than-life figure. Aliger was the first to shape Zoya's story into a heroic myth in her long poem *Zoya* (1943 Stalin Prize). She reworked the poem into the stage play *Tale of Truth* (1943–44), later an opera by Aram Khachaturyan and Nina Makarova (1947).

While *Zoya* made Aliger a famous wartime poet, her second major poem about the war, *Your Victory* (1944–45), became a stumbling block in Aliger's career. Published in *Banner* (*Znamia*) in September 1945 and as a separate book in 1946, this ambitious long poem of twenty-seven parts presented the experience of Aliger's generation at the war and home fronts by weaving the heroine's lyrical turmoil into the collective hardships and victories of her fellow citizens. The rhetorical power of the poem consisted in its transition from speaking to individual addressees (mother, lover) to addressing the "you" of Aliger's generation. Aliger concealed the identity of the man whom she addressed with passion, the gifted Soviet writer Aleksandr Fadeev (1901–1956). (An installment of Aleksandr Fadeev's novel *Young Guard* also appeared in the same issue of *Banner*. A major literary functionary and a member of the Communist Party Central Committee in 1939–44, Fadeev was general secretary and chairman of the board of the Writers' Union in 1946–54. Idolizing Stalin, Fadeev agonized over having to endorse his fellow-writers' verdicts. By the time Aliger's relationship with Fadeev began in 1942, her husband, composer Konstantin Makarov, the father of her elder daughter, Tatyana, had been killed in the first days of the war, and Fadeev's second wife, the actress Angelina Stepanova, was in evacuation. Aliger and Fadeev had a daughter, Maria, who was born during the war. Two months after the Twentieth Party Congress, at which Khrushchev delivered his "secret" anti-Stalin speech to the delegates in February 1956, Fadeev committed suicide.)

A gold mine for cultural historians, Aliger's *Your Victory* testifies to the extent to which Stalinist rhetoric had seeped into the works of the 1930s generation of Soviet poets. In chapter 20, centered on the Stalingrad battle, "Comrade Stalin" himself becomes the addressee of the exhausted fighters, and he inspires them: "But Stalin knew the only measure/of the strengths of the generation devoted [also: loyal] to him." In the revised, 1969, official version of *Your Victory*, Aliger deleted the Stalinist passage. The de-Stalinized version, published in Aliger's two-volume *Shorter and Longer Poems* (1970) and reprinted in the three-volume *Collected Works* (1984–85), also reflected the cowardly revisions Aliger had made in chapter 18, the Jewish chapter of *Your Victory* (text below).

Devoted to the plight of the Jewish people during the war and the Shoah, chapter 18 had caused Aliger serious troubles even though it was nearly politically correct in its Soviet presentation of the Jewish question. Aliger was severely criticized during the anticosmopolitan campaign, most tellingly by the diehard reactionary poet Nikolay Gribachev. In January 1949, writing in the pages of *Banner*, Gribachev labeled Aliger's poem "decadent." Speaking of Aliger's use of "alien" (a coded term) words to describe "our people," Gribachev also implied stereotypically antisemitic charges of his day: that Jews allegedly "fought" the war not on the front but in evacuation.

Aliger was traumatized but continued writing and publishing historically advantageous works. The reader gleans a suggestive dynamic in the titles of some of her poetry books: *First Omens* (1948), *The Beautiful Mecha River* (1953, a long poem about collective farms), *The Lenin Hills* (1953, about the construction of Moscow University), *To the Person on the Road* (1954), *Lyrical Poetry* (1955), *From a Notebook, 1946–1956, A Few Steps: New Poems, 1956–1960* (1962), *Yes and No* (1969), *The Blue Hour* (1970), *Yesterday and Tomorrow* (1977), *Quarter of a Century* (1981), and so forth. In 1956 Aliger coedited the collection *Literary Moscow* (*Literaturnaia Moskva*), a landmark of the Thaw. Having jumped on the bandwagon of post-Stalinist centrism, Aliger rode through the rest of the Soviet years as a token Soviet Jew officially paraded before the West. Aliger wrote less poetry in her latter years, concentrating on poetry translations. She identified the introspectively lyrical *The Blue Hour* as her best book. Aliger's books of prose included the travelogue *A Return to Chile. Two Journeys* (1966) and the memoir *Encounters and Partings* (1989).

Aliger was scared to treat Jewish themes, except very indirectly, in the 1960s poem "Nuremberg." In the 1970s and 1980s, eschewing associations with the exodus of Soviet Jews, she expressed no sympathy for the plight of refuseniks. Maria, her daughter by Fadeev, married the German poet Hans Magnus Enzensberger (b. 1929), left the Soviet Union with him, and settled in London in 1969. A translator of Osip

Mandelstam (in vol. 1) and Vladimir Mayakovsky into English, Maria Enzensberger committed suicide in 1991 after nearly returning to Russia. Margarita Aliger died in Moscow in 1992.

Aliger's discursive comments betray a disillusionment with the postwar generations—purportedly lacking the ideals of the 1930s. Was Aliger genuinely sincere in her continuous endorsement of the Soviet system? The difficulty of making such a judgment points to an inherent feature of Aliger's sensibility. An organic interlocking of the personal and lyrical with the ideological and epochal has rendered Aliger's legacy a poisoned symbol of Soviet cultural optimism.

Jewish themes entered Aliger's writings at the outbreak of World War II. By the time the poem "To a Jewish Girl" (text below) had appeared in Aliger's *Stones and Grasses* (1940), the Soviet Union had gained a large population of un-Sovietized Jews, standing in stark contrast to the Jews east of the old Polish–Soviet border. Aliger's propagandistic poem addressed her imaginary Jewish peer from Brest, in the recently annexed western Belorussia. In 1944 Aliger prepared the materials on the destruction of Brest's Jewish community in the Shoah for Ilya Ehrenburg and Vassily Grossman's *The Black Book* (Ehrenburg and Grossman in vol. 1).

Among Aliger's wartime publications were the lyrics of Rachel's aria "O My Native Land" from Rheinhold Glier's opera *Rachel* (1943–44); in 1944 the lyrics were published as a booklet along with the music. Based on Guy de Maupassant's novel *Mademoiselle Fifi* (1882) set during the French and Prussian War, the opera premiered on the radio in 1943. Its heroine, a Jewish-French prostitute, Rachel, kills a Prussian officer (compare Robert Wise's 1944 film).

Chapter 18 of *Your Victory* (1944–45) was the peak of Aliger's engagement with Jewish topics. Aliger's lyrical protagonist visits her mother, evacuated to a small town on the Kama River. In the context of their reunion, Aliger speaks about the plight of Jews in the Shoah. The English translation of chapter 18 follows the text published in 1945 and reprinted in 1946–47 (the first official version, OV1). As Isai Averbukh demonstrated in 1991, alternative versions of chapter 18 circulated widely in samizdat starting with the late 1940s. The footnotes highlight the fragments of Aliger's text that were missing in OV1. As Averbukh indicated, "The popularity of these uncensored verses was enormous [. . .]. But most people who read and distributed them in samizdat thought they were an independent poem and did not suspect that they were the unpublished version of a [published] fragment [. . .]." While disseminating Aliger's uncensored fragment, (re)copying and (re)typing it, Soviet Jews even clandestinely inserted it in library copies. They later recalled that in the 1940s and early 1950s it gave them a "feeling of pride," some even discerning, wistfully, an "argument in support of Zionism." Possession of the fragment could get one in trouble with universities and employers and result in persecution. An anonymous poetic "Reply to Margarita Aliger" began to circulate in Jewish samizdat in the late 1940s. Falsely attributed to Ilya Ehrenburg and inferior from an artistic point of view, the reply took issue with Aliger's muffled expression of Jewish pride, her lack of self-consciously Judaic religious awareness, and her view that she "had forgotten" about being Jewish until the Nazis reminded her. These were the last two lines of the anonymous reply: "I'm proud! Proud and not sorry,/that I'm a Jew, dear comrade Aliger."

In 1969 the Polish-born American author Alexander Donat, author of the memoir *The Holocaust Kingdom* (1965), visited the USSR as he prepared materials for his Russian-language anthology *The Burning Bush: Jewish Topics in Russian Poetry* (New York, 1973). Aliger refused to meet with Donat and denied authorship of the alternative fragment. Anthologizing Aliger's "uncensored" text, Donat was the first to note that "the changes, which the poetess felt necessary to introduce [in 1969], speak more eloquently than many volumes." Indeed, in the second official version of *Your Victory* (OV2), which Aliger published in 1970, references to Jewish pride were obliterated almost beyond recognition.

To a Jewish Girl

I could have grown up your next-door neighbor,
could have spoken in that very tongue,
if I had been born in Brest the same year,
in that spotless, murky little town.

I would have been just as clear and simple,
both hands tucked in my coquettish muff,
with a fluffy knitted hood, a little
slender, my hair interestingly coiffed.

And I would have lived and would have labored
with an eye to each next passing day.
Someone would have helped me find employment
as a salesgirl in a pharmacy.

In my breast, as quiet as a mouse does,
my heart would have dwelt, afraid to beat.
I'd have passed the Vilna theater posters,
never daring look at them or read.

I would not have known the point of mischief
or long-distance travel, that is true.
Sundays I would not have dared to venture
out to stroll the town's main avenue.

I'd have been afraid of high-school students,
carriages and silence, of daylight,
and for sure as summer was beginning
the war, too, would have given me a fright.

At night the roar of weapons would have reached me,
the wail of shells, the drone of fighter planes.
Then into our town would have marched—the
people they call Reds, down all the lanes.

Would I have been so quick to understand it,
from their posters glued to the damp wall,
from their speech and manner of commanding,
the way they treated me, or how they'd call?

Who, and when would be the one to say it,
that word that would turn the world about?
The first time I spread open a newspaper?
A little song? A good look at a painting?
Some commander lodging in our house?
So I'd have turned to see the earth's wide spaces,
for once I'd gaze straight out without a bow,
turned simple all at once, calm and courageous,
thoughtful and able, tender and vivacious,
—just the way I happen to be now.

1940

From *Your Victory*

18

Mama, mama, neither words nor tears.
Tears and words can't help us to survive.
You've lost shelter in your final years—
what's your joy, what helps you stay alive?
It turned out that you and I were strangers,
each lived with her very separate care.
But on the southern shore of Russia's ranges
I always knew my mother's home was there.
There you kept the dear old-fashioned dishes
and food as tasty as when I was small.
I always knew, if things got really vicious,
I could knock, could walk into your hall.
Children grow and move to other places,
but even so their blood sometimes reminds:
there's a safe place left on earth, and faces
glow with love that never doubts or bends.

Love that will forgive and never mention
the very worst offense that one could give,
love that is unable to imagine
how you could stop loving but still live,
a love that is unable to remember
some betrayal, lateness, or offense,
in that old house, in rooms so dim and somber,
it preserves your childhood's dearest scents.

So you lived, you hoped, your hair grew grayer,
you'd sit down as the kind proprietress,
always good, warm-spirited housekeeper
around the table with your many guests.

Suddenly, a ruthless clap of thunder
ruined all the life that you once knew.
You've been left without a home, you wander,
Bloodshot clouds burn, lower over you.
Not your calm nobility of visage—
when you turn to look at me I find
ancient looks, a charred resemblance, savage,
to those who had to leave their land behind;
those who faced a doom unjustly uttered
by the vile unrighteous magistrate,
came to a salt wave that roiled and shuddered,
and the sea that gasped and parted to make way;
for whom God's sun in generous effusion
baked on hot rocks the dry unleavened bread.
Did many, from Egypt as far as Russia,
Walk these miles, these centuries and fate?
Mama, mama, in a gloom unending,
on a thorny and untrodden strand,
how long did you stumble, unrelenting,
through the desert toward the promised land?
In the night you recognized that country,
kneeling on the sacred boundary
wept and whispered, "I'll continue searching.
I'll not spare my strength and love. I plead
for the pluming smoke of living settled,
a hearth where I can huddle and get warm."
Mama, mama, you're in your own country,
enemies have come to do us harm.
Battle thunders, war with wails and booming,
sirens cry. A dried-up autumn leaf,
mother's driven from her native homeland
eastward, by a dark and soaring breeze.
So here it is, the small town on the Kama,
In the Urals. Our fate for long?
Who is coming to pursue us, mama?
Who are we, to whom do we belong?
Stoking fire to warm her cold fingers,
arranging everything to live anew,
mother answered me, "So you forgot it?
How dare you let yourself?! We are Jews."

Yes, I dared, you understand, I dared to!
Life was just so cloudless all around.
I hadn't really thought of it since childhood.
Somehow there wasn't time, it wasn't found.
You don't choose the country where your home is
as you start to breathe and know and see,
all at once you just receive your homeland,
as your parents did, immutably.
Days were gray and smoky, and the rushing
chilly weather swept along the street . . .
I was born in autumn and in Russia,
Russia took me in and welcomed me.

Homeland mine! Both happiness and sorrow
blended in an endless bound with this!
Homeland! For in love you were my comrade,
ally in each battle or distress.
Homeland, tenderer than first caresses,
you have taught me to protect and guard
golden language in all Pushkin's treasures,
Gogol's magic, captivating word.
Clarity and space of nature's kingdom,
Broad horizons of the sky's expanse,
genuine liberty, the truest freedom,
endless flight of Lenin's outstretched hand.
You made me drunk on blood, rushing and restless,
like the waters of a living spring,
stung and stunned my body with the threat of
love from a wild Russian peasant man.[1]

---

1. In OV2 (1969; published 1970), Aliger replaced these two lines with the following two lines, given here in a literal translation without meter and rhyme: "As with frost, [the home-land] burnt me with the love/of a wild Russian peasant."

How I love the booming rolls of thunder,
the crackle and smooth surface of the frost,
sticky tears of birch trees, sprung from under
dazzling gleams of morning branches tossed,
winding babble of small waters tripping,
quiet evening fields, twilight above;
I throw wide my arms to you in greeting,
My own and only homeland, so well loved.

It was hard—and maybe even harder,
Only I'll have strength for everything.
Can there really be a land that's dearer
than where you first lived and came to sing,
land that raised me up into a woman,
land that let me grow up tall and proud?
Mama, it's true, I knew but had forgotten,
couldn't yet imagine or allow,
think that one could only glance in passing,
in secret, on the sly, to see the sky,
as behind us they are coming, chasing,
drive us to Treblinka barefoot, smother
us with gas, right there as we stand,
burn and shoot and hang us—as they murder,
tread our blood into the dirt and sand.[2]

"We are a people prostrate in the dust.
We are a people trodden by our foe . . ."
Why? And what for? Is that truly *us*?
My people, there is something else I know.
I recall the scholars and the poets
from other countries, dialects, and years,

---

2. In OV2 (1969; published 1970), Aliger replaced the next six lines with the following six lines, given here in a literal translation without meter and rhyme: "Churned into dust . . . Prostrate in the dust . . . /This is you and me? By what enemy?/Why? What the devil for?/I don't want to and I remember other things./I remember the poets and scholars,/those who have not been forgotten in the thunder of centuries [. . .]."

who loved life as little children know it,
noble jokers who through all their tears[3]
were generous with talents and ambitions,
didn't hoard the best strength of their soul.[4]

I know the doctors and musicians,
laborers—the great as well as small,
of the Maccabees the brave descendants,
flesh and blood sons of their ancestors,
thousands of Jews went into battle,
Russian commanders, Russian soldiers too.
I sing your praises, in the name of honor
of a tribe besieged for centuries,
boys missing in action, not returning,
boys who died in battle in those days.
A generation who grew up in freedom,
in our fatherland of youth and trust,
We did not recall that we're a people,
but the Fascists knew that fact for us.[5]

---

3. In the versions of chapter 18 that commonly circulated in Soviet samizdat (and were printed in several books in the West, including Tamar Dolzhanskaya's anthology *On the Same Wave: Jewish Motifs in Russian Poetry* [Tel Aviv, 1974] and Alexander Donat's anthology *The Burning Bush* [New York, 1973]), sixteen additional lines followed the line in OV1; they are given here in a literal translation without meter and rhyme, from Dolzhanskaya's text: "[. . .] Lorelei, a girl from the Rhine,/the green half-shades of the ancient streams./What was our guilt, Heinrich Heine?/What didn't we please [them] with, [Felix] Mendelssohn?/I'll ask [Karl] Marx and [Albert] Einstein,/both of them filled with great wisdom,/perhaps was revealed to them/the secret of our guilt before eternity?/The dear canvasses of [Isaac] Levitan—/the benevolent shining of the birches,/Charlie Chaplin from the pale screen/—you answer my question:/didn't we give away, without needless arguments,/all that we were rich in?/What is our guilt before the world?/[Ilya] Ehrenburg, [Eduard] Bagritsky, [Mikhail] Svetlov [. . .]"

4. In OV2 (1969; published 1970), Aliger replaced the next thirteen lines with the following thirteen lines, given here in a literal translation without meter and rhyme, from Dolzhanskaya's text: "I remember doctors and musicians/Laborers—the great and the small./I remember not the descendants of the Maccabees,/[but] the youths raised in the Komsomol,/thousands of fighting Jews—/Russian commanders and soldiers./You went together with the entire nation/under the same star, in the same formation./Boys who were missing in action,/boys who were killed in battle./Giving it all our heart and soul/we were growing up in our fatherland,/having forgotten we were Jews . . ."

5. In the versions of chapter 18 that commonly circulated in Soviet samizdat (and were printed in several books in the the West), ten additional lines followed this line in OV1; they are given here in a literal translation without meter and rhyme: "[. . .]The centuries-old smell of humiliation,/the lamentations of mothers and wives./In death camps of annihilation/my people were executed and burned./Children crushed with tanks,/the label 'Jude' and the insult 'Yid.'/ There are almost none of us left in the world,/but we know, time will resurrect [us]./We're Jews. In this word/How much bitterness and restless years [. . .]."

Battle began. Bluntly and severely
we regarded the divided world.
Does blood have a voice so one can hear it?
I know, though, that there's a color to blood.
All the earth was crimsoned with this color
by swine who'll live on in endless shame,
human blood spoke at the fatal hour
in every language and with every name.
Now I hear the voice of blood, a chorus,
My people's moaning, many million strong.
From underground it calls out with a summons,
strong and harsh, calls in a thunderous song.
It resounds, a single ceaseless ocean,
blending in its multiple refrain
with the suffering Slavs' united voices,
Poland, Belorussia, and Ukraine.[6]

Voice of blood! So tightly fused together
is our blood, that bright unfading blood.
Ours is a single road of vengeance,
common fury and a common love.
So much blood! The knot is drawn more tightly,
Binding us with an ancient bond and tie.
Bearing arms into the final battle,
we are one, impassioned and alive,
loving life, we seethe with passion, boiling,
enemies will never tread us down.
We're alive! We cannot fail to foil them!
I say it in plain Russian, hear the sound.
We're alive and breathing. See us, mama!

---

6. The four lines beginning with "It resounds . . ." were not present in the samizdat versions that commonly circulated.

Mama, see how children grow to men,
see your daughter standing with them, calmly,
on this crossroads, here in this great land
where so many of our tears have lighted,
so much labor, so much of our blood,
land that's rich, that is severe and mighty,
land we love, that we forever love.

1944–45

Translated from the Russian by Sibelan Forrester

LEV OZEROV

Lev Ozerov (1914–1996), poet, critic, and translator, was born Lev Goldberg in Kiev to a pharmacist's family. Ozerov worked as a turner, draftsman, book designer, and violinist before joining the staff of *Kiev Young Pioneer* (*Kievskii pioner*) in 1932. Ozerov wrote poetry from the age of fifteen, admiring the early Soviet modernists (Eduard Bagritsky [in vol. 1], Ilya Selvinsky [in vol.1], and Nikolay Zabolotsky); he was mentored in Kiev by the poet Nikolay Ushakov. By the early 1930s, Boris Pasternak (in vol. 1) had enthralled Ozerov.

Ozerov studied philology at the Moscow Institute of Philosophy, Literature, and History (MIFLI) in 1934–39. While pursuing a graduate degree at MIFLI in 1939–41, Ozerov worked at *Pravda*. Peers identified his aesthetics with the Lake School of English romanticism (in Russian, *ozernaia shkola*), hence his flight in 1935 to the (illusive) safety of the non-Jewish pseudonym Ozerov (literally "of the lakes"). Ozerov's first collection, *Environs of the Dnieper*, appeared in Kiev in 1940. Soon after the Nazi invasion, Ozerov was dispatched to the northern Caucasus with a Komsomol "brigade." He contributed to the army newspaper *Victory Shall Be Ours* (*Pobeda za nami*). Recalled to Moscow to defend his candidate's dissertation in 1943, Ozerov stayed to teach creative writing and in 1946 became poetry editor of *October* (*Oktiabr'*). Ozerov's wartime poems were gathered in *Rainfall* (Moscow, 1947; edited by Pavel Antokolsky [in vol. 1]. The collection bore a daring epigraph—the last two lines of the long poem *February* by Eduard Bagritsky (in vol. 1): "There'll be rainfalls, southern winds will blow,/Swans will make again their calls of passion." In 1948, during the "anticosmopolitan" campaign, Ozerov was fired from his teaching and editorial positions.

He resumed teaching at the Literary Institute in 1956, and his collection *Confession of Love* appeared in 1957. Shaken by the close call of 1948, Ozerov established himself as a liberal in the official camp of literature during the Thaw. He knew how to navigate the straights of post-Stalinist Soviet culture. A founder, in 1964, of the Oral Poet's Library at Moscow's Central House of Actors, Ozerov featured some poets with limited publishing opportunities (such as Yulia Neyman [in vol. 2]): "One must help talents/mediocrities will make it on their own," stated his classic aphorism. While assisting poets and helping return deleted names to print, he distanced himself from dissident and samizdat activity.

Ozerov published many books of verse, including *Chiaroscuro* (1961), *Unearthly Gravity* (1969; book design by Ozerov), *Evening Mail* (1974), *Selected Poems* (1974), *Behind the [Film] Shot* (1978), *Axis of the Earth* (1986), *Emergency Supply* (1990), and *Life's Abyss* (1996). He was a prominent translator of poetry, especially from

Lithuanian (he headed the Council on Lithuanian Literature at the Writers' Union) and Bulgarian, and produced such anthologies as *Song of Love* (1967; several reprints), coedited with Svetlana Magidson.

A professor at the Literary Institute and the author of a number of books of criticism, Ozerov also edited important literary works. He prepared the academic edition of Boris Pasternak's *Shorter and Longer Poems* (1965; Pasternak in vol. 1); the following year Ozerov escaped unscathed in another close call, when Andrey Sinyavsky, who wrote the introduction, was sentenced to hard labor along with his codefendant, Yuly Daniel (in vol. 2), for "anti-Soviet activity" in connection with their publications in the West. Ozerov was active as an author and editor until his last days. He died in Moscow in 1996. Following his death, Ozerov's unfinished memoirs in verse, *Portraits without Frames*, appeared in Moscow; the fifty chapters include verse portraits of the Yiddish writers David Hofshteyn, Leyb Kvitko, Perets Markish, Shmuel Halkin, and a number of other Jewish-Russian writers.

Formally elegant, entering into dialogue with other poets (such as Anna Akhmatova, Pasternak, and Goethe, whom Ozerov translated), Ozerov's poetry displays nature-philosophical features. He summed up his poetic predilections in a subtle, exemplary lyric about a nightingale (cf. "God *Nachtigal*" in the poem "To German Speech" [1932] by Osip Mandelstam [in vol. 1] and Ozerov's and Mandelstam's German romantic antecedents in the poetry of Goethe, Heine, and Theodor Storm), an "improviser," a poetic instrument of the universe, which Ozerov himself was not. Here is the last stanza in a literal translation: "We listened to him with bias/While thinking in thick darkness/That he possessed night space/The way we couldn't possess ourselves." "We" collectively stands for the Soviet poets of Ozerov's generation.

Babi Yar (Russ. literally "women's ravine") is the name of a wooded ravine on the outskirts of Kiev where approximately100,000 people, as many as 90,000 of them Jews, were murdered by the Nazis and local collaborators in September–November 1941. Jewish-Soviet authors turned to the subject of Babi Yar as early as 1943–44, the earliest examples including the Ukrainian poem "Abraham"(1943) by Sava Holovanivskyi (1910–19??); a 1944 article and a 1947 story in Yiddish by Itsik Kipnis (1896–1974); episodes in the epic *War* (Milkhome, 1943) by Perets Markish (1895–1952); Ilya Ehrenburg's poem "Babi Yar"(1945; text in vol. 1) and a scene in his novel *Storm* (1947); and Lev Ozerov's poem "Babi Yar." Other Soviet writers, including the non-Jews Yevgeny Yevtushenko (b. 1933) and Anatoly Kuznetsov (1929–1979), wrote about the Babi Yar massacre in the post-Stalinist years, but none with Ozerov's mournful power and piercing lyricism.

Ozerov contributed the essay "Kiev, Babi Yar" to the Ehrenburg–Grossman de-railed *Black Book* (see Ilya Ehrenburg and Vassily Grossman in vol. 1). He composed his poem "Babi Yar" in 1944–45, and it appeared in the April–May 1946 issue of *October*, and in 1947 in his *Rainfall*. Reprinted for the first time twenty years later in Ozerov's 1966 *Lyric: Selected Poems* (and again in 1974, 1978, and 1986), it remains the most profound treatment of the topic in Russian poetry. Ozerov revisited the topic in "Once again at Babi Yar," a short lyric against unremembrance.

Babi Yar

I have come to you, Babi Yar.
If grief were subject to age,
Then I would be too old by far.
Measure age by centuries?—too many to gauge.

Pleading, here at this place I stand.
If my mind can endure the violence,
I will hear what you have to say, land—
Break your silence.

What is that rumbling in your breast?
It makes no sense to me—
Either the water rumbles under the land
Or the souls lying in the Yar.

I ask the maple trees: reply.
You are witnesses—tell your story!
But all is quiet,
Only the wind—
Soughing in the leaves.

I implore the sky: speak your piece.
But its indifference is painful . . .
There was life, there will be life.
But your face gives no guidance.
Perhaps the rocks will have an answer.
No . . .

All is quiet.
In the coagulating dust—August.
A nag grazes in the sparse grass.
It chews a faded rusty-red blanket
—Perhaps you will answer me.
No . . .

But the nag kept its eye away from me.
A squirrel flashed by with its bluish whiteness,
And all at once—
My heart was filled by the quiet . . .

And I felt:
Twilight entering my mind
and Kiev on that autumn morning—
Before me . . .

                    *   *   *

Today they keep coming down Lvov Street.
The air is hazy.
On and on they come. Packed together, one against the other.
Over the pavement,
Over the red maple leaves,
Over my heart they go.

The streams merge into a river.
Fascists and local *Polizei*
Stand at every house, at every front yard.
Turning back? Impossible!
Turning aside? Not a chance!
Fascist machine gunners bar the way.

The diaphanous autumn day is riddled with sunlight.
The crowd flows—dark against the light.
Quietly quivering are the last candles of the poplar trees.
And in the air:
—Where are we? Where are they taking us?
—Where are they taking us? Where are they taking us today?
—Where?—ask their eyes in final supplication.
And the procession, long and relentless,
Plods along to attend its own funeral.

Beyond Melnik Street are hillocks, fences, and vacant land.
And the rusty-red wall of the Jewish cemetery. Halt . . .
Here the gravestones erected by death are parsimoniously dense,
And the exit to Babi Yar,
Like death, is simple.

It's all clear to them now. The pit gapes like a maelstrom,
And the horizon is brightened by the light of final minutes.
Death, too, has its dressing room.
The Fascists must get down to business.
They divest the newcomers of their clothes, which they
      arrange in piles.

And reality suddenly shatters
When assailed by a still greater reality:
The thousands frozen in their tracks,
The life of cherishing eyes,
The evening air,
And the sky.
With eyes boring into the land,
They look at that which we are given to see only
Once . . .

Now shooting, shooting, stars of sudden light,
As brother embraces sister one last time—
While a scuttling SS man snaps pictures of all this with his Leica.
Volley after volley.
The heavy gasps of those lying in the Yar.

People approach and fall into the pit like rocks . . .
Children tumbling on women, old people on kids—
Like tongues of flame, with arms clawing at the sky,
They grasp for air,
And, their strength failing, they gasp curses.

A girl, from below:—Don't throw dirt in my eyes—
A boy:—Do I have to take off my socks, too?—
Then he grew still,
Embracing his mother for the last time.

In that pit, men were buried alive.
But suddenly, out of the ground appeared an arm
And gray curls on the nape of a neck . . .
A Fascist struck persistently with his shovel.
The ground became wet,
Then smooth and hard . . .

* * *

I have come to you, Babi Yar.
If grief were subject to age,
Then I would be too old by far.
Measure age by centuries?—too many to gauge.

Here to this day lie bones,
Skulls turning yellow in the dust.
And lichen infecting the ground with its whiteness.
At that place where my brothers have laid themselves down.

In this blighted place grass refuses to grow.
And the sand is as white as a corpse.
And the wind's whistle is ever so slight:
That's my brother gasping for air.

It is so easy to fall into that Yar.
As soon as I step on the sand—
And the ground partly opens its maw.
My old granddad will ask for a drink of water.

My nephew will want to get up.
He will awaken his sister and mother.
They will want to work loose their arms,
And beg life for just a minute.

The ground gives beneath my feet:
Either bending or writhing.
Beyond the sacramental quiet
I hear a child saying:
—More bread please.

Where are you, little one—show yourself.
I am deafened by a dull pain.
I will give you my life, drop by drop—
I, too, could have ended up with you.

We could have embraced one another in the final sleep.
We could have fallen together to the bottom.
That thought will haunt me to my dying day.
That we did not share death.

I shut my eyes for a minute
And perked up my ears.
I heard voices:
—Where did you want to go? There?!

A beard jerked angrily.
Words reverberated from the empty pit:
—No, don't come here!
—Stay where you are!
Stop!

You have a future.
You must live out your life—and ours.
You don't hold grudges—start holding them.
You're forgetful—don't you dare forget!

And a child said:—Don't forget.
And a mother said:—Don't forgive.
And the earthen breast swung shut.
I was no longer at the Yar but on my way.

It leads to vengeance—that way
Along which I must travel.
Don't forget . . .
Don't forgive . . .

1944–45

Translated from the Russian by Richard Sheldon

PAVEL ANTOKOLSKY

Pavel Antokolsky (1896–1978), poet, translator, and essayist, was born in St. Petersburg to a lawyer's family. His grandfather was the great sculptor Mark Antokolsky (1843–1902), one of the first unconverted Jews to rise to the top of Russian culture. Living in Moscow since 1904, in 1915 Antokolsky entered the Law Faculty of Moscow University but left after two years. Starting from 1915 he acted on stage, and in 1920 he became a codirector of the theater studio of Evgeny Vakhtangov (see S. Ansky in vol. 1). Initially called the Third Studio of the Moscow Art Theater, it was renamed the Vakhtangov Theater in 1926. Antokolsky remained with the Vakhtangov Theater until 1934.

Antokolsky began to publish in 1918. His first collection, *Poems* (1922), and his second, *The West* (1926), were built around a 1923 trip to Sweden and Germany with the Vakhtangov troupe and featured Antokolsky's best poems. The texture of the verse in *The West* betrays the impact of Vladimir Mayakovsky and Marina Tsvetaeva, and also the influence of Boris Pasternak's (in vol. 1) *Themes and Variations*. A German expressionist atmosphere unites Antokolsky's "western" poems with the cycle *European Night* by Vladislav Khodasevich (in vol. 1). Although artfully constructed (the rhyming is especially masterful), Antokolsky's poems often lack lyricism.

A number of Antokolsky's histrionic poems—*Robespierre and Gorgona* (1930), *The Commune of 1871* (1933), and others—presented events in western history with revolutionary-romantic pathos. His collection *Dramatis Personae* (1932) marked a transition to poetry of ideological commission. Including such texts as "A Materialist's Catechism," it presented as a foreground the image of a stage of history where socialism was winning. Turning to the topics of Soviet daily life, Antokolsky published *Longer and Shorter Poems* (1934) and *Great Distances* (1936). He began to teach poetry at the Literary Institute and in 1938–39 served as poetry editor of *Novy mir*. His last prewar collection, *Poems 1933–1940*, features the unabashedly loyalist "October Poems," which end in the following manner (quoted in literal translation): "[. . .] But the boy finishes [playing the bugle]. And the red/Silk flutters. And Stalin/Smiles at him." It also includes the tasteless "If I Believed in God": "If I believed in God,/I would tell him this evening:— Lord, O Lord, how wretched is/Everything you can help me with!"

A *Komsomol Truth* (*Komsomol'skaia pravda*) correspondent during World War II, Antokolsky headed a front-line theater and composed patriotic ballads and long poems. His wartime collections include *Iron and Fire* and *Half a Year* (1942). In 1943 Antokolsky joined the Communist Party. He responded to the death of his son, a junior lieutenant, in battle with the moving and mournful long poem *Son* (1943; 1946 Stalin Prize). Antokolsky's postwar collections, including *The Third Book of War* (1946) and *Ten Years Later* (1953), treat the theme of memory and loss. His writings of the last Stalinist years include the long poem *Communist Manifesto* (1948). The conformist epic poem *In a Lane beyond Arbat Street* (1955) unfolded a collective biography of Antokolsky's generation, coming of age during World War I and (dialectically) embracing socialist construction.

During the Thaw, Antokolsky assumed the position of a minor Soviet classic. His collections include *Studio* (1958), *West–East* (1960), *High Voltage* (1962), *The Fourth Dimension* (1964), *A Cradle of Russian Poetry* (1976), *End of the Century* (1977), and others. His four-volume *Selected Works* appeared in 1971–73.

A translator from a number of languages, Antokolsky edited, with Leon Toom, *Estonian Poets of the Nineteenth Century* (1961) and other anthologies. His translations from the French were collected in *Civic Poets of France* (1955) and *From Beranger to Eluard* (1966).

A professor of poetry so much more than a "poet by God's gift" (as they say in Russian), Antokolsky was a mentor to several generations of Soviet poets and a living link with both the Silver Age and the seething Soviet 1920s.

Pavel Antokolsky coauthored with Veniamin Kaverin (in vol. 1) "The Uprising in Sobibor" for *The Black Book* (see Vassily Grossman and Ilya Ehrenburg in vol. 1). As was the case with other Soviet writers of Jewish origin otherwise disinclined to discuss Jewishness, the war and the Shoah compelled Antokolsky to turn to Jewish themes. In 1943 he wrote with piercing lyricism of the death of his son, "half-Russian, half-Jew." (Antokolsky's personal tragedy resonates through chapter 13 of Margarita Aliger's epic poem *Your Victory* [excerpt in vol. 1]). Before the introduction of a virtual ban on the discussion of the Shoah in Soviet culture, Antokolsky memorialized the victims of Nazism in several poems. One of them, "Death Camp," appeared in *Banner* (*Znamia*) in October 1945 and in his 1946 *Selected Works* and was reprinted in the USSR in Antokolsky's later volumes; its translation follows below. By calling the old Jewish-Polish woman Rachel and her murdered "boys" Joseph and Benjamin, Antokolsky evokes the biblical story of Jacob and his sons in the context of the Jewish Holocaust. In the 1946 *Selected Works*, "Death Camp" is sandwiched between a poem that ends with "long live Stalin" and another one, "Glory," where one finds the lines "Stalin! Stalin! To you/We give the oath of loyalty again!" Was that the price Antokolsky paid for being able to include his Holocaust poem?

Antokolsky's poem "Lost Are the Tracks" was published in the July 1946 issue of *Banner*. Through the evocation, in the last stanza, of the opening of the ancient prayer Shema, Israel! (Hear, O Israel!), Antokolsky called on the survivors to remain Jewish against all odds. The poem was not reprinted in the USSR.

Death Camp

And then that woman came, distressed,
Eighty, with lemon-sallow skin,
Wearing a shawl and quilted vest—
A feebly hobbling skeleton.
Her bluish wig of straggly strands
Must have been made before the Flood.
She pointed her thin blue-veined hands
Down at a ditch of oozing mud.

"Excuse me. I've walked very far
Through shtetls burnt down to the ground.
Sir, do you know where my boys are,
Where their dead bodies may be found?

"Excuse me. I've gone deaf and blind,
But maybe in this Polish glen
Among these broken skulls I'll find
My Joseph and my Benjamin,

"Because your feet aren't crunching stones
But blackened ashes of the dead,
The charred remains of human bones,"
Rachel, that ancient woman, said.

We followed, grievously aware
These were the fields of her despair.
The golden woods glowed bright and fair
In the late autumn Polish air.
A swath of grass was scorched and bare.
No scythes or sickles lingered there
But voices, voices everywhere,
Voices that whispered to declare,

"We're dead. We lie still and embrace.
To these loved ones and friends we cling,
But we tell strangers of this place.
To strangers we tell everything.

"You see how many hopes are dead
By counting ruts in this crushed grass,
How much they stole our sun and bread,
Here in these ashes, shards of glass,
A twisted toy, a shred of shirt,
And children's eyes covered with dirt,

"How much they sheared off the black hair
The girls had braided with such care,
Blood, phosphorus, and protein found
What value in this Fascist lair,
As the wind chased and whipped around
Our skirts and stockings along the ground.

"We are these stars, we are these flowers.
The killers hurried to be done,
Becoming blinded by the powers
Of naked lives, bright as the sun.

"The killers used their cans of gas.
Death in its beauty would soon pass
Down the highway from this morass,
Because in the new waving grass,
In evening dew and in birdsong,
In gray clouds over the world's grime,
You see, we are not dead for long
We have arisen for all time."

1945

Translated from the Russian by Maxim D. Shrayer and J.B. Sisson

YURY GERMAN

Yury German (1910–1967), prose writer, screenwriter, and playwright, was born in Riga to an educated Jewish-Russian family. His father, a lieutenant in the tsarist army, had apparently taken baptism; his mother taught Russian at a gymnasium. Throughout World War I, German accompanied his mother, who became a military nurse to follow German's father to the front. After the Revolution, German lived in Kursk, where he began to contribute to *Kursk Truth* (*Kurskaia pravda*) at the age of sixteen. In Dmitrov, a town north of Moscow, he headed an amateur drama studio and wrote his first novel, *Rafael from the Barber Shop* (Moscow, 1931), set during the NEP and featuring a Jewish theme.

In 1929 German enrolled at the Leningrad College of the Stage Arts. Unhappy with the course of study, he left and worked at a metal factory. German got to know *spetsy* ("specialists," usually engineers) from Germany working in the USSR and they became the subject of his novel *Introduction* (1931). German's novel *Poor Heinrich* (1934) also focused on western characters. In 1932 Maxim Gorky encouraged the twenty-one-year-old German in an article published in *Pravda*.

Becoming a full-time author, German composed the novel *Our Acquaintances* (1936), about a young Soviet woman's transition from a loveless marriage to a happy union with a security policeman. *Our Acquaintances* exemplifies German's prewar fiction, which avoided crude tendentiousness while constructing a Soviet prosaics "with a human face." Conservative critics nevertheless accused German of advocating "petit-bourgeois" virtues. German's tales about law-enforcement officers, *Lapshin* and *Aleksey Zhmakin*, appeared in a 1938 book; German worked the tales into the novel *One Year*, published in 1960. Starting with *The Iron Feliks* (1938), German published books about the founder of the Soviet security police (*Cheka*), Feliks Dzerzhinsky (1877–1926), helping to poison the minds of young Soviet readers. In 1939–40, mixing half-truths and half-lies, German published prose about his visit to the annexed eastern Poland; they included the essay "On Liberated Land," the short story "In the Shtetl," and the powerful novella "Hotel 'Voldemar'" about the "liberated" Jews of what the Soviets reinterpreted as "western Belorussia" and about Jewish–Polish relations. During World War II, German was a TASS and Sovinformburo correspondent with the Northern Fleet. His experiences informed the short novels *The Chilly Sea* (1943) and *The Far-Away North* (1943 and other works).

On 8 July 1946, German published a positive article about Mikhail Zoshchenko, a talented satirist. The 14 August 1946 Resolution of the Communist Party, "About the Journals *Star* [*Zvezda*] and *Leningrad*," vilified Zoshchenko and Anna Akhmatova; singling out several other writers, it commented on German's article: "*Leningrad Truth* committed an error in permitting a disgraceful laudatory review by Yury German about the writings of Zoshchenko [. . .]." Zhdanovshchina, the postwar onslaught of reaction known by this name after Andrey Zhdanov, Party secretary for ideology, flooded Soviet culture, and German was among its first victims. A year later, German published a pledge, "To Serve the Millions," in *Leningrad Pravda*, but that was not enough to deflect further attacks.

In January 1949, *Star* printed the first part of German's novel *Lieutenant Colonel of the Medical Corps*. The protagonist of the novel, a Jewish physician, was deemed too preoccupied with existential and personal issues. In the climate of the mounting antisemitic campaign, the serialization of German's novel was interrupted. German was forced to denounce his novel in a brief open letter, published in March 1949 in *Star*, followed on the same page by a denunciation of the novel by the editors. A complete version of *Lieutenant Colonel of the Medical Corps* did not appear until 1956, the turning-point year of the Thaw, in the relatively small print run of 30,000 copies.

Set in Petrine Russia, German's novel *Young Russia* (1952; revised 1954) suggested parallels with the suffering of the people in Stalinist Russia. Regaining faith in the Soviet system, German joined the Communist Party in 1957, following the Twentieth Party Congress. German's trilogy *The Task You Serve*, *My Dear Fellow*, and *I'm Responsible for Everything* (late 1950s–early 1960s) was suffused with post-Stalinist historical optimism.

German also wrote for screen and stage. Among his screen credits were *The Bold Seven* (1936, dir. Sergey Gerasimov), *Pirogov* (1947, dir. Grigory Kozintsev), *Belinsky* (1953, dir. Kozintsev), and *My Dear Fellow* (1958, dir. Iosif Kheifits). German's son, the filmmaker Aleksey German (b. 1938), adapted his father's works *Operation Happy New Year!* (1971; released 1986 as *Trial by Road*) and *My Friend Ivan Lapshin* (1984). German died in 1967 in Leningrad.

The generation of Soviet Jews who came of age after the Revolution was well represented in Yury German's prose. The naval physician Lieutenant Colonel (Commander) Aleksandr Levin, the protagonist of German's ill-fated novel of 1949, serves in the Northern Fleet during the war. In other works of fiction, German endowed fictional medical doctors with a Chekhovian humanism. A Jewish doctor was a cultural cliché in Soviet society. When German's novel finally appeared in 1956, the image of a Jewish physician evoked recent memories of the terror, lies, and humiliation of the so-called Doctors' Plot. The episode that follows occurs in the middle of German's novel and did not appear in the opening section published in 1949 in *Star*; it appeared for the first time in the 1956 edition of the novel. Of particular importance is the dramatic dialogue about "Judaic blood" between one of Levin's comrades-in-arms, the naval surgeon Barkan (presumably a Ukrainian), here representing Soviet internationalism, and the German pilot Stude, whose mind is infected with Nazi ideology.

From *Lieutenant Colonel of the Medical Corps*
(excerpt from Chapter 17)

This time they drew out the search, flying low over the water, with two fighter planes, sent by the commanding officer, patrolling above. The sea lapping below them was very gray, angry, with whitecaps; visibility got worse; then the fighter planes left—they were out of fuel. Bobrov kept flying and flying over the assigned squares, searching and searching, squinting his tired, teary eyes, and finally saw a figure in the water.

"All right," he said to himself and turned the plane.

A tiny boat sped beneath the plane; its crew let out wild yells and shot off a flare pistol. The green flare, curving, scattered into a shower and disappeared behind.

"All right," Bobrov repeated and righted the plane for landing.

The boat sped by close and again disappeared.

It turned dark suddenly. Large, soft snowflakes started adhering to the Plexiglas in front of Bobrov. Water spray instantly washed the snow away. The plane landed.

"Over to you, Comrade Lieutenant Colonel," shouted the medic, and with his long arms Aleksandr Markovich Levin caught hold of a lieutenant smiling in confusion. Then he took two more. One was shivering and groaning; Levin injected him with morphine. The other two he gave cognac, then returned to the first. Meanwhile Bobrov hadn't taken off; the plane was coasting along the water like a launch.

In a few minutes, a reconnaissance plane came along, humming like a bumblebee, and fired off a red flare. Bobrov banked his plane and kept coasting along the water.

"We better get to the base soon," said Lednev. "See that lightning again—we'll have snow squalls."

"With Bobrov at the helm," said Levin, "we're better off than in Tashkent. No problem. Let me have the probe and stop talking nonsense."

The navigator let out a yell.

"Stop yelling, my friend," said Levin. "That shrapnel of yours has almost worked itself out. You'll live to be a hundred and fifty, and each day you'll be embarrassed to recall how you yelled."

The gunner again scrubbed the upper hatchway clear and lowered himself by the outside companionway down to the water. Large snowflakes immediately clung to his face. A moderate swell was running, lapping along the side of the plane. Up above, the mechanic ran to the tail and, balancing there, threw down the line and called to the gunner:

"Lift slowly! Stepan! Lee-ee-ft!"

Lednev poked out of the hatchway up to his waist and suddenly said to those down below, in a whisper, like a secret:

"They got a German out of the water; honest to God, don't you believe me? A fritz, a fritz!"

No one could make out his words at first, but all, except for the wounded man, raised their heads. The medic climbed out. A few more moments went by, and water started pouring in from above. Then legs appeared, from which rivulets of water streamed down. Then a German with a thin face silently straightened out to attention before Levin.

The German wore an inflated vest, a yellow helmet blackened by the water; a pistol attached only by a cord hung down below his knee. The mechanic cut the cord with a penknife and stuck the pistol inside his jacket. The motors were already wailing, reaching the higher notes, as always before takeoff.

"*Sind Sie verwundet?*"[1] asked Levin very loudly.

The pilot mumbled something.

"*Wie fühlen Sie sich?*" said Levin still more loudly. "*Verstehen Sie mich? Ich frage, wie Sie sich fühlen? Sie sind nicht verwundet?*"[2]

The pilot kept staring at Levin. "This man may be mentally deranged," thought Levin, "maybe in a psychic trauma?"

And he reached out to take the German's pulse, but the latter jerked back and said he wished no services from a "*Jude.*"

"What?" Levin asked, flushing. He knew what the man had said, had heard everything word for word, but could not believe it. Over the years of Soviet power he had forgotten about this curse; he saw only in his nightmares how they squeezed "fat out of the little Yid"; he was a Red Army Lieutenant Colonel, and here this despicable creature reminded him again of those hateful times of the pogroms.

"What did he say?" asked the assistant medic.

"Oh, just some nonsense!" Levin answered, turning away from the German.

The pilot's mouth was quivering. Glancing around, he found a place on deck by the companionway and sat down, afraid that they would suddenly kill him. But no one intended to kill him; they just looked at him—how he sat down, how he drank water, and how he began to take off his wet clothes.

They gave him cognac; he drank it and moved all the available hot-water bottles closer to him. He could not get warm enough and could not take his eyes off the large white-faced Russian pilot who looked over his neighbor attentively, calmly, and seriously, every once in a while wincing with pain.

"Comrade Doctor!" the burly Russian called.

Levin bent down to him.

"We learned German in school," the pilot said. "The language of Marx and Goethe, Schiller and Heine, as our teacher Anna Karlovna told us. I understood what he . . . said to you . . . this . . . bastard . . . But don't you take offence, Comrade Doctor. To

---

1. (Ger.) = "Are you wounded?" In the original's footnotes, Yury German supplies translations from the German into Russian. These translations from German into English are by Helen Reeve. In the Russian original, German consistently translated the German adjective "Jüdisches" (as in Jüdisches Blut") as "Judaic" (iudeiskaia) rather than "Jewish" (evreiskaia). In speaking Russian Colonel Barkan also refers to blood as "Judaic" rather than "Jewish."

2. "How do you feel? . . . Do you understand me? I am asking how you feel. Are you not wounded?"

hell with him, with the vermin. Remember Korolenko and Maxim Gorky . . . how they fought against such filth. And I tell you another thing—let's shake hands, Lieutenant Shilov here . . ."

He raised his hand with difficulty. Levin pressed it.

"I figure that you need to forget this insult. Don't give a damn and forget it. This way . . . You see—he is looking at me. He's afraid I might shoot him dead. No, I won't shoot, the setting isn't right . . ."

Licking his dry lips, he slowly turned toward the other and began putting together German phrases, alternating with some Russian words:

"You better about this *Jude vergessen! Verstanden? Immer . . . Auf immer . . . Forever . . . Er ist . . . für dich Herr doktor. Verstanden? Herr* Lieutenant Colonel! *Und wirst sagen das . . . noch, werde schiessen dich im hospital*—I'll shoot you dead, you s.o.b.! *Das sage ich dir—ich*, Lieutenant Shilov Pyotr Semenovich. *Verstanden?* Got the picture?"[3]

"*Ja, ich habe verstanden. Ich habe es gut verstanden!*"[4] the German answered, barely moving his lips.

. . . Shilov was moved to room five, the German got a separate room, number eight. During the night he had a massive hemorrhage. Angelika, and Lora, and Vera, and Varvarushkina, and Zhakombai heard from Shilov how the Fascist had insulted the lieutenant colonel on the plane. They also told Barkan about it.

Frowning angrily, he entered number eight, where the prisoner lay.

"*Ich verblute*," softly, and with fear, said Lieutenant Kurt Stude. "*Ich bitte um sofortige Hilfe. Meine Blutgruppe ist hier angegeben.*" He pointed to his bracelet. "*Aber ich bitte Sie aufs dringlichste, Herr Doktor,—Ihr Gesicht sagt mir, dass sie ein Slave sind,—ich flehe Sie an: wenn Bluttransfusion notwendig ist . . . dass nur kein jüdisches Blut . . .*"[5]

Vyacheslav Viktorovich Barkan looked at the German sternly.

"*Verstehen Sie mich?*" asked Lieutenant Stude. "*Es geht um mein kuenftiges Schicksal, um meine Laufbahn, schliesslich um mein Leben. Keineswegs jüdisches Blut . . .*"[6]

Barkan frowned.

"*Haben Sie mich verstanden, Herr Doktor?*"[7]

---

3. "Forget this 'Jew' stuff! Got that? For good . . . once and for all. That's . . . *Herr Doktor,* Sir! to you. Got that? Lieutenant Colonel, Sir! And if you come out with that . . . again, just once more, I'll shoot you when we get to the hospital. This is me, telling you . . . me . . . Got it. . . ?"

4. "Yes. I understand. I understand very well."

5. "I am bleeding to death. I request immediate treatment. My blood type is written here . . . But I most urgently request, Doctor, Sir, by your face I see that you are a Slav. I implore you: if a blood transfusion is necessary—no Judaic blood . . ."

6. "Do you understand me? We're talking about my future, about my career, about my life, really. No Judaic blood, no matter what."

7. "Do you understand me, *Herr Doktor?*"

"Ja, ich habe Sie verstanden!" in a hoarse voice answered Barkan. *"Aber wir haben jetzt nur jüdisches Blut. So sind die Umstände. Und ohne Transfusion sind sie verloren . . ."*[8]

The pilot fell silent.

Barkan fixed him with a hard, unwavering gaze. He was seeing for the first time a genuine Fascist: my God, how shameful it was, how stupid, how crazy, how ugly. As if one could divide blood into Slavic, Aryan, Judaic. And this in the middle of the twentieth century . . .

"Ich hoffe, dass solche Einzelheiten in meinem Kriegsgefangenenbuch nicht verzeichnet werden. Das heisst, die Blutgruppe meinetwegen, aber nicht, dass es Jüdisches . . ."[9]

"Ich werde mir das Vergnuegen machen, alle Einzelheiten zu verzeichnen," said Barkan. *"Ich werde alles genau angeben."*[10]

"Aber warum denn, Herr Doktor? Sie sind doch ein Slave!"

"Ich bin ein Slave, und mir sind verhasst alle Rassisten. Verstehen Sie mich?" asked Barkan. *"Mir sind verhasst alle Antisemiten, Deutschhasser, mir sind verhasst Leute, die Neger lynchen, sind verhasst alle Obskuranten. Aber das sind unnuetze Worte. Was haben Sie beschlossen mit der Bluttransfusion?"*

"Ich unterwerfe mich der Gewalt!" said the pilot and pursed his lips.

"Nein, so geht es nicht. Bitten Sie uns um Transfusion beliebigen Blutes, oder bitten Sie nicht?"

"Dann bin ich gezwungen darum zu bitten."[11]

Barkan left the ward. In the hallway he said to Angelika:

"This scoundrel needs a transfusion. If he should inquire what kind of blood this is, tell him it's Judaic."

Angelika raised her eyebrows in wonder.

"Yes, yes, Judaic," repeated Barkan. "I am in my right mind and firm memory, but this will cut him down to size once and for all."

"You are doing this for Levin!" Angelika exclaimed in her deep voice. "Yes, don't deny it. That is splendid, Vyacheslav Viktorovich, that is wonderful. You are a marvel. I'm delighted . . ."

---

8. "Yes, understood! . . . But right now we have only Judaic blood. That's the situation. And without the transfusion, you'll die . . ."

9. "I hope the details won't get written down in my POW record. Well, the blood type of course, but not that . . . it's Judaic . . ."

10. "I'll take pleasure in writing down every detail! I'll write it all down exactly."

11. "But why, Herr Doktor? You're a Slav, after all!" "I'm a Slav, and I hate racists. Do you understand me? . . . I hate all antisemites, German-haters, I hate those who lynch Negroes. I hate reactionaries. However, there is no point talking. What have you decided about the blood transfusion?" "I submit to coercion!" . . . "No, that won't do. Are you asking for a transfusion of any kind of blood whatsoever, or not?" "Well then, I am being forced to ask for one."

"Glad to hear it!" growled Barkan.

That night Bobrov showed up in the clinic to see Levin.

"Plotnikov's plane didn't come back from the mission," he said, "the crew went down, and our Kurochka too."

"That's not possible!" said Levin.

His face turned gray.

Bobrov told him what details he knew. Many pilots saw the burning plane. No one managed to bail out. But still they had torpedoed the transport, and not a small one either—about ten tons, no less.

The phone on the table rang. A controlled voice warned:

"Lieutenant Colonel Levin? The general wishes to talk to you."

"Lieutenant Colonel Levin here," he said.

A tear slid down his cheek; embarrassed, he wiped it off with the sleeve of his lab coat and said again:

"Lieutenant Colonel Levin here."

Over the line came scratches and clicks. Then the general coughed and said in a very tired voice:

"I congratulate you, Lieutenant Colonel. You and your pilot Bobrov are awarded the Order of the Fatherland War, First Class. You accomplished a great deed, a great one."

Levin was silent. Another tear ran down from under his glasses.

"Ah, yes," said the general. "Well! Good night!"

"Thank you," answered Levin, and quickly hanging up, he turned away. Bobrov was looking at him, but Levin didn't want the pilot to see him crying.

They were quiet for a while, and then Levin went to his room and brought a book that Lednev had been reading recently. It was *War and Peace*. Over the cover, very worn and very dirty, spread a large ink stain.

"Your book?" he asked Bobrov.

The pilot's eye glistened avidly . . .

"For this I thank you," Bobrov said, "many thanks. Now, really, you've made me very happy . . . Well, get some rest, Aleksandr Markovich; I believe you're tired after today."

"Yes," Levin agreed, feeling guilty, "I'm very tired."

But Bobrov did not leave immediately; he sat around a bit, told Levin how the battle ended. The Fascist caravan, over all, was defeated. Four transports were sunk, a large barge with soldiers, and two escort ships.

Levin kept wiping off his tears.

1949

Translated from the Russian by Helen Reeve with Martha Kitchen

BORIS PASTERNAK

Boris Pasternak (1890–1960), poet, translator, and novelist, was born in Moscow, where his parents had moved from Odessa in 1889. A refined artistic milieu enveloped Pasternak and his three siblings: from his father, the visual artist Leonid Pasternak (1862–1945), Pasternak inherited a gift for seeing; from his mother, Rozalia Kaufman (1867–1939), a marvelously gifted pianist, Pasternak received his musical talents. The Pasternaks traced their lineage back to Sephardic Jews, to Don Isaac ben-Yehudah Abravanel (Abarbanel) (1437–1508). Although conversion to Christianity would have made things much easier for Pasternak's father at the beginning of his career, he never took the step on moral grounds. In 1894 Leonid Pasternak was invited to teach at the Moscow School of Painting, Sculpture, and Architecture; later the rank of Academician of Painting was bestowed upon him. In 1923 Leonid Pasternak's book *Rembrandt and Jews in His Work* appeared in Berlin in Russian and was later published in Hebrew translation. Bialik wrote admiringly of Leonid Pasternak as a Jewish artist.

The young Pasternak studied music theory and composition in 1903–9. Alexander Scriabin himself encouraged him, but the absence of perfect pitch hindered the musical career of the future poet. In 1913 Pasternak was graduated from the Historical-Philological Faculty of Moscow University, with a thesis on Hermann Cohen's philosophy. In May–August 1912, Pasternak attended summer school at the University of Marburg. Although Hermann Cohen asked him to stay on for graduate work, Pasternak refused the attractive offer.

In a letter to Jacqueline de Proyart dated 2 May 1959, Boris Pasternak spoke of having been baptized as an infant by his nanny in the Orthodox Church. Pasternak's leading biographers Lazar Fleishman and Christopher Barnes both suggest that the unconfirmed story of the infant Pasternak's conversion was a fantasy that the adult Pasternak cultivated in the 1940s and 1950s. As late as 1912, in his matriculation papers from Marburg University, Pasternak indicated his faith as "Mosaic." In 1922, when he married his first wife, the artist Evgenia Lurie, the marriage was certified by a Moscow rabbi. Although no evidence points to Pasternak's conversion at a later time, in the 1940s–1950s he regularly went to an Orthodox Church. Be this as it may, the argument in negotiating the Judaic–Christian and Jewish–Russian boundaries in Pasternak's worldview should not hinge on whether or not he was converted (a compensatory myth for the adult Pasternak) but on the Christian supersessionist beliefs and assimilationist convictions expressed in his writings, above all in *Doctor Zhivago* (1944–55; published 1957; excerpt below). Pasternak regarded his Jewish origin as an unfortunate complica-

591

tion. In a letter to the Judeophilic Maxim Gorky, dated 7 January 1928, he wrote, "With my place of birth, with my childhood circumstances, with my love, instincts, and inclinations, I should not have been born a Jew" (trans. Lazar Fleishman). Pasternak's poems first appeared in 1913; his first collection, *Twin in the Clouds*, came out a year later. With fellow poets Nikolay Aseev and Sergey Bobrov, Pasternak joined Centrifuge, a group of moderate Moscow futurists. His second collection, *Over the Barriers*, appeared in 1917, and that summer he finished *My Sister—Life*, which he considered his *first* book. Published only in 1922, Pasternak's astounding *My Sister—Life* was widely admired and vastly influential. Together with Pasternak's fourth collection, *Themes and Variations* (1923), *My Sister—Life* erected the pedestal on which his reputation as a great Russian poet was placed.

One of the most famous fellow travelers in the 1920s, Pasternak encountered criticism from official Bolshevik critics. Responding to the charges that he was an apolitical contemplator, Pasternak sought to inscribe vestiges of class struggle into his work. In the second, 1928, edition of the volume *Lofty Malady* (first edition 1923), he patched on a bit about Lenin. The epic poems of the 1920s, *1905* (1925–26) and *Lieutenant Schmidt* (1926–27), faired better as works by a sympathetic observer of revolutionary events. Yet Pasternak's best narrative poem, *Spektorsky* (1931), with a semiautobiographical protagonist-narrator who is a half-Jewish *intelligent*, communicated an ironic detachment from history. The year 1931 was an eventful one for Pasternak: he was attacked in connection with his autobiographical prose work *Safe Conduct* (1929; book edition 1931), he left his first Jewish wife for the non-Jewish Zinaida Neigauz (née Eremeeva), and he journeyed to the Caucasus. By 1929–30, the metaphorical fireworks and lexical and syntactic complexity of Pasternak's poetry had yielded to plainer verbal texture. Pasternak's 1932 collection *Second Birth* delivered topical poetry with details of the USSR going through five-year plans; this collection earned Pasternak official approval.

Nikolay Bukharin (1888–1938) was appointed editor of *Izvestia* in 1934 and recruited major talent for his paper; Pasternak was his favorite. In the summer of 1934, after turning to Bukharin for help following Osip Mandelstam's first arrest (O. Mandelstam in vol. 1), Pasternak received a telephone call from Stalin. Nadezhda Mandelstam reported the episode in a chapter of her *Hope Against Hope* (in vol. 2), along with Pasternak's cowardly response—both to Stalin's question about Mandelstam as a poet and to Mandelstam's poem against Stalin.

At the First Congress of Soviet Writers in September 1934 Pasternak was hailed as a leading *living* Soviet poet (the suicide Mayakovsky topped the official Soviet poetic pantheon, followed by the recently deceased Eduard Bagritsky [in vol. 1]). In the second edition of Pasternak's *Second Birth*, the poem "Waves" bore a dedication to Bukharin, the only time Pasternak dedicated anything to a Soviet leader. (Bukharin was arrested in 1937 and executed in 1938.) On 1 January 1936 *Izvestia* ran Pasternak's poem praising Stalin without naming him. The poem constituted the first part of the four-part cycle "The Artist," in which Stalin appeared as an "artist" of history; the loftiness of Pasternak's allegory and the quality of his verse had the potential to lend more aesthetic validity to the tyrant than hundreds of cultist hymns. The Great Purges of 1937–38 plunged Pasternak into despair. He wrote few original poems, focusing instead on translation work. The contributions of Pasternak the translator are numerous; his most celebrated translations included Shakespeare's *Hamlet* (1941), Goethe's *Faust* (1953), Schiller's *Maria Stuart* (1958), and the works of Georgian poets. After the Nazi invasion Pasternak was evacuated to Chistopol in Tatarstan; in 1941–1944 he contributed occasional poems, suffused with pressurized Russian patriotism, to Soviet periodicals. While he was not a principle target of the postwar anticosmopolitan campaign, he was chastised in print for being "alien to Soviet reality." Following his wartime patriotic upheaval, the collection *The Expanse of Earth* (1945), and a volume of *Selected Poems* (1945), no collections of Pasternak's appeared in the USSR until after his death.

With interruptions, Pasternak worked on the novel *Doctor Zhivago* throughout 1946–55. In 1946 Pasternak met Olga Ivinskaya (1912–1995), who became his last love. Rejecting *Doctor Zhivago* in 1956, the *Novy mir* editor, prominent Soviet writer Konstantin Simonov, and his staff wrote: "The spirit of your novel is the spirit of the nonacceptance of Socialist revolution." Published in Italian in 1957 and in Russian in 1958 by Feltrinelli Editore, *Doctor Zhivago* made Pasternak a world celebrity. In 1958 it competed with Vladimir Nabokov's *Lolita* on the American bestseller charts (Nabokov later described it as "melodramatic and vilely written"). Pasternak was awarded the Nobel Prize in Literature in 1958. In the Soviet Union the award brought forth an official campaign against him. The ostracism in the media began in Moscow's *Literary Gazette* (*Literaturnaia gazeta*) on 25 October 1958. The scoundrel journalist David Zaslavsky, a Jew by birth who had attacked Osip Mandelstam in the pages of *Literary Gazette* in 1929, distinguished himself again through sanctioned vilification of Pasternak in *Pravda* and *Literary Gazette*. Pasternak was expelled from the Union of Soviet Writers on 27 October. For different reasons a number of writers, including several in this anthology (such as Boris Slutsky [in vol. 2]), dirtied their hands in connection with the Pasternak affair. Calls, some laden with antisemitism, were made to expel Pasternak from the USSR. Harassed into turning down the Nobel Prize, on 31 October Pasternak wrote a penitent letter to Khrushchev (published 2 November) and an open letter to *Pravda*. He died in May 1960 in Peredelkino outside Moscow. A representative, albeit censored, edition of his poetry edited by Lev Ozerov (in vol. 1) came out in 1965 in the Poet's Library (Biblioteka poeta) series. Andrey Sinyavsky (1925–1997), himself about to go on trial for anti-Soviet activity alongside the writer Yuly Daniel (in vol. 2), wrote the introduction to the volume.

Pasternak's direct response to the Shoah was absent in prose and very limited in poetry. The two poems below were inspired by the main Soviet offensive launched in March 1944 in the south of Russia, Ukraine, and Belorussia. Soviet forces began an operation on 8 April 1944 aimed at the liberation of the Crimea and the surrounding areas, including Odessa. Dealing the Nazi and Romanian forces a powerful blow, the Soviet troops retook Sevastopol and had accomplished the operation by 13 May. By the summer of 1944, the Soviet troops had crossed the pre-1941 western frontier and moved into eastern Europe. Pasternak wrote both "In the Lowlands" and "Odessa" in the spring of 1944; they were published in the newspaper *Red Fleet* (*Krasnyi flot*) in March–April 1944. "In the Lowlands," dated 24 March 1944 in manuscript, was part of a fifteen-poem cycle "Poems about the War" and appeared in Pasternak's *The Expanse of the Earth* (1945), in which he apparently forgot to include "Odessa."

Nostalgically if faintly, the two poems paid tribute not only to the victims of the Nazi and Romanian atrocities during the occupation but also to the destruction—by Soviet history and by the war—of the Jewish-Russian Odessa that had nurtured Pasternak's parents and numerous other artists. Pasternak's "Odessa" appeared under the title "The Great Day" on 12 April 1944, just two days after the liberation of Odessa. The sixth stanza of the poem, which metaphorically evokes the faces of murdered Jews, was missing in the original publication.

In the Lowlands

Silted salt marsh's amber glare,
Black soil's glories,
Locals repairing tackle and gear,
Ferryboats, dories.
Nights in these lowlands, nights are rapt,
Dawns enter glowing.
Foam of the Black Sea glides over sand,
Swishing, slowing.
Quail in the swamps, cusk in the rivers,
Crawfish all over;
This way by shore the Crimea shimmers,
Ochakov the other.[1]

---

1. Ochakov—Black Sea port and district center presently in Ukraine, about 40 miles south of Nikolaev. Founded in the late fourteenth century, Ochakov had been a Turkish fortress and major military outpost until 1788, when it was captured by the Russian fleet during the Russo-Turkish war of 1787–91 and permanently ceded to the Russian Empire.

Beyond Nikolaev the salt marches stretch.[2]
Westward presses
A swell of fog-surges over the steppe
Toward Odessa.[3]
Did it happen, ever? Wrought in what style?
Where are those years?
Can they be returned? Legends revived?
That freedom be ours?
O how the ploughshare longs for the tilth,
Earth for the tillage,
The Sea for the Boug, south for the north,[4]
All for each village.
Peace, long awaited, is visibly near,
Round the bend of the bay.
Outlying landscapes promise—this year
The navy will have its say.

1944

---

2. Nikolaev—city and Black Sea port, major industrial center, and capital of Nikolaev Province in Ukraine. Site of a 1905 pogrom (see Isaac Babel's "The Story of My Dovecote"; Babel in vol. 1), prior to World War II, Nikolaev had a Jewish population of 30,000 people, of which about 25,000 escaped to the Soviet interior and 5,000 were massacred by the Nazis in 1941. Nikolaev was occupied by Nazi troops on 16 August 1941 and liberated by Soviet troops on 28 March 1944.

3. From 10 August 1941 to 16 October 1941, Soviet troops defended Odessa against an attack force consisting of sixteen Nazi divisions. Although the Soviet troops were outnumbered five to one, the siege lasted for seventy-three days before the city fell. By the time Odessa was occupied by Romanian and Nazi forces, about 90,000 Jews, including Odessan Jews and Jewish refugees from Bukovina, Bessarabia, and the western parts of Ukraine, had been concentrated in the city. In the first days of the occupation, over 8,000 Jews were murdered by Nazi and Romanian units. By February 1942, about 30,000 Jews remained in Odessa. In the course of the occupation, thousands of Jews were murdered in and on the outskirts of Odessa and transported to Transnistrian death camps. Odessa was liberated on 10 April 1944. Historians estimate that 2,000–3,000 Jews survived the occupation and remained in Odessa at the time of its liberation.

4. The Boug (Bug)—Pasternak is referring to the Southern Boug, a river in the southwestern region of Ukraine, originating in the Volhynian-Podolian elevation and falling into the Dnieper–Boug firth (liman) of the Black Sea.

Odessa

The land was a birthday girl, unsparingly
Kept waiting for that week's arrival
When the rescuer would break in daringly
As dusk set in or dawn was rising.

The tide roared out its gibberish, thundering
Among the splintered cliffs' recesses,
When, from above, we all heard suddenly
The rolling news, "We've won Odessa."

Down streets long empty of vehicular
Noise gushes the merry Russian humming,
Past sappers focused in particular
On doors and window frames' debugging.

Foot troops striding, cavalry cantering,
Long, horse-drawn carts, machine-gun mounted.
Midnight's still full of talk and bantering.
No one sleeps till the day's recounted.

But all's not well; a skull expressively
Leers from a nearby gulch. A savage
Cudgel here has mauled aggressively;
It's a waste Neanderthals have ravaged.

Small heads of immortelles peer cheerily[5]
Through empty sockets, nod and caper,
Inhabit the air with faces eerily,
Those of the dead mowed down last April.

---

5. *Immortelle* (Lat. *Helichrysum*)—also known as curry plant. Intent on alluding to the literal meaning of the flower's name, Pasternak opts for the foreign *immortelle* over the native Russian *bessmertnik* (lit. "deathless one = immortal one"), which to a native speaker's ear would invoke "death" and "immortality" much more prominently than the French *immortelle*.

Evil must be avenged with doubled blows
And the victim's widows and relatives
Eased in the moment of their family woes
By some new word that truly lives.

With all our Russian ingenuity
We swear, inspired by the great event,
To build the martyrs in perpetuity
A worthy peacetime monument.

1944

Translated from the Russian by Andrew von Hendy and Maxim D. Shrayer

Pasternak had completed parts 1–4 of book 1 of *Doctor Zhivago* by the summer of 1948, and the two excerpts that follow represent two of Pasternak's three main statements on Jews and Judaism found in the novel. The first appears at the very beginning of the novel; the episode describes Misha Gordon's journey to Moscow in 1903 in the course of which he witnesses the suicide of Yury Zhivago's father (book 1, part 1, chap. 7). The second, taking place in Galicia in the summer of 1915, depicts Gordon's visit to the eastern front, where his friend Zhivago is serving as a military doctor (book 1, part 4, chaps. 11–12). The third discussion of Jews and Judaism takes place in the middle of the novel, in two adjacent but not consecutive sections (book 2, part 9, chap. 15; book 2, part 10, chap. 3).

In October 1946, in a letter to his first cousin Olga Freidenberg, Pasternak wrote of his novel in progress: "In it I will square accounts with Judaism, with all forms of nationalism (including that which assumes the guise of internationalism), with all shades of anti-Christianity and its assumption that there are certain people surviving the fall of the Roman Empire from whose undeveloped national essence a new civilization could be evolved" (trans. Elliott Mossman and Margaret Wettlin). In addition to the sixteen prose parts of *Doctor Zhivago*, Pasternak included, as the novel's final, seventeenth part, "The Poems of Yury Zhivago." Whether or not "Zhivago's" poems, such as "Magdalene," treat the Gospel narratives with the freedom that the Jewish-born Christian Pasternak might have enjoyed is a question for a different forum. In *Doctor Zhivago*, Pasternak for the first time spoke openly of the Jews, exploring both the theological and the historical parameters of antisemitism and offering his authorial remedies.

The fact that Zhivago, who defends a Jew from a Cossack soldier, would be sympathetic to Jewish suffering proves nothing. How could Pasternak's idealized protagonist, doctor and poet, not defend a powerless old man? In this episode, the experience of anti-Jewish—and anti-Judaic—violence right in the heart of Hassidic Galicia adumbrates Pasternak's statement on the place of Judaism after the advent of Jesus of Nazareth. Writing after the Shoah and on the eve of the worst years for Jews of the Soviet Union (1948–53), Pasternak designates the Jewish-born Misha Gordon his spokesman; the Russian Yury Zhivago listens silently. Gordon's assimilationist— and supersessionist—beliefs are later echoed in Lara's monologue to Zhivago (book 2, part 9, chap. 15), who replies that he "had not thought about it" and that his friend Gordon is of "the same views." (Parts 9 and 10 of the novel were composed in 1949.) At the beginning of part 10, through the words of a tertiary character, Pasternak slipped in a further comment on the Jewish question. Returning home on the eve of "Great Thursday, the day of the Twelve Gospels" (the Orthodox equivalent of Holy Thursday), shopkeeper Galuzina thinks habitually antisemitic thoughts in connection with the town's small Jewish population but also acknowledges to herself that the Jewish question is hardly as central to Russian history as her fellow Russians tend to regard it. There is, perhaps, reason to suspect that Galuzina's confusion casts doubt on Lara's breathless call for Jews to "rise above themselves and dissolve without a trace among all the rest, whose religious foundation they themselves had laid and who would be so close to them, if only they knew them better."

From *Doctor Zhivago*
Book 1, Part 1, Chapter 7

7

In a second-class compartment of the train sat Misha Gordon, who was traveling with his father, a lawyer from Orenburg.[6] Misha was a boy of eleven with a thoughtful young face and big dark eyes; he was in his second year of gymnasium. His father, Grigory Osipovich Gordon, was being transferred to a new post in Moscow; [the boy was transferring to a Moscow gymnasium]. His mother and sisters had gone on some time before to get their apartment ready.

Father and son had been traveling for three days.

Russia, with its fields, steppes, villages, and towns, bleached lime-white by the

---

6. Orenburg—provincial capital on the Ural River; founded in 1735 as a military fortress, by the early twentieth century Orenburg had about 75,000 residents, including a Jewish community of about 1,300.

sun, flew past them wrapped in hot clouds of dust. Lines of carts rolled along the highways, occasionally lumbering off the road to cross the tracks; from the furiously speeding train it seemed that the carts stood still and the horses were marking time.

At big stations passengers jumped out and ran to the buffet; the sun setting behind the station garden lit their feet and shone under the wheels of the train.

Every motion in the world taken separately was calculated and purposeful, but, taken together, they were spontaneously intoxicated with the general stream of life which united them all. People worked and struggled, each set in motion by the mechanism of his own cares. But the mechanisms would not have worked properly had they not been regulated and governed by a higher sense of an ultimate freedom from care. This freedom came from the feeling that all human lives were interrelated, a certainty that they flowed into each other—a happy feeling that all events took place not only on the earth, in which the dead are buried, but also in some other region which some called the Kingdom of God, others history, and still others by some other name.

To this general rule, Misha was an unhappy, bitter exception. A feeling of care remained his ultimate mainspring and was not relieved and ennobled by a sense of security. He knew this hereditary trait in himself and watched with an alert diffidence for symptoms of it in himself. It distressed him. Its presence humiliated him.

For as long as he could remember he had never ceased to wonder why, having arms and legs like everyone else, and a language and a way of life common to all, one could be different from the others, liked only by few and, moreover, loved by no one. He could not understand a situation in which if you were worse than other people you could not make an effort to improve yourself. What did it mean to be a Jew? What was the purpose of it? What was the reward or the justification of this impotent challenge, which brought nothing but grief?

When Misha took the problem to his father he was told that his premises were absurd, and that such reasonings were wrong, but he was offered no solution deep enough to attract him or to make him bow silently to the inevitable.

And making an exception only for his parents, he gradually became contemptuous of all grownups who had made this mess and were unable to clear it up. He was sure that when he was big he would straighten it all out.

Now, for instance, no one had the courage to say that his father should not have run after that madman when he had rushed out onto the platform, and should not have stopped the train when, pushing Grigory Osipovich aside, and flinging open the door, he had thrown himself head first out of the express like a diver from a springboard into a swimming pool.

But since it was his father who had pulled the emergency release, it looked as if the train had stopped for such an inexplicably long time because of them.

No one knew the exact cause of the delay. Some said that the sudden stop had damaged the air brakes, other that they were on a steep gradient and the engine could not make it. A third view was that as the suicide was a prominent person, his lawyer, who had been with him on the train, insisted on officials being called from the nearest station, Kologrivovka, to draw up a statement. This was why the assistant engineer had climbed up the telegraph pole: the inspection handcar must be on its way.

There was a faint stench from the lavatories, not quite dispelled by eau de cologne, and a smell of fried chicken, a little high and wrapped in dirty wax paper. As though nothing had happened, graying Petersburg ladies with creaking chesty voices, turned into gypsies by the combination of soot and greasy cosmetics, powdered their faces and wiped their fingers on their handkerchiefs. When they passed the door of the Gordons' compartment, adjusting their shawls and anxious about their appearance even while squeezing themselves through the narrow corridor, their pursed lips seemed to Misha to hiss: "Aren't we sensitive! We're something special. We're cultured. It's too much for us."

The body of the suicide lay on the grass by the embankment. A little stream of blood had run across his forehead and, having dried, it looked like a cancel mark crossing out his face. It did not look like his blood, which had come from his body, but like a foreign appendage, a piece of plaster or a splatter of mud or a wet birch leaf.

Curious onlookers and sympathizers surrounded the body in a constantly changing cluster, while his friend and traveling companion, a thickset, arrogant-looking lawyer, a pure-bred animal in a sweaty shirt, stood over him sullenly with an expressionless face. Overcome by the heat, he was fanning himself with his hat. In answer to all questions he shrugged his shoulders and said crossly, without even turning around: "He was an alcoholic. Can't you understand? He did it in a fit of D.T.'s."[7]

Once or twice a thin old woman in a woolen dress and lace kerchief went up to the body. She was the widow Tiverzina, mother of two engineers, who was traveling third class on a pass with her two daughters-in-law. Like nuns with their mother superior, the two quiet women, their shawls pulled low over their foreheads, followed her in silence. [. . .] The crowd made way for them.

Tiverzina's husband had been buried alive in a railway accident. She stood a little away from the body, where she could see it through the crowd, and sighed as if comparing the two cases. "Each according to his fate," she seemed to say. "Some die by the Lord's will—and look what's happened to him—to die of rich living and mental illness."

All the passengers came out and had a look at the corpse and went back to their compartments only for fear that something might be stolen.

When they jumped out onto the track and picked flowers or took a short walk to stretch their legs, they felt as if the whole place owed its existence to the accident, and that without it neither the swampy meadow with hillocks, the broad river, nor the fine manor house and church on the steep opposite side would have been there.

Even the sun seemed to be a purely local feature. Its evening light was diffident, a little timid, like a cow from a nearby herd come to take a look at the crowd.

---

7. D.T.'s—medical abbreviation = *delirium tremens*; type of delirium typically experienced by alcoholics after rapid reduction or termination of alcohol consumption.

Misha had been deeply shaken by the event and had at first wept with grief and fright. In the course of the long journey the suicide had come several times to their compartment and had talked with Misha's father for hours on end. He had said that he found relief in the moral decency, peace, and understanding which he discovered in their world and had asked Grigory Osipovich endless questions about fine points in law concerning bills of exchange, deeds of settlement, bankruptcy, and fraud. "Is that so?" he exclaimed at Gordon's answers. "Can the law be as lenient as that? My lawyer takes a much gloomier view."

Each time that this nervous man calmed down, his traveling companion came from their first-class coach to drag him off to the restaurant to drink champagne. He was the thickset, arrogant, clean-shaven, well-dressed lawyer who now stood over his body, showing not the least surprise. It was hard to escape the feeling that his client's ceaseless agitation had somehow been to his advantage.

Misha's father described him as a well-known millionaire, [Zhivago], a good-natured profligate, not quite responsible for his actions. When he had come to their compartment, he would, unrestrained by Misha's presence, talk about his son, a boy of Misha's age, and about his late wife; then he would go on about his second family, whom he had deserted as he had the first. At this point he would remember something else, grow pale with terror, and begin to lose the thread of his story.

To Misha he had shown an unaccountable affection, which probably reflected a feeling for someone else. He had showered him with presents, jumping out to buy them at the big stations, where the bookstalls in the first-class waiting rooms also sold toys and local souvenirs.

He had drunk incessantly and complained that he had not slept for three months and that as soon as he sobered up for however short a time he suffered torments unimaginable to any normal human being.

At the end, he rushed into their compartment, grasped Gordon by the hand, tried to tell him something but found he could not, and dashing out onto the platform threw himself from the train.

Now Misha sat examining the small wooden box of minerals from the Urals that had been his last gift. Suddenly there was a general stir. A handcar rolled up on the parallel track. A doctor, two policemen, and a magistrate with a cockade in his hat jumped out. Questions were asked in cold businesslike voices, and notes taken. The policemen and the guards, slipping and sliding awkwardly in the gravel, dragged the corpse up the embankment. A peasant woman began to wail. The passengers were asked to go back to their seats, the guard blew his whistle, and the train started on.

Book 1, Part 4, Chapters 11–12

11

In this area the villages had been miraculously preserved.[8] They constituted an inexplicably intact island in the midst of a sea of ruins. [Gordon and Zhivago were on their way home in the evening. The sun was going down.] In one village [they passed through] they saw a young Cossack surrounded by a crowd laughing boisterously, as the Cossack tossed a copper coin in the air, forcing an old Jew with a gray beard and a long caftan to catch it. The old man missed every time. The coin flew past his pitifully spread-out hands and dropped into the mud. When the old man bent to pick it up, the Cossack slapped his bottom, and the onlookers held their sides, groaning with laughter: this was the point of the entertainment. For the moment it was harmless enough, but no one could say for certain that it would not take a more serious turn. Every now and then, the old man's wife ran out of the house across the road, screaming and stretching out her arms to him, and ran back again in terror. Two little girls were watching their grandfather out of the window and crying.

The driver, who found all of this extremely comical, slowed down so that the passengers could enjoy the spectacle. But Zhivago called the Cossack, bawled him out, and ordered him to stop baiting the old man.

"Yes, sir," he said readily. "We meant no harm, we were only doing it for fun."

Gordon and Zhivago drove on in the silence.

"It's terrible," said [Zhivago] when they were in sight of their own village. "You can't imagine what the [miserable] Jewish population [has been going] through in this war. The fighting happens to be in the [pale of their forced settlement]. And as if punitive taxation, the destruction of their property, and all their own sufferings were not enough, they are subjected to pogroms, insults, and accusations that they lack patriotism. And why should they be patriotic? Under enemy rule, they enjoy equal rights, and we do nothing but persecute them. This hatred for them, the basis of it, is irrational. It is stimulated by the very things that should arouse sympathy—their poverty, their overcrowding, their weakness, and this inability to fight back. I can't understand it. It's like an inescapable fate."

Gordon did not reply.

---

8. The military background of the scene was the spring 1915 campaign in Galicia, the Russian capture of Przemyśl, and advances in Austria followed by the German and Austrian counteroffensive, which, by October 1915, had undone most of the Russian gains. General Aleksey Brusilov's breakthrough in Austrian Poland did not occur until June 1916.

12

Once again they were lying [. . .] on either side of the long low window, it was night, and they were talking. Zhivago was telling Gordon how he had once seen the Tsar at the front. He told his story well.

It was his first spring at the front. The headquarters of his regiment was in the Carpathians, in a deep valley, access to which from the Hungarian plain was blocked by this army unit. At the bottom of the valley was a railway station. Zhivago described the landscape, the mountains overgrown with mighty firs and pines, with tufts of clouds catching in their tops, and sheer cliffs of gray slate and graphite showing through the forest like worn patches in a thick fur. It was a damp, dark April morning, as gray as the slate, locked in by the mountains on all sides and therefore still and sultry. Mist hung over the valley, and everything in it steamed, everything rose slowly— engine smoke from the railway station, gray vapors from the fields, the gray mountains, the dark woods, the dark clouds.

At that time the sovereign was making a tour of inspection in Galicia. It was learned suddenly that he would visit Zhivago's unit [. . .]. He might arrive at any moment. A guard of honor was drawn up on the station platform. They waited for about two oppressive hours, then two trains with the imperial retinue went by quickly one after the other. A little later the Tsar's train drew in.

Accompanied by the Grand Duke Nicholas, the Tsar inspected the grenadiers. Every syllable of his quietly spoken greeting produced an explosion of thunderous hurrahs whose echoes were sent back and forth like water from swinging buckets.

The Tsar, smiling and ill at ease, looked older and more tired than on the rubles and medals. His face was listless, a little flabby. He kept glancing apologetically at the Grand Duke, not knowing what was expected of him, and the Grand Duke, bending down respectfully, helped him in his embarrassment not so much by words as by moving an eyebrow or a shoulder.

On that warm gray morning in the mountains, Zhivago felt sorry for the Tsar, was disturbed at the thought that such [timorous] reserve and shyness could be the essential characteristics of an oppressor, that a man so weak could imprison, hang, or pardon.

"He should have made a speech—'I, my sword, and my people'—like the Kaiser. Something about 'the people'—that was essential. But you know he was natural, in the Russian way, tragically above these banalities. After all, that kind of theatricalism is unthinkable in Russia. For such gestures are theatrical, aren't they? I suppose that there were such things as 'peoples' under the Caesars—Gauls or Svevians or Illyrians and so on. But ever since, they have been mere fiction, which served only as subjects for speeches by kings and politicians: 'The people, my people.'

"Now the front is flooded with correspondents and journalists. They record their 'observations' and gems of popular wisdom, they visit the wounded and construct

new theories about the people's soul. It's a new version of Dahl[9] and just as bogus—
linguistic graphomania, verbal incontinence. That's one type—and then there's the
other: clipped speech, 'sketches and short scenes,' skepticism and misanthropy. I read
a piece like that the other day: 'A gray day, like yesterday. Rain since the morning,
slush. I look out of the window and see the road. Prisoners in an endless line. Wounded.
A gun is firing. It fires today as yesterday, tomorrow as today and every day and every
hour.' Isn't that subtle and witty! But what has he got against the gun? How odd to
expect variety from a gun! Why doesn't he look at himself, shooting off the same
sentences, commas, lists of facts day in, day out, keeping up his barrage of journalistic philanthropy as nimble as the jumping of a flea? Why can't he get it into his head
that it's for him to [do something new and] stop repeating himself—not for the gun—
that you can never say something meaningful by accumulating absurdities in your
notebook, that facts don't exist until man puts into them something of his own, a bit of
[free-ranging] human genius—of myth."

"You've hit the nail on the head," broke in Gordon. "And now I'll tell you what I
think about that incident we saw today. That Cossack tormenting the poor patriarch—
and there are thousands of incidents like it—of course it's an ignominy—but there's
no point in philosophizing [about it], you just hit it out. But the Jewish question as a
whole—there philosophy does come in—and then we discover something unexpected.
Not that I'm going to tell you anything new—we both got our ideas from your uncle.[10]

"You were saying, what is a nation? . . . And who does more for a nation—the one
who makes a fuss about it or the one who, without thinking of it, raises it to universal-
ity by the beauty and greatness of his actions, and gives it fame and immortality?
Well, [of course], the answer is obvious. And what are the nations now, in the Christian era? They aren't just nations, but converted, transformed nations, and what matters is this transformation, not loyalty to ancient principles. And what does the Gospel
say on this subject? To begin with, it does not make assertions: 'It's like this and like
that.' It is a proposal, naïve and timid: 'Do you want to live in a completely new way?
Do you want spiritual [bliss]?' And everybody accepted, they were carried away by it
for thousands of years. . . .

"When the Gospel [said] that in the Kingdom of God there are neither Jews nor
Gentiles, [did] it merely mean that all are equal in the sight of God? No—the Gospel
wasn't needed for that—the Greek philosophers, the Roman moralists, and the [Old
Testament] prophets had known this long before. But it said: In that new way of living
and new form of society, which is born of the heart, and which is called the Kingdom
of Heaven, there are no nations, there are only individuals.

---

9. Compiler of the remarkable *Reasoned Dictionary of the Living Russian Language* (1863–
66), the writer and lexicographer Vladimir Dahl (Dal') (1801–1872) was behind the authorship
of the notoriously antisemitic *Investigation of the Murder by Jews of Christian Infants and the
Use of Their Blood* (St. Petersburg, 1844).

10. Yury Zhivago was raised by his uncle after his father's suicide.

"You said that facts are meaningless, unless meanings are put into them. Well, Christianity, the mystery of the individual, is precisely what must be put into the facts to make them meaningful.

"We also talked about the mediocre [public figures] who have nothing to say to life and the world as a whole, of petty second-raters who are only too happy when some nation, preferably a small and [suffering] one, is constantly discussed—this gives them a chance to show off their competence and cleverness, and to thrive on their compassion for the persecuted. Well now, what more perfect example can you have of the victims of this mentality than the Jews? Their national idea has forced them, century after century, to be a nation and nothing but a nation—and they have been chained to this deadening task all through the centuries when all the rest of the world was being delivered from it by a new force which had come out of their own midst! Isn't that extraordinary? How can you account for it? Just think! This glorious holiday, this liberation from the curse of mediocrity, this soaring flight above the dullness of a humdrum existence was first achieved in their land, proclaimed in their language, and belonged to their race! And they actually saw and heard it and let it go! How could they allow a spirit of such overwhelming power and beauty to leave them, how could they think that after it triumphed and established its reign, they would remain as the empty husk of that miracle they had repudiated? What use is it to anyone, this voluntary martyrdom? Whom does it profit? For what purpose are these innocent old men and women and children, all these [sensitive], kind, humane people, mocked and [massacred] throughout the centuries? And why is it that all these literary friends of 'the people' of all nations are always so untalented? Why didn't the intellectual leaders of the Jewish people ever go beyond facile *Weltschmerz* and ironical wisdom? Why have they not—even if at the risk of bursting like boilers with the pressure of their duty—disbanded this army which keeps on fighting and being beaten up nobody knows for what? Why don't they say to them: '[You are the first and best Christians in the world.] Come to your senses, stop. Don't hold on to your identity. Don't stick together, disperse. Be with all the rest. You are the very thing against which you have been turned by the worst and weakest among you.'"

1946–(1955)

Translated from the Russian by Max Hayward and Manya Harari

BIBLIOGRAPHY OF PRIMARY SOURCES FOR VOLUME 1

The sources of the Russian originals are listed below in the same order as their English translations appear in the anthology and chronologically within each entry. In cases of excerpts from longer texts, the inclusive pages refer to the parts used in this anthology. The textual sources from which the translations were drawn are printed in boldface type. Where there are several sources listed, it is the source in boldface that provided the text from which our entry was translated.

This bibliography is not meant to be an exhaustive listing of all appearances of the anthologized texts in periodicals, individual collections and editions, and collective edited volumes. Of the numerous editions of some of the works, only the sources the editor consulted *de visu* are included below. While any previously unpublished original works have been excluded from this anthology by its selection criteria, alternative manuscript versions have been consulted, in several cases with the authors' assistance, where it was deemed necessary.

The textological challenges of works published under conditions of Soviet censorship have been dealt with in scholarship (e.g., in Herman Ermolaev's ground-breaking work), and they can be boundless. Those challenges, as demonstrated by post-Soviet scholarship (e.g., Arlen Blium's illuminating research), can be especially prohibitive for a historian of Jewish writing in the Soviet period. This is why, however helpful they may be, no Soviet-era academic editions of works by Jewish-Russian authors are fully reliable and/or complete. At the same time, while most works by émigré authors were not subjected to government censorship, the very limited conditions of their publication and distribution abroad frequently doomed them to obscurity. In seeking to represent the history of a given work's publication or to date the work, the editor in some cases had to check the later, modified versions against the original publications; significant differences have been accounted for in the notes to the texts. The editor frequently consulted the original publications, whether in periodical or in book form. Such consultation was not always possible as this information may not have been available, and the editor welcomes any suggestions and additions. The editor's task was made less arduous by the appearance in the 1990s of a number of reliable academic editions of Jewish-Russian works, both in the former Soviet Union and abroad, and by the generous help of the individuals listed in the acknowledgments.

If an English translation included in the anthology has appeared previously, the information about it follows the information about the Russian original.

A standard Library of Congress system of transliterating the Russian alphabet (without diacritical marks) is used throughout the bibliographical references.

The Beginning

Leyba Nevakhovich
From *Lament of the Daughter of Judah*: *Vopl' dshcheri iudeiskoi*, sochinenie Leiby Nevakhovicha, 27–43. St. Petersburg: pechatano v privilegirovannoi Breitkopfovoi Tipografii, 1803.

Gaining a Voice: 1840–1881

Leon Mandelstam
From "The People": "Narod," in L.I. Mandel'shtam, *Stikhotvoreniia*, 67–72. Moscow: V universitetskoi tipografii, 1841.

Afanasy Fet
"When my daydreams cross the brink of long lost days . . .": "Kogda moi mechty za gran'iu proshlykh dnei. . . ," in *Otechestvennye zapiski* 38 (1845): 94 (under the title "Elegiia");

"Sheltered by a crimson awning . . .": "Pod palatkoiu puntsovoi. . . ," in A. Fet, *Stikhotvoreniia*, 136–37. Moscow, 1850;

both in **A.A. Fet,** *Polnoe sobranie stikhotvorenii*, **ed. B.Ia. Bukhshtab, 82, 452. Leningrad: Sovetskii pisatel', 1959.**

Ruvim Kulisher
From *An Answer to the Slav*: *Otvet slavianinu*, *Perezhitoe* 3 (St. Petersburg, 1911): 365–77 (published, with introduction, by S.M. Ginzburg).

Osip Rabinovich
From *The Penal Recruit*: *Shtrafnoi*, in *Russkii vestnik* 6 (1859): 510–21;
in **Osip Rabinovich,** *Izbrannoe*, **ed. M. Vainshtein, 21–43. Jerusalem: Institut rossiiskogo evreistva, 1985.**

Lev Levanda
From *Seething Times: Goriachee vremia. Roman*, "Chast' pervaia. Na pravo ili na levo?" *Evreiskaia biblioteka*, vol. 1 (1871): 13–15; 22–25; 36; 50–55; 66–68;
in Lev Levanda. *Goriachee vremia: roman iz poslednego pol'skogo vosstaniia*, 14–16; 24–27; 40–41; 57–59; 59–63; 76–78. St. Petersburg: A.E. Landau, 1875;
English translation by Maxim D. Shrayer, forthcoming in *Polin* 20 (2007).

Grigory Bogrov
From *Notes of a Jew: Zapiski evreia*, in G. Bogrov, *Sobranie sochinenii*, 2nd ed., vol. 1, 55–81. Odessa: Knigoizdatel'stvo Shermana, 1912.

First Flowering: 1881–1902

Rashel Khin
From *The Misfit: Ne ko dvoru*, in R.M. Khin, *Siluety*, 203–10. Moscow: T-vo skoropechatni A.A. Levenson, 1895.

Semyon Nadson
From "The Woman": "Zhenshchina" (part 2: "Ros odinoko ia. Menia ne ograzhdala . . ."); "I grew up shunning you, O most degraded nation . . .": "Ia ros tebe chuzhim, otverzhennyi narod . . .";

both in **S.Ia. Nadson, *Stikhotvoreniia*, ed. F.I. Shushovskaia, 184–85, 262. Leningrad: Sovetskii pisatel', 1957.**

Nikolay Minsky
"To Rubinstein": "Rubinshteinu," in **N.M. Minskii, *Stikhotvoreniia*, 162–63. St. Petersburg: Tip. V.S. Balasheva, 1887**;
in *Polnoe sobranie stikhotvorenii*, vol. 1, 170–71. St. Petersburg: Izdanie M.V. Pirozhkova, 1907.

Simon Frug
"Song": "Pesnia" ("Ia eolova arfa doli narodnoi . . ."), in S.G. Frug, *Polnoe sobranie sochinenii*, vol. 6, 3. St. Petersburg: Izdanie zhurnala "Evreiskaia zhizn'," [1900?];

"Shylock": "Sheilok," in *Nauchno-literaturnyi sbornik "Budushchnost'*," 1 (1900): 94–96; in S.G. Frug, *Polnoe sobranie sochinenii*, vol. 6, 125–26. St. Petersburg: Izdanie zhurnala "Evreiskaia zhizn'," [1900?];

both in **S.G. Frug, *Polnoe sobranie sochinenii v 3kh tomakh*, 7th ed., vol. 3, 158–59. Odessa: Knigoizdatel'stvo Shermana, [1917]**;

"An Admirer of Napoleon": "Poklonnik Napoleona," in **S.G. Frug, *Polnoe sobranie sochinenii*, vol. 3, 3–6. St. Petersburg: Izdanie zhurnala "Evreiskaia zhizn'," [1900?].**

Ben-Ami
Author's Preface to vol. 1 of *Collected Stories and Sketches*: "Ot avtora," in **Ben-Ami, *Sobranie rasskazov i ocherkov*, vol. 1, v–viii. Odessa: Tipografiia G.M. Levinsona, 1898.**

Avraam-Uria Kovner
From *Memoirs of a Jew: Iz zapisok evreia*, chap. 5. *Istoricheskii vestnik* 92 (April 1903): 126–36. Signed "A.G."

On the Eve: 1903–1917

David Aizman

"The Countrymen": "Zemliaki," in D. Aizman, *Zemliaki. Rasskazy*, 201–44. Moscow: Priboi, 1929; in **D. Aizman, *Krovavyi razliv i drugie proizvedeniia*, ed. M. Vainshtein, 2 vols. Vol. 1, 230– 65. [Jerusalem], 1991**; English translation by Maxim D. Shrayer in *Commentary* 6 (2003): 30–40.

Semyon Yushkevich

From *The Jews: Evrei*, in Semen Iushkevich, *Evrei: povest'*, 188–204. Munich: Verlag Dr. J. Marchlewski, 1904; in Semen Iushkevich, *Evrei*, 158–69. St. Petersburg: Izdanie tovarishchestva "Znanie," 1906; in **Semen Iushkevich, *Evrei*, 203–16. Leningrad–Moscow: Kniga, 1928**.

Dmitry Tsenzor

"The Old Ghetto": "Staroe getto," in Dmitrii Tsenzor, *Staroe getto*, 3. St. Petersburg: Knigoizdatel'stvo "EOS," 1907; modified version in **Dmitrii Tsenzor, *Stikhotvoreniia 1903–1938*, 4. Leningrad: Sovetskii pisatel', 1940**;

"Father": "Otets," in **Dmitrii Tsenzor, *Stikhotvoreniia 1903–1938*, 87–88. Leningrad: Sovetskii pisatel', 1940**.

Vladimir Jabotinsky

"In Memory of Herzl": "Pamiati Gertslia," under the title "Hespêd," in *Evreiskaia zhizn'* 6.1 (1904): 8–10; in Vladimir Zhabotinskii, *Doktor Gertsl'*, 3–4. Odessa: Knigoizdatel'stvo "Kadima," 1905; in Vladimir (Zeev) Zhabotinskii, *Izbrannoe*, 7–8. Jerusalem: Biblioteka "Aliia," 1978 (with minor variations);

"An Exchange of Compliments": "Obmen komplimentov," in Vl. Zhabotinskii, *Fel'etony*, 181– 94. St. Petersburg: Tip. Akts. obshch. tipografsk. dela v Spb. "Gerol'd," 1913; in Vl. Zhabotinskii, *Fel'etony*, 3rd ed., 131–41. Berlin: Izdatel'stvo S.D. Zal'tsman, 1922; in **Vladimir (Zeev) Zhabotinskii, *Izbrannoe*, 104–15. Jerusalem: Biblioteka "Aliia," 1978**.

Leyb Jaffe

"In an Alien Tongue": "Na chuzhom iazyke"; "Off the Corfu Coast" (From Travel Notes): "U beregov Korfu" (Iz putevykh zametok), in *Molodaia Iudeia* [Ialta] 3–4 (June–July 1906): 69–70; in *Pesni Molodoi Iudei*, 19–20. Yalta: Izdanie zhurnala "Molodaia Iudeia," 1906; reprinted Tel-Aviv, 1969; both in **Lev Iaffe, *Ogni na vysotakh*, 7, 11–12. Riga: Splendid, 1938**.

Sasha Cherny

"The Jewish Question": "Evreiskii vopros"; "Judeophobes": "Iudofoby"; both in *Satirikon* 47 (1909): 2–3 ("Spetsial'nyi evreiskii nomer"); both in **Sasha Chernyi, *Sobranie sochinenii v piati tomakh*, ed. A.S. Ivanov, vol. 1, 335–37. Moscow: "Ellis Lak," 1996**.

Ossip Dymow

"The Guardian Press": "Okhranitel'naia pechat'," in Osip Dymov, *Veselaia pechal'. Iumoristicheskie rasskazy*, 45–49. St. Petersburg: Shipovnik, 1911.

S. An-sky

"The Book": "Kniga," in *Evreiskii mir* 5 (4 February 1910): 60–64; in S. An-skii, *Sobranie sochinenii*, vol. 1, 94–102. St. Petersburg: T-vo "Prosveshchenie," 1911.

Ilya Ehrenburg

"To the Jewish Nation": "Evreiskomu narodu," in Il'ia Erenburg, *Ia zhivu*, 51–52. St. Petersburg, 1911;

"Jews, I haven't strength to live with you . . .": "Evrei, s vami zhit' ne v silakh. . . ," in Il'ia Erenburg, *Staryi skorniak i drugie proizvedeniia*, ed. M. Vainshtein, 2 vols. Vol. 1, 342. Jerusalem, 1983;

both in Il'ia Erenburg, *Stikhotvoreniia*, ed. B.Ia. Frezinskii, 123, 135. St. Petersburg: Akademicheskii proekt, 2000.

Vladislav Khodasevich

"Evening": "Vecher," in Vladislav Khodasevich, *Schastlivyi domik*, 66–67. Moscow: Al'tsiona, 1914;

"Rachel's Tears": "Slezy Rakhili," in Vladislav Khodasevich, *Putem zerna*, 8. Moscow: Tvorchestvo, 1920;
in Vladislav Khodasevich, *Sobranie stikhov*, 10. Paris: Vozrozhdenie, 1927;
in Vladislav Khodasevich, *Sobranie stikhov (1913–1939)*, ed. Nina Berberova, 12. New Haven, CT: N. Berberova, 1961;
in Vladislav Khodasevich, *Stikhotvoreniia*, ed. Dzhon [John] Malmstad, 41–42. St. Petersburg: Akademicheskii proekt, 2001;

both in Vladislav Khodasevich, *Sobranie stikhov v dvukh tomakh*, ed. Iurii Kolker, vol. 1, 78, 84. Paris: La Presse Libre, 1982;
both in Vladislav Khodasevich, *Sobranie stikhov*, ed. A. Dorofeev and A. Lavrin, 89, 97. Moscow: Tsenturion Interpaks, 1992;

Rahel

"I love all temples—my own and others' . . .": "Ia liubliu vse khramy—svoi i chuzhie . . .";
"Tablets of the Past and Chains of the Past": "Skrizhali proshlogo i proshlogo verigi";

both in Rahel, *Lekha 've-'alekha*, ed. Binyamin Hachlili, 74, 77. Tel Aviv: Hakibbutz Hameuchad, 1987.

Samuil Marshak

"Palestine": "Palestina," in *U rek vavilonskikh: national'no-evreiskaia lirika v mirovoi poezii*, ed. L[ev] Iaffe, 129–35. Moscow: Safrut, 1917.

Sofia Parnok

"My anguish does the Lord not heed . . .": "Ne vnial toske moei Gospod' . . . ," in *Liricheskii*

krug: stranitsy poezii i kritiki, vol. 1, 19. Moscow: Severnye dni, 1922 (third of four-poem cycle numbered 1–4);
in Sofiia Parnok, *Loza*, 30. Moscow, 1923;
in *Novyi zhurnal* 138 (March 1980): 86 (incorrectly identified as "previously unpublished");

"Hagar": *"Agar'"*;
"Not for safekeeping for awhile . . .": "Ne na khranen'e do pory . . .";

all three in **Sofiia Parnok, *Sobranie stikhotvorenii*, ed. S. Poliakova, 250, 286, 291. St. Petersburg: Inapress, 1998.**

Revolution and Betrayal: 1917–1939

Leonid Kannegiser
"A Jewish Wedding": "Evreiskoe venchanie";
"Regimental Inspection": "Smotr";

both in *Leonid Kannegiser*; stat'i Georgiia Adamovicha, M.A. Aldanova, Georgiia Ivanova; iz posmertnykh stikhov Leonida Kannegisera, 77, 80–81. Paris, 1928.

Mikhail Gershenzon
Preface to *Jewish Anthology*: "Predislovie," in *Evreiskaia antologiia: Sbornik molodoi evreiskoi poezii*, ed. V.F. Khodasevich and L.B. Iaffe, 1st ed., v–viii. Moscow: Izdatel'stvo "Safrut," [1918];
in *Evreiskaia antologiia: Sbornik molodoi evreiskoi poezii*, **ed. V.F. Khodasevich and L.B. Iaffe, 3rd ed., 5–8. Berlin: Izdatel'stvo S.D. Zal'tsman, 1922.**

Elisheva
"Eretz-Israel": "Erez-Israel";
"I won't light a candle at the Sabbath hour . . . ": "V subbotnii chas mne svech ne zazhigat.' . .";

both in **E. Lisheva, *Tainye pesni: Stikhotvoreniia*, 14–15, 16. Moscow: Gatsida, 1919.**

Valentin Parnakh
"I will make your heaven as iron . . .": "Nebo vashe sdelaiu, kak zhelezo . . .";
"Deportees" (1914–1917): "Vyslannye, (1914–1917)" in Valentin Parnakh, *Vstuplenie k tantsam. Izbrannye stikhi*, 36. Moscow, 1925;
"Sabbetaians": "Sabbateiantsy," in Valentin Parnakh, *Vstuplenie k tantsam. Izbrannye stikhi*, 50. Moscow, 1925;
all three in **Valentin Parnakh, *Karabkaetsia akrobat*, 20, 30, 46. Paris: Izd-vo "Franko-russkaia pechat'," 1922.**

Ilya Selvinsky
"Bar Kokhba": in *Molodaia gvardiia* 9 (1924): 106–10;
in **Il'ia Sel'vinskii, *Rannii Sel'vinskii*, 212–24. Moscow–Leningrad: Gosudarstvennoe izdatel'stvo, 1929.**

Osip Mandelstam
"Slip back into your mother, Leah . . .": "Vernis' v smesitel'noe lono . . .";

"One Alexander Herzovich . . .": "Zhil Aleksandr Gertsevich, evreiskii muzykant . . .";
"Say, desert geometer, shaper . . .": "Skazhi mne, chertezhnik pustyni . . .";

all three in **O.E. Mandel'shtam, *Sobranie sochinenii*, ed. G.P. Struve and B.A. Filippov, vol. 1, 77, 162–63, 201. Moscow: Terra, 1991**;
all three in O. Mandel'shtam, *Polnoe sobranie stikhotvorenii*, ed. A.G. Mets, 149, 198, 229. St. Petersburg: Akademicheskii proekt, 1997;
English translation by Maxim D. Shrayer and J.B. Sisson, "Slip back into your mother, Leah. . . ," "Say, desert geometer, shaper. . . ," "One Alexander Herzovich. . . ," *AGNI* 55 (Spring 2002): 172–74;

"Judaic Chaos": "Khaos iudeiskii," in *Shum vremeni*, **O.E. Mandel'shtam, *Sobranie sochinenii*, ed. G.P. Struve and B.A. Filippov, vol. 2, 65–71. Moscow: Terra, 1991**.

Vladimir Lidin
"Jewish Luck": "Evreiskoe schast'e," in **Vladimir Lidin, *Myshinye budni*, 53–62. Moscow–Berlin: Gelikon, 1923.**

Lev Lunts
"Native Land": "Rodina," in *Evreiskii al'manakh*, **ed. B.I. Kaufman and I.A. Kleinman, 27–43. Petrograd–Moscow: Knigoizdatel'stvo Petrograd, 1923**;
in Lev Lunts, *Vne zakona*, ed. M. Vainshtein, 13–24. St. Petersburg: Kompozitor, 1994;
English translation by Gary Kern in *The Serapion Brothers: A Critical Anthology*, ed. Gary Kern and Christopher Collins, 35–45. Ann Arbor, MI: Ardis, 1975.

Veniamin Kaverin
"Shields (and Candles)": "Schity (i svechi)," in **Veniamin Kaverin, *Mastera i podmaster'ia*, 37–47. Moscow–Petersburg: Krug, 1923**;
English translation by Gary Kern in *Russian Literature of the Twenties: An Anthology*, ed. by Carl R. Proffer et al., 141–48. Ann Arbor, MI: Ardis, 1987.

Ilya Ehrenburg
From *Julio Jurenito*: in **Il'ia Erenburg, *Neobychainye pokhozhdeniia Khulio Khurenito i ego uchenikov. . . , 121–27. Moscow–Berlin: Gelikon, 1922**;
English translation by Anna Bostock in collaboration with Yvonne Kapp, in Ilya Ehrenburg, *Julio Jurenito*, 110–16. London: McGibbon and Kee, 1958.

Andrey Sobol
"The Count": "Schet," in **Andrei Sobol', *Kniga malen'kikh rasskazov: 1922–1925 gg.*, 51–61. Moscow: Moskovskoe tovarishchestvo pisatelei, 1925.**

Viktor Shklovsky
From *Zoo, or Letters Not about Love*: in **Viktor Shklovskii, *Zoo, ili pis'ma ne o liubvi*, 33–36, 50–52, 93–95. Berlin: Gelikon, 1923**;
English translation by Richard Sheldon in *Zoo, or Letters Not about Love*, 27–30, 44–46, 90–93. Ithaca: Cornell University Press, 1971.

Matvey Royzman
"Kol Nidre": "Kol Nidrei," in **Matvei Roizman, *Khevronskoe vino*, 3–12. Moscow: Vserossiiskii soiuz poetov, 1923**;

in *Poety-imazhinisty*, ed. E.M. Shneiderman, 375–79. St. Petersburg: Peterburgskii pisatel', 1997; Moscow: Agraf, 1997.

Isaac Babel

"The Rebbe's Son": "Syn rabbi," *Krasnaia nov'* 1 (1924): 69–71; "Awakening": "Probuzhdenie," in *Molodaia gvardiia* 17–18 (1931): 13–16; both in Isaak Babel', *Sochineniia*, ed. A.N. Pirozhkova, 2 vols. Vol. 2, 128–29, 171–78. Moscow: Khudozhestvennaia literatura, 1991–92; English translation by David McDuff in Isaac Babel, *Collected Stories*, 225–27, 59–67. Harmondsworth: Penguin, 1994.

Iosif Utkin

From *The Tale of Red-Headed Motele, Mr. Inspector, Rabbi Isaiah, and Commissar Blokh*: *Povest' o ryzhem Motele, gospodine inspektore, ravvine Isaie i komissare Blokh*, in **Iosif Utkin, Pervaia kniga stikhov, 2nd ed., 97–99. Moscow–Leningrad: Gosudarstvenoe izdatel'stvo, 1927;** in Iosif Utkin, *Povest' o ryzhem Motele, gospodine inspektore, ravvine Isaie i komissare Blokh*, 19–21. Moscow: OGIZ–Molodaia gvardiia, 1933; in Iosif Utkin, *Stikhotvoreniia i poemy*, 194–97. Moscow: Gosudarstvennoe izdatel'stvo khudozhestvennoi literatury, 1958.

Elizaveta Polonskaya

"Shop of Splendors": "Lavochka velikolepii"; "Enkounter": "Vstrecha";

both in **Elizaveta Polonskaia, Upriamyi kalendar', 77–79, 87–89. Leningrad: Izdatel'stvo pisatelei, 1929;**

"Encounter," untitled, in *Goda. Izbrannye stikhi*, 89–91. Leningrad: Izdatel'stvo pisatelei, 1935.

Yury Libedinsky

From *The Commissars*: *Komissary*, in **Iurii Libedinskii, *Komissary*, 2nd ed., 3–10. Leningrad: Priboi, 1926.**

Vera Inber

"The Nightingale and the Rose": "Solovei i roza," in *Prozhektor* 11 (1925): 15–18; in **Vera Inber, *Solovei i roza. Rasskazy*, 7–18. Kharkov: Proletarii, 1928;** in Vera Inber, *Izbrannye proizvedeniia*, 2 vols. Vol. 2, 7–13. Moscow: Gosudarstvennoe izdatel'stvo khudozhestvennoi literatury, 1955.

Mark Tarlovsky

"This Path": "Etot put'," in **Mark Tarlovskii, *Ironicheskii sad*, 24–28. Moscow–Leningrad: "Zemlia i fabrika," 1928.**

Mikhail Kozakov

From *A Man Is Brought to His Knees*: *Chelovek, padaiushchii nits*, in **Mikhail Kozakov, Chelovek, padaiushchii nits, 54–64. Leningrad: Priboi, 1930; reprinted Tel Aviv: Effect Publications, [1980].**

Viktor Fink
From *Jews on the Land*: "Propovedniki" and "Novaia kul'tura," both in **Viktor Fink, *Evrei na zemle*, 176–96. Moscow–Leningrad: Gosudarstvennoe izdatel'stvo, 1929.**

Semyon Kirsanov
"R": "Bukva R," in Semen Kirsanov, *Slovo predostavliaetsia Kirsanovu*. Moscow: Gosudarstvennoe izdatel'stvo, 1930;
in Semen Kirsanov, *Iskaniia*, **14–16. Moscow: Khudozhestvennaia literatura, 1967**;
English translation by Maxim D. Shrayer and J.B. Sisson, "The Letter 'R,'" *Sí Señor* 2 (Winter 2003): 40–43.

Eduard Bagritsky
"Origin": "Proiskhozhdenie," *Novyi mir* 11 (1930): 108;
in Eduard Bagritskii, *Pobediteli*, 3. Moscow: GIKhL, 1930;
in Eduard Bagritskii, *Stikhotvoreniia i poemy*, ed. E.P. Liubareva and S.A. Kovalenko, 107–8. Moscow: Sovetskii pisatel', 1964;
in **Eduard Bagritskii, *Stikhotvoreniia*, ed. G.A. Morev, 88–90. St. Petersburg: Akademicheskii proekt, 2000**;
English transaltion by Maxim D. Shrayer, "Origin," *AGNI* 52 (2000), 221–23;

From *February*: *Fevral'*, in ***Eduard Bagritskii. Al'manakh*, ed. Vladimir Narbut, 123–44. Moscow: Sovetskii pisatel', 1936**;
in Eduard Bagritskii, *Stikhotvoreniia i poemy*, ed. E.P. Liubareva and S.A. Kovalenko, 203–21. Moscow: Sovetskii pisatel', 1964;
in Eduard Bagritskii, *Stikhotvoreniia*, ed. G.A. Morev, 151–74. St. Petersburg: Akademicheskii proekt, 2000;
English translation by Maxim D. Shrayer, in Maxim D. Shrayer, *Russian Poet/Soviet Jew: The Legacy of Eduard Bagritskii*, 25; 27–30; 36–36. Lanham, MD: Rowman and Littlefield, 2000.

Ilya Ilf
"The Prodigal Son Retuns Home": "Bludnyi syn vozvrashchaetsia domoi," in *Ogonek* 2 (15 January 1930): 10;
in **Il'ia Il'f and Evgenii Petrov, *Neobyknovennye istorii iz zhizni goroda Kololanska*, ed. Mikhail Dolinskii, 209–11. Moscow: Knizhnaia palata, 1989.**

Ilya Ilf and Evgeny Petrov
From *The Golden Calf*: "Zolotoi telenok," in Il'ia Il'f, Evgenii Petrov, ***Novye pokhozhdeniia Ostapa Bendera: kniga vtoraia romana "Zolotoi telenok,"* 140–52. Riga: Zhizn' i kul'tura, 1931**;
in Il'ia Il'f, Evgenii Petrov, *Dvenadtsat' stul'ev. Zolotoi telenok*, 566–76. Kiev: Radian'skii pis'mennik, 1957;
in Il'ia Il'f i Evgenii Petrov, *Zolotoi telenok*, ed. M. Odesskii and D. Fel'dman, 299–307. Moscow: Vagrius, 2000.

Mark Egart
From *Scorched Land*: *Opalennaia zemlia*, in **Mark Egart, *Opalennaia zemlia: kniga vtoraia*, 25–40. Moscow: Sovetskii pisatel', 1934**;
in Mark Egart, *Opalennaia zemlia*, 171–86. Moscow: Sovetskii pisatel', 1937 (with significant modifications).

Arkady Shteynberg
"David awoke in an unfamiliar bedroom . . .": "David prosnulsia. . . ," in *Arion* **1 (1997): 45–46;**
"One night I saw the Black Sea in a dream . . . ": "Ia videl more Chernoe vo sne. . . ," in **Arkadii Shteinberg,** *K verkhov'iam,* **254–55. Moscow: Soglasie, 1997.**

Emigrations: 1917–1967

Vladislav Khodasevich
"Not my mother but a Tula peasant woman . . .": "Ne mater'iu, no tul'skoiu krest'iankoi. . . ,"
in Vladislav Khodasevich, *Tiazhelaia lira: Chetvertaia kniga stikhov, 1920–1922,* 21–22.
Moscow–Petrograd: Gosudarstvennoe izdatel'stvo, 1922;
in Vladislav Khodasevich, *Tiazhelaia lira: Chetvertaia kniga stikhov,* 10–11. Berlin-Petrograd:
Izdatel'stvo Z.I. Grzhebina, 1923;
in Vladislav Khodasevich, *Sobranie stikhov,* 68–69. Paris: Vozrozhdenie, 1927;
in Vladislav Khodasevich, *Sobranie stikhov (1913–1939),* ed. Nina Berberova, 66. New Haven, CT: N. Berberova, 1961;
in Vladislav Khodasevich, *Sobranie stikhov v dvukh tomakh,* ed. Iurii Kolker, vol. 1, 134–35.
Paris: La Presse Libre, 1983;

"In Moscow I was born. I never . . .": "Ia rodilsia v Moskve. Ia dyma . . . ;"

both in Vladislav Khodasevich, *Sobranie stikhov v drukh tomakh,* ed. Iurii Kolker, vol. 2, 78.
Paris: La Presse Libre, 1983 (incomplete version of second poem);
both in **Vladislav Khodasevich,** *Sobranie stikhov,* **ed. A. Dorofeev and A. Lavrin, 158–59, 365. Moscow: Tsenturion Interpaks, 1992;**
both in Vladislav Khodasevich, *Stikhotvoreniia,* ed. Dzhon [John] Malmstad, 85–86, 163–64.
St. Petersburg: Akademicheskii proekt, 2001.

Mark Aldanov
"The Assassination of Uritsky": "Ubiistvo Uritskogo," in *Leonid Kannegiser,* **7–37. Paris, 1928;**
in M.A. Aldanov, *Sobranie sochinenii v shesti tomakh,* ed. Andrei Chernyshev, 486–516. Moscow: Pravda, 1991 (significantly longer version).

Evgeny Shklyar
"Shield of David, crescent or ikon . . .": "Pred shchitom-li Davida, pred sviatoi-li ikonoi. . . ,"
in **Evgenii Shkliar,** *Ogni na vershinakh. Tret'ia kniga liriki,* **14. Berlin: Otto Kirschner, 1923;**

"Where's Home?": "Gde dom?" in **Evgenii Shkliar,** *Posokh. V sbornik stikhov,* **48. Riga, 1925;**

English translation by Andrew von Hendy and Maxim D. Shrayer, in *Bee Museum* 3 (2005): 83–85.

Dovid Knut
"I, Dovid-Ari ben Meir . . .": "Ia, Dovid-Ari ben Meir . . . ," in Dovid Knut, *Moikh tysiacheletii,* 7–10. Paris: K-vo Ptitselov, [1925];

"A Kishinev Burial": "Kishinevskie pokhorony," in Dovid Knut, *Parizhskie nochi*, 35–39. Paris: Izd-vo "Rodnik," 1932 (published as untitled);

"Haifa": "Khaifa";
"Tsfat";
"The Land of Israel": "Zemlia izrail'skaia";

all five in Dovid Knut, *Izbrannye stikhi*, 9–11; 107–10; 171–72; 175–76; 181–82. Paris, 1949; all five in **Dovid Knut, *Sobranie sochinenii v dvukh tomakh*, ed. V[ladimir] Khazan, vol. 1, 77–78, 159–61, 199, 200, 202–3. Jerusalem: The Hebrew University of Jerusalem, 1997.**

Don-Aminado
"Autumn in the Provinces": "Provintsiia," in **Don-Aminado, *Nakinuv plashch: Sbornik liricheskoi satiry*, 64–66. Paris: Knigoizdatel'stvo "Neskuchnyi sad," 1928.**

Raisa Blokh
"A snatch of speech came floating on the air . . .": "Prinesla sluchainaia molva . . .";
"How can I find you again, holy names . . .": "Kak mne vernut'sia k vam, sviatye imena . . .," in Raisa Blokh, *Zdes' shumiat chuzhie goroda*, 90. Moscow: Izograf, 1996; both in Raisa Blokh, Mikhail Gorlin, *Izbrannye stikhotvoreniia*, 39, 44. Paris: Rifma/Izdatel'stvo imeni Iriny Iassen, 1959;

"Remember, father would stand . . .": "Pomnish', otets, byvalo . . . ," in *Nevod. Tretii sbornik stikhov berlinskikh poetov*, 63. Berlin: Slovo, 1933;
in Raisa Blokh, *Zdes' shumiat chuzhie goroda*, 89. Moscow: Izograf, 1996;

all three in **Raisa Blokh, *Tishina: Stikhi 1928–1934*, 47, 52, 53. Berlin: Petropolis, 1935.**

Anna Prismanova
"Grandmother": "Babushka";
"Eyes": "Glaza";
"Shine": "Sianie," in *Russkie zapiski* 14 (1939): 73–74, part two of the three-part cycle "Pepel";

all three in Anna Prismanova, *Bliznetsy*, 17, 58–59, 28. Paris: Izdatel'stvo Ob"edineniia poetov i pisatelei, 1946;
in **Anna Prismanova, *Sobranie sochinenii*, ed. Petra Couvée, 45, 51, 69–70. The Hague: Luexenhoff Publishing, 1990** (dedication appears in *Bliznetsy*).

Sofia Dubnova-Erlich
"Shtetl": "Mestechko," in *Novosel'e* 3 (1943): 64–67;
"Scorched Hearth": "Na pepelishche," in *Novosel'e* 11 (1944): 70–73.

Sofia Pregel
"Pharaoh's Daughter": "Doch' faraona";
"In the Ghetto": "V getto";
"You Shall Not Forget": "Vy pripomnite";

all three in **Sofiia Pregel', *Berega. Chetvertaia kniga stikhov*, 95, 98, 92–93. Paris: Novosel'e, 1953.**

Yuly Margolin
From *A Jewish Tale*, "The Exodus from Poland": "Iskhod iz Pol'shi" and "On the Way," "V doroge" in **Iulii Margolin, *Evreiskaia povest'*, 121–39. Tel Aviv: Maaian, 1960.**

Andrey Sedykh
From *The Promised Land*: "If I forget you, O Jerusalem . . .": "Esli ia zabudu tebia, Ierusalim. . . ," in **Andrei Sedykh, *Zemlia obetovannaia*, 144–58. New York: [Novoe russkoe slovo], 1966.**

War and Terror: 1939–1953

Boris Yampolsky
From *Country Fair:* "Mr. Dykhes and Others": "Gospodin Dykhes i drugie," in Boris Iampol'skii, *Iarmarka, Krasnaia nov'* 3 (March 1941): 34–87;
in **Boris Iampol'skii, *Iarmarka*, 128–54. Moscow: Sovetskii pisatel', 1942**;
in Boris Iampol'skii, *Arbat, rezhimnaia ulitsa*, ed. Vladimir Prikhod'ko, 321–41. Moscow: Vagrius, 1997.

Ilya Ehrenburg
"Rachels, Hayims, and Leahs wander . . .": "Brodiat Rakhili, Khaimy, Lii . . .";
"Because remembrance of Esther's sultry midday . . .": "Za to, chto znoi poludennyi Esfiri . . .";
"To this ghetto people will not come . . .": "V eto getto liudi ne pridut . . .";
"Babi Yar": "Babii Iar," in *Novyi mir* 1 (1945): 16 (published as untitled);
all four in Il'ia Erenburg, *Staryi skorniak i drugie proizvedeniia*, ed. M. Vainshtein, 2 vols. Vol. 1, 350, 352, 353, 353–54. Jerusalem, 1983;
all four in **Il'ia Erenburg, *Stikhotvoreniia*, ed. B. Ia. Frezinskii, 482, 513, 513, 512. St. Petersburg: Akademicheskii proekt, 2000**;

"To the Jews": "Evreiam";
"Jews": "Evrei";
"The Triumph of a Man": "Torzhestvo cheloveka";
all three in **Il'ia Erenburg, *Staryi skorniak i drugie proizvedeniia*, ed. M. Vainshtein, 2 vols. Vol. 2, 251–52, 253–55, 271–75. Jerusalem, 1983.**

Vassily Grossman
"The Old Teacher": "Staryi uchitel'," in *Znamia* 7–8 (1943): 95–110;
in Vasilii Grossman, *Staryi uchitel': povesti i rasskazy*. Moscow: Sovetskii pisatel', 1962; 472–500.
in Vasilii Grossman, *Na evreiskie temy: Izbrannoe v dvukh tomakh*, vol. 1, 111–43. Jerusalem: Biblioteka "Aliia," 1985.

Margarita Aliger
"To a Jewish Girl": "Evreiskoi devushke," in *Znamia* 3 (1940): 7–8;
in **Margarita Aliger, *Kamni i travy*, 38–39. Moscow: Sovetskii pisatel', 1940**;

From *Your Victory*: Tvoia pobeda (chap. 18), in *Znamia* 9 (1945): 16–17;
in Margarita Aliger, *Tvoia pobeda*, 55–61. Moscow: Sovetskii pisatel', 1946;
in **Margarita Aliger, *Izbrannoe*, 176–80. Moscow: Sovetskii pisatel', 1947**;

in *Stikhotvoreniia i poemy*, 2 vols. Vol. 1, 259–64. Moscow: Khudozhestvennaia literatura, 1970; in *Sobranie sochinenii v trekh tomakh*, vol. 1, 354–58. Moscow: Khudozhestvennaia literatura, 1984.

Lev Ozerov

"Babi Yar": "Babii Iar," in *Oktiabr'* 3/4 (1946): 160–63; in **Lev Ozerov, *Liven'*, ed. P. Antokol'skii, 25–32. Moscow: Molodaia gvardiia, 1947**; in Lev Ozerov, *Lirika: Izbrannye stikhotvoreniia*, 25–32. Moscow: Sovetskii pisatel', 1966.

Pavel Antokolsky

"Death Camp": "Lager' unichtozheniia," in *Znamia* 10 (1945): 34; in **Pavel Antokol'skii, *Izbrannoe*, 174–76. Moscow: Molodaia gvardiia, 1946**; in Pavel Antokol'skii, *Sobranie sochinenii*, 4 vols. Vol. 2, 81–82. Moscow: Khudozhestvennaia literatura, 1971.

Yury German

From *Lieutenant Colonel of the Medical Corps*: *Podpolkovnik meditsinskoi sluzhby*, in Iurii German, *Podpolkovnik meditsinskoi sluzhby*, 109–116. Leningrad: Sovetskii pisatel', 1956. in Iurii German, *Podpolkovnik meditsinskoi sluzhby. Nachalo. Butsefal. Lapshin. Zhmakin. Vospominaniia*, 110–17. Leningrad: Sovetskii pisatel', 1968; in **Iurii German, *Podpolkovnik meditsinskoi sluzhby*, 107–14. Moscow: Sovetskii pisatel' 1972**; in Iurii German, *Podpolkovnik meditsinskoi sluzhby*, 110–116. Moscow: ACT/Olimp, 2001.

Boris Pasternak

"In the Lowlands": "V nizov'iakh," in Boris Pasternak, *Zemnoi prostor: stikhi*, 41. Moscow: Sovetskii pisatel', 1945; "Odessa"; both in **Boris Pasternak, *Stikhotvoreniia i poemy*, ed. L.A. Ozerov, 422–23, 568–69. Moscow–Leningrad: Sovetskii pisatel', 1965**;

From *Doctor Zhivago*, in **Boris Pasternak, *Doktor Zhivago: roman*, 19–24, 140–45. Paris: Société d'Edition et d'Impression Mondiale, 1959**; English translation by Max Hayward and Manya Harari, in Boris Pasternak, *Doctor Zhivago*, 12–16, 118–23. New York: Pantheon, 1958.

OUTLINE OF JEWISH-RUSSIAN HISTORY

PART I: 1772–1953

John D. Klier

The Jews did not come to Russia; Russia came to the Jews during the partitions of 1772, 1793, and 1795. Through the forcible annexation of large portions of the Polish–Lithuanian Commonwealth—the lands that today comprise all or part of the states of Poland, Belarus, Ukraine, and Lithuania—the Russian Empire acquired the largest Jewish population in the world, almost one million people. Bessarabia, the present state of Moldova, was acquired in 1815. Before 1772, Jews had been barred from even entering the Russian Empire, as the Russian empress Elizabeth Petrovna perceived them as "the enemies of Christ," who would work spiritual and physical harm upon her subjects. Ironically, one of the foremost servitors of her father, Peter the Great, was Baron Pyotr Shafirov, the scion of a converted Jewish family. Settlements of Jews in classical times actually predated the Slav presence in eastern Europe. The first Slavic state, Kievan Rus, had paid tribute to the Khazars, a Turkic people who were converts to Judaism and who participated in the legendary debate surrounding the choice of a monotheistic religion, Orthodox Christianity, by Kiev's Grand Prince Vladimir in 988.

At the time of the late-eighteenth-century annexations, Russia was ruled by the tolerant Empress Catherine II ("The Great"). In her first act regarding the Jews in 1772, Empress Catherine recognized their usefulness as a mercantile population by guaranteeing them all the rights they had enjoyed under Polish rule. The key to Jewish life in Poland–Lithuania was the exercise of communal autonomy. As long as it fulfilled its

John D. Klier is Corob Professor of Modern Jewish History in the Department of Hebrew and Jewish Studies at University College London. Among his numerous publications on the history of Russian Jewry are *Russia Gathers Her Jews: The Origins of the Jewish Question in Russia, 1772–1825* (DeKalb, IL, 1986) and *Imperial Russia's Jewish Question, 1855–1881* (Cambridge, 1996).

fiscal obligations to the state, each legally constituted local Jewish community, or *kahal*, was allowed extensive self-government. Jewish society within the *kahal* was governed by religious traditions and cultural values that had evolved over centuries and were safeguarded and enforced by voluntary bodies known as fellowships (the *hevrah*; pl. *hevrot*). The *hevrot* oversaw communal welfare, such as assistance to the poor, and religious devotion, such as the upkeep of synagogues and study houses. The variety and importance of these institutions were without equal elsewhere in Europe.

Judaism assigned distinct roles to women and men, awarding a higher status to the latter in terms of worship and in the central obligation to study Torah—broadly conceived, the body of Jewish sacred texts and commentaries written in Hebrew and Aramaic. A network of private schools (the *heder*), each led by a teacher (the *melamed*), provided primary religious instruction for all Jewish males. A community with higher aspirations might also have supported a center for more advanced study, a yeshiva, and the Lithuanian lands became famous for theirs. While women were not educated to study the sacred texts, many were literate. A body of secular and religious materials in the Yiddish vernacular served their needs.

The period of the partitions witnessed the rise of a mass religious movement, Hassidism, inspired by the semi-legendary religious leader Israel ben Eliezer, the Ba'al Shem Tov (the *BeShT*, c. 1700–1760). Hassidic doctrine emphasized ecstatic prayer and the leading role of a religious leader known as a *tzaddik*, whose status was determined not by his learning and legal skills but by his charismatic personality. At the turn of the eighteenth century, east European Jewry was plagued by a religious civil war between the adherents of Hassidism and their opponents, the so-called Mitnagdim. Hassidism had the largest number of adherents in the Ukraine and Belorussia, while its strongest foes were in Lithuania.

Jews had initially been invited to settle in the region in the Middle Ages by Polish kings who hoped to benefit from their trade and commercial acumen. After 1569, Polish noblemen received large landholdings in the newly colonized Ukraine. They succeeded in binding the peasantry to the land and imposing a feudal economy in which Jews played a major role as agents, serving in the capacity of estate managers and leaseholders of the numerous feudal privileges possessed by the nobility, in particular the monopoly on the distillation and sale of spirits. The large landowners (the magnates) offered land to Jews for settlement. The typical settlement became the small Jewish market town, or shtetl, a distinctive feature of Jewish life in eastern Europe.

Jewish prosperity was tied to the welfare of Poland–Lithuania as a whole. Jews thrived during the buoyant years of the sixteenth and early seventeenth centuries, when east European grain was an important resource for the rest of Europe, and in turn experienced economic distress when the Polish–Lithuanian Commonwealth suffered political and economic decline due to the rise of powerful and aggressive neighbors such as Russia, Sweden, and Prussia.

When Russian rulers first encountered the Jews in 1772, they sought to use their mercantile abilities and granted them extensive trade and commercial rights. Gradually, Russian officials became aware of the additional role played by Jews as middlemen in the village, especially as tavern keepers, which they identified as exploitation of the peasantry. The perception of the Jews as a harmful economic force caused the Russian state to restrict Jewish movement within the empire through laws that created a Jewish "Pale of Settlement" in the northwestern and southwestern provinces and barred most Jews from residence in the Russian interior. The Pale was variously strengthened and relaxed throughout the nineteenth century, but it endured until the outbreak of war in 1914.

Russian administrators also looked to the experience of western states. The dominant assumption of eighteenth-century Enlightenment thinkers was that the Jews were religious fanatics whose beliefs alienated them from all non-Jews. It was said that Jews employed their mercantile skills to deceive and exploit their peasant neighbors. The western solution to the "Jewish Question" thus lay in reducing Jewish fanaticism through education and eliminating exploitation by directing the Jews into productive work. Russian officials sought to follow this western lead, most famously through the work of the Jewish Committee of 1802–4 and in the Statute for the Jews of 1804. Falling short of extending all civil liberties to the Jews, the 1804 statute allowed them to enter all Russian state educational institutions and offered various privileges to Jews who undertook agriculture or manufacturing. The statute also attempted to re-settle Jews from the countryside into nearby towns, an initiative that was unsuccessful but that nonetheless caused much economic dislocation and distress for the Jews.

Russian attempts to reform the Jewish population were aided by a small group of Jews eager to assist. These were the followers of the Haskalah, the Jewish version of the European-wide Enlightenment movement of the eighteenth century. The Haskalah took many forms, but its key element in eastern Europe was a belief in the need for Jews to move away from the exclusive study of Jewish texts. By learning from the "wisdom of the Gentiles," they believed, Jews could engage with the modern world. The followers of Haskalah, known as the *maskilim*, hoped to turn the Jews into a productive class, especially by directing them into agriculture. The language of the western Haskalah was German; forced by necessity, east European *maskilim* had to use the language of the masses, Yiddish, a Germanic language with Hebrew, Slavic, and Romance additions that was derided by intellectuals as a nonliterary "jargon." *Maskilim* in eastern Europe, such as Isaac Ber Levinson (1788–1860) were confident, with some justification, that Russian officials shared their goals. The mass of east European Jews, on the contrary, scorned the *maskilim* and considered the government initiatives to be little more than attempts at conversion or persecution.

Jewish traditionalists saw this view validated by the policies that marked the reign of Tsar Nicholas I. Nicholas ordered the drafting of Jews into the Russian army in 1827, ending a previous exemption. Jewish communities were required to choose the recruits themselves and were allowed to draft boys between the ages of 11 and 17;

community officials who did not meet their recruitment targets could be drafted themselves. These boys entered special "cantonist schools" for preliminary training before beginning their twenty-five-year term of active service. Although not the original intent of the policy—Nicholas believed the harsh discipline of the army could correct the perceived shortcomings of the Jews—military commanders conducted missionary activity among the recruits, often using coercive methods, and it is estimated that one-third, about 25,000, of Jewish recruits were converted to Christianity. Upon completion of their term of service, "Nicholas's soldiers," as they were called, did receive certain benefits, such as the right to reside outside the Pale. Military recruitment was just part of a wider scheme to "make the Jews more productive." Nicholas also encouraged agricultural colonization (without much success) and imposed restrictions upon those he saw as "unproductive" Jews. Nicholas abolished the *kahal* system in 1844, ostensibly to promote Jewish integration, but this goal might have been better served by abolishing the Pale of Settlement. Nicholas also placed restrictions on traditional Jewish dress.

One of Nicholas's most interesting reforms was motivated by a desire to wean the Jews from what Russians saw as "religious fanaticism." This reform was devised by a high-level committee, headed by Count P.D. Kisilev after its creation in 1840, called the Committee to Develop Measures for a Fundamental Transformation of the Jews. In 1844 Nicholas ordered the creation of a state-sponsored Jewish school system designed to rival the traditional heders and yeshivas. The state Jewish school system, which numbered about one hundred institutions, met great resistance in the Jewish communities, which viewed it as a direct threat to Judaism and its traditions, and only enrolled some five thousand students. The schools nevertheless opened the way for some Jews to enter the mainstream of Russian culture and society, with graduates moving into journalism and the legal and medical professions. The system educated the pioneer creators and consumers of Jewish literature in Russian, who may collectively be called the Jewish-Russian intelligentsia. The same drive toward modernity led other writers to create a modern Jewish literature in other languages: Avraham Mapu, Peretz Smolenskin, and Reuben Asher Braudes in modern Hebrew, S.Y. Abramovich (Mendele Mokher Sefarim) in Hebrew and Yiddish; and Shalom Rabinovich (Sholem Aleichem) and Isaac Leyb Perets in Yiddish.

The reality of acculturation, symbolized by the Jewish-Russian intelligentsia, was mirrored in the Jewish population as a whole; it was not motivated by ideology but was generated by the processes of modernization. The decisive date was 1861, when the Russian serfs—peasants who were bound to the land and virtually the slaves of the landowners—were emancipated. The social changes associated with emergent capitalism produced new ideologies, variously calling for liberal democracy or socialism. The Russian government was slow to respond to the need to create new political and legal systems, resulting in the rise of political dissent and revolutionary activism, including terrorism.

Jews were directly influenced by the social, economic, and political changes that were taking place around them. The abolition of serfdom made superfluous the role of Jews as middlemen; the creation of a rail network put many Jewish teamsters and innkeepers out of work; the reorganization of the spirit trade reduced the role of the Jewish tavern keeper. At the same time, industrialization created jobs for Jewish factory workers, although often under brutal conditions. These changes encouraged a movement of Jews from the countryside and the shtetl to the new industrial centers of Odessa, Warsaw, and Lołz. But Jews, like non-Jews, found that industry did not grow rapidly enough to absorb Russia's surplus labor. The Jewish population of the Russian Empire in particular increased fivefold between 1800 and 1900, numbering over five million in the first national Russian census of 1897.

In 1881, in the unsettled atmosphere following the assassination of Emperor Alexander II, a series of anti-Jewish riots, or pogroms, broke out in the southwestern provinces of the empire in major centers like Kiev and Elizavetgrad (present-day Kirovohrad). In its efforts to control this popular violence, the government reversed the policies designed to promote Jewish integration that it had followed for over seventy-five years: the so-called May Laws of 1882 endeavored to restrict Jews from residence in the countryside, and quotas were imposed upon Jewish access to higher education and to the professions. The pogroms and legal restrictions intensified the trend of Jewish out-migration already generated by poverty, and by 1914 over two million Jews had left the empire to settle in the Americas, Europe, South Africa, and Palestine.

Some acculturated Jews, such as the sculptor Mark Antokolsky, the painter Isaac Levitan, and the composer Anton Rubinstein, made notable contributions to modern Russian culture. Yet no phenomenon reveals the extent of Jewish acculturation in the late empire as much as the participation of Jews in the Russian revolutionary movement. Specialists differ as to why Jews were overrepresented in all branches of the movement, even as the mass of Jews remained politically quiescent. Revolutionaries of Jewish descent played active, even leadership roles in the revolutionary struggle: the populist (*narodnik*) theoretician Mark Natanson, the Socialist-Revolutionary Party leader Gregory Gershuni, the Menshevik leader Yuly Martov, the Bundists Arkady Kremer and Vladimir Medem, and, most famously, Leon Trotsky, who became one of Lenin's closest collaborators, the director of the revolution in Petrograd, and the founder of the Red Army. Before 1917, the tsarist government depicted the Jews as the carriers of revolution into Russia and encouraged the extremist Right to make Jews the target of physical and verbal attacks. In contrast to Jewish socialists, a tiny number of Jews, such as the banker Horace Ginzburg and the railway contractor Samuel Poliakov, became immensely rich capitalists. Playing to the right-wing obsession with Jewish conspiracies, officials of the Russian secret police fabricated the infamous "Protocols of the Learned Elders of Zion" (first published in 1903), purporting to reveal an international Jewish plot for world domination. After the Revolution of 1905, antisemitic groups, known collectively as the "Black Hundreds," carried out violent attacks on Jews.

The early twentieth century saw no improvement in the situation of the Jews. They were the target of pogroms in Kishinev in 1903 and throughout the revolutionary period of 1905–6. Jews derived little benefit from the creation of a constitutional monarchy following the October Manifesto (dated 17 October and issued by Nicholas II on 30 October 1905). There was little improvement in their legal position, and they were the object of hostile propaganda and provocations, most notably the trial of the Jew Mendel Beilis on a trumped-up charge of ritual murder in 1913. In contrast, liberal parties such as the Constitutional Democrats, some of whose leading members, notably Maxim Vinaver and Iosif Gessen, were Jewish, called for the grant of full civil rights to the Jews.

The immediate causes of the revolution that forced the abdication of Nicholas II on 15 March 1917 were the social and economic strains of the Great War and Russia's inability to capitalize on its natural advantages in manpower and resources. The Provisional Government that came to power in February/March 1917 attempted to reform the empire by promising land to the peasantry and satisfying the aspirations of national minorities, and one of its first actions was to remove all restrictions on the Jews, including restrictions on residence and education. The Provisional Government also actively—and unsuccessfully—continued the war. The failure of Russian arms and the delay of promised reforms undermined the Provisional Government's position and facilitated the October/November coup led by V.I. Lenin's Bolsheviks.

The Bolsheviks acted quickly to withdraw Russia from the war, to announce the distribution of land to the peasants, and to permit dissident national groups to secede from the empire. When the Great War ended in November 1918, Russia was consumed by a fierce civil war whose major participants were the Reds (the Bolsheviks and their left-wing allies), the Whites (the monarchist Volunteer Army), the Greens (peasant anarchists), as well as bandits, brigands, and various national armies (primarily in Ukraine). In the midst of the civil war, the new Soviet state also fought a war with Poland.

The Great War and the civil war were disastrous for the empire's Jewish population. Major Jewish settlements were located in the middle of the zone of conflict. Early in the war, Russian military commanders evicted large numbers of Jews, forcing them to move into the Russian interior. The civil war marked the complete breakdown of state authority. Marauding armies terrorized Jews, and also non-Jews, with pogroms, arson, and looting. For this reason, some Jews in the Pale welcomed the victory of the Red Army, while tens of thousands fled the country altogether. When the Reds triumphed in 1921–22, all the citizens of the Russian state, Jews and non-Jews, confronted a state whose economy was crippled and that was led by a small party of political radicals who were isolated from the rest of the world.

To paraphrase the famous joke, Soviet rule up to 1945 may be characterized as "good for the Jew, but bad for the Jews." In other words, Jews as individuals were able to participate in the economic development of the Soviet state and were offered sweeping opportunities for educational and social advancement. On the other hand, Judaism as a religion was almost destroyed, and traditional Jewish culture was demolished. The new Soviet state desperately needed personnel, or "cadres" in Soviet terminology, a resource that the Jews could provide. Any servitor of the old regime (bureaucrats, educators, and police and army personnel) was considered politically unreliable. Jews, a target of tsarist discrimination, were frequently viewed as reliable simply by virtue of being Jewish. This implicit loyalty was reinforced by the Whites' use of antisemitic propaganda against the Communists. Conveniently, many Jews possessed high levels of literacy and education, which were in short supply among the workers and peasants, the core supporters of the new Soviet state. Some Jews from other revolutionary parties, especially the Bund, were willing to throw in their lot with the victorious Bolsheviks. In the early twenties, therefore, Jews were well represented in the Communist Party, in the Soviet bureaucracy, in the officer corps of the Red Army, and in the ranks of the security forces and secret police. Many members of Lenin's first government, such as Lev Kamenev, Grigory Zinoviev, Yakov Sverdlov, and Leon Trotsky, were of Jewish descent. Their attitude to this "accident of birth" was well illustrated by a legendary meeting of Trotsky with a Jewish delegation that appealed to him for help on the basis of his Jewish origins. Trotsky corrected them: He was not a "Jew" but a "Social Democrat." In the future, antisemites would attribute Jewish support for the regime to Russophobia or to an alleged destructive, revolutionary spirit in Judaism. A more reasonable and unbiased explanation was that Jews, like other Soviet citizens, sought a livelihood in troubled times, since the war and revolution left the majority of Jews destitute.

Despite his own origins, Karl Marx had scant respect for the Jews, and classic Marxist dogma considered the Jews as little more than ethnic debris whose identity was created by discrimination and persecution. Once these disabilities were removed, it was assumed that Jews would assimilate into the majority population, and the "Jewish Question" would disappear. Reality intruded into this wishful thinking. In 1918 Russia had a Jewish population of over two and a half million persons. Jewish political parties, such as the socialist Bund and the vigorous Zionist parties, sought to mobilize Jewish identity. The new Soviet state responded by co-opting or abolishing these rivals and by granting the Jews the same prerogatives as the other national minorities that comprised the new Union of Soviet Socialist Republics created in 1923. The Jews were assigned an identity, *evrei*, defined as an east European national group (there being no such thing as "world Jewry" in Soviet eyes) with a common historical experience, a common Germanic language, Yiddish, and a common folk culture, expressed in music, art, and literature. The term *evrei* (Jew) is used in modern literary Russian primarily in reference to the ethnic and historical origin of the Jews, whereas *iudei* (Hebrew, "Judean") is used primarily in reference to the religious tradition of Judaism. Other segments of the Jewish population of the USSR, such as the Georgian-speaking Jews of the Caucasus, were either erroneously assigned to the same category as the Ashkenazic, Yiddish-speaking Jews or given a separate national identity altogether, as in the case of the so-called Mountain Jews, who spoke Judeo-Tat, a Hebrew-Persian language. Judaism and anything linked to it, such as the Bible and the Hebrew language, were decried as nonessential and counterrevolutionary. The recognition of the Jews as a national minority was of vital importance, for nationality was a central organizing principle of the new regime. Yet while *evrei* (ethnic Jews) were officially tolerated as a national minority, Judaism, Hebrew, and the millennia-old religious culture of the Jews was increasingly persecuted.

The regime recruited Jewish cadres "to bring the revolution to the Jewish street" by implementing the ideological program of Communism among the Jewish masses. For this purpose, special Jewish sections were created in the Party (the *Evsektsii*) and the state bureaucracy (the *Evkomy*). These institutions combated Jewish religious culture and created a network of Yiddish-language schools organized along the Communist principle of "national in form, socialist in content," which meant that, whatever the language, Soviet ideological guidelines had to be followed. Sympathetic writers were encouraged to publish in Yiddish, and a substantial body of Soviet Yiddish poetry and prose appeared, while Yiddish theatres operated in Moscow and major provincial centers. In the economic realm, the Soviet state sought to make the Jews more "productive" by encouraging agricultural colonization, largely with the assistance of foreign Jewish bodies such as Agro-Joint and ORT. By 1930, such programs had moved over 5 percent of the Soviet Jewish population into agriculture, most notably in the Crimea and the Ukraine.

Perhaps the most idiosyncratic move of the Soviet state in regard to the Jews as an ethnic group was the creation, in 1930, of a national territory for them in Birobidzhan, a remote and undeveloped territory on the Soviet–Chinese frontier. Despite efforts to resettle Jews in this region, Jews never constituted a majority of Birobidzhan's population, and the Jewish Autonomous Region always functioned more as an illusory Jewish "Potemkin village" than a Soviet Zion.

Having won the battle for leadership of the Communist Party in 1928, Stalin presided over a dramatic new program, later known as the First Five-Year Plan. It is best summarized as a program to modernize the national economy through total state control in order to produce unprecedented rates of growth. A parallel change was the forced reorganization of all peasants into collective farms, where they could be easily controlled and exploited by the regime. Economic centralization placed unprecedented power in the hands of the Communist Party, and Stalin used this accumulated power to purge all real or potential rivals within the Party through a series of dramatic show trials. The so-called Great Terror was extended to the general population. Tens of thousands were executed, while millions more were sent to corrective labor camps— the gulags.

Jews, like the Soviet population as a whole, were significantly transformed during the period from 1929 to 1939. The economic aspects of the tsarist-era "Jewish Question" were resolved, as Jews moved into all sectors of the USSR's modernizing economy. Culturally, a new generation of Soviet Jews emerged, well-acculturated Soviet citizens who also maintained a distinct Jewish identity, albeit one largely stripped of religious culture. In fact, Jews increasingly abandoned Yiddish and displayed high rates of intermarriage. By law, antisemitism was illegal, but it remained widespread among the general population.

During the 1930s, Stalin consolidated total political control over the Communist Party, the army, and the secret police. Although a number of prominent individuals of Jewish origin perished in the purges of high-ranking officials, including former Party leaders Lev Kamenev, Grigory Zinoviev, former secret police chief Genrikh Yagoda, and Red Army general Yona Yakir, the Great Terror of 1937–38 did not have a specifically anti-Jewish coloration.

The USSR was able to postpone war with Nazi Germany by signing a nonaggression pact with Hitler in 1939. The pact effectively divided eastern Europe into spheres of influence and allowed the USSR to occupy or annex eastern Poland, the Baltic states, and parts of Romania and Finland, all but the last of which had substantial Jewish populations. When Nazi Germany invaded the USSR in June 1941, the Jewish population in Soviet-controlled territories numbered over five million.

The war was a disaster for the Soviet population, and approximately twenty-five million Soviet citizens perished. The war was even more catastrophic for the Jews, as it provided the opportunity for the Nazis to implement their Final Solution—a high-priority effort to murder all the Jews of Europe. The Nazi program of mass shootings and mechanized slaughter numbered as many as two million Soviet Jews among the estimated six million Jewish victims of the Shoah. There was a substantial degree of participation in the mass murder by collaborators in the German-occupied territories, especially the Baltic states and the Ukraine.

Soviet Jews, however, were not merely passive victims. They served with distinction in the Red Army, and Jews were fifth among Soviet nationalities in the total number of wartime decorations received, far in excess of their percentage of the Soviet population. Jews also played a role on the propaganda front as journalists (Ilya Ehrenburg, Vassily Grossman) and broadcasters. Particularly successful was the Jewish Antifascist Committee (JAC), composed of prominent Jewish-Soviet cultural leaders, including the writers Dovid Bergelson, Der Nister (Pinhas Kahanovich), Perets Markish, and Itsik Fefer, and headed by the celebrated Yiddish actor Shloyme Mikhoels. The JAC publicized the Soviet war effort among Jewish groups abroad, sought support for a second front, and advocated financial and material aid to the USSR. The JAC accidentally became the "Jewish address" in the USSR, as Jews contacted its headquarters to seek help, to search for missing family members, or to report events on the home front, especially incidents of antisemitism.

At the end of the war, Jews, like the rest of the population, expected the Party to deliver on its war-time promises of reconstruction, the end of political repression, and a higher standard of living. Instead, the outbreak of political and ideological rivalry between the USSR and its western allies gave rise to the cold war. The Soviet government tightened ideological controls and censorship (particularly directed against anything Western), renewed political repression, and returned to the worst excesses of state economic planning.

The period of late Stalinism was especially ominous for Soviet Jews. The JAC, with its numerous links to the West, fell under suspicion. Mikhoels was murdered by the secret police in 1948, while the JAC was closed down and many of its leading members arrested. The Soviet anti-Western campaign made a special target of "rootless cosmopolitans," who lacked ideological loyalty and were not to be trusted. Jews were increasingly placed in this category, and many Jewish writers and critics working in Yiddish, Russian, and Ukrainian were repressed.

The Soviet Union had supported the partition of Palestine and the creation of the state of Israel in 1948. But the subsequent orientation of Israel to the West and the public support for the new Jewish state voiced by many Soviet Jews compromised them in the eyes of Stalin. Many Jews had responded to the Shoah with a heightened sense of their Jewish identity and called for the rebuilding of Jewish communal life in the USSR. In the atmosphere of the late 1940s, the secret police easily depicted such activity as "bourgeois nationalism." Stalin apparently came to question the loyalty and political reliability of all Soviet Jews despite their almost total removal from most of the higher echelons of the Party, with the exception of a few symbolic figures such as Lazar Kaganovich.

In 1952, the leaders of the JAC, under arrest since 1948, were tried on charges of spying for the West and Israel and for bourgeois nationalist deviations. A total of fourteen defendants were secretly tried and all but one, Dr. Lina Shtern, were executed on 12 August 1952, the "Night of the Murdered Poets." This judicial murder of many of the leaders of modern Yiddish literature, including P. Markish, I. Fefer, Leyb Kvitko, and D. Bergelson, was a devastating blow to Yiddish culture. The attack on Soviet Jews began to spread wider. On 13 January 1953, it was announced that a number of prominent Soviet physicians who staffed the elite medical clinic in the Kremlin that served the Soviet leadership were "assassins in white coats" linked to foreign intelligence operations. Most of the accused at the center of this Doctors' Plot, such as Professor Miron Vovsi, were Jews. Rumors were rife in Moscow and Leningrad, the veracity of which is still debated by scholars, that the trial of the doctors would provide the pretext for a massive anti-Jewish pogrom, which would be followed by the exile of much of the Jewish population of the USSR to camps in Soviet Central Asia. At this juncture, Stalin suffered a stroke and died on 5 March 1953. One of the first actions of the new collective leadership was to denounce the Doctors' Plot as a provocation and to release all the accused. Jews, even more than other Soviet citizens, viewed this as a miraculous escape. Nonetheless, the legacy of war, the Shoah, and the purges put paid to the claim that Soviet Russia was ruled by Jews.

The Jews in Russia and the Soviet Union, 1772–1953
A Selected Bibliography

Jews in Tsarist Russia: 1772–1917

Aronson, I. Michael. *Troubled Waters: The Origins of the 1881 Anti-Jewish Pogroms in Russia.* Pittsburgh: University of Pittsburgh Press, 1990.

Berk, Stephen M. *Year of Crisis, Year of Hope: Russian Jewry and the Pogroms of 1881–1882.* Westport, CT: Greenwood Press, 1985.

Frankel, Jonathan. *Prophecy and Politics: Socialism, Nationalism, and the Russian Jews, 1862–1917.* Cambridge: Cambridge University Press, 1981.

Judge, Edward H. *Easter in Kishinev: Anatomy of a Pogrom.* New York: New York University Press, 1992.

Klier, John D. *Imperial Russia's Jewish Question, 1855–1881.* Cambridge: Cambridge University Press, 1996.

———. *Russia Gathers Her Jews: The Origins of the Jewish Question in Russia, 1772–1825.* DeKalb: Northern Illinois University Press, 1986.

Klier, John D., and Lambroza, Shlomo, eds. *Pogroms: Anti-Jewish Violence in Modern Russian History.* Cambridge: Cambridge University Press, 1991.

Levitats, Isaac. *The Jewish Community in Russia, 1844–1917.* Jerusalem: Posner, 1981.

Mendelsohn, Ezra. *Class Struggle in the Pale: The Formative Years of the Jewish Workers' Movement in Tsarist Russia.* Cambridge: Cambridge University Press, 1970.

Nathans, Benjamin. *Beyond the Pale: The Jewish Encounter with Late Imperial Russia.* Berkeley: University of California Press, 2002.

Rogger, Hans. *Jewish Policies and Right-Wing Politics in Imperial Russia.* London: Macmillan, 1986.

Stanislawski, Michael. *Tsar Nicholas I and the Jews: The Transformation of Jewish Society: 1825–1855.* Philadelphia: The Jewish Publication Society of America, 1983.

Zipperstein, Steven J. *The Jews of Odessa: A Cultural History, 1794–1881.* Stanford: Stanford University Press, 1985.

Jews in the Soviet Union: 1917–1945

Abramson, Henry. *A Prayer for the Government: Ukrainians and Jews in Revolutionary Times, 1917–1920.* Cambridge: Harvard University Press, 1999.

Altshuler, Mordechai. *Soviet Jewry on the Eve of the Holocaust: A Social and Demographic Profile*. Jerusalem: Hebrew University Centre for Research of East European Jewry, 1998.

Aronson, Gregor, ed. *Russian Jewry, 1917–1967*. Trans. Joel Carmichael. New York: Thomas Yoseloff, 1969.

Baron, Salo Wittmayer. *The Russian Jew under Tsars and Soviets*. New York: Macmillan, 1976.

Emiot, Israel. *The Birobidzhan Affair: A Yiddish Writer in Siberia*. Philadelphia: The Jewish Publication Society of America, 1981.

Gilboa, Yehoshua A. *A Language Silenced: The Suppression of Hebrew Literature and Culture in the Soviet Union*. New York: Associated University Presses, 1982.

Gitelman, Zvi. *Jewish Nationality and Soviet Politics: The Jewish Sections of the CPSU*. Princeton: Princeton University Press, 1972.

Goldman, Guido G. *Zionism under Soviet Rule (1917–1928)*. New York: Herzl Press, 1960.

Gurevitz, Baruch. *National Communism in the Soviet Union, 1918–28*. Pittsburgh: University of Pittsburgh Press, 1980.

Kagedan, Allan Laine. *Soviet Zion: The Quest for a Russian Jewish Homeland*. Houndmills: Macmillan, 1994.

Klier, John D. "Russian Jews and the Soviet Agenda." In *Reinterpreting Russia*, ed. Geoffrey Hosking and Robert Service, 183–97. London: Arnold, 1999.

Kochan, Lionel, ed. *The Jews in Soviet Russia since 1917*. 3d ed., rev. Oxford: Oxford University Press, 1978.

Levin, Nora. *The Jews in the Soviet Union since 1917: Paradox of Survival*. 2 vols. New York: I.B. Tauris, 1988.

Miller, Jack, ed. *Jews in Soviet Culture*. New Brunswick, NJ: Transaction Books, 1984.

Pinkus, Benjamin. *The Jews of the Soviet Union: The History of a National Minority*. Cambridge: Cambridge University Press, 1988.

———. *The Soviet Government and the Jews, 1948–1967: A Documented Study*. Cambridge: Cambridge University Press, 1984.

Ro'i, Yaacov, ed. *Jews and Jewish Life in Russia and the Soviet Union*. Ilford: Frank Cass, 1995.

Rothenberg, Joshua. *The Jewish Religion in the Soviet Union*. New York: Ktav, 1971.

Sawyer, Thomas E. *The Jewish Minority in the Soviet Union*. Boulder, CO: Westview Press, 1979.

Weinberg, Robert. *Stalin's Forgotten Zion: Birobidzhan and the Making of a Soviet Jewish Homeland. An Illustrated History, 1928–1996*. Berkeley: University of California Press, 1998.

The Shoah: 1941–1945

Dawidowicz, Lucy. *The War against the Jews, 1933–1945*. New York: Holt, Rinehart and Winston, 1975.

Dobroszycki, L., and Gurock, J., eds. *The Holocaust in the Soviet Union: Studies and Sources on the Destruction of the Jews in Nazi-Occupied Territories of the USSR, 1941–1945.* Armonk, NY: M.E. Sharpe, 1993.

Ehrenburg, Ilya, and Grossman, Vasily, eds. *The Complete Black Book of Russian Jewry.* New Brunswick, NJ: Transaction Publishers, 2002.

Garrard, John, and Garrard, Carol. *The Bones of Berdichev: The Life and Fate of Vasily Grossman.* New York: Free Press, 1996.

Gilbert, Martin. *The Holocaust. A History of the Jews During the Second World War.* London: Fontana, 1986.

Hilberg, Raul. *The Destruction of the European Jews.* 3 vols. New York: Holmes and Meier, 1985.

Levin, Nora. *The Destruction of European Jewry, 1933–1945.* New York: Schocken, 1973.

Porter, Jack Nusan, ed. *Jewish Partisans: A Documentary of Jewish Resistance in the Soviet Union During World War II.* 2 vols. Washington, DC: University Press of America, 1982.

The Jews and Postwar Stalinism: 1945–1953

Gilboa, Yehoshua A. *The Black Years of Soviet Jewry, 1935–1953.* Boston: Little, Brown and Company, 1971.

Gitelman, Zvi, ed. *Bitter Legacy: Confronting the Holocaust in the USSR.* Bloomington: Indiana University Press, 1997.

Kostyrchenko, Gennadi V. *Out of Red Shadows: Antisemitism in Stalin's Russia.* Amherst, NY: Prometheus Books, 1995.

Krammer, Arnold. *The Forgotten Friendship: Israel and the Soviet Bloc, 1947–1953.* Champaign: University of Illinois Press, 1974.

Rapoport, Louis. *Stalin's War against the Jews: The Doctors' Plot and the Soviet Solution.* New York: Free Press, 1990.

Redlich, Shimon. *Propaganda and Nationalism in Wartime Russia: The Jewish Anti-Fascist Committee in the USSR, 1941–1948.* Boulder, CO: Eastern European Monographs, 1982.

———. *War, Holocaust and Stalinism. A Documented History of the Jewish Anti-Fascist Committee in the USSR.* Luxembourg: Harwood Academic Publishers, 1995.

Vaksberg, Arkady. *Stalin against the Jews.* New York: Knopf, 1994.

INDEX OF TRANSLATORS

INDEX OF AUTHORS

K

L

M

ABOUT THE EDITOR

Maxim D. Shrayer is Professor of Russian and English at Boston College, where he is chair of the department of Slavic and Eastern Languages, and co-director of the Jewish Studies Program. He was born in 1967 in Moscow and in 1987 immigrated to the United States with his family. He completed his undergraduate education at Brown University and master's studies at Rutgers, and then earned an M.A. and PhD at Yale. His publications include *The World of Nabokov's Stories* (1999), *Nabokov: Themes and Variations* (2000), *Russian Poet/Soviet Jew* (2000), *Genrikh Sapgir: An Avant-Garde Classic* (2004, with David Shrayer-Petrov), and also three collections of verse. Shrayer is the editor and cotranslator of *Jonah and Sarah: Jewish Stories of Russia and America* (2003) and *Autumn in Yalta: A Novel and Three Stories* (2006), by David Shrayer-Petrov. Shrayer has been the recipient of fellowships from the National Endowment for the Humanities, the Rockefeller Foundation, and the Bogliasco Foundation. His English-language prose, poetry, and translations have appeared in *Absinthe*, *Agni*, *Commentary*, *Kenyon Review*, *Massachusetts Review*, *Partisan Review*, *Southwest Review*, *Tiferet*, and other magazines. He lives in Chestnut Hill, MA with his wife, Dr. Karen E. Lasser, and daughter Mira Isabella Shrayer.